MARIJUANA
Horticulture
The Indoor/Outdoor
MEDICAL
Grower's Bible

by JORGE CERVANTES

This book is written for the purpose of supplying information to the public. The publisher and the author, or anyone associated with the production of this book, do not advocate breaking the law.

You are encouraged to read any and all information available about cannabis to develop a complete background on the subject.

The author and the publisher have tried to the best of their ability to describe the most current cannabis growing methods. However, there may be some mistakes in the text that the author and publisher were unable to detect. This book contains current information up to the date of publication.

Published by Van Patten Publishing

Cover Design: Chris Payaso
Cover Photos: The greenhouse at Eddy Lepp's Medicinal Gardens is by Chris Payaso.
 The `Thaitanic' bud in full bloom is by Gato.
Artwork: Christopher Valdes, Chris Payaso
Book Design and Layout: Chris Payaso
Back Cover Photos: Jorge Cervantes
Photos: Jorge Cervantes, Gato, Jorge, Gregorio Fernandez, Hugo, William, Eirik,
 Chris Payaso
Editors: Linda Meyer, Estella Cervantes
Contributors: Dr. John McPartland, Chimera, Therese Blanco, Chris Payaso

Copyright 2006, Jorge Cervantes
ISBN-13: 978-1-878823-23-6
ISBN-10: 1-878823-23-X

12 13 14 15

Printed in China

For wholesale orders please contact the following:
United Kingdom: Avalon Wholesale: www.avalonheadshop.co.uk, Tel: 44-23-9283-2383
North America: Homestead Books: www.homesteadbook.com, 1-800-426-6777
North America: Quick Distribution: 1-510-527-7036
North America: Ingram Books: www.ingrambook.com
See our website: www.marijuanagrowing.com for more distributors.

In Memoriam:
Steven McWilliams

Scared of possible jail time, in constant pain and tired of battling for medical marijuana patients' rights, Steven McWilliams committed suicide in San Diego on Monday July 11, 2005, on his 51st birthday.

Mr. McWilliams was famous nationwide for his efforts and the legitimacy he lent to the medical marijuana movement. Not taken seriously at first, McWilliams did not give up, working for the movement since as early as 1996 when California state voters approved Proposition 215, allowing patients to use marijuana for medical purposes when prescribed by a doctor.

Steven McWilliams worked to implement Proposition 215 locally in San Diego. Showing up weekly for City Council meetings carrying a marijuana plant, he urged the local politicians to come up with a plan for the distribution of marijuana. As a result the city came up with standards for the number of plants allowed by users. Mr. McWilliams served on a city-organized committee for a time that dealt with these issues. He ran for city council a few times, when he wasn't alternately suing the city.

In spite of all this, he was convicted in 2003 for illegal cultivation, and sentenced to a six-month federal prison term. Still out on appeal at the time of his suicide, he was in chronic and serious pain–the judge had ordered that he not use marijuana. Mr. McWilliams suffered severe

Dedication

This book is dedicated to Sebastain Orfali; Roger Watanabe; my mother, father, wife and family; all cannabis medical patients; and all the people who have suffered the effects of the War on (prohibited cannabis) Drugs. We share a common affliction. Some law enforcement and political agents have shared our pain; others are in different stages of denial. May the Christian God, Buddha, Allah, Sheba, and the God you worship, bless you all.

side effects from the use of standard prescription painkillers. He left a note saying that the pain was too much to bear, and he hoped his suicide would help change the government's position towards marijuana as a medicine.

Memorial services were held in San Diego at City Hall, white roses were passed to the attendees.

Steph Sherer, executive director of Americans for Safe Access said, "Steve McWilliams was tortured by the federal government because of the medication he needed."

The Native Suns Dispensary opened in San Diego on June 6, 2005, in defiance of the Supreme Court's ruling against individual states' medical marijuana laws. In a 6-3 split-decision, Justice Paul Stevens said that Congress has a moral responsibility to change the nation's laws regarding cannabis use for medical patients. In writing the decision, Justice Stevens did find that the federal government did not exceed its authority under law when federal officers raided medical marijuana patients with California state prescriptions.

Credits

Some information in this book was extrapolated from the "Frequently Asked Questions" and "Forums" from the closed site, www.overgrow.com. This list contains OG member names and some of the many people who made this book possible.

It has been a long and winding road. Many, many wonderful people have helped make this book a reality. I have listed everybody in alphabetical order. To clarify, some of the people below provided inspiration, others hard facts, and among them, some gave much more than others. We know who we are. and we are together!

Extra special thanks to Chimera who added precision and knowledge to the breeding chapter. He is an expert!

10K
Adam (Hempworks/THSeeds)
Al (Insta Print)
Alan Dronkers (Sinsi)
Albert (Sensi)
Aleen
Alex (not Lying Sack of Shit Alex)
Allen St. Pierre, (NORML)
Amadeo (Spain)
André Grossman (*High Times*)
Annie
Apollo11Genius
Arjan (Greenhouse)
Aurora
Badar
Balta
Barbas
Barge
Barry (Australian Hydroponics)
Bean (*High Times*)
Ben Dronkers (Sensi)
Bernard Rapaz (*Valchanvre*)
Bev
Beverly Potter
Biddy
BigIslandBud
Bill
Bill C.
Bill Drake (Author)
Bill K.
Bill R.
BOG
Boy Ramsahai (*High Life* and *Soft Secrets*)
Breeder Steve (Spice of Life)
Brian (SNB)
Bubbasix
Bubble Man
Buko
Buddy (Nirvana), Holland
Buddy R.
Bud-E
Carlos Cholula
Carlos Hernandez
Cezar Doll (*Cañamo*)
Charlie
Charlie F.
Chimera (Chimera Seeds)
Chris Conrad
Chris I.
Chris Payaso

Chris Simunek (*High Times*)
Cliff Cremer (*High Life* and *Soft Secrets*)
Connie (*Hanf*)
Consuelo
Cosmic Jimmy
Crow
Crystal (Kind Seeds)
Crystalman (Joop Dumay), Holland Culture)
Curt (Advanced Nutrients, Holland)
D. B. Turner
D. C.
D.J. Short (DJ Short Seeds)
DaChronicKing
Dan (Vancouver, BC)
Dana Larson (*Cannabis Culture*)
Darryll (Kind Seeds)
Daryll
Dave Bienenstock (*High Times*)
David
David Garcia (Translator)
David Strange (*Heads*)
David T.
David W.
David Watson
Dennis (*Grass Times*)
Dennis Peron
Dennis S.
Dennos
Derry (Barney's)
Deva
Dieter Hagenbach
Dirk Rehahn (*Canna*)
Doc Ontario
Doctor Dangerous
Don Collins
Donny
Doug (Hempworks/THSeeds)
Dr. John McPartland (*Hemp Diseases and Pests*)
Drew Bennie
Dutch Grown
Eagle Bill (RIP)
Ed Borg, Holland
Ed Rosenthal (Author)
Ed S. (Canada)
Eddie (Flying Dutchmen)
Eirik
Elizabeth
Eddy Lepp

Elmar (BTT)
Emilio Gómez
Enric
Ernesto (*Cañamo*)
Estelita, Spain
Evie
Farmer in the Sky
Fatima
Felipe
Felipe Borallo (Makoki)
Felix Kaatz (Owl's Production)
Feran (Good House Seeds)
Fergetit
Flick
Fluus
Foz
Frank
Frank (Canna)
G. I. Joe
Gaspar Fraga (*Cañamo*)
Gato
George
Gillis (Canna)
Gisela
Glass Joe
Gloria (Kind Seeds)
Gonz
Gordon
Grant
Green Man
Gregorio (Goyo) Fernandez
Guido (Hanfblatt)
Gurney
Gypsy Nirvana (Seeds Direct)
Hank
Harmon D.
HashMan
HempHappy
Henk (Dutch Passion)
Henk & Siglinde (HESI)
Hillary Black
Hugo (Soft Secrets)
Ivan (Ivanart)
ixnay007
J. D., Spain
Jack Herrer
Jaime Prats (*Cañamo*)
Jan
Jan Sennema
Jason King (Author)
Javi

Javi (The Plant)
Javis
Jerry
Jim
Jim from Chicago
Jim R.
Jimmy Chicago
JJ Jackson (Advanced Hydroponics)
JJ Turner
Joan Melendez
John
John (Avalon)
Johnny Sage from Ocean Beach
Joint Doctor (Low Ryder)
Jordi Bricker (*Cañamo*)
Josete (*Cañamo*)
Juan
Juan (The Plant)
Juaquin (El Conde) Bucati
K. Trichome Technologies
Karen (The Amsterdam)
Karulo (l'Interior)
Kees (Super Sativa Seed Club)
Keith Stroop (NORML)
Kelly
Ken
Kevin
Kinny
Kyle (Kind Seeds)
Kyle Kushman (*High Times*)
Larry Armantrout
Larry Turner
Lars
Laurence Cherniac (author)
Leaf
Lee Bridges
    (The Cannabis Poet, RIP)
Liam (Pollinator)
Linda
Lock
Lord of the Strains
Lorna (Cannabis College)
Loti, Swiss
Luc (Paradise)
Lyndon (CC Newz)
Madelena (Flying Dutchmen)
Mani, Spain
Marc
Marc Emery (*Cannabis Culture*)
Marco Kuhn (CannaTrade)
MarcusVonBueler
Mario Belandi (Reyna Madre)
Martin Palmer (Avalon)
Martin Trip
Mary Anderson
Matt (*High Times*)
Matt (THSeeds), Holland
Mauk (Canna)
Max M.
Mel Frank
    (*Marijuana Grower's Guide*)
Michael

Michael A.
Michka (Mama Editions)
Mickey
Miguel
Miguel Gemino
Mike
Mike
Mike Edison (*High Times*)
Mila (Pollinator)
Moisés Lopéz (*Cañamo*)
Moño
Mr. Beaner
Mr. Ito
Murphy Stevens (Author)
Napoleon (Martin)
Natalia
Neil Wilkinson
Neville (The Seed Bank)
Nick (*Redeye Express*)
Nol Van Schaik (Willie Wortel's)
Noucetta
Ocean
Olaf (Greenhouse)
Oli, Swiss
Opti
Oscar (Osona)
Patricia
Patrick, Swiss
Patty Collins
Paul
Pepe Poblacion
Phil (*Weed World*)
Pim (Super Sativa Seed Club)
PREMIER
Psychotropic Nomad
R.C. (overgrow.com Founder)
Ravi Dronkers (Sensi)
Red (Legends Seeds)
Reeferman
Renaté
Rick
Rick Cusick (*High Times*)
Roach from Spain
Rob
Rob Clarke (*Marijuana Botany*)
Robbie (Agromix)
Roberto C.
Roger
Roger (*Nacht-Schatten Verlag*)
Roger Botlanger (*Hanf*)
Roger Watanabe (RIP)
Rolf
Romulan Joe
Ron (Baba) Turner (Last Gasp)
Ron Wilks
Ross
Rubio
Sam S.
Sammy
Saskia
Saskia (Canna)
SC

Scott
Sebastain Orfali RIP
Secrets)
Sergi Doll (*Cañamo*)
Shantibaba (Mr. Nice)
Simon (Serious Seeds)
Sita
Sixfinger
Skip
Skip Higdon
Skip Stone
Snoofer
Soma (Soma Seeds)
Spanish Hash Guy
Spence (Cannabis College)
Steve
Steve Bloom (*High Times*)
Steve from Amsterdam
Steve from OZ
Steve Hagar (*High Times*)
Steve R.
Steve Solomon
Sus
Susan L.
T.
Taylor (Kind Seeds)
Ted B.
Ted Zitlau, RIP
Tigrane (Mama Editions)
Tim G.
Times)
Tom (*Sinsemilla Tips*)
Tom Flowers
    (*Marijuana Flower Forcing*)
Tony (Sagarmatha)
Tony B.
Twofingered
Uncle Ben
Vansterdan
Wally Duck
Wayne O.
Wernard Bruining
Whirly
William
Willie (Hanfblatt Tuner)
Winnie (*Grow!*)
Wismy (*Yerba*)
Xavi
Xus
Yorg, Swiss
Yorgos
Ztefan (CannaTrade)

Countless growers and cannabis afficionados (that were not named above) helped with this book. They provided valuable input and support over the last 20 years to make this book possible.

The War on Drugs

The War on Drugs in "America, Land of the Free" is out of control. This War on American citizens and many other unfortunate souls around the world continues to be driven by fear and misinformation that is spun by numerous US and foreign government agencies.

The War on Drugs concentrates on encarcerating cannabis users and is headed by a drug czar.

Czar is defined by Webster's Dictionary, as 1. A former Russian emperor. 2. An autocrat. 3. Informal. One in authority: Leader. From these definitions we know that a Drug Czar is not one to listen to any opposition. Is this the basis of democracy?

The most infamous American Drug Czars include: William Bennet (a tobacco smoker, alcohol drinker and compulsive gambler) General Barry McCaffrey (the most decorated US General and instigator of failed "anti-cannabis media propaganda"), and John Walters (a career bureaucrat who labels peaceful cannabis consumers as terrorists). All past and present Drug Czars profess "high moral standards."

Many official Government and private reports have recommended legalization or decriminalization of cannabis including:

1928: Le Dain Commission (Canada) recommended to decriminalize or legalize small amounts of marijuana.

1972: the Safer Commission, appointed by President Nixon, reported that laws regarding marijuana should be decriminalized. Nixon rejected that recommendation, and instead endorsed the creation of the US Drug Enforcement Agency (DEA).

1990: California Advisory Panel (appointed by the State of California) recommended that California legalize marijuana. State Attorney General John Van de Kamp refused to publish the report.

2005: The Budgetary Implications of Marijuana Prohibition report is released. The Harvard University report by 500 US economists headed by economist Milton Friedman endorses legalizing and taxing cannabis.

Cannabis has been used medicinally for more than 10,000 years. Cannabis is being legally dispensed medicinally in 10 US states, Canada, the Netherlands and Spain. Still the US Government classifies cannabis as a Schedule I drug along with heroin as having no medical value.

The July 30, 2004 editon of the *Seattle Times* reported "Marijuana smuggling case first local use of Patriot Act provision. The US attorney in Seattle, WA charged 15 people in a marijuana smuggling operation. The undercover snitch, a U.S. Immigration and Customs Enforcement agent, posed as a middle man who actually smuggled money from the US to Canada.

The alleged cannabis and money smugglers were charged under the Patriot Act. The Patriot Act was passed into law in the US in order to thwart international terrorism after the September 11 attacks on the World Trade Center towers in New York City. However according to US attorney Todd Greenberg in Seattle, "there is no indication these defendants are connected to terrorism."

Here are a few well documented facts:

Cause of Death	Annual Deaths
Tobacco	435,000
Poor Diet and Physical Inactivity	365,000
Alcohol	85,000
Microbial Agents	5,000
Toxic Agents	55,000
Motor Vehicle Crashes	26,347
Adverse Reactions to Prescription Drugs	32,000
Suicide	30,622
Incidents Involving Firearms	29,000
Homicide	20,308
Sexual Behaviors	20,000
All Illicit Drug Use, Direct and Indirect	17,000
Non-Steroidal Anti-Inflammatory Drugs Such as Aspirin	7,600
Marijuana	0

This confirmed information for the year 2000 in the USA is from: http://www.drug warfacts. org/causes.htm .

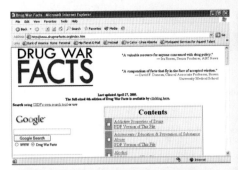

www.drugwarfacts.org

www.stopthedrugwar.org

www.cannabisconsumers.com

www.druglibrary.org

YEAR	MARIJUANA ARRESTS
2001	723,627
2000	734,498
1999	704,812
1998	682,885
1997	695,200
1996	641,642
1995	588,963
1994	499,122
1993	380,689
1992	342,314

88.6 percent of arrests in 2001 were for possession only.

With ever increasing prohibition we are growing more cannabis around the world than ever before. Most of the photographs and much of the information was collected outside of the USA. The cannabis laws in the "Land of the Free" are some of the most horrifying and repressive in the world. However, with the artificial "cannabis price support program in a free market" spawned by the US government, the rest of the world is benefiting. Growers from all over the world, including the ones that are willing to risk their freedom and assets in the USA, are able to cash in on this defacto program.

Here is how the program works. Cannabis is illegal. This creates an artificially high price for cannabis because the supply is limited and the demand high. Aggressive entrepreneurs see the opportunity and fill the need in the marketplace. When harsh laws are enforced, entrepreneurs give way to thugs and organized crime who fill the orders for cannabis. Any first year economics student can figure this out!

This information has caught the eye of a few politicians. A growing number of politicians are finding the integrity and moxie required to risk "political suicide" and endorse medical cannabis.

Table of Contents

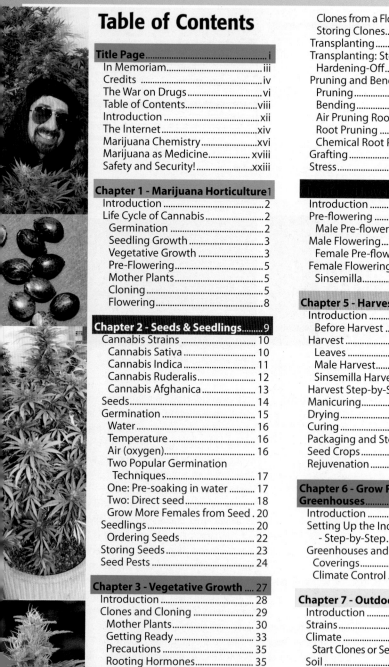

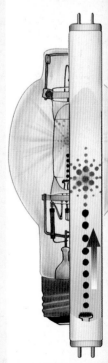

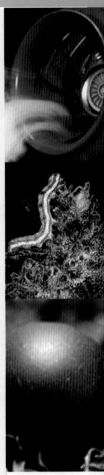

Introduction

The "Bible" has gone through a complete metamorphosis since the first edition in 1983. The First Edition was just 96 pages, black and white and bound with a pair of staples. I wrote the book on a Kaypro II computer. To typeset I hooked my Kaypro to a VAX mainframe computer. The typeset "galleys" were pasted up into "hard copy." I printed the book on a Multilith press. My wife and I collated pages and stapled them together to form the first *Indoor Marijuana Horticulture* book. The book immediately became a best-seller among indoor growers and has remained on top ever since!

The book covers below are some of the many published by Jorge.

Original Indoor Marijuana Horticulture 1983

The Second Edition (1985) grew to 288 pages and was christened "The Bible" by indoor growers. The Third Edition (1993) grew to 320 pages and the Fourth Edition (2001) tipped the scales at 432 pages and contained 200 color photos and drawings. The Bible is published in Dutch, German, French, English, and Spanish. There is also a special UK Edition. The Australian Edition was banned by the Australian Government, but lofty Auzzies still find ways to bring in the Bible.

The Fifth Edition has a little larger format (6 x 8.25 inches [150 x 210 cm]), 512 pages and is full-color throughout with more than 1100 full color photographs, drawings, charts, and graphs. It is completely rewritten to reflect the changes in cannabis cultivation and medicine in recent years. Sections on medical cannabis, seeds, seedlings, vegetative growth, cloning, flowering, breeding and hash have been amplified substantially. All-new sections have been added on greenhouses and outdoor growing. Photos and precise color drawings augment text to simplify information so that it is easier to assimilate.

Indoor Marijuana Horticulture Second Edition

Digital cameras, fast computers with big hard disks, and fast Internet connections have transformed the Bible into a much more complete work.

We were able to hold the price at $21.95 from 1993 until 2005, 12 years. The expense of adding color to each and every page, hiring editors, travel, office overhead, and inflation have made it necessary to sell a minimum of advertising as well as increase the price to $29.95.

If you would like to learn more about advertising in the Bible, please hit our website: www.marijuanagrowing.com.

Case studies follow the text. They show exactly how different growers grew super smoke for pennies a day. All of their growing statistics - watts, varieties, calendar, cost, harvest weight, etc. - are also listed. See how growers invest a minimum of cash and harvest pound after pound of outstanding bud 365 days a year!

IMH Second Edition Revised

A garden "Calendar" and "Checklist" in the book lend additional organization for all indoor horticulturists.

- Jorge Cervantes

IMH Dutch First Edition

IMH Fourth Edition

Marijuana Indoors:
Five Easy Gardens

IMH Third Edition

IMH Fourth Edition
German

Marijuana Outdoors:
Guerilla Growing

IMH Banned!

IMH Fourth Edition
Spanish

Marijuana Outdoors:
Guerilla Growing -
Spanish Edition

Marihuana Drinnen

IMH Fourth Edition UK

Marijuana Jorge's Rx

The Internet

Grow Info FREE!

Information and the velocity at which it travels is the most important innovation in marijuana growing during the last five years.

The Internet allows millions of growers all over the world to share information. US growers can still ask and answer anonymous grow questions on line and download information about cannabis use. Here is a short list of some of my favorite web sites.

1. www.cannabiscafe.com was started with a ".com" domain by a Mexican cowboy who had an accident. He stayed busy building the site while recuperating. Now the site is maintained by the Asociación de Internautas del Cannabis Café who also organize the annual Cannabis Parade in different places in Spain.

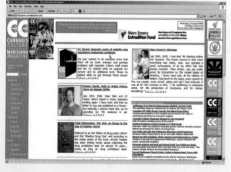

2. www.cannabisculture.com is the website for *Cannabis Culture* magazine. It has a full array of cannabis information including a good

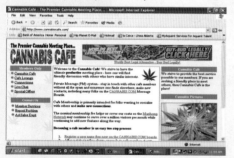

deal about cultivation. Highlights include current and recent news.

3. www.cannabisworld.com, is a must for the serious grower. This is an advanced cultivation site.

4. www.weedfarmer.com is full of grow forums that stay very active! Packed with information!

5. www.hightimes.com is the official High Times magazine site. This site has a full array of politics, news, cultivation, and more! This very high-traffic site has everything for the cannabis enthusiast. Put this site on your "Favorites" list.

6. www.marijuanagrowing.com is Jorge Cervantes' official site. It is packed with current information on marijuana cultivation with pages and pages of up-to-date cultivation information, plus Jorge's articles and numerous tips on growing in today's world.

7. www.naturescontrol.com is not a cannabis site, but is packed with beneficial insect information

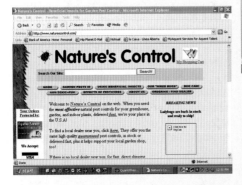

8. www.overgrow.com (top right) was the absolute best grow site on the Internet. Canadian authorities shut this site and www.cannabis-world.com down early in 2006. At press time we were still waiting to find out the fate of the popular site. We all miss the hundreds of thousands of images, StrainGuide, forums, and up to date information!

9. www.seedbankupdate.com (below) rates seed companies with the most reliable information on the Internet. This outstanding site is updated weekly.

10. www.solocannabis.com This Spanish site has the biggest member base and the most hits of any Spanish language site-definitely the biggest site in the Spanish language. This site is run by a dedicated cannabis afficionado and good friend from a small town in Northeastern Spain.

The Internet was developed by the DOD (Department of Defense) in the latter half of the 20th century. Government geeks and spooks developed the World Wide Web for national security reasons. It is easy to set up a proxy server along with a few other safety precautions to surf with safety so the government cannot track your every move.

Be very careful when surfing the Internet. Check out www.webopedia.com/TERM/p/proxy_server.html for more information about surfing safely.

Smart growers, especially from countries with draconian laws, do not e-mail about growing or surf grow sites on a computer located in a grow house. Remember, a person never knows who is peeking at transparent e-mail. "Firewall" software alerts and protects the user against another party tracking a surfing path or to unauthorized entry into their computer. Ask at your local software store for security software to keep unwanted computer spooks subdued.

Check out www.proxyblind.org/ for more information on surfing anonymously.

Do not frequent marijuana sites or talk shop on the net unless you have taken appropriate security measures.

Internet information can be great or it can be packed with problems. All growers and "authorities" have the same status on the Internet, and can post "facts" to their site or news group. Many times unverified, poorly researched "facts" are either self-serving or untrue. Always ask yourself if the information you are reading makes sense. If it sounds too good to be true, it probably is. I often surf through many sites and pages before finding something worth retaining. "Free" often means the material is sales oriented. News groups provide an excellent forum to share grow stories.

Marijuana Chemistry

Cannabis is the only plant that produces chemicals called cannabinoids. However, with gene splicing and genetic engineering, it is only a matter of time until cannabinoids are added to other plants. Cannabinoids are ingredients unique to cannabis; the psychoactive cannabinoids are responsible for the mind-bending effects of marijuana. Some cannabinoids get you high. Around 40 cannabinoids have been confirmed to exist, but most are not psychoactive. Here is a short rundown on the six most prominent cannabinoids.

Δ^9 THC, the main ingredient that gets you high, is called: Δ^9-trans-tetrahydrocannabinol. All cannabis, whether industrial hemp or drug marijuana, contains some Δ^9 THC. Industrial hemp cannabis contains infinitesimal amounts while dried flower tops (buds) of potent marijuana can contain up to 25 percent Δ^9 THC. In potent varieties of marijuana, perhaps all of the mind-bending effects are derived from Δ^9 THC. Δ^8 THC is found in very low concentrations in cannabis. It also gets you high, but there is so little Δ^8 THC in most cannabis that researchers, breeders, and growers concentrate on the more abundant and potent Δ^9 THC. To simplify matters we will refer to both Δ^9 THC and Δ^8 THC as THC.

Cannabidiol, known as CBD, also appears in virtually all varieties of cannabis. The amount of CBD varies enormously, from a trace to more than 95 percent of all cannabinoids present in a plant. CBD generally has a sedative effect regarding the high you experience. CBD, when combined with THC, tends to postpone the beginning of the high, but the good part is that CBD can make it last twice as long. Whether CBD increases or decreases the force of the high is subjective and must be discerned by each smoker.

Cannabinol, or CBN, is produced as THC oxidizes or degrades. Only a trace of CBN exists in fresh bud. Stored and cured tops or hashish have higher levels of CBN that has converted from THC. Marijuana with high levels of CBN generally makes the toker feel disoriented, often sleepy or groggy, referred to as a stupefying high. At best, CBN contains only 10 percent of the psychoactive potency of the original THC.

Tetrahydrocannabivarin, called THCV, is the shorter three-carbon propyl that replaces the five-carbon pentyl chain. This compound is associated with the fragrance of the plant. In other words, very pungent-smelling marijuana normally contains THCV. Warmer temperatures bring out more smell. THCV is found in very potent marijuana that originates in Southeast and Central Asia as well as regions in Africa. Concentrations of THCV usually make the high come on quicker and disappear sooner. There is still much research to do on this cannabinoid.

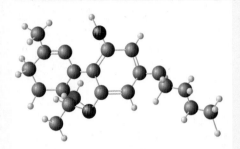

Here is a look at a THC molecule.

Cannabichromene, or CBC, may make up to 20 percent of the cannabinoid profile in a plant. Little study has been done on this cannabinoid. So far, researchers believe it may interact with THC to make the high more intense.

For a complete background on cannabinoids, including chemical diagrams, resin profiles, and production of cannabinoids, see the classic book, *Marijuana Grower's Guide*, by Mel Frank, Redeye Press, 1997, 330 pages.

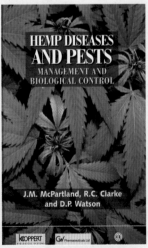

Three excellent reference books that all indoor marijuana horticulturists should have on hand are: the Marijuana Grower's Guide, by Mel Frank (Redeye Press), Marijuana Botany, by Robert Connell Clarke (Ronin Press), and Hemp Diseases and Pests by J. M. McPartland, R. C. Clarke, and D. P. Watson (CABI Publishing). The books are classic cultivation and breeding guides. For more valuable background information on gardening, read some of the 20 magazines we list in the back of this book, and hit the Internet sites listed in this chapter. You may also want to attend some of the cannabis fairs listed in the Introduction. Also, read such publications as Organic Gardening, Sunset, Mother Earth News, etc., and the gardening section of your local newspaper.

The Reverend Charles Eddy Lepp of Eddy's Medicinal Gardens and Multi-Denominational Ministry of Cannabis and Rastafari.

Tgranne and Mishka of Mama Productions and Jack Herrer (The Emperor Wears No Clothes) enjoy a moment at the Cannabis Cup in Amsterdam.

Lorna, director of the Cannabis College in Amsterdam, educates thousands every year about the proper use and benefits of medical marijunana and cannabis.

Marijuana as Medicine
by Dr. John McPartland

Cannabis (marijuana, hashish) has long been used for recreational and medicinal purposes-for 10,000 years or more. Its medical indications are manifold, including glaucoma, muscle spasticity (e.g., multiple sclerosis), movement disorders (e.g., Huntington's disease), and a variety of pain syndromes. Marijuana reduces nausea and vomiting and enhances appetite, so it helps people with AIDS and opposes the side effects of cancer chemotherapy. Research shows it can prevent the death of injured neurons. And everyone knows it alleviates anxiety and depression.

Marijuana research is one of the fastest-moving fields of medical science, so any books we suggest may soon be outdated. In the 2000 edition of *Indoor Marijuana Horticulture*, we recommended the book *Marijuana and Medicine* (National Academy Press, 1999). This classic book has been updated by *Cannabis and Cannabinoids* (Haworth Press, 2002) and *The Medicinal Uses of Cannabis and Cannabinoids* (Pharmaceutical Press, 2004). *Marijuana Medicine* by Christian Rätsch (Healing Arts Press, 1998) is a beautiful book that focuses on ethnobotany and the historical uses of cannabis. Notable web sites include www.maps. org, www.medicalmj.org, www.medmjscience. org, and links posted at www.druglibrary.org/ schaffer/hemp/medical/medical.htm. For regular updates on the "Science, Politics and Law" surrounding medical marijuana, subscribe to O'Shaughnessy's-*The Journal of Cannabis in Clinical Practice* (www.ccrmg.org/journal.html).

Despite marijuana's unambiguous medical benefits, the USA Drug Enforcement Administration (DEA) classifies marijuana as a prohibited Schedule 1 drug ("no currently accepted medical use"). However, tetrahydrocannabinol (THC), the primary active ingredient in marijuana, is classified as a synthetic Schedule III drug (dronabinol, Marinol®). The DEA's hypocritical classification is rejected by many Americans. Currently ten states in the USA allow patients to possess marijuana for medical use, contingent upon a physician's recommendation, but possession remains illegal under Federal law.

Because marijuana remains illegal under Federal law, its source remains the black market. Patients must obtain their medicine from unregulated producers. You, dear reader, may be one such unregulated producer. Patients depend upon your ethics and expertise to supply them with high-quality medicine, free from contaminants. Jorge and I reckon that dishonorable laws create honor among outlaws, so we entreat all growers to supply only the best organically grown marijuana. The methods for cultivating pharmaceutical-grade herb are outlined in this book. Grow the healthiest plants possible by paying careful attention to the basics: light, nutrients, water, and air. Everything must be in balance, especially nutrients. If you get the balance right, you won't need to read the chapters on insect and mold control. The most common contaminants of marijuana are molds or pesticides. Optimal cultivation eliminates the possibility of these contaminants.

Of course, optimal cultivation may sometimes elude even the best grower. This book details the use of natural pesticides such as oils and soaps. Better yet, this book promotes the use of biocontrols—commercially available organisms that combat pests and diseases (ladybugs versus aphids being a classic example). For more information regarding the use of natural pesticides and biocontrols, consult the "bible," *Hemp Diseases and Pests* (see page xv). Despite all this great information, we still preach the bottom line: "An ounce of prevention is worth a pound of cure." Even "natural" chemicals may cause problems in some people. The latest edition of O'Shaughnessy's details the case of a woman who fell ill while manicuring marijuana that had been sprayed with abamectin. Abamectin is a natural compound produced by a soil bacterium. It is approved for use in organic gardens, but, nevertheless, it nearly killed the woman. Grow well and avoid chemicals.

This medical marijuana patient is tending a garden while seated in a wheelchair. Gardening can produce a patient's medicine and provide therapy.

So how does marijuana work as medicine? The question is a proverbial onion, with many layers to peel before we get to the core. The first layer is the medicine's herbal essence, which is at odds with current medical science. The DEA and FDA criticize the use of herbs as medicines, saying plants contain a variable mix of compounds and cannot provide a precisely defined drug effect. According to the pharmaceutical industry, medicines are synthetic, single-ingredient "silver bullets" that focus upon solitary metabolic pathways in our physiological systems. Herbalists, on the other hand, applaud the polypharmacy of herbal remedies and claim two advantages over single-ingredient drugs:

1. The many constituents in herbs may work by multiple mechanisms to improve therapeutic activity in a cumulative or synergistic manner.

2. Herbs may also contain compounds that mitigate the side effects of their predominant active ingredients.

Thus, marijuana has been characterized as a "synergistic shotgun," in contrast with synthetic, single-ingredient "silver bullets." The many ingredients in marijuana modulate our health via several metabolic pathways, gently nudging our system towards homeostasis. This kind of "multitasking" makes marijuana impossible to evaluate, according to the pharmaceutical industry. But multitasking avoids the unbalanced distortion of solitary metabolic pathways, as produced by synthetic, single-ingredient silver bullets such as Vioxx.

First and foremost in marijuana's list of ingredients is THC. Tetrahydrocannabinol (THC) is a "new" molecule, produced by cannabis, which evolved within the past 34 million years. Many botanists speculate that THC initially evolved as a toxin to deter herbivores. But this evolutionary strategy was diverted when THC became attractive to humans–the "botany of desire" described by Michael Pollan. THC works in humans by mimicking an endogenous compound that our own bodies make, called anandamide. THC binds to anandamide's receptors, called cannabinoid (CB) receptors. Research indicates that CB receptors originally evolved in primitive organisms about 600 million years ago! However, as with all chicken-and-egg questions, the story of CB receptors and cannabis began long before the current pair of protagonists appeared in evolutionary time. It is probable that both CB receptors and cannabis had evolutionary predecessors. They may date to "deep time," before plants and animals diverged in the primordial soup. Over many eons, CB receptors may have become "vestigial," analogous to an appendix, only to be reactivated when *Homo sapiens* discovered cannabis. Humans have interacted and coevolved with cannabis for millennia, creating a complex heterogenous medicine by selecting plants that provide maximal benefits and minimal side effects. The success of 10,000 or more years of human refinement

with this botanical medication will be difficult to replicate in modern laboratories. This deconstruction of pharmacological theory is radical, and may herald the reintroduction of herbal medicines into modern medical pharmacopeias, with marijuana leading the way.

When THC or anandamide activate CB receptors, the CB receptors activate G-proteins. G-proteins are microscopic messengers that migrate around cells and modulate a variety of ion channels and enzymes. Cannabinoid receptors associate with different subtypes of G-proteins, such as Gi and Gs subtypes. The "i" and "s" abbreviate "inhibitor" and "stimulator," which describe the opposite effects these G-proteins have on their targets. Research has shown that different cannabinoids preferentially activate different subtypes of G-proteins. This may explain why different strains of marijuana produce different highs. For example, Afghani plants produce a lot of cannabidiol (CBD), and perhaps CBD preferentially activates Gi and causes an inhibitory, stony, narcotic-like effect. Whereas plants from Thailand contain tetrahydrocannabivarin (THCV, a propyl analogue of THC) that might preferentially activate Gs and cause that speedy, buzzy, Thai high.

Thanks to its mix of ingredients, marijuana causes fewer psychological side effects (such as anxiety and panic reactions) than pure, synthetic THC (Marinol). Clinical trials have shown that CBD reduces the anxiety provoked by THC, and CBD demonstrates antipsychotic effects. Anxiety from THC may also be alleviated by terpenoids present in marijuana. Many terpenoids are volatile and possess sedative properties when inhaled, including limonene, linalool, citronellol, and terpineol. Terpenoids may also mitigate memory loss caused by pure THC. Limonene, terpinene, carvacrol, and pulegone increase brain acetylcholine activity. This mechanism is shared by tacrine, a drug used for the treatment of Alzheimer's disease. Terpenoids act on other receptors and neurotransmitters. Some terpenoids act as serotonin uptake inhibitors (as does Prozac®), and augment the neurotransmitter GABA (as does Valium). Terpenoids produce anti-inflammatory effects in the respiratory tract. Their presence in marijuana smoke may explain why inhaling marijuana smoke causes less airway irritation and inflammation than inhaling pure THC. Limonene blocks the carcinogenesis induced by "tar" generated from the combustion of herb. Limonene is currently undergoing tests for the treatment of several types of cancer. Terpenoids rock.

Dr. Ethan Russo described "endocannabinoid deficiency syndrome," and suggested that the administration of THC and CBD corrected for deficiencies of either anandamide or CB receptors. The administration of THC and CBD seems to kick-start our endocannabinoid system. For example, THC stimulates the release of anandamide, and CBD inhibits the breakdown of anandamide. One study has shown that acute administration of THC may increase the density of CB receptors in the central nervous system. Tolerance and addiction to marijuana is uncommon, in part, because THC is a "partial agonist." Agonists are compounds that stimulate receptors, and partial agonists can only partially activate receptors. Perhaps the best medicines are partial agonists–they steer us away from disease, but our innate healing mechanisms are still required to restore us to complete health. We recall the sheep farmer analogy: when the farmer finds a sheep on the wrong side of the fence, the farmer corrects the situation by placing the sheep on the other side of the fence, not by carrying the sheep over the fence and all the way to the center of the pasture.

In conclusion, marijuana as medicine is becoming accepted around the world, even among scientists and physicians. Professor John Graham was not far off when he predicted in 1976, "The drug has been frowned upon, officially banned, but the interest of the medical profession is slowly reviving. It is not impossible that a limited but respectable niche will be established for it in therapeutics by the end of the century" (*Marijuana and Health*, by J. D. P. Graham, Academic Press, 1976).

For regular updates on the "Science, Politics and Law" surrounding medical marijuana, subscribe to *O'Shaughnessy's - the Journal of Cannabis in Clinical Practice* (www.ccrmg.org/journal.html).

More Information on Medical Marijuana

Visit www.marijuanagrowing.com or any of these other web sites:

www.drugpolicy.org/marijuana/medical/

www.americanmarijuana.org

www.cannabislink.ca/

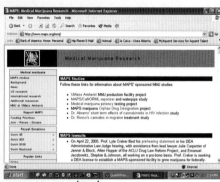

www.maps.org/mmj

www.crrh.org

www.medicalmarijuana.org

www.erowid.org

www.treatingyourself.com

www.thecompassionclub.org

www.wamm.org

Safety and Security!

Unfortunately we must include a security chapter in this book. You must keep your crop secure from police and thieves alike. Ironically, the police will cause you more problems than thieves!

Successful indoor growers are good citizens and keep a low profile. They keep their yard and home clean and in excellent repair. They always drive a street-legal car and there are no outstanding warrants on the drivers. Remember, an overdue traffic ticket turns into a warrant for the violator's arrest. Smart growers pay bills on time, are nice to neighbors, and do not throw noisy, wild, crazy parties.

Do not throw out any garbage that could prove that you grow. Cops pick through it like rats to find evidence to make a case against gardeners. Growers live by the motto "loose lips sink ships."

Never have seeds or grow products sent directly to your home.

Growers and tokers have been made into "the enemy" by the American government in the War on Drugs. It is the job of law enforcement to arrest the flower-growing enemy. To wage this war on US citizens, law enforcement wields an impressive arsenal, including draconian laws, misinformation and high-tech surveillance gizmos.

The cardinal rule of growing is: Never tell anybody about any garden.

Clandestine growing is as simple as the name implies. The name of the game is secrecy. Tell nobody and cause no suspicion. Countless underground growers have been harvesting crop after crop for decades in Drug War-torn America. These benevolent souls supply much of America today.

Stay away from other grow houses, wild parties, real criminals, etc. Always take a friend's car to the grow store and go seldom. Travel with others whenever possible. Your car is easy to trace and follow. Keep your consumption habits reasonable; don't show large cash income. Buy large assets, houses and cars, over time. Don't ever tell anybody you are growing or even joke about growing. Always have a job and a reason for your activities. Keep a low profile.

Keep your home and surrounding property in good repair. Make sure the house is painted, lawn mowed, and garbage picked up. Keep electrical use to a reasonable amount, and keep the air clean around the house. Have very few visitors, and keep to yourself. Have minimal conversations with neighbors.

Never trust anybody–friends, family–brother, sister, children, even your mother! In America, "Land of the Free," a grower can go to jail just for giving another grower advice! The Racketeer Influenced and Corrupt Organizations [Act]

A guard dog is one of the best deterrents against thieves.

(RICO) conspiracy laws were enacted to break up the Mafia. Today RICO laws are used against growers and non-growers alike. Under the law, a person that advises a grower to "water in the morning" is equally guilty of growing the marijuana garden, even if he never saw the garden. RICO laws tread on the very essence of the American Constitution.

The new Homeland Security Act further erodes personal rights of individuals.

Never visit or telephone other growers. If visiting another grow room, that grower can implicate you with circumstantial evidence, and you are considered as guilty as the grower!

DO NOT use booby traps, bear traps, firearms attached to tripwires, etc., to protect your crop

I know of people who use infrared systems that take pictures and/or start recording video when an object of particular size/temperature enters the vicinity.

Depending upon the country in which you live, law enforcement must first have a search warrant to use infrared or thermo imaging devices to secure a search warrant. But if they have a search warrant, such high-tech snooping is perfectly legal. If you want to take a look at what they see, rent heat-sensitive night-vision

glasses from your local military supply store, or take a photo of the outside of your grow operation with infrared film. You can also add a filter to your digital camera and convert the photographs with a few clicks of Photoshop to show heat signatures.

Law enforcement has sophisticated telephone bugging devices, super-sensitive directional microphones, infrared scopes, thermal imaging, etc. They can also subpoena telephone, Internet, and electrical company records. Intimidating cops coerce electric company employees to break the law and give them the records of unsuspecting consumers. Tracking telephone numbers, including location, is very easy. There has been more than one case where US law enforcement illegally acquired telephone records and placed illegal taps on garden store telephones. American police use telephone records to target grow houses. Always use pay telephones with an untraceable phone card or pay with coins. Lazy narcs also watch garden store parking lots and follow clients home.

Pay all bills and make all purchases with cash. Cash tells no tales and leaves no trails. Pay for mail order merchandise with a money order. Have the merchandise sent to a "safe" address.

If you want to take photos of your garden, use a digital camera. Using an old-fashioned film camera, you risk discovery when getting the film developed.

Growers who cultivate cannabis, including medical cannabis, should never show their grow show to anyone! Never tell anyone you are growing. Deny growing to everyone, always! You immediately change from a Weed Warrior to a helpless victim subject to extortion the instant anybody knows you are growing in the USA. When the cops arrest a "friend" that has seen your grow show, they can legally use deception and intimidation to trick your "friend" into squealing on you. Beware! Interrogations can last for months!

Law enforcement rewards jealous, hateful, and vindictive "friends," lovers, and enemies for implicating a grower under the RICO laws and Homeland Security Act. Hundreds of thousands of growers have had their lives ruined in a matter of moments on testimony from a vindictive "friend."

Cannabis indica plant with its characteristic broad leaf and short stature.

All electrical outlets, fuses, and connections must be grounded. Inspect electrical connections for signs of heat-blackened wires, melted connections, and smelly wiring.

Have a current fire extinguisher rated to put out wood, paper, grease, oil, and electrical fires.

When law enforcement has "evidence" of a growing operation, they look for more. In the USA they look at telephone, electric, and shipping records, for starters. A thermal imaging camera is most often used at this point. Occasionally they use dogs trained to sniff out marijuana. The information is used against the grower to obtain a search warrant. If there are plants discovered at the house, they continue to build the case against the grower by using anything the grower says. The police collect most of the information on the grower from the grower!

Surround your property with a bed of cedar shavings instead of bark chips in the flowerbeds. Cedar shavings disguise other odors. Use a carbon filter and an ozone generator to neutralize the marijuana fragrance. Have a ready reason for extra electrical consumption. Unload grow supplies a little bit at a time or from within a locked garage.

Remember the quote from Bart Simpson: "I didn't do it. Nobody saw me. You can't prove a thing!"

Absentee owners are the best landlords. Make sure home inspections are done before you move into the home and the rental agreement should allow for an advance notification of inspections. Put the telephone, electricity, garbage, etc., in a friend's name. Grow in a rented home. If you have bank accounts and stocks, own property such as a home, automobile, ATV, etc., in the USA, they are often forfeited if you are "suspected" of growing. You do not need to be convicted of any crime for your assets to be confiscated!

Curb noise and odors by sealing and insulating the grow room with "sound board." Similar to sheetrock, sound board muffles sounds well. Install rubber feet or grommets on fan feet.

Security Checklist:
- Regular schedule
- Simple lifestyle
- Very little contact with neighbors
- Always be pleasant
- Never open the grow room door for anybody!
- Electric bill should be about the same as the neighbors and previous tenants
- Garden and grounds should be tidy and similar to neighbors
- No light leaks whatsoever
- Use friend's car to visit grow store
- No noise–humming, fan on/off at night, etc.–is audible day and night
- No strange odors, including ozone smell

Build an extra room or box (allow for airflow) around ballasts to muffle noise. Place a thick pad under ballasts to absorb vibrations. In-line fans are much quieter and more efficient than squirrel-cage blowers. If light escapes from vents, give venting a 90-degree turn and paint the vent black where it turns. This will eliminate unsightly light leaks. Ozone-treated air should discharge through a roof vent or chimney to decrease ground-level odors. See "Ozone Generators" in Chapter Thirteen. Be careful when installing a ceiling vent or when venting out chimney. Light shining out the chimney and around roof vents looks very suspicious!

"All electric" homes are few and far between. Electrical use information from previous tenants might be available from the electric company. On the average, growers in the USA can use one 1000-watt lamp per bedroom. This means a two bedroom home can host 2000 watts, a three bedroom home 3000 watts, etc. Unhook the dryer and other appliances that draw much electricity. Turn the water heater down to 120 degrees, and take showers at the gym.

Stealing power from the electric company causes even more exposure than paying for it! The extra risk is insane, and it's wrong to steal!

For more information on Internet, personal, and grow show safety, check out the cannabis grow sites listed earlier in this chapter.

Now, relatively inexpensive (less than $10,000) thermal imaging devices are becoming more affordable for smaller police forces. Thermal imaging devices have been used legally to measure the heat signature escaping from structures. This invasive "evidence" is used with other "evidence" to secure a search warrant.

According to US police sources, the devices are legal only to find heat escaping from windows, vents, etc. Most often narcs use the cameras illegally to secure a search warrant. They slither around the neighborhood early in the morning or under the cloak of darkness to snap the hot shots. The law stipulates specific parameters for the camera, and the technology is relatively arcane. The "approved" imaging devices are able to record differences in heat levels outside of buildings. In the USA, it is illegal to search the inside of a structure for the "heat signature." However, today there are devices that can actually "see through walls" to provide an image based on the heat a person emits.

Avoid thermal imaging problems by turning grow lights on during the daytime. The daytime heat and light make accurate measurement of

Keep air conditioner water from draining outside. The water is packed with potent cannabis fragrance.

heat coming from vents and windows impossible. Thermal imaging cameras are rendered useless; the technology will not work during the daytime. Shield and insulate walls and windows from heat loss from lamps. Store ballasts in separate rooms, and channel the heat away from the grow room. Cool grow room air before exhausting outdoors. Air vented out underneath a structure is nice and cool before mixing with the outdoor environment.

Growers having problems with thermal imaging should contact NORML, 1001 Connecticut Ave. NW, suite 710, Washington, DC 20036, Tel: 1-202-483-7205. They have an excellent study on thermal imaging devices and legal aspects compiled by Carlos Ghigiotti. This information could save another lawyer a lot of time.

In June of 2001, the Supreme Court decided a case brought against Oregon resident Danny Kyllo. The decision determined that the use of a thermal imaging device constitutes an illegal search. High-tech thermal imaging devices often get as much press as police bullying tactics. Law enforcement officials can legally lie, cheat, and steal to acquire evidence against peaceful, plant-loving growers. Deception is one of their biggest weapons, and snitches their best allies. Law enforcement legally coerces terrified growers into squealing on their friends and family. The lesson here is simple; do not tell anybody, under any circumstances, that you are growing in the United States of America. Growers are arrested daily on "hearsay" evidence from an arrested informant. Stay away from the heat.

One last bit of simple security detail: grow efficiently! Growers in a Drug War-torn America should harvest 0.5 grams of dried bud every month for each watt of light in the flowering room. Growers that do not harvest this much are cheating themselves and need to master the basics of growing. Always grow fewer than 99 total plants in America. Federal laws require a five-year minimum sentence with no parole when convicted of growing 100-1000 plants.

Always keep a fire extinguisher nearby.

Put rubber feet on fans and blowers to shunt vibrations and noise.

A carbon filter will remove the fragrance of cannabis before expelling grow room air.

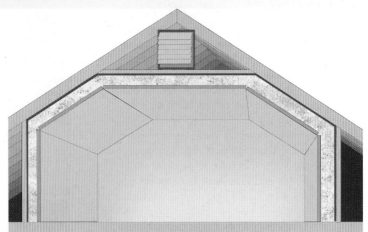

Heavy insulation will keep grow room temperature easier to control and will help keep the heat signature inside.

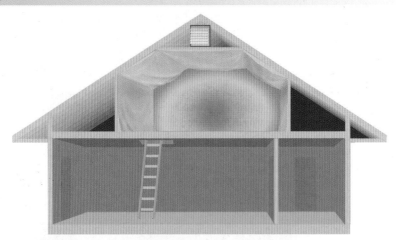

This grow room has been lined with a material to keep the heat signature inside. For more information check www.hysupply.nl.

I would like to exchange e-mail with every reviewer that reviews my works. If you make a review on any of the websites that we have on our list, (please add those that are not listed below) I would like to give you a personal answer to your concerns about your review.

www.amazon.com
www.amazon.ca
www.amazon.co.uk
www.amazon.co.jp
www.amazon.de

www.amazon.fr
www.barnesandnoble.com

Our goal in making the Bible, is to give you the absolute best information in the world.

We are looking for ways to make this book the best possible! Do you have anything to add? If so, please hit our website, www.marijuanagrowing.com, for instructions.

If we use your information and you leave your name (alias is OK) you will receive credit in our next edition!

- Jorge Cervantes

With a little care you too can have a beautiful crop of 'Power Plant' indoors or outdoors!

Introduction

The key to successful indoor cannabis cultivation is to understand how cannabis produces food and grows. Cannabis, whether cultivated indoors or out, has the same requirements for growth. It needs light, air, water, nutrients, a growing medium, and heat to manufacture food and to grow. Without any one of these essentials, growth stops and death soon results. Indoors, the light must be of the proper spectrum and intensity; air must be warm, arid, and rich in carbon dioxide; water must be abundant but not excessive, and the growing medium must contain the proper levels of nutrients for vigorous growth. When all these needs are met consistently at optimum levels, optimum growth is the result.

Cannabis is normally grown as an annual plant, completing its life cycle within one year.

A seed that is planted in the spring will grow strong and tall through the summer and flower in the fall, producing more seeds. The annual cycle starts all over again when the new seeds sprout the following year. In nature, cannabis goes through distinct growth stages. The text and photos below show each stage of growth.

Life Cycle of Cannabis

After 3-7 days of germination, plants enter the seedling growth stage which lasts about a month. During the first growth stage the seed germinates or sprouts, establishes a root system, and grows a stem and a few leaves.

Germination

During germination moisture, heat, and air activate hormones (cytokinins, gibberellins, and auxins) within the durable outer coating of the seed. Cytokinins signal more cells to form and gibberellins to increase cell size. The embryo

Strong healthy 'Chronic' seeds from Serious Seeds germinated after being soaked in water overnight.

Sprouted seed was placed between two pieces of a rockwool seed block and caused virtually no transplant shock.

Strong healthy seedling emerges from a Jiffy™ cube. The sprouted seed was carefully inserted into a hole with the taproot pointing down.

Sweet Purple (Paradise) seedling shows perfect symmetrical growth. Leaflets will increase from three to as many as eleven during vegetative growth.

expands, nourished by a supply of stored food within the seed. Soon, the seed's coating splits, a rootlet grows downward, and a sprout with seed leaves pushes upwards in search of light.

Seedling Growth

The single root from the seed grows down and branches out, similar to the way the stem branches up and out above ground. Tiny rootlets draw in water and nutrients (chemical substances needed for life). Roots also serve to anchor a plant in the growing medium. Seedling should receive 16-18 hours of light to maintain strong healthy growth.

Vegetative Growth

Vegetative growth is maintained by giving plants 16-24 hours of light every day. As the plant matures, the roots take on specialized functions. The center and old, mature portions contain a water transport system and may also store food. The tips of the roots produce elongating cells that continue to push farther and farther into the soil in search of more water and food. The single-celled root hairs are the parts of the root that actually absorb water and nutrients. Without water, frail root hairs will dry

This 'Marley's Collie' (Sensi Seeds) is planted in a 5-gallon (19L) bucket and was grown in a greenhouse.

MIDDLE: Strong healthy roots are vibrant white. Feeder roots are fuzzy white. This rooted clone is ready to transplant.

LEFT: Male pre-flowers (a small nub above the fourth internode) develop on plants after about four weeks of vegetative growth.

This close-up shows female pre-flowers, white pistils growing from newly formed green calyx. Female pre-flowers usually sprout after male pre-flowers.

This large mother plant is growing in a 10-gallon (38 L) container. She can provide more than a hundred clones every month.

up and die. They are very delicate and are easily damaged by light, air, and klutzy hands if moved or exposed. Extreme care must be exercised during transplanting.

Like the roots, the stem grows through elongation, also producing new buds along the stem. The central or terminal bud carries growth upward; side or lateral buds turn into branches or leaves. The stem functions by transmitting water and nutrients from the delicate root hairs to the growing buds, leaves, and flowers. Sugars and starches manufactured in the leaves are distributed through the plant via the stem. This fluid flow takes place near the surface of the stem. If the stem is bound too tightly by string or other tie-downs, it will cut the flow of life-giving fluids, thereby strangling and killing the plant. The stem also supports the plant with stiff cellulose, located within the inner walls. Outdoors, rain and wind push a plant around, causing much stiff cellulose production to keep the plant supported upright. Indoors, with no natural wind or rain present, stiff cellulose production is minimal, so plants develop weak stems and may need to be staked up, especially during flowering.

Once the leaves expand, they start to manufacture food (carbohydrates). Chlorophyll (the substance that gives plants their green color) converts carbon dioxide (CO_2) from the air, water, and light energy into carbohydrates and oxygen. This process is called photosynthesis. It requires water drawn up from the roots, through the stem, into the leaves where it encounters carbon dioxide. Tiny breathing pores called stomata are located on the underside of the leaf and funnel CO_2 into contact with the water. In order for photosynthesis to occur, the leaf's interior tissue must be kept moist. The stomata open and close to regulate the flow of moisture, preventing dehydration. Marijuana leaves are also protected from drying out by an outer skin. The stomata also permit the outflow of water vapor and waste oxygen. The stomata are very important to the plant's well being and must be kept clean to promote vigorous growth.

Dirty, clogged stomata would breathe about as well as you would with a sack over your head!

Pre-Flowering

Cannabis grown from seed dawns pre-flowers after the fourth week of vegetative growth. They generally appear between the fourth and sixth node from the bottom of the plant. Cannabis plants are normally either all male or all female. Each sex has its own distinct flowers. Pre-flowers will be either male or female. Growers remove and destroy the males (or use them for breeding stock) because they have low levels of cannabinoids (THC, CBD, CBN, etc.). Female plants are cultivated for their high cannabinoid content.

Once the branch tip has been cut, bottom leaves are trimmed off before planting the clone, an exact replica of the mother plant.

Mother Plants

Growers select strong, healthy, potent mother plants they know are female. Mothers are given 18-24 hours of light daily so they stay in the vegetative growth stage. Growers cut branch tips from the mother plants and root them. The rooted cuttings are called "clones." Cultivating several strong, healthy mother plants is the key to having a consistent supply of all-female clones.

Clones grow a strong root system in 14-21 days under fluorescent light. Once rooted, they spend from 7-30 days in vegetative growth.

Cloning

Branch tips are cut and rooted to form clones. Clones take 10-20 days to grow a strong healthy root system. Clones are given 18-24 hours of

`Haze Heaven' female is starting to flower heavily. Branch internodes are shorter and white female pistils grow from calyxes.

Male plants flower before females. Males show signs of flowering after receiving a week or more of 12/12 day/night photoperiod.

Many receptive female pistils on this 'Hash Plant' await pollination from male pollen. Left unfertilized, female plants continue to produce more and more cannabinoids.

`Purple #1`

light so they stay in the vegetative growth stage. Once the root system is established, clones are transplanted into larger containers. Now they are ready to grow for 1-4 weeks in the vegetative growth stage before being induced to flower.

Flowering

Cannabis flowers outdoors in the fall when days become shorter and plants are signaled that the annual life cycle is coming to an end. At flowering, plant functions change. Leafy growth slows, and flowers start to form. Flowering is triggered in most commercial varieties of cannabis by 12 hours of darkness and 12 hours of light every 24 hours. Plants that developed in tropical regions often start flowering under more light and less darkness. Flowers form during the last stage of growth. Left

This pollinated female is packed with seeds. Once fertilized with male pollen, females put the bulk of their energy into producing strong, healthy seeds.

unpollinated, female flowers develop without seeds, "sinsemilla." When fertilized with male pollen, female flower buds develop seeds.

Unpollinated, female cannabis flowers continue to swell and produce more resin while waiting for male pollen to successfully complete their life cycle. After weeks of heavy flower and cannabinoid-laden resin production, THC production peaks out in the unfertilized, frustrated sinsemilla!

Cannabis has both male and female plants. When both male and female flowers are in bloom, pollen from the male flower lands on the female flower, thereby fertilizing it. The male dies after producing and shedding all his pollen. Seeds form and grow within the female flowers. As the seeds are maturing, the female plant slowly dies. The mature seeds then fall to the ground and germinate naturally or are collected for planting next spring.

Grow out as many seedlings as possible to select the best mothers.

The main bud on this 'Thai' plant growing under the tropical sun appears to be much denser that it actually is.

Leaf from the strain 'Thaitanic' demonstrates the classic C. sativa characteristics–long, thin blades or fingers.

Cannabis Strains

Technically and legally, all cannabis, whether rope or dope, is classified as *Cannabis sativa*. Regardless of origin, all cannabis is considered *Cannabis sativa* (*C. sativa*) under international law. However, according to *Hemp Diseases and Pests,* Dr. J. M. McPartland, R. C. Clarke, and D. P. Watson, CAB International, *Cannabis sativa* can be further classified as: *Cannabis sativa* (= *C. sativa* var. *sativa*), *Cannabis indica* (= *C. sativa* var. *indica*), *Cannabis ruderalis* (= *C. sativa* var. *spondanea*), *Cannabis afghanica* (= *C. sativa* var. *afghanica*). Each has distinct growth patterns, look, smell, taste, etc.

Cannabis Sativa

Cannabis sativa (= *C. sativa* var. *sativa*), originated predominately in Asia, the Americas, and Africa. Each area of origin has specific characteristics, but all have the following general traits: tall, leggy stature with spacious internodal length, a large sprawling root system, large narrow-bladed leaves, and somewhat sparse flowers when grown indoors under lights. *Sativas* bloom several weeks to months later than *indica* strains. While good producers outdoors, often growing to 15 feet (4.5 m) or more, indoors pure *sativa* strains often grow too tall too fast–some up to ten feet in three months–to be practical for grow room cultivation. An HID bulb is unable to efficiently illuminate tall plants, and the yield-per-watt-of-light or yield-per-square-foot-of-space is very low. Mexican, Columbian, Thai, and Jamaican strains can be very potent, with a high THC to CBD ratio that produces a soaring, energetic, "speedy" high. But potency can also be minimal, with low levels of THC. Most exported Columbian, Mexican, Thai, and Jamaican marijuana is poorly treated throughout life and abused when dried and packed. This abuse causes more rapid degradation of THC. Consequently, seeds from fair smoke are often more potent than the parent.

Central African *sativas,* including the THC-potent 'Congolese', grow similarly to Columbian strains, with a tall leggy stature, often growing more than 15 feet (4.5 meters) tall with loosely packed buds.

South Africa has major seaports. Sailors brought *Cannabis sativa* from many different places and planted it in South Africa. Consequently, potency of South African weed can be very high or very low, and can grow short, tall, leggy, bushy, etc. The famous 'Durban Poison' yields potent, pale-green, early buds and is the best-known South African strain.

Asian *sativas,* including Thai, Vietnamese, Laotian, Cambodian, and Nepalese, have diverse growth characteristics and vary significantly in potency. While Thai and other *sativas* from the area are often super THC-potent, they are some of the most difficult to grow indoors and the slowest to mature. Thai strains produce very light, wispy buds after flowering for about four months on plants with large, sprawling branches. Thai, Vietnamese, Cambodian, and Laotian *sativas* are more prone to grow into hermaphroditic adults.

Nepalese *sativas* can grow oversized leaves on tall leggy plants that produce sparse, late-blooming buds, but other strains from this region develop into short, compact plants that bloom earlier. Tetrahydrocannabinol (THC) production and potency is often quite high, but can also be second-rate.

Hemp strains are all considered to be *Cannabis sativa.* Hemp, affectionately referred to as "rope," is *Cannabis sativa* grown for fiber content. Hemp is often seeded and contains very, very low levels of THC.

This leaf from an industrial hemp plant came from the French entity Chanvre & Co. Industrial "no high" cannabis will pollinate drug cannabis.

Cannabis Indica

Cannabis indica (= *C. sativa* var. *indica*) originated in Pakistan and India. *Indica* is prized by indoor growers and breeders for its squat, bushy growth; condensed root system; stout stems; broad leaves; and dense, THC-laden, fat heavy flowers. Foliage is very dark green, and in some strains, leaves around buds turn reddish to purple. Short, whitish pistils turn reddish to purplish in hue. A few *indicas* from this part of the world have narrower leaves, long white pistils, and pale green foliage. *Indica* strains generally contain a higher ratio of CBD to THC, which causes an effect often described as a heavy, incapacitating "sit-on-your-head" stone. Potency of the "high" ranges from fair to stupefying. Some *indicas* have a distinctive odor similar to that of a skunk or cat urine, while others smell sweet and exotic. Heavily resin-laden plants tend to be the most fungus- and pest-resistant. Few *indicas* with heavy, dense, compact buds are resistant to gray (bud) mold.

Cannabis indica *plant.*

Cannabis Ruderalis

Cannabis ruderalis (= C. sativa var. spon-danea) was first brought to Amsterdam from Central Europe in the early1980s by the Seed Bank to enhance their breeding program. Very similar, if not the same "*ruderalis*" plants grow from Minnesota north through Manitoba and Saskatchewan, Canada. C. ruderalis is a short, weedy, scrubby plant containing very, very little THC, but it starts the flowering cycle after a few weeks growth. Photoperiod does not induce flowering in C. ruderalis. Sometimes confused with more potent indicas, pure C. ruderalis is true ditch weed. It yields a headache rather than a high! Today a few breeders have incorpo-rated the early flowering C. ruderalis genes with other early blooming C. sativa, C. indica, and C. afghanica.

Cannabis indica *leaf has broader blades than* C. sativa *leaves, but not as broad as* C. afghanica.

'Lowryder' is one of the few C. ruderalis crosses that is auto-flowering and THC-potent.

Cannabis Afghanica

Cannabis afghanica (= C. sativa var. afghanica) originated near present day Afghanistan. It is quite short, seldom reaching six feet, with distinctive, broad, dark-green leaflets and leaves. Dense branching and short internodes, most often with long leaf stems (petioles), dominate the profile of C. afghanica. The most common examples of pure C. afghanica include the many different hash plants and Afghani strains. C. afghanica is cultivated exclusively for drugs with much of the resin being made into hashish. It is known for the high cannabinoid content. Many growers and breeders do not distinguish C. afghanica from C. indica, lumping them both into the C. indica category.

'Hash Plant', of which there are many, is one of the classic C. afghanica strains.

One of the first Seed Bank catalogs from 1987 shows a C. ruderalis plant alongside the highway in Hungary. Many breeders mistakenly hailed this plant as the "Holy Grail" of cannabis.

C. afghanica has very wide and distinctive leaflets and leaves.

Close-up of 'Power Plant' seeds.

Close-up of 'Eclipse' seeds.

'Kali Mist' seeds are spotted and mottled.

Seeds

Explosive growth of seed breeders and legal seed sales in the Netherlands, the United Kingdom, Canada, France, Switzerland, Spain, etc., has given way to more strains of cannabis than ever before. Most popular strains of cannabis are a combination of two or more of the following: *C. sativa, C. indica, C. ruderalis,* and *C. afghanica.* But there are also many seeds with the genes from just one of the above. These strains of cannabis are bred to grow best indoors. Others grow best in greenhouses, and still others outdoors in specific climates. See Chapter Sixteen, "Breeding," for information about hybrid seeds including F1, F2, F3, etc., hybrids.

A seed contains all the genetic characteristics of a plant. Seeds are the result of sexual propagation and contain genes from each parent, male and female. Some plants, known as hermaphrodites, bear both male and female flowers on the same plant. The genes within a seed dictate a plant's size; disease and pest resistance; root, stem, leaf, and flower production; cannabinoid levels; and many other traits. The genetic makeup of a seed is the single most important factor dictating how well a plant will grow under artificial light or natural sunlight and the levels of cannabinoids it will produce.

Strong, healthy parents and proper care yield strong seeds that germinate well. Strong seeds produce healthy plants and heavy harvests. Seeds stored too long will germinate slowly and have a high rate of failure. Vigorous seeds initiate growth within seven days or sooner. Seeds that take longer than a month to germinate could always be slow and produce less. However, some seeds take longer to germinate even under the best conditions.

The cask, or outer protective shell, on some seeds never properly seals, which allows moisture and air to penetrate. It also

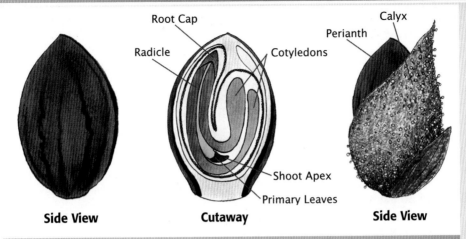

Root Cap

Radicle

Cotyledons

Perianth

Calyx

Shoot Apex

Primary Leaves

Side View   **Cutaway**   **Side View**

The cutaway drawing in the center shows how the seed will develop into different plant parts.

causes hormone concentrations to dissipate and make seeds less viable. Permeable seeds signal diseases and pests to move in. Such seeds are immature, white, fragile, and crush easily with slight pressure between finger and thumb. These are weak seeds and do not have enough strength to grow well.

Typically, a grower who acquires a bag of ten quality seeds from a reputable seed company germinates them all at once. Once germinated, the seeds are carefully planted and grown to adulthood. By and large, of the ten seeds, some will be male, some will be weak and grow poorly, and two or three seeds will grow into strong, super females. Of these "super" females, one will be more robust and potent than her siblings. This super female is selected to be the mother of countless super clones.

A simple picture of a seed reveals an embryo containing the genes and a supply of food wrapped in a protective outer coating. Mature seeds that are hard, beige to dark brown, and spotted or mottled have the highest germination rate. Soft, pale, or green seeds are usually immature and should be avoided. Immature seeds germinate poorly and often produce sickly plants. Fresh, dry, mature seeds less than a year old sprout quickly and grow robust plants.

Germination

Cannabis seeds need only water, heat, and air to germinate. They do not need extra hormones to germinate. Seeds sprout without light in a wide range of temperatures. Properly nurtured seeds germinate in two to seven days, in temperatures from 70-90°F (21-32°C). Temperatures above 90°F (32°C)

Seeds in this seeded female swell and break open the seed bract.

Timeline for germinating seeds

At 55-72 hours
Water is absorbed
Root tip (radicle) is visible

At 10-14 days
First roots become visible

At 21-30 days
At least half of seeds are rooted by day 21. Seeds not rooted by day 30 will probably grow slowly.

Once seeds are rooted, cell growth accelerates; stem, foliage, and roots develop quickly. Seedlings develop into full vegetative growth within four to six weeks of germination.

impair germination. At germination, the outside protective shell of the seed splits, and a tiny, white sprout (radicle) pops out. This sprout is the root or taproot. Cotyledon, or seed leaves, emerge from within the shell as they push upward in search of light.

Seeds are prompted to germinate by:
Water
Temperature
Air (oxygen)

Water
Soaking seeds in water allows moisture to penetrate the protective seed shell within minutes. Once inside, moisture continues to wick in to activate the dormant hormones. In a few days, hormones activate and send enough hormone signals to produce a radicle. The radicle emerges upward to bring a new plant into the world. Once a seed is moist, it must receive a constant flow of

moisture to carry nutrients, hormones, and water so that it can carry on life processes. If germinated seeds are allowed to suffer moisture stress now seedling growth will be stunted.

Temperature
Cannabis seeds grow best at 78°F (25°C). Low temperatures delay germination. High temperatures upset seed chemistry causing poor germination.
Seeds germinate best under the native conditions where they were grown.
Once germinated, move seedlings to a slightly cooler growing area, and increase light levels. Avoid high temperatures and low light levels, which cause lanky growth.

Air (oxygen)
Seeds need air to germinate. Moist, soggy growing mediums will cut off oxygen supplies and the seed will literally drown. Seeds germinate poorly when planted too deeply. Tender seedlings do not have sufficient stored energy to drive through deep layers of soil when sprouting. Sew seeds twice as deep as the width of the seed. A 0.125-inch (3 mm) seed should be planted 0.25-inch (6 mm) deep.
Household water contains enough dissolved solids (food) to nourish seeds through their first few weeks of life. Although seeds need only 30-50 ppm of nitrates before they germinate, any more will disrupt internal chemistry. Some growers choose to use distilled water that contains practically no dissolved solids to germinate seeds. In fact, a high concentration of dissolved solids (salts) in the water will actually pull moisture out of the seed!
Start feeding two to four weeks after seedlings have sprouted. Some growers wait until leaves yellow to begin feeding. Use a mild quarter-strength solution. If yellowing persists, give seedlings a little more fertilizer.

Some seeds have a very hard outer shell, testa, and must be scarified to allow water to penetrate. To scarify, line a matchbox with a piece of fine-grain sandpaper or emery board. Put the seeds in the matchbox and shake for about 30 seconds. Remove the seeds, and make sure they have been scuffed a bit. Just a little scuffing will allow water to enter and set germination in motion.

To scarify seeds, place a small emery board inside a matchbox along with seeds.

Two Popular Germination Techniques:
One: Pre-soaking in water

Soak seeds overnight in a glass of water. Make sure seeds get good and wet so growth is activated. Do not let seeds soak more than 24 hours, or they might get too wet, suffer oxygen deprivation, and rot. Once soaked, seeds are ready to be placed between moist paper towels to sprout or be planted in a root cube or fine, light soilless mix.

Close the match box with the seeds and emery board inside.

In a warm location (70-90°F, [21-32°C]), place seeds in a moist paper towel or cheesecloth, making sure they are in darkness. Set the moist cloth or paper towel in a vertical position (so tap root grows down) on a grate (for drainage) on a dinner plate.

Water the cloth daily, and keep it moist. Let excess water drain away freely. The cloth will retain enough moisture to germinate the seed in a few days. The seed contains an adequate food supply for germination. Prevent fungal attacks by watering with a mild two-percent bleach or fungicide solution. Once seeds have sprouted and the white sprout is visible, carefully pick up the fragile sprouts (with tweezers) and plant them. Take care not to expose the tender rootlet to prolonged intense light or air. Cover the germinated seed with 0.25–0.5-inch (1-2 cm) of fine planting medium with the white root tip pointing down.

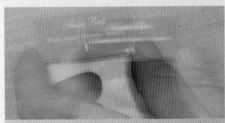

Shake the box for about 30 seconds to rough up and scuff the seeds, so water can penetrate the outer shell.

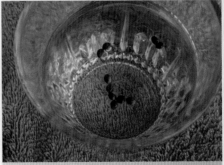

Soak seeds in water overnight to germinate before planting.

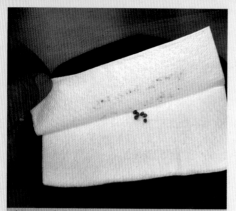

Place seeds between leaves of a paper towel on a plate to germinate.

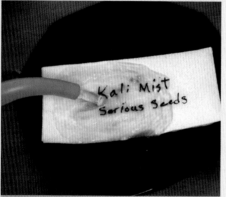

Add water to moisten the paper towel. Tip plate to drain off excess moisture.

Jiffy pellets expand when water is added. They make excellent pop-up pots to grow seedlings. They are also very easy to transplant.

Two: Direct seed

One of the problems with rockwool can be that the seeds heave out before germinating. This is why it is best to germinate seeds before putting them into the rockwool substrate.

Once seeds have sprouted and the white sprout is visible, carefully pick up the fragile sprouts (with tweezers) and plant them in a pre-drilled hole in the rockwool with the white root tip pointing down. Take care not to expose the tender rootlet to prolonged intense light or air. Cover the germinated seed with one-quarter to one-half inch of moist rockwool. Keep the rockwool evenly moist. Once the taproot sprouts, small fuzzy feeder roots will grow in 12-14 days.

Water penetrates the outer protective shell, continues to wick in, and activates dormant hormones that induce germination. Once a seed receives moisture, there must be a constant stream of moisture to transport nutrients, hormones, and water to carry on life processes. Letting germinated seed suffer moisture stress now will stunt or stop seedling growth. The black tip of the root tells me this is what has happened.

Soggy growing mediums cut oxygen supplies and cause seeds to drown. Planting seeds too deeply causes poor germination. Seedlings do not have enough stored energy to force through too much soil before

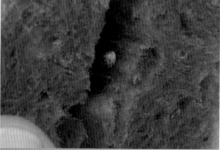

Seeds set inside rockwool blocks often heave up and out. Germinate seeds before planting to avoid this common problem.

sprouting. Plant seeds twice as deep as the width of the seed. eighth-inch (4 mm) seed one-quarter (8 mm) inch deep.

Seeds do not need any extra hormones to germinate. Average household water contains enough dissolved solids to feed seeds through their first few weeks of growth. Supplemental nutrients will disrupt internal chemistry. Some growers prefer to use distilled water which contains virtually no dissolved solids to germinate seeds.

Sow (direct seed) or move the sprout into a shallow planter, small seed pot, peat pellet, or rooting cube. Keep the planting medium evenly moist. Use a spoon to contain the root ball when transplanting from a shallow planter. Peat pellets or root cubes may be transplanted in two to three weeks or when the roots show through the sides. Feed with a dilute, quarter-strength fertilizer solution.

Construct a moisture tent over the seedling container to help retain even grow-medium moisture. To build, place a baggie or piece of cellophane over the seeded soil. The cover will keep the humidity and temperature elevated. Seeds usually need only one initial watering when under a humidity tent. Remove the cover as soon as the first sprout appears aboveground. Leaving the tent on after seeds sprout through soil will lead to damping-off and other problems.

Place planted seeds under an HID lamp to add dry heat while germinating. The heat dries soil, which requires more frequent watering. Place a heat pad or soil heating cables below growing medium to expedite germination. Marijuana seeds germinate and sprout quickest when the soil temperature is

This outdoor grower made a seedbed from fine potting soil. He has started hundreds of seeds in this seedbed.

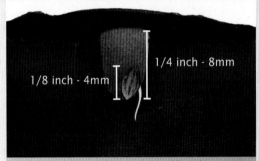

1/4 inch - 8mm

1/8 inch - 4mm

Plant seeds twice as deep as the seed is wide.

between 78-80°F (24-27.5°C) and the air temperature is 72-74°F (22-23°C). But stems will stretch between internodes if temperatures exceed 85°F (29°C) for long.

Over-watering and under-watering are the biggest obstacles most growers face when germinating seeds and growing seedlings. Keep the soil uniformly moist, not waterlogged. Do not let the growing medium surface dry for long. Keep it evenly moist. Setting root cubes or planting flats up on a grate allows good drainage. A shallow flat or planter with a heat pad underneath may require daily watering, while a deep, one-gallon pot will need watering every three days or more. A properly watered flat of rockwool cubes needs water every three to five days when sprouting seeds. When the surface is dry (0.25-inch [7 mm] deep) it is time to water. Remember, there are few roots to absorb the water early in life, and they are very delicate.

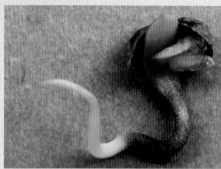

This germinated seed was allowed to dry out for a little more than an hour. Notice how the tip of the root has shriveled. This seemingly small oversight caused the resulting plant to have a very slow start in life.

Grow More Females from Seed

Environmental factors start influencing sex the moment the seedling has three pairs of true leaves (not counting cotyledons). Environmental factors that influence sex determination of cannabis include but are not limited to:

Increasing the level of nitrogen makes more female plants. Lower the nitrogen level to create more male plants. Increase the level of potassium to increase male tendencies; lowering the potassium level encourages female plants. A higher nitrogen level and a lower potassium level for the first two weeks increases females.

Low temperatures increase the number of female plants. Warm temperatures make more male plants.

High humidity increases the number of female plants. Low humidity increases male plants.

Low growing-medium moisture increases males.

More blue light increases the number of female plants. More red light increases male tendencies.

Fewer hours of daylight (e.g. 14 hours) increases the number of females. Longer days (e.g. 18 hours) make more male plants.

Stress: any environmental stress tends to yield more male plants when growing from seed.

Henk, owner of Dutch Passion Seeds, http://www.dutch-passion.nl, was kind enough to allow us to adapt this information from his archives.

See Chapter Sixteen, "Breeding," for information on producing feminized seeds.

Seedlings

When a seed sprouts, the white taproot emerges. Soon afterward, the cotyledon, also known as seed or seedling leaf, appears. The seed leaves spread out as the stem elongates. Within a few days, the first true leaves appear, and the little plant is now officially a seedling. This growth stage lasts for three to six weeks. During seedling growth, a root system grows rapidly while green aboveground growth is slow. Water and heat are critical at this point of development. The new, fragile root system is very small and requires a small but constant supply of water and warmth. Too much water will drown roots, often leading to root rot and damping-off. Lack of water will cause the infant root system to dry up. As the seedlings mature, some will grow faster, stronger, and appear healthy in general. A little heat now will help nurture small seedlings to a strong start. Other seeds will sprout slowly and be weak and leggy. Cull sickly, weak plants, and focus attention on the remaining strong survivors. Seedlings should be big enough to thin out by the third to fifth week of growth. Thinning out seedlings is very difficult for growers who pay $300 dollars for a few seeds!

Seedlings need at least 16 hours of light daily. They require less intense light now and grow well under fluorescent tubes for the first two to three weeks. Compact fluorescent and HID light can also be used. The compact fluorescent should be 12-18 inches (30-45 cm) and the HID 3-4 feet (90-120 cm) above seedlings for best growth.

The seedling stage is over when rapid foliage growth starts. Rapid growth above ground is the beginning of the vegetative growth stage. Plants need more room to grow; transplanting into a larger container hastens development.

Strong, healthy seedlings like this 'White Widow' are the key to a heavy harvest.

Seedlings emerging from peat pots develop seed (cotyledon) leaves before growing their first set of "true leaves."

'Blue Satellite' seedlings are flourishing in this Styrofoam cup. They were transplanted the day the photo was taken.

Small 'Thaitanic' is at the end of the seedling stage of growth.

Deep plugs grow a deeper root system. This seedling was transplanted outdoors and grew very well.

Ordering Seeds

Ordering seeds via a magazine ad or the Internet is commonplace. Many reputable companies advertise. You are most secure to order from a company you can contact by telephone. Speak to a qualified representative who will provide good answers to your questions. Companies with an e-mail address and web site are usually okay to order from, but make sure they answer your e-mails promptly. Do not be afraid to call several companies and ask them specific questions about the strains they sell. If you live in a country where seeds are illegal, call from a public telephone and use a calling card. Do not call the seed company from a telephone located at a grow house.

Communicating via e-mail can leave a trail to the computer if you do not use a proxy server. Learn more about proxy servers at: http://www.webopedia.com/TERM/p/proxy_server.html

Some seed companies produce their own seed and sell it directly to the public. Most seed producers sell their seed to a reseller such as the seed companies that can be found at www.seedbankupdate.com.

Check www.marijuanagrowing.com to find more information about growing specific strains. Once you decide on what to order and have communicated with the company, you are ready to place your order. Do not use a credit card if security is a concern. Companies normally bill your credit card discreetly and do not charge your credit card with "Cannabis Seeds." However, if you decide to use a credit card, discuss the matter with the retailer. You may decide to use an international money order. Cash tells no tales and leaves no trails. Wrap the cash in carbon paper so that it cannot be seen. Allow a reasonable amount of time, two to four weeks, for the order to arrive. Do not forget that sometimes packages are lost, misplaced, and mislabeled.

You may want to set up a "safe address" such as a PO Box under an assumed name. Hit Green Man's page, http://www.seedbankupdate.com. He regularly updates the page and lists seed companies' performance levels.

If US Customs seizes your order of seeds, they will send you a note informing you of that fact. We have never heard a report of a law enforcement official showing up at your door.

Buy ten seeds, and germinate half of them at once. Then, when and if they germinate, start the rest of the seeds.

Boy Ramsahai, owner of High Quality Seeds and Black Label Seeds, shows off his high-tech refrigerator for seed storage. The refrigerator keeps humidity levels below five percent to ensure safe long-term storage.

Storing Seeds

Store seeds in a cool, dark, dry place. Make sure to label containers! Some seeds will remain viable for five years or longer when stored properly. When 50 percent of the stored seeds do not germinate, the average storage life is over. But seeds a year old or older often take longer to sprout and have a lower rate of germination.

Seed hormones–ABA, cytokinins, and gibberellins–are primed to respond to moisture, which is the first signal to germinate. Prevent moisture from signaling seeds to germinate by keeping them dry. Small amounts of moisture in the form of condensation can give seeds a false start on germination and cause them to expend all their stored energy. Avoid moisture levels above five percent to ensure viable seed. Moisture levels above five percent will cause germination levels to decrease rapidly. Seal seed in an airtight container, and place silicon crystal packages in the container to absorb excess moisture.

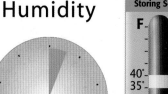

Humidity

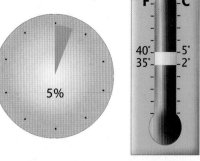

5%

Seeds store for a long time when humidity is less than 5 percent and temperature is 35-40° F (2-5° C).

Cannabis seeds need enough moisture to initiate this process within 48 hours.

Hit our site, www.marijuanagrowing.com for updated information about seeds.

Dry seeds are temperature-sensitive; they can be disinfected with a short application of heat. Low temperatures slow internal seed activity so are best for preserving seeds. You can use super-cold liquid nitrogen and cryogenics to store seeds for a long time.

Air, once it enters the outer seed shell, signals seeds to germinate. Viable seeds are preserved longer when vacuum-packed to remove all oxygen.

Seeds with a thin, outer protective shell never truly go dormant, because moisture and air are always present within. This moisture and air cause hormone levels to slowly dissipate. Such seeds do not store well for a long time.

Seed Pests

Seed pests become active when there is more than ten percent moisture content. When the growing medium contains more than fifteen percent moisture, fungi become active. Excess fertilizer slows seedling growth and promotes fungus attacks.

Temperatures from 68-85°F (20-30°C) promote Pythium (damping-off) and rhixoctonia fungi. Cannabis seeds grow best at 78°F (25°C). Most fungi reproduce fastest in a temperature range of 68-86°F (20-30°C).

Keep a wary eye on problems. Nutrient overdose burns leaf tips and fringes, which can look like damping-off to the untrained eye. Do not fertilize. Applying a fungicide now will make the problem worse.

Rooms like this supply a B.C. seed breeder with female breeding stock.

A lovely 'Hempstar' bud.

`Northern Lights #5 x Haze.'

Strong, healthy vegetative growth is the key to a heavy harvest.

Introduction

The seedling growth stage lasts for about two to three weeks after seeds have germinated. Once a strong root system is estab-

This seedling is in the early stages of vegetative growth.

This 'Euphoria' female has been in the vegetative growth stage for more than two months.

lished and foliage growth increases rapidly, seedlings enter the vegetative growth stage. When chlorophyll production is full speed ahead, a vegetative plant will produce as much green, leafy foliage as it is genetically possible to manufacture as long as light, CO_2, nutrients, and water are not limited. Properly maintained, marijuana will grow from one-half to two inches per day. A plant stunted now could take weeks to resume normal growth. A strong, unrestricted root system is essential to supply much needed water and nutrients. Unrestricted vegetative growth is the key to a healthy harvest. A plant's nutrient and water intake changes during vegetative growth. Transpiration is carried on at a more rapid rate, requiring more water. High levels of nitrogen are needed; potassium, phosphorus, calcium, magnesium, sulfur, and trace elements are used at much faster rates. The larger a plant gets and the bigger the root system, the faster the soil will dry out. The key to strong vegetative growth and a heavy harvest is supplying roots and plants with the perfect environment.

Vegetative growth is maintained with 16 or more hours of light. I used to believe a point of diminishing returns was reached after 18 hours of light, but further research shows that vegetative plants grow faster under 24 hours of light. Marijuana will continue vegetative growth a year or longer (theoretically forever), as long as an 18-hour photoperiod is maintained.

Cannabis is photoperiodic-reactive; flowering can be controlled with the light and dark cycle. This allows indoor horticulturists to control vegetative and flowering growth. Once a plant's sex is determined, it can become a mother, clone, or breeding male, and can be harvested or even rejuvenated.

Note: Plants show early male or female "pre-flowers" about the fourth week of vegetative growth. See "Pre-flowering" in Chapter Four and the sections here on pre-flowering male and female.

Cloning, transplanting, pruning, and bending are all initiated when plants are in the vegetative growth stage.

Clones and Cloning

Marijuana can be reproduced (propagated) sexually or asexually. Seeds are the product of sexual propagation; cuttings or clones are the result of asexual or vegetative propagation. In its simplest form, taking a cutting or clone involves cutting a growing branch tip and rooting it. Technically, cloning is taking one cell of a plant and promoting its growth into a plant. Marijuana growers commonly refer to a clone as meaning a branch of a cannabis plant that has been cut off and rooted.

Cloning reduces the time it takes for a crop to mature. Productive growers have two rooms, a vegetative/cloning room, about a quarter the size of a second room used for flowering. Smaller vegetative plants take up less space than older flowering plants. For example, a 250- or 400-watt metal halide could easily illuminate vegetative plants and clones that would fill a flowering room lit by three 600-watt HP sodiums. If the halide is turned off, fluorescent and compact fluorescent lamps are more economical and work well to root clones.

Combine eight-week flowering/harvest cycles with continuous cloning to form a perpetual harvest. One easy-to-implement scenario is to take two clones every four days, and harvest one ripe female every other day. Every time a plant is harvested, one or two rooted clones are moved from a constantly supplied vegetative room into the flowering room. This regimen gives a grower 30 flowering clones that are on a 91-day schedule. It takes 91 days from the time a clone is cut from the mother plant until the day it is harvested. Using this schedule, a grower would have 30 clones, 10 vegetative plants, and 30 flowering plants growing at all times. See chart next page.

Swiss retailers sold clones over-the-counter until the law changed in 2001. Now, Swiss growers have gone underground.

Clone production room in the basement of a Swiss retail store.

Growth Stage	Time	Number of plants
Clone	3 weeks	30
Vegetative	2 weeks	10
Flower	8 weeks	30
	Total	70

A sea of clones share all genetic characteristics. They will all grow up to look like their mothers.

Two 'Queen Mother' plants will soon bear many, many clones.

Induce clones to flower when they are four to twelve inches tall to make most efficient use of HID light. Artificial light diminishes to the square of the distance, which means that *foliage four feet away from the bulb receives one fourteenth as much light as if it were one foot away!* Foliage that is shaded or receives less light grows slowly and looks spindly.

Short crops of clones in small containers are much easier to move and maintain than big plants in big containers. Short clones are also easy and efficient to grow in greenhouses and outdoors.

Well-illuminated, strong clones grow fast and have less chance of being affected by pests and diseases. Fast-growing clones develop more quickly than spider mites can reproduce. By the time a spider mite infestation is noticed and sprayed, the plants are a few weeks from harvest. Clones are also easy to submerge in a miticide when small.

Experiments with clones are consistent and easy to control. Genetically identical clones respond the same to different stimuli, such as fertilizer, light, bending, etc. After experimenting on several crops of clones from the same mother, a grower has a very good idea what it takes to make them grow well.

Mother Plants

Any plant can be cloned, regardless of age or growth stage. Take clones from mother plants that are at least two months old. Plants cloned before they are two months old may develop unevenly and grow slowly. Clones taken from flowering plants root quickly but require a month or longer to revert back to vegetative growth. Such rejuvenated clones occasionally flower prematurely, and buds are more prone to pest and disease attacks.

Any female can become a mother. She can be grown from seed or be a clone of a clone. I interviewed several growers who made clones of clones more than 20 times! That is, clones (C-1) were taken from the original female grown from seed. These clones were grown in the vegetative stage, and clones (C-2) were taken from the first clones (C-1). Blooming was induced in (C-1) two weeks later and (C-2), grown in the vegetative stage. Then, clones (C-3) were taken from the second clones (C-2). This same growing technique is still going on with clones of clones well past (C-20) and there has been no apparent breakdown in the potency or the vigor of the clone. However, if mothers suffer stress, they produce weak clones. Mothers that are forced to flower and revert back to vegetative growth not only yield less, they are stressed and confused. Clones that grow poorly are generally the result of poor, unsanitary cloning practices.

A clone is an exact genetic replica of the mother plant. Each mother's cell carries a DNA blueprint of itself. Radiation, chemicals, and poor cultural practices can damage this DNA. Unless damaged, the DNA remains intact.

This young 'Shaman' has already shown female pre-flowers and can become a mother plant.

A female plant will reproduce 100 percent females, all exactly like the mother. When grown in the exact same environment, clones from the same mother look alike. But the same clones subjected to distinct environments in different grow rooms will often look different.

A six-month old plant produces more cannabinoids than a one-month old plant. By cloning, a horticulturist is planting a THC-potent plant that will continue to grow in potency at a very rapid rate. A month-old rooted clone acts exactly like a four-month-old plant and can be induced easily to flower with a 12-hour photoperiod.

Keep several mother plants in the vegetative stage for a consistent source of cloning stock. Start new mothers from seed every year. Give mother plants 18-24 hours of light per day to maintain fast growth. For best results, give mothers about ten percent less nitrogen, because less nitrogen promotes rooting in clones.

Swiss greenhouse grower nurtures clones in lower beds and keeps mothers in bright light in upper bed.

Young mother plant is given the best of care. A few weeks ago, this clone was taken from a mother plant.

Mother plants must stay very healthy to be able to produce many clones. The roots on this mother are very healthy!

Mother plants are growing in large, individual hydroponic containers for easy culture and maintenance.

The root system on this heavily producing mother plant is white–very strong and healthy.

Negative points

Clones grow slower than F1 hybrid plants grown from seed. An F1 hybrid is the heterozygous first filial generation–pollen and ovule. F1 hybrids have "hybrid vigor" which means that this cross will grow about 25 percent bigger and stronger than cuttings. Hybrid vigor also makes plants less susceptible to pest and disease problems.

Always start with the best mothers you can find. A mother plant yields clones in her image. If the mother plant lacks potency, harvest weight, or is not pest and disease resistant, the clone shares her drawbacks. These weaknesses are compounded when growing only one strain. An unchecked pest or disease infestation could wipe out the entire crop.

Some growers have a difficult time learning to make clones. If this is the case, continue to work through the little problems one step at a time, and you will learn. Some people have a little longer learning curve when cloning is involved. Take five to ten practice clones before making a serious cloning. You can also work with strains that are easy to clone.

Plants that are easy to clone

Most Skunk and Indica strains are easy to clone.

Growers and sick plants cause most clone rooting problems. Weak plants that lack vigor provide slow-rooting weak clones. Poor growing conditions also affect clone strength.

Harder to clone:

Ruderalis Indica and Ruderalis Skunk do not make suitable mother plants due to their auto-flowering capability. Outdoor strains with a slight tendency to pre-sex in an 18hr photoperiod include: Early Girl, Early Skunk and many others. Check with seed companies for details. But early flowering does not exclude them as mother plants.

Getting Ready

Cloning is the most traumatic incident cannabis plants can experience. Clones go through an incredible transformation when they change from a severed growing tip to a rooted plant. Their entire chemistry changes. The stem that once grew leaves must now grow roots in order to survive. Clones are at their most tender point in life now.

Clones quickly develop a dense system of roots when stems have a high carbohydrate and low nitrogen concentration. Build carbohydrate levels by leaching the growing medium with copious quantities of water to flush out nutrients. The growing medium must drain very well to withstand heavy leaching without becoming waterlogged. Reverse foliar feeding will leach nutrients from leaves, especially nitrogen. To reverse foliar feed, fill a sprayer with clean water and mist mother heavily every morning for three or four days. Older leaves may turn light green; growth slows as nitrogen is used and carbohydrates build. Carbohydrate and hormonal content is highest in lower, older, more mature branch-

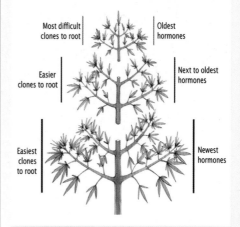

Clones from lower branches root the easiest because they contain more of the proper hormones.

Integrity in parents:
1. Maintain 18-24-hour day photoperiod
2. Keep plants healthy
3. Grow for 6-9 months
4. Repot
5. Grow hydroponically

es. See drawing on previous page. A rigid branch that folds over quickly when bent is a good sign of high carbohydrate content.

Hormone content is different in different parts of a plant. Root growth hormones are concentrated near the base of the plant close to the main stem. This is the oldest portion of the plant and is where most root hormones are located. The top of the plant contains older hormones; cuttings taken from this part root slowly.

While rooting, clones require a minimum of nitrogen and increased levels of phosphorus to promote root growth. Sprays should be avoided during rooting as they compound cloning stress. Given good instruction and a little experience, most growers achieve a consistent, 100 percent clone survival rate.

Large cuttings with large stems packed with starch grow roots slower than small clones with small stems. The excess starch in moist substrate also attracts diseases. Thin-stemmed clones have fewer reserves (accumulated starch), but they only need enough reserve energy to initiate root growth.

Small clones with few leaves root faster than big cuttings with many leaves. At first leaves contain moisture, but after a few days, the stem is no longer able to supply enough moisture to the leaves, and the clone suffers stress. A small amount of leaf space is all

These 'Ortega' clones were taken on August 25. Now they are rooted and ready to transplant.

	Cut from Young	Cut from Old
Cell division starts	Day 4	Day 6
First root nubs form	Day 6	Day 10
Roots start to grow	Day 7	Day 20
Enough roots to transplant	Day 14	Day 28

This chart shows average times for roots to grow from the cambium. Note: Clones taken from younger growth root about twice as fast as those taken from older growth.

that is necessary for photosynthesis to supply enough energy for root growth.

Precautions

An embolism is a bubble of air that gets trapped in the hole in the stem. Embolisms occur when you take big clones and lay them on the counter before placing in water or a growing medium. When an embolism happens, fluid flow stops, and clones die. After taking cuttings, immediately dip them in water or a growing medium to prevent air from getting trapped in the hollow stems. Eliminate the threat of an embolism by taking cuttings under water.

Clones root well within a pH range of five to six. Aeroponic clone gardens normally do best with a pH of five to five and a half. Most diseases grow poorly below these pH levels. Always make sure there is plenty of air in the rooting medium; this will stimulate root growth.

Do not kill clones with kindness and fertilizer. At best, giving clones an excess dose of fertilizer causes rooting to be delayed. In fact, a good dose of ammonium nitrate, a common fertilizer, will stop root hairs from growing.

If an infestation occurs, apply aerosol pyrethrum. Remember, all pesticides, natural or not, are phytotoxic. Spraying cuttings is a bad idea in general. If you must use sprays, use natural organic sprays, apply them when it is cool, and keep their use to a minimum.

Use anti-desiccant sprays sparingly, if at all, and only if a humidity dome is unavailable. Anti-desiccant sprays clog stomata and can impair root growth in clones.

Do not over-water clones. Keep the medium evenly moist, and do not let it get soggy.

Any kind of stress disrupts hormones and slows rapid growth.

Keep the cloning area clean. Do not take clones where fungus spores and diseases are hiding! Pythium is the worst! Pythium flourishes in high temperatures and excessive moisture. Mites, whiteflies, thrips, etc., love weak tender clones. Remove infested

Do not use fertilizers on clones or seedlings.

clones from the room. Cooler conditions, 65-78°F (18-25°C), slow mite and fungal spore reproduction and allow you to avert an infestation.

Rooting Hormones

Root-inducing hormones speed plant processes. When the stem of a cutting develops roots, it must transform from producing green stem cells to manufacturing undifferentiated cells and, finally, to fabricating root cells. Rooting hormones hasten growth of undifferentiated cells. Once undifferentiated, cells quickly transform into root cells. Three substances that stimulate undifferentiated growth include napthalenaecetic acid (NAA), indolebutyric acid (IBA) and 2, 4-dichlorophenoxyacetic acid (2, 3 DPA). Commercial rooting hormones contain one, two, or all of the above synthetic ingredients and often include a fungicide to help prevent damping-off.

Rooting hormones are available in liquid, gel, or powder form. Liquid and gel types penetrate stems evenly and are the most versatile and consistent. Powdered rooting hormones adhere inconsistently to stems, penetrate poorly, spur uneven root growth, and yield a lower survival rate.

Rooting Hormone	Contents	Notes
Algimin® Maxicrop	Dry kelp product Liquid seaweed	NO IBA or NAA. Soak cuttings overnight in a solution of two ounces Algimin® to one gallon of water. After planting, continue watering with this solution.
Clonex®	First cloning gel	Blend of seven vitamins, eleven minerals, two anti-microbial agents, 3000 ppm rooting hormones. Gel seals cutting tissues, reducing chance of infection and embolisms.
Dip-N-Grow®	IBA, NAA, anti-bacterial	Cost is one penny per 100 cuttings.
Earth Juice Catalyst®		Organic, derived from oat bran, kelp, molasses, vitamin B complexes, amino acids, hormones, and low levels of nutrients.
Hormex	IBA based powder	Available in six different strengths ranging from 1000 ppm to 45,000 ppm.
Hormodin®	IBA	Powder available in three strengths: 1000, 3000, and 8000 ppm.
Nitrozyme®	Natural product	Seaweed extract, contains cytokinins, auxins, enzymes, gibberellins, and ethylenes. Spray Nitrozyme on mothers two weeks before taking cuttings.
Olivia's Cloning Solution® Olivia's Cloning Gel	IBA, anti-fungal agents, nutrients	Very high success rate.
Rhizopon AA® (Rhizopon B.V.)	IBA	World's largest company devoted to research and man-ufacture of rooting products. Powder and water-soluble tablets in strengths from 500 to 20,000 ppm.
Rootex	IBA vitamins, hormones	From Tecknaflora is one of the favorite products in North America.
Vita Grow	IBA NAA.	Customers say "you could root a popsicle stick"

Warning! Some products are not recommended for use with edible plants. Read the label carefully before deciding to use a product.

Liquid rooting hormones can be mixed in different concentrations. Always mix the most dilute concentration for *softwood* cuttings. Apply any rooting hormone containing IBA *only once*. If exceeded in concentration or duration, IBA applications impair root formation. As soon as cuttings are taken, clones start dispatching rooting hormones to the wound. They arrive in full force in about a week. The artificial rooting hormone fills the need until natural hormones take over.

Give cuttings a 5-15 second dip in concentrated solutions of IBA and NAA, 500-20,000 ppm. With a quick dip, stems evenly absorb the concentrated hormone.

Relatively new to the market, gels have caught on everywhere. They are easy to use and practical, but are not water soluble. Once applied, gels hold and stay with the stem longer than liquids or powders.

Rooting powders are a mixture of talc and IBA and/or NAA and are less expensive than liquids or gels. To use, roll the moistened end of your cutting in the powder. Apply a thick, even coat. To avoid contamination, pour a small amount into a separate container, and throw away any excess. Tap or scrape excess powder off the cutting; excess hormones can hinder root growth. Make a hole bigger than the stem in the rooting medium. If the hole is too small, the rooting powder gets scraped off upon insertion.

You can also spray clones with a single foliar spray of dilute IBA (50-90 ppm). Be careful to spray just enough to cover leaves. Spray should not drip off leaves. An IBA overdose slows growth, makes leaves dwarf, and could even kill the clone.

Some growers soak their cuttings in a dilute solution (20-200 ppm IBA and/or NNA) for 24 hours. But I have seen few growers use this time-consuming technique.

To determine the rooting hormone concentration in parts per million, multiply the percentage listed by the manufacturer by 10,000. For example, a product with 0.9% IBA contains 9000 ppm IBA.

An all-natural, root-inducing substance is willow (tree) water. The substance in all willow trees that promotes rooting is unknown, but repeated experiments have proven willow water promotes about 20 percent more roots than plain water. This willow water is mixed with commercial rooting hormones for phenomenal results.

To make willow water rooting compound, find any willow tree and remove some of this year's branches that are about one and a half inches in diameter. Remove the leaves, and cut the branches into one-inch lengths. Place one-inch willow sticks on end, so a lot of them fit in a water glass or quart jar. Fill the jar with water, and let it soak for 24 hours. After soaking, pour off the willow water, and use it for rooting hormone. Soak the marijuana clones in the willow water for 24 hours, then plant in rooting medium. If using a commercial liquid rooting hormone,

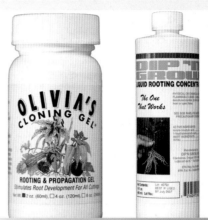

Cloning gels are very popular because they keep root-inducing hormones evenly distributed along the subterranean stem.

Get all cloning supplies ready before starting.

substitute the willow water in place of regular water in the mix.

Canna products and several other commercial products contain *Trichoderma* bacteria. The bacterium causes roots to grow and absorb nutrients better. To learn more about it, check out the Canna web site www.canna. com.

Grow More Roots

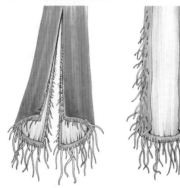

Split the stem of clones to expose more of the cambium layer just under the "skin" of the stem. It is the only place that generates new roots.

Exposing the cambium layer causes many roots to grow there. Lightly scraping away the outer layer of the stem to expose only the cambium allows hormones to concentrate where roots start. Splitting the clones' stem exposes more surface area to grow roots. Both practices increase the number of healthy roots, but rooting time is a few days longer.

After the cutting has been trimmed and scraped, dip the bare stem into a rooting hormone. Now it is ready to "stick" into the substrate.

Split the stem to initiate more surface area for roots to grow.

Avoid problems:

Keep the work area clean. Wash work surfaces and tools before starting.

Have grow medium ready.

Prepare mother plant (scion).

Take clones.

Store unused clone.

Insert (stick) cutting in growing medium or aeroponics system.

Place clones under humidity tent.

Look for root growth.

Transplant when roots emerge from root cube or medium.

Harden-off by gradually exposing to new environment.

This beautiful 'Stinky Pinky' mother is just two and a half months old.

Before Making Clones

Making clones or cuttings is the most efficient and productive means of cannabis propagation for small growers, both indoors and out. Once females have been distinguished, you are ready to practice the simple, productive art and science of cloning.

Disinfect all tools and working surfaces to kill bacteria, fungi, viruses, and other diseases already present. Use sharp scissors, razor, or razor blade dipped in alcohol, vinegar, or bleach (five to ten percent solution). Wash your hands thoroughly beforehand.

Make a 45-degree cut across the stem to cut the clone.

Make sure to have all cloning supplies within arm's reach–rooting cubes, hormone, razor or scissors, humidity dome, etc.–before you start to take clones.

Cloning: Step-by-Step

Step One: Choose a mother plant that is at least two months old. Some varieties give great clones even when pumped up with hydroponics and fertilizer. If a variety is difficult to clone, leach the soil with two gallons of water for each gallon of soil every morning for a week before taking clones. Drainage must be good. Or mist leaves heavily with plain water every morning. Both practices help wash out nitrogen. Do not add fertilizer.

Trim off one or two sets of leaves.

Step Two: With a sharp blade, make a 45-degree cut across firm, healthy 0.125-0.25-inch-wide (3-6 mm) branches, two to four inches (3-5 cm) in length. Take care not to smash the end of the stem when making the cut. Trim off two or three sets of leaves and growth nodes so the stem can fit into the soil. There should be at least two sets of leaves above the soil line and one or two sets of trimmed nodes below ground. When cutting, make the slice halfway between the sets of nodes. Immediately place the cut end in water. Store cut clones in water while making more clones.

Hold cut clones in a glass of water until you are ready to dip in hormone and plant.

Dip trimmed stem into the rooting gel or liquid hormone. Make sure stem is covered with the proper amount of rooting hormone.

Place the stem covered with rooting hormone into the root cube.

Pinch the top of the root cube so that growing medium is in full contact with the stem.

Step Three: Rockwool and Oasis™ root cubes are convenient and easy to maintain and transplant. Fill small containers or nursery flats with coarse, washed sand, fine vermiculite, soilless mix, or, if nothing else is available, fine potting soil. Saturate the substrate with water. Use an unsharpened pencil, chop stick, nail, etc., to make a hole in the rooting medium–a little larger than the stem. The hole should stop about one-half inch (1.5 cm) from the bottom of the container to allow for root growth.

Place a tray containing rooting cubes or plugs into a standard nursery rooting flat. If none exist, make holes through three-fourths of the cube for clone stems.

Fill rockwool tray with water, pH 5-6. Always use strong plastic trays.

Grow clones until they are well-rooted. Always remember to label clones when planting.

Step Four: Use a rooting hormone, and mix (if necessary) just before using. For liquids, use the dilution ratio for softwood cuttings. Swirl each cutting in the hormone solution for 5-15 seconds. Place the cuttings in the hole in the rooting medium. Pack rooting medium gently around the stem. Gel and powder root hormones require no mixing. Dip stems in gels as per instructions or roll the stem in the powder. When planting, take special care to keep a solid layer of hormone gel or powder around the stem when gently packing soil into place.

Step Five: Lightly water until the surface is evenly moist. Keep cuttings moist at all times. Clones have no roots to bring water to leaves. Water arrives from leaves and the cut stem until roots can supply it. Water as needed to keep growing medium evenly moist. Do not let it get soggy.

Step Six: Clones root fastest with 18-24 hours of fluorescent light. If clones must be placed under an HID, set them on the perimeter of the garden so they receive less intense light; or shade them with a cloth or screen. A fluorescent tube six inches (18 cm) above clones or a 400-watt metal halide 4-6 feet (1.2-1.8) away supplies the perfect amount of light for clones to root. Cool white fluorescents (or a combination of warm and cool white) are excellent for rooting.

Rooting Clones

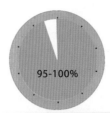

95-100%

Roots/Air

80°   27°
75° Roots 24°
65°   Air   18°

Above: Best humidity ranges for cloning.

Right: Best temperature range for growing medium.

A fogger in the cloning room will ensure humidity stays above 95 percent.

Humidity domes fit over flats of clones to retain humidity. The domes on the right are covered with lightweight Agronet to lower light on new clones.

To lower transpiration, cut clone leaves in half before sticking.

An incandescent light bulb attached to a rheostat provides exacting control of bottom heat.

This large clone has been rooting for a week. The expert grower makes sure the climate is perfect, so clones suffer no stress.

Strong clone in an aeroponic clone garden has a mass of roots and is ready to plant.

Step Seven: Clones root fastest when humidity levels are 95-100 percent the first two days and gradually reduced to 80-85 percent during the following week. A humidity tent will help keep humidity high. Construct the tent out of plastic bags, rigid plastic, or glass. Remember to leave openings for air to flow in and out so little clones can breathe. If practical, mist clones several times a day as an alternative to the humidity tent. Remove any sick, rotting, or dead foliage.

Cut leaves in half to lower transpiration surface and to keep them from overlapping. Moisture that could foster fungus is often trapped between overlapping leaves. Keep the grow medium evenly moist so there is enough moisture to prevent cut leaves from bleeding out plant sugars that attract diseases.

Step Eight: Clones root faster when the growing medium is a few degrees warmer than the ambient air temperature. A warmer substrate increases underground chemical activity, and lower air temperature slows transpiration. For best results, keep the rooting medium at 75-80°F (24-27°C). Growing medium temperatures above 85°F (29°C) will cause damage. Keep the air temperature 5-10°F (3-5.5°C) cooler than the substrate. A warmer growing medium coupled with cooler ambient temperature slows diseases and conserves moisture. Misting clones with water also cools foliage and slows transpiration to help traumatized clones retain moisture unavailable from nonexistent roots.

Put clones in a warm place to adjust air temperature and use a heat pad, heating cables, or an incandescent light bulb below rooting cuttings.

Step Nine: Some cuttings may wilt but regain rigidity in a few days. Clones should look close to normal by the end of the week. Cuttings that are still wilted after seven days may root so slowly that they never catch up with others. Cull them out, or put them back into the cloning chamber to grow more roots.

Step Ten: In one to three weeks, cuttings should be rooted. Signals they have rooted include yellow leaf tips, roots growing out drain holes, and vertical growth of the clones. To check for root growth in flats or pots, carefully remove the root ball and clone to see if it has good root development. For best results, do not transplant clones until a dense root system is growing out the sides and bottom of rooting cubes.

This cutting needs to grow a bigger root system before transplanting.

Cuttings are always strong and healthy-looking after you take them. After five or six days, leaves may start to change color. Leaves stay small and often turn a deeper shade of green. After about a week, lower leaves may start to yellow if their nutrient levels dissipate.

A week after being taken, clones' stems will develop stubby callused roots called primordia. The primordia are semi-transparent to white and should look healthy. Clones produce very little green growth during this process. Once the root and vascular transport system is in place and working properly, clones are able to experience explosive growth with the proper care.

This mass of roots is from a clone with a split stem; the outer layer of the stem was scraped away to expose the cambium.

Rooting clones can handle increasingly more light as roots grow. Move the fluorescent lamps to two to four inches above plants when roots form. Fertilize with a mild fertilizer solution when all clones have started vegetative growth.

Any sign of slime, pests, or disease means there are problems, and clones should be removed from the garden.

Transplant only the strongest, well-rooted clones. (See "Transplanting.") Slow-rooting clones should be kept in the cloning chamber or culled out. Do not move clones below bright light until they have fully developed root systems. Once transplanted, clones are ready to harden-off (see "Transplanting").

Plenty of roots are growing from this clone rooted in a Jiffy cube. It is ready to transplant.

Sequence of cloning for sex

1. Make 2 cuttings

2. Label each cutting

12 Hours

3. Give 12 hours of light while rooting

4. Cutting will determine sex in 2-3 weeks

Cloning the apex of the tip

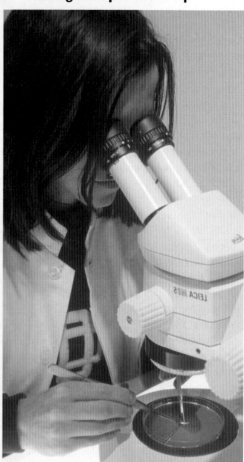

Swiss cloning expert is removing the tip of a mother plant to clone in an agar solution. Such clones are easy to maintain for long periods.

Set up a vegetative pre-growing area that is lit with an HID or bright compact fluorescent lamp for the rooted clones. Place them in this area to let them grow the first week or two of vegetation. This area needs to be just big enough to accommodate plants from the time they are a few inches tall until they are about a foot tall and ready to be moved into the flowering room.

Air layering

There is a good sequence of air layering in *Marijuana Botany*, by Robert C. Clarke. To date, I have never seen anybody use this technique. It is interesting, but normally not necessary. Cannabis is easy to root or clone.

Cloning for Sex

Determine plant sex accurately, 100 percent of the time, by "cloning for sex." To clone for sex, take two cuttings (in case one dies) from each parent plant in question. Use waterproof labels and an indelible marker to identify sets of clones and corresponding parents.

Give rooting clones a 12-hour light/dark regimen. After a 12-hour day, set clones in a dark closet, or place a box over them. The dark period must be total and uninterrupted to induce flowering. Clones usually show sex within two weeks. Cull out all males except those used for breeding. Flower little females, and keep their mothers growing under 18-24 hours of light.

Growers with only one room root clones in a nursery flat, and cover it with a light-tight cardboard box for 12 hours every night. Remove the cardboard box after the lights go out to increase air circulation and ventilation.

Clones from a Flowering Female

You can clone a favorite flowering plant, but it is difficult. Clones take longer to root, and results are not always the best. Powerful flowering hormones must be reversed, and rooting hormone signals must be sent. Now is the time to give plants 24 hours of light to signal them to grow.

Cut clones from the lower green branch tips. Cut a one to two-inch-long (3-5 cm) stem. Trim off flowers and lower leaves. Keep two or three green leaves. If leaves have yellowed, survival chances diminish exponentially.

You can take clones from flowering plants and revert them to vegetative growth once rooted.

The earlier in the flowering stage cuttings are taken, the more rapid the rooting and the re-vegetation rate. Once a plant reaches the senescence point, growth hormones have dissipated, leaving not enough to initiate roots.

Storing Clones

To store cuttings for later use, wrap recently cut and trimmed stems in a damp cloth or paper towel. Put the wrapped clones into a plastic bag, and store in the refrigerator. On a daily basis, remove the water that condenses inside the bag in the cool refrigerator. Keep the temperature above 40°F (5°C). Temperatures below this level may cause plant cells to rupture. Cuttings should last in the refrigerator for about three weeks.

Clonex Root Matrix, a Growth Technology product, is a gel that allows cut clones to root and be held until they are needed.

Transplanting

Mix the clone dip, and use a rag to cover and contain soil when dipping.

Submerge the entire clone in the dip to ensure miticide covers all foliage.

Remove the clone, and shake off excess dip before transplanting.

Dip rooted clones into a miticidal/ fungicidal solution before transplanting and before moving into the flowering room.

Mix a miticidal/fungicidal dip (I like Einstein Oil) to disinfect clones before sticking them in the growing medium. Fill a container with low pH water (5-6) and add a natural fungicide such as hydrogen peroxide in a two percent solution. Or include a ten percent mix of chlorine or vinegar. **Do not mix vinegar and chlorine! The resulting gas is hazardous.** See "Transplanting."

Transplanting

When plants are too big for their containers, they must be transplanted to continue rapid growth. Inhibited, cramped root systems grow sickly, stunted plants. Signs of root bound plants include slow, sickly growth and branches that develop with more distance between limbs. Severely root-bound plants tend to grow straight up with few branches that stretch beyond the sides of the pot. To check for root-bound symptoms, remove a plant from its pot to see if roots are deeply matted on the bottom or surrounding the sides of the pot.

When growing short plants that reach full maturity in 90 days, there is little need for containers larger than three gallons (11 L). Large mother plants will need a large pot if they are kept for more than a few months.

In this container, roots are growing mainly around the sides and along the bottom. This plant is ready to be transplanted.

Transplant into the same type or similar growing medium; otherwise, a water pressure differential could develop between the different mediums, which slows water movement and causes slow root growth. Starting seeds and clones in root cubes or peat pots makes them easy to transplant. Set the cube or peat pot in a hole in the growing medium, and make sure growing medium is in firm contact. Remember to keep root cubes and substrates evenly moist after transplanting.

Transplanting is the second most traumatic experience after cloning. It requires special attention and manual dexterity. Tiny root hairs are very delicate and may easily be destroyed by light, air, or clumsy hands. Roots grow in darkness, in a rigid, secure environment. When roots are taken out of contact with the soil for long, they dry up and die.

Transplanting should involve as little disturbance to the root system as possible. Water helps the soil pack around roots and keeps them from drying out. Roots need to be in constant contact with moist soil in order to supply water and food to the plant.

Roots showing through a rooting cube means cuttings are ready to transplant.

After transplanting, photosynthesis and chlorophyll production are slowed, as are water and nutrient absorption via roots. Transplant late in the day so transplanted plants will have all night to recover. Transplants need subdued light, so foliage can grow at the rate roots are able to supply water and nutrients. Give new transplants filtered, less-intense light for a couple of days. If there is a fluorescent lamp handy, move transplants under it for a couple of days before moving them back under the HID or outdoors to harden-off.

Ideally, plants should be as healthy as possible before being traumatized by transplanting. But, transplanting a sick, root-bound plant to a bigger container has cured more than one ailing plant. Once transplanted, cannabis requires low levels of nitrogen and potassium and increased quantities of phos-

phorus. Any product containing *Trichoderma* bacteria or Vitamin B_1 will help ease transplant shock. Plants need a few days to settle in and re-establish a solid flow of fluids from the roots throughout the plant. When transplanted carefully and disturbed little, there will be no signs of transplant shock or wilt.

Double potting is a simple transplanting technique that disturbs roots very little. To double pot a plant, cut the bottom out of a root-bound pot, and set on top of another bigger pot of soil. Roots grow down into second pot.

Transplanting Step-by-Step

Step One: Water clone with half-strength *Trichoderma* bacteria or Vitamin B_1, two days before transplanting.

Step Two: Fill the three-gallon (11 L) container with rich potting soil or soilless mix to within two inches (5 cm) of the top.

Step Three: Water growing medium with a mild, quarter-strength hydroponic fertilizer solution until saturated and solution drains freely out the bottom.

Step Four: Carefully remove the root ball from the container. Place your hand over top of container with the stem between your fingers; turn it upside down, and let root ball

Carefully remove seedlings from containers. These seedlings were kept moist and moved quickly to minimize exposure to air and light. Growers used Vitamin B$_1$ solution to ease transplant shock.

slip out of pot into your hand. Take special care at this point to keep the root ball in one integral piece.

Step Five: Carefully place the root ball in the prepared hole in the three-gallon (11 L) container. Make sure all roots are growing down.

Step Six: Backfill around the root ball. Gently, but firmly, place soil into contact with root ball.

Step Seven: Water with half-strength fertilizer containing *Trichoderma* bacteria or Vitamin B$_1$. Soil should be saturated–not waterlogged–and drain freely. If rooting cube and new substrate are not identical, pay special attention to moisture levels. Let rockwool dry out enough so that roots penetrate new growing medium in search of moisture.

Step Eight: Place new transplants on the perimeter of the HID garden or under a screen to subdue sunlight for a couple of days. Once transplants look strong, move them under full light.

Step Nine: Fertilize soilless mixes after transplanting with a complete hydroponic fertilizer that contains soluble chelated nutrients. New potting soil usually supplies enough nutrients for a couple of weeks before supplemental fertilization is necessary.

Transplanting this clone grown in rockwool into soil or soilless mix is simple and easy. Remove the rockwool's plastic covering before setting the clone in a pre-made hole in substrate.

This clone grew in a four-inch (10-cm) pot and is ready to be transplanted.

Step Ten: Minimum Container Size chart below.

Minimum Container Size	
Plant age	**Container size**
1-3 weeks	root cube
2-6 weeks	4-inch (10 cm) pot
6-8 weeks	2-gallon (7.5 L) pot
2-3 months	3-gallon (11 L) pot
3-8 months	5-gallon (19 L) pot
6-18 months	10-gallon (38 L) pot

Seedlings and clones can also be transplanted directly into a three- to five-gallon (11-19 L) pot, a system which requires fewer containers and involves less work and less possible plant stress. The larger volume of soil holds water and nutrients longer and requires less frequent watering. When clones and seedlings are transplanted directly into a five-gallon (19 L) container, the roots grow down, out, and around the container walls and bottom. In fact, the majority of roots grow out of the soil and form a layer behind the container wall.

To encourage roots to develop a dense compact system, transplant just before they have outgrown their container. Transplanting a well-rooted clone in a root cube into a four-inch (10-cm) pot and transplanting the four-inch (10-cm) pot into a three-gallon (11 L) pot or grow bag causes roots to develop a more extensive system in a small ball of growing medium. Successful transplanting causes minimal stress. Most marijuana crops are in the ground for such a short time that bungled transplanting costs valuable recuperation time and loss in production.

Transplant clones and seedlings into raised beds and large planter boxes directly from four-inch (10-cm) pots. As many as 20 plants can be transplanted into a 24 × 24 × 12-inch (61 × 61 × 30 cm) planter, but six to twelve plants will yield about the same dry weight of buds. Once plants start crowding and shading one another, bend stems outward and tie them to a trellis attached to the planter. Large planters require less mainte-

This clone was transplanted directly into a large container at the Cannabis College in Amsterdam.

nance. The larger mass of soil retains water and nutrients much longer and more evenly. One downside is that all plants must receive the same water and diet.

Three-gallon (11 L) containers are the ideal size for two- to three-foot-tall (60-90 cm) plants. Larger pots are usually unnecessary because plants grow no longer than a week or two in the vegetative stage and six to ten weeks flowering. Smaller three-gallon (11 L) pots are easy to move and handle. Roots also grow less during flowering. By the time a plant is potbound, it is ready to harvest. I used to recommend up to a five-gallon (19 L) container for plants that are harvested after 90 total days of life. I now believe this is a waste. While the smaller containers require daily watering, they produce harvests com-

Hardening-off

Hardening-off is the process of toughening-up clones and seedlings. During the rooting process, leaves supplied much of the moisture for the clone. Now, healthy white new roots are supplying moisture to the clone. Check for root damage. Brown roots are rotting and lack oxygen. Thin hair-like dark roots are dried out. Once damaged, roots remain damaged. New roots must grow to replace damaged roots. Cull out any clones with damaged roots, because they will grow slowly. The protective wax coating must also grow back on leaves. It is best to acclimate rooted clones to the grow room over the course of a week. Gradually hardening-off clones will assure they suffer a minimum of stress and continue to grow rapidly.

Harden off the strong ones, and introduce them to the real world–the grow room where they will see photosynthetically active response (PAR) at full value and nutrients that make their cells quiver. Now is the time to pre-grow clones before placing them into the flowering room.

Foliage loses its protective wax coating when it is pampered during cloning, so it is very tender now. New roots must start to transport water via the stems to the leaves.

These beautiful little seedlings were started indoors under a fluorescent lamp. The grower moves them outdoors for a few hours every day to harden-off and acclimate to the outdoor environment.

The roots and moisture-transport system start to work on strong, healthy clones first. Clones that lag behind now should be tossed out, because they will always be slow. You can let them root longer and not transplant them until adequate roots develop.

This female was pruned and bent to keep a low profile and open up the center of the plant.

parable to those of five-gallon (19 L) containers.

Mother plants are much larger, grow longer, and can require containers up to 30 gallons (115 L) in size. However, mother plants grow quite well in five or ten-gallon (19-38 L) hydroponic containers for a year or longer. If you plan to keep a mother plant for more than a few months, grow it hydroponically in its own container for best results.

Pruning and Bending

Pruning and bending a plant redirects growth hormones. Pruning affects the plant more drastically than bending. Selective pruning and bending allow us to manipulate auxin hormone levels in branch and flower tips. Removing or bending a branch or branch tip causes hormonal balances to shift. Cutting the meristem (top growth tip) of a cannabis plant will diffuse auxins and cause greater concentrations in lower branch tips. Bending a growing tip changes hormone concentrations less than pruning.

Pruning

Always use clean instruments when pruning. A straight razor, single-edge razor blade, a sharp pair of pruners, or a pair of scissors all work well. Sanitize clippers and blades between cuts by dipping in rubbing alcohol. Use indoor pruners *only* in the indoor garden. Pruners used outdoors have everything from spider mites to fungus spores on them. If outdoor clippers must be used, dip in rubbing alcohol to sterilize before making cuts.

After pruning, the open wound invites diseases and pests. Wash your hands and tools before and after pruning. Make cuts at a 45-degree angle to discourage moisture from sitting on wounds.

Avoid pruning up to a month before inducing flowering. Since pruning diffuses floral hormones, flowering is retarded. If heavily pruned shortly before flowering, peak maturation is delayed for a week or longer. It takes a month or longer for hormones to build up to pre-pruning concentrations.

Leave leaves alone! Removal of healthy leaves hacks up a healthy plant. Removing large fan or shade leaves DOES NOT make plants more productive even though this practice supplies more light to small leaves and growing tips. Plants need all their leaves to produce the maximum amount of chlorophyll and food. Removing leaves slows chlo-

There are a few basic techniques to pruning marijuana, including:

Prune off the top of the plant below the first set or two of branches to drive hormones to lower branches. Pruning off more of the main stem will increase the effect.

Prune off the tip of plants to diffuse hormones and make lower branches grow more.

Prune the tips of all branches except the main tip to make plants tall.

Remove lower branches that do not receive light. Plants will direct energy into buds.

Pruning off all lower branches makes inspecting irrigation fittings easy and diminishes problems associated with weak growth.

rophyll production, stresses the plant, and stunts its growth. Stress is a growth inhibitor. Remove only dead leaves or leaves that are more than 50 percent damaged.

Remove spindly branches and growth that is not collecting light energy, including dead and dying leaves. Pruning lower branches concentrates auxins in upper branches which forces growth upwards. Cut lower branches off cleanly at the stem so no stub is left to rot and attract pests and diseases. If you must harvest a little smoke prematurely, removing a few lower branches will diminish the harvest the least.

Pruning out spindly branches and growth inside plants opens up the interior and provides more and better air circulation. It also allows light to reach deeper inside plants.

Not pruning has several advantages. Floral hormones are allowed to concentrate in tips of branches causing buds to grow stronger and denser. Unpruned plants are crammed into a small area. Crowded plants have less space to bush out laterally and tend to grow more upright. Clones are set into the flowering room after 1-30 days in the vegetative

No pruning was done in this room. Buds were so big in this room that plants were staked with bamboo sticks.

Pruned plants often seal themselves, but problems can still arise when there is an appealing opening for pests.

room. All the little clones are packed tightly together in three-gallon pots. Each one of the plants is taking up the minimum amount of space for the minimum amount of time to produce the maximum amount of marijuana. Light is much more intense, and the entire plant grows flower tops with few fan leaves.

Most successful growers do not prune at all, especially if growing a short clone crop that is only two to three feet (61-91 cm) tall. Short clone crops require no pruning to increase light to bottom leaves or to alter their profile. "No pruning" is the easiest and most productive method when growing short crops.

Pinching back or pruning tops (branch tips) causes the two growing shoots just below the cut to grow stronger and bigger. This increases the number of top or main buds. Pruning tops also diffuses floral hormones. These hormones (auxins) prevent the lateral buds from growing very fast. All lower branches develop more rapidly when the terminal bud is removed. The further a branch is from hormones at the plant tip, the less effect the auxins have.

To pinch back a branch tip, simply snip it off below the last set or two of leaves. Pinching off tender growth with your fingers helps seal the wound and is often less damaging to plants than cutting. When the main stem is pinched back, side and lower growth is stimulated. When all the tops are pinched back, lower growth is encouraged. Continually pinching back, as when taking clones from a mother, causes many more little branches to form below the pruned tips. Eventually, the plant is transformed into a hedge-like shape. Most growers do not pinch plants back, because it diminishes the yield of prime, dense tops; but it may not affect the overall weight of dried smoke.

Supercropping is a form of pinching back or pruning branch tips. We are not sure who or when the term or buzzword was coined. We do know that there are several differ-

The main growing tips of this large patio plant were pruned off, which stimulated lower growth.

ent versions of supercropping "invented" by innovative growers.

Supercropping can also incorporate FIM pruning which is explained below. It can be combined with bending, too. Some people

Floral hormones are concentrated in four main branches.

go to the point of mutilating plants by breaking branches a few inches below main buds. Removing healthy leaves so that "budding sites get more light" is also practiced by some supercroppers. See "Stress" in this chapter for more information.

Pruning all the branches or removing more than 20 percent of the foliage in a short time frame stresses plants too much and diminishes harvest. But if taking clones, some growers effectively prune a mother down to stubby branches and let her recuperate for a month or longer.

Pruning too much over time may alter hormonal concentrations, causing spindly growth. This is often the case with mother plants that provide too many clones. The mother must rest and gain girth, because small, spindly branches root poorly.

Remove all but the four main branches. The meristem (central stem) is removed just above the four lowest (main) branches. Removing the central leader concentrates the floral hormones in the four remaining branches. Fewer branches are stronger and bear a larger quantity of dense, heavy flower tops. Remove the stem above the four main branches; do not remove leaves on the main branches. Select plants with three sets of branch nodes about six weeks old, and pinch or prune out the last set of nodes so that two sets of branches remain. Move plants into the flowering room when they are about 12 inches tall. 'Skunk #1' and similarly robust bloomers should be set in the flowering room when about six to eight inches tall.

The FIM Technique was coined by an anonymous *High Times* reader from South Carolina in the July 2000 issue of the magazine. The technique became legendary on www.overgrow.com, ever since the grower wrote: "this pruning technique could revolutionize indoor gardening." The South Carolina grower tried to pinch the tip of a plant and said "Fuck, I Missed!" when he did not remove the entire bud and coined the acronym FIM.

FIM Technique

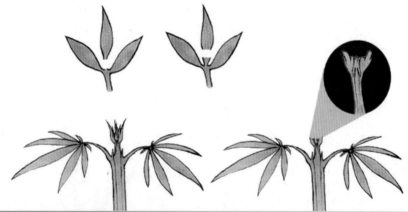

The drawing on the left shows the traditional method to top a plant. The entire growing shoot just below the bud is removed. When the entire growing shoot is removed, the two buds located directly below the cut grow faster and stronger. The drawing in the center and the close-up on the right show the FIM pruning technique – the bottom ten percent of the bud remains intact. This is the key to FIM pruning. Many different flowering tops form as a result of this single pruning. According to FIM afficionados, terminal buds put on much more weight and are more dense.

Bending

Bending is similar to pruning, in that it alters the flow of hormones. Bending efficiently neutralizes the effect of the growth-inhibiting hormone. Bending is much easier on plants than pruning. To bend, lean a branch in the desired direction and tie it in place. Branches can take a lot of bending before they fold over or break. Even if a branch folds, tie it in place; if necessary, use a wooden splint. The stem will heal itself. Young, supple branches take bending much better than old, stiff ones. Bending branches horizontally will encourage the buds to grow vertically towards the light. Each bud will turn into an impressive top, because they all receive more light. A wooden planter box with a lattice trellis alongside makes a great anchor to tie bent plants to.

Wire ties, the kind used to close bread sacks, can be purchased at a nursery. Wire ties are either pre-cut or cut to length by the grower. Plastic-coated electronic and telephone cable wire also work well. They are fastened with a simple twist and stay rigid, leaving the stem breathing room. But if applied too tightly around a stem, the liquids cannot flow, and death could result.

Be gentle when bending, even though cannabis can take much abuse. Sometimes a crotch will separate or a branch will fold over, cutting off fluid flow. These mishaps are easily fixed with a small wooden splint snugly secured with wire ties or duct tape to support the split and broken stem.

Growers also combine bending and pruning. It is easy to prune too much, but it is hard to over bend.

Bending plants will give them a low, inconspicuous profile.

Air Pruning Roots

When roots grow to the end of the container and are exposed to air, they stop growing. The air naturally prunes roots. They cannot grow out the end of the pot, because the climate with little moisture and lots of air is too inhospitable.

Root Pruning

Root pruning could be necessary to give new life to potbound plants outdoors or in greenhouses. Removing roots will not make plants grow faster; in fact, it will slow growth for about two weeks. Once new roots start to grow, growth rebounds. About mid-summer, root-prune plants that must stay in the same size container. Root pruning will keep plants manageable and much easier to maintain.

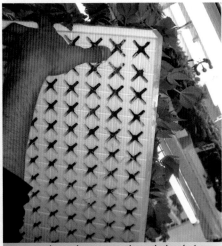

Two plants growing in this ten-gallon (38 L) pot have been trained to grow along a wall just out of the neighbor's field of vision.

Roots on these clones grow through the drainage holes. Once they hit the air, growth stops. Roots are "air pruned."

Bending branches lowers the garden profile and allows sunshine to reach smaller buds.

Chemical Root Pruning

Chemical root pruning is an excellent way to control root growth inside containers. Commercial nursery people have been using chemical root pruning for many years with outstanding results. This passage is condensed from an excellent FAQ article on chemical root pruning with great photos by Uncle Ben, a charter member of the shut down site www.overgrow.com.

Uncle Ben used a product called Griffin's Spin-Out that consists of copper hydroxide suspended in a carrier. To use, simply spray-paint the inside of the containers with two coats of Griffin's Spin-Out. Roots grow to within a fraction of an inch of the copper hydroxide, then stop. Roots will not touch the unpleasant compound. The result is similar to what happens aboveground when new, lower growth is stimulated as branch tips are pruned. When pruned with copper hydroxide paint, more roots develop overall, and they grow in the *entire* root ball, especially in the center. Plants with a dense root system dispersed evenly throughout the root ball are easier to maintain, and they grow bigger in smaller containers.

To remove large plants from containers, use a knife or blade to separate roots from the inside of the container. Move the blade up and down all the way around the inside of the container to break roots away.

The roots in this potbound plant form a mass around the interior and bottom of the container. Roots that grow out drainage holes are "pruned" when they come into contact with air. This plant needs repotting.

Remove the root ball from the container.

Grafting

Little is known about grafting cannabis. Yes, it is possible to graft cannabis to hops. Most often the hop stem is grafted to a cannabis rootstock. The plant will live; however, it will not produce THC.

I asked a number of growers if they had experimented with grafting, and none had. Grafting an *indica* stem to a large *sativa* rootstock would be an interesting experiment. The larger root system could easily supply water and nutrients to the smaller *indica* plant. The resulting plant would be drought resistant.

Stress

Cannabis grows best and produces heaviest when it is given a stable environment. Stressed plants produce less than unstressed plants. Stress-induced trauma include withholding water, photoperiod fluctuation, low light intensity, ultraviolet light, nutrient toxicities and deficiencies, cold and hot soil, ambient temperatures and mutilation. In addition, any overt applications of growth hormones such as B9 hormone, gibberellins, cytokinins, abscisic acid, ethylene, colchicine, etc., cause stress.

Gently remove a portion of the soil from the root ball. I like to remove the part in the center of the root ball where few roots reside.

Once 30-40% of the soil has been removed, lay a base of fresh soil in the bottom of the container and fit remaining root ball on top of it. Fill the container with fresh potting soil and gently pack in place. After transplanting, water heavily with a Vitamin B1 solution.

Stress can cause plants to produce more resin, but it simultaneously causes odd and/or reduced growth. For example, Felix, a Swiss outdoor grower, grew a field of cannabis at 900 feet (300 meters) and another at 4200 feet (1300 meters). The upper field suffered stress, because it is exposed to cooler temperatures and more ultraviolet radiation. Plants there produce about 25 percent more resin-packed THC than plants in the lower field. But, plants that grow at 900 feet (300 meters) yield at least 25 percent or more dry weight than plants at the 4200-foot elevation.

Removing large green shade leaves allows more light to shine on smaller leaves, but it also causes growth to slow and harvest to diminish. Remove only leaves that are more than half damaged by pests or diseases. Often, partially yellow leaves green up once stress is eliminated. Removing spindly, dimly lit lower branches stresses plants much less than removing leaves to speed growth of upper foliage.

Mutilating plants by breaking the trunk, driving a stake through the trunk, torturing or slapping them around might increase resin production, but most often the stress retards growth and causes other problems.

Insides of pots have been painted with Griffin's Spin-Out containing copper hydroxide to prune roots.

This close-up of a root ball shows a spot scraped away with roots behind. This demonstrates the roots will not grow into the copper hydroxide coating.

Stressed plants with wounded stems and vegetation grow slower and invite pests and diseases.

This photo of the foot-long fibrous mass of roots was taken after Uncle Ben shook off much of the semi-dry soil.

Withholding water may also cause more resin production, but it impairs growth and diminishes leaf, stem, and flower production. Water stress slows or stops clones from rooting. If clones have too many leaves and are too busy transpiring, root growth is very slow. Conversely, waterlogged rooting mediums harbor no air, and rooting is also slowed to a crawl.

Stress can also affect plants' sex. See Chapter Sixteen, Breeding, for more information.

This little plant, nicknamed "Lola," was stressed and stunted by lack of water. Although a beautiful little female, the harvest weighed in at a meager 0.08 ounce (2.3 gm).

Phyllotaxy - Branching changes when a seedling enters the flowering stage. The vegetative plant on the left has symmetrical branching. Branching changes to asymmetrical when plants enter the flowering growth stage.

Introduction

Cannabis must flower and produce seeds to successfully complete its annual life cycle. Marijuana is a dioecious plant, being either male (pollen producing) or female (ovule producing). However, hermaphrodite (bisexual) plants with both male and female flowers can also occur.

In nature, cannabis flowers in the fall, after the long hot days of summer. The long nights and short days of autumn signal marijuana to start flowering. Plants are normally either male or female. Cannabis produces male or female pre-flowers after four weeks of vegetative growth. For more information, see "Pre-flowering" in this chapter.

Growth patterns and chemistry change during flowering: stems elongate; leaves grow progressively fewer blades; cannabinoid production slows at first then accelerates; and flower formation is rapid at first then slows. Nutrient needs change as growth stages change. Plants focus on flower production rather than vegetative growth. Green chlorophyll production,

Plants grown from seed support symmetrical branches during seedling and vegetative growth.

Asymmetrical branching occurs as plants grown from seed begin to flower.

requiring much nitrogen, slows. Phosphorus and potassium uptake increase to promote floral formation. Shortly before the flowering stage, growers change to a "super bloom" fertilizer formula with less nitrogen and more potassium and phosphorus.

Induce flowering in greenhouses, outdoors, and indoors by giving plants more hours of total darkness and fewer hours of light. Give cannabis 12 hours of uninterrupted darkness and 12 hours of light to induce visible signs of flowering in two weeks or less. This program is effective in all but the latest blooming pure *sativa* strains. Growers with a vegetative room illuminated 18-24 hours a day and a flowering room with 12-hour days and 12-hour nights, create environments that mimic the photoperiod in summer and fall. With this simple combination, growers crank out a crop of outstanding buds every six to ten weeks all year long.

The top of this bud from an unknown strain is a mass of white, fuzzy, hair-like pistils.

When a low-nitrogen super bloom fertilizer with more phosphorus and potassium is used, fan leaves yellow during flowering.

This flowering male plant is in full bloom. Pollen-laden flowers continue to open and shed pollen for two weeks or longer.

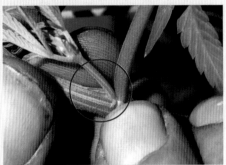

Image shows a male plant after 24 days of vegetative growth at 18/6 day/night. Staminate flowers are located at the node between the stipule and emerging branch.

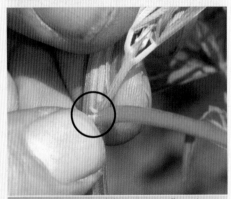

This is another view of the same pre-flowering male plant so you can get a better view.

Staminate
Primordia

The red arrow shows where pre-flowers develop on both male and female plants.

Inducing flowering in cannabis grown from seed with a 12/12 day/night photoperiod will cause plants to show sex, male or female. Once the sex of the plant is guaranteed, males are almost always harvested before they shed pollen, and females are coaxed into higher yields. Once the photoperiod is set, disrupting it will cause plants to suffer stress. If they suffer enough stress, hermaphrodite tendencies increase.

Water intake of flowering plants is usually somewhat less than in the vegetative stage. Adequate water during flowering is important for plants to carry on internal chemistry and resin production. Withholding water to "stress" a plant will actually stunt growth and diminish yield.

Removing large fan leaves to allow more intense light to reach small buds or to stress plants is crazy! Large leaves are necessary to keep plants healthy. Indoors and in greenhouses where the hours of darkness are controlled, cannabis flowers for six to ten weeks or longer. This is a very short time. Hacking off branch tips to initiate more budding sites diffuses floral hormones and retards growth. Remove only leaves that are 50 percent or more damaged by diseases, pests, and cultural practices.

Upon pollination, one of the many, tiny grains of pollen from the male (staminate) flower pod, lands on a pistil of the female (pistillate) flower. Female flower tops are a mass of calyxes with each calyx harboring an ovule and a protruding set of pistils. Actual fertilization takes place when the grain of male pollen slides down the pistil and unites with the female ovule deep within the female calyx. Once fertilization takes place, pistils turn brown and a seed forms within the seed bract. Seeds are the result of this sexual propagation and contain genetic characteristics of both parents. In nature there is a 50/50 chance for a seed to produce a male or female plant. Once fertilized with male pollen, female plants put the bulk of their energy into producing strong, viable seeds. When flowers are full of ripe, mature seeds, the female will die, having successfully completed her life cycle. The male completes his life cycle and dies after producing and dispersing all of his pollen into the wind, in search of receptive female pistils.

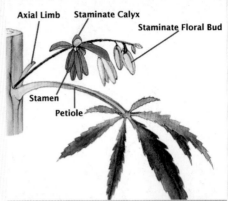

Botanical drawing of all male parts and overall view of the male flower.

Pre-flowering

Pre-flowers, described by Robert Clarke in *Marijuana Botany* as "primordial," are the first indication of a plant's sex. The pre-flowers grow at branch internodes just behind the leaf spur or stipule about the fourth week of vegetative growth, when the plant is six to eight weeks old. This is the point of sexual maturity, the first sign a plant is preparing for flowering–the next stage in life.

You can see pre-flowers with the naked eye, but a 10 to 30X magnifier will make viewing easier. You can accurately determine plant sex after eight weeks. Using this method, you can distinguish sex before inducing flowering.

Early male flowers are easy to spot with the naked eye. They are located at branch internodes.

Male Pre-flowering

Male pre-flowers are normally visible when plants are six to eight weeks old, after the fourth week of vegetative growth. The pre-flowers emerge behind the stipule at the fourth to fifth branch internodes and generally do not turn into full flowers. But, according to Bongaloid (www.overgrow.com, now shut down) "a male plant will develop mature staminate flowers after prolonged periods of vegetative growth."

Always wait to induce flowering until after pre-flowers appear. Inducing flowering with 12 hours of uninterrupted darkness and 12 hours of light before pre-flowers develop will stress the plant. This stress could cause peculiar growth, and plants might develop into hermaphrodites. Inducing flowering before

Male pollen sacks hang like little balls. Each pollen sac has enough pollen to pollinate all the females in the average grow room.

Male flowers develop quickly on the tip of this male plant. Keep an eye out for male plants, and separate them from females as soon as they are spotted.

pre-flowers form will not expedite flowering. In fact, flowering will occur at about the same time as if you had waited for pre-flowers to show!

Plants grown from seed under a 24/0 photoperiod will generally show pre-flowers after plants that are given a 18/6 day/night photoperiod. Once pre-flowers are distinguishable as male or female, plants can be induced to flower with a 12/12 day/night photoperiod.

A word of caution from bc-trichome-farmer (the extinct site, www.overgrow.com): "Do not try to sex a seedling based on the very first pre-flower. Wait and make sure. The time

This beautiful male flower has dispersed its yellowish pollen into the air.

This male plant is in full bloom. Flowers open over the course of a week or longer to ensure females are completely pollinated.

Grains of pollen are miniscule. This close-up of a grain of male pollen is magnified 4000 times. Cannabis cohort Eirik captured this image on a scanning electron microscope.

between using a 25X (loupe) to spot the very first pre-flower and the plant dropping pollen is at least 10+ days away, so it's safe."

Male Flowering

When given a 12/12 day/night photoperiod, male cannabis reaches maturity and flowers one to two weeks before females. However, male plants do not necessarily need a 12/12 day/night photoperiod to dawn flowers and shed pollen. Males can flower under long days and short nights as well, but they generally produce fewer flowers. Once male calyxes show, pollen develops quickly and can disperse within a very short time. There is always an early opener that sheds pollen, often within 24 hours or less! To avoid pollination problems, remove males as soon as they are distinguished. If growing male plants, always isolate them from females, so they will not be pollinated. See Chapter 5, "Harvest," for more information on harvesting males.

Males continue flowering and shedding yellowish, dust-like pollen from bell-shaped pollen sacks well into the females' flowering stage, which ensures pollination. If you are making seeds, pollinating females too early, before the girls have developed many receptive female pistils, will result in a small seed crop. See Chapter Sixteen, "Breeding," for more information.

Male flowers are about one quarter-inch (6 mm) long and pastel green to yellowish in color. Flowers first develop near the top of the plant. Pollen sacks develop on a short spike and hang in clusters at the base of branches. Gradually, flowers develop towards the bottom of the plant. After two to six weeks of the 12-hour photoperiod, fully formed floral sacks split open and shed pollen.

Males are usually taller than females and have stout stems, sporadic branching, and fewer leaves. In nature, wind and gravity carry pollen from taller males to fertilize (pol-linate) receptive females. Male plants produce fewer flowers than females, because one male plant can pollinate many females. Males also contain less THC and overall lower cannabinoid levels.

Males fertilize females, causing them to stop high THC production and start seed formation. Remove and destroy males, except those used for breeding, as soon as their sex has been determined. The instant they show sex, separate male plants used for breeding from females. Do not let them shed pollen. Premature pollen sacks often form and open early or are hidden under foliage and go unnoticed until it is too late. If growing from seed, take special care to ferret out male flowers and plants.

Growers have reported that bouncing the photoperiod around and dynamically raising or lowering the temperature have the effect of producing more male plants. Note that each stimulus involves creating a climate that causes plants to suffer stress. Also, the stressful environment does not necessarily turn the entire plant male; it turns it hermaphrodite. The most susceptible plants already

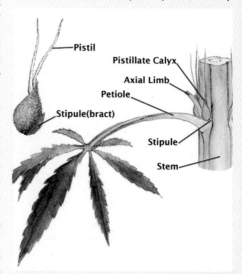

This drawing shows the main parts of a female cannabis plant.

The green calyx supports two very small pistils on this pre-flowering 'Flo' from DJ Short.

The pre-flower on this 'Mr. Bubble' female is very easy to spot with the naked eye.

Pre-flowers on this 'Puna Budder' from THSeeds are nearing the end of the pre-flowering stage that lasts about two weeks.

have a predisposition to hermaphrodism. See Chapter Sixteen, "Breeding," for more information.

There are several ways to promote male or female plants during seedling growth. (See "Grow More Female Plants from Seed" in Chapter Two.) During vegetative growth you can get a good idea of a plant's sex from its genetic background and growth characteristics. The most dependable way to deduce sex is "Cloning for Sex" (see Chapter Three). For a complete discussion, see Chapter Sixteen, "Breeding."

Female Pre-flowering

Near the end of normal vegetative growth, plants grown from seed develop pre-flowers. This is when female calyx formation initiates, and it is not contingent upon photoperiod. It occurs when a plant is old enough to show signs of sexual maturity, about the fourth week of vegetative growth, or six to eight weeks from germination. The pre-flowers emerge behind the stipule at the fourth to fifth branch internodes.

A pre-flower looks like a regular female flower; most have a pair of white fuzzy pistils. Pistils normally form after the light green seed bract part of the pre-flower has formed. Wait until pistils have formed to ensure the plant is a female and not a male. The pre-flowering stage lasts from one to two weeks. A little patience is in order now!

Plants grown from seed under an 18/6 day/night photoperiod will usually show pronounced pre-flowers before plants given a 24/0 day/night photoperiod. And, under a 16/8 day/night regimen pre-flowers show more quickly and are often more pronounced. As soon as you can distinguish pre-flowers as male or female, plants can be induced to flower with a 12/12 day/night photoperiod.

Wait to induce flowering until pre-flowers have appeared. Inducing flowering with 12 hours of uninterrupted darkness and 12 hours of light before pre-flowers set will stress the plant. Such stress could cause strange growth, and plants may grow into hermaphrodites. Inducing flowering before pre-flowers develop does not make plants flower faster. Plants will flower about the same time as if you had waited for pre-flowers to develop.

'Chocolate Chunk' in early flowering

Female Flowering

Female cannabis is prized for heavy, potent resin production and weighty flower yield. Ideal female plants grow squat and bushy with branches close together on the stem and dense foliage on branches. In most strains, the first signs of female flowers appear one to three weeks after inducing flowering with the 12-hour photoperiod. Female flowers initially appear near the top of the terminal bud and gradually develop on lower branches starting at the tips and moving downward. Flowers have two small one-quarter to one-half inch (6-12 mm) fuzzy, white hairs, called pistils that form a "V." The set of pistils is attached at the base to an ovule, which is contained in a light green pod, called a calyx. Pistil-packed calyxes form dense clusters or buds along stems. A cluster of buds is often called a top or cola.

'Chocolate Chunk' in full flower

The masses of calyxes develop rapidly for the first four or five weeks, after which they grow at a slower rate. Buds put on much of their harvest weight as they swell during the last two or three weeks of growth. Pure sativas, including Thai varieties, can flower for four months or longer! Once the ovule has been fertilized by male pollen, rapid calyx formation and resin production slow, and seed growth starts.

When females' flowering is at their zenith, pistils swell and swell. Soon they change in color, most often from white to amber and, eventually, to reddish brown.

'Flo' in early flowering

'Flo' in full flower

Sinsemilla

Sinsemilla (pronounced sin-semiya) is derived from two Spanish words: "sin" = without and "semilla" = seed. Sinsemilla is the word that describes flowering female cannabis tops that have not been fertilized by male pollen.

Highly prized sinsemilla buds are the most potent part of any strain, with a proportionately large volume of THC per flower bud, and it's all smoke, no seeds! Unpollinated female plants continue to flower until calyx formation and resin production peak out, six to ten weeks after turning the lights to 12 hours. During six to ten weeks of flower-

'Mr. Bubble' in early flowering

'Haze Heaven' in early flowering

'Haze Heaven' in full flower

'Nebula' in early flowering

'Stinky Pinky' in early flowering

'Shaman' in early flowering

ing, calyxes develop and swell along the stem, yielding more high quality buds than pollinated, seeded flowers.

Make any female marijuana sinsemilla by removing male plants as soon as they are identified. Removing males virtually guarantees that male pollen will not fertilize succulent female pistils. Sometimes a few early grains of pollen are shed by premature male flowers. Pollen dispersed from wild or cultivated male cannabis plants could also be floating in the air. Sometimes a hermaphrodite with a few male flowers will sprout on a predominately female plant. See "Intersexuality" in Chapter Sixteen, Breeding.

'Nebula' in full flower

'Warlock Passion' in early flowering

'Stinky Pinky' in full flower

'White Russian' in early flowering

'Warlock' in full flower

'White Russian' in full flower

'Shaman' in full flower

'Mr. Bubble' in full flower

Inspect resin crystals with a 30X microscope to discern the exact time to harvest.

This 'Thaitanic' is not ready for harvest. The white pistils are just starting to turn color.

This 'Thaitanic' is at the point of harvest. Note that many of the pistils are turning color.

Introduction

The payoff for all the research, work, risk, expense, and the long, patient wait is a bountiful harvest. Strong, healthy, well-grown clones and seedlings yield the heaviest harvests. A well-organized pre-harvest and harvest are essential to preserve cannabis quality and decrease the workload.

Harvest when plants are at peak ripeness. Depending upon the high you like, which is discussed below, harvest timing is critical. The peak harvest window is open for about five to seven days.

Once harvested, most growers manicure buds before drying them slowly and evenly so THC is preserved. After drying, buds should cure to achieve full aroma and flavor. Like a fine wine, aging or curing improves taste and fragrance. Once cured, proper storage will ensure buds retain all of their essential qualities.

Before Harvest

Fragrance is often a problem before, during, and after harvest. Control fragrance by keeping drying and manicuring rooms well-vented. If possible, allow plenty of fresh circulating air to pass through the drying room to remove odors quickly. If air in and around drying and manicuring room is stagnant, odors linger and accumulate. Keep temperatures below 70°F (21°C) so essential oils in cannabis do not volatize and release pleasant but unwanted fragrances. Contain cannabis fragrance in sealed drying and manicuring rooms. Filter air before expelling with a carbon filter. See "Odor" in Chapter Thirteen for more information on controlling fragrance.

Avoid the taste of organic or chemical fertilizers in harvested buds by flushing with plain water or a clearing solution to remove any residuals and chemicals that have built up in soil or plant foliage. Ten to fourteen days before harvesting, flush the garden with distilled water or water treated with reverse osmosis. Use a clearing solution such as Final Flush® if you have to use plain tap water that contains dissolved solids. Some growers fertilize until three to four days before harvest and use a clearing solution to remove fertilizer residues. Apply this water just as you would apply nutrient solution. Always let at least ten percent, preferably more, drain out the bottom of containers. If using a recirculating hydroponic system, change the water after the first four to six days of application. Continue to top off the reservoir with "clean" water.

Do not water for one or two days before harvest. The soil should be fairly dry, but not dry enough that plants wilt. This will speed drying

> **How to tell when fertilizer will affect taste.**
> 1. Leaf tips and fringes are burned.
> 2. Leaves are brittle at harvest.
> 3. Buds crackle when burning.
> 4. Buds smell like chemicals.
> 5. Buds taste like fertilizer.

time by a day or more and not affect the quality of the end product.

Harvest

Growth stops at harvest and the THC content cannot increase. It will stay the same or decrease after harvest. Proper handling is the key to retaining THC potency. Prolonged periods of light, temperatures above 80°F (27°C), friction from fondling hands, and damp, humid conditions should be avoided because they all degrade the THC.

The THC chemical is produced in leaves, flowers, and stalked glandular trichomes, lovingly referred to as "resin glands" or simply "trichomes." Stems and roots may smell like they should be smoked, but contain few mind-bending cannabinoids, if any, and the resin is not very psychoactive. Male plants contain much less THC and are harvested before they pollinate females. Female plants are harvested when trichomes show peak ripeness. Leaves are harvested first.

Growers hang plants upside down because it is simple, convenient, and effective— not to drain existing THC-potent resin into the buds. Also, boiling roots to extract THC is crazy!

Leaves

Once the large leaves are fully formed, THC potency has generally peaked out. Smaller leaves around buds continue to develop resin until buds are ripe. Peak potency is retained, as long as leaves are healthy and green; nothing is lost by leaving them on the plant. Harvest leaves if they show signs of disease or rapid yellowing that fertilizer has failed to cure. Once

Manicuring plants takes a long time. One pound (454 gm) takes four to six hours to manicure by hand with scissors and one to two hours to manicure with an automatic trimmer.

they start to yellow and die, potency decreases somewhat. This is true especially with fan leaves that grow before the buds. The large leaves turn yellow when nitrogen-rich fertilizer is withheld during flowering.

Cut the entire leaf, including the leaf stem (petiole) and toss it into a bag. Paper bags breathe well and can be closed by folding over the top. Plastic bags do not breathe, so the top must be left open. If the petiole is left on the stem, it shrivels and dies back. This little bit of dead plant attracts moisture and mold. Removing it will avoid mold problems.

Keep the paper bag in a closet or area with 40-60 percent humidity and 60-70°F (15-21°C) temperature. Reach into the bag once or twice a day and stir leaves by hand. Leaves should be dry to the touch in five to seven days. Once dry, place in the freezer to get ready to make Ice-O-Lator hash.

Male Harvest

Male flowers can produce pollen as early as two weeks after changing lights to the 12-hour day/night schedule. Watch out for early openers. Three to six weeks after initiating flowering, pollen sacks open and continue producing flowers for several weeks after the first pods have begun to shed pollen. Once male flowers are clearly visible but not yet open, THC production is at peak levels. (See "Sinsemilla Harvest" for information on trichome glands.) This is the best time to harvest. Once males release pollen, the degradation process speeds up and flowers fall.

Put leaves in an open plastic bag to dry. Stir once or twice daily to mix moist and dry leaves.

Trim large leaves from plants before manicuring small leaves around buds. Make sure to remove leaves including petiole at main stem to avoid promoting mold.

These big bags of dried leaf and trimmings are ready to be made into hash.

Harvest males carefully, especially if close to females. Cut the plant off at the base, taking care to shake it as little as possible. To help prevent accidental pollination by an unnoticed

open male flower, carefully cover the male plant with a plastic bag, and tie it off at the bottom before harvesting. Or, if you can see an open pollen sack, spray it with water to make pollen unviable. Keep males used for breeding as far from flowering females as possible. Make sure to install fine screens for air coming into the flowering room and wet them down regularly to discourage rogue pollen. Isolate males until needed. After a month, the male will start reverting to vegetative growth even though it retains viable sacks of pollen. Males can also be cloned and held in the vegetative stage until needed. Induce flowering about three weeks before viable pollen is needed. Within three to five weeks, the male will be full of viable pollen sacks.

Prolong male harvest by removing flowers with tweezers or fingernails as they appear. New flowers soon emerge after plucking old ones. Continue to remove pollen sacks until females are two weeks from full bloom. Picking off individual male flowers is a tedious, time consuming process, and it is easy to miss a few.

Harvesting most of the branches, leaving only one or two pollen-bearing limbs, is practical. A single male flower contains enough pollen to fertilize many female ovules; a single branch full of male flowers is necessary to produce enough pollen for most home breeding needs.

Spray male plants with water to deactivate pollen before harvest.

Sinsemilla Harvest

Sinsemilla flowers are mature from 6-12 weeks after the photoperiod has been changed to 12 hours. The best time to harvest sinsemilla is when THC production has peaked but not yet started the degradation process. Established indoor varieties are bred so the entire plant reaches peak potency at the same time. Lower flower tops that received less light are not as heavily frosted with resin as upper branches and could be slower to mature. Varieties that ripen all at once tend to go through four to five weeks of rapid bud formation before growth levels off. The harvest is taken one to three weeks after growth slows. Pure *indica* varieties and many *indica/sativa* crosses are picked six to ten weeks after inducing flowering, while *indica* crosses with more dominant *sativas*, such as 'Skunk #1', may not be ready for ten weeks. Commercial growers often pick immature six-week-old buds so they can harvest one more crop every year.

Pure *sativa* varieties, especially Thai and Asian strains that were grown from native seed, take longer to bloom after turning the light to 12 hours. They could take four months to finish blooming! These types tend to form buds at an even rate throughout flowering with no marked decline in growth rate. Few indoor growers have the time or patience to grow pure *sativa*

Cut a male branch from the plant to store and use later before harvesting.

Cover male plants with a plastic bag to help contain pollen before removing from the garden.

Store male branches in a glass of water for several days. The pollen sacks will continue to open.

Carefully inspect buds for peak ripeness.

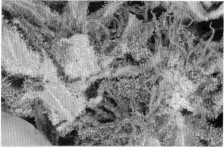

Long thin trichomes are common on most sativa-dominant strains. The underside of this leaf is packed with clear glands, some of which are turning amber.

Trichomes in the center of the photo have turned amber, and many have lost the ball on top. The plant was harvested to curtail further trichome degradation.

Trichomes fight for limited leaf space on this ripe bud. Notice all the pistils have died back and the trichomes are at peak maturity for harvest.

varieties because of their long flowering period, leggy stature, and low yield. Buds at the top of the plant often reach peak potency a few days to a couple of weeks before lower buds. Long-blooming equatorial *sativas* may require several harvests.

Pistils turn from white to brown or brownish-red as the flower tops ripen. Pistils changing color indicates plants are turning ripe; however,

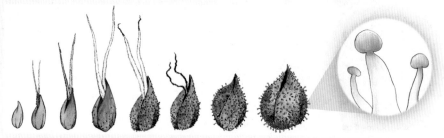

Female calyx development is shown in early, middle, and late stages.

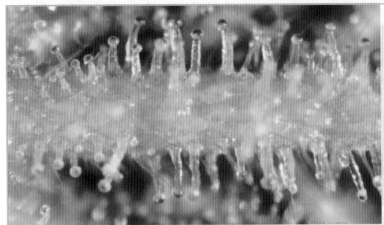

Early Harvest: These resin glands are in the early stages of formation. Harvest when the trichomes start to turn milky white to amber for the most potent THC.

Late Harvest: Colored light in this photo accentuates the amber color trichomes turn as the harvest window fades.

Photos on this page courtesy of Joop Dumay, the "Crystalman." www.crystalman.nl

Peak Harvest: Resin glands start to turn creamy white after trichomes are fully formed. These trichomes signify harvest time!

it is not the best indicator of peak ripeness. After more hands-on research, I have learned that it is difficult to tell peak ripeness by the color of pistils in all strains. The best gauge of peak ripeness is the color of the resin glands or trichomes.

Resin glands change colors as they ripen. At first, glands are clear. As they continue to mature, they turn a translucent milky color and, finally, they turn amber. Resin glands that are bruised from being squeezed or jostled about deteriorate quickly. All glands do not change color simultaneously on the same bud or plant. The process is gradual, and individual resin glands change at different rates. Of course there

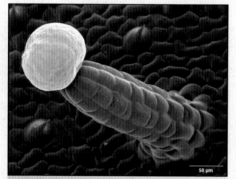

are exceptions such as the strain 'Blueberry,' which bears darker, even purplish resin glands.

To get a close-up look at resin glands, use a 10X magnifying glass, jeweler's loupe, or a 20-50X hand-held microscope. My preference is a 30X hand-held microscope with a battery-powered lamp used by stamp collectors. Look at resin glands without harvesting buds, or take a small, thin, resinous portion of a ripe bud and place it under the microscope at a low 30X magnification setting. If the microscope does not have a lamp, a flashlight will be necessary for an un-shadowed view.

Resin gland development will be in one of three stages—clear, translucent or milky white, and amber.

Harvest when the majority of glands are clear and a few glands have started to turn milky white. Harvesting plants too early, before a few of the glands turn milky, will make them less psychoactive, because they hold less THC. Harvesting at this point will yield a cerebral, soaring, heady stone. The body will be less affected. Pure *sativa* and *sativa*-dominant strains are perfect for this harvest scenario.

Close-up of a single resin gland was shot with a scanning electron microscope at 370X. THC is concentrated at the base of the "ball." 370X electron scanning photo courtesy Eirik.

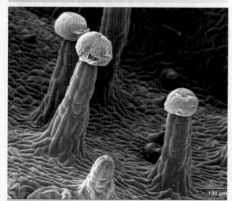

Trichomes are very delicate and can be ruptured easily. Note the torn head on one trichome and the one in the foreground has lost its head completely! 80X electron scanning photo courtesy

This scientist from Canna measures the exact THC content of harvested buds with a gas chromatograph.

A trichome is a "plant hair." The trichomes found on drug cannabis are glandular and secretory in character. These stalked glandular trichomes are comprised of a stalk with a resin head. They look like a post with the knob at the top. They form on buds and small leaves. The highest concentration of THC is located at the base of the resin head. The best time to harvest is when these trichomes have developed a spherical head and are transparent to creamy white. Senescing glands start to turn amber and later brown and get smaller; they are decomposing, and THC content diminishes. Check buds every day starting the sixth week of flowering. Check several buds from different plants to ensure the maximum amount of trichomes are ripe for harvest.

Cystolith trichomes have a pointed tip and are often long and hair-like. These protective trichomes are most common on leaf undersides. Cystolith glands exude insecticidal and miticidal substances to gum up pest mouthparts and repel them, but they have no THC.

The glandular trichomes in this photo are short and stout. Crystalman added color to this photo to provide perspective.

Photos on this page courtesy of Joop Dumay, the "Crystalman." www.crystalman.nl

This close up photo by Crystalman shows a single long tall resin gland that is perfectly ripe.

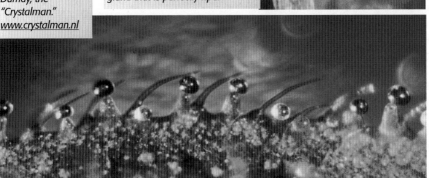

You can clearly see stalked trichomes, the clear column with a ball on top that contains much THC. Hair-like pointed cystolith hairs contain virtually no THC.

Harvest when half (50 percent) of the trichomes have turned a creamy translucent color for absolute peak ripeness. At this point, the high will be both cerebral and physical with a good head and body stone.

Harvest when the majority of trichomes have turned amber for a body stone. Pure *indica*, *afghani*, and *indica*-dominant strains harvested at this late point will possess a heavy body, or couch-lock, stone. Waiting to harvest pure *sativa* and *sativa*-dominant varieties until this stage will not take advantage of the strains. Such strains are best harvested when resin glands are clear to milky colored.

Harvest Step-by-Step

Step One: Stop fertilization seven to ten days prior to harvest. Latent nutrient accumulation in foliage imparts a fertilizer-like taste. Leach nutrients from the growing medium seven to ten days before harvest. Some growers continue to fertilize until three days before harvest if using a product such as Final Flush®. Such products expedite flushing built-up chemicals from cannabis plants.

Step Two: If sprays have been applied during the last week (not recommended), mist plants heavily to wash off undesirable residues that may have accumulated on foliage. The bath will not affect resin production. Gently jiggle buds after rinsing to shake off any standing water. To prevent fungus and bud blight, wash the garden early in the day to allow excess water on leaves to dry before nightfall. If bud mold (*botrytis*) is a threat, DO NOT wash buds.

Step Three: You may want to give plants 24 hours of total darkness before harvest. Many growers do this and say the buds are a little more resinous afterward.

Step Four: Harvest in the morning when THC content is at its peak. Harvest entire plant or one branch at a time by cutting near the base with pruners. Jerking the root ball creates a mess and is unnecessary. All of the THC is produced in the foliage, not in the roots.

Step Five: It is not necessary to hang plants upside down so all the resin drains into the foliage. Once formed, resin does not move. However, drying the entire plant by hanging it upside down is very convenient. When stems are left intact, drying is much slower.

Step Six: To harvest entire plants and/or branches:

a. Remove large leaves one or two days before actually cutting the plants down. Or remove leaves after cutting plants. Harvesting large leaves early gets them out of the way and makes manicuring easier and faster.

b. Harvest entire plants by cutting them off at the base before manicuring.

c. Or cut each branch into lengths of 6-24 inches. Manicure the freshly harvested tops, trimming away leaves with clippers or scissors. Hang the manicured branches until dry. Once dry, cut the tops from the branches, taking special care to handle tender buds as gently as possible.

d. Or leave larger leaves on branches to act as a protective sheath to flower buds. Tender resin glands are protected from bruises and rupture until final manicuring, but, manicuring is much slower and more tedious when trimming dry foliage.

Manicuring

Once harvested, carefully manicure buds by cutting large leaves where they attach to the stem. Leaving the petiole (leaf stem) can cause mold to grow. Snip off smaller, low-potency leaves around buds that show little resin, so a beautiful THC-potent bud remains.

Manicuring is easiest when leaves are soft and supple immediately after harvest. Trimming off leaves now will also speed drying. Waiting until foliage is dry to manicure will make manicuring buds a tedious, time-consuming job.

Manicuring is easiest with a good pair of trimming scissors that has small blades to facilitate reaching in and snipping off leaf petioles at the main stem. An ergonomic pair of scissors with comfortable handles is indispensable when manicuring cannabis for hours.

Manicure over a fine silkscreen (see Chapter 15, "Hash") or a glass table. Scrape up fallen resin glands on the table or under the screen. This potent resin can be smoked immediately or pressed into blocks of hash.

Wear inexpensive rubber gloves to collect "finger hash." After trimming for a few hours, remove accumulated finger hash on gloves by bathing in a small portion of isopropyl alcohol. Set the hash-laden alcohol on the counter overnight to evaporate. Scrape up the remaining hash after all the alcohol has evaporated. Or put the rubber gloves in a freezer for a few hours. Cooling will make it easier to scrape and rub the accumulated hash from the gloves.

Scrape accumulated resin from scissors when it impairs blade movement. Use a small knife to remove built-up resin from blades. Ball up small bits of scraped resin by rubbing it together between fingers. The ball of hash will grow as manicuring progresses.

Budget enough time to harvest and manicure your crop. Properly manicuring one pound (454 gm) takes from four to six hours by hand with scissors and one to two hours when using an automatic trimmer.

Remove large leaves by cutting the petiole where it meets the main stem.

Looking at a wall of buds is impressive, but it tends to loose its luster after manicuring by hand for a few days.

Cut the main stalk at the base to harvest entire plant at once.

Remove individual branches and hang from drying lines after manicuring to speed drying and reduce workload.

Drying

After harvest, marijuana must dry before smoking. Drying converts THC from its non-psychoactive, crude, acidic form to its psychoactive neu-

tral form. In other words, fresh green marijuana will not be very potent. Drying also converts 75 percent or more of the freshly harvested plant into water vapor and other gases.

When you cut a plant or plant part and hang it to dry, the transport of fluids within the plant continues, but at a slower rate. Stomata close soon after harvest, and drying is slowed since little water vapor escapes. The natural plant processes slowly come to an end as the plant dries. The outer cells are the first to dry, but fluid still moves from internal cells to supply moisture to outer cells which are dry. When this process occurs properly, plants dry evenly throughout. Removing leaves and large stems upon harvest speeds drying; however, moisture content within the "dried" buds, leaves, and stems is uneven. If buds are dried too quickly, chlorophyll and other pigments, starch, and nitrates are trapped within plant tissue, making it taste "green," burn unevenly, and taste bad.

When dried relatively slowly, over five to seven days or longer, moisture evaporates evenly into the air, yielding uniformly dry buds with minimal THC decomposition. Slowly dried buds taste sweet and smoke smooth. Taste and aroma improve when pigments break

The Aardvark trimmer attaches to a vacuum which whisks all trim into a tidy bag. Put flexible hose in the freezer and shake out accumulated resin an hour later.

Bonsai electric scissors work on AC or DC current. This great invention for guerilla and indoor growers cuts trimming time by two thirds or more. The poster in the background is Napoleon on the cover of Newsweek magazine!

down. Slow even drying–where moisture content is the same throughout stems, foliage and buds– allows enough time for the pigments to degrade. Hanging entire plants to dry allows this process to take place over time.

To speed drying time, remove large leaves and stems upon harvest. Fresh supple leaves are easier to work with than when dry. When you are looking at manicuring 10 pounds (4.5 kg), you make it as easy as possible!

Plants with outer "fan" leaves intact take longer to dry and require much more time to manicure. The outer leaves form a sheath that helps protect delicate trichomes when drying, but this practice turns trimming dry leaves into a tedious, messy, two-step job.

Circulation and ventilation fans will help control heat and humidity and keep them at proper levels. You can also use a dehumidifier to control humidity. An air conditioner is ideal to "dial in" temperature and humidity in warm climates. Large drying areas may require a heater to raise temperature and lower humidity. Do not train fans directly on drying plants; it causes them to dry unevenly.

For best results, drying should be slow. Ideal air temperature is between 65 and 75°F (18-24°C) and humidity from 45 to 55 percent. Temperatures below 65°F (18°C) slow drying, and humidity often climbs quickly. Humidity above 80 percent extends drying time and makes the threat of bud mold imminent. Temperatures above 75°F (24°C) may cause buds to dry too fast, and humidity can also fall below the ideal 50 percent level more easily. Temperatures above 85°F (29°C) cause buds to dry so fast that smoke becomes harsh. Relative humidity below 30-40 percent causes buds to dry too fast and retain chlorophyll, giving them a "green" taste. Fast-dried buds become crispy and crumble. Low humidity also causes buds to lose flavor and odor. If humidity is between 30 and 40 percent, allow for minimum air movement to slow drying. Always use an accurate maximum/minimum thermometer and hygrometer to ensure temperature and humidity are kept in the ideal range.

The Grass Chopper is one of the many new medium-sized bud trimmers that feature vacuum leaf removal.

Scrape resin from scissors and ball up into hash. Remove accumulated resin from gloves with alcohol or put in the freezer to facilitate separation.

Trim buds over a screen or glass table to collect resin glands. Scrape up glands and press into hash.

This ingenious grower made a bud trimmer by duct taping a couple of pieces of metal and a drill to a workbench.

This grower dried his one-pound (450 gm) crop in a small closet. Two levels of drying lines were stretched across the closet.

Small harvests can easily be dried in a closet, cabinet, or a cardboard box that is a fraction of the growing area's size. Large harvests require much more room. If drying space is a problem, a staggered planting schedule, or planting varieties that ripen both early and late, carries over to a staggered harvest that frees up drying space as buds dry.

Large outdoor and indoor crops need large spaces in which to dry. You can use the grow area as a drying room if not growing any plants. Do not dry plants in the same room in which plants grow. Different climates are required for growing marijuana and drying it. Fungus and spider mites can also migrate from dead plants to live ones. Inspect drying buds daily for any signs of fungus, mold, and spider mites. Smear Tanglefoot™ around the end of drying lines to form a barrier which keeps mites from migrating to live plants. Mites congregate at the barrier and are easy to smash.

A cardboard or wooden box makes an excellent drying space to hang small harvests. The air flow in the enclosed area is diminished, and buds and leaves must be turned daily to even out the moisture content and discourage mold. Thread a large needle with dental floss, and string the floss back and forth through the box near the top to make drying lines. If the box is tall enough, you can install several levels of drying lines. Lock the flaps on the box and set it in a closet or spare room. Open flaps to allow air circulation as needed. Or, cut holes near the bottom and top

Shantibaba (Mr. Nice Seeds) constructed drying racks from Mecalux angleiron and put wheels on the bottom to facilitate handling and storage.

This harvest took longer to dry because it was not manicured until after it dried.

of the box to allow air exchange and circulation. Check daily to see how buds are drying. If tops dry too fast, open the box-top and set the box in a cooler location.

Hanging plants is a labor-saving way to facilitate slow, even drying. Large, moist stems can also be removed and small branches hung from the ceiling to cut drying time by a few days.

Use clothespins to attach branches to drying lines, or poke a paper clip through the base of branches and hang clip from line. Another option is to trim branches to form a hook and hang from the "hook."

Use a portable foldable clothesline to make a quick mobile drying room. Unfold clothesline, hang buds from lines, and cover with a large, black bed sheet or cloth. The cloth sheet allows the exchange of air and maintains darkness. Train a fan on the outside of the sheet so air circulates underneath and dries buds.

Building a small drying room is as easy as tacking some plywood together at right angles and hanging lines across the enclosure. Or you can make walls from black Visqueen™ plastic by tacking or taping it to the ceiling and floor to form walls.

Drying a large harvest can require a large space. If you have a large space such as a bedroom, barn, shed, etc., cut plants at the base and remove large leaves, and hang on drying lines in the room. Cut branches from 12-40 inches (30-100 cm). Manicure each branch and hang on drying lines to complete the drying process.

Save space by building or buying drying racks for the buds. Make drying racks from window screen or plastic agricultural netting. Stretch the screen or netting over a wooden frame and secure with staples. Put three- to six-inch (8-15-cm) spacers between framed screens to allow adequate airflow. Or build a drying box with removable screens. See photo above.

Hang manicured buds to dry for a day or two before placing on drying screens to allow the bulk of the moisture to dissipate. Once on screens, buds should be turned daily to ensure even drying.

A simple drying box is easy to make. Wooden spacers between boxes allow for adequate air flow.

Manicured buds can also be placed in boxes to dry. Move buds daily so new surfaces are exposed to air. Buds dry slower, because the air flow is reduced. Line boxes with plastic or aluminum foil to contain for collection resin glands that fall to the bottom. To contain resin glands, seal cracks in boxes with tape.

Drying time depends upon temperature, humidity, and bud density. Most buds will be dry enough to cure in five to seven days. Big, fat, dense buds can take three to four days longer. Gently squeeze buds after they dry for a few days to check for moisture content. Bend stems to see if they are done. If the stem breaks rather than folds, it is ready to cure.

Check for dryness by bending a stem. *The stem should snap rather than fold when bent.* The bud should be dry to touch, but not brittle. The bud should burn well enough to smoke when dry.

Light (UV rays), heat, and friction hasten biodegradation and are dry and drying, marijuana's biggest enemies. Keep dried marijuana off hot car dashboards and away from heat vents, etc. Friction and rough handling bruise and knock

Spanish grower wrapped newspaper around plants to protect them from light.

This outdoor crop is hanging in the entrance to a barn. A breeze flowing through the opening carries away evaporated moisture and fragrance.

This chest of drawers has screens on the bottom. Place buds on screens to dry.

off resin glands. Even with proper drying and curing, brutal handling of harvested marijuana will diminish THC content. Baggies and fondling hands rupture millions of tiny resin glands in the world every minute! To keep dried marijuana in mint condition, store it in a dark, airtight, glass container, and place it in the refrigerator. Ordinary canning jars allow buds to be admired as well as protected. Glass containers do not impart any plastic or metal odors and contain the pungent fragrance of fresh marijuana buds. Placing an orange or lemon peel in the jar will add a citrus aroma to the bouquet.

Curing

Curing allows buds to continue to dry slowly. The first week of curing affects potency in that it evenly removes moisture within the bud so virtually all the THC is psychoactive. Curing also allows buds to dry enough that mold does not grow when buds are stored. Well-cured buds have an even glow when burned and smoke smooth.

After plants, branches, and/or buds have dried on screens or hung in a drying room for five to seven days and appear to be dry, they still contain moisture inside. This moisture affects taste and potency. Curing will remove this excess moisture. Curing makes the bud uniformly dry and converts virtually all THC into its psychoactive form.

Cut stems into manageable lengths–less than 12-18 inches (30-45 cm)–and place them in an airtight container. Airtight glass containers with a rubber or similar seal are the best. Avoid Ziploc and other plastic bags that are not airtight. Plastic bags used for long-term storage are airtight. The "reflection anti-detection barrier foil bags" available from Hy Supply (www.hy supply.nl) are airtight and infrared-proof. Some growers avoid plastic containers such as Rubbermaid™ bins and Tupperware™, saying the plastic imparts an undesirable flavor to the buds. But when curing large amounts, such plastic bins are the best option because stuffing 10 pounds (4.5 kg) or more into small canning jars would be laborious and impractical.

Enclose buds in a container to create a micro-climate that allows moisture to even out within the buds. Internal moisture will migrate to the dry portions of the bud. Gently pack as many buds into container as possible without forcing and damaging them. Leave the containers in a cool, dry, dark place. Check in two to four hours to see if buds have "sweated" moisture. Check buds by gently squeezing to feel if they are moister than they were a few hours before. Be careful when squeezing buds; resin glands bruise easily.

If stems fold instead of snapping when bent, and buds are still moist to the touch, remove them from the container and gently place in the bottom of a paper bag. They can be stacked in the paper bag as high as six inches (15 cm). Fold the top of the bag once or twice to close. Check the buds two to three times during the day to monitor drying. Carefully turn them in the bag so that different sides are exposed. Remove when they are dry and place back into the sealed container. Check them the next day to see if they are evenly dry. Stems should snap when bent. If too moist, put them back in the paper bag until dry. When dry, return to the curing container.

If buds appear to have fairly low moisture content, and stems snap when bent, leave them in the container and let excess moisture escape out the top. Open the container for a few minutes every few hours to let the excess moisture escape before closing the lid again. At this point you can add an orange or lemon peel to the container to impart a slight citrus aroma.

Check the container several times daily. Leave the top off for five to ten minutes so moisture evacuates. Depending upon moisture content, buds should be totally dry in a few days to two weeks. Once they are evenly dry, they are ready to seal in an airtight container for storage.

To find the approximate moisture content of dry buds, weigh a specific bud upon harvest when it is wet. Weigh it again during the drying

Lay small buds in a box to dry. Turn them daily to promote even drying and prevent mold.

Exact conditions that are best for drying

1.	Temperature	65–75°F (18-24°C)
2.	Humidity	45–55 percent
3.	Light	None
4.	Handling	Minimum
5.	Leaves	Remove at harvest
6.	Manicured buds	Hang until dry

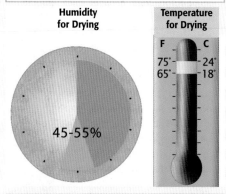

Humidity for Drying

45-55%

Temperature for Drying

F   C
75° — 24°
65° — 18°

Humidity and temperature that are best for drying.

Fast Drying

Here are six ways to dry buds quickly. Remember, buds that dry quickly burn hot; the smoke is harsh, and they taste "green" when smoked.

One: Manicure fresh buds and remove all branches. Spread them out evenly and wrap in paper or enclose in an envelope. Place the paper or envelope on a warm refrigerator, radiator, television, etc. Depending upon heat level, buds will be dry in a few hours to overnight. Buds will be a bit crispy when dry. Place buds in an airtight container until they sweat. Put back in the paper and dry until dehydrated enough to burn well.

Two: Cut up fresh buds and/or foliage. Place on a 12-inch (30 cm) square of tinfoil. Hold or place it over a 60-100-watt light bulb. Stir every 15-30 seconds. It will be dry enough to smoke in one to three minutes.

Three: Place diced buds and/or foliage on a cookie sheet in an oven at 150°F (65°C) for 10-15 minutes. Check regularly and stir if needed until dry. Do not increase temperature above 200°F (93°C) or the THC will vaporize into the air.

Four: Place cut up buds and/or foliage in a microwave oven. Turn the microwave on in short, weak (50 percent power) bursts of 15-30 seconds each. Recycle until dry, and stir if necessary.

Five: Cut buds and/or foliage into small pieces, and place in a glass jar with an airtight lid. Place several silica gel desiccant packs (the kind that come with electronic devices and cameras) into the glass jar and seal. Moisture will migrate to the silica gel in a few hours. Remove the packets and dry using dry heat source. Replace silica packs until marijuana is dry enough to smoke. Find silica gel packs at auto parts or electronics stores.

Six: Drying buds in a food dehydrator for 24-48 hours is the next best option. Food dehydrators are a series of stackable screens. Place bud and leaf on screens and stack. A fan blows air gently upward to dry the marijuana quickly. One friend used this technique and the buds smoked OK, but it was the only dope around, and this could have colored my taste perceptions!

Freeze Drying

Dry ice is frozen carbon dioxide. When it warms, CO_2 converts from a frozen solid to a gas, without turning into a liquid. When moist marijuana is enclosed with dry ice (frozen CO_2) at virtually zero relative humidity, water molecules migrate from the cannabis to the dry ice. This causes the relative humidity of the CO_2 to increase and the moisture content of the marijuana to decrease. This process occurs below 32°F (0°C), and it preserves cannabis.

Place equal amounts of dry ice and bud into a container. Put the dry ice on the bottom and bud on top. Seal with a lid. Make a few small holes in the lid of the container for excess gas to exit. Place in your kitchen freezer. Check every 12-24 hours. When the dry ice is gone, the buds should be completely dry. If not dry, add more dry ice until cannabis is dry. Conserve dry ice by partially drying buds for a few days before enclosing with dry ice.

This method retains potency and freshness and causes very little degradation of resin glands from heat, light, air, and fondling hands. The smoke has a mint-like taste because the chlorophyll does not break down.

and curing process to learn how much moisture it has lost. For example, a bud that weighs 10 grams (0.36 oz) upon harvest, will weigh 2.5 grams (0.09 oz) when it has lost 75 percent of its moisture. In general, a dry bud will weigh 75 percent less than its wet weight at harvest.

Packaging and Storage

Storing cannabis in an airtight environment will preserve aroma, taste, and potency. Use a vacuum sealer to evacuate air in glass jars. Inexpensive vacuum sealers are available in the canning section of grocery and variety stores. Growers report that containers sealed with inexpensive vacuum sealers lose the vacuum after a few days. More expensive vacuum sealers such as the one available at www.deni.com work much better. When properly vacuum-packed, buds will stay as fresh as the day they were sealed in the airtight jar.

Vacuum seal the jar, and place it in the refrigerator for storage. Leave it in the refrigerator or a cool, dark, dry place for a month or longer. The taste and potency will be tops! Refrigeration slows decomposition, but, remember, refrigerators have a high humidity level, so the container must be sealed airtight. I just checked the relative humidity and temperature in my refrigerator—65 percent relative humidity and 40°F (5°C). Do not place it in the freezer. Freezing draws moisture to the surface of buds, which can harm resin glands on the surface.

Place sealed containers in a cool, dry, dark place. Some growers prefer to keep airtight, sealed containers in the refrigerator. If the seal is not airtight, the low temperature in the refrigerator creates a condition of high humidity. Dry buds stored in a container that is not airtight attract moisture in the high-humidity environment. Before long, the buds are so moist that they must be dried again.

Seed Crops

Harvest seed crops when seeds are big and ripe. Often, seeds actually split open their containing seed bract. Flowering females grow

This grower lets buds dry slowly in a large cedar box before moving them to a glass container for the final cure.

Remove the lid of a jar two or three times a day to allow moisture to escape during the curing process.

Curing jars with a rubber seal keep the environment inside airtight.

Buds are bagged after weighing.

Bagged buds are then put into the vacuum/sealing machine.

Once in place, air is removed and the bag of buds is hermetically sealed.

The end result is a compact, airtight bag of buds.

many ready, receptive calyxes until pollination occurs. Seeds are fully mature within six to eight weeks. Once pollinated, the majority of the female's energy is directed toward seed production. Tetrahydrocannabinol (THC) content is usually of minimum importance. Seed crops can be left in the ground until seeds "rattle in the pod," but most growers harvest them before then. Watch for and control insects, mites, and fungus that attack the weakening female and her cache of ripe seeds.

Home breeders often pollinate only one or two branches. The unpollinated branches are sinsemilla. The sinsemilla tops are harvested when ripe. Seeded branches continue to mature for another week or two until ripe. When seeds are mature, remove them from the pods by rubbing seeded buds between your hands over a container. To separate seeds from marijuana, place harvested seeds and accompanying foliage in a large tray with sides. Move the tray back and forth and tip so the seeds congregate in one corner. Remove excess marijuana by hand and repeat the process. Rub seeds together in

Seeds in this 'Blueberry' female from Dutch Passion are split open, resin-coated calyxes.

your hands to remove traces of calyxes that still adhere to seeds. Agitate tray and tip to congregate seeds and separate from chaff.

Store seeds in a cool, dry, dark place. The seeds are viable and ready for planting as soon as they are harvested, but they may grow sickly plants. Let the seeds dry out a month or two before planting. Seeds with a hard outer cask are the most likely to sprout and grow well. See "Storing Seeds" in Chapter Two.

Rejuvenation

This photo of a seeded 'TNT' female was snapped in Gypsy Nirvana's grow room before the police harvested her.

Rejuvenate harvested females by leaving several undeveloped lower branches with foliage on plants. Give her an 18/6 day/night photoperiod. The female will stop flowering and rejuvenate and revert back to vegetative growth stage.

Give the harvested, leafy, buddy stubs an increased dose of high-nitrogen fertilizer to promote green, leafy growth. This will help the harvested plant grow more foliage as it reverts back to vegetative growth in four to six weeks. New, green, leafy growth will sprout from the branches and flower tops. Leaves will continue to grow more and more "fingers" as re-vegetation progresses. Let the rejuvenated plants grow until they are the desired size before inducing flowering with a 12-

Let seeds develop until they are big and strong. Most often some of the seeds will actually split open the containing calyx.

hour photoperiod. If second crops are allowed to grow too tall, they produce sparse buds. Remember, these plants are already root bound and when given dim light, sparse buds result.

Here is a possible scenario to rejuvenate plants. For example, a person who grew a beautiful crop of females and knew each plant by name, had to harvest. Instead of starting from seed again, the grower decided to leave a few leaves and buds on the harvested stubby branches. He induced vegetative growth with 18-hour days and 6-hour nights the day after harvesting. A month later, he took many clones from these original favorite females. He induced the original mothers to flower a month after the clones were taken. The clones were rooted, transplanted, and moved into a flowering room. The original harvest was taken on January 1st. The second harvest was April 1st. The second harvest weighed less, and the buds were smaller. Taking clones from rejuvenated plants also diffuses hormones and severely stresses plants.

Rejuvenated plants take from a month to six weeks to develop new vegetative growth.

This female received 18 hours of light daily. A mistake made it receive a 12/12 day/night schedule for three days, which induced flowering. The grower put it back on an 18/6 day/night photoperiod. The plant took 6 weeks to resume normal vegetative growth. The light stress also caused leaves to grow in circles!

Female plants in this Colombian greenhouse are sheltered from daily rains.

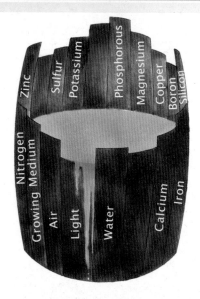

This barrel full of water shows that cannabis will grow only as fast as its most limiting factor. Light is most often the factor that limits growth indoors.

Air   20%
   Temperature
   Humidity
   CO_2 and O_2 content

Light   20%
   Spectrum (color)
   Intensity
   Photoperiod (hours of light per day)

Water   20%
   Temperature
   pH
   EC
   Oxygen content

Nutrients   20%
   Composition
   Purity

Growing Medium   20%
   Air content
   Moisture content

Introduction

The best location for a grow room is in an obscure corner of a basement, where the temperature is easy to keep constant year round. Basements are well insulated by concrete walls and soil. A basement room can be enclosed and camouflaged with junk, a double wall, workbench, or shelving.

Added security is afforded by installing a false door in a closet. The grow room is located behind the secret door. Another good secret location, except for the possible heat build-up, is the attic. Few people venture to an attic that is difficult to access. Some growers locate their gardens below a trapdoor covered with a rug.

Law enforcement cannot use the electricity bill as sole grounds for a search warrant. But, they can use it along with other "evidence" such as remnants of indoor growing visible outdoors, thermal image heat signatures, snitch testimony, etc., to secure a search warrant. As long as the marijuana grown is not sold or shown to a snitch, there should be no reason for any suspicion. Thermal image technology is easy to outwit. Just keep the lights on during daylight hours to confuse the technology. Or, cool exhaust air and expel it under the well-insulated grow house so it does not leave a heat trail.

Outbuildings, garages, and barns not

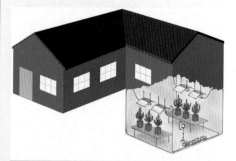

This cutaway basement grow room shows a real scenario. Plants on tables stay warmer and are easy to maintain.

attached to homes are some of the worst places to grow cannabis. Thieves and law enforcement often do not regard entering a barn or garage as a crime, though they would not consider entering a home. Security is much better when the garden is within the home.

Although less common, there are even grow rooms on wheels! Some innovative growers have remodeled trailer houses and buses into grow rooms. One of my favorite grow rooms was in a tricked-out trailer. Another was in a 60-foot (18 m) sailing yacht!

The grow room's size determines the size and the number of lamps. High intensity discharge (HID) lamps that work well to grow marijuana are available in wattages of 150, 175, 250, 400, 600, 1000, and 1100. Smaller wattages from 150-400, work well in closets or spaces with 9-21 square feet (0.8-2 m²) of floor space. Use 600-watt and larger bulbs for larger areas.

The drawings (pages 108-109) show several grow room floor plans. As the floor plans demonstrate, there are several basic approaches to grow room design and production. Most growers start out with a crop grown in a single room. After they harvest the crop, they introduce a new batch of clones. The photoperiod is switched back to 18 hours, and the cycle continues.

The most productive setups utilize two rooms. The first room is for vegetative growth, mother plants, and rooting clones. This room should be about one-quarter the size of the flowering room. When the flowering room crop is harvested, plants from the vegetative room are moved into the flowering room.

Super productivity is achieved with a perpetual crop. Several clones are taken every day or every week. Every day a few plants are harvested. For every plant harvested, a new cutting takes its place.

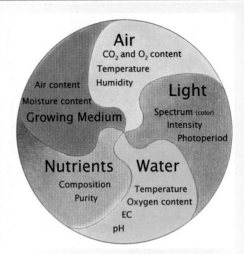

Air
CO_2 and O_2 content
Temperature
Humidity

Air content
Moisture content
Growing Medium

Light
Spectrum (color)
Intensity
Photoperiod

Nutrients
Composition
Purity

Water
Temperature
Oxygen content
EC
pH

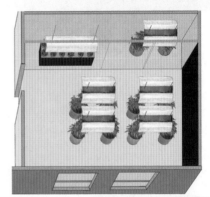

This indoor setup has a big flowering room, a vegetative room, and a clone chamber.

This productive grow room is located in a closed-off corner of the basement.

Take a little time to set up your grow room so all the space is used efficiently.

This closet grow room has everything necessary to grow a crop–lights, fans, and cannabis! A 400-watt HID lights the 3 × 4- foot (90 ×120 cm) flowering room above, and two 55-watt CFLs in one reflector illuminate mothers and clones in this perpetual harvest setup.

Setting Up the Grow Room- Step-by-Step

Set up the grow room before introducing plants. Construction requires space and planning. A grow room under construction offers a terrible environment for plants. Once the grow room is set up and totally operational, it will be ready for plants.

Step One: *Choose an out-of-the-way space with little or no traffic. A corner of the basement or a spare bedroom are perfect. A 1000-watt HID, properly set up, will efficiently illuminate up to a 6 × 6-foot (1.8 x 1.8 m) room. The ceiling should be at least five feet (1.5 m) high. Keep in mind that plants in containers are set up at least one foot (30 cm) off the ground, and the lamp needs about a foot (30 cm) of space to hang from the ceiling. This leaves only three feet (90 cm) of space for plants to grow. If forced to grow in an attic or basement with a low four-foot (120 cm) ceiling, much can be done to compensate for the loss of height, including cloning, bending, pruning, and using smaller wattage lamps.*

Step Two: Enclose the room, if not already enclosed. Remove everything that does not pertain to the garden. Furniture, drapes, and curtains may harbor fungi. An enclosed room allows easy, precise control of everything and everyone that enters or exits, as well as who and what goes on inside. For most growers, enclosing the grow room is simply a matter of tacking up some plywood

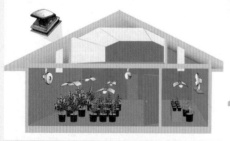

A single 1000-watt metal halide can grow enough mothers, clones, and vegetative plants to support 4000 watts of flowering HID light. This design allows pungent odors to waft upward before being evacuated via roof fans. A third area in the attic is used as a heat buffer in hot climates.

This attic grow room has access via a retractable ladder. The grower uses the dead airspace above the room for his ozone generator to exchange air before expelling.

or fabricating plastic walls in the basement or attic and painting the room flat white. Make sure no light is visible from outside. If covering a window, do so discreetly–it should not look boarded up. Insulate windows and walls so a telltale heat signature does not escape. Basement windows often are painted to look like the foundation. Place some stuff–books, personal effects, household goods, etc.–in front of the window, and build a box around the things so a natural scene is visible from the outside. At night, bright light leaking through a crack in an uncovered window is like a beacon to curious neighbors or bandits.

This attic grow room is insulated with Styrofoam and reflection/anti-detection barrier foil available at www.hysupply.nl, which keeps the heat signature from showing.

Step Three: Cover walls, ceiling, floor–everything–with a highly reflective material like flat white paint or Mylar. The more reflection, the more light energy available to plants. Good reflective light will allow effective coverage of an HID lamp to increase from 10 to 20 percent, just by putting a few dollars worth of paint on the walls. Reflective white Visqueen® plastic is inexpensive and protects walls and floors.

Step Four: See "Setting Up the Vent Fan" in Chapter Thirteen. Constant air circulation and a supply of fresh air are essential but often inadequate. There should be at least one fresh-air vent in every grow room. Vents can be an open door, window, or duct vented to the outside. An exhaust fan vented outdoors or pulling new air through an open door usually creates an adequate flow of air. An oscillating fan works well to circulate air. When installing such a fan, make sure it is not set in a fixed position and blowing too hard on tender plants. It could cause windburn and dry out plants, especially seedlings and clones. If the room contains a heat vent, it may be opened to supply extra heat or air circulation.

Step Five: The larger your garden becomes, the more water it will need. A 10 × 10-foot (3 × 3 m) garden could use more than 50 gallons (190 L) per week. Carrying water is

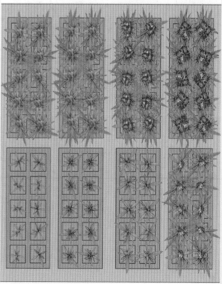

In this simple Sea of Green layout, there are ten plants in each tray (80 total plants) illuminated by a single 1000-watt HID. Each week one tray of ten plants is harvested, and ten new plants are started.

These plants are growing in 3-gallon (11 L) pots and spaced on 6-inch (15 cm) centers. The 5-foot (2 m) high walls are covered with white Visqueen plastic.

Keeping heat inside the room is as important as keeping it out! Insulation will keep heat out, and the heat generated inside the room will be easy to control.

hard, regular work. One gallon (3.8 L) of water weighs eight pounds (3.6 kg); 50 × 8 = 400 pounds (180 kg) of water a week! It is much easier to run in a hose with an on/off valve or install a hose bib in the room than to schlep water. A three-foot (90 cm) watering wand attached to the hose on/off valve makes watering easier and saves branches from being broken when watering in dense foliage. Hook up the hose to a hot and cold water source so the temperature is easy to regulate.

Step Six: Ideally, the floor should be concrete or a smooth surface that can be swept and washed down. A floor drain is very handy. In grow rooms with carpet or wood floors, a large, white painter's drop cloth or thick, white Visqueen plastic, will protect floors from moisture. Trays placed beneath each container add protection and convenience.

Step Seven: Mount a hook strong enough to support 30 pounds (14 kg) for each lamp. Attach an adjustable chain or cord and pulley between the ceiling hook and the lamp fixture. The adjustable connection makes it easy to keep the lamp at the proper distance from plants and up out of the way during maintenance.

Step Eight: There are some tools an indoor gardener must have and a few extra tools that make indoor horticulture much more precise and cost effective. The extra tools help make the garden so efficient that they pay for themselves in a few weeks. Procure all the tools before bringing plants into the room. If the tools are there when needed, chances are they will be put to use. A hygrometer is a good example. If plants show signs of slow, sickly growth due to high humidity, most growers will not identify the exact cause right away. They will wait and guess, wait and guess, and maybe figure it out before a fungus attacks and the plant dies. When a hygrometer is installed before plants are brought into the grow room, the horticulturist will know from the start when the humidity is too high and causing sickly growth.

Step Nine: Read and complete: "Setting Up the HID Lamp" at the end of Chapter Nine.

Step Ten: Move seedlings and rooted clones into the room. Huddle them closely together under the lamp. Make sure the HID is not so close to small plants that it burns their leaves. Position 400-watt lamps 18 inches (45 cm) above seedlings and clones. Place a 600-watt lamp 24 inches (60 cm) away and a 1000-watt lamp 30 inches (75 cm) away. Check the distance daily. Hang a precut string from the hood to measure distance.

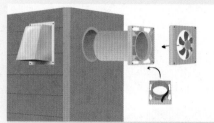

This drawing shows how to install a vent fan. Adding rubber feet or padding around the fan will dampen noise.

Greenhouses and Cold Frames

This simple overview of greenhouses and cold frames will give you a feeling of what to look for and how to plan your project and reap a heavy harvest. Several links below will help you tap into the wealth of information on greenhouses and cold frames.

A vent fan and an oscillating circulation fan are essential to maintain a healthy environment.

Greenhouses, cold frames, and hot frames are all useful in extending the growing season and/or protecting new plants and seedlings. Which type of structure you select depends on the size and location of your growing area, how much money you have to spend, how much time you have to grow, and security issues. Simple cold frames and hot frames can be assembled from common materials like old framed window panes and hay bales. Greenhouses are generally larger and more complex. They can be expensive to build and maintain but offer more flexibility for growing time and building use.

When deciding on a growing structure, first carefully analyze the project on paper. Consider how much space you have for the footprint and how many plants you can grow safely. Cold frames are small and can be as simple as a glass or plastic frame set on the ground with no artificial heat source. Their

A watering can works well in small gardens and to apply small amounts of fertilizer.

This carpeted bedroom is completely lined with reflective Visqueen plastic. Duct tape works very well to hold the overlapping Visqueen together even under moist conditions.

This Swiss grower anchored a strong steel beam to the ceiling from which he suspended all the lights.

basic function is to protect young plants and seedlings from wind and cold in the early spring, but they can also be blacked out to induce early flowering and harvest. Hot frames are similar in size and structure but provide heat through manure, electricity, steam, or a hot-water pipe (radiant heat). You may use a hot frame to raise early seedlings and clones, after which the structure can be converted into a cold frame. Both frames share the advantages of economy, simplicity, small size, and portability.

Both large and small greenhouses cost more money, time, and space. With the exception of the lightweight "hoop" house or miniature greenhouse, they are also more permanent. The type of greenhouse selected will be determined by the planned use of the space and where it will be located. A lean-to or attached greenhouse will probably be smaller and less expensive to build than a freestanding structure.

Total area of the greenhouse is determined by the number of plants you intend to grow. Allow one square yard (90 cm^2) per mature plant. Do not forget to allow about

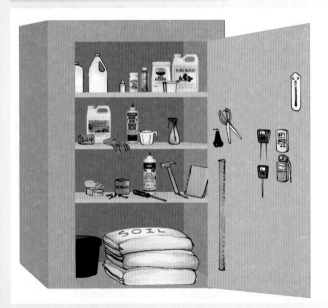

Necessary Tools:

Thermometer
Spray bottle
pH tester
Liquid biodegradable soap
Hygrometer
Pruners or scissors
Wire ties
Sheetrock screws
Screwdriver
Measuring cup and
    spoons
Pencil and notebook
Moisture meter
Light meter
Yardstick to measure
    growth!

six inches (15 cm) space for air circulation between benches and side-walls. Add space for walkways–standing room only or room for a wheelbarrow–and possibly a center bench. Glass, plastic panels, and sheeting all come in standard widths, and it is easier to build in a size compatible with these units rather than have to cut the panels down. For example, an eight-foot (2.4 m) house can be made with two 48-inch (120 cm) wide fiberglass panels. Center height depends on the level of the eaves. Low growing plants can take an eave of five feet (1.5 m); tall plants need six or seven feet (1.8 or 2.1 m). After determining eave height, a simple formula will give you the center height: Center height = eave + 0.25 width (a twelve-foot wide (3.6 m) house with a five-foot (1.5 m) eave will have a center height of eight feet (2.4 m).

These vegetative clones were transplanted a week earlier and grown out under 24 hours of light before being moved into the flowering room.

Budget, building skills, and security will weigh heavily in the decision making process. The least expensive structure per square foot (m²) is an even-span 16-foot (4.8 m) wide that will house two side beds or benches, two walks, and a wide center bed or bench. An 8 to 12 foot (2.4 to 3.6 m) wide lean-to with wide beds or benches and a central walk is the least expensive option overall. Whichever option you choose, building it yourself will be cheaper and more secure than hiring a contractor. You can purchase much of the plumbing and electricity installations in kits or pre-assembled to avoid compromising security. Here is an excellent web site for the do-it-yourselfer: http://www.buildeazy.com/greenhouse.html Or consider a kit: http://www.greenhouse kit.com/frame.htm.

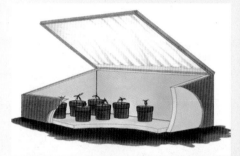

This cutaway shows the Styrofoam lining to retain heat. The Styrofoam insulates small containers from cold ground. The top is hinged to give complete access and when raised, it acts as an efficient vent.

Climate will play a role in choosing your greenhouse. For example, a cold frame in the mild Pacific Northwest can give you a six-week jump on the growing season. This would not work in a colder region like the upper Midwest. Likewise, a hot or tropical area will require more shade and water. While the large cold frame is the most eco-

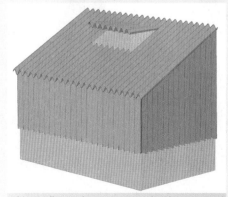

This small greenhouse is covered with corrugated fiberglass. A vent on the top is all the ventilation necessary. Enough light penetrates the fiberglass to foster plant growth and keep out of public view.

Hoop houses are very easy to construct from plastic or metal pipe. Some growers use rebar. Arches can easily be made with PVC plastic pipe up to 8 feet (2.4 m) tall. You can also make tunnels hug the ground with a height of less than 3 feet (90 cm).

Black plastic mulch conserves moisture and stops weeds in this hoop house.

This photo was taken in Nijmegen, Netherlands, in late November, 1985, at the original Cannabis Castle started by Neville, owner of the Seed Bank. Plants grow in small squares of rockwool. The white box at right is a heater.

nomical of structures, it will not function as a cold-climate garden. Location and exposure will depend on climate, but in general, you will want the greenhouse to be sheltered from curious eyes and strong winds and to be away from any areas where falling limbs or other debris might be a problem.

There are a number of external design options. Cold frames can be as simple as a window sash laid over a rectangle of straw bales or a piece of plastic stretched over a metal or PVC pipe frame and held in place with clamps. Duct tape also works wonders to keep plastic in place. The advantage to plastic sheeting is that it can be removed during the day to take advantage of fresh air and the sun's warmth and then replaced at night to protect plants from cold air. The cold frame can easily be converted to a hot frame by installing electric heat and a watering/misting system.

Greenhouses can be attached (lean-to, window-mount, even-span) or free-standing. A lean-to uses an existing structure for one or more sides and is limited to single or double-row plant benches with a total width of seven to twelve feet (2.1-3.6 m) and length up to that of the building. Without considering security, the advantages of the lean-to are its proximity to electricity, water, and heat, but on the downside are its limited size, light, ventilation, and temperature control.

A window-mount replaces an existing window providing a relatively low-cost way to grow short plants, small seedlings, or clones. It can be installed fairly simply with common household tools. The disadvantages are its small size and possibly public view.

Low profile greenhouses are perfect for crops of short plants. It is easy to set up a low profile hoop house or a greenhouse alongside a building that gets full sun. The short greenhouse or cold frame is simple to darken during full summer and lets you reap the benefits of the harvest early!

Small greenhouses and cold frames also work well on patios, balconies, and rooftops. They protect plants from wind and prying eyes of neighbors.

An even-span can be an attractive option. Like the window-mount or lean-to, the even-span is attached to the house and bears similar limitations of size, light, ventilation, and temperature. Unlike the lean-to or window-mount, the even-span can be larger and can open into the house–providing heat and humidity–or even function as a conservatory, an attractive place to relax. It is, however, more expensive to heat and maintain. Such greenhouses are most popular where security is a minimum concern.

The freestanding greenhouse offers the most flexibility in size and location. It can be built to take full advantage of the sun, but it does not retain heat well and can be expensive to keep warm. Many frame types and coverings are available in kits or raw materials. There are also a number of good web sites such as http://www.wvu.edu/~agexten/hortcult/greenhou/building.htm to help you choose the plan that works best for you.

Framing can be in wood or metal. You may select a panel frame which is more expensive to build (panels are individual units) but has the advantage of quick installation and breakdown for storage. If portability is an issue, there are miniature greenhouses and hoop houses which can be purchased as a kit for under $300. These structures, because they can be picked up and moved, are usually considered temporary by municipalities and often do not require permits. For more information on types and prices, visit web sites such as www.hoophouse.com .

The female seedling transplants in this greenhouse have just been watered. Even though they were transplanted late, they still grew out well.

Coverings

Options for coverings are more extensive than those for framing. The traditional greenhouse is glass. Glass, besides compromising security, is heavy, expensive, and easily broken. Plastics and fiberglass can provide safe, economical alternatives.

Early-flowering crop in a greenhouse shows these ladies touching leaves. They are 3 feet (90 cm) tall.

This backyard greenhouse near Paris, France was recently planted.

Two months after planting, the grower used black plastic to induce flowering with a 12/12 day/night photoperiod.

The long 12-hour nights induce visible signs of flowering in about two weeks. These plants have been flowering for almost a month.

Plastic is much cheaper than glass (a sixth to a tenth of the cost), can be heated as effectively as glass, and is equal to glass in producing quality plants and buds. Polyethylene (PE) is low cost, lightweight, provides ample light, and can withstand fall, winter, and spring weather. It does not tolerate summer UV levels, however, and must be replaced annually. Ultra-violet inhibited PE lasts longer, but both types lose heat more quickly than glass. During the day, this can help keep plants cooler, but at night the heat loss requires the use of an artificial heat source. Poly Weave™ is a plastic fabric made of 8-mil polyethylene reinforced with nylon mesh. It transmits up to 90% sunlight, can be sewn or taped, and has a lifespan of up to five years.

Polyvinyl chloride (PVC) is two to five times more expensive than PE but can last five years or longer. Polyvinylchloride is pliable, transparent or translucent, and comes in four to six foot (1.2-1.8 m) widths which can be sealed together to provide a super-wide piece. Ultraviolet inhibited corrugated plastic panels provide another option. The panels can be used in cold frames, propagation houses, and greenhouses to provide excellent wind and snow protection and optimal solar heat collection. UV inhibited corrugated plastic also has insulating properties (2.5 R insulation/3.5 mm panels, 3.0 R/5.0 mm panels).

Corrugated fiberglass is lightweight, strong, and comes in eight to twelve foot (2.4-3.6 m) panels. Poor grades will discolor, reducing light penetration, but a good grade of clear fiberglass can cost as much or more than glass. Its lower weight is an advantage, and it is more difficult to see through!

Lexan™ http://www.geplastics.com/gelexan/ is a thermoplastic that lasts for years and transmits almost as much light as glass while retaining heat. Clear panels like those in glass or Lexan™ may require shading during the heat of the day. Again, there are a number of options. You may select a roll-up shade of wood or aluminum, or a shading compound that is painted onto the outside of the glass. Vinyl plastic is a flexible film that installs easily against wet glass inside the structure and is reusable.

Framework and covering are only the beginning. Growing plants in a greenhouse is often more demanding than growing plants indoors. Air temperature, humidity, light, and air quality must all be controlled in relation to a constantly changing greenhouse climate.

Big strong buds are a few weeks from harvest.

Climate Control

Even the best greenhouses will lose heat through radiation, conduction, convection through glass, walls, and floor (or soil), and also through vents, doors, and cracks. To counteract external variables, the internal structure of the greenhouse is, in some ways, more complex than the selection of framing and covering materials.

All greenhouses need ventilation and most need fans. Look for an extraction fan with the capacity to change the air once every minute. Capacity refers to the amount of power needed to circulate the air volume of your structure.

Calculate the volume by multiplying the square footage of your greenhouse by the height. Multiply the volume by sixty air changes per hour to get the cubic feet per minute (cfm) capacity of the greenhouse.

For example a greenhouse with the following:
8 × 12 × 7 feet (2.4 × 3.6 × 2.1 m) greenhouse requires a fan with a cfm of 40,320
8 × 12 × 7 feet × 60 minutes = 40,320
Here is a similar metric example:
2.5 × 3.5 × 2 = 17.5 m^2 × 60 minutes = 1050 m^3

The combination of louvers and fan will force the hottest, most humid air out while protecting the plants from draft. See Chapter Thirteen, "Air," for more information.

Vents control temperatures in all seasons and improve growing conditions. Hand-operated roof vents will require frequent checks, or you may install automatic vents with an electric motor and thermostat that will respond to conditions around the clock. Venting is important with a cold frame, too. The high-end models have wax-filled vents that operate automatically, opening when the

This good looking 'Mekong Haze' is an outstanding sativa cross.

heat rises in the frame and contracting as the temperature cools. You can find the paraffin-filled "Optivent" and many other greenhouse supplies at www.charleysgreenhouse.com.

Heating systems are important to keep plants healthy during cold nights. Cannabis grows well with night temperatures of 60-65°F (16-18°C), but colder nights will require an additional heat source for sustained growth.

You can turn a cold frame into a hot frame by insulating it with manure or heating it with steam, hot water pipes, or electricity. To make the most efficient use of electricity, purchase soil-heating tape or cable, with a thermostat that will automatically control the temperature. Lay the cable on the soil at the bottom of the bed or on a bed of sand or vermiculite and cover with about two inches (5 cm) of sand. You will need to provide 10-15 watts of electric heat for every square foot (30 cm^2) of growing area. Heat cables are also useful in greenhouses for warming seedlings, clones, or flowering plants without the cost of heating the entire structure.

Small greenhouses can be heated relatively economically with an electric space heater, or more effectively with thermostatically controlled forced air using ducts or plastic tubing to distribute the heat. Larger units may be

This Swiss clone greenhouse was converted from a greenhouse that grew bedding flowers and vegetables.

heated with forced air or by a coal or natural hot-water or steam system. Steam can also be used to sterilize growing beds and potting soils. Then there is the low-tech method of greenhouse warming: compost. A grower in Portland, Oregon, stacks organic matter on the sides of the greenhouse to a height of about five feet (1.5 m) inside and out. As the compost decomposes, it gives off heat keeping the structure warm at a very low cost.

Evaporative cooling eliminates excess heat and adds humidity, reducing water needs. Moist air circulates through the structure while warm air is expelled through roof vents or exhaust fans. Properly installed, a cooler can reduce the interior temperature as much as 30-40°F (15-23°C) in hot, dry climates, less in wetter areas. As with fans, the size of the cooler is determined by the size of the greenhouse. A general guideline is to find a cooler equal to the total cubic space of the structure plus 50%. To provide both cooling and humidifying effects, the cooler must be installed on the outside of the greenhouse; otherwise, it simply humidifies without dropping the temperature. Turner greenhouses has a handy site (http://www.turnergreenhouses.com/Cooling/cool_tip.html) with some quick tips on selecting a cooling system for your greenhouse. Other great greenhouse sites include: http://www.igcusa.com/greenhousecooling_information.htm for some helpful graphics and http://www.cpjungle.com/nuecool.htm for a detailed explanation of cooling needs and resources.

Misting and watering are also important components of greenhouse gardening. Extended periods of growing and higher sustained temperatures make adequate water essential. Again, there are methods to suit every temperament from low-tech to automatic.

Most companies offer watering and misting systems by component, which can be mixed and matched to suit the grower's needs.

Automatic systems will have a timer that triggers the mist or water at preset intervals. You may want a toggle switch that allows you to rotate between manual and automatic watering. For more information on specific uses and types of watering systems, go to a website such as www.cloudtops.com which covers a variety of topics pertaining to the internal greenhouse environment.

A lower-tech method of mist and watering control consists of a series of screens that tilt downward with the weight of the water shutting off the flow then raising to restart the cycle as the screens dry. It is fully automated by the weight of the water or lack thereof. Of course, there is also hand-watering which is very effective and requires no mechanical intervention. Automatic systems, both high and low-tech, are alternatives to hand-watering that can be most helpful during a gardener's absence.

Heating and watering devices depend on that other cost of greenhouse keeping: how much time the grower has to spend tending plants. You can keep equipment costs to a minimum if you plan to spend a lot of time in the greenhouse. For growers who are away from the structure for long periods, automatic systems are a good investment.

In addition to shelter, heat, water, and ventilation, plants need light. This section will offer a brief treatment of lighting, since it is covered in greater depth in Chapter Nine. Fluorescent light offers higher efficiency with low heat and is the most widely used. Incandescent light– 60-500 watts–may be used to extend daylength. High-intensity discharge (HID) offers long life, and the sodium lamps emit the best light to be combined with natural sunlight. Regardless of light source selected, you may want to purchase a light meter ($30-50). It will be very useful in setting the light level in your greenhouse for maximum efficiency.

Carbon Dioxide (CO_2) is another important aspect of the greenhouse environment that will be only touched upon in this section.

Over the last decade, the soil in this Spanish glasshouse has been regularly amended with organic matter. The growers put lightweight hydroclay on soil surface as mulch that does not decompose.

This beautiful greenhouse was grown by the legendary Shantibaba in Switzerland. After an extended stint in Swiss prison, he is free!

Greenhouse buds in all directions!

Closed greenhouses often have too little CO_2 during the day for plants to be able to use light effectively. Enhancing the levels of CO_2 will accelerate plant growth; methods for doing so range from expensive CO_2 equipment with infrared sensors to block dry ice kept in a pressure bottle until needed. More detailed information on CO_2 can be found in Chapter Thirteen, "Air."

Security is always a concern when growing cannabis. There are several ways to camouflage the greenhouse such as growing other plants with the cannabis. Paint the walls with sun-blocking paint so light still enters but prying eyes do not. Go to the discount store and purchase artificial flowers. Put the artificial flowers on and around the cannabis plants so it looks like they are growing from the cannabis. Remember to pay attention to other plants that could be blooming during this time and follow suit.

Planting in the earth floor of the greenhouse allows you to use organic methods. The plants cannot be moved easily, but they grow bigger and require less maintenance than container-grown plants. Without containers, plants also retain a lower profile. Growing in Mother Earth is always better than planting in pots! Most all the principles that apply to outdoor growing apply to growing in a greenhouse, too. Check out Chapter Seven, "Outdoors" and Chapter Ten, "Soil & Containers" for more information.

Seeded female from Next Generation seeds in British Colombia, Canada is one of the new and upcoming companies.

Greenhouses can be darkened to induce flowering during mid summer. This practice will allow you to harvest up to three crops a year! Cannabis plants flower when nights are long (12 hours) and days are short (12 hours). Darken the greenhouse so that plants receive 12 hours of uninterrupted darkness every day to induce flowering. When the greenhouse is darkened daily so that plants receive 12 hours of darkness, a crop of clones planted May 1st can be harvested by the middle of July.

Automatic darkening machinery is available for large commercial greenhouses. Smaller greenhouses are normally covered with black plastic to "black out" the interior for 12 hours.

When combined with natural sunlight, artificial light is optimally used during non-daylight hours. Greenhouse growers turn the HID lights on when sunlight diminishes (30 minutes before sunset) and off when sunlight strengthens (30 minutes after sunrise). Turn on the HID when the daylight intensity is less than two times the intensity of the HID. Measure this point with a light meter. Turn off the HID when the daylight intensity is greater than two times the intensity of the HID. A simple photocell that measures light intensity can be used to turn the lights on and off automatically.

Supplementary lighting has greatest effect when applied to the youngest plants. It is least expensive to light plants when they are small.

Many different types of coverings are available for greenhouses and cold frames. The best greenhouse films are UV (ultraviolet) resistant and still transmit plenty of light. Lexan is rigid and full of thermo-storing

This Swiss grower moves the covering over plants in the afternoon and opens it after dark. The coverings slide over smooth wires strung between wooden posts.

channels. It is one of the best greenhouse plastics available. Lexan lasts for years and transmits almost as much light as glass while retaining greenhouse heat. The only problem with Lexan is that it is clear! Some growers disguise greenhouse cannabis by wiring ornamental plastic flowers to the branches visible to passers by, which is advisable where neighbors are not curious and laws lax.

Regulating heat in a greenhouse is much more difficult than in an enclosed grow room. Greenhouses heat up quickly on sunny days and cool equally fast when the sun ducks behind a cloud or drops below the horizon. This fluctuation in heat is difficult and expensive to control. Hot and cold dips also affect the ratio of nutrient to water plants need and use, which makes growing in a greenhouse more demanding than growing indoors.

Adding a complete greenhouse chapter here is beyond the scope of this book. A

Automatic greenhouse darkening system in a greenhouse at the Cannabis Castle in the Netherlands "blacks out" gardens to induce flowering. The covering also serves to insulate the greenhouse during the short days of winter.

couple of my favorite books on greenhouse growing include *Gardening Under Cover*, by William Head, Sasquatch Books, $16.95, and *Gardening in Your Greenhouse*, by Mark Freeman, Stackpole Books, $18.95.

Keep the lights on at night if days are short in the winter or if you live in a tropical climate. These South American growers use incandescent light to prevent plants from flowering when days are short.

Good looking bud matures in light filtered through Agrolene greenhouse covering.

Gregorio (Goyo), cannabis photographer and writer demonstrates a field of flowering females in Switzerland.

Peek-a-boo! This beautiful 'Jamaican Pearl' was planted in an obscure corner of the back yard.

The grower is peeking through this plant in his guerilla patch.

Introduction

Much of the information that pertains specifically to outdoor cultivation is in this chapter. Many of the subjects within this chapter are covered in great detail in other chapters of the book. References to these chapters are made in the appropriate places.

Outdoor growing is more popular than indoor growing in countries with lax cannabis laws. The reason is simple–sunshine is free; lights and electricity cost money. More people grow outdoors than indoors for this simple reason.

Cannabis is a strong plant that can be grown successfully almost anywhere. As long as you pay attention to security, virtually any growing area can be altered enough, often with little effort, to grow a healthy crop.

Do your research before planting. Read garden columns and talk to local growers about the best time to plant and grow tomatoes or similar vegetables, then plan accordingly. Also inquire about common pests and insects. Collect publications on local growing conditions. These are often available at nurseries or through your local department or ministry of agriculture.

You can grow anywhere. For example, one of the first guerilla crops I planted was on a freeway on-ramp in a city in the Northwest U.S. in the 1970s. I planted seedlings in a clay soil in a blackberry infested environment in late June. I gave the plants a single application of time release fertilizer. By late September there were short little female plants with dense little buds to smoke. The harvest weighed in at just under a pound of fragrant but leafy little buds. Everybody called it "homegrown."

My first big guerilla crop was planted and harvested in the California foothills. I hiked up one of the many canyons carrying a 3.5 hp engine that weighed 30 pounds, (14 kg) plus the pump (another 30 pounds) and the plumbing connections that made it attach to a 2-inch (5 cm) inlet and a 1.5-inch (3.5 cm) outlet. Schlepping four, 30-gallon (115 L) plastic garbage cans to act as reservoirs, 10-foot (3 m) lengths of PVC pipe, and 200 feet (60 m) of hose was a challenge!

I made these trips carrying conspicuous supplies at four in the morning. The hard part was carrying it all back down when I closed down the grow show!

After many trips up the canyon, I harvested six pounds of Colombian and Mexican bud. The quality was fair, but I harvested early and had the only fresh buds in town in mid-September.

In "the good old days," rural real estate for sale in northern California often advertised the number of marijuana growing holes that had already been amended.

Now Park Rangers carry guns and have the authority to arrest "suspected" growers. Latin mafias have also moved into the National Forests installing illegal immigrants with guns to grow and defend large patches of guerilla grass. The War on Drugs has turned much of America into an unsafe place to live and grow.

Australia, Canada, much of Europe, and many other parts of the world are significantly different; growers can plant in their backyards, greenhouses, or in remote locations with little fear of arrest.

Cannabis strains mature at different times. Choose strains that grow well in your climate and that ripen before days grow cold and wet.

Strains

Selecting the right strains for your climate is just as important as finding the perfect location. This section on strains is adapted from a thread started by Leaf, a member of www.overgrow.com and an expert outdoor grower with tons of experience. One of the Case Studies is also adapted from posts by Leaf. Much more information is also available on the site.

This is a quick rundown on some popular outdoor strains. The strains are grouped in five different categories distinguished by their finishing times. For more information on strains, check our website, www.marijuanagrowing.com.

It is a good idea to grow several different strains with different finishing times to spread out the work and drying over the course of time. If you grow a spring crop, you can harvest much of the season.

'Hash Plant', available from many seed companies, is ready to harvest in late August when grown outdoors.

'Early Riser', true to its name, is ready to harvest from late August to mid-September.

'Jack Herer' finishes from mid- to late-September.

1. 'Hash Plant', 'Afghani', 'Hindu Kush', etc., are great varieties that finish mid- to late-August. The yield and potency are quite high, but the fragrance is high, too! These strains are for experienced growers. They need lots of intense sunlight and must be watered from below, not from above with rain. These varieties start to bud when the days are long and the sunlight is intense. The buds fatten up quickly on plants with a short, squat growth habit. Rain followed by hot sunny days can foster mold, which could decimate the crop in a short time. Leaf has seen dried, cured buds the size of softballs that were packed with mold. They were thrown away. To avoid mold problems, he suggests harvesting when about 10 percent of the pistils have died back. Even heavy dew can cause a moldy disaster! Leaf loves 'Hash Plant'.

2. 'Early Pearl', 'Early Queen', 'Early Riser', etc., 'Manitoba Poison', and similar strains finish from late-August to early-September at latitude 49° north. They are potent and yield a little better than the plants listed above. They grow from six to nine feet (1.8-2.7 m) tall and are quite bushy. Most of these strains are mold resistant and easy to grow–excellent choices for novices or growers with little time to look after their plants.

3. 'Mighty Mite', 'Durban Poison', 'Jack Herer', etc., finish mid- to late-September. The yield and potency are very good, and the odor is not too intense. All the plants grow a huge, dominant main cola with several large terminal buds on main branches. They may need trellising to avoid broken branches. Topping appears to increase yield. These strains are fairly low-maintenance, but the more love you give, the more they return. These plants grow well if left alone until mid-September and have a good harvest as long as they do not dry out or fall over. 'Mighty Mite' is another favorite.

4. 'Blueberry', 'White Widow', 'White Rhino', 'Super Silver Haze', 'Pure Power Plant', etc., tend to finish mid- to late-October. Yields and

potency are very high! They do not smell a lot while growing, but that changes when they are cut! They grow seven- to ten-feet (2-3 m) tall and yield heavily. They require some attention to get the best crop. 'Super Silver Haze' and 'Pure Power Plant' can be a bitch to grow because they often develop mold near harvest when the weather is damp. However, a mild to moderate frost tends to bring out some nice (purple) colors. They all do well outdoors but grow even better indoors.

5. 'Skunk #1', 'Northern Lights #5', 'Big Bud', and pure or nearly pure *sativas* finish from late-October to early-November. Sometimes *sativas* do not finish if the weather cools too much and snow comes. One year, on November 15th, the first snowfall had to be shaken off at harvest! About 50 percent of the pistils had died back. 'Skunk #1' is extremely smelly; the wind can literally carry the skunk scent for a mile. All of the plants in this group have a large to huge yield capable of producing several pounds each. 'Big Bud' yields an enormous amount; the bottom branches must be tied or staked to avoid breaking from bud weight. Potency is superb in all plants in this category except for 'Big Bud.'

All plants grow tall. 'Big Bud' and 'Skunk #1' grow 10-14 feet (3-4 m) tall. 'Northern Lights' are often taller! A few *sativas* can grow to 20 feet (6 m)!

Fungus can become a problem with these late-flowering plants. They withstand rain and light frost well; many can take a few light snowfalls. After all, they grow like weeds!

Climate

Outdoor grow shows are dominated by climate, soil, and water supply whether you are planting in a remote mountain patch, a cozy garden in your backyard, or on your balcony.

Microclimates are mini climates that exist within larger climates. Maps are available of these areas. Many maps such as the United States Department of Agriculture (USDA) Hardiness Zone map, www.usna.usda.gov/

'White Russian' and others from the "White" family are ready to harvest from mid- to late-October.

'Northern Lights #5 x Haze' is one of the most potent and tasty strains. This cross is ready to harvest from late-October through early-November.

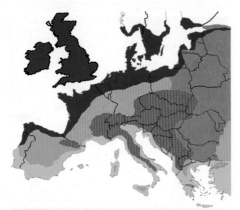

ABOVE: Rough climate map of Europe.
BELOW: Rough climate map of North America.
The legend is the same in both illustrations.

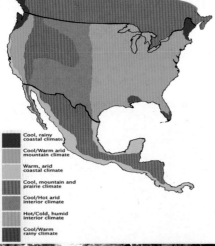

Cool, rainy
coastal climate

Cool/Warm arid
mountain climate

Warm, arid
coastal climate

Cool, mountain and
prairie climate

Cool/Hot arid
interior climate

Hot/Cold, humid
interior climate

Cool/Warm
rainy climate

Flanked by a fig tree, this flowering female was
grown in Ticino, the "Banana Belt," of Switzerland.

Hardzone/ushzmap.html, detail limited climatic boundaries. The map divides North America into ten zones plus zone 11 to represent areas that have average annual minimum temperatures above 40°F (4.4°C) and are frost free. Look into detailed microclimate maps for your grow zone. One of the most detailed climate maps can be found in Sunset's *Western Garden Book*, Sunset Publishing. The map details 26 distinct climate zones in 13 Western States and British Colombia and Alberta, Canada. This is the best climatic map available for the area.

Europe and other countries have much climatic information available via the Internet. Check out rainfall, temperature, and humidity charts for virtually all large cities in the world and most geographic regions. Visit www.weather.com for specific information on your local weather.

Temperature, rainfall, and sunlight vary widely across the globe, providing unique growing environments and countless microclimates. Look for specific information for your climate at local nurseries and in regional gardening books and magazines or through the department of agriculture (County Extension Agents) in your area. Here is a brief rundown on the qualities of different climates.

Coastal climates like those found in the Northwestern United States, British Columbia, Canada, Northern Coastal Europe, and the United Kingdom, etc., are cool and rainy. Annual rainfall most often exceeds 40 inches (103 liters per m³) and can be as high as 100 inches (253 per m³)! Winter blows in early in these areas bringing a chilling rain and low light levels. The more northern zones experience shorter days and wet cold weather earlier than the southern zones. Growing outdoors here is challenging because the temperature seldom drops below freezing, which contributes to larger insect populations. Some of these cold coastal rain-forests are packed with lush but invasive foliage and fungal growth brought on by the cold and damp.

Clay soil with a low pH is common in moist coastal zones. See "Soil" on the next page for more information.

Start Clones or Seedlings Indoors

Get a jump on the season by starting clones and seedlings under lights indoors. Move small containerized plants into heated greenhouses to start hardening-off. Transplant to a backyard or secure guerilla patch once they have become hardened-off and are more resistant to environmental stress.

Beat the cold; start seedlings and cuttings indoors and move them into a heated greenhouse in March or April. A 400-watt HP sodium lamp on a timer can augment the less-intense natural light of early spring. Seedlings and clones will need at least 14 hours of artificial and natural light per day until plants are transplanted outdoors.

Alpine mountain climates are cold much of the year. Freezing temperatures, mineral-heavy acidic soil, and wind top the list of grower concerns.

Summer temperatures in the mountains can dip to 30°F (-1°C) or lower in the summer, at as low as 2000 feet (610 m) elevation. Temperatures below 50°F (10°C) virtually stop growth, and temperatures below 40°F (5°C) can cause foliage tissue damage in many strains. Low temperatures cause stress in plants and a reduction in harvest weight. On the other hand, plants in high alpine climates tend to produce more resin and 10-20 percent more THC than those in lower gardens.

Most alpine soils lack humus, and strong winds will dry out the plants. For best results, look for patches where pasture grass grows.

You can help your plants deal with mountain stress by backfilling planting holes with a mix of peat moss, soil, polymer crystals, and slow-acting layers of organic fertilizer.

Cold wind causes moisture loss, and plants dry out quickly. This causes stress which can weaken plants and leave them open to attack by disease and insects.

Guerilla-grown buds suffer many days of wind, rain, hot sun, and cool nights. Such stressful conditions often impair resin production.

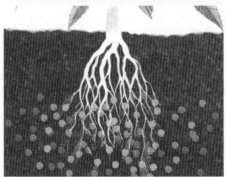

Polymer crystals mixed in the soil absorb water and release it over time.

Cool mountain environments, like those in Switzerland or the Rocky Mountains of North America, usually experience first frost in September and last frost during May.

Spring and fall months are rainy with a dry period in July and August. Cold rains in the fall can cause mold. Planting early-maturing strains helps avoid weather problems.

Rain and wind coupled with heavy buds broke this plant. Tied together with nylon rope, buds were supplied with enough fluids to produce a healthy harvest.

Tropical climates are generally warm to hot and humid. Rainy and dry seasons vary by location. Most jungle and tropical climates have daily rains. Protecting flowering females from rain with a greenhouse will help avoid bud mold and other problems. The closer to the equator, the less deviation there is between the length of days and nights. Extra hours of artificial light are necessary to keep plants in the vegetative growth stage. Tropical *sativa* strains are often favored in these regions because they are acclimated and require little special care.

Nighttime temperatures and humidity are often high. In fact, extended nighttime temperatures above 85°F (28°C) will cause plants to stop growing. Nighttime cooling could be necessary to keep plants growing well.

Soil

Soil is of three main types and all shades of gray and brown in between. Soil is the product of millions of years of geology.

Clay soil, also known as "heavy soil" or "adobe" in North America, is common in coastal areas and is very widespread inland. It is difficult to work with.

Clay soils hold water well and provide slow, even drainage. Clay soils are slow to warm in the spring, but hold warmth well into autumn when sunlight is fading. The density of clay does not allow for proper air circulation, and root growth is inhibited. For more information on clay soil, see Chapter Ten, "Soil & Containers."

Prepare clay soil at least a month before planting, adding lots of compost and manure. Clay soils can hold water too well, which can smother roots. Adding organic matter will "lighten"

the heavy soil, thus creating air pockets, improving drainage, and promoting root growth.

The month delay gives the manure a chance to "cool" so it won't burn the plants.

Use low sodium manure that contains few salts. Cows are given sodium nitrate to make them gain weight, but that same salt in their manure can lock up nutrients available to the plants, stunting their growth.

Do not be fooled by anyone who suggests adding sand to break up clay soil. Sand and clay create cement; add straw to make bricks!

One gardener had a backhoe operator excavate a pit 10 feet square by 2 feet (3 m × 60 cm) deep, built a 2-foot (60 cm) retaining wall around it, then filled it in with 400 cubic yards of river loam. This expensive, laborious soil transformation paid off in one outstanding crop after another over the years.

A long-term option is to annually till in compost, manure, and other organic amendments.

Raised beds are an excellent option for clay soil. Till the clay when it is damp and workable, and add manure/compost in heaps; plant directly in the mounds.

Pile subsoil in a ring around the plant, making a bowl to catch rain water.

Sandy soil is found near large bodies of water, in deserts, and in many inland areas. It is comprised of small, medium, and large particles and is easy to till even when wet. Plants can achieve excellent root penetration. Sandy soil feels and looks gritty.

Sand is easy to work and warms quickly in the spring, but it does not hold fertilizer well, especially when over-watered—the nutrients wash out. Compost helps bind the large particles providing food and air circulation, but in hot climates the organic matter decomposes rapidly and is soon consumed by bacteria and other soil organisms.

For best results keep sandy soil cool, retain moisture with mulch, and cultivate often, adding additional compost. Winter season cover crops will hold moisture and prevent runoff while retaining life in the soil.

Loam soil has all the advantages of clay and sand; it holds moisture and water like clay but is quick to warm and has good drainage and a work-friendly structure like sand. It is the perfect growing medium.

Most soils are a combination of sand and clay. Silty loam falls in between and feels almost greasy when rubbed in your hand, though it is less slippery than clay. The ultimate soil for growing plants is loam found in ancient river bottoms and lake beds where sedimentary soil builds up. It is dark, fertile, and crumbly in the hand.

Forest soils vary greatly in pH and fertility. The needles and deadfall from the trees usually make the soil acidic.

Most of the forests remaining in North America and Europe are on hillsides. Flat land is used for farming, recreation, and urban sprawl.

Long-needle pines grow in poor soils such as those found in mountainous and tropical regions. They have deep roots to look for all the elements in the soil. When a layer

Once you have amended soil so it holds plenty of water and nutrients but still drains well, you can take it easy.

of humus evolves, short-needle conifers dominate. The roots on these trees spread out on the surface to search for nourishment and bury roots to anchor it in place.

Jungles are usually low-growing, hot, moist, and dense. The soil is shallow and alive. The hot weather makes all foliage that falls to the ground decompose quickly. Often nutrients are available to plants, but the soil does not have a chance to build density. Layers of tropical soils can be very thin. However, through much of Mexico and Central America volcanic eruptions brought much rock and minerals to the surface. Mountain valleys and lowlands are full of alluvial plains that are packed with nutrient-rich soil.

Grasslands often have wonderful soil that recycles nutrients. Sunshine is likely to be good, but detection could be a problem in wide-open spaces. Plant in areas that are protected from wind and curious eyes.

Mountain soils are often very rich in minerals but lack humus. Alpine valleys hold the best alluvial-plain soil that is the product of volcanic rock erosion. Hillsides are generally less fertile, and soil must be amended to grow a good crop.

Bog soils are moist and spongy. Bogs are filled with vegetation and often have very rich soil. They present a perfect place to grow individual plants. Cut a square yard (90 cm^2) of moist sod from the ground, turn it over, and plant. Marsh ground supplies sufficient water on its own. Add a bit of time-release fertilizer during transplanting and another handful of "flowering" formula during a check-up in early August.

Turn over the top layer of grass to prepare moist soils for planting.

Most often, it is easiest to change or amend native soil that will produce scrawny plants. You can grow in containers so you can control all factors, but just remember, containers require more maintenance. See "Terrace Growing" for more information.

Amendments improve soil, root penetration, soil water retention, etc. See Chapter Ten, "Soil," for a complete discussion of amendments.

Maintain a compost pile. See "Compost" in Chapter Ten for more information.

Worms work wonders with soil. Grow your own crop of worms in a worm bin. Worms grow and reproduce in layers of food scraps, soil, and manure. They produce worm castings, an excellent fertilizer/amendment or compost tea ingredient. For more information about worms, check out the classic book, *Worms Eat My Garbage: How to Set Up & Maintain a Worm Composting System*, by Mary Appelhof, Flower Press.

Soil and water pH levels are exceptionally important. Cannabis does best with a soil pH of about 6.5. Soil pH is easy to change. See Chapter Ten for a complete discussion of pH.

Lime amendments will raise pH and lower acidity, but too much lime can burn roots and make nutrients unavailable. If you need more than one full point of pH adjustment, check with local farmers, nurseries, or agricultural agencies for recommendations on lime application.

Lime application differs based on soil type. Some guidelines are:

35 pounds/300 square yards (16 kg/251 m²) very sandy soil
50 pounds/300 square yards (23 kg/251 m²) sandy soil
70 pounds 300 square yards (32 kg/251 m²) loam
80 pounds/ 300 square yards (36 kg/251 m²) heavy clay soil
*1 cubic yard = 27 cubic feet (1 m³ = 106 cm³) (1 cubic yard = 105 cm³)
* rule of thumb: add 1-2 pounds (0.5-0.9 kg) of dolomite lime to each cubic foot (0.03 cm³) of soil

Raising alkaline levels is somewhat easier than raising the acid level. If your soil is too alkaline, 1.2 oz (34 gm) of finely ground rock sulfur per square yard (90 cm²) of sandy soil will reduce soil pH by one point. Other types of soil will need 3.6 oz (100 gm) per square yard (90 cm²). Well-decomposed sawdust, composted leaves, and peat moss also help to acidify soil and lower pH.

Hardpan

Hardpan is a condition whereby a layer of soil beneath the soil surface is hard and impermeable to both water and roots. Caliche is a hardpan common in the southwest USA. It consists of a layer of calcium carbonate (lime) located below the topsoil. The texture of caliche varies from granular to solid cement-like rock and can be from a few inches to many feet thick.

To plant in any hardpan area, you must bore through it to provide drainage. An auger will work to bore a hole, but a pick and shovel are practical, too. All other planting techniques remain the same. Discard the hardpan bored out of the hole and replace with compost or high-quality garden soil.

Prepare Soil

Help reduce the stress by growing seedlings in tall containers (three-inch square by six-inch tall) (8 cm² × 15 cm) which will produce a strong root system and a plant that has a better chance of surviving in tough conditions. Adding water-absorbing polymers in the plant mix is an excellent defense against desiccation, too. The crystals expand up to 15 times when watered, making moisture available to the roots for longer periods of time. Slow-release crystals will allow an extended period between watering. This is very helpful if your patch is in a remote location that you cannot visit often.

Mountain areas can have poor soil and will need to be improved before planting for best results. Dig holes at least 18 inches (46 cm) wide by 18 inches (46 cm) deep for each plant. Place a handful of blood meal (see warnings in Chapter Eleven) on the bottom and three to four inches (8-10 cm) of soil on top of it before transplanting the cuttings or seedlings, then water heavily. A little effort preparing the planting holes will result in healthier plants and a heavier harvest.

On an incline, planting holes must be terraced into the hillside and be large enough to catch runoff water. Dig extra gullies to channel runoff to growing plants, and make a "dish" around the plants to hold water.

Plants remain smaller in rocky terrain but often go unseen because they are grown where no one expects to see them.

Clay forms an excellent underground planting container. After a good rain, dig large planting holes. Fill holes with lots of good dirt and compost. Backfill in layers; for example, fill a three-foot (90 cm) deep hole with an eight-inch (20 cm) layer of steamed bone-meal (see warnings in Chapter Eleven) and soil. The balance is made up of a thin layer of topsoil mixed with a rich compost-manure-straw mixture, rock phosphate, and seaweed meal. Mound compost and soil about a foot above ground level. It will settle during growing season. See "Organic Fertilizers" in Chapter Eleven for more information.

Prepare to plant by digging a big hole and placing boards at the bottom to stop downward water flow. Add compost, peat moss, coco peat, good soil, organic nutrients, polymers, and

Hardpan

Porous Soil

Cut through hardpan so water can drain.

dolomite lime—all will help soil hold water—then top with a concave bowl of soil that will catch rain and irrigation water.

Raised beds

Raised beds are wonderful for growing in the backyard. Cultivation and weed control are easier, and soil quality is simpler to maintain.

Build a raised bed on top of clay soils. Planting in a bed raised six to eight inches (15-20 cm) eliminates the necessity of trying to dig in clay while providing the early warmth and good drainage clay lacks. Plants can be put into the ground two weeks to a month early and may even produce an early spring crop.

One friend plants on top of the compost pile. He plants six, 12-inch-tall (30 cm) clones into three to four inches (8-10 cm) of good soil that is on top of a two- to three-foot (60-90 cm) high compost heap. By the time the roots penetrate into the compost, it has cooled enough

Dig big, deep planting holes and backfill with amended soil.

Place a board at the bottom of fast-draining soils to hold water longer.

3ft.

Make raised beds up to 3-feet (90 cm) tall. Layers of fresh plant debris below decompose and release heat as a by-product.

that the roots are safe from burning. He places a portable greenhouse over the plants. The compost keeps plants warm while the structure protects foliage. This works exceptionally well to coax a spring harvest.

Another grower prepares a vegetable garden by dumping three cubic yards (90 cm³) of finished compost and manure with a dose of dolomite lime into a raised bed, then he roto-tills and plants. When the vegetables are growing well, he transplants hardened-off clones to blend in alongside vegetables.

Mulch

Mulch attracts and retains soil moisture and smothers weeds. Mulch is a layer of decomposing foliage, straw, grass clippings, weeds, etc. and/or paper, rocks, plastic, etc., laid around plants.

Native foliage is an excellent and convenient mulch. My favorite mulch is dry grass clippings, which are free. Fill your backpack with light-weight grass clippings before every trip to the patch. Always pile the mulch as high as you can (6-12+ inches (15-30+ cm), because it biode-grades over time.

Biodegradable plastic breaks down into frayed strips that flap in the wind after continued exposure to sunlight. Plan to use it one year only and remove it before it shreds into unsightly pieces of long plastic.

Rock or rock dust makes excellent mulch. Use rock mulches where they are readily available. They become hot to touch on sunny days, but they still protect the soil from evaporative moisture loss.

Newspaper or brown paper shopping bags make excellent mulch. Slightly wet paper is easier to work with and less likely to blow around. Inexpensive and readily available, newspaper layers should be at least six pages thick (preferably a dozen or more), before adding a soil or mulch covering to hold it in place.

Woven weed barriers or strips of scrap carpet let water drain but will not let the weeds grow through. Cover these barriers with rock or bark chips.

1 2 in.

Planting in a thick layer of mulch is a good way to conserve moisture.

Cover the entire garden bed with black plastic and cut holes through which seedlings are planted. A soaker hose can be laid underneath the plastic to irrigate. Make sure to cut large enough holes so that plant stems do not touch the plastic. Black plastic gets very hot during the day but actually warms the soil very little. When a young, tender plant stem touches the hot, black plastic, it will literally cook at the soil line.

Fertilizers

Plants can be fertilized enough to make them respond and grow well within a temperature range of 60-90°F (15-32°C), reasonable humidity, adequate sunshine, and moderate wind.

Be sparing with fertilizer the first month after transplanting. Depending upon the fertilizer, application could be as often as every watering or as seldom as every week or two.

If fertilizing with every watering, you may need to dilute the food to half-strength or less until you figure out the proper dosage.

Fertilize with a mild, soluble flowering solution for germination and seedling growth. Change to a high-nitrogen formula during the vegetative stage and back to a "super-bloom" when the long nights induce flowering.

Use granular concentrated fertilizers or organic fertilizers that are lightweight and not bulky to transport and store.

Build organic soils using different natural substances. Always use the most readily available form of the element. See Chapter Eleven, "Water and Nutrients," for complete information on fertilizers.

For more complete information about soil, see *Soil Science Simplified*, by Helmut Kohnke and D. P. Franzmeier, Waveland Press, 4th edition.

Water

Clean rainwater is the best for irrigation. To make sure it is not too acidic (acid rain) and harmful to plants, take the pH and parts per million (ppm) reading from collected rainwater before using.

Sodium-heavy water builds up in the soil causing slow growth and shorter plants with smaller leaves. At low levels, sodium appears to benefit plants and may even make up for potassium deficiency, but too much leads to "sodium stress." Roots lose the ability to absorb water and other nutrients and will dry out even with heavy watering. It is very important to test your water for sodium and other dissolved solids and take appropriate action if the reading reaches more than 50 ppm. Sodium is more of a problem when growing in containers than when growing in well-drained soil.

See Chapter Eleven for more information on sodium and water quality.

Local farmers or the Department of Agriculture have information about water solids in your area, and many areas have low-cost, state-certified labs that can test your water for you.

Often, if the sodium content is below 300 ppm, a good flushing every month will keep sodium and other salts from building up to toxic levels.

Drip irrigation is a very efficient way to irrigate.

Water small plants by hand until they are established.

There are several easy, inexpensive options to improve water quality.

Irrigate seedlings, clones, and mother plants with rainwater (or 50 percent rainwater with tap water) to dilute dissolved solids.

Flush container gardens with three quarts (3 L) of water for each dry quart (liter) of soil.

Water once with tap water and always afterwards with tap water augmented with ammonium sulfate.

Clean tap water by filling barrels and setting 2-3 feet (60-90 cm) off the ground. Add ammonium sulfate to settle out the sodium, then siphon water from the top of the barrel, refilling after each watering to allow the chlorine to evaporate. Chlorine, like sodium, is beneficial in small amounts. It is essential to the use of oxygen during photosynthesis and is necessary for root and leaf cell division. But too much chlorine causes leaf tips and margins to burn and leaves to turn a bronze color.

Empty the barrel periodically, and scrub out residues and sediments. Clean rainwater is an excellent choice for irrigation. Collect runoff by placing a barrel under a downspout. Mix the

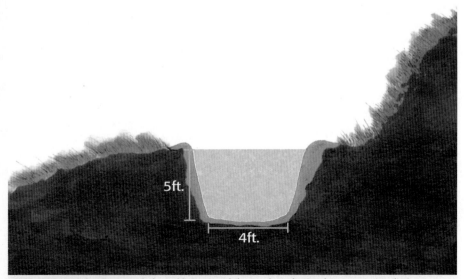

Make a reservoir by digging a hole and lining it with heavy-duty plastic. Always cover it to limit evaporation and animal access.

Siphon water you haul in to a receptacle located downhill. Always plan trips carefully and avoid problems.

rainwater with barrels of tap water to dilute the dissolved solids. Roofs and terraces can accumulate trash, which will pollute the otherwise clean rainwater. Covering your catch-barrel will prevent evaporation and keep out trash.

Sodium, calcium, and magnesium can be harmful in the soil, too. Excess calcium, for example, keeps the pH level too high and blocks uptake of several nutrients including iron and potassium. Fertilizer with chelated iron will

Secret Tunnel

Blackberries

Planting inside a patch of blackberries or other sticker bushes will deter many curious hikers and other animals.

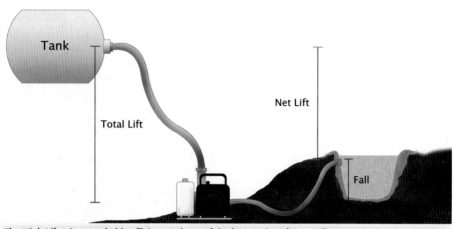

The High Lifter is remarkably efficient and one of the best options for guerilla growers.

Right: Drill powered pump that uses a rechargeable battery. Attach a pump to the end of the drill. Remove cord and make battery powered.

Below: A ram pump is one of the original low-tech methods to lift water with the force of gravity.

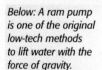

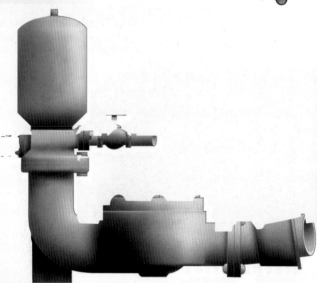

Above: The Grobot is an outstanding invention! This battery-powered pump delivers water to three plants quietly and efficiently.

counteract this problem. Too much magnesium creates rapid uptake of trace elements but does not usually cause a problem.

The fertilizer comes in liquid or wettable crystal form and can also be used in soil to alleviate problems caused by bad water. Several commercial hydroponic fertilizer formulations for "hard water" are available and work very well.

Check the garden daily, if possible, and water when soil is dry one inch (3 cm) below the surface. Irrigate containers until 10-20 percent of the water comes through the drainage holes. Irrigate plants in the ground until they are completely wet.

Many different types of receptacles and reservoirs can store irrigation water. Use the biggest storage unit that you can manage; you will always need water. One good option for storing a lot of water is to dig a nice big hole and line it with a pond liner. For all kinds of water storage devices, see www.realgoods.com.

Pumps

Pumps move water long distances and uphill. Pumps can be operated by hand, batteries, gasoline, gravity, and with pressure from moving water.

Gasoline-powered pumps are reliable and can lift much water uphill quickly, but they are noisy. You can purchase a pump already attached to the motor or connect them yourself and mount them on a board. Check your local *Yellow Pages* for a good supplier.

Noise is a major factor in starting up a small gasoline-powered engine in the middle of a quiet mountainous area. An oversized muffler and small baffle will deaden most of the exhaust sound.

Set up the pump so that the intake will be able to gather water easily. Make a small dam only if it is discreet.

A ram pump pumps water from a source of flowing water above the pump. The force of gravity is all the power needed. Ram pumps are rugged and dependable, but noisy. www.rampumps.com.

A gasoline-powered pump moves much water uphill, but they are noisy!

Build a baffle around gasoline-powered motors to muffle noise.

The High Lifter Water Pump is water-powered and will work with a low flow of water. The unique design uses hydraulic pressure and is self-starting and self-regulating. If inlet water stops, so does the pump; the pump starts by itself as soon as water flow begins. www.realgoods.com.

Manual-powered pumps require a lot of physical energy to operate and are impractical for moving a large volume of water uphill.

Solar energy is an outstanding way to move water. On a sunny day a 75-watt solar panel supplies enough power to a pump to move 75 gallons (285 L) of water 35 feet (10.5 m) uphill and more than 400 feet (120 m) away to a reservoir. www.otherpower.com.

Cold-affected plants develop few calyxes but still frost with resin.

Cold temperatures turned this plant purple and curled the leaves.

Siphoning water downhill will move a lot of water. Finding a water source above the garden is the key!

Lightweight hose will not disturb foliage. If you can find it in black, it will be more difficult to spot. Most garden hose is a bright green color!

Temperature

The best way to control temperature outdoors is to plant in the right place. Normally hot temperatures are common during midday in full sun. Cannabis virtually stops growing at 85°F (29°C). If you are planting in a hot climate, make sure plants receive filtered sunlight during the heat of the day. Also, plant them in natural breezeways so a breeze will cool them during the heat of the day.

You can create shade over your patch by bending tree branches and tying them in place.

Cold temperatures can be avoided by planting at the proper times—well after last frost. Harvest before first frost!

See Chapter Thirteen, "Air," for more specific information about temperature.

A shade house covered with "shade cloth" (synthetic sun-blocking material) or lath house, which is built from thin, narrow strips of wood, are great places to protect plants. Lath houses can provide 25 percent shade or more depending on the placement of the laths. Shade cloth is available in different meshes that filter out 10, 20, 30, etc., percent of the sunlight. Shade or lath houses are also a great place to pass summer days!

Wind

Wind is one of the strongest forces outdoors. Sustained wind will suck moisture from plants. Wind causes plants to draw moisture from the roots and shed it through the leaves in a defensive mechanism to regulate internal temperature and chemistry. It creates a problem if the water supply is limited.

For example, Southern Spain and other arid regions are subject to strong desert winds that transport abrasive sand and other particles. We call it "kalmia" in Spain because the grit is mixed with saline air from the Mediterranean. These winds can destroy crops. If your climate is plagued by such abrasive winds, protect plants with windbreaks. Wash foliage with plenty of water to remove the particles after windstorms.

Moderate sustained winds will dry out container- and field-grown crops within a few hours. Container crops suffer the most. For example, plants grown in five-gallon (20 L) containers on a terrace that receives full sun and constant moderate winds uses about two gallons (7.5 L) of water daily! Indoors, the same plant would use 75 percent less water!

Plant in protected areas so the garden suffers little effect from strong wind.

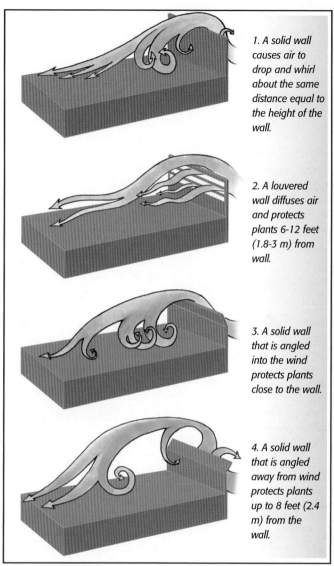

1. A solid wall causes air to drop and whirl about the same distance equal to the height of the wall.

2. A louvered wall diffuses air and protects plants 6-12 feet (1.8-3 m) from wall.

3. A solid wall that is angled into the wind protects plants close to the wall.

4. A solid wall that is angled away from wind protects plants up to 8 feet (2.4 m) from the wall.

Pests and Predators

Once your plants are in the ground, well-fed, and watered, check them weekly (if possible) for pest and fungal damage. Inspect the top and bottom of leaves for stippling (small spots) from mites or damage from chewing insects and slugs and snails. First identify the pest, and then determine a course of action.

Properly grown outdoor cannabis has few problems with pests. See Chapter Ten, "Soil & Containers," for more information on a wide array of diseases and pests that attack cannabis.

Low-tech, natural approaches to pest control work well. A few large pests like caterpillars and snails can be hand-picked from the foliage. Caterpillar populations can be reduced at the source by installing bat houses. Resident bats will eat moths and decrease the number of chewing caterpillars. Birds will eat caterpillars too, as well as aphids and other insects. Attract birds with suet, bird houses, baths, and feeders but cover tender seedlings and clones with wire or nylon mesh to protect from birds, too! Ladybugs and Praying Mantis are good options for insect control and can be purchased from nursery supply stores.

Barns owls eat mice, gophers, and voles but are hard to come by in the city. If you are lucky enough to have them nearby, take advantage of their ability to eat plant pests. On the other hand, some rodents, like moles and shrews, help your garden by dining on slugs, insects, and larvae.

Marigold cultivars of the *Tagetes erecta* and *T. patula* species, will repel nematodes, also known as eelworms, from the soil for two to three years if they are planted in an infested area and then tilled under. Just planting them in an area doesn't accomplish anything. Numerous tests indicate that they do not have an effect on insects above the ground.

Frogs and Toads

Frogs and toads eat insects and slugs. The frogs will need a water source, while toads are more terrestrial. Large snakes in the garden will eat gophers, squirrels, and mice as well as the moles and shrews. Snakes can give you a good scare if you come across one unexpectedly! The snake will also want to eat your frog. Plan carefully before committing to any mini-predator solution to pest infestation.

Birds

Although most birds are welcome guests in most gardens, there are some that can make quick work of tender seedlings or new clones.

The most effective way to keep birds from freshly planted seed and transplants is to cover plants with plastic wire or plastic netting. When installing the netting, make sure it is securely fastened around the perimeter of plants so hungry birds do not get underneath.

Deer and Elk

Deer and elk love newly formed growth on cannabis plants. In addition, they may destroy crops by trampling them. Elk are somewhat of a problem, and deer are a problem!

A cage around plants is the best deterrent. But remember, the wire may be easy to spot if it is not discreet in color. Deer are repelled by the smell of blood and human hair. Place handfuls of dried blood meal in cloth sacks and dip in water to activate the smell. Hang sacks from a tree to discourage dogs and other predators from eating them.

Handfuls of human hair can be placed in small cloth sacks and hung from a fence or tree branch as a deterrent. Do not use your own hair; it could turn into evidence for police! Scented soaps have repelled deer from some gardens. But if deer are very hungry, the smell of blood meal, human hair, scented soap, or anything else will not deter them.

Always urinate in several locations around the perimeter of the garden so animals take your presence seriously. Some growers save urine all week and disperse it at regular visits to their patch.

Deer easily bound over eight-foot (2.4 m) fences. A good deer fence is eight feet (2.4 m) tall with the top foot (30 cm) sloping outward, away from the garden at a 45 degree angle. Electric fences and large dogs are also excellent deterrents.

Gophers

Pocket gophers are small burrowing rodents that eat plant roots and foliage. These herbivores find fleshy roots a real treat and occasionally attack  cannabis. Should a family of gophers move into your area, get rid of them as soon as possible! Females can

Gopher Trap

bear up to five litters of four to eight offspring a year. A family of gophers can clean out a large garden in a matter of weeks.

The only sure way to get rid of gophers is by trapping. There are several gopher traps available, including ones that capture them alive. It will take some skill before you are regularly able to catch gophers with traps. You must avoid getting human scent on any part of the traps. If gophers sense the human odor, they will simply push soil over the trap to spring it or render it otherwise ineffective. Traps are put in gopher runways and so don't need to be baited.

A fence of poultry wire or 0.5-inch (1.5 cm) hardware cloth buried one foot (30 cm) deep and standing 3 feet (90 cm) above the ground will exclude gophers. Line planting holes with chicken wire before filling with soil. Driving metal sheets around the perimeter of planting holes will also prevent gopher damage.

Mice and Voles

Mice and voles can chew bark from around the base of cannabis plants (girdling). If this is a problem, keep mulch a foot away from plants, and install a wire mesh around the trunks. Mice and voles make nests in large piles of mulch, and they are attracted to stored water. Cover all water sources to exclude them, but keep in mind that they might chew through the container if water is super scarce.

The best mouse deterrent is a cat that is serious about hunting. Mousetraps also work well on smaller populations. Removing a large number of mice with traps can be tedious and unpleasant.

DO NOT USE POISON! Scavenger animals will eat the dead rodents and may become poisoned themselves.

Moles

Moles are minor pests. They are primarily insectivores that eat cutworms and other soil grubs, but their tunnels may dislodge cannabis roots.

Repel moles with castor plants or gopher (mole) plants (*Euphorbia lathyris*). Castor bean leaves and castor oil, as well as applications of tobacco and red pepper, will repel moles if put into their main runs.

Blend two tablespoons (3 cl) of castor oil with three tablespoons of dish soap concentrate and ten tablespoons (18 cl) of water. Mix in a blender. Use this as a concentrate at the rate of two tablespoons per gallon (4 ml per liter) of water. Apply as a soil drench directly over mole holes.

Barrel traps, scissor traps, and guillotine traps are effective and kill moles instantly.

Rabbits

Rabbits eat almost anything green, and they multiply like rabbits! Repel rabbits with a light dusting of rock phosphate on young leaves or dried blood sprinkled around the base of plants. Manure tea sprayed on leaves and soil may keep them from dining on your plants. Rabbits find plants dusted with hot pepper or a spray of dilute fish emulsion and bone meal repulsive. There also are a number of commercial rabbit repellents, but be wary of using these on consumables!

A dog will help keep rabbits in check, but the only surefire way to keep rabbits out of the garden is to fence them out with one-inch (3 cm) poultry wire. The poultry wire should be buried at least six inches (15 cm) in the ground to prevent burrowing and rise two or three feet (60-90 cm) aboveground. Wrap trunks with a wire mesh or aluminum foil to keep rabbits from chewing bark in winter or early spring.

Rogue Pollen

Rogue pollen from commercial hemp farms and wild or cultivated males can threaten sinsemilla cannabis grown outdoors or in greenhouses. Undesired pollen can drift from a few feet to hundreds of miles to pollinate flowering females and cause them to grow seeds.

Large clouds of pollen blow across the Mediterranean Sea from the Riff Mountains in Morocco dropping pollen on Spain and Portugal. In fact, local weather reports always include the cannabis pollen statistics. The reports are directed at people with allergies but are also used by marijuana growers.

Make inquiries into air quality including cannabis pollen. Some growers develop "allergies" in order to get the most information from officials. Researching wind direction relative to your crop and closest hemp plants will help you select sites less likely to be contaminated.

Wind-shadows (large divots in a hillside) protect plants from wind and anything it brings along.

If rogue pollen is a problem, plant early crops or late crops that flower before or after male plants. Usually June and July are the worst months for pollen, but it could also spill into August.

A backyard garden is not always a security risk.

Remove the bottom of containers and plant in the garden to avoid transplant shock.

You may be able to grow indoors until the industrial hemp is done flowering and males are no longer releasing pollen, or plant out of the wind pattern. If pollen is severe, keep plants in a greenhouse. Cover the intake opening with a moist towel–humidity makes pollen unviable. Put one edge of the towel in a bucket of water to wick moisture. Wetting down the exterior of the greenhouse will also help incapacitate any wild pollen.

Backyard Growing

Lucky growers who live in countries that tolerate cannabis can safely plant a crop in their backyard and give their garden the tender loving care it deserves. You can pay close attention to your plants' soil, water, and nutrient needs. Growing cannabis in your flower and vegetable garden is ideal because you can care for all your plants at the same time.

Prepare soil in the fall; remove weeds and dig

Small 'AK-47' plants are easy to move and give a 12/12 day/night schedule during the summer.

planting holes or garden beds. Turn it over and make sure it has plenty of amendments (see Chapter Ten). Always put a heavy layer of mulch on any soil that will be planted! A 12-inch-plus (30 cm+) layer of mulch will keep soil elements intact as well as attract moisture. Bare soil loses most of its valuable topsoil to erosion during winter months.

In the spring, mulched amended soil should be well-mixed and ready for planting. You can transplant cannabis seedlings or clones in the garden just like you would tomatoes. If your soil is poor, or you didn't begin cultivation in fall, dig large holes, three feet (90 cm) in diameter by three feet (90 cm) deep, and fill with your best compost, potting soil, or planting mix. Otherwise, break up the top six to eight inches (15-20 cm) of soil in a six-foot (1.8 m) radius to provide room for root branching.

Bury containers in a garden bed so they do not stick out too much. They can be easily moved indoors at night or to a remote location.

Put pots inside another container to protect roots from being cooked by heat from the sun.

Terrace Growing

Growing in containers on a terrace, balcony, or roof is very rewarding. A small sunny location, good genetics, containers, and good soil are the basic needs.

Your gardening techniques will depend upon the location of the grow show. City building rooftops, terraces, and balconies tend to be windy. The higher the garden, the more wind. Wind dries plants quickly. See "Wind" in this chapter.

Beautiful plants line this protected Spanish terrace.

Patio gardens are most often protected from strong winds and strong sunlight.

An automatic watering system is often a good idea in such gardens to ensure they receive adequate water, especially if you are gone for a few days.

Pots will also need to be shaded from sunlight. Hot sun beating down on pots cooks plant roots. See Chapter Six "Grow Rooms & Greenhouses" and Chapter Ten "Soil & Containers" for more information.

Containers with wheels are much easier to move, especially if you are moving them back and forth from indoors to outdoors.

Even with adequate security, the standard issues of water, soil, and fertilizer apply. For a successful crop, daily maintenance is essential during hot and windy weather.

Wind can carry rogue male pollen or industrial hemp pollen creating problems for terrace growers. Plan ahead. See "Rogue Pollen" on page 145.

This cannabis plant is growing on a terrace between an ancient church and a high-rise office building.

Large containers require less maintenance and grow big plants.

This terrace garden obscures the door!

Avoid planting too early in the year or lower growth will be spindly.

This short crop was planted and harvested in just 3.5 months!

Basque growers planted this crop in a natural clearing in early summer.

Here is a shot of the same garden (above) a couple months later.

Coastal winds tend to flow inland during the day creating cool zones denoted by blue lines.

Coastal breezes generally carry air from land out to sea at night. Valleys and exposed hillsides experience more wind.

Guerilla Growing

Guerilla growing, a term coined in the early 1970s, requires strategy, time, and most often, physical prowess. Depending upon your location and local laws, clandestine guerilla growing in remote locations could be your only option.

Location and security are the main concerns for a guerilla grower. Choose a location that has limited public access. Check regulations for hunting and recreation, and think of who might be using the area: hunters, mushroomers, other marijuana growers, hikers, dirt-bikers, Boy Scouts, etc. Select a remote site unlikely to be used casually.

Look for a site that already has big green stands of vegetation. Marijuana is a vigorous plant with a large root system, and a flowering female will stand out if surrounding vegetation dies back before harvest. Stands of thorny blackberry bushes, ferns, and meadow grass are good options.

Prepare your marijuana patch up to six months before planting. Remove green vegetation in the fall for a spring garden. Clear a few patches to allow sufficient sunshine, cut back roots of competing plants, and till planting holes two- to three-feet square (60-90 cm^2). If possible, allow amended soil to sit for a month or longer before planting. Remote locations are hard to visit on a regular basis, so proper planning and preparation is important. If your home and guerilla gardens are similar, you can plant an indicator crop like tomatoes as a backyard guide to your hidden plants' condition.

Ample water is an important factor for site selection. If you cannot count on rainfall, locate your garden near a water source that does not dry up in the summer; doing so will make watering easier and cut the chance of being spotted hauling water. Exclusive access by boat will reduce the risk of discovery, but make sure your plants cannot be seen from the boat. Many people use waterways and explore land bordering rivers.

Cool air tends to sit in natural and man-made valleys which are often a few degrees cooler.

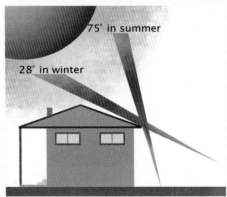

75° in summer

28° in winter

The angle of the sun climbs during the summer, and it is also brighter.

Planting in a corn field offers plenty of cover.

Cannabis plants easily blend into other foliage when planted properly.

Plants need a minimum of five to six hours of sunshine a day. Scout sites in the winter and try to visualize how the trees will cast shadows during the summer months. Remember that the sun takes a higher path in the spring and summer. Five hours of direct midday sun per day is essential for acceptable growth. More is better. Rocky terrain, hillside terraces, and grasslands all receive good amounts of sunlight.

Wind patterns will affect your garden and influence where plants are located. Do your homework. Research average wind direction and force. Windbreaks protect plants from heat and water loss.

Security

A secure location is the number one concern for most guerilla growers. Indoor growers can rent an apartment, house, or warehouse in the name of another person to avoid discovery. Guerilla gardens planted on public land risk detection by hikers, fishermen, or other outdoor enthusiasts. Remember, they are interested in specific sports and recreation. They will not go out of their way to find your patch unless you lead them to it.

Plant in a secure location that is out of sight! A greenhouse or a field of cannabis is vulnerable to both thieves and law enforcement.

Choose a site that does not make your plants the focal point of the garden. Make everything blend into surroundings so there is virtually no trace of a grow show. Hide cannabis among other plants that are of similar size and foliage. Stinging nettles camouflage cannabis well, and if you are unlucky enough to brush up against them, they seem to reach out and bite you, giving a burning sensation for about 20 minutes.

Park your vehicle in a discreet place away from the trailhead to your guerilla patch.

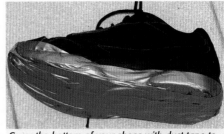

Cover the bottom of your shoes with duct tape to camouflage the pattern on the sole of your shoes.

Paint containers black, dark green, or camouflage. There are also camouflage sleeves available to cover pots.

You can see how cannabis stands out when surrounding foliage dries out in the summer.

Plant 'Ducks Foot' in your garden to fool casual observers into believing it is not cannabis!

A big dog will keep bandits at bay!

Plant on a tree stand to make plants harder to detect.

Be prepared with a believable story about why you are hiking around. Some possible ideas include bird watching, fishing, wildflower photography, etc. Make sure to have some props: fishing pole, camera, bird identification book, etc., to corroborate your story. Stay alert; this is risky business!

Some growers prefer to visit their patch late in the afternoon when the bulk of visitors are most likely to be in the forest. Now you will have plenty of time to complete tasks, and when the sun sets, you can return under the secure veil of twilight.

If you prefer to visit your grow show in the early morning when it is dark, a flashlight with a red or green lens helps your eyes adjust.

Always carry a cell phone to call for help or to communicate with a partner while at the patch. Turn the ringer off!

Prevent making a distinguishable path to the patch by taking a different route every visit. Walk

on logs, rocks, and up stream beds to avoid detection. Rapid growth of native plants will erase any obvious trail. You can fertilize to assist in repairs, but be careful with application as wild plants are easily over-fertilized. Remember, in late summer and early fall, most native plants in dry climates will not regrow.

Bring growing supplies to the patch and stockpile them over time–PVC pipe, gasoline-powered pumps, water tanks, soil, bricks of coconut fiber, compost, etc.–and hide them discreetly. You can take a few things to the patch each time. Make these trips count; plan ahead.

Prevent the style, size, and sole pattern of your shoes from leaving discernible tracks that could lead thieves and cops to your patch. Your shoe print could be used as evidence against you if your patch is busted!

Camouflage plants by bending, pruning, or splitting the stem down the middle. Bending branches is the least traumatic and has more subtle effects on hormones, liquid flow, and physical shape. See "Pruning and Bending" in Chapter Three. You can split the main stem (and the plant) down the middle and stretch the halves horizontally to create an espalier. Pruning produces the strongest effect because it removes the high concentrations of hormones in the terminal buds and stimulates lateral growth. Pruning several main stems may make the plants less obvious but does not improve harvest. Think carefully about desired outcome before cutting.

Grow in sticker bushes or other unpleasant foliage such as poison oak, poison ivy, stinging nettles, etc, to discourage intruders. Look for bushes that are dense and high enough to shelter the patch from view. This deters large animals or people from wandering into the site. Protect yourself from these plants with a slick rain suit and gloves. Wash after each visit to remove irritating toxic oils and thorns.

Some growers plant where there are a lot of mosquitos or wasps, and at least one grower I know plants near a skunk's den. The pungent spray keeps people and animals at bay.

Some growers climb 30 feet or higher up into the trees to plant on stands in the canopy or use deer and elk stands as growing platforms.

Set up a pulley system to lift large containers and potting soil up to the platform. Install an irrigation hose from the base of the tree up to the planting area and arrange around the pots so you can perform weekly watering with a battery powered pump rather than climbing the tree. Find a partner to stand lookout when you are working in the canopy, and be sure to use safety lines. Do not overextend yourself. I used to climb trees for a living, and my hard and fast rule was to spend no more than four hours climbing per day. When you get tired, accidents happen. If you hurt yourself, you will not be able to care for your plants!

Drought Growing

If you do not have access to a water source, dry land crops are possible if the area gets at least one good rain every one to four weeks.

In general, *sativa* strains have a bigger root system than *indica* strains and are more drought resistant.

Plants pull water and nutrients from the soil. Acceptable soil will hold one inch (3 cm) of water per one square foot (30 cm²) of area and grow a plant seven- to eight-feet (2.1 to 2.4 m) tall with roots five feet (1.5 m) across and six feet (1.8 m) deep. Insufficient water results in small buds. A five-foot (1.5 m) plant may produce only one to six ounces (30-180 gm) of smokable bud. By contrast, a plant in good soil with ample water will be more robust and yield two to ten times more than those in poor soil, making attention to soil and water quality essential.

An easy, inexpensive way to feed and water your plants is to cut a 3/16-inch (5 mm) hole in the bottom of a five-gallon (19 L) bucket and fill with water and water-soluble fertilizer. Place one bucket by each plant with the hole oriented near the stem. Buckets should be refilled every ten days during the hottest weather. You will be

Rig up a backpack so that it is easy to carry many clones.

Remove the lower leaves on spindly seedlings and plant deep.

This seedling will develop roots along the subterranean stem in a few weeks.

Remove male plants as soon as they are distinguished.

Beautiful outdoor harvest is drying in a remote concrete pump house.

Beautiful Spanish guerilla garden is close to harvest.

able to get through the summer with as few as four to six buckets of water. This is very inexpensive and the extra water and nutrients will really pay off when it is time to harvest.

Planting and Maintenance

Start clones in rockwool, Jiffy, or soilless grow cubes for three weeks, and then transplant into four-inch (10 cm) pots of organic soil mix. Water transplants heavily to encourage root growth. Grow under an HID or CF lamp for two weeks. Harden-off before moving outside into the garden or secret garden.

One grower I know keeps a stream of plants moving from indoors to his outdoor gardens. He plants the first crop of clones in three-gallon (11 L) pots in a greenhouse, hardens them off, and moves them to their final location. The second crop is moved into the greenhouse when the first crop is moved out. He repeats this process three to four times during the season.

A complete low-maintenance setup is the goal for most guerilla growers. Loosen the soil, amend it, and throw in a handful of polymers to retain moisture. A thick layer of mulch, early in the year, will attract water, keep the soil cool, and prevent evaporation. Bury clones deep in the ground to promote a deep root system that will not require a lot of additional water.

Some growers transplant one-foot (30 cm) tall clones with smaller root systems by removing the first few sets of leaves and burying the root ball deeper with only six inches (15 cm) of foliage left above ground. Roots will grow along the underground stem in a few weeks. Deep roots will create more self-sufficient plants. This is of particular importance in extremely remote areas that are hard to get to and in the mountains where the rainfall may be sporadic.

Pest prevention is crucial for guerilla crops, because the patch is too difficult to maintain every day or week. It is easier to keep pests from attacking plants in the first place than to try and do damage control later.

Water and fertilize as needed. See chapters in this book that pertain to specific outdoor needs.

Harvest

Harvest before cold, damp, autumn weather sets in. This weather causes fungus–*botrytis* (bud mold) and powdery mildew. Many plants can take a short mild freeze (30-32°F [-1-0°C]). But if the temperature stays below freezing for more than a few hours, it could kill plants. Pay close attention to weather forecasts and apply the information to the microclimate where your plants are growing. Be ready to harvest quickly if weather dictates.

Law enforcement can force a harvest, too. Limit potential discovery by hunters, hikers, and cops by harvesting at night. Find out when police or rangers are in the area, and plan to be there at a different time. Police scanners that pick up local police activities can come in handy for determining their location.

Take a sharp pocket knife and a backpack to haul your crop incognito. If you are harvesting more than one variety, put them in separate bags or wrap in newspaper before they go in the backpack.

Determine a believable story to explain your presence in the area, including proximity to the garden, should you be discovered. Offer nothing, explain little, and keep it simple so you don't slip. Always remember Bart Simpson's words, "I didn't do it. Nobody saw me. You can't prove a thing!"

Check Chapters Four and Five for more information on flowering and harvest timing.

Extending Seasons

Many products protect plants from cold weather and high winds, allowing growers to cultivate earlier and later in the year than would normally be possible.

The easiest and most cost-effective approach to extending the growing season is to locate and take advantage of microclimates such as areas that warm up faster or retain heat longer. Orientation to the sun, wind breaks, and walls made out of materials–bricks, mortar, stone– that will hold the heat and can even prevent

Note the small white pen next to the trunk of this 8-month-old 'Thai' plant ready for harvest.

You can use any transparent container to protect plants from cold. Always make sure they have a little ventilation.

To make a cloche, cut the bottom out of a plastic milk container and remove the lid for ventilation.

A Wall O' Water will keep plants warm when temperatures freeze.

They are easy to use and stack well for storage.

The Wall O' Water is a plant lifesaver. It is a water-filled teepee which uses the heat-emitting properties of water to shield plants from excess heat and keep them warm in the cold. It holds three gallons (11.5 L) of water and fits over the plant. During the day, the water absorbs the heat of the sun, moderating the temperature inside the teepee. At night, as the air temperature drops, the water releases its heat, keeping the plant comfortable. The Wall O' Water does its best work in the spring when there is still a chance of freezing. As water freezes, it releases more heat into the teepee and can protect plants down to 20°F (-7°C).

freeze-thaw cycles all play a part in evaluating microclimates.

Dark rocks can moderate temperature in a very small area by soaking up the heat of the day then releasing it slowly as the evening temperature cools.

Dark walls and soil will absorb and hold more heat than their light-colored counterparts. Or use plastic mulch which will shade weeds, prevent moisture loss, and raise the temperature of the soil by 5-15°F (3-8°C) on a sunny day. As plants grow, the leaves will shade the plastic and stop the warming effects.

A lake, pond, or small creek will also moderate air temperature, keeping it warmer in winter and cooler in the summer.

Cloches are individual protective coverings that keep plants warm at night. A simple cloche is a milk container with the bottom cut off and the lid removed. Placed over a plant, the plastic will capture and retain heat while allowing ventilation through the open top. You can make cloches out of wax paper, glass, and jars, or buy them. Commercial units are made of rigid transparent plastic or heavy-duty wax paper.

Covers protect early plants and can help produce a spring crop. The most uncomplicated cover is a sheet or blanket spread over the plant and held down with stones or soil. A low wattage electric light bulb carefully placed under the cover will raise the temperature 10-15°F (5.5-8°C) above that of the rest of the garden. Be very careful that the light bulb does not touch any part of the cover, or it may start a fire. Products such as Agronet™ and Reemay™ are spun-fiber with sun-protection properties that can be used as covers in place of the sheet or blanket.

Row tunnels can be made of clear corrugated fiberglass that is bent into an arch and secured over the garden. Commercial row covers come in many sizes from large enough for dwarf fruit trees to smaller units for pepper plants and rose bushes. Those made with polypropylene will protect plants down to 25°F (-5°C).

Inspect plants carefully every day.

Case Study –
Energy Efficient Organic Sea of Green

Growing Statistics

Yield 1: 8.4 pounds (3.8 kg) in ten weeks, initial grow in room half the size of other grows.

Yield 2: 27.6 pounds (12.5 kg) in nine weeks for second grow.

Yield 3: 30.2 pounds (13.7 kg) in nine weeks for third grow.

Cost: First Crop / Initial setup + power: USD $5647 (Eur $4500) - USD $672 per pound (Eur $1184 per kg)

Second Crop / Improvements + power: USD $8220 (Eur $6550) - USD $298 per pound (Eur $524 per kg)

Third Crop / Reap the rewards: USD $1882 (Eur $1500) - USD $62 per pound (Eur $106 per kg)

Space: First grow: 16' 5" × 7' 10" (5 × 2.4 m), **Second and third grows:** 33' × 7' 10" (10 × 2.4 m)

Watts: First grow - 6000 watts, second and third grows - 8400 watts.

Cloning: 100 clones (first crop) and 400 clones (second and third crops) purchased from an outside source and ready for planting. Clones were purchased for USD $3.15 each (Eur $2.50 each). The strain supplied was Power Plant.

Vegetative: First crop - 100 clones were planted directly into flowering room and given 18 hours of light per day for a period of 14 days. For the second and third crops, 400 clones were used. Because the number of plants grown per square meter was doubled, only seven days of vegetative growth were needed pre-flowering.

Flowering: The young plants, when acclimatized to their new home and growing well, were switched to a 12-hour light cycle for eight weeks.

Harvest: Mature plants reached an average height of 23 inches (60 cm) with multiple branches.

The First Crop

Nigel and Terry lived together in Central London and worked for the same large British company. When both were offered a transfer to a new firm in Holland, they jumped at the chance. The new company was in the west, near the coast, and in close proximity to some picturesque rural districts. They rented a house in the countryside where they could enjoy the solitude and reduce the stress associated with corporate life.

The house they rented was on a large piece of land, not in direct view of any neighbors. Near the house was a big shed once used to service farm equipment. It had power, water, and a functioning toilet and shower. Interesting?

After settling in at work and making the house comfortable, Nigel and Terry got to thinking. "That shed's just sitting there empty, and wouldn't it be just perfect for a hydro setup?" As it turned out, the property they rented was owned by an elderly woman who lived in Belgium. The rent was paid to a real estate agent in town, and no neighbors had even spoken to them in the six weeks since they moved in, so they figured the place was pretty safe. After a few nights sitting up and discussing their prospects, the lads decided to capitalize on their good fortune, and "go for the grow!!"

At the back of the shed was a storage area that had been partitioned off from the rest. It spanned the entire width of the building, about 33 feet (10 m) and was approximately 10 feet (3 m) wide. This seemed like an ideal place for the new project, but a few questions arose. Exactly how big were they going to make this thing? How much cash were they willing to invest? What were the consequences of success versus failure, or worse, discovery? Being corporate minded, the lads decided to make an executive decision. Seek advice from a professional.

Holland is world-renowned for its indoor weed production; consequently, grow shops are abundant. Nigel and Terry found the staff at their nearest "grow-op" to be open, professional, and well equipped to deal with their specific inquiries. After an enlightening chat, the boys decided to play it safe and use only half the area of the storage room 16 feet 6 inches × 10 feet (5 × 3 m). They figured that organic was the way to go, and the simplest growing method (pots and soil) would be best for starters.

They bought enough timber and other materials to construct two benches 16 feet 6 inches long × 4 feet wide (5 × 1.2 m). They bought 100 1.3-gallon (5 L) plastic pots, ten 13-gallon (50 L) bags of organic potting soil, and enough white, laminated wooden panelling to cover the walls (approximately 36 sq ft [30 sq m]). The idea was to construct the basic room, fill the pots with soil, place them on the benches, and check that the design was solid before progressing further. All went together well, total expense USD $780 (Eur $620).

This system was relatively easy to set up. The inline fan was installed high up on the rear wall. Its job was to expel hot air from the grow room and create enough draw to pull cool air in through a vent (large gap) between the opposite wall and the grow room floor. When and if smell became a problem, the carbon filter could be connected to the Torin and its fan speed increased to maintain constant odor-free airflow. The two pedestal fans would be incorporated to increase air movement but not until all else was set up. The lamps were arranged to cover an area of approximately 3 feet 3 inches × 3 feet 11 inches (1.0 × 1.2 m) each. The reflectors supplied with the lighting kits were cheap, half-octagon, aluminium horizontal hoods. However, they were lightweight and seemed very bright when the lights were turned on.

Clones were potted and placed on the benches (ten under each lamp). For the first five or six days, the lights were kept about one meter above the plants, then gradually lowered to about half that height as growth became healthy and vigorous. Watering was done by hand, and because the soil was a premixed organic blend, no extra fertilizer was added for the first week.

Nigel and Terry hovered over this first crop like proud fathers. They adhered to a daily schedule of watering, monitoring pH, and inspecting leaves for signs of insect attack and nutrient imbalance. As a result, the plants developed quickly and were ready to begin flowering by the end of the second week. To induce flowering, the lights were set back from 18 to 12 hours per day. About this time, they began to add organic nutrient supplements to the daily soak. As the plants developed further, they worked up quite a thirst; all pots were watered until their individual drip trays nearly overflowed.

The carbon filter was connected around week 6, in an effort to prevent odors escaping the shed. This tactic worked well, but it reduced airflow. As the plants increased in size and density, it became increasingly difficult to keep grow room temperatures below 86°F (30°C). On a couple of occasions, the temperature rose above 91°F (33°C), and bud development definitely suffered. The guys remember one time when every plant stopped growing for three or four days after the room overheated.

As their crop approached maturity, Nigel and Terry noticed something strange going on. Most plants were finishing off nicely, but some (generally the biggest) didn't seem to be maturing properly. The buds on the plants growing right under the lamps were big but didn't seem as solid or as resinous as those on the other plants. This condition became more noticeable as time progressed. By the 8-week mark, the larger plants started to go a bit yellow and drop leaves. It was time to pull the pin on this caboose!

The crop was harvested a few days later and hung to dry. In general, the smaller plants produced better quality buds than the larger plants. The yield was 8.4 pounds (3.8

kg) of very nice weed, and with that in hand, who was going to complain?

Actually, the boys were very happy with their first result, as everything ran quite smoothly. They had a few problems with heat, but they learned a lot and gained the confidence (and the $) to expand their room to its full potential, 33 feet × 10 feet (10 × 3 m).

The Second Crop

This was a time of change and serious improvement. Over the past three months, Nigel and Terry had visited the local hydro store on many occasions and had struck up a friendship with one of the owners who worked there. He had given them heaps of useful advice, and the boys realized that without his input, the first crop could have easily ended in failure.

The storeowner (we'll call him Bob) offered to help the boys design their new double-sized room, provided they purchase all their new equipment from him, of course. He insisted that the system they were currently running used too much power, generated too much heat, and was too labor-intensive to be successfully doubled in size and maintained by two guys already working full-time jobs. As usual, Bob was talking sense, so Nigel and Terry decided it was a safe bet to play it Bob's way and part with the necessary cash. The total cost of Bob's proposed improvements weighed in at USD $7552 (Eur $6000). Calculating at a rate of Eur $2200/kilo, the first crop paid for itself and more than half the expenses of the proposed expansion and improvements. Cool!

Bob's plan was to: 1. Double the length of the existing two benches and line the walls of the other half of the storage area with white laminated wood; 2. Set up an automatic watering system with a large reservoir to reduce manual labor; 3. Plant double the amount of clones per area to reduce time in vegetation by a week; 4. To achieve adequate air flow, install a new 5000 cu/hr fan for air extraction, and use their existing 3200 cu/hr fan for air intake; 5. Make use of current advancements in reflector technology to decrease the number of lights required–from 20 to 14–and consequently reduce the power usage and heat generation by the same ratio; 6. Bob also suggested ditching the pot idea in favor of cocopeat slabs. "Just supply the plants with a top-quality organic nutrient, and the garden will be state-of-the-art and organic."

The room was set up pretty much as Bob had planned. Look at the photo on page 162 to see an example. Five Danish-made plastic 6 foot 6 inch × 3 foot 3 inch (2 × 1 m) trays were loaded up with coco mats and placed on each 33 foot (10 m) long bench top. Each tray was installed with a 3-degree tilt to promote drainage. An elaborate system of drippers and drainage pipes was constructed and each bench was run as a separate entity with its own 400-liter reservoir and 6000 L/hr pump. Both pumps were timed to run x times a day for y minutes, and nutrient runoff was pumped out of the grow room and into the shower drain.

The fans were installed placing the 5000 cu/hr fan high at one end of the room and the 3200 cu/hr fan down low at the other. The 5000 removed air via the vent in the upper central part of the room. The vent was box-shaped and permanently connected to the carbon filter. When the filter was not required, a cover on the under side of the box was removed, and air was drawn out through the exposed opening. The 3200 forced cool air through ductwork that ran along the floor under each bench. This air entered the room in four places under each bench, equally spaced along their length. Four pedestal fans were used to mix the air and push it in the general direction of the outlet vent.

The room was lit using fourteen 600-watt lamps, each covering an area of 4 feet 8 inches × 3 feet 11 inches (1.43 × 1.2 m). This was achieved by using high-tech adjust-able double-parabolic reflectors (Adjust-a-Wings). These flexible "wings" were highly reflective and could spread light evenly and broadly at a range of heights above the plants. They were rated to cover areas of 4 feet 11 inches × 4 feet 1 inch (1.5 × 1.25 m) and above with 600-watt lamps, so 4 feet 8 inches × 3 feet 11inches (1.43 × 1.2 m) was within prescribed limits. Another lighting product was used in conjunction with the wings and referred to as a Super Spreader. These fit below the lamp and spread excess light and heat from that hot area across the light's entire footprint. They allow lamps to be close to plants to produce rapid growth but keep growth rate and plant size even.

When compared to the first, this crop almost seemed to grow itself! The irrigation system alone (reservoir size, how many days reserve, nutrient dosing, the coco/Danish tray/run to waste system) saved Nigel and Terry about two hours a day.

The ventilation design combined well with the simple, effective lighting strategy. Air was pumped in and pushed up from below, cooling plants and lights on its way up. The heated air would rise naturally, be trapped by the ceiling, sucked towards the vent/filter, and exhausted from the room. With a small amount of adjustment, the air temperature could be maintained at 80-82°F (27°C to 28°C) even when the plants formed a dense mass across the whole room.

The wing reflectors could be adjusted to provide even lighting when they were close to the plants (growth and flowering phases) and when they were farther away (early vegetative and final maturation phases). When reflectors were hung low over the plants, the spreaders dealt with any hot spots and insured even lighting.

Nigel and Terry's second crop grew vigorously and evenly all the way through to maturity. They had a small problem early on with spider mites. Seems the clones they bought had a few mites onboard. The mites were dealt with organically and effectively.

Bob had suggested the boys use Ecolizer organic nutrients and follow their program exactly. The program suggested misting clones regularly with their "Bugs Away" foliar feed. This solution contains nutrition plus essential oils that coat mite eggs and suffocate them. No chemicals and it worked!

After a total of nine weeks growing, the room was filled with plants that formed a dense layer of evenly developed, sticky, fat bud. The room resembled a "sea of green" rather than a collection of plants of assorted size and shape. As they harvested, Nigel and Terry joked about mowing down a mass of sticky green corn cobs. Cutting, hanging, drying, and particularly manicuring this much weed was one hell of a job and took them a month to finish. The final yield was 12.5 kilos and the quality was A+.

At this point, the boys had covered all their expenses, they were almost half way into their third crop (which was growing strong), and were already 10 kilos in the black. This had been an ambitious project. Nigel and

Terry had not achieved success without significant risk and a lot of hard work! Guess who was planning a well deserved "holiday in da sun"?

Comparing Statistics:

First Crop, 8.4 pounds (3.8 kg) / 6000 watts = 0.02 ounces (0.63 g) / watt

8.4 pounds (3.8 kg) / 14.4 square yards (12 m sq) = 11.1 ounces (316 g) / m sq

Second Crop, 27.6 pounds (12.5 kg) / 8400 watts = .05 ounces (1.49 g) / watt

27.6 pounds (12.5 kg) / 28.7 square yards (24 m sq) = 18.4 ounces (521 g) / m sq

– Bob's advice helped the boys increase their power efficiency (g / watt) by 137 percent.

– Bob's advice helped the boys increase their space efficiency (g / m sq) by 65 percent.

Nigel and Terry grew their entire third crop for only $52 per pound (106 euros per kilo).

Calendar and Checklist

A calendar helps growers know what to do and when to prepare to do it. A checklist adds necessary routine to the process. The calendar outlines the average three-month life cycle of clones. It notes major points of interest during each stage in life. The weekly checklist consists of a few things that must be done every week to ensure a successful crop.

Savvy growers read and consider each and every point on the calendar weekly. They mark each point with a check when finished with it.

Growers should spend at least 10 minutes per day, per lamp, to have a productive garden. This is enough time to complete all the stuff on the weekly calendar. Much of gardening is simply watching and paying attention, but it takes time to have a decent, productive garden. If using CO_2 enrichment or hydroponics, allow 20 minutes per day for maintenance.

Large chunks of time will be spent setting up the grow room and harvesting. These are not included in the 10-20 minute daily schedule.

Calendar

The calendar starts on January 1st and is only three months long. Two weeks for clones to stick (root), two weeks of vegetative growth, and eight weeks of flowering. This indoor calendar can be started any day of the year, no matter which direction the wind is blowing or what the weatherman says.

If the garden is full of clones grown with CO_2 enrichment or hydroponically, the calendar could move up one week, depending on how fast the garden grows. Remember, light intensity substantially diminishes over four feet away from the bulb.

Weekly Checklist

Check the following to see if they function properly:

- Air ventilation
- Air circulation
- Humidity: 40-60 percent - flowering
- Humidity: 60-70 percent - vegetative
- Temperature: day 70-75°F (21-24°C); night 60-65°F (16-19°C)
- Soil moisture (dry pockets) water as needed
- Cultivate soil surface
- Check pH
- Rotate (turn) plants
- Check for spider mites under leaves
- Check for fungi
- Check for nutrient deficiencies
- Regular fertilization schedule
- Check HID system for excessive heat at plug-in, timer, ballast, and near ceiling
- Cleanup!
- Cleanup!
- Check walls and ceiling for mold
- Move lamp up, 12-36 inches above plants

Examine your plants carefully under a magnifying eyepiece to see if they are ready for harvest.

First Month
January 1st, First Week

Take clones and root clones. They root in 1-4 weeks.

Sow seeds. Make sure they are warm for speedy germination.

Mix dolomite lime into soil before planting.

Prepare grow room. Read "Setting up the Grow Room" and "Setting up the Lamp."

Set timer for 18-hour days and 6-hour nights.

January 15th, Third Week

Make sure the vegetative room is perfect before bringing in the clones.

Move in rooted clones or sprouted seedlings, place 24-36 inches under HID. Keep soil surface moist.

Fertilize seedlings and clones. Use an ALL PURPOSE fertilizer. Start regular fertilization schedule.

Special care should be given to soil. Moisture damping-off and dry soil pockets could stunt plants now!

Second Month

February 1st,
Fifth Week

Vegetative plants should be 6-12 inches tall with broad, firm, green leaves.

Grow rooted cuttings under metal halide light.

Take cuttings from strong mother plants.

When vegetative plants are big enough, induce flowering.

Continue regular supplemental fertilization program.

Move HID 12-36 inches above month-old seedlings and clones.

Thin and transplant seedlings into larger pots.

Irrigate as needed.

February 15th, Seventh Week

Move vegetative clones into 12-hour flowering room.

Change to superbloom fertilizer.

Plants should be 12-24 inches tall.

No leaves should be yellowing. If they are, fine-tune the weekly checklist.

Over-watering is sometimes a problem now. Check the soil with a moisture meter.

Increased air circulation and ventilation are essential.

Mist the garden with water to wash leaves.

Iron, magnesium, and nitrogen deficiencies could show up now.

Supplemental trace element mix should be applied.

Third Month March 1st, Ninth Week

The plants are two months old and 18-36 inches tall.

Females should dawn

Watch out for diseases and pests.

Plants need plenty of light to flower well.

Continue to water and fertilize your garden.

white, hair-like pistils.

Male pollen sacks develop. Remove or save males for breeding.

Take clones for the next crop.

If there are any leaves yellowing and dying, fine-tune the weekly check list.

Air circulation, ventilation, and relative humidity are very important now!

Leach soil to wash away any excess fertilizer salt residues.

Seedlings only two-months old should be given another month of growth before flowering is induced.

Cloning for sex may now be practiced.

Soil will dry out rapidly now; watch for dry soil pockets.

Bend and tie plants over to give garden an even profile.

Prune plants that are shadowing other plants (optional).

Heavily planted rooms should be ready for a second lamp. Add another lamp to increase harvest.

This is the time of peak THC production. During the next one to four weeks, the tops will double in size and potency!

Lower leaves may yellow. If many leaves are yellowing, fine-tune the checklist.

After fine-tuning checklist, remove yellowing leaves only if they are clearly going to die.

Garden might still be using quite a bit of water; make sure to check it daily if needed.

Plants grow tall as they reach for the light.

This is the last chance for spraying and fertilizing, if you plan to harvest within two weeks. If there are any nutrient, fungi, or insect disorders, this is the last chance you will have to use sprays to combat them.

March 15th, Eleventh Week

Tops elongate, making the garden's profile about 6-12 inches taller than two weeks ago.

Continue fertilizing with a high-bloom fertilizer.

Older leaves may start to drop a little faster, due to decreased nitrogen in the super-bloom fertilizer or if only an HP sodium lamp is used.

Inspect for bud (gray) mold.

Check all factors listed on the checklist.

Buds should be oozing with resin by now.

Some shade-leaf yellowing is normal.

Indica and early-maturing buds are nearly ripe now. Harvest if ready.

Water as needed.

No insecticides!

No fungicides!

No fertilizer!

Check for bud blight or bud mold.

Females show white, fuzzy pistils when they flower.

Fourth Month
April 1st, Twelfth week

The only change will be in growth of more and heavier calyxes on the flower buds.

Continue to water as needed.

Bud (gray) mold could become a problem. Constant scrutiny is a must! It shows up overnight, so watch out!

Everything should be ready for harvest by now. If it is not, consider growing an earlier-maturing strain of cannabis.

Harvest now or within a couple of weeks.

THC content is on its way downhill when resin glands turn amber.

Let "seed crops" go until the seeds are big and healthy before harvesting.

Harvest and clean up.

Move in rooted clones for next crop.

This big 'Kahuna' will be ready soon.

Huge buds adorn this garden a week from harvest.

Mouth-watering 'S.A.G.E.'

A single handle raises and lowers an entire room full of lights!

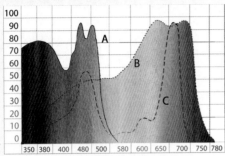

Spectrum of A. Photosynthetic response, B. Light spectrum humans use to see, C. Chlorophyll synthesis

This graph shows the exact level at which A. Phototropic response, B. Photosynthetic response, and C. Chlorophyll synthesis take place.

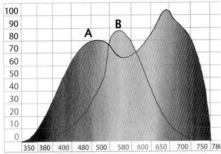

The single humped line in the center of the graph represents the visible light spectrum humans see. The dual humped line represents the spectrum cannabis needs to grow.

Kelvin Scale

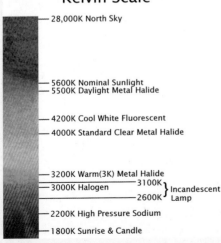

- 28,000K North Sky

- 5600K Nominal Sunlight
- 5500K Daylight Metal Halide

- 4200K Cool White Fluorescent
- 4000K Standard Clear Metal Halide

- 3200K Warm(3K) Metal Halide
- 3000K Halogen ⎫ 3100K
-                ⎬ Incandescent
-                2600K ⎭ Lamp
- 2200K High Pressure Sodium
- 1800K Sunrise & Candle

Introduction
Light, Spectrum, and Photoperiod

Marijuana needs light to grow. The light must have the proper spectrum and intensity to ensure rapid growth. Light is comprised of separate bands of colors. Each color in the spectrum sends the plant a separate signal. Each color in the spectrum promotes a different type of growth.

PAR and Light Spectrum

Plants need and use only certain portions of the light spectrum. The most important colors in the spectrum for maximum chlorophyll production and photosynthetic response are in the blue and red range. The main portion of light used by plants is between 400 and 700 nanometers (nm).* This region is called the Photosynthetically Active Radiation (PAR) zone.**

"PAR watts" is the measure of the actual amount of specific photons a plant needs to grow. Photons are a measure of light energy. Light energy is radiated and assimilated in photons. Photosynthesis is necessary for plants to grow and is activated by the assimilation of photons. Blue photons are worth more PAR watts than red photons, but scientists have difficulty measuring the exact difference.

*One nanometer (nm) = one billionth (10^{-9}) of a meter. Light is measured in wavelengths; the wavelengths are measured in nanometers.
**Some scientists still disagree as to the exact PAR zone and make their calculations based on 350 to 750 nanometers. PAR watts measured with this scale will be a little higher.

Bulb Rating	CCT Rating in degrees Kelvin
Warm	3000
Neutral	4000
Cool	6000

Bulb	Kelvin Temp	CRI
Cool White	4150 K	62
Lite White	4150 K	62
Warm White	300 K	52
Deluxe Daylight	8500 K	84
Vitalight	5500 K	96
Noon Sunlight	5300 K	100

Each color of light activates different plant functions. Positive tropism, the plant's ability to orient leaves toward light, is controlled by spectrum. Light bulbs deliver only a part of the necessary light marijuana needs to grow. However, they deliver enough! Most of marijuana's light needs can be met by artificial means.

Measuring Light

Virtually all light is measured in foot-candles, lux, or lumens. Foot-candles and lux measure light visible to the human eye. The human eye sees much less of the light spectrum than plants "see." The eye is most sensitive to light between 525-625 nanometers. The importance of the blue and red portions in the spectrum is diminished greatly when light is measured in foot-candles, lux, or lumens. A foot-candle is a unit of illumination equal to the intensity of one candle at a distance of one foot. The lux scale is similar to that of the foot-candle; one foot-candle is equal to 10.76 lux.

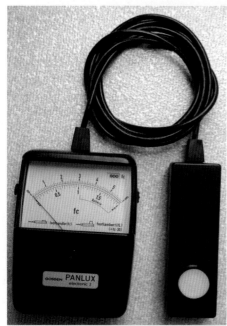

Although this simple light meter measures light in foot-candles rather than PAR, it still gives an accurate idea of light distribution.

Humans see light differently than plants do. Compare the graphs (page 170) to see how the light you see differs from the light plants use to grow. Plants use the photosynthetically active response (PAR) portion of the spectrum. Humans use the central portion of the spectrum, while plants are able to use large portions of the spectrum not measured by light meters that record foot-candles, lux, and lumens.

Light is also measured in spectrum with Kelvin temperature which expresses the exact color a bulb emits. Bulbs with a Kelvin temperature from 3000 to 6500 are best for growing marijuana. The PAR section explains that plants use specific portions of the spectrum–a complete range from blues to reds. Lamps with a spectrum similar to PAR-rated bulbs can use Kelvin temperature of a bulb to ascertain the approximate PAR rating of the lamp. Color spectrum results from a specific mix of different colors. High intensity discharge bulbs are very similar in spectrum. Making these safe assumptions, a rough PAR rating could be extrapolated from a Kelvin temperature rating.

The Color Corrected Temperature (CCT) of a bulb is the peak Kelvin temperature at which the colors in a bulb are stable. We can classify bulbs by their CCT rating which tells us the overall color of the light emitted. It does not tell us the concentration of the combination of colors emitted. Companies use a Color Rendering Index (CRI). The higher the CRI, the better the bulb is for growing.

Light Meters

Most commercial light meters measure light in foot-candles or lux. Both scales measure light to which the human eye reacts to "see." They do not measure photosynthetic response to light in PAR watts.

Light measurements in this book are made in foot-candles and lux. This information is still valuable, because it records the amount of light spread over a specific surface. The information is then coupled with the PAR rating of different bulbs. Regardless of the lamp, the amount of light emitted is constant. It only makes sense to use the proper reflective hood with a high PAR-rated bulb to grow the best garden.

Bulb	Model	Mfrg	MH/HPS	Watts	Initial Lumens	Color Deg. K
Sunmaster	Warm Deluxe	V	MH	1100	133000	385 PAR
AgroSun	AgroSun	V	MH	1000	117000	3250
Multivapor	HO	GE	MH	1000	115000	3800
MultiMetal	Super	I	MH	1000	115000	4200
Metal Halide	Metal Halide	Ph	MH	1000	110000	3700
Solarmax	Veg	V	MH	1000	85000	7200
Super Metalarc	Super	O	MH	1000	115000	3600
Sunmaster	Warm Deluxe	V	MH	1000	117000	315 PAR
Sunmaster	Natural Deluxe	V	MH	1000	117000	315 PAR
Sunmaster	Cool Deluxe	V	MH	1000	80000	315 PAR
Solarmax	Veg / Conversion	V	MH	600	55000	7200
Solarmax	Veg	V	MH	400	32000	7200
Sunmaster	Warm Deluxe	V	MH	400	40000	110 PAR
Sunmaster	Natural Deluxe	V	MH	400	40000	110 PAR
Sunmaster	Cool Deluxe	V	MH	400	32500	110 PAR
Super Metalarc	Super	O	MH	400	40000	4200
Super Metal Halide	Super	Ph	MH	400	4000	4300
AgroSun	AgroSun	V	MH	400	4000	3250
Multivapor	HO	GE	MH	400	40000	4200
Sunmaster	Warm Deluxe	V	MH	250	22000	85 PAR
Sunmaster	Natural Deluxe	V	MH	250	23000	85 PAR
Sunmaster	Cool Deluxe	V	MH	250	21500	85 PAR
Super Metalarc	Super	O	MH	250	23000	4200
Super Metal Halide	Super	Ph	MH	250	23000	4300
Multivapor	HO	GE	MH	250	23000	4200
Hortilux	Super		HPS	1000	145000	2100
Solarmax	Super HPS	V	HPS	1000	147000	2100
Lucalox	HPS	GE	HPS	1000	140000	2100
Sunlux	HPS	I	HPS	1000	140000	2100
Lumalux	HPS	O	HPS	1000	140000	2100
Ceramalux	HPS	Ph	HPS	1000	140000	2100
Solarmax	Super HPS	V	HPS	600	95000	2100
Sunmaster	Super HPS Deluxe	V	HPS	600	85000	358 PAR
Lumalux	Super	O	HPS	600	9000	2200
SonAgro	Plus	Ph	HPS	600	9000	2100
Hortilux	Super	I	HPS	430	58500	2100
Hortilux	Super	I	HPS	400	55000	2100
Solarmax	Super HPS	V	HPS	400	55000	2100
Lucalox	HPS	GE	HPS	400	41000	4000
Sunlux	HPS	I	HPS	400	50000	2100
Lumalux	HPS	O	HPS	400	50000	2100
Ceramalux	HPS	Ph	HPS	400	50000	2100
Hortilux	Super	I	HPS	250	32000	2100
Lucalox	HPS	GE	HPS	250	30000	2100
Sunlux	HPS	I	HPS	250	29000	2100
Lumalux	HPS	O	HPS	250	29000	2100
Ceramalux	HPS	Ph	HPS	250	28500	2100

After all the talk about PAR watts, industry officials are unable to agree on a common scale of measurement. For this reason, we have decided to rely on Kelvin color temperature to measure lamp spectrum.

Photoperiod

The photoperiod is the relationship between the duration of the light period and dark period. Most strains of marijuana will stay in the vegetative growth stage as long as an 18 to 24-hour light and a 6 to 0-hour dark photoperiod are maintained. However, there are exceptions. Eighteen hours of light per day will give marijuana all the light it needs to sustain vegetative growth.

Flowering is most efficiently induced with 12 hours of uninterrupted darkness in a 24-hour photoperiod. When plants are at least two months old–after they have developed sexual characteristics–altering the photoperiod to an even 12 hours, day and night, will induce visible signs of flowering in one to three weeks. Older plants tend to show signs of flowering sooner. Varieties originating in the tropics generally mature later. The 12-hour photoperiod represents the classic equinox and is the optimum daylight-to-dark relationship for flowering in cannabis.

This ruderalis *cross is blooming in the middle of summer. The photoperiod does not induce flowering in this plant.*

Research has proven that less than 12 hours of light will not induce flowering any faster and reduces flower formation and yield. More than 12 hours of light often prolongs flowering. Some growers have achieved higher yields by inducing flowering via the 12-hour photoperiod, then changing to 13-14 hours of light after two to four weeks. However, flowering is often prolonged. I spoke with growers who increase light by one hour two to three weeks after flowering is induced. They say the yield increases about 10 percent. Flowering takes about a week longer, and different varieties respond differently.

A relationship exists between photoperiod response and genetics. We can make generalizations about this relationship, because little scientific evidence documents the extent to which specific strains of cannabis are affected by photoperiod. For example, *sativa*-dominant plants that originated in the tropics respond to long days better than *indica*-dominant plants. On the equator, days and nights are almost the same length year-round. Plants tend to bloom when they are chronologically ready, after completing the vegetative growth stage. However, most growers are familiar with the pure *sativa* strain, 'Haze', which flowers slowly for three months or longer, even when given a 12-hour photoperiod. You can start 'Haze' on a 12/12 day/night schedule, but it still must go through the seedling and vegetative stages before spending three months or longer flowering. Plants grow more slowly in 12-hour days than when given 18 hours of light, and inducing flowering takes longer.

Indica-dominant varieties that originated in northern latitudes tend to flower sooner and respond more quickly to a 12-hour photoperiod. Many *indica* varieties will flower under a 14/10 or 13/11 day/night

> Give plants 36 hours of total darkness just before inducing flowering with the 12/12 photoperiod. This heavy dose of darkness sends plants an unmistakable signal to flower sooner. Growers using this technique report that plants normally show signs of flowering, such as pistil formation, within two weeks and develop pistils after a week of flowering.
>
> Growers have experimented with giving plants up to 48 hours of total darkness to jump-start flowering and have found that 36 hours–three contiguous 12-hour nights–is most effective.

Half of this 'Haze' plant received light from a streetlamp, causing it to remain in the vegetative growth stage. The other half of the plant received total darkness at night and flowered!

Turn on a green light bulb to work in the indoor garden at night. Green light will not affect the photoperiod of flowering plants.

photoperiod. Again, the hours of light necessary to induce flowering in an *indica*-dominant plant is contingent upon the genetics in the strain. More hours of light during flowering can cause some strains to produce bigger plants with reduced flowering time, but some growers have reported looser, leafier buds as a result.

Giving any cannabis variety less than 12 hours of uninterrupted darkness will not make it flower faster. Instead, the plant will take longer to mature, its buds will be smaller, and the overall harvest will be lessened.

Genetically unstable strains could express hermaphroditic tendencies if the photoperiod bounces up and down several times. If you plan to give plants a photoperiod of 13/11 day/night, stick to it. Do not decide you want to change the photoperiod to 15/9. Such variation will stress plants and could produce hermaphrodites.

Some growers experiment with gradually decreasing daylight hours while increasing hours of darkness. They do this to simulate the natural photoperiod outdoors. This practice prolongs flowering and does not increase yield.

The photoperiod signals plants to start flowering; it can also signal them to remain in (or revert to) vegetative growth. Marijuana must have 12 hours of *uninterrupted*, total darkness to flower properly. Dim light during the dark period in the pre-flowering and flowering stages prevents marijuana from blooming. When the 12-hour dark period is interrupted by light, plants get confused. The light signals plants, "It's daytime; start vegetative growth." Given this signal of light, plants start vegetative growth, and flowering is retarded or stopped.

Marijuana will not stop flowering if the lights are turned on for a few minutes once or twice during the flowering cycle. If a light is turned on for a few minutes–long enough to disrupt the dark period–on two or three consecutive nights, plants will start to revert to vegetative growth. Less than one half of one foot-candle of light will prevent cannabis from flowering. That is a little more light than reflected by a full moon on a clear night. Well-bred *indica*-dominant plants will revert within three days. *Sativa*-dominant plants take four to five days to revert to vegetative growth. Once they start to re-vegetate, it takes four to six additional weeks to induce flowering!

When light shines on a green object, green pigment in the object absorbs all spectrum colors but green, and the green light is reflected. This is why we see the color green.

The smart way to visit a grow room during the dark period is to illuminate it with a green light. Marijuana does not respond to the green portion of the light spectrum, thus a green bulb is usable in the grow room at night with no ill effects.

Some growers leave the HID on 24 hours a day. Marijuana can efficiently process 16 to 18 hours of light per day, after which it reaches a point of diminishing returns, and the electricity is wasted. (See Chapter Sixteen Breeding*)*

I talked with Dutch and Canadian growers who claim their plants flower under a 6-hour dark and 12 hour light photoperiod. This expedited, 18-hour photoperiod regimen is supposed to work, but I'm not sold on it. Growers say that their

You can put outdoor plants in a closet daily to induce flowering with 12 hours of uninterrupted *darkness*.

harvest is undiminished, and that they are getting 25 percent more marijuana in the same time. I have not visited their grow rooms to verify these claims. No electricity is saved by adopting this regimen.

Intensity

High intensity discharge lamps are bright–very, very bright. Growers who properly manage this intense brightness harvest more weed per watt. Intensity is the magnitude of light energy per unit of area. It is greatest near the bulb and diminishes rapidly as it moves away from the source.

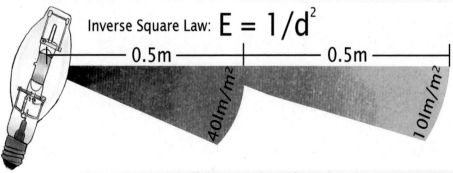

Inverse Square Law: $E = 1/d^2$

The Inverse Square Law dictates light intensity in relation to distance.

Tie a string 12 to 36 inches long to the HID reflector. Use the string to measure the distance between the bulb and plant canopy.

For example, plants that are two feet from a lamp receive one-fourth the amount of light received by plants one foot away! An HID that emits 100,000 lumens produces a paltry 25,000 lumens two feet (60 cm) away. A 1000-watt HID that emits 100,000 initial lumens yields 11,111 lumens three feet (90 cm) away. Couple this meager sum with a poorly designed reflective hood, and beautiful buds suffer big time! The closer marijuana is to a light source,

Leaves reach for the light. Strong, well-illuminated plants orient foliage to catch the maximum amount of light possible.

This `Chronic' cola received plenty of bright PAR watts. It developed super-thick, dense, heavy buds.

Loose buds like this form when they do not receive enough light.

the more PAR watts it receives and the better it grows, as long as it is not so close that heat from the lamp burns foliage.

The Inverse Square Law

The relationship between light emitted from a point source (bulb) and distance are defined by the inverse square law. This law affirms that the intensity of light changes in inverse proportion to the square of the distance.

$I = L/D^2$

Intensity = light output/distance^2

For example:

= light output/distance^2

100,000 = 100,000/1

25,000 = 100,000/4

11,111 = 100,000/9

6250 = 100,000/16

Link to the best light handbook on the Internet http://www.intl-light.com/handbook.html

A 1000-watt standard metal halide emits from 80,000 to 110,000 initial lumens and 65,000 to 88,000 average (mean) lumens. One lumen is equal to the amount of light emitted by one candle that falls on one square foot of surface one foot away. Super halides emit 115,000 initial lumens and 92,000 mean lumens. A 1000-watt HP sodium emits 140,000 initial lumens, and a 600-watt HP sodium emits 90,000; watt for watt, that's seven percent more lumens than the 1000-watt HPS. Lumens emitted are only part of the equation. Lumens received by the plant are much more important.

Lumens received are measured in watts-per-square-foot or in foot-candles (fc). One foot-candle equals the amount of light that falls on one square foot of surface located one foot away from one candle.

Watts-per-square-foot (or m^2) is easy to calculate, but is an erroneous way to determine usable light for a garden. It measures how many watts are available from a light source in an area. For example, a 400-watt incandescent bulb emits the same watts-per-square-foot as a 400-watt metal halide. Mounting height is not considered in watts-

	175w	250w	400w	600w	1000w	
30cm	1200-2000	2000-3500	3500-5500	5400-9000	9000-12000	1 ft
60cm	500-1000	800-1700	1400-3000	3300-4800	5500-8000	2 ft
90cm	250-400	500-800	600-1200	1000-2000	2500-4000	3 ft
1.2m		100-200	300-500	450-800	1500-2000	4 ft
1.5m					500-1200	6.5ft

- A 175-watt HID yields enough light to grow a 2 × 2-foot (60 x 60 cm) garden well. Notice how fast light intensity diminishes more than a foot from the bulb.
- A 250-watt HID will illuminate up to a 3 x 3 foot (90 x 90 cm) area. Keep the bulb from 12 to 18 inches (30-45 cm) above plants.
- A 400-watt HID delivers plenty of light to illuminate a 4 × 4-foot (1.2 x 1.2 m) area well. Hang the lamp from 12 to 24 inches (30-60 cm) above the canopy of the garden.
- A 600-watt HP delivers enough light to illuminate a 4 × 4-foot (1.2 x 1.2 m) area well. Hang the lamp from 18 to 24 inches (30-60 cm) above plants.
- A 1000-watt HID delivers enough light to illuminate a 6 × 6-foot (1.8 x 1.8 m) area well. Some reflective hoods are designed to throw light over a rectangular area. Large 1000-watt HIDs can burn foliage if located closer than 24 inches (60 cm) from plants. Move HIDs closer to plants when using a light mover.

Plants are spaced evenly in this bed of contiguous growing medium.

Each bud in this Swiss garden grows from a clone that is spaced one foot (30 cm) apart.

This Adjust-A-Wing spreads light evenly and plants can be placed very close to the bulb without burning.

per-square-foot; the lamp could be mounted at any height from four to eight feet. Nor does it consider PAR watts or efficiency of the bulb.

Calculating foot-candles or lux is a more accurate way to estimate the amount of light plants

---

The benefits of using lower wattage bulbs include:

More point sources of light

More even distribution of light

Able to place bulbs closer to garden

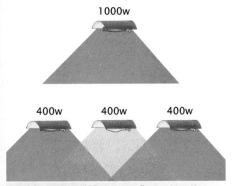

Using three 400-watt bulbs can actually cover 30 to 40 percent more growing area than one 1000-watt bulb. The 400's can also be hung closer to plants.

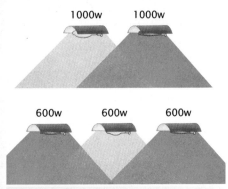

Three 600-watt HIDs actually deliver more light to plants than two 1000-watt HIDs. Smaller HIDs provide three points of light and can be located closer to plants.

receive, but it still lacks the precision of measuring how much light is used by plants. If you start with a bulb that is rated in PAR watts, using a foot-candle or lux meter will suffice.

To demonstrate how dim light intensity retards plant development, check out an outdoor vegetable garden. Have you ever planted 65-day broccoli that took 100 days to mature? Most gardeners have suffered this fate. Did the plants get full sun all day long? The seed vendor assumes seeds were planted under perfect conditions–full sun and perfect temperature range. Plants that received less PAR light matured slowly and produced less than plants getting full sun all day long. It is the same in an indoor marijuana garden; plants that receive less light grow poorly.

Lamp Spacing

Light intensity virtually doubles for every six inches (15 cm) closer an HID is to the canopy of a garden. When light intensity is low, plants stretch for it. Low light intensity is often caused by the lamp being too far away from plants. Dim light causes sparse foliage and spindly branches that are further apart on the stem.

1000-watt: LPW = 140	
1 foot (30 cm) away	140,000 lumens
2 feet (60 cm) away	35,000 lumens
3 feet (90 cm) away	15,555 lumens
4 feet (120 cm) away	9999 lumens

1000-watt HP sodium @ 4 feet = 10,000 lumens
$4 \times 4 = 16$ square feet, 1000 watts / 16 square feet = 62.5 watts per square foot.
1000 watts / M^2 = 100 watts per cm^2

1000-watt: LPW = 115	
1 foot (30 cm) away	115,000 lumens
2 feet (60 cm) away	28,750 lumens
3 feet (90 cm) away	12,777 lumens
4 feet (120 cm) away	8214 lumens

1000-watt metal halide @ 3.25 feet = 10,000 lumens
$3.25 \times 3.25 = 12.25$ square feet, 1000 watts / 12.25 = 81.6 watts per square foot.
1000 watts / m^2 = 10 watts per cm^2

600-watt: LPW = 150	
1 foot (30 cm) away	90,000 lumens
2 feet (60 cm) away	22,500 lumens
3 feet (90 cm) away	9,999 lumens
4 feet (120 cm) away	6428 lumens

600-watt HP sodium @ 3 feet = 10,000 lumens
$3 \times 3 = 9$ square feet, 600 watts / 9 = 66 watts per square foot
600 watts / m^2 = 6 watts per cm^2

400-watt: LPW = 125	
1 foot (30 cm) away	50,000 lumens
2 feet (60 cm) away	12,500 lumens
3 feet (90 cm) away	5,555 lumens
4 feet (120 cm) away	3571 lumens

400-watt HP sodium @ 2.25 feet = 10,000 lumens
$2.25 \times 2.25 = 5$ square feet, 400 watts / 5 square feet = 80 watts per square foot.
400 watts / m^2 = 4 watts per cm^2

400-watt: LPW = 100	
1 foot (30 cm) away	40,000 lumens
2 feet (60 cm) away	10,000 lumens
3 feet (90 cm) away	4,444 lumens
4 feet (120 cm) away	2857 lumens

400-watt metal halide @ 2 feet = 10,000 lumens
$2 \times 2 = 4$ square feet, 400 watts / 4 = 100 watts per square foot
400 watts / m^2 = 4 watts per cm^2

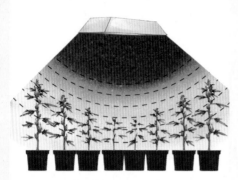

Light intensity is brightest directly under the bulb. To promote even growth, arrange plants under lamps so they receive the same intensity of light.

This gardener is able to rotate and move plants around within the garden beds. Wheels on the bed make it easy to rotate or remove entire beds.

A large bed on casters is easy to maintain.

Increase yield by giving growing area uniform light distribution. Uneven light distribution causes strong branch tips to grow toward the intense light. Foliage in dimly lit areas is shaded when light distribution is uneven.

Reflective hoods ultimately dictate lamp placement–distance between lamps and above the plants. Nearly all stationary lamps have bright (hot) spots that plants grow toward.

Growers prefer high-wattage lamps–400, 600, 1000, or 1100 watts–because they have lumens-per-watt and their PAR rating is higher than smaller bulbs. Plants receive more light when the lamp is closer to the garden. Even though 400-watt lamps produce fewer lumens-per-watt than a 1000-watt bulb, when properly set up, they actually deliver more usable light to plants. The 600-watt bulb has the highest lumen-per-watt conversion (150 LPW) and can be placed closer to the canopy of the garden than 1000 or 1100-watt bulbs. When the 600-watt bulb is closer to plants, they receive more light.

A 1000-watt HID emits a lot of light. It also radiates a lot of heat. The bulb must be farther away from the plants to avoid burning them. In many cases it is more effective to use smaller wattage bulbs. For example, two 400-watt bulbs can be placed closer to plants than one 1000-watt bulb, and the 400-watt bulbs emit light from two points. The disadvantage is that two 400-watt systems cost more than one 1000-watt system.

Check out the diagrams that show the difference in usable light in different sized growing areas. Growers who use these drawings fine-tune the area with a hand-held light meter.

Look at the simple mathematical examples below to see how much more efficient 400 and 600-watt lamps are than 1000-watt lamps.

For example, a 1000-watt lamp that produces 100,000 lumens at the source produces the following:

The goal is to give plants 10,000 lumens.

If you use three 600-watt HP sodium lamps, you get a total of 270,000 lumens at a cost of $0.18 per hour (cost per kWh = $0.10). If you use two 1000-watt HP sodium lamps, you get a total of 280,000 lumens at a cost of $0.20 per hour.

Use the examples above to see the 1000-watt HP sodium offers more watts per square foot and m² to achieve the desired lumen output of 10,000 lumens. However, the bulb also produces a hot spot near the center of the illuminated area. Plants tend to grow into the hot spot and shade other plants.

Although 400-watt lamps have a lower lumen-per-watt conversion, when used properly they may be more efficient than higher wattage bulbs. One 1000-watt halide produces 115,000 initial lumens and a 400-watt halide only 40,000. This means each 400-watt lamp must be located closer to the canopy of the garden to provide a similar amount of light. It also means that several different point sources sustain more even, intense light distribution.

Side Lighting

Side lighting is generally not as efficient as lighting from above. Vertically oriented lamps without reflectors are efficient, but require plants to be oriented around the bulb. To promote growth, light must penetrate the dense foliage of a garden. The lamps are mounted where light intensity is marginal–along the walls–to provide sidelight.

Compact fluorescent lamps are not a good choice for side lighting when using HID lamps. (See "Compact Fluorescent Lamps" for more information.)

Tall lanky buds are easy to grow in small containers.

Rotating Plants

Rotating the plants will help ensure even distribution of light. Rotate plants every day or two by moving them one-quarter to one-half turn. Rotating promotes even growth and fully-developed foliage.

Move plants around under the lamp so they receive the most possible light. Move smaller plants toward the center and taller plants toward the outside of the garden. Set small plants on a stand to even out the garden profile. Arrange plants in a concave shape (stadium method) under the lamp so all plants receive the same amount of light. Containers with wheels are easier to move.

Take advantage of the different levels of light below the HID. Place seedlings and cuttings requiring low light levels on the perimeter and flowering plants needing higher light levels under bright bulbs.

Some clones grow so fast that the harvest is ready before plants shade one another.

You can really pack plants into a garden when they receive a lot of bright light.

Plant Spacing

When light shines on a garden, the leaves near the top of plants get more intense light than the leaves at the bottom. The top leaves shade the bottom leaves and absorb light energy, making less light energy available to lower leaves. If the lower leaves do not receive enough light, they will yellow and die. Tall six-foot (1.8 m) plants take longer to grow and have higher overall yields than shorter four-foot (1.2 m) plants, but the yield of primo tops will be about the same. Due to lack of light, the taller plants have large flowers on the top three to four feet (90-120 cm) and spindly buds nearer the bottom. Tall plants tend to develop heavy flower tops whose weight the stem cannot support. These plants need to be tied up. Short plants better support the weight of the tops and have much more flower weight than leaf weight.

At least 99 two-week-old seedlings or clones can be huddled directly under a single 400-watt HID. The young plants will need more space as they grow. If packed too closely together, plants sense the shortage of space and do not grow to their maximum potential. Leaves from one plant shade another plant's foliage and slow overall plant growth. It is very important to space young plants just far enough apart so their leaves do not touch or touch very little. This will keep shading to a minimum and growth to a maximum. Check and alter the spacing every few days. Eight to sixteen mature females three to four months old will completely fill the space under one 1000-watt HID.

Plants can absorb light only if it falls on their leaves. Plants must be spaced so their leaves do not overlap too much. Yield increases very little when plants are crowded. Plants also stretch for light, which makes less efficient use of intense light.

Best number of plants per square foot or m² is often a matter of experimenting to find the magic number for your garden. In general, each 40-inch-square (m²) space will hold from 16 to 32 plants.

Reflective Hoods

Some reflective hoods reflect light more evenly than others. A reflector that distributes light evenly–with no hot spots–can be placed closer to plants without burning them. These hoods are most efficient, because the lamp is closer and the light more intense. The farther the lamp is from the garden, the less light plants receive. For example, a 1000-watt reflector with a "hot spot" must be placed 36 inches (90 cm) above the garden. A 600-watt lamp with a reflector that distributes light evenly can be placed only 18 inches above the garden. When placed closer, the 600-watt lamp shines as much light on the garden as the 1000-watt bulb!

The proper reflective hood over the lamp and reflective walls can double the growing area. Growers who use the most efficient reflective hoods harvest up to twice as much as those who don't.

Seedlings, cuttings, and plants in the vegetative growth stage need less light than flowering plants, because their growth requirements are different. For the first few weeks of life, seedlings and clones can easily survive beneath fluorescent lights. Vegetative growth requires a little more light, easily supplied by a metal halide or compact fluorescent lamps.

Reflective hoods are made from steel sheet metal, aluminum, even stainless steel. The steel is either cold-rolled or pre-galvanized before a reflective coating is applied. Pre-galvanized steel is more rust resistant than cold-rolled steel. This metal can be polished, textured or painted, with white being the most common paint color. Premium hood manufacturers apply

Maximum Light Requirements for Plants

Growth Stage	Foot-candles	Lux	Hrs. of Light
Seedling	375	4000	16-24
Clone	375	4000	18-24
Vegetative	2500	27,000	18
Flowering	10,000	107,500	12

These guidelines will give plants all the light they need to form dense buds.
Less light will often cause looser, less-compact buds to form.

The ballast box is attached to the reflector in this greenhouse fixture.

The Wide reflector from Hortilux was one of the first European reflectors to use a deflector below the bulb.

Double fixture greenhouse fixture has the ballasts between bulbs.

This air-ventilated tube is very inefficient, leaving a "hot spot" below.

Place Hortilux 1000-watt fixture 4 feet (1.2 m) above garden.

You can put the Super Wide reflector very close to plants.

This fixture is designed to be mounted next to a wall. It reflects light down and away from the wall.

This Ecotechnics Diamond reflector from Spain is very efficient.

Hortilux sets the standard with their line of reflectors. The Deep model is to be mounted high in greenhouses.

The Adjust-A-Wing is one of my favorite reflectors because it delivers the most light! The deflector under bulb allows it to be super close to plants.

Parabolic dome reflectors orient bulbs vertically. Although less efficient these hoods work well to grow vegetative plants.

Gavita invented a lamp with the reflector inside the bulb! The reflector is the most efficient I have seen!

The Medium reflector from Hortilux is a favorite in Europe.

The Hydrofarm reflector is one of the best values in North America. It reflects a lot of light and "breathes" well.

The "cone" reflector is one of the least efficient available. Much reflected light is wasted.

The Butterfly reflector and deflector is one of the most interesting designs I have seen, but I have no idea about efficiency!

Hortilux Midi reflector spreads light well.

The hammered-finish specular interior of this lamp/ballast fixture diffuses light well.

This vertical reflector is covered in plastic. The bulb hangs between plants.

This reflector from Easy Green has holes for forced-air ventilation and can be placed close to plants.

white paint in a powder-coating process. Note: there are different shades of white, and some whites are whiter than others. Flat titanium white is the most reflective color and diffuses light most effectively. Glossy white paint is easy to clean but tends to create hot spots of light. Sheet metal hoods are less expensive than the same size aluminum hood, because of reduced materials expense.

The pebble and hammer-tone surfaces offer good light diffusion and more surface area to reflect light. Hot spots are commonplace among highly polished, mirror-like surfaces. Mirror-polished hoods also scratch easily and create uneven lighting.

Horizontal Reflective Hoods

Horizontal reflectors are most efficient for HID systems, and are the best value for growers. A horizontal lamp yields up to 40 percent more light than a lamp burning in a vertical position. Light is emitted from the arc tube. When horizontal, half of this light is directed downward to the plants, so only half of the light needs to be reflected. Horizontal reflectors are inherently more efficient than vertical lamps/reflectors, because half of the light is direct and only half of the light must be reflected.

Horizontal reflective hoods are available in many shapes and sizes. The closer the reflective hood is to the arc tube, the less distance light must travel before being reflected. Less distance traveled means more light reflected.

Vertical parabolic dome reflective hoods distribute light evenly over a large area and are perfect for vegetative growth.

Horizontal reflective hoods tend to have a hot spot directly under the bulb. To dissipate this hot spot of light and lower the heat it creates, some manufacturers install a light deflector below the bulb. The deflector diffuses the light and heat directly under the bulb. When there is no hot spot, reflective hoods with deflectors can be placed closer to plants.

Horizontally mounted HP sodium lamps use a small reflective hood for greenhouse culture. The hood is mounted a few inches over the horizontal HP sodium bulb. All light is reflected down toward plants, and the small hood creates minimum shadow.

Vertical Reflective Hoods

Reflectors with vertical lamps are less efficient than horizontal ones. Like horizontal bulbs, vertically mounted bulbs emit light from the sides of the arc tube. This light must strike the side of the hood before it is reflected downward to plants. Reflected light is always less intense than original light. Light travels farther before being reflected in parabolic or cone reflective hoods. Direct light is more intense and more efficient.

Parabolic dome reflectors offer the best value for vertical reflectors. They reflect light relatively evenly, though they throw less overall light than horizontal reflectors. Large parabolic dome hoods distribute light evenly and reflect enough light to sustain vegetative growth. The light spreads out under the hood and is reflected downward to plants. Popular parabolic hoods are inexpensive to manufacture and provide a good light value for the money. Four-foot parabolic hoods are usually manufactured in nine parts. The smaller size facilitates shipping and handling. The customer assembles the hood with small screws and nuts.

Four-foot cone hoods are usually manufactured in four parts. The smaller size facilitates shipping and handling. The customer assembles the pieces with small screws and nuts. Cone-shaped reflectors using a vertical bulb waste light and are very inefficient. Growers who try to save money by purchasing cone-shaped reflectors pay even more in lost efficiency.

For example, say you bought a cone reflective hood for $20 instead of the top of the line horizontal reflector for $40. First, let's look at efficiency. The cone hood produces at 60 percent efficiency and the horizontal reflector at 100 percent, or 40 percent more. Each lamp costs $36 per month to operate 12 hours daily at $0.10 per kilowatt-hour (kWh). If 100 percent = $0.10 per kilowatt-hour, then 60 percent efficiency = $0.06, or a loss of $0.04 for each kilowatt-hour. With this information we can deduce that $36/$0.04 = 900 hours. In 900 hours (75 12-hour days) the horizontal reflector has recouped the extra $20 cost. Not only does the vertical cone yield 40 percent less light, it costs 40 percent more to operate! When this 75-day break-even point is reached, you will be stuck with an inefficient reflective hood that costs more for fewer lumens every second the lamp is using electricity!

Lightweight reflective hoods with open ends dissipate heat quickly. Extra air flows directly through the hood and around the bulb in open-end fixtures to cool the bulb and the fixture. Aluminum dissipates heat more quickly than steel. Train a fan on reflective hoods to speed heat loss.

Artificial light fades as it travels from its source (the bulb). The closer you put the reflector to the bulb, the more intense the light it reflects.

Enclosed hoods with a glass shield covering the bulb operate at higher temperatures. The glass shield is a barrier between plants and the hot bulb. Enclosed hoods must have enough vents; otherwise, heat build-up in the fixture causes bulbs to burn out prematurely. Many of these enclosed fixtures have a special vent fan to evacuate hot air.

Air-Cooled Lamp Fixtures

Several air-cooled lights are available. Some use a reflective hood with a protective glass face and two squirrel cage blowers to move air through the sealed reflective hood cavity. The air is forced to travel around corners, which requires a higher velocity of airflow. Other air-cooled reflectors have no airflow turns, so the air is evacuated quickly and efficiently.

Air-cooled fixtures use blowers to direct heat generated by the bulb out ducting.

Water-Cooled Lamp Fixtures

Water-cooled and air-cooled lamp fixtures are somewhat popular in hot climates. These lamps run cooler and can be moved closer to plants. Water-cooled bulbs are difficult for thermal imaging equipment to detect. Air-cooled fixtures are inexpensive to operate and easy to set up. Keep outer jacket clean and avoid scratching.

Growers decrease bulb heat by 80 percent with a properly set up water-cooled bulb. The water and outer jacket account for a ten percent lumen loss. Growers make up for the loss by moving bulbs closer to plants. On an average day, a 1000-watt bulb uses about 100 gallons of water to keep cool, if the water runs to waste. To recirculate the water requires a big, big reservoir. The water in the reservoir that serves a recirculating cooling system must also be cooled. Reservoir coolers can easily cost $1000.

No Reflective Hood

One option is to remove the reflective hood. With no hood, the lamp burns cooler and emits only direct light.

Reflective Hood Study

I constructed a black room, everything black inside, to measure the amount of light reflective hoods yield. The room was 10 × 10-foot square (3 m2). The floor was covered with black tar paper. Less than three percent light could be reflected from the black surfaces–there was no extra light in this room. Measurements were

In this experimental system, a hoodless HID travels up and down vertically between tiered tubes of budding females. Growers are trying every possible means to grow more in less space and get the highest yield per watt.

made every 12 inches (30 cm) on a matrix marked on the floor. The walls had one-foot increments marked.

I tested five different lamps: a 1000-watt clear super metal halide, a 1000-watt HP sodium, a 600-watt HP sodium, a 400-watt super metal halide, and a 400-watt HP sodium. I positioned the bulb exactly three feet from the floor. Every lamp was warmed up for 15 minutes before taking measurements.

The foot-candle readings on the floor were taken every 12 inches (30 cm) and the results posted to a spreadsheet program. I used a simple spreadsheet graph program to present the graphic results.

The studies show a huge difference between reflective hoods. Some companies do not test their hoods before putting them on the market. To protect yourself and your plants, set up tests like the ones I did here to find out which reflector is the best for your needs.

When a reflector distributes light evenly, the lamp can be placed closer to plants.

In general, the larger the wattage of the bulb, the more efficient it is. Since light intensity dimin-

The Cage from THC BC in Vancouver, BC is one of the most productive gardens per square foot (m²).

Plants grow in vertical slabs and are irrigated from above in this recirculating garden.

ishes so quickly, bulbs must be close to plants. Consequently, more lamps or point sources of light are necessary for even distribution of bright light.

Operating costs for three 600-watt HPS lamps are lower than for two 1000-watt HPS lamps. The 600-watt lamps produce more lumens for the same amount of money, plus they can be closer to plants. There are also three point sources of light, which evens out distribution.

A heat vent outlet around the bulb helps dissipate heat into the atmosphere. Excessive heat around the bulb causes premature burnout.

The studies show the light distribution of several types of light reflectors. The graphs on page 187 clearly show that horizontal reflectors deliver many more lumens than vertical setups.

Check out the "Light Measurement Handbook" available free on the Internet. The 64-page technical book answers endless light questions. Download the book in a few minutes, photos and all: www.Intl-Light.com/handbook/.

Reflective Light

Flat white contains little or no light-absorbing pigment, so it absorbs almost no light and reflects almost all light. Do not use glossy white. It contains varnish that inhibits reflective light. A matte texture provides more reflective surface.

Foylon is a reflective material that reflects light and heat in an evenly dispersed pattern. It is durable, and it reflects about 95 percent of the light that

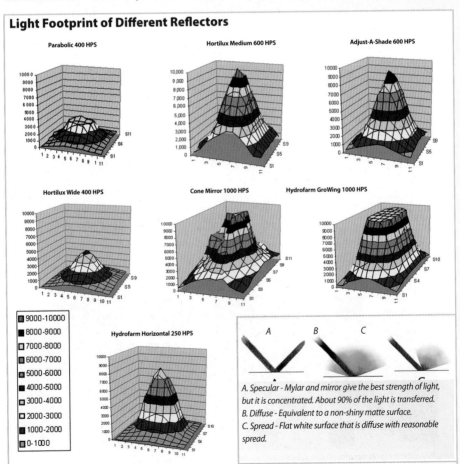

A. Specular - Mylar and mirror give the best strength of light, but it is concentrated. About 90% of the light is transferred.
B. Diffuse - Equivalent to a non-shiny matte surface.
C. Spread - Flat white surface that is diffuse with reasonable spread.

Reflective Chart

Material	Percent Reflected
Foylon	94-95
Reflective Mylar	90-95
Flat white paint	85-93
Semi-gloss white	75-80
Flat yellow	70-80
Aluminum foil	70-75
Black	less than 10

How to add light without using more electricity.

Any unused light is wasted. There are several ways to get the most out of your light without adding more watts, including:

Use several 400 or 600-watt lamps instead of 1000's.
Manually rotate plants regularly.
Add a shelf.
Install rolling beds.
Grow a perpetual crop.
Use a light mover.

hits it. The material is plied with rip-stop fiber and is thick enough to act as an insulator. It's also heat and flame resistant. For more information on Foylon, see www.greenair.com.

Reflective Mylar provides one of the most reflective surfaces possible. Mylar looks like a very thin mirror. Unlike light-absorbing paint, Reflective Mylar reflects almost all light. To install Reflective Mylar, simply tape or tack to the wall. To prevent rips or tears, place a piece of tape over the spot where the staple, nail or tack will be inserted. Although expensive, Mylar is preferred by many growers. The trick is to position it flat against the wall. When loosely affixed to surfaces, light is poorly reflected. To increase its effectiveness, keep Reflective Mylar clean.

Aluminum foil is one of the worst possible reflective surfaces. The foil always crinkles up and reflects light in the wrong directions-actually wasting light. It also reflects more ultraviolet rays than other surfaces, which are harmful to chloroplasts in leaves.

Mirrors also reflect light, but much less than Mylar. Light must first pass through the glass in the mirror, before it is reflected back through the same glass. Light is lost when passing through the glass.

Move small plants to shelves around the perimeter of the grow room. Remember, plants grow wherever light shines!

More Free Growing Light

Even though the lumens-per-watt conversion is lower with 400-watt bulbs than 1000-watt bulbs, hanging ten 400-watt lamps over the same area that four 1000-watt lamps cover, provides more even distribution of light and minimizes shading. Three 600-watt lamps that produce 270,000 lumens from three point sources, instead of two 1000-watt HP sodiums yielding 280,000 lumens from two points, lower total light output by 10,000 lumens, but increases the number of sources of light. Lamps can be placed closer to plants, increasing efficiency even more.

Manually rotating plants helps them fill out better, promoting more even development. The longer plants are in the flowering growth stage, the more light they need. During the first three to four weeks of flowering, plants process a little less light than the last three to four weeks. Plants flowering during the last three to four weeks are placed directly under the bulb where light is the brightest. Plants that have just entered the flowering room can stay on the perimeter until the more mature plants are moved out. This simple trick can easily increase harvests by five to ten percent.

When plants get big, it can become laborious to rotate them. Difficult jobs often go undone. Save the strain and use a light mover, or put the containers on wheels.

Add a shallow shelf around the perimeter of the garden to use light that is eaten by the walls. This sidelight is often very bright and very much wasted. Use brackets to put up a four to six-inch-wide shelf around the perimeter of the garden. The shelf can be built on a slight angle and lined with plastic to form a runoff canal. Pack small plants in six-inch pots along the shelf. Rotate them so they develop evenly. These plants can either flower on the short shelf or when moved under the light.

Installing rolling beds will remove all but one walkway from the garden. Greenhouse growers learned long ago to save space. We can use the same information to increase usable grow space in a grow room. Gardens with elevated growing beds often waste light on walkways. To make use of more growing area place two, two-inch (6 cm) pipes or wooden dowels below the growing bed. The pipe allows the beds to be rolled back and forth, so only one walkway is open at a time. This simple trick usually increases growing space by about 25 percent.

Growing a perpetual crop and flowering only a portion of the garden allows for more plants in a smaller area and a higher overall yield. More plants

Reliable linear light movers offer an exceptional value to indoor growers. Light intensity increases exponentially when bulbs are moved closer to the garden using a light mover.

A single light mover transports all four 1000-watt HP sodium lamps over this rockwool garden of flowering females.

receive intense light, and no light is wasted in such a garden.

Light Movers

Replicate the movement of the sun through the sky with a motorized light mover. A light mover is a device that moves lamps back and forth or in circles across the ceiling of a grow room. The linear or circular path distributes light evenly. Use a light mover to get lights closer to plants. Keep plants at least 12 inches away from a lamp on a light mover. The closer a lamp is to plants without burning them, the more light plants get!

Light movers make bright light distribution more even. Uniform light distribution makes cannabis grow evenly. Budding branches tend to grow toward and around stationary HIDs. These extra-tall spikes of buds shade other foliage. More plants receive more intense light with a lamp moving overhead. This is not a substitute

Benefits of a light mover:

Bulbs can be placed closer to the canopy of the garden.

Increases bright light to more plants.

Delivers light from different angles providing even lighting.

Increases intense light coverage 25 percent or more.

Light is closer to plants.

Economical use of light.

Watch out for the following:

Stretched or leggy plants.

Weak or yellowing plants.

Foliage burned directly under the bulb.

Uneven lighting.

Light mover binding or getting hung up.

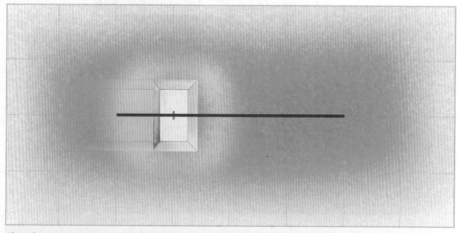

This is the approximate coverage of a linear light mover. Note the brightest light is close to the reflector.

for more lumens from an additional lamp. It is a more efficient way to use each HID, especially 1000-watt lamps. A lamp that is directly overhead casts more direct, intense light to a greater number of plants.

Slower-moving light movers are generally more reliable. Fast-moving light movers can cause light-weight reflectors to wobble or list.

Light from a stationary bulb always shines with the same intensity in the same spot. If upper foliage shades lower leaves, growth slows and is uneven. Light, received by plants from several directions, shines more intensely on more foliage. The light energy is being processed by more foliage and promotes even growth. In nature, as the sun arcs overhead, the entire plant gets full benefit of the light. Most varieties of cannabis grow into a classic Christmas tree shape. This is the most efficient configuration for the plant's growth. Light reaches the center of the plant as well as all outside parts.

Commercial light movers supply more intense light to more plants for less money. Growers report that light movers make it possible to use fewer lamps to get the same yield. Light movers increase intense light coverage by 25 to 35 percent. According to

---

Setting up a Light Mover

Step-by-Step

Step One: Choose the right place.

Step Two: Affix board to the ceiling. Mount light mover track on board. Attach Sun Twist units to a board that is screwed into ceiling joists.

Step Three: Run electrical cord via timer to light mover.

Step Four: Attach supporting electrical wires with cable ties alongside track. You may want to install eyebolts alongside the light track.

Step Five: Reduce vibrations by backing the mounting board with a vibration-absorbing material.

---

some growers, three lamps mounted on motorized light mover(s) will do the job of four lamps.

Motorized light movers keep an even garden profile. The HID draws about 9.2 amperes (A). If this lamp is on a 15 or 20 ampere circuit, you can easily add a light mover that draws one more ampere to the circuit with no risk of overload.

Affix a sturdy board to the ceiling. Mount a light mover on the board with joist below. Run electrical cord via timer to light mover.

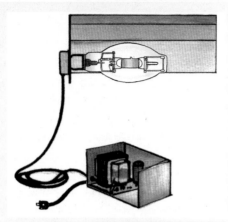

A simple cutaway drawing of a metal halide reveals the transformer and capacitor in a protective metal box. The bulb and hood are attached to the ballast with 14/3-wire and a mogul socket.

Linear systems move in a straight line simulating the sun's path through the heavens. A linear system increases intense light to plants in a linear oval. The area covered by a light mover depends on the length of the track and the number of lamps. The systems use a track that affixes to the ceiling. The lamp moves back and forth across the ceiling, guided by the track. The lamp is fastened to the mover with an adjustable chain or cord. These units vary in length and the speed at which the lamp travels. Some are designed for one lamp, while others are able to move six lamps efficiently. A six-foot linear light mover increases optimum coverage of light from 36 to 72 square feet (3.3 to 6.5 m2)

Young clones and seedlings might stretch and become leggy if the lamp travels too far away. Start using the light movers after the plants are 12 inches (30 cm) tall and have several sets of leaves.

Planter boxes or containers on wheels offer a good alternative to light movers. Containers are rotated daily; wheels make this job a snap. Light reaches every corner of the garden without having to move the lamp. This method has a similar effect as moving the lamp overhead, but is more work because all plants have to be moved, rather than only one or two lamps.

High Intensity Discharge (HID) Lights

Growers use HID lamps to replace natural sunlight indoors and grow outstanding cannabis. High intensity discharge lamps out-perform all other lamps in their lumens-per-watt efficiency, spectral balance, and brilliance. The spectrum and brilliance of HIDs help growers replicate growth responses induced in cannabis by natural sunlight. Compare charts on HID spectral emission with the chart on photosynthetic response, chlorophyll synthesis, and positive tropism.

The HID lamp family contains mercury vapor, metal halide, High Pressure (HP) sodium, and conversion bulbs. Metal halide, HP sodium, and conversion lamps have a spectrum similar to actual sunshine and can be used to grow marijuana. Mercury vapor lamps were the first HIDs on the market. Obsolete mercury vapor lamps are inefficient electrically and produce a poor spectrum for plant growth. Now most all mercury vapor lamps have been retrofitted with more efficient HIDs.

Researchers have created a few better bulbs with a higher PAR rating, but there is no new technology in sight. The latest glass covers of the bulbs have become slightly better at letting light through, but there have been very few major technical advances in these bulbs for the last 20 years.

Popular HID wattages include 150, 175, 250, 400, 430, 600, 1000, and 1100. A 1500-watt metal halide is also available but is not practical for growing. The 1500-watt lamp is designed for stadium lighting and generates too much heat and light to be used efficiently indoors. Smaller 150-250-watt bulbs are popular for small gardens measuring up to three feet square. Brighter 400-1100 lamps are favorites for larger gardens. The 400 and 600-watt bulbs are most popular among European growers. North American growers favor 600 and 1000-watt bulbs. Super efficient 1100-watt metal halides were introduced in 2000.

Incandescent bulbs are the least efficient; 600-watt HP sodium lamps are the most efficient. The brightest bulbs measured in lumens-per-watt are the metal halide and HP sodium bulbs.

Originally developed in the 1970s, metal halides

and HP sodium bulbs were characterized by one main technical limitation—the larger the bulb, the higher the lumens-per-watt conversion. For example, watt for watt, a 1000-watt HP sodium produces about 12 percent more light than a 400-watt HPS and about 25 percent more light than a 150-watt HPS. Scientists overcame this barrier when they developed the 600-watt HP sodium. Watt for watt, a 600-watt HPS produces seven percent more light than the 1000-watt HPS. The "pulse start" metal halides are also brighter and much more efficient than their predecessors.

High intensity discharge lamps produce light by passing electricity through vaporized gas enclosed in a clear ceramic arc tube under very high pressure. The dose, or combination of chemicals, sealed in the arc tube determines the color spectrum produced. The mix of chemicals in the arc tube allows metal halide lamps to yield the broadest and most diverse spectrum of light. The spectrum of HP sodium lamps is somewhat limited because of the narrower band of chemicals used to dose the arc tube. The arc tube is contained within a larger glass bulb. Most of the ultraviolet (UV) rays produced in the arc tube are filtered by the outer bulb. Never look at the arc tube if the outer bulb breaks. Turn off the lamp immediately. Some bulbs have a phosphor coating inside the bulb. This coating makes them produce a little different spectrum and fewer lumens.

General Electric, Iwasaki, Lumenarc, Osram/Sylvania, Philips, and Venture (SunMaster) manufacture HID bulbs. These companies construct many bulbs with the exact same technical statistics. According to some gardeners, certain brands of bulbs are better than others because of where they are manufactured. They usually came to this conclusion because they purchased two different brands of (1000-watt) bulbs and had better luck using one brand. What these gardeners don't know is that many of the manufacturers buy and use the same components, often manufactured by competitors!

Pulse-start metal halides commonly use 240 volts and harbor the starter in the ballast box, not in the arc tube. These systems employ physically smaller reactor ballasts that keep original line voltage within ten percent of the voltage in the arc tube.

Reflective walls increase light in the growing area. Less intense light on the perimeter of gardens is wasted unless it is reflected back onto foliage. Up to 95 percent of this light can be reflected back toward plants. For example, if 500 foot-candles of light is escaping from the edge of the garden and it is reflected at the rate of 50 percent, then 250 foot-candles will be available on the edge of the garden.

Reflective walls should be 12 inches (30 cm) or less from the plants for optimum reflection. Ideally, take walls to the plants. The easiest way to install mobile walls is to hang the lamp near the corner of a room. Use the two corner walls to reflect light. Move the two outside walls close to plants to reflect light. Make the mobile walls from lightweight plywood, Styrofoam, or white Visqueen plastic.

Using white Visqueen plastic to "white out" a room is quick and causes no damage to the room. Visqueen plastic is inexpensive, removable, and reusable. It can be used to fabricate walls and partition rooms. Waterproof Visqueen also protects the walls and floor from water damage. Lightweight Visqueen is easy to cut with scissors or a knife and can be stapled, nailed, or taped.

To make the white walls opaque, hang black Visqueen on the outside. The dead air space between the two layers of Visqueen also increases insulation.

The only disadvantages of white Visqueen plastic are that it is not as reflective as flat white paint, it may get brittle after a few years of use under an HID lamp, and it can be difficult to find at retail outlets.

Using flat white paint is one of the simplest, least expensive, most efficient ways to create optimum reflection. Artists' titanium white paint is more expensive, but more reflective. While easy to clean, semi-gloss white is not quite as reflective as flat white. Regardless of the type of white used, a nontoxic, fungus-inhibiting agent should be added when the paint is mixed. A gallon of good flat white paint costs less than $25. One or two gallons should be enough to "white out" the average grow room. But do not paint the floor white—the reflection is detrimental to tender leaf undersides. Use a primer coat to prevent bleed-through of dark colors or stains or if walls are rough and unpainted. Install the vent fans before painting. Fumes are unpleasant and can cause health problems. Painting is labor-intensive and messy, but it's worth the trouble.

HID Ballasts

A ballast regulates specific starting requirements and line voltage for specific HID lamps. Wattages from 150-1100 use old-fashioned coil transformer-type ballasts. Smaller wattages– below 100–use energy-efficient electronic ballasts. Electronic ballasts run cool and quiet. Scientists continue to develop electronic ballasts for larger wattage HIDs, but the failure rate is still very high. It is very important to buy the proper ballast for your HID. Smart growers buy the entire HID system–ballast, lamp, socket, connecting wiring, and timer–at the same time from a reputable supplier to ensure the ballast and lamp go together.

Be careful when purchasing ballasts that are made in China or Asia, in general. Many of these ballasts are poorly made and do not meet local safety standards. Do not be tricked by misleading sales phrases such as "all components UL or CSA approved."

Of course, each of the components could be UL or CSA approved, but when the components are used together to operate a lamp, they are not UL or CSA approved. Furthermore, chances are that if components are approved, they are not approved for the specific application. Cheap transformers, capacitors, and starters are cheap because they are of inferior quality.

Do not try to mix and match ballasts and lamps. Just because a lamp fits a socket attached to a ballast, does not mean it will work properly in it. If you use the wrong ballast, capacitor, or starter with a lamp, the lamp will not produce the rated amount of light, and it will burn out sooner. The wrong lamp plugged into the wrong ballast adds up to a burnout!

The "core," or transformer, consists of metal plates stuck together by resin and wound with copper wire. The capacitor can is on the right under the connecting wires.

More economical ballast kits contain a transformer core, capacitor (HPS and some metal halides), starter, containing box, and, sometimes, wire. You can purchase components separately from an elec-

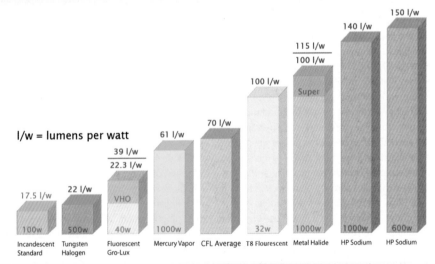

I/w = lumens per watt

The above bar graph shows the lumens-per-watt conversion of different lamps. Notice that except for the 600-watt HPS, the lumens-per-watt conversion factor increases with higher wattage bulbs. The lumens-per-watt formula is used to measure the lamps' efficiency–the amount of lumens produced for the quantity of watts (electricity) consumed.

trical supply store, but it's a bigger hassle than it's worth. If unfamiliar with electrical component assembly and reading wiring diagrams, purchase the assembled ballast in a package containing the lamp and hood from one of the many HID distributors.

Do not buy used parts from a junkyard or try to use a ballast if unsure of its capacity. Just because a bulb fits a socket attached to a ballast, does not mean that it is the proper system. One of the most miserable gardens I have ever seen was grown with mercury vapor streetlights and makeshift reflective hoods. The grower was low on money, so he pilfered all the street lamps, ballast and all, in front of his house.

Even though HIDs have specific ballasting requirements, the ballasts have a good deal in common.

Plastic Visqueen is easy to clean, and it covers walls completely.

Reflective walls are easy to set up.

Movable reflective walls are easy to remove for maintenance, and they give the maximum reflection.

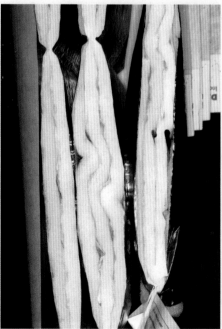

Insulated greenhouse mobile blankets also make great grow room partitions.

Ballast designs are more simple now than ever before. Above, you see two new European ballast designs.

The ballast is attached to the bulb and reflective hood in this greenhouse fixture.

Attach ballasts to the wall on a plank for easy inspection and troubleshooting.

Place ballasts up on shelves so they stay out of the way and out of the splash-range of water.

The most common characteristics ballasts share are noise and heat. This noise could drive some people to great fits of paranoia! Ballasts operate at 90-150°F (32-60°C). Touch a "strike anywhere" kitchen match to the side to check if it is too hot. If the match lights, the ballast is too hot and should be taken into the shop for assessment. A ballast that runs too hot is noisy and could cause problems or burn out. Heat is the number one ballast destroyer. Many ballasts are manufactured with a protective metal box. This outer shell safely contains the core, capacitor (starter), and wiring. If you build another box around a ballast to dampen noise, make sure there is plenty of air circulation. If the ballast runs too hot, it will be less efficient, burn out prematurely, and maybe even start a fire!

More expensive ballasts are equipped with ventilation fans to maintain cool operating temperatures. Air vents allow a ballast to run cooler. The vents should protect the internal parts and prevent water from splashing in.

Some industrial ballasts are sealed in fiberglass or similar material to make them weatherproof. These ballasts are not recommended. They were designed for outdoor use where heat buildup is not a problem. Indoors, the protection of the sealed unit from weather is unnecessary and creates excessive heat and inefficient operation.

A handle will make the ballast easy to move. A small 400-watt halide ballast weighs about 30 pounds (14 kg), and a large 1000-watt HP sodium ballast tips the scales at about 55 pounds (25 kg). This small, heavy box is very awkward to move without a handle.

Most ballasts sold by HID stores are "single tap" and set up for 120-volt household current in North America or 240-volts in Europe, Australia, and New Zealand. North American ballasts run at 60 cycles per minute, while European, Australian, and New Zealand models run at 50 cycles per minute. A ballast from Europe, Australia, or New Zealand will not work properly at 60 cycles per minute. Some "multi-tap" or "quad-tap" ballasts are ready for 120 or 240-volt service. Single-tap ballasts accommodate only one voltage, usually 120. Multi-tap ballasts accommodate either 120 or 240-volt service.

It is generally easiest to use the regular 120-volt systems, because their outlets are more common. The 240-volt systems are normally used in Europe, Australia, and New Zealand or in North America when several lamps are already taking up space on other 120-volt circuits. Changing a "multi-tap" ballast from 120 volts to 240 volts is a simple matter of moving the wire from the 120-volt tap to the 240-volt tap. "Single-tap" ballasts cannot change operating voltages. Consult the wiring diagram found on each transformer for specific instructions. There is no difference in the electricity consumed by using either 120 or 240-volt systems. The 120-volt system draws about 9.6 amperes, and an HID on a 240-volt current draws about 4.3 amperes. Both use the same amount of electricity. Work out the details yourself using the chart below.

This grower lost the crop! He also almost lost his life! Pay attention to electrical connections, ampere ratings for wire, breaker switches, and connectors.

The ballast has a lot of electricity flowing through it. Do not touch the ballast when operating. Do not place the ballast directly on a damp floor or any floor that might get wet and conduct electricity. Always place it up off the floor, and protect it from possible moisture. The ballast should be suspended in the air or on a shelf attached to the wall. It does not have to be very high off the ground, just far enough to keep it dry.

Place the ballast on a soft foam pad to absorb vibrations and lower decibel sound output. Loose components inside the ballast can be tightened to further deaden noise caused by vibrations. Train a fan on ballasts to cool them. Cooler ballasts are more efficient, and bulbs burn brighter.

Ballasts can be attached to the light fixture remote. The remote ballast offers the most versatility and is the best choice for most indoor grow shows. A remote ballast is easy to move. Help control heat by placing it on or near the floor to radiate heat in a cool portion of the grow room, or move the ballast outside the garden to cool the room. Attached ballasts are fixed to the hood; they require more overhead space, are very heavy, and tend to create more heat around the lamp.

Ballasts may be manufactured with an attached timer. These units are very convenient, but the timer should be constructed of heavy-duty heat-resistant

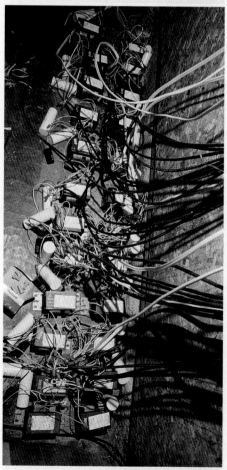

Stoners have a way of making simple things complex.

materials. If it is lightweight plastic, it could easily melt under the heat of the ballast.

Ballasts with a switch allow growers to use the same ballast with two different sets of lights. This wonderful invention is perfect for running two flowering grow rooms. The lights go on for 12 hours in one grow room while they are off in a second room. When the lights turn off in the first room, the same ballasts hooked to another set of lights in the second room are turned on. This setup is very popular in Canada.

There are also ballasts to run both metal halide and HP sodium systems. These dual-purpose ballasts are not a good idea. They will work, but they generally over-drive the metal halide bulb causing it to burn out prematurely after accelerated lumen output loss. I do not recommend these types of ballasts. If you have a limited budget and can only afford one transformer, use conversion bulbs to change spectrum. (See Conversion Bulbs).

HID Bulbs

Many new HID bulbs have been developed in the last few years. The most notable have been the 430-watt HP sodium, pulse start metal halides, the AgroSun, SunMaster PAR bulbs, and the 1100-watt metal halide. These HID bulbs are also available with many different outer envelopes, so bulbs can fit into more confining reflective hoods.

High intensity discharge bulbs are rated by wattage and by the size of the outer envelope or bulb.

High intensity discharge bulbs come in different shapes and sizes. Below each bulb are the numbers industry uses to define their shape and size.

In general, HID bulbs are designed to be tough and durable. New bulbs are tougher than used bulbs. Once the bulb has been used a few hours, the arc tube blackens, and the internal parts become somewhat brittle. After a bulb has been used several hundred hours, a good bump will substantially shorten its life and lessen its luminescence.

Never remove a warm lamp. Heat expands the metal mogul base within the socket. A hot bulb is more difficult to remove, and it must be forced. Special electrical grease is available to lubricate sockets (Vaseline works too). Lightly smear a dash of the lubricant around the mogul socket base to facilitate bulb insertion and extraction.

The outer arc tube contains practically all of the ultraviolet light produced by HIDs. If an HID should happen to break when inserting or removing, unplug the ballast immediately and avoid contact with metal parts to prevent electrical shock.

Always keep the bulb clean. Wait for it to cool before wiping it off with a clean cloth every two to four weeks. Dirt will lower lumen output substantially. Bulbs get covered with insect spray and salty water vapor residues. This dirt dulls lamp brilliance just as clouds dull natural sunlight.

Hands off bulbs! Touching bulbs leaves them with your hand's oily residue. The residue weakens the bulb when it is baked onto it. Most growers clean bulbs with Windex or rubbing alcohol and use a clean cloth to remove filth and grime, but Hortilux Lighting advises cleaning bulbs with a clean cloth only.

Lumen output diminishes over time. As the bulb loses brilliance, it generates less heat and can be moved closer to the garden. This is not an excuse to use old bulbs; it is always better to use newer bulbs. However, it is a way to get a few more months out of an otherwise worthless bulb.

Write down the day, month, and year you start using a bulb so you can better calculate when to replace it for best results. Replace metal halides after 12 months of operation and HP sodium bulbs after 18 months. Many growers replace them sooner. Always keep a spare bulb in its original box available to replace old bulbs. You can go blind staring at a dim bulb trying to decide when to replace it. Remember, your pupils open

Ohms Power Law:

Volts × Amperes = Watts

115 volts × 9 amperes = 1035 watts

240 volts × 4 amperes = 960 watts

and close to compensate for different light levels! One way to determine when to replace a bulb is to examine the arc tube. When the arc tube is very cloudy or very blackened, it is most likely time to replace it.

Bulb Disposal

1. Place the bulb in a dry container, and then place it in the trash.
2. Lamps contain materials that are harmful to the skin. Avoid contact, and use protective clothing.
3. Do not place the bulb in a fire.

Metal Halide Systems

The metal halide HID lamp is the most efficient source of artificial white light available to growers today. It comes in 175, 250, 400, 1000, 1100, and 1500-watt sizes. They may be either clear or phosphor coated, and all require a special ballast. The smaller 175 or 250-watt halides are very popular for closet grow rooms. The 400, 1000 and 1100-watt bulbs are very popular with most indoor growers. The 1500-watt halide is avoided due to its relatively short 2000 to 3000 hour life and incredible heat output. American growers generally prefer the larger 1000-watt lamps, and Europeans almost exclusively favor 400-watt metal halide lamps.

The main metal halide manufacturers include General Electric (Multivapor), Osram/Sylvania (Metalarc) and Westinghouse (Metal Halide), Iwasaki (Eye), Venture (SunMaster), and Philips (Son Agro). Each manufacturer makes a super halide which fits and operates in standard halide ballasts and fixtures. Super metal halides produce about 15 percent more lumens than standard halides. Super halides cost a few dollars more than standards but are well worth the money.

SunMaster, a division of Venture Lighting, has developed new horticultural metal halide bulbs. The new bulbs are brighter and provide a spectrum better suited to plant growth. Growers prefer the Warm Deluxe bulbs. Check out their web site: www.sunmastergrowlamps.com.

Clear halides are most commonly used by indoor growers. Clear super metal halides supply the

BC growers run flowering rooms 24 hours a day with half as many ballasts. This box is made for three transformers, capacitors, and starters to run six 1000-watt HP sodiums. Three lamps run for 12 hours; the other three lamps run for the next 12 hours.

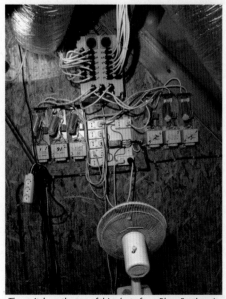

The switch on the top of this photo from Blues Brothers is running twelve 600-watt lamps in a zigzag pattern. A fan is trained on the ballasts and switch to keep them cool.

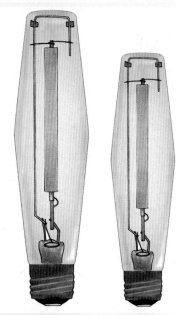

High Pressure Sodium Bulbs

Metal Halide Bulbs

bright lumens for plant growth. Clear halides work well for seedling, vegetative, and flower growth.

Phosphor coated 1000-watt halides give off a more diffused light and are easy on the eyes, emitting less ultraviolet light than the clear halides. They produce the same initial lumens and about 4000 fewer lumens than the standard halide and have a slightly different color spectrum. Phosphor-coated halides have more yellow, less blue and ultraviolet light. Phosphor-coated bulbs used to be popular among growers, but this trend has waned over the last ten years because they are not as bright as clear bulbs.

The 1000-watt super clear halides are the most common halides used to grow marijuana in North America. Compare energy distribution charts and lumen output of all lamps to decide which lamp offers the most light for your garden. Typically, a home grower starts with one super metal halide.

Construction and Operation

Metal halide lamps produce light by passing or arcing electricity through vaporized argon gas, mercury, thorium iodide, sodium iodide, and scandium iode within the quartz arc tube. After they are in their proper concentrations in the arc tube, the characteristic bright white light is emitted. This process takes about three to five minutes. The metal halide arc system is very complex and requires a seasoning period of 100 hours operation for all of its components to stabilize. If a power surge occurs and the lamp goes out or is turned off, it will take five to fifteen minutes for the gases inside the arc tube to cool before restarting.

The outer bulb functions as a protective jacket that contains the arc tube and starting mechanism, keeping them in a constant environment as well as absorbing ultraviolet radiation. Protective glasses that filter out ultraviolet rays are a good idea if you spend much time in the grow room, or if you are prone to staring at the HID!

When the lamp is started, incredible voltage is necessary for the initial ionization process to take place. Turning the lamp on and off more than once a day causes unnecessary stress on the HID system and will shorten its life. It is best to start the lamp only once a day, and always use a timer.

The metal halides operate most efficiently in a vertical ± 15-degree position (see diagram page 202). When operated in positions other than ± 15-degrees of vertical, lamp wattage, lumen output, and life decrease; the arc bends, creating non-uniform heating of the arc tube wall, resulting in less efficient operation and shorter life. There are special lamps made to operate in the horizontal or any other position other than ± 15 degrees (see diagram page 202).

These bulbs have "HOR" stamped on the crown or base which refers to horizontal.

Lumen Maintenance and Life

The average life of a halide is about 12,000 hours, almost two years of daily operation at 18 hours per day. Many will last even longer. The lamp reaches the end of its life when it fails to start or come up to full brilliance. This is usually caused by deterioration of lamp electrodes over time, loss of transmission of the arc tube from blackening, or shifts in the chemical balance of the metals in the arc tube. Do not wait until the bulb is burned out before changing it. An old bulb is inefficient and costly. Replace bulbs every 10-12 months or 5000 hours. Electrode deterioration is greatest during start-up. Bulbs are cheap! Throw another one in, and you will be happy!

The halide may produce a stroboscopic (flashing) effect. The light will appear bright, then dim, bright, dim, etc. This flashing is the result of the arc being extinguished 120 times every second. Illumination usually remains constant, but it may pulsate a little. This is normal and nothing to worry about.

Metal Halide Ballasts

Read "About Ballasts." The ballast for a 1000-watt halide will operate standard, clear, and phosphor-coated and super, clear, and phosphor-coated halides on a 120 or 240-volt current. Different ballasts are required for each lamp wattage; 150, 250, 400, 1000, 1100, and 1500. The ballast for each wattage will operate all halides (super or standard, clear or phosphor coated) of the same wattage. Each ballast must be specifically designed for the 150, 250, 400, 1000, 1100, or 1500-watt halides, because their starting and operating requirements are unique.

Metal Halide Bulbs

Universal metal halide bulbs designed to operate in any position, vertical or horizontal, supply up to ten percent less light and often have a shorter life.

SunMaster Warm Deluxe Grow Lamps emit balanced light similar to a 3000 Kelvin source. The enhanced orange-red component promotes flowering, stem elongation, and germination while a rich blue content assures healthy vegetative growth.

Venture manufactures the AgroSun for Hydrofarm. It is an enhanced metal halide bulb with more yellow/orange in the spectrum. To find out more about this lamp, hit the site www.growlights.com.

High Pressure Sodium Systems

The most impressive fact about the 600-watt high-pressure sodium lamp is that it produces 90,000 initial lumens. The HP sodium is also the most efficient HID lamp available. It comes in 35, 50, 70, 100, 150, 200, 250, 310, 400, 600, and 1000 wattages. Nearly all of the HP sodium bulbs used in grow rooms are clear. All HP sodium vapor lamps have their own unique ballast. High pressure sodium lamps are manufactured by: GE (Lucalox), Sylvania (Lumalux), Westinghouse (Ceramalux), Philips (Son Agro), Iwasaki (Eye), and Venture (High Pressure Sodium). American growers use 1000 and 600-watt HP sodiums most often, while European growers love 400 and 600-watt HPS lamps.

High pressure sodium lamps emit an orange-tinged glow that could be compared to the harvest sun. The color spectrum is highest in the yellow, orange, and red end. For many years, scientists believed this spectrum promoted flower production. However, with the new PAR technology, scientists are rethinking old theories. Marijuana's light needs change when flowering; it no longer needs to produce so many vegetative cells. Vegetative growth slows and eventually stops during blooming. All the plant's energy and attention is focused on flower production so it can complete its annual life cycle. Light from the red end of the spectrum stimulates floral hormones within the plant, promoting flower production. According to some growers, flower volume and weight increase when using HP sodium lights. Other compelling evidence shows the SunMaster halides to be superior. Growers using a 10 × 10-foot (3 m²) room often retain the 1000-watt halide and add a 1000-watt sodium during flowering. Flowering plants need more light to produce tight, full buds. Adding an HP sodium lamp not only doubles available light, it increases the red end of the spectrum. This 1:1 ratio (1 halide and 1 HP sodium) is a popular combination for flowering.

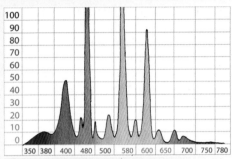

Color spectrum of Cool Deluxe Sunmaster bulb

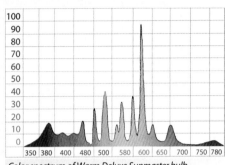

Color spectrum of Warm Deluxe Sunmaster bulb

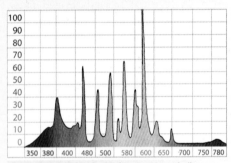

Color spectrum of Neutral Deluxe SunMaster bulb

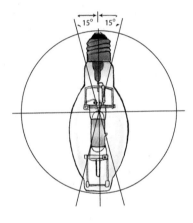

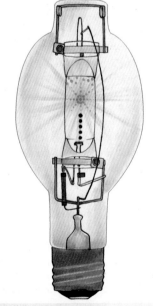

Metal Halide bulb showing reaction.

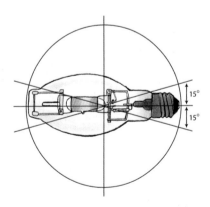

Base Up (BU) and Base Down (BD) metal halide lamps must be vertical to operate properly. Horizontal (H) lamps must orient the arc tube horizontally to burn brightest.

Operation and Construction

High pressure sodium lamps produce light by passing electricity through vaporized sodium and mercury within an arc tube. The HP sodium lamp is totally different from the metal halide in its physical, electrical, and color spectrum characteristics. An electronic starter works with the magnetic component of the ballast to supply a short, high-voltage pulse. This electrical pulse vaporizes the xenon gas and initiates the starting process that takes three to four minutes. Electricity passes, or arcs, between the two main electrodes. If the lamp is turned off, or power surge occurs and the lamp goes out, the gases in the tube will usually need to cool three to fifteen minutes before restarting is possible.

Similar to the metal halide, the HP sodium has a two-bulb construction, with an outer protective bulb and inner arc tube. The outer bulb, or jacket, protects the arc tube from damage and contains a vacuum, reducing heat loss from the arc tube. The sodium, mercury, and xenon gas are contained within the arc tube and have a constant operating temperature. The lamp may be operated in any position (360 degrees). However, most prefer to hang the lamp overhead in a horizontal operating position.

Life and Lumen Maintenance

High pressure sodium lamps have the longest life and best lumen maintenance of all HIDs. Eventually, the sodium bleeds out through the arc tube. Over a long period of daily use, the sodium to mercury ratio changes, causing the voltage in the arc to rise. Finally, the arc tube's operating voltage will rise higher than the ballast is able to sustain. At this point, the lamp will start, warm-up to full intensity, and go out. This sequence is then repeated over and over, signaling the end of the lamp's life. The life of a 1000-watt HP sodium lamp will be about 24,000 hours, or five years, operating at 12 hours per day. Replace HPS bulbs after 18 to 24 months to keep the garden bright.

HP Sodium Ballasts

Read "About Ballasts." A special ballast is specifically required for each wattage of HP sodium lamp. Each wattage lamp has unique operating voltages and currents during start-up and operation. These voltages and currents do not correspond to similar wattages of other HID lamps. Sodium ballasts contain a transformer that is larger than that of a metal halide, a capacitor, and an igniter or starter. Purchase complete HID systems rather than a component kit.

HP Sodium Bulbs

High pressure sodium bulbs are used for industrial, residential, and horticultural lighting. The bulbs are inexpensive and readily available. Discount building stores often carry 250 and 400-watt lamps. All HP sodium lamps will grow cannabis. Even though they are brighter, the spectrum contains little blue and more yellow/orange. Lack of color balance makes plants stretch between internodes, but does not necessarily diminish overall harvest.

Philips designed and manufactures the 430-watt Son Agro specifically to augment natural sunlight and grow plants. The bulb produces a little more blue light in the spectrum. Adding a touch more blue light helps prevent most plants from becoming leggy. The other enhanced performance HP sodium bulb is the Hortilux by Eye (Iwasaki).

The 600-watt HP sodium increased the lumens-per-watt (LPW) efficiency of high intensity bulbs by seven percent. The 600-watt HP sodium is the most efficient lamp on the market. The 430-watt Son Agro HP sodium bulbs have more blue in the spectrum and run a little hotter than their 400-watt counterpart. The Son Agro bulbs are the choice of European growers.

Conversion Bulbs

Conversion, or retrofit, bulbs increase flexibility. One type of conversion bulb allows you to utilize a metal halide (or mercury vapor) system with a bulb that emits light similar to an HP sodium bulb. The bulb looks like a blend between a metal halide and an HP sodium. While the outer bulb

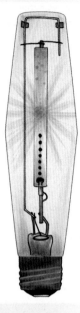

HPS + Reaction

looks like a metal halide, the inner arc tube is similar to that of an HP sodium. A small igniter is located at the base of the bulb. Other conversion bulbs retrofit HP sodium systems to convert them into virtual metal halide systems.

Conversion bulbs are manufactured in 150, 215, 360, 400, 880, 940, and 1000-watt sizes. You do not need an adaptor or any additional equipment. Simply screw the bulb into a compatible ballast of comparable wattage. Conversion bulbs operate at a lower wattage and are not as bright as HP sodium bulbs. Although conversion bulbs have less blue, they are up to 25 percent brighter than metal halide systems and their lumens-per-watt conversion is better than that of super metal halides. The 940-watt conversion bulb has a lumens-per-watt rating of 138. Similar to the HP sodium lamp, the conversion bulb has a life expectancy of up to 24,000 hours. Unlike most high-pressure sodium lamps which flicker on and off near the end of their lives, conversion bulbs go off and remain off at the end of their lives.

Although conversion bulbs are not inexpensive, they are certainly less expensive than an entire HP sodium system. For gardeners who own a metal halide system, or who deem metal halide the most appropriate investment for their lighting needs, conversion bulbs offer a welcome alternative for bright light. In the United States, CEW Lighting distributes Iwasaki lights. Look for their Sunlux Super Ace and Sunlux Ultra Ace lamps.

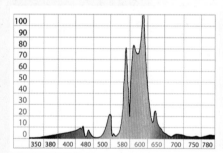

Color spectrum of Spectrum HPS Super bulb

Venture, Iwasaki, and Sunlight Supply manufacture bulbs for conversion in the opposite direction, from high-pressure sodium to metal halide. Venture's White-Lux and Iwasaki's White Ace are metal halide lamps which will operate in an HP sodium system. The 250, 400, 1000-watt conversion bulbs can be used in compatible HPS systems with no alterations or additional equipment. If you own a high-pressure sodium system but need the added blue light which metal halide bulbs produce, these conversion bulbs will suit your needs.

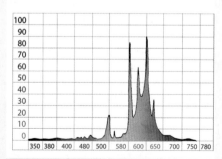

Color spectrum of Son Agro bulb

Many gardeners have great success using conversion bulbs. If you have a metal halide system but want the extra red and yellow light of an HP sodium lamp to promote flowering, simply buy a conversion bulb. Instead of investing in both a metal halide and an

HP sodium system, you can rely on a metal halide system and use conversion bulbs when necessary, or vice versa.

HP Sodium to Metal Halide

The Sunlux Super Ace and Ultra Ace (Iwasaki) and Retrolux (Philips) produce an HP sodium spectrum with a metal halide system. These bulbs make it possible to use a metal halide ballast and get the same spectrum as an HP sodium lamp. Lumens-per-watt efficiency is traded for the convenience of using these bulbs. A 1000-watt HP sodium bulb produces 140,000 initial lumens. A MH to HPS conversion bulb produces 130,000 initial lumens. If you only want one lamp, a conversion bulb is a fair choice.

Metal Halide to HP Sodium

The White Ace (Iwasaki) and White Lux (Venture) are conversion bulbs. They have a metal halide spectrum and are used in an HPS system. The bulb converts from HPS to MH and produces 110,000 initial metal halide lumens.

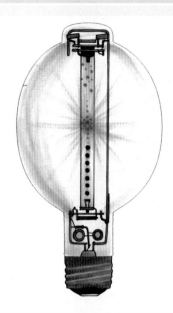

Conversion bulbs make it possible to have both metal halide and HP sodium spectrums at the expense of electrical efficiency.

Mercury Vapor Lamps

The mercury vapor lamp is the oldest and best-known member of the HID family. The HID principle was first used with the mercury vapor lamp around the turn of the 20th century, but it was not until the mid 1930s that the mercury vapor lamp was really employed commercially.

Mercury vapor lamps produce only 60 lumens-per-watt. A comparison of the spectral energy distribution of the mercury vapor and the photosynthetic response chart will show this is a poor lamp for horticulture. It is expensive to operate and produces a spectrum with a low PAR value.

Lamps are available in sizes from 40 to 1000-watts. Bulbs have fair lumen maintenance and a relatively long life. Most wattages last up to three years at 18 hours of daily operation.

Bulbs usually require separate ballasts, however there are a few low wattage bulbs with self-contained ballasts. Uninformed growers occasionally try to scrounge mercury vapor ballasts from junk yards and use them in place of the proper halide or HP sodium ballast. Trying to modify these ballasts for use with other HIDs will cause problems.

Fluorescent Lamps

Fluorescent lamps have gone through major changes in recent years. New bulbs produce more light. Most growers use fluorescents to grow clones and small vegetative plants and maintain mother plants. Some growers even use them to flower a crop. Fluorescents are available in many different spectrums, some almost identical to natural sunlight.

Fluorescent lamps are long glass tubes that come in a wide variety of lengths, from one to twelve feet. The two- and four-foot tubes are the easiest to handle and most readily available. Two four-foot fluorescent bulbs in a shop light fixture cost from $20 to $30.

Fluorescent lamps work very well for root cuttings. They supply cool, diffused light in the proper color spectrum to promote root growth. Use any "daylight spectrum" fluorescent lamp to root cuttings. Fluorescents produce much less light than HIDs and must be very close (two to four inches) to the plants for best results.

Using fluorescents along with HIDs is awkward and problematic. When using them in conjunction with HIDs, fluorescents must be very close to plants to provide enough intense light to do any good. Fixtures may also shade plants from HID light and generally get in the way.

Plants will flower under fluorescent lights. The buds will be small and light, but, with enough fluorescent light, you can grow a mature crop. The grow show will have to literally be lined with fluorescents.

Fluorescent tubes are available in so many different wattages or outputs that they are hard to track! All fluorescents require specific ballasts. The old standard (T12) tubes use about 10 watts per linear foot. A two-foot tube uses about 20 watts, four-foot: 40 watts, etc. The most common bulbs used for growing are available in lengths from 15 inches (38 cm) to four feet (120 cm). Lamps are available in very low to more than 50 watts. Circular fluorescent tubes are available but used by few growers.

Power twist, or groove type, lamps offer additional lumens in the same amount of linear space. The deep wide grooves give more glass surface area and more light output. Several companies market variations of power twist fluorescents.

Black light fluorescent lamps emit ultraviolet (UV) rays through a dark filter glass bulb, but they are not used to grow cannabis. Ultraviolet light is supposed to promote more resin formation on buds. However, all known experiments that add artificial UV light in a controlled environment have proven that it does not make any difference.

Most of the major lighting manufacturers–GE, Osram/Sylvania, and Philips–make fluorescent lamps in a variety of spectrums. The most common are Warm White, White, Cool White, Full Spectrum, and Daylight. See chart for Kelvin temperatures. Sylvania has the GroLux and the Wide Spectrum GroLux. The Standard GroLux is the lamp to use for

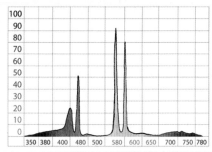

Color spectrum of Mercury Vapor Spectrum bulb

Full Spectrum?

The term full-spectrum was coined in the 1960s by photo-biologist Dr. John Ott to describe electric light sources that simulate the visible and UV spectrum of natural light. Today there are many fluorescent lamps advertised as "full-spectrum." All fluorescent bulbs marketed as "full-spectrum" grow lights are tri-phosphor-coated. Until photo-biologist Dr John Ott began producing and selling the first "color-corrected" bulbs, all fluorescent lamps were halo-phosphor or deluxe halo-phosphor blends, which did not render the reds well. Tri-phosphor-coated lamps emit the visible light spectrum in spectrums from 2700 K to 6400 K. They simulate colors by mixing the three colors associated with the three cone types in our eyes "specially formulated to replicate all the wavelengths in the visible spectrum."

The term "full-spectrum" has been successful to help sell overpriced lights. Now the market is rampant with hype about the lights. Resellers purchase tri-phosphor bulbs from manufacturers and market them as "Grow Lites." Major lamp manufacturers do not sell tri-phosphor-coated lights as "full-spectrum."

starting clones or seedlings. It is designed for use as the only source of light, having the full spectrum necessary for photosynthesis and chlorophyll production. The Wide Spectrum GroLux is designed to supplement natural light and covers the blue to far-red regions. Westinghouse has the AgroLight that produces a very similar spectrum to the sun. Warm White and Cool White bulbs used together make excellent lamps to root clones.

Type/model	Kelvin Temperature
Warm White	2700 K
White	3000 K
Neutral	3500 K
Cool White	4100 K
Full Spectrum	5000 K
Daylight	6500 K

Fluorescent bulbs are further classified by diameter and come in the sizes T12 (1.5 inch [5 cm]), T8 (1 inch [3 cm]), T5 (0.625 inch [1.5 cm]) and CFL (see "Compact Fluorescent Lamps"). The T12 uses old-fashioned magnetic ballasts. The T8 and the T5 (technically CFLs) use electronic ballasts. Growers prefer slimmer T8 and T5 bulbs with electronic ballasts because they run cooler, electricity cycles faster, and lights do not flicker.

The average lumen output of a 40-watt T12 is 2800 lumens, about 68 lumens per watt.

A 32-watt T8 bulb yields 100 lumens per watt and cranks out 100 average lumens.

A 54-watt T5 throws 5000 average lumens, which means it produces 92 lumens per watt.

Construction and Operation

Fluorescent lamps create light by passing electricity through gaseous vapor under low pressure.

Like the HID family, fluorescents require an appropriate fixture containing a small ballast to regulate electricity and household electrical current. The fixture is usually integrated into the reflective hood. There are several types of fixtures. The most common fluorescent bulbs used for growing are hooked to sockets with bi-pin connectors. If purchasing new tubes, make sure the bulb fits the fixture. The fixture may contain one, two, or four tubes.

A ballast radiates almost all heat produced by the system. The ballast is located far enough away from fluorescent tubes that plants can actually touch them without being burned.

Ballasts will normally last 10-12 years. Used fluorescent fixtures are generally acceptable. The end of a magnetic ballast's life is usually accompanied by smoke and a miserable chemical odor. Electronic ballasts simply stop. When the ballast burns out, remove it and buy a new one to replace it. Be very careful if the ballast has brown slime or sludge on or around it. This sludge could contain carcinogenic PCBs. If the ballast contains the sludge, dispose of it in an approved location. Most modern fluorescents are self-starting, but older fluorescents require a special starter. This starter may be integrated into the body of the fixture and hidden from view, or be a small metal tube (about 1 inch [3 cm] in diameter and 0.5-inch long [1 cm]), located at the end of the fixture on the underside. The latter starters are replaceable, while the former require a trip to the electrical store.

If your fluorescent fixture does not work, and you are not well versed in fluorescent troubleshooting, take it to the nearest electric store and ask for advice. Make sure they test each component and tell you why it should be replaced. It might be less expensive to buy another fixture.

The tubular glass bulb is coated on the inside with phosphor. The mix of phosphorescent chemicals in the coating and the gases contained within determine the spectrum of colors emitted by the lamp. Electricity arcs between the two electrodes located at each end of the tube, stimulating the phosphor to emit light energy. The light emission is strongest near the center of the tube and somewhat less at the ends. If rooting just a few cuttings, place them under the center of the fixture for best results.

Once the fluorescent is turned on, it will take a few seconds for the bulb to warm-up before an arc can be struck through the tube. Fluorescents blacken with age, losing intensity. Replace bulbs when they reach 70 percent of their stated service life listed on the package or label. A flickering light is about to burn out and should be replaced. Life expectancy ranges from 9000 hours (15 months at 18 hours daily operation).

Compact Fluorescent Lamps

Available since the early 1990s, compact fluorescent lamps (CFL) are finally available in larger wattages. The larger CFLs are having a major impact

Fluorescent lamps are great for rooting cuttings. Some people even use them to grow cannabis. Buds that flower under fluorescents lack density and weight.

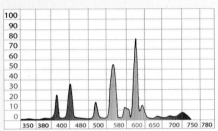

Light spectrum of Warm White (2700 K) fluorescent bulb

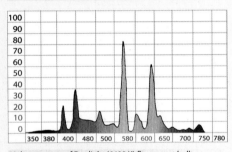

Light spectrum of Daylight (6400 K) fluorescent bulb

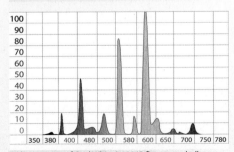

Light spectrum of Cool White (4100 K) fluorescent bulb

on small indoor grow shows. CFLs are similar to long-tube fluorescents but boast increased power, smaller size, and an electronic ballast that ensures longevity and precise spectrum rendition. Although not as bright as HIDs they are available in Cool White and Warm White spectrums and generate little heat. Compact fluorescent lamps are perfect for growers with a limited budget and a small space. They run cooler than HIDs and require minimal ventilation.

When CFLs were first introduced, wattages were too small, and bulbs did not emit enough light to grow cannabis. New large-wattage CFLs are much brighter than smaller, low-wattage CFLs. Several years ago, European companies started selling 55-watt CFLs and Home Depot began to sell a 65-watt CF flood light for $30. Soon afterward 95, 125, and 200-watt CF lamps made in China became available in North America and Europe. The new lamps changed the way growers looked at CFLs. *The new CFLs provide enough light to grow cannabis from seed to harvest.*

Compact fluorescent lamps used to grow cannabis are available in two basic styles and shapes. Modular CFLs have independent bulbs and ballasts that can be replaced separately. The bulb is shaped like a long "U" with a two- or four-pin fixture (these lamps are designated "1U"). The 20-inch (50 cm) long "1U" 55-watt, dual-pin base bulbs are common in Europe. Normally, two 55-watt lamps are placed in a reflective hood. Shorter U-shaped bulbs are common in North America, the United Kingdom, Europe, Australia, and New Zealand.

The second type consists of miniaturized fluorescent tubes packaged with an attached (electronic) ballast. The short lamps consist of several U-shaped tubes (designated 4U, 5U, 6U, etc., for the number of U-shaped tubes) that measure from eight to twelve inches (20-30 cm) not including the two- to four-inch (5-10 cm) attached ballast and threaded base. Smaller wattages fit into household incandescent light bulb sockets. Larger 95, 125, 150, and 200-watt bulbs require a larger mogul socket. Common wattages used for growing cannabis include 55, 60, 65, 85, 95, 120, 125, 150, and 200.

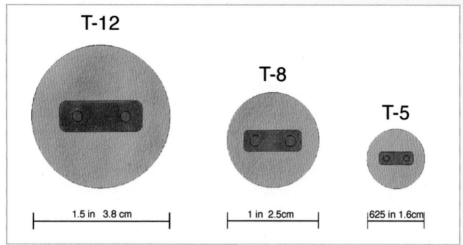

This end view of different sized fluorescent lamps shows their diameters.

Watts	Initial Lumens
26	1800
55	3500
60	4000
65	4500
85	6000
95	7600
12	9000
125	9500
150	12,000
200	15,000

Fluorescent lamps are great for rooting cuttings. Some people even use them to grow cannabis. Buds that flower under fluorescents lack density and weight.

Lighting and specialty stores sell CF lamps, but often charge more than discount warehouse stores. Look for deals at Home Depot and other similar discount stores. Check the Internet, for example, www.lightsite.net is an outstanding site that also has a retail store locator. Philips is producing some of the higher wattage lamps. Their PL-H bulb is a 4U bulb available in 60, 85, and 120 wattages with Kelvin ratings from 3000 to 4100.

Beware of manufacturer and reseller web sites making outrageous claims about CFL performance. The most common exaggerated claim is found at the Lights of America site about the 65-watt Florex security light. The package claims the lamp produces 6825 lumens, but an asterisk directs you to the bottom of the box and explains these are "brightness lumens" not "photometric lumens." A look at their website www.lightsofamerica.com claims the 65 watt Florex produces 4550 lumens. We tested them and we can agree with 4500 lumens.

Furthermore, manufacturers commonly compare the output of CFLs with incandescent lamps. But the comparison is misleading. They claim the 65 watt CFL is equivalent to a 500 watt incandescent. A 65 watt CFL produces the same number of lumens as a 500 watt incandescent bulb. Given this information many people assume that a 65 watt lamp produces as much light as all 500 watt bulbs. Not true.

Cool White CFLs have a kelvin (K) temperature of

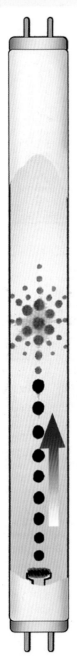

The arc tube of a fluorescent lamp is long, emitting light along its entire length.

4100, with more blue in the spectrum, which lessens internodal branching space in plants. Cool White CFLs are perfect to grow short, stout seedling and vegetative plants. Warm White CFLs (2700 K) have more red in the spectrum and can be used alone but are best used in conjunction with Cool White lamps to avoid internodal stretching during flowering. A 95- to 120-watt lamp will illuminate a space of about two square feet (60 cm2).

Light from CFLs fades fast and must be placed close to the plants. The bulb produces very little heat and can be mounted about two inches (5 cm) away from foliage to achieve the best results.

Short U-shaped bulbs are most efficient when vertically oriented. When mounted horizontally under a reflective hood, much light is reflected back and forth between the bulb's outer envelope and the hood, which markedly lowers efficiency. Heat also builds up from the ballast. Both conditions lessen efficiency.

Save electricity in the grow house and replace incandescent bulbs with compact fluorescents. Compact fluorescents use about 75 percent less energy than incandescent lamps, and emit 90 percent less heat for the same amount of light. If you replace ten 100-watt incandescent bulbs, you will save 750 watts of electricity!

Construction and Operation

Compact fluorescent lamps create light by passing electricity through gaseous vapor under low pressure. Compact fluorescent bulbs are coated inside with tri-phosphor which further expands light emission. CFLs must warm up about five minutes so the chemicals become stable before they come to full brightness. Like all fluorescents, CFLs require an appropriate fixture containing a small electronic ballast to regulate electricity and household electrical current. Ballasts are either attached to the lamp (self-ballasted) or integrated into the reflective hood. Smaller self-ballasted lamps screw into a household incandescent bulb socket. Larger bulbs screw into a mogul socket. Each 1-U bulb is hooked to sockets with bi-pin connectors.

Compact fluorescent lamps will normally last 10-20,000 hours (18-36 months at 18 hours daily use). The life of a CF ballast is from 50,000 to 60,000 hours (seven to nine years at 18 hours daily use). Lamps with attached ballast burn out three to six times faster than the ballast. When the lamp's life is over, the lamp and the attached ballast are both thrown away, which means you are throwing away a perfectly good ballast! My preference is to use the long CFLs that are not attached to a ballast.

Compact fluorescent lamps can also be used to supplement the reddish-yellow spectrum from HP sodium lamps. However, the outer case covering the attached ballast is susceptible to deterioration from UV light. When used in conjunction with other HID lamps that produce UV rays, the ballast case deteriorates more quickly. Attached ballasts are not designed for humid grow room applications. Couple this weakness to humidity with a bit of UV light, and bulbs burn out more quickly.

The end of ballast life is signaled when it stops. When the ballast burns out, remove and replace it.

Although CFLs are not considered hazardous waste, they still contain a little mercury and should be disposed of properly to avoid contaminating the environment. Place CFL bulbs in a sealed plastic bag and dispose the same way you do batteries, oil-based paint, motor oil, etc. at your local Household Hazardous Waste (HHW) Collection Site.

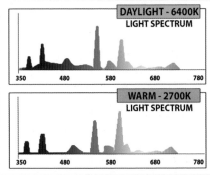

CFL light spectrums are perfect for growing plants, even cannabis!

Other Lamps

Several other lamps deserve a mention, however, they grow marijuana poorly. Incandescent lamps are inefficient, tungsten halogen lamps are bright but inefficient, and low-pressure sodium lamps are efficient but have a limited spectrum.

Incandescent Lamps

Incandescent lamps were invented by Thomas Edison. Light is produced by sending electricity through the filament, a super fine wire inside the bulb. The filament resists the flow of electricity, heating it to incandescence, causing it to glow and emit light. The incandescent bulbs work on ordinary home current and require no ballast. They come in a wide range of wattages and constructions.

Most incandescent lamps have a spectrum in the far-red end, but there are some incandescent grow lamps that have an enhanced blue spectrum. They are expensive to operate and produce few lumens-per-watt. They are most efficiently used as a source of rooting medium heat for clones rooting under cool fluorescents.

Tungsten Halogen Lamps

The tungsten halogen lamp is a poor grow light. It was originally called Iodine Quartz lamp. The outer tube is made of heat-resistant quartz. The main gas inside the quartz tube was iodine, one of the five halogens. Today, Bromine is used most often in the lamps. Similar to incandescent lamps, they use a tungsten wire filament and a sealed bulb and are very expensive to operate. Their lumens-per-watt output is very low. They run on a household current and require no ballast. Tungsten bulbs are as inefficient to operate as are the incandescent lamps. Their color spectrum is in the far-red end with 10-15 percent in the visible spectrum.

LP Sodium Lamps

Low Pressure (LP) sodium lamps are monochromatic. Do not use these lamps to grow cannabis. They produce light in a very narrow portion of the spectrum, at 589 nanometers, and emit a yellow glow. They are available in wattages from 55 to 180. Their lumens-per-watt conversion is the highest of all lamps on the market today. Their main use in industry has been for security or warehouse light.

Lamps require specific ballasts and fixtures according to wattage. The fixture for a 180-watt lamp is just a little larger than a fixture for two 40-watt, four-foot (120 cm) fluorescent tubes.

After visiting hundreds and hundreds of grow rooms over the last 20 years, I have seen only one LP sodium lamp in use.

Electricity & Safety

You don't need to understand the basics of electricity to grow indoors or in a greenhouse, but understanding the basics will save you money, time, and possibly the shock of your life.

Before you touch anything electrical, please remember to work backwards when installing electrical components or doing wiring. Start at the bulb, and work towards the plug-in. Always plug in the cord last!

Ampere (amp): is the measure of electricity in motion. Electricity can be looked at in absolute terms of measurement just as water can. A gallon is an absolute measure of a portion of water; a coulomb is an absolute measure of a portion of electricity. Water in motion is measured in gallons per second, and electricity in motion is measured in coulombs per second. When an electrical current flows at one coulomb per second, we say it has one ampere.

Breaker Switch: ON/OFF safety switch that will turn the electricity OFF when the circuit is overloaded. Look for breaker switches in the breaker panel or breaker box.

Circuit: the circular path that electricity travels. If this path is interrupted, the power will go off. If this circuit is given a chance, it will travel a circular route through your body!

Conductor: something that is able to carry electricity easily. Copper, steel, water, and your body are good electrical conductors.

Fuse: Electrical safety device consisting of a fusible metal that melts and interrupts the circuit when overloaded. Never replace fuses with pennies or aluminum foil! They will not melt and interrupt the circuit when overloaded. This is an easy way to start a fire.

Ground: means to connect electricity to the ground or earth for safety. If a circuit is properly grounded and the electricity travels somewhere it is not supposed to, it will go via the ground wire into the ground (earth) and be rendered harmless. Electricity will travel the path of least resistance. This path must be along the ground wire.

The ground is formed by a wire (usually green, brown, or bare copper) that runs parallel to the

circuit and is attached to a metal ground stake. Metal water and sewer pipes also serve as excellent conductors for the ground. Water pipes conduct electricity well and are all in good contact with the ground. The entire system, pipes, copper wire, and metal ground stake conduct any misplaced electricity safely into the ground.

The ground wire is the third wire with the big round prong. The ground runs through the ballast all the way to the hood. High intensity discharge systems must have a ground that runs a continual path from the socket through the ballast to the main fuse box, then to the house ground.

GFI: Ground Fault Interrupt outlets are required anywhere water is used in a home or business. Install GFI outlets in grow rooms to provide an instant, safe electrical shut-off when necessary.

Hertz: Irregular fluctuations or cycles in electricity within a conductor (wire). In the United States, electricity runs at 60 hertz (Hz), or cycles, per second.

Ohm's Power Law: A law that expresses the strength of an electric current: volts × amperes = watts.

Short Circuit: A short or unintentional circuit formed when conductors (wires) cross. A short circuit will normally blow fuses and turn off breaker switches.

Volts: Electricity is under pressure or electrical potential. This pressure is measured in volts. Most home wiring is under the pressure of approximately 120 or 240 volts.

Watts: are a measure of work. Watts measure the amount of electricity flowing in a wire. When amperes, (units of electricity per second) are multiplied by volts (pressure), we get watts. 1000 watts = 1 kilowatt.

A halide lamp that draws about 9.2 amperes × 120 volts = 1104 watts. Remember Ohm's Power Law:

Overload Chart

Rating	Available	Overload
15	13	14
20	16	17
25	20	21
30	24	25
40	32	33

Connect only one 1000-watt HID to a 15, 20, or 25 ampere 120-volt (North American) circuit.

Connect two 1000-watt HIDs to a 15 ampere 240-volt (European) circuit.

Type/model	Kelvin Temperature
Warm White	2700 K
White	3000 K
Neutral	3500 K
Cool White	4100 K
Full Spectrum	5000 K
Daylight	6500 K

amps × watts = volts. This is strange; the answer was supposed to be 1000 watts. What is wrong? The electricity flows through the ballast, which uses energy to run. The energy drawn by the ballast must amount to 104 watts.

Watt-hours: measure the amount of watts that are used during an hour. One watt-hour is equal to one watt used for one hour. A kilowatt-hour (kWh) is 1000 watt-hours. A 1000-watt HID will use roughly one kilowatt per hour, and the ballast will use about 100 watts. Electrical bills are charged out in kWh.

Each of the 20-inch (50-cm) bulbs uses 55 watts of electricity.

Electrical wire comes in many thicknesses (gauges) indicated by number. Higher numbers indicate smaller wire and lower numbers indicate larger wire. Most household circuits are connected with 14-gauge wire. Wire thickness is important for two reasons–ampacity and voltage drop. Ampacity is the amount of amperes a wire is able to carry safely. Electricity flowing through wire creates heat. The more amps flowing, the more heat created. Heat is wasted power. Avoid wasting power by using the proper thickness of well-insulated wire (14-gauge for 120-volt applications and 18-gauge for 240-volts) with a grounded wire connection.

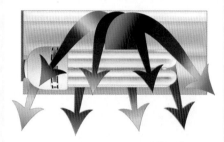
A horizontal reflector is not as efficient as vertical operation with no reflector with this bulb.

Using too small of a wire forces too much power (amperes) through the wire, which causes voltage drop. Voltage (pressure) is lost in the wire. For example: by forcing an 18-gauge wire to carry 9.2 amperes at 120 volts, it would not only heat up, maybe even blowing fuses, but the voltage at the

The ballast is attached to the lamp in this compact fluorescent.

Compact fluorescent lamp box shows 65 actual watts. That is comparable to a 500-watt incandescent.

CF lamps produce plenty of light of the proper spectrum to grow and flower a decent crop.

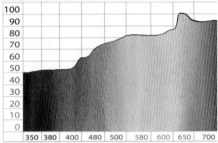

The inside of an electronic CFL ballast is compact and creates very little heat.

The light spectrum of an incandescent lamp. It will grow plants but is best suited to generating heat.

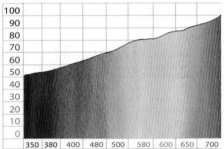

Light spectrum of tungsten halogen lamp. The red end of the spectrum is high but they are very inefficient.

Tungsten halogen lamps are a poor choice to grow cannabis.

outlet would be 120 volts, while the voltage ten feet away could be as low as 108. This is a loss of 12 volts that you are paying for. The ballast and lamp run less efficiently with fewer volts. The further the electricity travels, the more heat that is generated and the more voltage drops.

A lamp designed to work at 120 volts that only receives 108 volts (90 percent of the power it was intended to operate at), would produce only 70 percent of the normal light. Use at least 14-gauge wire for any extension cords, and if the cord is to carry power over 60 feet, use 12-gauge wire.

When wiring a plug-in or socket:
- The hot wire attaches to the brass or gold screw.
- The common wire attaches to the aluminum or silver screw.
- The ground wire always attaches to the ground prong.
- Note: Keep the wires from crossing and forming a short circuit.

Plugs and outlets must have a solid connection. If they are jostled around and the electricity is allowed to jump, electricity is lost in the form of heat; the prongs will burn, and a fire could result. Periodically check plugs and outlets to ensure they have a solid connection.

If installing a new circuit or breaker box, hire an electrician or purchase *Wiring Simplified* by H. P. Richter and W. C. Schwan. It costs about $10 and is available at most hardware stores in the USA. Installing a new circuit in a breaker box is very easy, but installing another fuse in a fuse box is more complex. Before trying anything of this scope, read about it, and discuss it with several professionals.

Electricity Consumption

It is not a crime to use electricity that has been legally purchased. No sensible judge would issue a search warrant on the basis of suspicious electricity consumption. However, not all judges are sensible, and small communities with bored police officers or special marijuana task forces often take it upon themselves to investigate whatever information they are able to weasel out of electric company employees. Larger police forces do not have the desire, time, or money to look for small-time marijuana growers. I once went to check on the electricity consumption of a home I was thinking about renting; I went to the electric company and asked how much electricity the current tenant was using. The electric company employee called up the address on the computer and spun the screen around for me to examine. I could see the electrical consumption for the past few years as well as all the personal information about the tenant! If this is what I can do with a simple question and a smile, imagine what law enforcement officials can do with intimidation!

There are many ways to deal with the increase in consumption of electricity. One friend moved into a home that had all electric heat and a fireplace. He installed three HID lamps in the basement that also generated heat. The excess heat was dispersed via a vent fan attached to a thermostat/humidistat. He turned off the electric heat, bought a fireplace insert,

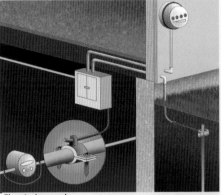

Electrical ground

Water and electricity don't mix. Always work with a grounded system, and keep all standing water off the floor!

Breaker switches have their ampere rating printed on the face.

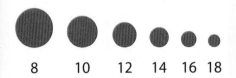

8   10   12   14   16 18

The diameter of electrical wire grows thicker as the gauge number decreases. Notice how much thicker a 14-gauge wire is than 16-gauge.

Avoid scenes like this, and never operate lamps on an overloaded circuit.

A ground fault interrupt (GFI) outlet contains a breaker switch and will turn off electricity when tripped.

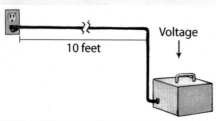

Voltage

10 feet

The voltage drops if electricity travels more than ten feet (3 m) from the outlet to the ballast. The longer the distance, the greater the voltage drop. Ballasts are underpowered when voltage is low, causing the bulb to dim.

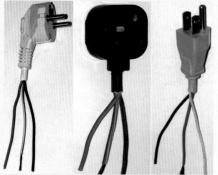

Left European 240-volt grounded plug. Center UK 240-volt grounded plug that contains a fuse. Right Grounded US and Canadian plug. The green or green-striped wires are ground wires.

and started heating with wood. Even running three lamps, consuming three kilowatts per hour, the electric bill was less than it had been with electric heat! Electric bills are controlled with and generated by a computer system. Monthly energy consumption is often displayed on a bar graph for the previous 12 months. This graph makes it easy to see fluctuations in electricity consumption.

A one- to three-bedroom home can run two to three 1000-watt lamps, and a four- to five-bedroom home can operate three to five lamps with little or no suspicion regarding electrical consumption. Powering any more lamps usually requires adding new incoming circuits, or the use of present circuits will be severely limited.

The amount of electricity consumption and the size of the home are proportional. Often, an increase in electric consumption is normal. For example, electric bills always increase if there is a baby in the home or if there are more residents living there. Changing to gas or wood heat and a gas stove and water heater will also lower the electricity bill. Some friends bought a new, efficient water heater and saved $17 per month! Just by changing water heaters, they were able to add another 600-watt lamp. Another grower set her water heater for 130°F (54°C) instead of 170°F (77°C). This simple procedure saved about 25 kWh per month. But do not turn the water heater any lower than 130°F. Harmful bacteria can grow below this safe point.

The electric company might call to ask if you were aware of your increased electricity bill. This is nothing to worry about. Simply reply that you are aware of the electricity being used. If you like to make excuses, some appliances that draw a lot of electricity are: electric pottery kiln, arc welder, and hot tub. If the situation warrants, take showers at a friend's house or at a gym, use a Laundromat, and never use any electrical appliances.

The meter reader may think it is strange to see the electric meter spinning like a top during the middle of the day when nobody is home. Change the daylight cycle to be on at night, so the meter reader sees the meter when the lamps are off. Growers tend to know exactly when the meter reader is coming around. Now meter readers are using high-tech telescopes to read the dials on the meter and storing the readings in an integrated digital entry device. The information is then dumped into the larger computer at the central office. One friend had his meter replaced by the power company. The company had noticed a major change in electricity consumption at the residence and thought that it could be due to a defective meter, so the meter was changed, but no difference was realized. Large electricity consumers may use a heavy-duty commercial power meter.

Cost of Electricity Chart

Cost per	12-hour days			18-hour days	
kWh	day	month		day	month
$0.05	$0.60	$18.00		$0.90	$27.00
$0.06	$0.72	$21.60		$1.08	$32.40
$0.07	$0.84	$25.20		$1.26	$37.80
$0.08	$0.96	$28.80		$1.44	$43.20
$0.09	$1.08	$32.40		$1.62	$48.60
$0.10	$1.20	$36.00		$1.80	$54.00
$0.15	$1.80	$54.00		$2.70	$81.00
$0.20	$2.40	$72.00		$3.60	$108.00
$0.25	$3.00	$90.00		$4.50	$135.00

(In US Dollars)

Some people bypass the meter or figure out some other way to steal electricity. This is a bad idea. If you are stealing electricity from a power company, they might find out. Stealing electricity is a very good way to call unnecessary attention to your growing operation. If you steal electricity, you are making it easy for someone from the power company to investigate you. Of course, some people have stolen electricity for years and gotten away with it, and they might get away with it forever. Ironically, one of the main reasons that people steal electricity in the first place is because of security. If conspicuous electricity consumption is a problem, a generator will help.

Generators

Generators can supply all the electricity necessary for a grow room, and you can grow "off the power grid." Reliability, ampere output, and noise are important to consider when shopping for a generator.

Buy the generator new. It should be water cooled and fully automated. Start it up, and check its noise output before purchasing. Always buy a generator that is big enough to do the job. A little extra cushion will be necessary to allow for power surges. If it fails, the crop could fail! Allow about 1300 watts per lamp to be run by the generator. The ballast consumes a few watts as does the wire, etc. A 5500-

A circuit with a 20-amp fuse, containing the following items
1400-watt toaster oven
  100-watt incandescent light bulb
+ 20 watt radio
1520 total watts
1520/120 volts = 12.6 amps in use
or
1520/240 volts = 6.3 amps in use

The above example shows 12.6 amps are being drawn when everything is on. By adding 9.2 amps, drawn by the HID to the circuit, we get 21.8 amps, an overloaded circuit!

There are three solutions:
1. Remove one or all of the high-amp–drawing appliances and plug them into another circuit.
2. Find another circuit that has few or no amps drawn by other appliances.
3. Install a new circuit. A 240-volt circuit will make more amps available per circuit.

This generator produces 4000 watts at full capacity.

watt Honda generator will run four lamps.

Honda generators are one of the most common found in grow rooms because they are reasonably priced, dependable, and quiet. But, they are not designed to work for long periods. One grower I met hooked up a generator to a six-cylinder gasoline motor. It could run five lamps with ease, but it guzzled a lot of gas. Diesel motors are more economical to run, but noisy, and the toxic fumes reek. Always make sure gasoline or diesel-powered generators are vented properly. The exhaust produces carbon monoxide, which is toxic to plants and humans.

Gasoline generator motors can be converted to propane, which burns much cleaner,

This generator on wheels provides complete "off the grid" security. Check into their consumption and maintenance before purchasing. Some models make quite a bit of noise that must be muffled. You can park it anywhere!

If you must wire your own grow room electricity, make sure to plan ahead of time. Attach junction boxes, timers, etc., to a board, and mount the board on the wall once the appliances are in place.

Grow room controllers make dialing in the exact temperature and humidity for your grow show easy.

The timer on the right controls the entire lighting system in the grow room.

The mechanical timer on the left will operate several lamps at the same time. The digital timer on the right operates a single 1000-watt HID.

Place ballasts on shelves so that they are up and out of the way.

Wiring your own grow room is relatively easy. This grower hardwired a separate breaker box and timer that supports four lamps.

Fixing all wiring and electric devices to a control panel makes control and troubleshooting easy.

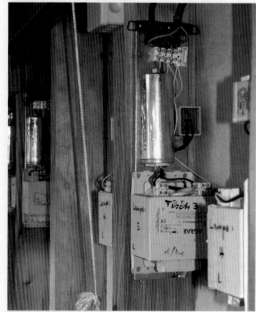

Attach ballasts to the wall so they are out of the way in the garden.

and the exhaust may be used as a source of CO_2.

Diesel generators for truck and train car refrigerators are fairly easy to acquire and last for years. Once set up, one of these "Big Bertha" generators can run many, many lights. Check with wholesale railway and truck wrecking yard outlets for such generators. The generators are usually moved to a belowground location and covered with a building. With a good exhaust system and baffling around the motor, the sound is soon dissipated. Muffling the exhaust and expelling the fumes is a little complex but very effective. The exhaust must be able to escape freely into the atmosphere.

Maintaining a generator that runs 12 hours a day is a lot of work. The generator will need fuel and must be monitored regularly. If the generator shuts down prematurely, plants stop growing.

I once interviewed a grower who ran a generator for six years. He seemed to know a lot about the idiosyncrasies of the machine. He also had the innate feeling that the machine would do something outrageous if he were not there to make it right. This underlying theme dominated the entire interview. Running the generator motor–making sure it had oil, fuel, and ran quietly–was all he thought about when he was growing in the country with "Big Bertha," who produced 20 kilovolts of electricity. Check this site for more information, www. hardydiesel.com.

Timers

A timer is an inexpensive investment that turns lights and other appliances on and off at regular intervals. Using a timer ensures that your garden will receive a controlled light period of the same duration every day.

Purchase a heavy-duty grounded timer with an adequate amperage and tungsten rating to meet your needs. Some timers have a different amperage rating for the switch; it is often lower than that of the timer. Timers that control more than one lamp are more expensive, because they require the entire force of electricity to pass through them. Many pre-wired timers are available at stores that sell HID lights.

How many lights (total watts) will the timer handle? If you are running more than 2000 or 3000 watts, you may want to attach the lamps to a relay, and control the relay with a timer. The advantage of a relay is it offers a path for more electricity without having to change the timer. There are numerous sophisticated timers on the market that will solve every last need you have.

Setting up the HID System - Step-by-Step

Step One: Before setting up the HID system, read "Setting Up the Grow Room" in Chapter Six, and complete the step-by-step instructions.

Step Two: Both the lamp and ballast radiate quite a bit of heat. Take care when positioning them, so they are not so close to plants or flammable walls and ceiling that they become hazardous. If the room has limited space with a low ceiling, place a protective, non-flammable material like metal between the lamp and ceiling to protect from heat. An exhaust fan will be necessary to keep things cool. It is most effective to place the remote ballast near the ceiling to keep things cool. Place it outside the grow room if the room is too hot. When hanging the lamp on the overhead chain or pulley system, make sure electrical cords are unencumbered and not too close to any heat source.

Step Three: Buy and use a good timer to keep the photoperiod consistent. A decent timer costs from $20 to $30 and is worth its weight in buds!

Step Four: To plug in the HID lamp, it will be necessary to find the proper outlet. A 1000-watt HID lamp will use about 9.5 amperes (amps) of electricity on a regular 120-volt house current.

A typical home has a fuse box or a breaker box. Each fuse or breaker switch controls an electrical circuit in the home. The fuse or breaker switch will be rated for 15, 20, 25, 30, or 40-amp service. Circuits are considered overloaded when more than 80 percent of the amps are being used. (See: "Overload Chart" on page 212). The fuse will have its amp rating printed on its face, and the breaker switch will have its amp rating printed on the switch or on the breaker box. To find out which outlets are controlled by a fuse or breaker switch, remove the fuse or turn the breaker switch off. Test each and every outlet in the home to see which ones do not work. All the outlets that do not work are on the same circuit. All outlets that work are on another circuit. When you have found a circuit that has few or no lights, radios, TVs, stereos, etc., plugged into it, look at the circuits' amp rating. If it is rated for 15 amps, you can plug one 1000-watt HID into it. A leeway of 5.5 amps is there to cover any power surges. If the circuit is rated for 20 or more amps, it may be used for the 1000-watt HID and a few other low-amp appliances. To find out how many amps are drawn by each appliance, add up the number of total watts they use, and divide by 120.

Never put a larger fuse in the fuse box than it is rated for. The fuse is the weakest link in the circuit. If a 20-amp fuse is placed into a 15-amp circuit, the fuse is able to conduct more electricity than the wiring. This causes wires to burn rather than the fuse. An overloaded circuit may result in a house fire.

Use an extension cord that is at least 14-gauge wire or heavier if the plug will not reach the outlet desired. Thick 14-gauge extension cord is more difficult to find and may have to be constructed. Smaller 16- or 18-gauge cord will not conduct adequate electricity and will heat up, straining the entire system. Cut the 14-gauge extension cord to the exact length. The further electricity travels, the weaker it gets and the more heat it produces, which also strains the system.

Step Five: Always use a three-prong grounded plug. If your home is not equipped with working three-prong grounded outlets, buy a three-prong grounded plug and outlet adapter. Attach the ground wire to a grounded ferrous metal object like a grounded metal pipe or heavy copper wire driven into the earth to form a ground, and screw the ground into the plug-in face. You will be working with water under and around the HID system. Water conducts electricity about as well as the human body.

Step Six: Once the proper circuit is selected, the

A bulb hanging crookedly under a reflective hood causes light to be reflected unevenly, which creates "hot spots" and "cold spots" of light in the garden.

socket and hood are mounted overhead, and the ballast is in place (but not plugged in), screw the HID bulb finger-tight into the socket. Make sure the bulb is secured in the socket tightly, but not too tight, and make certain there is a good connection. When secure, wipe off all smudges on the bulb to increase brightness.

Step Seven: Plug the three-prong plug into the timer that is in the OFF position. Plug the timer into the grounded outlet, set the timer at the desired photoperiod, and turn the timer on. Shazam! The ballast will hum; the lamp will flicker and slowly warm up, reaching full brilliance in about five minutes.

This garden is filled with happy plants under an air-cooled lighting system that not only ventilates, but keeps the room cooler. The lmaps are suspended from yo-yo's and are easily adjusted as the canopy height rises.

This plant is growing in sandy soil 30 feet (10 m) below sea level in Amsterdam

This cutaway drawing shows how the roots penetrate the soil. Note: There must be enough air trapped in the soil to allow biological activity and absorption of nutrients.

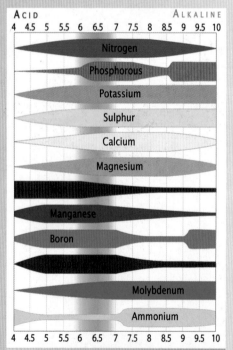

This pH Chart shows the Safe Zone for soil gardens is between 5.8 and 6.8.

Introduction

Soil is made up of many mineral particles mixed together with living and dead organic matter that incorporates air and water. Three basic factors contribute to the cannabis root's ability to grow in a soil: texture, pH, and nutrient content.

Soil texture is governed by the size and physical makeup of the mineral particles. Proper soil texture is required for adequate root penetration, water, and oxygen retention and drainage as well as many other complex chemical processes.

Clay or adobe soil is made up of very small, flat mineral particles; when it gets wet, these minute particles pack tightly together, slowing or stopping root penetration and water drainage. Roots are unable to breathe because very little or no space is left for oxygen. Water has a very difficult time penetrating these tightly packed soils, and once it does penetrate, drainage is slow.

Sandy soils have much larger particles. They permit good aeration (supply of air or oxygen) and drainage. Frequent watering is necessary because water retention is very low. The soil's water- and air-holding ability and root penetration are a function of texture.

Loam soil is ideal for growing cannabis. It contains a mix of clay, silt, and sand. The different sized particles allow a large combination of pore spaces, so it drains well and still retains nutrients and moisture.

To check soil texture, pick up a handful of moist (not soggy) soil and gently squeeze it. The soil should barely stay together and have a kind of sponge effect when you slowly open your hand to release the pressure. Indoor soils that do not fulfill these requirements should be thrown out or amended. See "Soil Amendments."

pH

The pH scale, from one to 14, measures acid-to-alkaline balance. One is the most acidic, seven is neutral, and 14 most alkaline. Every full point change in pH signifies a ten-fold increase or decrease in acidity or alkalinity. For example, soil or water with a pH of five is ten times more acidic than water or soil with a pH of six Water with a pH of five is one hundred times more acidic than water with a pH of seven. With a ten-fold difference between each point on the scale, accurate measurement and control is essential to a strong, healthy garden.

Cannabis grows best in soil with a pH from 6.5 to 7.0. Within this range marijuana can properly absorb and process available nutrients most efficiently. If the pH is too low (acidic), acid salts chemically bind nutrients, and the roots are unable to absorb them. An alkaline soil with a high pH causes nutrients to become unavailable. Toxic salt buildup that limits water intake by roots also becomes a problem. Hydroponic solutions perform best in a pH range a little lower than for soil. The ideal pH range for hydroponics is from 5.8 to 6.8. Some growers run the pH at lower levels and report no problems with nutrient uptake. The pH of organic soil mixes is very important because it dictates the ability of specific pH-sensitive bacteria.

Measure the pH with a soil test kit, litmus paper, or electronic pH tester, all of which are available at most nurseries. When testing pH, take two or three samples and follow instructions supplied by the manufacturer "to the letter." Soil test kits measure soil pH and primary nutrient content by mixing soil with a chemical solution and comparing the color of the solution to a chart. Every one of these kits I have seen or used is difficult for novice gardeners to achieve accurate measurements. Comparing the color of the soil/chemical mix to the color of the chart is often confusing. If you use one of these kits, make sure to buy one with good, easy-to-understand instructions and ask the sales clerk for exact recommendations on using it.

An inexpensive electronic pH tester is easy to use.

When planting, add one cup of fine dolomite lime to each cubic foot (one ounce per gallon [30 ml per 4 L]) of planting medium to stabilize the pH and provide calcium and magnesium.

For an accurate pH test with an electronic pH meter:

- Clean the probes of the meter after each test and wipe away any corrosion.
- Pack the soil around the probes.
- Water soil with distilled or neutral pH water before testing.

If using litmus paper, collect samples that demonstrate an average of the soil. Place the samples in a clean jar, and moisten the soil samples with distilled water. Place two pieces of the litmus paper in the muddy water. After ten seconds, remove one of the strips of litmus paper. Wait a minute before removing the other one. Both pieces of litmus paper should register the same color. The litmus paper container should have a pH-color chart on the side. Match the color of the litmus paper with the colors on the chart to get a pH reading. Litmus paper will accurately measure the acidity of the substance to within a point. The pH readings will not be accurate if altered by water with a high or low pH, and the litmus paper could give a false reading if the fertilizer contains a color-tracing agent.

Electronic pH testers are economical and convenient. Less expensive pH meters are accurate enough for casual use. More expensive models are quite accurate. Pay special attention to the soil moisture when taking a pH test with an electronic meter. The meters measure the electrical current between two probes and are designed to work in moist soil. If the soil is dry, the probes do not give an accurate reading. I prefer electronic pH meters over the reagent test kits and litmus paper because they are convenient, economical, and accurate. Once purchased, you can measure pH thousands of times with an electronic meter, while the chemical test kits are good for about a dozen tests. Perpetual pH-metering devices are also available and most often used to monitor hydroponic nutrient solutions.

Check the pH of irrigation water. In dry climates, such as the desert Southwest United States,

Spain, Australia, etc., irrigation water is often alkaline with a pH above 6.0. The water in rainy climates, such as the Pacific Northwest of North America, the United Kingdom, Netherlands, and maritime Northern Europe, is often acidic with a pH below 6.0. The pH and electrical conductivity (EC) of water supplies in municipalities and cities can also change throughout the year in some countries. After repeated watering, water with a pH that is too high or low will change the pH of the growing medium, especially in organically amended soils. Raw-water pH above 6.0 helps keep fertilizer mixes from becoming too acidic. Climatic conditions can also affect irrigation water pH. For example, the pH can become more acidic in late autumn, when leaves fall and decompose. Large municipalities carefully monitor and correct the pH, and there are few water-quality problems. Check the pH at least once a week.

Cannabis will grow in almost any soil*, but it flourishes when the pH is between 6.5 and 7. Commercial potting soil almost never has a pH above 7.5. A lower pH is more common, even as low as 5.5. Some potting soils purchased at a nursery are pH balanced and near a neutral 7. However, most potting soils have a tendency to be acidic. The easiest way to stabilize soil pH is to mix in one cup of fine dolomite lime per cubic foot (10 liters) of potting soil. Mix dolomite lime thoroughly into dry soil. Remix the soil in the container after it has been watered.

Fine Dolomite Lime has long been a favorite pH stabilizer for gardeners. It is difficult to apply too much as long as it is thoroughly mixed into soil. Dolomite has a neutral pH of 7, and it can never raise the pH beyond 7.0. It stabilizes the pH safely. Compensate for acidic soil by mixing dolomite with soil before planting. It will help

Cannabis is a well-known accumulator plant that takes in heavy metals and sequesters toxins in vacuoles, which are impermeable. The heavy metals remain toxic. Cannabis was planted around Chernobyl, the toxic nuclear site in Russia, to absorb toxic heavy metals.

keep the pH stable, and maintain the correct pH when applying mild acidic fertilizers. Dolomite, a compound of magnesium (Mg) and calcium (Ca), is popular among indoor and outdoor growers in rainy climates with acidic soil. Dolomite does not prevent toxic-salt accumulation caused by impure water and fertilizer buildup. A proper fertilizer regimen and regular leaching helps flush away toxic salts. When purchasing, look for dolomite flour, the finest fast-acting dust-like grade available. Coarse dolomite could take a year or more before it becomes available for uptake by roots. Mix dolomite flour thoroughly with the growing medium before planting. Improperly mixed, dolomite will stratify, forming a cake or layer that burns roots and repels water.

The pH of these large sativa *plants growing on a terrace is kept at 6.5 to 6.8.*

Hydrated Lime contains only calcium and no magnesium. As the name hydrated implies, it is water-soluble. Fast-acting hydrated lime alters the pH quickly. Mix it thoroughly with warm water and apply with each watering for fast results. Many growers use a mix of 0.25 cup (6 cl) hydrated lime and 0.75 cup (18 cl) dolomite lime. Hydrated lime is immediately available, whereas the slower acting dolomite buffers the pH over the long term. Do

not use more than 0.5 cup (12 cl) of hydrated lime per cubic foot (30 L) of soil. The larger quantity is released so fast that it can toxify soil, and stunt or even kill plants. The beauty of hydrated lime is that it washes out of the soil in about two weeks. Leach it quicker by flushing pots with copious quantities of water. Hydrated lime is also used as a grow room fungicide. Sprinkle it on the floor and around the room. It kills fungus on contact.

Do not use **quicklime**; it is toxic to plants. Calcic lime (quicklime) contains only calcium and is not a good choice. It does not have the buffering qualities of dolomite nor does it contain any magnesium.

Raise the pH of a growing medium or irrigation water by adding some form of alkali, such as calcium carbonate, potassium hydroxide, or sodium hydroxide. Both hydroxides are caustic and require special care when handling. These compounds are normally used to raise the pH of hydroponic nutrient solutions but can be used to treat acidic nutrient solutions when applied to soil. The easiest and most convenient way to raise and stabilize soil pH is to add fine dolomite lime and hydrated lime before planting. To raise the pH one point add 3 cups (65 cl) of fine dolomite lime to one cubic foot (30 L) of soil. An alternate fast- acting mix would be to add 2.5 cups (590 cl) of dolomite and 0.5 cup (12 cl) of hydrated lime to one cubic foot of soil.

Pulverized eggshells, clam or oyster shells, and wood ashes have a high pH and help raise soil pH. Eggshells and oyster shells take a long time to decompose enough to affect the pH; wood ashes have a pH from 9.0-11.0 and and are easy to overapply. Ashes are often collected from fireplaces or wood stoves that have been burning all kinds of trash and are, therefore, unsafe. Do not use wood ashes on indoor

Outdoors, the soil temperature can climb quickly when sunshine warms the containers.

Soil

70° – – 21°
65° – – 18°

Soil temperature should stay between 65-70°F (18-24°C) for best results.

Aspirin also lowers the pH. However, hormonal reactions appear to be triggered by aspirin. Some growers have reported more hermaphrodites when using aspirin to alter the pH.

Humates Chelate

Humic and fulvic acids chelate metallic ions making them readily transportable by water. This ability is dependent upon the pH level. Copper, iron, manganese, and zinc are difficult to dissolve. When mixed in a chelated form, they become readily available for absorption.

gardens unless you know their origin, pH, and nutrient content. You can add cottonseed meal, lemon peels, coffee grounds, or a high-acidity fertilizer to lower pH in soil to below 7.0.

Commercial potting soils and soilless mixes are often acidic and the pH seldom needs to be lowered. If new soil pH is under 6 or above 8, it is easier and less expensive in the long run to change soil rather than experiment with changing the pH. Fertilizers are naturally acidic and lower the pH of the growing medium. Sulfur will lower the pH, if necessary, but it is tricky to use. I advise using an acid to alter the pH. Add distilled white vinegar at the rate of one teaspoon per gallon (1.2 ml per L) of irrigation water, allow the water to sit for a few minutes, and then recheck it. The pH should drop by a full point. If it does not, add more vinegar in small increments. Often when using vinegar, the pH drifts up overnight. Check the pH the next day. Hydroponic growers use phosphoric and nitric acid to lower pH. Calcium nitrate can also be used, but is less common. Keep a close eye on the pH and control it accordingly. After altering the pH, check it, and then check it again daily to make sure it remains stable.

Soil Temperature

Raising the soil temperature speeds the chemical process and can hasten nutrient uptake. Ideally, the soil temperature should range from 65-70°F (18-24°C) for the most chemical activity. Warm the soil with soil-heating cables or a heating pad. Fasten heating cables to a board or table and set a heat-conducting pad on top of the cables to distribute heat evenly. Set cuttings and seedlings in shallow flats or growing trays on top of the heat-conducting pad. The added heat speeds root growth when soil temperature is below 65°F (18°C).

Soil heating cables cost much less than soil heating pads but must be installed, whereas the pads are ready to use. Most commercial nurseries carry cables, and hydroponic stores carry heating pads. When rooting clones, a heating pad or cables virtually ensure success and expedite root growth.

Cold soil slows water and nutrient uptake and stifles growth. Growers often overwater when the soil is too cold or the room cools unexpectedly, which further slows growth. Pots on cold concrete floors stay as cold as the concrete, which is always colder than the ambient temperature. Increase soil temperature by moving pots up off the floor a few inches. Set them on an insulating board or piece of Styrofoam™.

Soil temperatures that climb above 75°F (39° C) dehydrate roots, and at higher temperatures the roots actually cook! It is relatively easy to heat the soil in a pot. If the light or any heat source is too close to small pots, it can easily heat up the outside layer of soil where the majority of the feeder roots are located. Once destroyed, roots take one or two weeks to grow back. Two weeks accounts for one quarter of the flowering cycle!

The more *feeder root hairs* there are to absorb water and nutrients, the faster and stronger plants will grow. Once roots go beyond their comfort zone, they send stress signals to foliage and stomata via hormones to close and conserve moisture.

Oxygen is essential for clones that are growing roots. Water holds under one percent dissolved oxygen at 70°F (21°C). Bump the temperature up to 85°F (29°C) and it holds less than 0.5 percent oxygen.

Root temperatures below 40°F (4°C) make water expand, which causes cell damage.

Temperatures above 92°F (33°C) cause excessive vapor pressure within the roots, which can cause damage. At high temperatures roots send stress signals to shut the leaves down before damage can occur.

Potting Soil

Potting soil fresh out of the bag often fulfills all requirements for a growing medium: good texture that allows good root penetration, water retention, and good drainage, a stable pH between 6 and 7, and a minimum supply of nutrients.

Premium fast-draining soils with good texture that will not break down quickly are the best choice. Potting soils found at nurseries are often formulated with a wetting agent and retain water and air evenly, drain well, and allow easy root penetration. Organic potting soils are very popular. These soils are often fortified with organic nutrients including readily available high-nitrogen worm castings. Potting soils are very heavy, and transportation costs tend to keep them somewhat localized. There are many good brands of high-quality potting soil. Ask your nursery person for help in selecting one for fast-growing vegetables.

Stay away from discount brands of low-quality potting soil. These soils can be full of weed seed

Quality potting soil

Quality organic potting soil

Mushroom Compost

and diseases, hold water unevenly, and drain poorly. Ultimately, saving a few pennies on soil will cost many headaches and a low yield later.

Many potting soils supply seedling transplants and clones with enough food (fertilizer) for the first two to four weeks of growth. After that, supplemental fertilization is necessary to retain rapid, robust growth. Add fine-grade dolomite lime to buffer and stabilize the pH. Trace elements in fortified soil and soilless mixes can leach out and should be replenished with chelated nutrients, if deficiency signs occur. Organic growers often add their own blends of trace elements in mixes that contain seaweed, guanos, and manures.

Although some growers reuse their potting soil, I do not recommend it. If used for more than one crop, undesirable microorganisms, insects and fungi start growing; nutrients are depleted; water and air retention are poor, causing compaction and poor drainage. Some growers mix their old potting soil with new potting soil to stretch their mix. Cutting corners this way most often costs more in production than is saved in soil.

Potting soil or soilless mix that contains more than 30 percent lightweight pumice or perlite may float and stratify when saturated with water before planting. Mix water-saturated soil thoroughly with your hands until it is evenly mixed before planting or transplanting, if necessary.

Mushroom Compost

Mushroom compost is an inexpensive potting soil and soil amendment that is packed with organic goodies. Mushroom compost is sterilized chemically to provide a clean medium for mushroom growth. After serving its purpose as a mushroom growing medium, it is discarded. Laws usually require that it sit fallow for two years or more to allow all the harmful sterilants to leach out. After lying fallow for several years, mushroom compost is very fertile and packed with beneficial microorganisms. The high-power compost could also foster antifungal and antibacterial properties in foliage and below the

soil line, which helps guard against disease. Mushroom compost is loaded with beneficial bacteria that hasten nutrient uptake. The texture, water holding ability, and drainage in some mushroom compost should be amended with perlite to promote better drainage. Check your local nursery or extension service for a good source of mushroom compost. Some of the most abundant harvests I have seen were grown in mushroom compost.

Soilless Mix

Soilless mixes are very popular, inexpensive, lightweight, and sterile growing mediums. Commercial greenhouse growers have been using them for decades. The mixes contain some or all of the following: pumice, vermiculite, perlite, sand, peat moss, and coconut coir. Premixed commercial soilless mixes are favorites of countless growers. These mixes retain moisture and air while allowing strong root penetration and even growth. The fertilizer concentration, moisture level, and pH are very easy to control with precision in soilless mix.

Soilless mixes are the preferred substrate for many bedding plant and vegetable seedling commercial growers. Soilless mixes have good texture, hold water, and drain well. Unless fortified with nutrient, soilless mixes contain no nutrients and are pH balanced near 6.0 to 7.0. Coarse soilless mixes drain well and are easy to push plants into growing faster with heavy fertilization. The fast-draining mixes can be leached efficiently so nutrients have little chance of building up to toxic levels. Look for ready-mixed bags of fortified soilless mixes such as Jiffy Mix®, Ortho Mix®, Sunshine Mix®, Terra-Lite®, and ProMix®, etc. To improve drainage, mix 10-30 percent coarse perlite before planting. Fortified elements supply nutrients up to a month, but follow directions on the package.

Soilless components can be purchased separately and mixed to the desired consistency. Ingredients always blend together best when mixed dry and wetted afterwards using a wetting agent to make water more adhesive. Mix small amounts right in the bag. Larger batches should be mixed in a wheelbarrow, concrete slab, or in a cement mixer. Blending your own soil or soilless mix is a dusty, messy job that takes little space. To cut down on dust, lightly mist the pile with water several times when mixing. Always wear a respirator to avoid inhaling dust.

The texture of soilless mixes–for rapid-growing cannabis–should be coarse, light, and spongy. Such texture allows drainage with sufficient moisture and air retention, as well as providing good root penetration qualities. Fine soilless mix holds more moisture and works best in smaller containers. Soilless mixes that contain more perlite and sand drain faster, making them easier to fertilize heavily without excessive fertilizer-salt buildup. Vermiculite and peat hold water longer and are best used in small pots that require more water retention.

The pH is generally near neutral, 7.0. If using more than 15 percent peat, which is acidic, add appropriate dolomite or hydrated lime to correct and stabilize the pH. Check the pH regularly every week. Soilless mixes are composed mainly of mineral particles that are not affected by organic decomposition, which could change the pH. The pH is affected by acidic fertilizers or by water with a high or low pH. Check the pH of the runoff water to ensure the pH in the medium is not too acidic.

Propagation Cubes & Mixes

Rockwool root cubes, peat pellets, and Oasis® blocks are pre-formed containers that make rooting cuttings, starting seedlings, and transplanting them easy. Root cubes and peat pots also help encourage strong root systems. Peat pots are small, compressed peat moss containers with an outer wall of expandable plastic netting. The flat pellets pop up into a seedling pot when watered.

Place a seed or cutting in a moist peat pot or root cube. If the little container does not have a planting hole, make one with a chopstick, large nail, or something similar. Set the seed or clone stem in the hole. Crimp the top over the seed

Lightweight horticultural perlite is available in large bags.

This soilless mix contains 50 percent perlite and 50 percent coco. Drainage is rapid and water retention is good. This mix must be watered daily.

This soilless mix contains 10 percent perlite and 90 percent peat moss. It holds water very well and the perlite assists drainage.

Make a seedbed from fine-screened soil.

Seedling trays are easy to use.

Small rockwool plugs are fast to plant and easy to maintain.

Rockwool plugs grow strong root systems in about two weeks.

Coarse perlite is lightweight.

or around the stem so it makes constant contact with the medium. In one to three weeks, roots grow and show through the side of the cube. Cut the nylon mesh from peat pots before it gets entangled with roots. To transplant, set the peat pot or root cube in a pre-drilled hole in a rockwool block or into larger pot. Clones and seedlings suffer little or no transplant shock when transplanted properly.

Check moisture levels in peat pots and root cubes daily. Keep them evenly moist but not drenched. Root cubes and peat pots do not contain any nutrients. Seedlings do not require nutrients for the first week or two. Feed seedlings after the first week and clones as soon as they are rooted.

Coarse sharp sand, fine vermiculite, and perlite work well to root cuttings. Sand and perlite are fast draining, which helps prevent damping-off. Vermiculite holds water longer and makes cloning easier. A good mix is one third of each: sand, fine perlite, and fine vermiculite. Premixed seed starter mixes sold under such brand names as Sunshine Mix and Terra-Lite are the easiest and most economical mediums in which to root clones and start seedlings. Soilless mix also allows for complete control of critical nutrient and root stimulating hormone additives, which are essential to asexual propagation.

Soil Amendments

Soil amendments increase the soil's air-, water-, and nutrient-retaining abilities. Soil amendments fall into two categories: mineral and organic.

Mineral amendments are near neutral on the pH scale and contain few, if any, available nutrients. Mineral amendments decompose through weathering and erosion. Add mineral amendments to augment air and increase drainage. They have the advantage of creating no bacterial activity to alter nutrient content and pH of the growing medium. Dry mineral amendments are also very lightweight and much easier to move in and out of awkward spaces.

Perlite is sand or volcanic glass expanded by heat. It holds water and nutrients on its many irregular surfaces, and it works especially well for aerating the soil. This is a good medium to increase drainage during vegetative and flowering growth, and it does not promote fertilizer-salt build-up. Versatile perlite is available in three main grades: fine, medium and coarse. Most growers prefer the coarse grade as a soil amendment. Perlite should make up one third or less of any mix to keep it from floating and stratifying the mix.

Pumice is lighweight.

Pumice, volcanic rock, is very light and holds water, nutrients, and air, in its many catacomb-like holes. It is a good amendment for aerating the soil and retaining moisture evenly. But like perlite, pumice floats and should constitute less than a third of any mix to avoid problems.

Hydroclay is used more and more as a soil amendment in containers. The large expanded clay pellets expedite drainage and hold air within the growing medium. See Chapter Twelve "Hydroponic Gardening" for more information.

Vermiculite is lightweight and absorbent.

Vermiculite is mica processed and expanded by heat. It holds water, nutrients, and air within its fiber and gives body to fast-draining soils. Fine vermiculite holds too much water for cuttings, but does well when mixed with a fast-draining medium. This amendment holds more water than perlite or pumice. Used in hydroponic wick systems, vermiculite holds and wicks much moisture. Vermiculite comes in three grades: fine, medium, and coarse. Use fine vermiculite as an ingredient in cloning mixes. If fine is not available, crush coarse or medium vermiculite between your hands, rubbing palms back and forth. Coarse is the best choice as a soil amendment.

Organic soil amendments contain carbon and break down through bacterial activity, slowly yielding humus as an end product. Humus is a soft, spongy material that binds minute soil particles together, improving the soil texture. New, actively composting organic soil amendments require nitrogen to carry on bacterial decomposition. If they do not contain at least

Some growers use organic potting soil as a soil amendment.

This bag of soil amendments contains well-rotted mulch and chicken manure.

1.5 percent nitrogen, the organic amendment will get it from the soil, robbing roots of valuable nitrogen. When using organic amendments, make sure they are thoroughly composted (at least one year) and releasing nitrogen rather than stealing it from the soil. A dark, rich color is a good sign of fertility.

Peat moss is available in bags or compressed bales.

Coco bricks are ideal for guerilla growers. They expand to nine times their original size when wet.

Coconut peat is becoming very popular among growers.

Rent a commercial cement mixer to mix large quantities of soil.

Rich, thoroughly composted organic matter amends texture and supplies nutrients. Leaf mold, garden compost (at least one year old), and many types of thoroughly composted manure usually contain enough nitrogen for their decomposition needs and release nitrogen rather than using it. Purchase quality organic amendments at a reputable nursery. Look carefully at the descriptive text on the bag to see if it is sterilized and is guaranteed to contain no harmful insects: larvae, eggs, and fungi or bad microorganisms. Contaminated soil causes many problems that are easily averted by using a clean mix.

Garden compost and leaf mold are usually rich in organic nutrients and beneficial organisms that speed nutrient uptake, but they can be full of harmful pests and diseases, too. For example, compost piles are a favorite breeding ground for cutworms and beetle larvae. Just one cutworm in a container means certain death for the defenseless marijuana plant. Garden compost is best used in outdoor gardens and not indoors. See below for more information on garden compost.

Manure: Barnyard manure, a great fertilizer for outdoor gardens, often contains toxic levels of salt and copious quantities of weed seeds and fungus spores that disrupt an indoor garden. If using manure, purchase it in bags that guarantee its contents. There are many kinds of manure: cow, horse, rabbit, and chicken, etc. See Chapter Eleven for a complete rundown on manures, all of which help retain water and improve soil texture when used as soil amendments. When mixing manures as amendments, do not add more than 10-15 percent, to avoid salt buildup and overfertilization. The nutrient content of manures varies, depending upon the animal's diet and the decomposition factors.

Peat is the term used to describe partially decomposed vegetation. The decay has been slowed by the wet and cold conditions of the northern United States and Canada where it is found in vast bogs. The most common types of peat are formed from sphagnum and hypnum mosses. These peats are harvested and used to amend soil and can be used as a growing medium. Peat moss is very dry, and difficult to wet the first time, unless you bought it wet. Wet peat is heavy and awkward to transport. When adding peat moss as a soil amendment, cut your workload by dry-mixing all of the components before wetting. Use a wetting agent. Another trick to mixing peat moss is to kick the sack a few times to break up the bale before opening.

Peat tends to break down and should be used for only one crop.

Sphagnum peat moss is light brown and the most common peat found at commercial nurseries. This bulky peat gives soil body and retains water well, absorbing 15 to 30 times its own weight. It contains essentially no nutrients of its own, and the pH ranges from 3-5. After decomposing for several months, the pH could continue to drop and become very acidic. Counter this propensity for acidity and stabilize the pH by adding fine dolomite lime to the mix.

Hypnum peat moss is more decomposed and darker in color with pH from 5.0 to 7.0. This peat moss is less common and contains some nutrients. Hypnum peat is a good soil amendment, even though it cannot hold as much water as sphagnum moss.

Coconut fiber is also called palm peat, coco peat, cocos, kokos, and coir. Coir is coconut pith, the fibery part just under the heavy husk. Pith is soaked in water up to nine months to remove salts, natural resins, and gums in a process called retting. Next, they beat the straw-brown coir to extract the husk.

Coir is biodegradable and a good medium for propagation through flowering and fruit growth. Coir holds lots of water while maintaining structure. It is durable, rot-resistant, and a good insulator, too. It is inexpensive, easy to control, and holds lots of air.

Washed, pressed blocks or bricks of coir are virtually inert. Bricks weigh about 1.3-2.2 pounds (0.6-1 kg.) The pH is between 5.5 and 6.8. Some of the best coconut coir is from the interior of the Philippine Islands, where the environment is not packed with coastal salts. Quality coconut coir is guaranteed to have sodium content of less than 50 ppm.

Growers use coir by itself or mixed 50/50 with perlite or expanded clay to add extra drainage to the mix. Some growers sprinkle coconut coir on top of rockwool blocks to keep the top from drying out.

Flake dry bricks of coconut coir apart by hand or soak the bricks in a bucket of water for 15 minutes to expand and wet. One brick will expand to about 9 times its original size. Growing in coconut coir is similar to growing in any other soilless medium. Coconut coir may stay a little too wet and require more ventilation and air circulation.

Hit the site www.canna.com for more information on coconut fiber and growing marijuana.

Soil Mixes

Outdoor soil mixes that incorporate garden soil, compost, manure, coco peat, and rock powders grow some of the best plants in the world. Outdoor soil mixes can be mixed a few months early and left in the hole to blend and mature. Outdoor organic soil mixes are alive, and controlling the soil life is a matter of paying attention to a few details.

Indoors, outdoor soil mixes often create more trouble than they are worth. Too often misguided novices go out to the backyard and dig up some good-looking dirt that drains poorly and retains water and air unevenly. The problems are compounded when they mix the dirt with garden compost packed with harmful microorganisms and pests. This lame soil mix grows bad dope. By saving a few bucks on soil, such growers create unforeseen problems and pay for their savings many times over with low-harvest yields. Avert problems with soil mixes by purchasing all of the components. Use garden soil or compost only if they are top quality and devoid of harmful pests and diseases. Use only the richest, darkest garden soil with a good texture. Amend the soil by up to 80 percent to improve water

Solarize used soil to kill pests and diseases.

Compost piles must be at least 3 feet (90 cm) square in order to retain more heat than they give off.

Soil mixes with compost:

0.5 compost
0.5 soilless mix

0.3 compost
0.3 soilless mix
0.3 coco coir

0.5 compost
0.5 coco coir

0.3 compost
0.3 soilless mix
0.16 worm castings
0.16 perlite

retention and drainage. Even a soil that drains well in the outdoor garden needs amending to drain properly indoors. Check the pH of the garden soil before digging to ensure it is between 6.0 and 7.0. Add fine dolomite to stabilize and buffer pH. Check pH several times after mixing to ensure it is stable.

Solarize garden soil by putting it out in the sun in a plastic bag for a few weeks. Turn the bag occasionally to heat it up on all sides. Make sure the bag receives full sun and heats up to at least 140°F (60°C). This will kill the bad stuff and let the beneficial bacteria live.

You can also sterilize soil by laying it out on a Pyrex plate and baking it at 160°F for 10 minutes, or microwave it for two minutes at the highest setting. It is much easier and more profitable in the end to purchase good potting soil at a nursery.

Compost

Compost is outstanding. It solves most problems outdoors. Compost is an excellent soil amendment. It holds nutrients and moisture within its fiber. However, using backyard compost indoors is tricky.

Some growers have no trouble with organic composts, but others have bad luck and even lose their entire crop when growing in backyard compost. Good compost recipes are available from monthly publications such as *Sunset, Organic Gardening, National Gardening,* etc., or from the companies specializing in organic composts. Outdoor growers love compost. It is inexpensive, abundant, and works wonders to increase water retention and drainage. It also increases nutrient uptake because of biological activity. Indoors, compost is not very practical to use in containers. It could also have unwanted pests. If using compost indoors, make sure it is well-rotted and screened.

A good compost pile includes manure–the older the better. Manure from horse stalls or cattle feedlots is mixed with straw or sawdust bedding. Sawdust uses available nitrogen and is also acidic and not recommended. Look for the oldest, and most-rotted manure. Well-rotted manure is less prone to have viable weed seeds and pests. Fresh nitrogen-packed grass clippings are one of my favorites to use in a compost pile. Put your hand down deep into a pile of grass clippings. The temperature one or two feet down in such a pile ranges from 120° to 180°F (49° to 82°C). Heat generated by chemical activity kills pests, breaks down the foliage, and liberates the nutrients.

Build compost piles high, and keep turning them. Good compost pile recipes include the addition of organic trace elements, enzymes, and the primary nutrients. The organic matter used should be ground up and in the form of shredded leaves and grass. Do not use large woody branches that could take years to decompose.

Before using compost indoors, pour it through 0.25-inch mesh hardware cloth (screen) to break up the humus before mixing with soil. Place a heavy-duty framed screen over a large garbage can or a wheelbarrow to catch the sifted compost. Return earthworms found on the screen to the medium and kill cutworms. Make sure all composts are well rotted and have cooled before mixing with indoor soil. For more information about composting, see *Let It Rot!, Third Edition*, by Stu Campbell, Storey Press, Prowal, VT.

Some growers mix up to 30 percent perlite into organic potting soil that contains lots of worm castings. Heavy worm castings compact soil and leave little space for air to surround roots. Adding perlite or similar amendments aerates the soil and improves drainage.

Used Soil

- Let soil dry.
- Screen to separate roots, stems, and foliage from the soil.
- Pack in plastic bags.
- Remove soil from property.
- Dispose of discreetly.

Growing Medium Disposal

Disposing of used growing medium can be as big a problem as finding the proper soil. Most soilless mixes and soils contain perlite, which leaves white telltale traces when dumped anywhere. Grow soil is also packed with incriminating cannabis roots. The plug was pulled on more than one grow-show because soil residuals were found in the back yard.

Dry soil is easier to work and transport. Press and rub dry soil through a 0.25 to 0.5-inch screen to remove roots, stems, and foliage. Screening also transforms the cast-container shape of the soil to an innocuous form. Once the roots are removed, dry, used soil can be bagged up or compacted. Place the dry soil in a trash compactor to make it smaller and more manageable. Do not throw the spent growing medium into your trash can. Remember, it is not a crime for law enforcement in America to dig through your garbage. In fact, picking through a suspected grower's garbage is a tactic often used by American authorities to secure a search warrant. Remove the depleted soil from the property. Take it to the dump or dispose of it in a very discreet locale. Never throw away the transporting bags with the used soil. Reuse the bags.

Used indoor growing mediums make excellent outdoor amendments when mixed with compost and garden soil. Do not reuse the depleted soil in outdoor pots. Many of the same problems that occur indoors will happen in outdoor pots.

Grow Medium Problems

These maladies are caused by growing medium problems but manifest as nutrient problems. The solution is found within the growing medium.

When water is abundant in the growing medium, roots easily absorb it. Roots use more energy to absorb more water as it becomes scarce. Finally, the point comes when the substrate retains more moisture than it surrenders, and the roots receive no water. A good growing medium readily yields its bank of stored water and nutrients. A poor medium does not pass enough nutrients to a plant's roots. The more easily cannabis absorbs nutrients, the higher the yield.

The cation-exchange-capacity (CEC) of a growing medium is its capacity to hold cations that are available for uptake by the roots. The CEC is the number of cation charges held in 3.5 ounces (100 gm) or 100 cc of soil and is measured in milli-Equivalents (mEq) or Centi-Moles/kg on a scale from 0-100. CEC of 0 means the substrate holds no available cations for roots. CEC of 100 means the medium always holds cations available for root uptake. Growing mediums that carry a negative electrical charge are the best.

Containers

Container preference is often a matter of convenience, cost, and availability. But the size, shape, and color of a container can affect the size and the health of a plant as well as the versatility of the garden. Containers come in all shapes and sizes and can be constructed of almost anything–clay, metal, plastic, wood, and wood fiber are the most common. Cannabis will grow in any clean container that has not been used for petroleum products or deadly chemicals. Clay fiber and wood containers breathe better than plastic or metal pots. Heavy clay pots are brittle and absorb moisture from the soil inside, causing the soil to dry out quickly. Metal pots are also impractical for grow rooms because they oxidize (rust) and can bleed

Visible Signs of Grow Medium Stress

- Dry, crispy, brittle leaves
- Patchy or inconsistent leaf color
- Yellow leaf edges that worsen
- Crispy, burnt leaf edges
- Chlorosis–yellowing between veins
- while veins remain green
- Irregular blotches on leaves
- Purple stems and leaf stems
- Leaf edges curl up or down
- Leaf tip curls down
- Super-soft pliable leaves
- Branch tips stop growing
- Leggy growth

CEC of popular growing mediums measured in Milli-Eq/100 grams

Compost	90
Sunshine Mix	90
Peat moss	80
Garden soil	70
Expanded clay	20
Vermiculite	20
Perlite	0
Rockwool	0

This chart shows different growing mediums' ability to hold positive charges that are ready for root uptake. Note the zero CEC of perlite and rockwool. Roots must be constantly bathed in nutrients. Other mediums do not provide a constant flow of nutrients and the CEC regulates the ability to hold a positive charge to make nutrients available for root uptake.

Ceramic containers are durable but heavy.

off harmful elements and compounds. Wood, although somewhat expensive, makes some of the best containers, especially large raised beds and planters on wheels. Plastic containers are inexpensive, durable, and offer the best value to indoor growers.

Rigid plastic pots are the most commonly used containers in grow rooms. Growing in inexpensive, readily available containers is brilliant because they allow each plant to be cared for individually. You can control each plant's specific water and nutrient regimen. Individual potted plants can also be moved. Turn pots every few days, so plants receive even lighting and foliage will grow evenly. Huddle small, containerized plants tightly together under the brightest area below the HID lamp, and move them further apart as they grow. Set small plants up on blocks to move them closer to the HID. Individual plants are easily quarantined or dipped in a medicinal solution. Weak, sick, and problem plants are easy to cull from the garden.

Grow bags are economical, lightweight, and reusable.

Grow bags are one of my favorite containers. Inexpensive, long-lasting grow bags take up little space and are lightweight. A box of 100 3-gallon (13 L) bags weighs less than 5 pounds (2.3 kg) and measures less than a foot square. One hundred 3-gallon (13 L) grow bags can be stored in two 3-gallon (13 L) bags. Imagine storing 100 rigid pots in the same space!

White pots reflect light and heat. Black pots set inside the white pots keep roots in a dark environment.

The potting soil bag can also be used as a container.

Grow bags are very easy to wash and reuse. Empty out the soilless mix and submerge bags in a big container of soapy water overnight. Wash each one by hand the next day and fill with soil. I like them much better than rigid pots because they are so practical.

The potting soil sack can be used as a container. The moist soil inside the bag holds its shape well, and the bags expand and contract with the soil, lessening the chance of burned root tips that grow down the side of pots.

Fiber and paper-pulp pots are popular with growers who move their plants outdoors. The bottoms of the pots habitually rot out. Painting the inside of the fiber container with latex paint will keep the bottom from rotting for several crops.

Set large pots on blocks or casters to allow air circulation underneath. The soil stays warmer and maintenance is easier. Planters should be as big as possible but still allow easy access to plants. The roots have more room to grow and less container surface for roots to run into and grow down. With large pots, roots are able to intertwine and grow like crazy.

Grow beds can be installed right on the earthen floor of a garage or basement. If drainage is poor, a layer of gravel or a dry well can be made under the bed. Some growers use a jackhammer to remove the concrete floor in a basement to get better drainage. An easier option is to cut a hole in the basement floor and install a dry well. Knocking holes in basement floors could

Woven coco fiber pots from General Hydroponics breathe well, do not compact, can be used several times, and are biodegradable.

Containers on casters are easy to move and stay warmer when up off the floor.

Containers must be:

• Clean

• Have adequate drainage holes

• Big enough to accommodate plant

Planting directly in the floor of a basement or building gives roots plenty of space to expand.

cause water seepage, where water tables are high. When it rains, the water may collect underneath; the garden seldom needs watering, but plants are kept too wet.

A raised bed with a large soil mass can be built up organically after several crops. To hasten organic activity within the soil, add organic seaweed, manure, and additives. When mixing soil or adding amendments, use the best possible organic components and follow organic principles. There should be good drainage and the soil should be as deep as possible, 12-24 inches (30-60 cm).

At the Cannabis College in Amsterdam, Netherlands, they are growing in large soil beds set on a concrete floor. The basement beds are below sea level and filled with outstanding Dutch cannabis. They are able to treat the beds similar to outdoor soil beds, but when watered heavily, water runs out on the floor and it must be mopped up. They also have a problem with ventilation. The ambient climate is naturally humid and the extra water in the large basement increases humidity to above 90 percent, day and night. They employ a large extraction fan and a relatively small intake fan. Air is pulled

You can find this raised bed garden in the grow room at the Cannabis College in Amsterdam.

Install a dry well to evacuate excess runoff.

Flush containers with three times as much water volume of soil to leach out excess fertilizer salts. Flush containers every month to avoid many problems.

Flush containers with a mild nutrient solution every month.

through the long narrow basement room quickly and efficiently to evacuate moisture and lower the humidity. Even with this much soil, they have to flush individual beds at least once every four weeks to avoid nutrient buildup.

Much heat can be generated by decomposing organic matter, and it warms the room. Ventilation lowers heat and humidity, and helps keep the room free of pests and diseases. An organic garden sounds great, but it is a lot of work to replicate the great outdoors. Most organic growers opt for organic liquid fertilizers and a bagged commercial organic soil mix.

Another drawback to raised beds is that the crop will take a few days longer to mature than if it were grown in containers. But the longer wait is offset by a larger harvest.

Drainage

All containers need some form of drainage. Drainage holes allow excess water and nutrient solution to flow freely out the bottom of a container. Drainage holes should let water drain easily, but not be so big that growing medium washes out onto the floor. Containers should have at least two half-inch (1.2 cm) holes per square foot of bottom. Most pots have twice this amount. To slow drainage and keep soil from washing out of the large holes, add a one-inch (3 cm) layer of gravel in the bottom of the pot. Surface tension created by the varying sizes of soil and rock particles cause water to be retained at the bottom of the container. Line pots with newspaper if drainage is too fast or if soil washes out drain holes. This will slow drainage, so be wary!

Put trays under containers to catch excess water. Leaving water-filled saucers under pots often causes root rot. To avoid water-logging soil and roots, set containers up an inch or two on blocks when using trays.

Nursery trays used for rooting cuttings and growing seedlings must have good drainage throughout the entire bottom. Once clones and seedlings are in place in the tray, the tray should always drain freely with no standing water in the bottom.

Container Shape, Size, and Maintenance

Popular pot shapes include rectangular and cylindrical. Growers prefer taller pots rather than wide, squat containers because the cannabis root system penetrates deeply. Of all the gardens I have visited, squat pots were few and far between. Growers I queried said squat pots may hold more soil for their stature, but they do not produce as extensive a root system.

The volume of a container can easily dictate the size of a plant. Cannabis is an annual; it grows very fast and requires a lot of root space for sustained, vigorous development. Containers should be big enough to allow for a strong root system, but just big enough to contain the root system before harvest. If the container is too small, roots are confined, water and nutrient uptake is limited, and growth slows to a crawl. But if the container is too big, it requires too much expensive growing medium and becomes heavy and awkward to move.

Marijuana roots develop and elongate quickly, growing down and out, away from the main taproot. For example, about midsummer, nurseries have unsold tomato plants that are still in small 4-inch (10 cm) pots and one-gallon (4 L) containers. The stunted plants have blooming flowers and ripe fruit. But few branches extend much beyond the sides of the container; the plants are tall and leggy with curled down leaves and an overall stunted, sickly appearance. These plants are pot- or root-bound. Once a plant deteriorates to this level, it is often easier and more efficient to toss it out and replace it with a healthy one.

Roots soon hit the sides of containers where they grow down and mat up around the bottom. The unnatural environment inside the container often causes a thick layer of roots to grow alongside the container walls and bottom. This portion of the root zone is the most vulnerable to moisture and heat stress and is the most exposed.

When soil dries in a pot, it becomes smaller, contracting and separating from the inside of the container wall. This condition is worst in smooth plastic pots. When this crack develops, frail root hairs located in the gap quickly die when they are exposed to air whistling down this crevice. Water also runs straight down this crack and onto the floor. You may think the pot was watered, but the root ball remains dry. Avoid such killer cracks by cultivating the soil

Large pots hold a lot of soil and require irrigation less frequently.

Large square pots are perfect for this hydroponic garden.

This room full of 3-gallon (11 L) pots is packed in so tight that you can walk on the pots.

Square containers are easy to bunch together when plants are small.

Deep containers are ideal for seedlings that will be planted outdoors.

Soil shrinks when dry; it causes a gap to form alongside the container wall.

Selecting Container Size

Plant age	Container size
0 – 3 weeks	root cube
2 – 6 weeks	4-inch pot
6 – 8 weeks	2-gallon pot
2 – 3 months	3-gallon pot
3 – 8 months	5-gallon pot
6 – 18 months	10-gallon pot

Allow 1 to 1.5 gallons (4 to 7 L) of soil or soilless mix for each month the plant will spend in the container. A 2- to 3-gallon (7.5-11 L) pot supports a plant for up to three months. 3- to 6-gallon containers are good for three to four months of rapid plant growth.

Roots grow quickly and soon encircle the inside of the container.

Cultivate the top layer of soil with a fork to break up the crusty surface.

surface and running your finger around the inside lip of the pots. Cultivate the soil in pots every few days and maintain evenly moist soil to help keep root hairs on the soil perimeter from drying out.

Do not place containers in direct heat. If soil temperature climbs beyond 75°F (24°C), it can damage roots. Pots that are in direct heat should be shaded with a piece of plastic or cardboard.

A 1 to 2-inch (3-5 cm) layer of hydro clay mulch on soil surface keeps soil surface moist. Roots are able to grow along the surface, and the soil does not need to be cultivated. The

Feeder roots grow near the soil surface, just under the expanded clay mulch.

Lightly cultivate the soil surface, so water penetrates evenly. Be careful not to disturb roots.

mulch also decreases evaporation and helps keep irrigation water from damaging roots or splashing.

Green Roots

White containers reflect light and keep soil cooler. Always use thick, white containers so light does not penetrate and slow root growth. If roots around the outside of the root ball start turning green, you know they are receiving

Roots turn green and grow poorly when they receive direct light.

direct light. Remedy the problem by painting the inside of the container with a non-toxic latex paint.

These outdoor plants are thriving in Canada.

Introduction

Water provides a medium to transport nutrients necessary for plant life and make them available for absorption by the roots. Water quality is essential for this process to work at maximum potential. The laws of physics govern plant water uptake. Applying these laws, a grower can provide precise, properly balanced components to grow outstanding marijuana indoors.

Microscopic root hairs absorb water and nutrients in the oxygen present in the growing medium and carry them up the stem to the leaves. This flow of the water from the soil through the plant is called the *transpiration stream*. A fraction of the water is processed and used in photosynthesis. Excess water evaporates into the air, carrying waste products along with it via the stomata in the leaves. This process is called *transpiration*. Some of the water also returns manufactured sugars and starches to the roots.

The roots support the plants, absorb nutrients, and provide the initial pathway into the vascular system. A close-up look at a root reveals the xylem and phloem core, vascular tissue that is enveloped by a cortex tissue or the layer between the internal vascular and the external epidermal tissue. The microscopic root hairs are located on the epidermal tissue cells. These tiny root hair follicles are extremely delicate and must remain moist. Root hairs must be protected from abrasions, drying out, extreme temperature fluctuations, and harsh chemical concentrations. Plant health and well-being is contingent upon strong, healthy roots.

The nutrient absorption begins at the root hairs, and the flow continues throughout the plant via the vascular system. Absorption is sustained by diffusion. In the process of diffusion, water and nutrient ions are uniformly distributed throughout the plant. The intercellular spaces–apoplasts and connecting protoplasm, symplast–are the pathways that allow the water and nutrient ions and molecules to pass through the epidermis and the cortex to the xylem and phloem's vascular bundles. The xylem channels the solution through the plant while phloem tissues distribute the food manufactured by the plant. Once the nutrients are transferred to the plant cells, each cell accumulates the nutrients it requires to perform its specific function.

The solution that is transported through the vascular bundles or veins of a plant has many functions. This solution delivers nutrients and carries away the waste products. It provides pressure to help keep the plant structurally sound. The solution also cools the plant by evaporating the water via the leaves' stomata.

Water Quality

The concentration of calcium (Ca) and magnesium (Mg) indicate how "hard" the water is. Water containing 100 to 150 milligrams of calcium ($CaCO_3$) per liter is acceptable to grow marijuana. "Soft" water contains less than 50 milligrams of calcium per liter and should be supplemented with calcium and magnesium.

Look at a rooting clone. Check out the fine, fuzzy roots closely. You can see the minute hair-like feeder roots.

Roots on this clone have reached the wall of the container.

Water with high levels of chloride frequently contains high levels of sodium, but the opposite is not true. Water with high levels of sodium does not necessarily contain excessive levels of chloride (chlorine).

At low levels sodium appears to bolster yields, possibly acting as a partial substitute to compensate for potassium deficiencies. But when excessive, sodium is toxic and induces deficiencies of other nutrients, primarily potassium, calcium, and magnesium.

Chloride (chlorine) is essential to the use of oxygen during photosynthesis, and it is necessary for root and leaf cell division. Chloride is vital to increase the cellular osmotic pressure, modify the stomata regulation, and augment the plant's tissue and moisture content. A solu-

tion concentration of less than 140 parts per million (ppm) is usually safe for marijuana, but some varieties may show sensitivity when foliage turns pale green and wilts. Excessive chlorine causes the leaf tips and margins to burn and causes the leaves to turn a bronze color.

Simple water filters do not clean dissolved solids from the water. Such filters remove only debris emulsified (suspended) in water; releasing dissolved solids from their chemical bond is more complex. A reverse-osmosis machine uses small polymer, semipermeable membranes that allow pure water to pass through and filter out the dissolved solids from the water. Reverse-osmosis machines are the easiest and most efficient means to clean raw water.

Check the pH of the irrigation water and adjust when

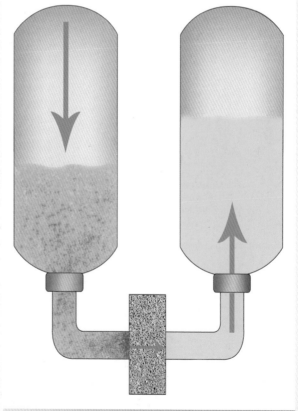

The drawing shows that pure water with no salts or dissolved solids migrates to the solution with more dissolved solids.

Osmosis

The roots draw the nutrient solution up the plant by the process of osmosis. Osmosis is the tendency of the fluids to pass through a semi-permeable membrane and mix with each other until the fluids are equally concentrated on both sides of the membrane. Semipermeable membranes located in the root hairs allow specific

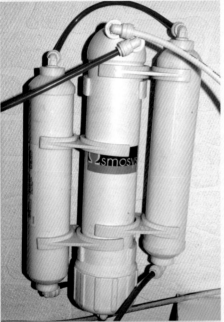

This reverse osmosis machine transforms water with a high ppm or EC into water with less than 10 ppm.

nutrients that are dissolved in the water to enter the plant while the other nutrients and impurities are excluded. Since salts and sugars are concentrated in the roots, the electrical conductivity (EC) inside the roots is (almost) always higher than that outside the roots. Transporting the nutrients by osmosis works, because it depends on relative concentrations of each individual nutrient on each side of the membrane; it does not depend on the total dissolved solids (TDS) or EC of the solution. For nutrients to be drawn in by the roots via osmosis, the strength of the individual elements must be greater than that of the roots.

But, the transport of water (instead of nutrients) across the semipermeable membrane depends on EC. For example, if the EC is greater outside the roots than inside, the plant dehydrates as the water is drawn out of the roots. In other words, salty water with a high EC can dehydrate the plants.

Reverse-osmosis machines are used to separate the dissolved solids from the water. These machines move the solvent (water) through the semipermeable membrane, but the process is reversed. It moves from lower concentrations to higher. The process is accomplished by applying pressure to the "tainted" water to force only "pure" water through the membrane. The water is not totally "pure" with an EC of "0," but most of the dissolved solids are removed. The efficiency of reverse osmosis depends on the type of membrane, the pressure differential on both sides of the membrane, and the chemical composition of the dissolved solids in the tainted water.

Unfortunately, common tap water often contains high levels of sodium (Na), calcium (Ca), alkaline salts, sulfur (S), and chlorine (Cl). The pH could also be out of the acceptable 6.5 to 7 range. Water containing sulfur is easily smelled and tasted. Saline water is a little more difficult to detect. Water in coastal areas is generally full of salt that washes inland from the ocean. Dry regions that have less than 20-inches-annual rainfall also suffer from alkaline soil and water that is often packed with alkaline salts.

Table salt, sodium chloride (NaCl), is added to many household water systems. A small amount of chlorine, below 140 ppm, does not affect marijuana growth, but higher levels cause foliage chlorosis and stunt growth. Do not use salt-soft-

STORE IN A COOL DRY PLACE AWAY FROM DIRECT SUNLIGHT

TYPICAL ANALYSIS

	mg/l		mg/l
CALCIUM	55	SULPHATE	13
MAGNESIUM	19	NITRATE	<0.1
POTASSIUM	1	IRON	0
SODIUM	24	ALUMINIUM	0
BICARBONATE	248	DRY RESIDUE	
CHLORIDE	37	AT 180°C	280

pH AT SOURCE............7.4

The dissolved solids in this bottled water are measured in milligrams per liter (m/l).

ened water. Salty, brackish, salt-softened water is detrimental to cannabis. Chlorine also tends to acidify soil after repeated applications. The best way to get chlorine out of the water is to let it sit one or two days in an open container. The chlorine will evaporate (volatilize) as a gas when it comes in contact with the air. If chlorine noticeably alters soil pH, adjust it with a commercial "pH UP" product or hydrated lime.

The metric system facilitates the measurement of "dry residue per liter." Measure the dry residue per liter by pouring a liter of water on a tray and allowing it to evaporate. The residue of dissolved solids that remains after all of the water evaporates is the "dry residue per liter." The residue is measured in grams. Try this at home to find out the extent of impurities. Fertilizers have a difficult time penetrating root tissue when they must compete with resident dissolved solids.

Flushing plants with plain water will wash out most built-up toxic salts. Flush again with a diluted nutrient solution.

Water that is loaded with high levels of dissolved solids (salts in solution) is possible to manage but requires different tactics. Highly saline water that contains sodium will block the uptake of potassium, calcium, and magnesium. Salt-laden water will always cause problems. If water contains 300 ppm or less dissolved solids, allow at least 25 percent of the irrigation water to drain out of the bottom of containers with each watering. *If raw water contains more than 300 ppm of dissolved solids, use a reverse-osmosis device to purify the water.* Add nutrients to pure water as a way to avoid many nutrient problems.

Dissolved salts, caused by saline water and fertilizer, quickly build up to toxic levels in container gardens. Excessive salts inhibit seed germination, burn the root hairs and tips or edges of leaves, and stunt the plant. Flush excess salt buildup from growing mediums by applying two gallons of water per gallon of medium and repeat leaching using a mild pH-corrected fertilizer solution. Leach growing medium every two to four weeks, if using soft water or saline water. Hard water and well water in dry climates are often alkaline, and usually contain notable amounts of calcium and magnesium. Cannabis uses large quantities of both nutrients, but too much calcium and magnesium can build up in soil. In general, water that tastes good to people also tastes good to cannabis.

Plants in small containers require more frequent watering.

Irrigation

Large plants use more water than small plants, but there are many more variables than size that dictate a plant's water consumption. The age of the plant, container size, soil texture, temperature, humidity, and ventilation all contribute to water needs. Change any one of these variables, and the water consumption will change. Good ventilation is essential to promote a free flow of fluids, transpiration, and rapid growth. The healthier a plant, the faster it grows and the more water it needs.

When they are small, plants in medium-sized containers can be watered every other day.

A water meter takes the guesswork out of watering. Remember to keep probes clean for an accurate reading.

Tip the containers to check if they are heavily laden with water. Irrigate the light containers.

Add a few drops of biodegradable liquid dish soap concentrate to the irrigation water. Detergent makes the water penetrate the soil more thoroughly.

Small plants with a small root system in small containers must be watered often. Water frequently–as soon as the soil surface dries out. If exposed to wind, the small plants will dry out very quickly.

Irrigate soil and soilless mixes when they are dry one-half inch below the surface. As long as the drainage is good, it is difficult to overwater fast-growing cannabis. Four-week-old clones flowering in 2- to 3-gallon (7.5 to 11 L) containers need to be irrigated once or twice daily. In fact, most growers prefer smaller containers because they are easier to control.

Irrigate larger plants in the vegetative and flowering stages when soil is dry one-half inch below the surface. Flowering marijuana uses high levels of water to carry on rapid floral formation. Withholding the water stunts the flower formation.

Plants that are exposed to wind dry out much faster. Outdoor, terrace, and patio plants will use up to three or four times more water on a hot, windy day. Keeping up with the watering is difficult and time-consuming. Use an automated watering system or break the wind to lessen its impact on the plants. Mulch will also lessen the evaporation from the soil.

Use plenty of water, and allow up to 10 percent runoff during each watering. The runoff will prevent the fertilizer from building up in the soil. Water early in the day, so excess water will evaporate from the soil surface and the leaves. Leaving the foliage and the soil wet overnight invites a fungal attack.

Moisture meters take most of the guesswork out of irrigating. They can be purchased for less than $30 and are well worth the money. The meter measures exactly how much water the soil contains at any level or point. Often the soil will not hold the water evenly, and it develops dry pockets. Checking the moisture with a finger provides an educated guess but disturbs the root system. A moisture meter will give an exact moisture reading without disturbing the roots.

Cultivate the soil surface to allow the water to penetrate evenly and guard against dry soil pockets. It also keeps the water from running down the crack between the inside of the pot and the soil and out the drain holes. Gently break up and cultivate the top half inch of the soil with your fingers or a salad fork. Be careful not to disturb the tiny surface roots.

After you develop some skill at knowing when the plants need water, you can check to see how heavy they are simply by tipping them. Once you get the hang of it, all you will have to do is tip each container.

It is easier to keep pots in straight lines when growing and watering, and it is much easier to keep track of watered pots when they are in a straight line.

Overwatering is a common problem, especially with small plants. Too much water drowns the roots by cutting off their supply of oxygen. If you have symptoms of overwatering, buy a moisture meter! It will let both you and your garden breathe easier. Sometimes, parts of the soil are overwatered and other soil pockets remain bone-dry. Cultivating the soil surface, allowing even water penetration, and using a moisture meter will overcome this problem. One of the main causes of overwatering is poor air ventilation! The plants need to transpire water into the air. If there is nowhere for this wet, humid air to go, gallons of water are locked in the grow room air. Well-ventilated air carries this moist air away, replacing it with fresh, dry air. If using trays to catch runoff water, use a turkey baster, large syringe, or sponge to draw the excess water from the tray. Signs of overwatering are: leaves curled down and yellowed, waterlogged and soggy soil, fungal growth, and slow growth. Symptoms of overwatering are often subtle, and inexperienced gardeners may not see any blatant symptoms for a long time.

Put a saucer under the plants to retain irrigation water, if they run out of water quickly.

Marijuana does not like soggy soil. Soil kept too wet drowns the roots, squeezing out the oxygen. This causes slow growth and possible fungal attack. Poor drainage is most often the cause of soggy soil. It is compounded by poor ventilation and high humidity.

Underwatering is less of a problem; however, it is fairly common if small (1-2 gallon) pots are used and the grower does not realize the water needs of rapid growing plants. Small containers dry out quickly and may require daily watering. If forgotten, water-starved plants become stunted. Once tender root hairs dry out, they die. Most growers panic when they see their prize-marijuana plants wilt in bone-dry soil. Dry soil, even in pockets, makes root hairs dry up and die. It seems to take forever for the roots to grow new root hairs and resume rapid growth.

Plants in small containers require more frequent watering.

Add a few drops (one drop per pint) of a biodegradable, concentrated liquid soap like Castille® or Ivory® to the water. It will act as a wetting agent by helping the water penetrate the soil more efficiently, and it will guard against dry soil pockets. Most soluble fertilizers contain a wetting agent. Apply about one-quarter to one-half as much water/fertilizer as the plant is expected to need, and then wait 10 to 15 minutes for it to totally soak in. Apply more water/fertilizer until the soil is evenly moist. If trays are underneath the pots, let excess water remain in the trays a few hours or even overnight before removing it with a large turkey baster.

Another way to thoroughly wet pots is to soak the containers in water. This is easy to do with small pots. Simply fill a 5-gallon (19 L) bucket with 3 gallons (11 L) of water. Submerge the smaller pot inside the larger pot, for a minute or longer, until the growing medium is completely saturated. Wetting plants thoroughly insures against dry soil pockets.

Having a readily accessible water source is very convenient, and it saves time and labor. A 4 × 4-foot garden containing 16 healthy plants in 3-gallon (11 L) pots needs 10 to 25 gallons

AIR   AIR

A water wand with a breaker head mixes air with irrigation water just before applying.

A water wand with an air breaker head oxygenates water and splits it into many streams.

Use a filter with drip systems!

Spaghetti tubing is anchored in the growing medium with a spike. A stream of nutrient solution flows out the tubing and percolates down through the growing medium.

(40-100 L) of water per week. Water weighs eight pounds a gallon (1 kg per L). That's a lot of containers to fill, lift, and spill. Carrying water in containers from the bathroom sink to the garden is okay when plants are small, but when they are large, it is a big, sloppy, regular job. Running a hose into the garden saves much labor and mess. A lightweight, half-inch hose is easy to handle and is less likely to damage the plants. If the water source has hot and cold water running out of the same tap, and it is equipped with threads, attach a hose and irrigate with tepid water. Use a dishwasher coupling if the faucet has no threads. The hose should have an on/off valve at the outlet, so water flow can be controlled while watering. A rigid water wand will save many broken branches while leaning over to water in tight quarters. Buy a water wand at the nursery or construct one from plastic PVC pipe. Do not leave water under pressure in the hose for more than a few minutes. Garden hoses are designed to transport water, not hold it under pressure, which may cause it to rupture.

To make a siphon or gravity-fed water system, place a barrel, at least four feet high, in the grow room. Make sure it has a lid to reduce the evaporation and the humidity. If the grow room is too small for the barrel, move it to another room. The attic is a good place because it promotes good pressure. Place a siphon hose in the top of the tank, or install a PVC on/off valve near the bottom of the barrel. It is easy to walk off and let the barrel overflow. An inexpensive device that measures the gallons of water added to the barrel is available at most hardware stores. You can also install a float valve in the barrel to meter out the water and retain a constant supply.

Drip systems deliver nutrient solution one drop at a time or in low volume, via a low-pressure plastic pipe with friction fittings. Water flows down the pipe and out the emitter one drop at a time or at a very slow rate. The emitters that are attached to the main hose are either spaghetti tubes or a nozzle dripper actually emitting from the main hose. Drip irrigation kits are available at garden stores and building centers. You can also construct your own drip system from component parts.

Drip systems offer several advantages. Once set up, drip systems lower watering maintenance. Fertilizer may also be injected into the irrigation system (fertigation); naturally, this facilitates fertilization but gives the same amount of water and nutrient to each plant. If setting up a drip system, make sure the growing medium drains freely to prevent soggy soil or salt buildup. If you are growing clones that are all the same age and size, a drip system would work very well. However, if you are growing many different varieties of plants, they may need different fertilizer regimens.

I interviewed several growers that loved the convenience and constant feeding-ability of their drip systems. All the growers irrigated (fertigated) with mild nutrient solution. They mixed the nutrient solution in a reservoir and pumped it through plastic feeder hoses. They also grew clones in smaller containers and kept root growth to a minimum by keeping the nutrients and the water in constant supply.

A drip system attached to a timer disperses nutrient solution at regular intervals. If using such a system, check the soil for water application daily. Check several pots daily to ensure they are watered evenly and that all the soil gets wet. Drip systems are very convenient and indispensable when you have to be away for a few days. However, do not leave a drip system on its own for more than four consecutive days, or you could return to a surprise!

Drip systems cost a few dollars to set up, but with the consistency they add to a garden, their expense is often paid off by a bountiful yield. Be careful! Such an automated system could promote negligence. Remember that gardens need daily care. If everything is automated, the garden still needs monitoring. All the vital signs: moisture, pH, ventilation, humidity, etc., still need to be checked and adjusted daily. Automation, when applied properly, adds consistency, uniformity, and usually a higher yield.

One indoor grower I met was out of town for five consecutive days every week. He watered and fertilized his plants. He put containerized plants in a tray with 2-inch-tall (6 cm) sides and watered the plants from above until the tray was full of water. He left for five days, and the plants needed no watering while he was gone. He used regular potting soil and added about 10 percent perlite. His plants needed maintenance when he returned, but the plants grew quite well.

Misdiagnosed Disorders

Many indoor garden problems, and to a lesser degree outdoor problems, are misdiagnosed as a lack of fertilizer. Often, disease and insects cause such problems. Other times, problems are caused by an imbalanced pH of the growing medium and water. A pH between 6.5 and 7 in soil and 5.8 to 6.5 in hydroponics will allow nutrients to be chemically available; above or below this range, several nutrients become less available. For example, a full point movement in pH represents a tenfold increase in either alkalinity or acidity. This means that a pH of 5.5 would be ten times more acidic than a pH of 6.5. In soil, a pH below 6.5 may cause a deficiency in calcium, which causes root tips to burn and leaves to get fungal infections and dead spots on foliage. A pH over 7 could slow down the plant's iron intake and result in chlorotic leaves causing veins to yellow.

Heat stress makes calyxes stretch up and grow beyond a compact bud.

Light burned this leaf. It appeared only on one leaf under the light.

Light burned this bud. Light burn could be mistaken for overfertilization or fungus. The dead foliage makes a perfect place for bud mold to start!

Water and heat stress caused our little "Lolita" to dwarf. The roots cooked in the hot sun which arrested development.

Incorrect pH contributes to most serious nutrient disorders in organic-soil gardens. Many complex biological processes occur between organic fertilizers and the soil during nutrient uptake. The pH is critical to the livelihood of these activities. When the pH fluctuates in a hydroponic garden, the nutrients are still available in the solution for uptake, and the pH is not as critical. Electrical conductivity is the most critical indicator of plant health and nutrient uptake in hydroponics.

Once a plant shows symptoms, it has already undergone severe nutritional stress. It will take time for the plant to resume vigorous growth. Correct identification of each symptom as soon as it occurs is essential to help plants retain vigor. Indoor, greenhouse, and some outdoor marijuana crops are harvested so fast that plants do not have time to recover from nutrient imbalances. One small imbalance could cost a week of growth. That could be more than 10 percent of the plant's life!

Here is another prime example of heat stress coupled with salt buildup and a lack of Zn, Fe, and Mn.

Big ridges between veins along with curled leaf fringes signify temperature stress coupled with salt build up.

Leaf fringe standing up – Leaf fringes that point up mean the leaf is trying to dissipate as much moisture as possible, but it is unable to. This could be caused by toxic salt buildup, lack of water, or heat stress.

Chapter ELEVEN

Do not confuse nutrient deficiencies or toxicities with insect and disease damage or poor cultural practices.

The temperature within the leaves can climb to an excess of 110°F (43°C). It happens easily because the leaves store the heat radiated by the lamp. At 110°F (43°C), the internal chemistry of a marijuana leaf is disrupted. The manufactured proteins are broken down and become unavailable to the plant. As the internal temperature of the leaves climbs, they are forced to use and evaporate more water. About 70 percent of the plant's energy is used in this process.

The basic elements of the environment must be checked and maintained at specific levels to avoid problems. Check each of the vital signs–air, light, soil, water, temperature, humidity, etc.– and fine-tune the environment, especially ventilation, before deciding that plants are nutrient deficient.

Nutrient deficiencies are less common when using fresh potting soil fortified with micronutrients. If the soil or water supply is acidic, add dolomite lime to buffer the soil pH and to keep it sweet. Avoid nutrient problems by using fresh planting mix, clean water, and a complete nutrient solution. Maintain the EC and pH at proper levels, and flush the system with mild nutrient solution every four weeks.

COMMON CULTURAL PROBLEMS

Here is a short list of some of the most common cultural problems. Some of them result in nutrient deficiencies.

1. Lack of ventilation: Leaves are stifled and unable to function, causing slow growth and poor consumption of water and nutrients.
2. Lack of light: Nutrients are used poorly, photosynthesis is slow, stems stretch, and growth is scrawny.
3. Humidity: High humidity causes the plants to use less water and more nutrients. Growth is slow because stomata are not able to open and increase the transpiration. Low humidity stresses the plants because they use too much water.
4. Temperature: Both low and high temperatures slow the growth of plants. Large fluctuations in temperature–more than 15 to 20°F (8 to 10°C)–causes slow growth and slows the plant's process.
5. Spray application damage: Sprays are phytotoxic, and they can burn the foliage if the spray is too concentrated or if sprayed during the heat of the day.
6. Ozone damage: See Chapter Thirteen "Air" for more information on ozone damage.
7. Overwatering: Soggy soil causes a menagerie of problems. It cuts the air from the roots, which retards the nutrient intake. The plant's defenses weaken. Roots rot when severe.
8. Underwatering: Dry soil causes nutrient transport to slow severely. It causes nutrient deficiencies and sick foliage, and the roots die.
9. Light burn: Burned foliage is susceptible to pest and disease attack.
10. Indoor air pollution: This causes very difficult-to-solve plant problems. Always be aware of chemicals leaching or vaporizing from the pressboards and other building materials. Such pollution causes plant growth to slow to a crawl.
11. Hot soil: Soil over 90°F (32°C) will harm the roots. Often, outdoor soil that is used in the containers warms up to well over 100°F (38°C).
12. Roots receiving light: Roots turn green if the light shines through the container or the hydroponic system. Roots require a dark environment. Their function slows substantially when they turn green.

Nutrients

Nutrients are elements that the plant needs to live. Carbon, hydrogen, and oxygen are absorbed from the air and the water. The rest of the elements, called *nutrients*, are absorbed from the growing medium and nutrient solu-

Chart of Mobile and Immobile Nutrients

Nitrogen (N)	mobile
Phosphorus (P)	mobile
Potassium (K)	mobile
Magnesium (Mg)	mobile
Zinc (Zn)	mobile
Calcium (Ca)	immobile
Boron (B)	immobile
Chlorine (Cl)	immobile
Cobalt (Co)	immobile
Copper (Cu)	immobile
Iron (Fe)	immobile
Manganese (Mn)	immobile
Molybdenum (Mo)	immobile
Selenium (Se)	immobile
Silicon (Si)	immobile
Sulfur (S)	immobile

I would like to thank the scientists at CANNA Research, Breda, Netherlands for information about nutrient deficiencies and toxicities in cannabis. The research team at Canna has been experimenting with cannabis in their fully-equipped scientific laboratory for 20 years. Mauk, head scientist, has made numerous discoveries, and proven them scientifically, about the nutritional needs of the cannabis plant. Hit their web site at

www.canna.com

tion. Supplemental nutrients supplied in the form of a fertilizer allow marijuana to reach its maximum potential. Nutrients are grouped into three categories: macronutrients or primary nutrients, secondary nutrients, and micronutrients or trace elements. Each nutrient in the above categories can be further classified as either *mobile* or *immobile*.

Mobile nutrients–nitrogen (N), phosphorus (P), potassium (K), magnesium (Mg), and zinc (Zn)–are able to translocate, move from one portion of the plant to another as needed. For example, nitrogen accumulated in older leaves translocates to younger leaves to solve a deficiency. The result, deficiency symptoms appear on the older, lower leaves first.

Immobile nutrients–calcium (Ca), boron (B), chlorine (Cl), cobalt (Co), copper (Cu), iron (Fe), manganese (Mn), molybdenum (Mo), silicon (Si) and sulfur (S)–do not translocate to new growing areas as needed. They remain deposited in their original place in older leaves. This is the reason deficiency symptoms appear first in the upper, new leaves on top of the plant.

Mobile nutrients translocate within a plant. They move to the specific part of the plant where they are needed; this causes the older leaves to show deficiencies first.

Macronutrients

Nitrogen (N) - mobile

Practical Information: Marijuana loves nitrogen and requires high levels of it during vegetative growth but lower levels during the balance of life. Nitrogen is easily washed away and must be replaced regularly, especially during vegetative growth. Excess levels of nitrogen in harvested plants cause the dried marijuana to burn poorly.

Technical Information: Nitrogen regulates the cannabis plant's ability to make proteins essential for new protoplasm in the cells. Electrically charged nitrogen allows the plant to tie proteins, hormones, chlorophyll, vitamins, and enzymes together. Nitrogen is essential for the production of amino acids, enzymes, nucleic acids, and chlorophyll and alkaloids. This important nutrient is mainly responsible for leaf and stem growth, as well as overall size and vigor. Nitrogen is most active in young buds, shoots, and leaves. Ammonium (NH_4^+) is the most readily available form of nitrogen. Be careful when using too much of this form; it can burn the plants. Nitrate (NO_3^-)–the nitrate form of nitrogen–is much slower to assimilate than ammonium. Hydroponic fertilizers use this slower-acting nitrogen compound and mix it with ammonium.

Deficiency: Nitrogen is the most common nutrient deficiency. The symptoms include slow growth. Lower leaves cannot produce chlorophyll and become yellow between the veins while the veins remain green. Yellowing progresses through the entire leaf, eventually causing it to die and drop off. Stems and the leaves' undersides may turn reddish-purple, but this can also be a sign of a phosphorus deficiency. Nitrogen is very mobile, and it dissipates into the environment quickly. It must be added regularly to sustain fast-growing gardens.

Progression of deficiency symptoms at a glance:
Older leaves yellow between the veins (interveinal chlorosis).
Older bottom leaves turn entirely yellow.
More and more leaves yellow. Severely affected leaves drop.
Leaves might develop reddish-purple stems and veins on leaf undersides.
Progressively younger leaves develop interveinal chlorosis.
All foliage yellows and the leaf drop is severe.

Treat deficiency by fertilizing with N or a complete N-P-K fertilizer. You should see results in four to five days. Fast-acting organic sources of nitrogen include seabird guano, fish emulsion, and blood meal. Growers also report excellent results by adding bio-fertilizers (see "Additives" page 285) to stimulate the uptake of nitrogen.

Toxicity: An overdose of nitrogen will cause excessively lush foliage that is soft and susceptible to stress, including insect and fungal attacks. The stems become weak and they may fold over easily. The vascular transport tissue breaks down, and water uptake is restricted. In severe cases, leaves turn a brownish-copper

color, dry, and fall off. Roots develop slowly, and they tend to darken and rot. Flowers are smaller and sparse. Ammonium toxicity is most common in acidic soils, while nitrate toxicity is more prevalent in alkaline soil.

Progression of toxicity symptoms at a glance:
Excessively lush, green foliage.
Weak stems that fold over.
Slow root development.
Flowers become wispy.

Beginning of N deficiency.

Leaves brown, dry, and fall off.

Treat toxicity by flushing the growing medium of the affected plants with a very mild, complete fertilizer. Severe problems require that more water be flushed through the growing medium to carry away the toxic elements.

Progression of N deficiency.

Flush a minimum of three times the volume of water for the volume of the growing medium. Do not add more fertilizer that contains nitrogen for one week so the excess nitrogen in foli-

Later stage of N deficiency.

Early stage of N overdose.   *Later stage of N overdose.*

age can be used. If the plants remain excessively green, cut back on the nitrogen dose.

Phosphorus (P) - mobile

Practical Information: Cannabis uses the highest levels of phosphorus during germination, seedling, cloning, and flowering. Super Bloom fertilizers, designed for flowering, have high levels of phosphorus.

Technical Information: Phosphorus is necessary for photosynthesis and provides a mechanism for the energy to transfer within the plant. Phosphorus–one of the components of DNA, many being enzymes and proteins–is associated with overall vigor, resin, and seed production. The highest concentrations of phosphorus are found in root-growing tips, growing shoots, and vascular tissue.

Early stage of P deficiency.

Deficiency A lack of phosphorous causes stunted growth and smaller leaves; leaves turn bluish-green and blotches often appear. Stems, leaf stems (petioles), and main veins turn reddish-purple starting on the leaf's underside. NOTE: The reddening of the stems and the veins is not always well pronounced. The leaf tips of older leaves turn dark and curl downward.

Progression of P deficiency.

Severely affected leaves develop large purplish-black necrotic (dead) blotches. These leaves later become bronzish-purple, dry, shrivel up, contort, and drop off. Flowering is often delayed, buds are uniformly smaller, seed yield is poor,

Later stage of P deficiency.

and plants become very vulnerable to fungal and insect attack. Phosphorus deficiencies are aggravated by clay, acidic, and soggy soils. Zinc is also necessary for proper utilization of phosphorus.

Deficiencies are somewhat common and are often misdiagnosed. Deficiencies are most common when the growing-medium pH is above 7 and phosphorus is unable to be absorbed properly; the soil is acidic (below 5.8) and/or there is an excess of iron and zinc; the soil has become fixated (chemically bound) with phosphates.

Progression of deficiency symptoms at a glance:
Stunted and very slow-growth plants.
Dark bluish-green leaves, often with dark blotches.
Plants are smaller overall.
When blotches overcome the leaf stem, the leaf turns bronzish-purple, contorts, and drops.

Treat deficiency by lowering the pH to 5.5-6.2 in hydroponic units; 6 to 7 for clay soils; and 5.5-6.5 for potting soils so phosphorus will become available. If the soil is too acidic, and an excess of iron and zinc exists, phosphorous becomes unavailable. If you are growing in soil, mix a complete fertilizer that contains phosphorus into the growing medium before planting. Fertigate with an inorganic, complete hydroponic fertilizer that contains phosphorus. Mix in the organic nutrients–bat guano, steamed bone meal, natural phosphates, or barnyard manure–to add phosphorus to soil. Always use finely ground organic components that are readily available to the plants.

Toxic signs of phosphorus may take several weeks to surface, especially if excesses are buffered by a stable pH. Marijuana uses a lot of phosphorus throughout its life cycle, and many varieties tolerate high levels. Excessive phosphorus interferes with calcium, copper, iron, magnesium, and zinc stability and uptake. Toxic symptoms of phosphorus manifest as a deficiency of zinc, iron, magnesium, calcium and copper; zinc is the most common.

Treat toxicity by flushing the growing medium of affected plants with a very mild and complete fertilizer. Severe problems require more water to be flushed through the growing medium. Flush a minimum of three times the volume of water for the volume of the growing medium.

Potassium (K) - mobile

Practical Information: Potassium is used at all stages of growth. Soils with a high level of potassium increase a plant's resistance to bacteria and mold.

Technical information: Potassium helps combine sugars, starches, and carbohydrates, which is essential to their production and movement. It also is essential to growth by cell division. It increases the chlorophyll in the foliage and helps to regulate the stomata openings so plants make better use of the light and air. Potassium is essential in the accumulation and translocation of carbohydrates. It is necessary to make the proteins that augment the oil content and improve the flavor in cannabis plants. It also encourages strong root growth and is associated with disease resistance and water intake. The potash form of potassium oxide is (K_2O).

Deficiency Potassium-starved plants initially appear healthy. Deficient plants are susceptible to disease. Symptoms include the following: older leaves (first tips and margins, followed by whole leaves) develop spots, turn dark yellow, and die. Stems often become weak and sometimes brittle. Potassium is usually present in the soil, but it is locked in by high salinity. First, leach the toxic salt out of the soil and then apply a complete N-P-K fertilizer. Potassium deficiency causes the internal temperature of the foliage to climb and the protein cells to burn or degrade. Evaporation is normally highest on leaf edges, and that's where the burning takes place.

The progression of the deficiency symptoms at a glance:

Plants appear healthy with dark green foliage. The leaves lose their luster.

Branching may increase, but the branches are weak and scrawny.

Leaf margins turn grey and progress to a rusty-brown color, and then curl up and dry.

Yellowing of the older leaves is accompanied by rust-colored blotches.

The leaves curl up, rot sets in, and the older leaves drop.

The flowering is retarded and greatly diminished.

Early stage of K deficiency.

Treat deficiency of potassium by fertilizing with a complete N-P-K fertilizer. Occasionally, a grower will add potassium directly to the nutrient solution. Organic growers add potassium in the form of soluble potash (wood ashes) mixed with water. Be careful when using wood ash, the pH is normally above 10. Use a pH-lowering mix to bring the pH to around 6.5 before application. Foliar feeding to cure a potassium deficiency is not recommended.

Progression of K deficiency.

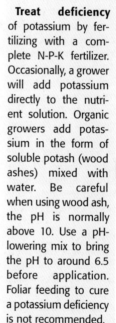

Toxicity occurs occasionally and is difficult

Later stage of K deficiency.

to diagnose because it is mixed with the deficiency symptoms of other nutrients. Too much potassium impairs and slows the absorption of magnesium, manganese, and sometimes zinc and iron. Look for signs of toxic-potassium buildup when symptoms of magnesium, manganese, zinc, and iron deficiencies appear.

Treat toxicity by flushing the growing medium of affected plants with a very mild and complete fertilizer. Severe problems require that more water be flushed through the growing medium. Flush with a minimum of three times the volume of water for the volume of the growing medium.

Secondary Nutrients

The secondary nutrients–magnesium, calcium, and sulfur–are also used by the plants in large amounts. Rapid-growing indoor marijuana crops are able to process more secondary nutrients than most general-purpose fertilizers are able to supply. Many growers opt to use high quality two- and three-part hydroponic fertilizers to supply all necessary secondary and trace elements. But be careful, these three nutrients may be present in high levels in the ground water. It is important to consider these values when adding nutrient supplements. If growing in a soil or soilless mix with a pH below 7 such as Peat-Lite, incorporating one cup of fine (flour) dolomite lime per gallon of medium ensures adequate supplies of calcium and magnesium.

Macronutrients are the elements that the plants use most. The fertilizers usually show nitrogen (N), potassium (P), phosphorous (K) as (N-P-K) percentages in big numbers on the front of the package. They are always listed in the same N-P-K order. These nutrients must always be in an available form to supply marijuana with the building blocks for rapid growth.

Magnesium (Mg) - mobile

Practical Information: Marijuana uses a lot of magnesium, and deficiencies are common, especially in acidic (pH below 7) soils. Adding dolomite lime to acidic potting soils before planting will stabilize the pH, plus it will add magnesium and calcium to the soil. Add Epsom salts with each watering to correct magnesium deficiencies, if no dolomite was added when planting. Use Epsom salts designed specifically for plants rather than the supermarket-type.

Technical Information: Magnesium is found as a central atom in every chlorophyll molecule, and it is essential to the absorption of light energy. It aids in the utilization of nutrients. Magnesium helps enzymes make carbohydrates and sugars that are later transformed into flowers. It also neutralizes the soil acids and toxic compounds produced by the plant.

Deficiency: Magnesium deficiency is common indoors. The lower leaves, and later the middle leaves, develop yellow patches between dark, green veins. Rusty-brown spots appear on the

leaf margins, tips, and between the veins, as the deficiency progresses. The brownish leaf tips usually curl upward before dying. The entire plant could discolor in a few weeks, and if severe, turn a yellow-whitish tinge before browning and dying. A minor deficiency will cause little or no problem with growth. However, minor deficiencies escalate and cause a diminished harvest as flowering progresses. Most often, magnesium is in the soil but is unavailable to the plant because the root environment is too wet and cold or acidic and cold. Magnesium is also bound in the soil if there is an excess of potassium, ammonia (nitrogen), and calcium (carbonate). Small root systems are also unable to take in enough magnesium to supply heavy demand. A high EC slows the water evaporation and will also diminish magnesium availability.

Early stage of Mg deficiency.

Progression of deficiency symptoms at a glance:

No deficiency symptoms are visible during the first three to four weeks.

In the 4th to the 6th week of growth, the first signs of deficiency appear. Interveinal yellowing and irregular rust-brown spots appear on older and middle-aged leaves. Younger leaves remain healthy.

Progression of Mg deficiency.

Leaf tips turn brown and curl upward as the deficiency progresses.

Rust-brown spots multiply and interveinal yellowing increases.

Rust-brown spots and yellowing progress, starting at the bottom and advancing to the top of the entire plant.

Later stage of Mg deficiency.

Younger leaves develop rust-colored spots and interveinal yellowing.
The leaves dry and die in extreme cases.

Treat deficiency by watering with two teaspoons of Epsom salts (magnesium sulfate) per gallon of water. For fast results, spray the foliage with a 2 percent solution of Epsom salts. If the deficiency progresses to the top of the plant, it will turn green there first. In four to six days, it will start moving down the plant, turning lower leaves progressively more green. Continue a regular watering schedule with Epsom salts until the symptoms totally disappear. Adding Epsom salts regularly is not necessary when the fertilizer contains available magnesium. Use a foliar spray of Epsom salts for a fast cure. Another option is to apply magnesium sulfate monohydrate in place of Epsom salts. Add fine dolomite lime to soil and soilless mix to add a consistent supply of both calcium and magnesium over the long term. Always use the finest dolomite available.

Control the room and root-zone temperatures, humidity, pH, and EC of the nutrient solution. Keep root zone and nutrient solution at 70 to 75°F (21-24°C). Keep ambient air temperature at 75°F (21°C) day and 65°F (18°C) night. Use a complete fertilizer with an adequate amount of magnesium. Keep the soil pH above 6.5, the hydroponic pH above 5.5, and reduce high EC for a week.

The extra magnesium in the soil is generally not harmful, but it can inhibit calcium uptake. Signs of excess magnesium are described below.

Toxicity: Magnesium toxicity is rare and difficult to discern with the naked eye. If extremely toxic, the magnesium develops a conflict with other fertilizer ions, usually calcium, especially in hydroponic nutrient solutions. The toxic buildup of magnesium in soil that is able to grow marijuana is uncommon.

Calcium (Ca) - immobile

Practical Information: Cannabis requires nearly as much calcium as other macronutrients. Avert deficiencies in the soil and in most soilless mixes by adding fine dolomite lime or using soluble-hydroponic fertilizers containing adequate calcium.

Technical Information: Calcium is fundamental to cell manufacturing and growth. Calcium is necessary to preserve membrane permeability and cell integrity, which ensures proper flow of nitrogen and sugars. It stimulates enzymes that help build strong cell and root walls. Cannabis must have some calcium at the growing tip of each root.

Deficiency of calcium is somewhat uncommon indoors, but not uncommon in fiber hemp. Frequently, plants can process more calcium than is available. It also washes out of the leaves that are sprayed with water. Deficiency signs may be difficult to detect. They start with weak stems, very dark green foliage, and exceptionally slow growth. Young leaves are affected, and they show the signs first. Severe calcium deficiency causes new, growing shoots to develop yellowish to purple hues and to disfigure before shriveling up and dying; bud development is inhibited, the plants are stunted, and harvest is diminished. Growing tips could show signs of calcium deficiency if the humidity is maxed out. At 100 percent humidity, the stomata close, which stops the transpiration to protect the plant. The calcium that is transported by transpiration becomes immobile.

Treat deficiencies by dissolving one-half teaspoon of hydrated lime per gallon of water. Water the deficient plants with calcium-dosed water as long as the symptoms persist. Or use a complete hydroponic nutrient that contains adequate calcium. Keep the pH of the growing medium stable.

Progression of deficiency symptoms at a glance:
Slow growth and young leaves turn very dark green.
New growing shoots discolor.
New shoots contort, shrivel, and die.
Bud development slows dramatically.

Toxicity is difficult to see in the foliage. It causes wilting. Toxic levels also exacerbate deficiencies of potassium, magnesium, manganese, and iron. The nutrients become unavailable, even though they are present. If excessive amounts of soluble calcium are applied early in life, it can also stunt the growth. If growing hydroponically, an excess of calcium will precipitate with sulfur in the solution, which causes the nutrient solution to suspend in the water and to aggregate into clumps causing the water to become cloudy (flocculate). Once the calcium and sulfur combine, they form a residue (gypsum $Ca(SO_4)\cdot 2(H_2O)$) that settles to the bottom of the reservoir.

Sulfur (S) - immobile

Practical Information: Many fertilizers contain some form of sulfur, and for this reason, sulfur is seldom deficient. Growers avoid elemental (pure) sulfur in favor of sulfur compounds such as magnesium sulfate. The nutrients combined with sulfur mix better in water.

Technical Information: Sulfur is an essential building block of many hormones and vitamins, including vitamin B_1. Sulfur is also an indispensable element in many plant cells and seeds. The sulfate form of sulfur buffers the water pH. Virtually all ground, river, and lake water contains sulfate. Sulfate is involved in protein synthesis and is part of the amino acid, cystine, and thiamine, which are the building blocks of proteins. Sulfur is essential in the formation of oils and flavors, as well as for respiration and the synthesis and breakdown of fatty acids. Hydroponic fertilizers separate sulfur from calcium in an "A" container and a "B" container. If combined in a concentrated form, sulfur and calcium will form crude, insoluble gypsum (calcium sulfate) and settle as residue to the bottom of the tank.

Deficiency: Young leaves turn lime-green to yellowish. As shortage progresses, leaves yellow interveinally and lack succulence. Veins remain green, and leaf stems and petioles turn purple. Leaf tips can burn, darken, and hook downward. According to literature, youngest leaves should yellow first. But Mauk from Canna Coco in the Netherlands, who has conducted detailed scientific experiments with nutrients, says, "We have repeatedly noticed that the symptoms were most obvious in the older leaves." Sulfur deficiency resembles a nitrogen deficiency. Acute sulfur deficiency causes elongated stems that become woody at the base.

Sulfur deficiency occurs indoors when the pH is too high or when there is excessive calcium present and available.

Progression of deficiency symptoms at a glance:
Similar to nitrogen deficiency: older leaves turn a pale green.
Leaf stems turn purple and more leaves turn pale green.
Entire leaves turn pale yellow.
Interveinal yellowing occurs.

Acute deficiency causes more and more leaves to develop purple leaf stems and yellow leaves.

Treat deficiency by fertilizing with a hydroponic fertilizer that contains sulfur. Lower the pH to 5.5 to 6. Add inorganic sulfur to a fertilizer that contains magnesium sulfate (Epsom salts). Organic sources of sulfur include mushroom composts and most animal manures. Make sure to apply only well-rotted manures to avoid burning the roots.

Toxicity: An excess of sulfur in the soil causes no problems if the EC is relatively low. At a high EC, the plants tend to take up more available sulfur which blocks uptake of other nutrients. Excess sulfur symptoms include overall smaller plant development and uniformly smaller, dark-green foliage. Leaf tips and margins could discolor and burn when severe.

Treat toxicity by flushing the growing medium of affected plants with a very mild and complete fertilizer. Check the pH of the drainage solution. Correct the input pH to 6. Severe problems require more water to be flushed through the growing medium. Flush a minimum of three times the volume of water for the volume of the growing medium.

Early stage of S deficiency.

Progression of S deficiency.

Later stage of S deficiency.

MICRONUTRIENTS

Zinc, iron, and manganese are the three most common micronutrients found deficient. Deficiencies of these three micronutrients plague many more grow rooms than I had imagined. Often deficiencies of all three occur concurrently, especially when the soil or water pH is above 6.5. Deficiencies are most common in arid climates– Spain, the Southwestern United States, Australia, etc.–with alkaline soil and water. All three have the same initial symptom of deficiency: interveinal chlorosis of young leaves. It is often difficult to distinguish which element– zinc, iron, or manganese–is deficient, and all three could be deficient. This is why treating the problem should include adding a chelated dose of all three nutrients.

Micronutrients

Micronutrients, also called *trace elements* or *trace nutrients*, are essential to chlorophyll formation and must be present in minute amounts. They function mainly as catalysts to the plant's process and utilization of other elements. For best results, and to ensure a complete range of trace elements is available, use fertilizers designed for hydroponics. High quality hydroponic fertilizers use food-grade ingredients that are completely soluble and leave no residues. If using an inexpensive fertilizer that does not list a specific analysis for each trace element on the label, it's a good idea to add soluble trace elements in a chelated form. Chelated micronutrients are available in powdered and liquid form. Add and thoroughly mix micronutrients into the growing medium before planting. Micronutrients are often impregnated in commercial potting soils and soilless mixes. Check the ingredients on the bag to ensure that the trace elements were added to the mix. Trace elements are necessary in minute amounts but can easily reach toxic levels. Always follow the manufacturer's instructions to the letter when applying micronutrients, because they are easy to over-apply.

Zinc (Zn) - mobile

Practical Information: Zinc is the most common micronutrient found deficient in arid climates and alkaline soils.

Technical Information: Zinc works with manganese and magnesium to promote the same enzyme functions. Zinc cooperates with other elements to help form chlorophyll as well as

---

A **chelate** (Greek for *claw*) is an organic molecule that forms a claw-like bond with free electrically charged metal particles. This property keeps metal ions such as zinc, iron, and manganese, etc., soluble in water, and the chelated metal's reactions with other materials is suppressed. Roots take in the chelated metals in a stable, soluble form that is used immediately.

Natural chelates such as humic acid and citric acid can be added to organic soil mixes. Roots and bacteria also exude natural chelates to promote the uptake of metallic elements. Man-made chelates are designed for use in different situations. DTPA is most effective in a pH below 6.5, EDDHA is effective up to a pH of 8, and EDTA chelate is slow to cause leaf burn.

Chelates decompose rapidly in low levels of ultraviolet (UV) light including light produced by HID bulbs and sunlight. Keep chelates out of the light to protect them from rapid decomposition.

Chelate - combining nutrients in an atomic ring that is easy for plants to absorb.

This information was condensed from Canna Products, www.canna.com.

prevent its demise. It is an essential catalyst for most plants' enzymes and auxins, and it is crucial for stem growth. Zinc plays a vital part in sugar and protein production. It is fairly common to find zinc-deficient cannabis. Deficiencies are most common in soils with a pH of 7 or more.

Deficiency: Zinc is the most common micronutrient found deficient. First, younger leaves exhibit interveinal chlorosis, and new leaves and growing tips develop small, thin blades that contort and wrinkle. The leaf tips, and later the margins, discolor and burn. Burned spots on the leaves could grow progressively larger. These symptoms are often confused with a lack of manganese or iron, but when zinc deficiency is severe, new leaf blades contort and dry out. Flower buds also contort into odd shapes, turn crispy dry, and are often hard. A lack of zinc stunts all new growth including buds.

Early stage of Zn deficiency.

Progression of deficiency symptoms at a glance:

Interveinal chlorosis of young leaves.

New leaves develop thin, wispy leaves.

Leaf tips discolor, turn dark, and die back.

Progression of Zn deficiency.

New growth contorts horizontally.

New bud and leaf growth stops.

Treat zinc-deficient plants by flushing the growing medium with a diluted mix of a complete fertilizer containing chelated trace elements, including zinc, iron,

Later stage of Zn deficiency.

and manganese. Or add a quality-brand hydroponic micronutrient mix containing chelated trace elements.

Toxicity: Zinc is extremely toxic in excess. Severely toxic plants die quickly. Excess zinc interferes with the iron's ability to function properly and causes an iron deficiency.

Manganese (Mn) - immobile

Practical Information: Manganese deficiency is relatively common indoors.

Technical Information: Manganese is engaged in the oxidation-reduction process associated with the photosynthetic electron transport. This element activates many enzymes and plays a fundamental part in the chloroplast membrane system. Manganese assists nitrogen utilization along with iron in chlorophyll production.

Deficiency: Young leaves show symptoms first. They become yellow between veins (interveinal chlorosis), and the veins remain green. Symptoms spread from younger to older leaves as the deficiency progresses. Necrotic (dead) spots develop on severely affected leaves which become pale and fall off; overall plant growth is stunted, and maturation may be prolonged. Severe deficiency looks like a severe lack of magnesium.

Treat deficiency: Lower the pH, leach the soil, and add a complete, chelated micronutrient formula.

Progression of deficiency symptoms at a glance:

Interveinal chlorosis of young leaves forms.

Interveinal chlorosis of progressively older leaves forms.

Dead spots develop on acutely affected leaves.

Toxicity: Young and newer growth develop chlorotic, dark orange to dark, rusty-brown mottling on the leaves. Tissue damage shows on young leaves before progressing to the older leaves. Growth is slower, and overall vigor is lost. Toxicity is compounded by low humidity. The additional transpiration causes more manganese to be drawn into the foliage. A low pH can cause toxic intake of manganese. An excess of manganese causes a deficiency of iron and zinc.

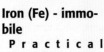

Early stage of Mn deficiency.

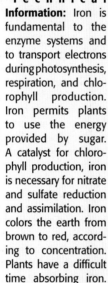

Progression of Mn deficiency.

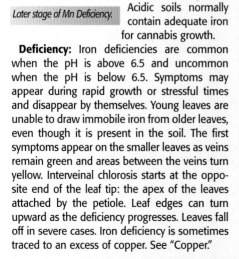

Later stage of Mn Deficiency.

Iron (Fe) - immobile

Practical Information: Iron is available in a soluble chelated form that is immediately available for absorption by the roots. Deficiency indoors is common in alkaline soils.

Technical Information: Iron is fundamental to the enzyme systems and to transport electrons during photosynthesis, respiration, and chlorophyll production. Iron permits plants to use the energy provided by sugar. A catalyst for chlorophyll production, iron is necessary for nitrate and sulfate reduction and assimilation. Iron colors the earth from brown to red, according to concentration. Plants have a difficult time absorbing iron. Acidic soils normally contain adequate iron for cannabis growth.

Deficiency: Iron deficiencies are common when the pH is above 6.5 and uncommon when the pH is below 6.5. Symptoms may appear during rapid growth or stressful times and disappear by themselves. Young leaves are unable to draw immobile iron from older leaves, even though it is present in the soil. The first symptoms appear on the smaller leaves as veins remain green and areas between the veins turn yellow. Interveinal chlorosis starts at the opposite end of the leaf tip: the apex of the leaves attached by the petiole. Leaf edges can turn upward as the deficiency progresses. Leaves fall off in severe cases. Iron deficiency is sometimes traced to an excess of copper. See "Copper."

Progression of deficiency symptoms at a glance:

Younger leaves and growing shoots turn pale green and progress to yellow between the veins starting at the petiole but the veins remain green.

More and more leaves turn yellow and develop interveinal chlorosis.

Larger leaves finally yellow and develop interveinal chlorosis.

In acute cases, leaves develop necrosis and drop.

Treat deficiency by lowering the soil pH to 6.5 or less. Avoid fertilizers that contain excessive amounts of manganese, zinc, and copper, which inhibit iron uptake. High levels of phosphorus compete with the uptake of iron. Improve the drainage; excessively wet soil holds little oxygen to spur iron uptake. Damaged or rotten roots also lower iron uptake. Increase root-zone temperature. Apply chelated iron in liquid form to root zone. Chelates are decomposed by light and must be thoroughly mixed with the growing medium to be effective. Exposing the nutrient solution to light causes depleted iron. Sterilizing the nutrient solution with UV light causes iron to precipitate. Leaves should green up in four or five days. Complete, balanced, hydroponic nutrients contain iron, and deficiencies are seldom a problem. Organic sources of iron, as well as che-

Early stage of Fe deficiency.

Progression of Fe deficiency.

Later stage of Fe deficiency.

lates, include cow, horse, and chicken manure. Use only well-rotted manures to avoid burning plants.

Toxicity: Excess of iron is rare. High levels of iron do not damage cannabis, but it can interfere with phosphorus uptake. An excess of iron causes the leaves to turn bronze accompanied by small, dark brown leaf spots. If iron chelate is over applied, it will kill the plant in a few days.

Treat excess iron by leaching plants heavily.

The following group of micronutrients is seldom found deficient. Avoid deficiencies by using a high-quality hydroponic fertilizer that contains chelated micronutrients.

Boron (B) - immobile

Practical Information: Usually causes no problems, but boron must be available during the entire life of a plant.

Technical Information: Boron deficiencies seldom occur indoors. Boron is still somewhat of a biochemical mystery. We know that boron helps with calcium uptake and numerous plant functions. Scientists have collected evidence to suggest boron helps with synthesis, a base for the formation of nucleic acid (RNA uracil) formation. Strong evidence also supports boron's role in cell division, differentiation, maturation, and respiration as well as a link to pollen germination.

Deficiency: Stem tip and root tip grow abnormally. Root tips often swell, discolor, and stop elongating. Growing shoots look burned and may be confused with a burn from being too close to the HID light. First leaves thicken and become brittle, top shoots contort and/or turn dark, which is later followed by progressively lower-growing shoots. When severe, growing tips die, and leaf margins discolor and die back in places. Necrotic spots develop between leaf veins. Root steles (insides) often become mushy–perfect hosts for rot and disease. Deficient leaves become thick, distorted, and wilted with chlorotic and necrotic spotting.

Treat deficiency: Boron-deficient plants with one teaspoon of boric acid per gallon of water. You can apply this solution as a soil drench to be taken up by the roots, or apply hydroponic micronutrients containing boron. Hydroponic

gardeners should keep boron dosage below 20 parts per million (ppm), because boron quickly becomes toxic if it is concentrated in the solution.

Toxicity: Leaf tips yellow first, and as the toxic conditions progress, leaf margins become necrotic toward the center of the leaf. After the leaves yellow, they fall off. Avoid using excessive amounts of boric acid-based insecticides.

Chlorine (Chloride) (Cl) - immobile

Practical Information: Chloride is found in many municipal water systems. Cannabis tolerates low levels of chlorine. It is usually not a component of fertilizers and is almost never deficient in gardens that grow cannabis.

Technical Information: Chlorine, in the form of chloride, is fundamental to photosynthesis and cell division in the roots and the foliage. It also increases osmotic pressure in the cells, which open and close the stomata to regulate moisture flow within the plant tissue.

Deficiency: It is uncommon to be deficient. Young leaves pale and wilt, and roots become stubby. As the deficiency progresses, leaves become chlorotic and develop a characteristic bronze color. The roots develop thick tips and become stunted. NOTE: Both severe deficiency and excess of chloride have the same symptoms: bronze-colored leaves.

Treat deficiency: Add chlorinated water.

Toxicity: Young leaves develop burned leaf tips and margins. Very young seedlings and clones are the most susceptible to damage. Later, the symptoms progress throughout the plant. Characteristic yellowish-bronze leaves are smaller and slower to develop.

Treat toxicity: Let heavily chlorinated water sit out overnight, stirring occasionally. Chlorine will volatize and disappear into the atmosphere. Use this water to mix the nutrient solution or to irrigate the garden.

Cobalt (Co) - immobile

Practical Information: This nutrient is seldom mentioned as necessary for plant growth, and most fertilizer labels do not include cobalt. Cobalt is virtually never deficient in indoor cannabis gardens.

Technical Information: Cobalt is necessary

for countless beneficial bacteria to grow and flourish. It is also vital for nitrogen absorption. Scientific evidence suggests this element is linked to enzymes needed to form aromatic compounds.

Deficiency: When deficient, the problems with nitrogen availability occur.

Copper (Cu) - immobile

Practical Information: Copper is concentrated in the roots. It is also used as a fungicide.

Technical Information: Copper is a component of numerous enzymes and proteins. Necessary in minute amounts, copper helps with carbohydrate metabolism, nitrogen fixation, and the process of oxygen reduction. It also helps with the making of proteins and sugars.

Deficiency: Copper deficiencies are not rare. Young leaves and growing shoots wilt, leaf tips and margins develop necrosis and turn a dark, copper-gray. Occasionally, an entire copper-deficient plant wilts, drooping even when adequately watered. Growth is slow and the yield decreases. A small deficiency can cause new shoots to die back.

Treat deficiency: Apply a copper-based fungicide such as copper sulfate. Do not apply if the temperature is above 75°F (24°C) to avoid burning the foliage. Apply a complete hydroponic nutrient that contains copper. Cannabis plants seldom develop a copper deficiency.

Toxicity: Copper, although essential, is extremely toxic to the plant even in minor excess. Toxic levels slow the overall plant growth. As the toxic level climbs, symptoms include interveinal iron chlorosis (deficiency) and stunted growth. Fewer branches grow, and the roots become dark, thick, and slow growing. Toxic conditions accelerate quickly in acidic soils. Hydroponic gardeners must carefully monitor their solution to avoid copper excess.

Treat toxicity: Flush the soil or the growing medium to help expel the excess copper. Do not use copper-based fungicides.

Molybdenum (Mb) - immobile

Practical Information: Molybdenum is seldom deficient.

Technical Information: Molybdenum is a part of two major enzyme systems that convert nitrate to ammonium. This essential element is used by cannabis in very small quantities. It is most active in roots and seeds.

Deficiency: This micronutrient is almost never found deficient in cannabis. Deficiency promotes nitrogen shortage. First, the older and middle-aged leaves yellow, and some develop interveinal chlorosis; then the leaves continue to yellow and develop cupped or rolled-up margins as the deficiency progresses. Acute symptoms cause the leaves to become severely twisted, die, and drop. Overall growth is stunted. Deficiencies are worst in acidic soils.

Toxicity: Excess is uncommon in marijuana gardens. An excess of molybdenum causes a deficiency of copper and iron.

Silicon - (Si)

Practical Information: Silicon is readily available in most soils, water, and as far as I know, it does not cause cannabis any complications due to deficiencies or excesses.

Technical Information: Silicon is absorbed by the plants as silicic acid. Silicon assists in keeping iron and manganese levels consistent. It is found mainly in the epidermal cell walls where it collects in the form of hydrated amorphous silica. It also accumulates in the walls of other cells. Adequate and soluble silicon guarantees stronger cell walls that resist pest attacks and increase heat and drought tolerance.

Deficiency: A lack of silicon has been proven to decrease yields of some fruits and cause new leaves to deform.

Excess: Never heard of a problem.

NOTE: Pests and diseases have a difficult time penetrating the plants that are sprayed with a silicon-based repellent/insecticide.

Nickel - (Ni)

Enzymes require nickel to break down and use the nitrogen from the urea. It is also essential to iron absorption. Seldom deficient and subtly mixed with other nutrient deficiencies, most commonly nitrogen.

Fertilizers show the N-P-K in big letters on the front of the package.

potting soil will supply all the necessary nutrients for the first month of growth, but the development might be slow. After the roots have absorbed most of the available nutrients, more must be added to sustain vigorous growth. Unless fortified, soilless mixes require fertilization from the start. I like to start fertilizing fortified soilless mixes after the first week or two of growth. Most commercial soilless mixes are fortified with trace elements.

Marijuana's metabolism changes as it grows and so do its fertilizer needs. During germination and seedling growth, intake of phosphorus is high. The vegetative growth stage requires larger amounts of nitrogen for green-leaf growth, and phosphorus and potassium are also necessary in substantial levels. During this leafy and vegetative growth stage, use a *general purpose* or a *grow* fertilizer with high nitrogen content. In the flowering stage, nitrogen takes a backseat to potassium, phosphorus, and calcium intake. Using a *super bloom* fertilizer with less nitrogen and more potassium, phosphorus, and calcium promotes fat, heavy, dense buds. Cannabis needs some nitrogen during flowering, but very little. With no nitrogen, buds do not develop to their full potential.

Now we come to the confusing part about the

Sodium - (Na)

This is one of the problem elements. A little bit will go a long way! Sodium is taken up by the roots very quickly and in small amounts (50 ppm). It can block enough other nutrients causing severe deficiencies to result. When mixed with chlorine, it turns into table salt, which is the worst possible salt to put on the plants. Be very careful to measure your input water to ensure that it contains less than 50 ppm sodium. The less sodium in the solution, the better.

Fluoride - (F)

Some water systems are abundant with fluoride. If concentrated, fluoride can become toxic. I have yet to see fluoride toxicity or deficiency cause problems in an indoor grow room.

Fertilizers

The goal of fertilizing is to supply the plants with the proper amounts of nutrients for vigorous growth, without creating toxic conditions by overfertilizing. A 2-gallon (8 L) container full of rich, fertile *guaranteed analysis* of commercial fertilizer mixes. Federal and state laws require nutrient concentrations to appear prominently on the face of the fertilizer packages, even though the accuracy of the values is dubious.

Do you think the N-P-K numbers on the label give the percentages of nitrogen, phosphorous, and potassium? Well, yes and no. The scale measures nutrients with different scales. Nitrogen is listed as *total combined elemental*. Most hydroponic fertilizers break nitrogen into slow-acting nitrate (NO_3) and ammonium (NH_4). Phosphoric anhydride (P_2O_5) is listed as the form of phosphorus, but this figure understates phosphorus content by 44 percent. It gets worse! The balance (56 percent) of the phosphorus molecule is comprised of oxygen. Twenty percent P_2O_5 is 8.8 percent actual phosphorous. Potassium (K) is listed in the potash form of potassium oxide (K_2O) of which 83 percent of the stated value is actually elemental potassium.

The rest of the mineral nutrients are listed in their elemental form that represents the actual content. Most often, the mineral elements used in the fertilizer formulas are listed in chemical compounds on the label. Look at the fertilizer labels to ensure that the elements, especially trace elements, are chelated and readily available for root absorption. Also, be careful about having too much sodium in your water/nutrient solution. The sodium will block potassium and several other nutrients, causing deficiencies and slow growth.

Nutrients in the United States are measured in parts-per-million (ppm), even though they are expressed as a percentage concentration on the label. The ppm scale is simple and finite–almost. The basics are simple: one part per million is one part of 1,000,000, so divide by one million to find parts per million. To convert percentages into ppm, multiply by 10,000 and move the decimal four (4) spaces to the right. For example: two percent equals 20,000 ppm. For more information on ppm and Electrical Conductivity, see Chapter Twelve, "Hydroponic Gardening."

Fertilizers are either water-soluble or partially soluble (gradual-release). Both soluble and gradual-release fertilizers can be organic or chemical.

These are the suggested soluble-salts fertilizer recommendations for indoor cannabis cultivation. The values are expressed in parts per million.

Chemical Fertilizers

The diversity of hydroponic fertilizers is amazing. Local shop owners know which ones work best in the local climate and water. Local storeowners know a lot about the local water and the growers' needs. They are in a perfect position to develop their own nutrient solution or adapt one that works well with their water. A few manufacturers do not do their homework and make bad nutrients. Most manufacturers are conscious and manufacture excellent fertilizers. As always, read the entire fertilizer label and follow the directions.

Soluble-chemical fertilizers are an excellent choice for indoor container cultivation. Soluble fertilizers dissolve in water and are easy to control, and they can be easily added or washed (leached) out of the growing medium. Control the exacting amounts of nutrients available to the plants in an available form with water-soluble fertilizers. The soluble fertilizer may be applied in a water solution onto the soil. In general, high-quality hydroponic fertilizers that use completely soluble food-grade nutrients are the best value. Avoid low-quality fertilizers that do not list all necessary micronutrients on the label.

Chemical granular fertilizers work well but can easily be over applied, creating toxic soil. They are almost impossible to leach out fast enough to save the plant.

Osmocote™ chemical fertilizers are time release and are used by many nurseries because they are easy to apply and only require one application every few months. Using this type of fertilizer may be convenient, but exacting control is lost. They are best suited for ornamental, containerized plants where labor costs and uniform growth are the main concerns.

Organic Fertilizers

Organically grown cannabis has a sweeter taste, but implementing an organic indoor garden requires horticultural know-how. The limited soil, space, and the necessity for sanitation

Element	Average	Limits
Nitrogen	150 – 1000	250
Calcium	100 – 150	200
Magnesium	50 – 100	75
Phosphorus	50 – 100	80
Potassium	100 – 400	300
Sulfur	200 – 1000	400
Copper	0.1 – 0.5	0.5
Boron	0.5 – 5.0	1.0
Iron	2.0 – 10	5.0
Manganese	0.5 – 5.0	2.0
Molybdenum	0.01 – 0.05	0.02
Zinc	0.5 – 1.0	0.5

These are the suggested soluble-salts fertilizer recommendations for indoor cannabis cultivation. The values are expressed in parts per million.

must be considered when growing organically. Outdoors, organic gardening is easy because all of the forces of nature are there for you to seek out and harness. Indoors, few of the natural phenomena are free and easy. Remember, you are Mother Nature and must create everything! The nature of growing indoors does not lend itself to long-term organic gardens, but some organic techniques have been practiced with amazing success.

Most indoor organic gardens use potting soil high in worm castings, peat, sand, manure, leaf mold, compost, and fine dolomite lime. In a container, there is little space to build the soil by mixing all kinds of neat composts and organic nutrients to cook down. Even if it were possible to build the soil in a container, it would take months of valuable growing time and it could foster bad insects, fungi, etc. It is easier and safer to throw old, depleted soil outdoors, and start new plants with fresh organic soil.

Organic nutrients, manure, worm castings, blood and bone meal, etc., all work very well to increase the soil nutrient content, but nutrients are released and available at different rates. The nutrient availability may be tricky to calculate, but it is somewhat difficult to over-apply organic fertilizers. Organic nutrients seem to be more consistently available when used in combination with one another. Usually, growers use a mix of about 20 percent worm castings with other organic agents to get a strong, readily available nitrogen base. They fertilize with bat guano, the organic super bloom, during flowering.

An indoor garden using raised beds allows true organic methods. The raised beds have enough soil to hold the nutrients, promote organic activity, and when managed properly, ensure a constant supply of nutrients. The raised beds must have enough soil mass to promote heat and fundamental organic activity.

Outdoor organic gardens are easy to implement and maintain. Using compost tea, manures, bulky compost, and other big, smelly things is much easier outdoors.

Several common chemical fertilizers from the hydroponic industry.

Organic Teas

Compost teas not only contain soluble organic nutrients diluted in water, but they support a potent elixir that is loaded with beneficial microbes that fight off pests and diseases. For example, a quarter teaspoon of a well-made compost tea holds more than a billion bacteria and at least 15 feet of fungi strands! A good compost tea also contains thousands of different species of protozoa, nematodes, and mycorrhizal fungi.

Disease-causing organisms are unable to compete with beneficial bacteria and fungi. Beneficial bacteria also work to break down plant residues and toxic materials, plus they improve soil structure and water-holding ability.

The best teas are made from well-rotted compost, because it contains a complex collection of microbes and nutrients. Just make sure the compost pile has heated to 135°F (52°C) for at least 3 days to ensure it is free of most diseases. You can usually buy quality compost at the local nursery. If using manure, make sure it has been well-composted.

You can brew the tea in a 5-gallon (19 L) bucket. Add about a gallon (3.8 L) of rotted compost or manure to 4 gallons (15 L) of water. Stir well, and let the mix sit for several days. You can also put sifted compost into a nylon stocking, and submerge it in the bucket. To stir, simply bounce the stocking around in the water. Stir the mixture gently several times a day to integrate oxygen and remove microbes from the compost. Adequate oxygen keeps the brew fresh. If it starts to smell foul, anaerobic bacteria are present. Add fresh water and stir more often. The good aerobic bacteria re-establish as soon as they have an ample supply of oxygen.

Dilute the tea at the rate of 1 to 5 with water. Add more water to the same bucket, and continue to brew 3 to 4 more batches before starting a new batch.

Organic Nutrients Chart

Alfalfa meal has 2.5 percent nitrogen, 5 percent phosphorus, and about 2 percent potash. Outdoor growers use pelletized animal feed as a slow-release fertilizer.

Blood and bone meal are wonderful organic fertilizers, but could transport Mad Cow Disease and other maladies. I can't recommend these with a clear conscience.

Blood (dried or meal) is collected at slaughterhouses, dried, and ground into a powder or meal. It's packed with fast-acting soluble nitrogen (12 to 15 percent by weight), about 1.2 percent phosphorus, and under one-percent potash. Apply carefully because it's easy to burn foliage. We advise avoiding use of any dried blood or blood meal that could carry Mad Cow Disease.

Bone meal is rich in phosphorus and nitrogen. The age and type of bone determine the nutrient content of this pulverized slaughterhouse product. Older bones have higher phosphorus content than young bones. Use

Here are just a few of the numerous fertilizers available for cannabis cultivation.

bone meal in conjunction with other organic fertilizers for best results. Its lime content helps reduce soil acidity and acts fast in well-aerated soil. We advise avoiding any bone meal that could carry Mad Cow Disease.

Raw, unsteamed bone meal contains 2 to 4 percent nitrogen and 15 to 25 percent phosphorus. Fatty acids in raw bone meal retard decomposition. We advise avoiding any bone meal that could carry Mad Cow Disease.

Steamed or cooked bone meal is made from fresh animal bones that have been boiled or steamed under pressure to render out fats. The pressure treatment causes a little nitrogen loss and an increase in phosphorus. Steamed bones are easier to grind into a fine powder, and the process helps nutrients become available sooner. It contains up to 30 percent phosphorus and about 1.5 percent nitrogen. The finer the bone meal is ground, the faster it becomes available.

Cottonseed meal is the leftover by-product of oil extraction. According to the manufacturer, virtually all chemical residues from commercial cotton production are dissolved in the oil and not found in the meal. This acidic fertilizer contains about 7 percent nitrogen, 2.5 percent phosphorus, and 1.5 percent potash. It should be combined with steamed bone meal and seaweed to form a balanced fertilizer blend.

Chicken manure is rich in available nitrogen, phosphorus, potassium, and trace elements. Indoor growers most often prefer to purchase dry, composted chicken manure in a bag. Use it as a topdressing or mix it with the soil before planting. Often chicken manure collected from farms is packed with feathers, which contain as much as 17 percent nitrogen; this is an added bonus. The average nutrient content of wet chicken manure is as follows: N – 1.5%, P – 1.5%, K – 0.5%; and dry chicken manure, N – 4%, P – 4%, K – 1.5%. Both have a full range of trace elements.

Coffee grounds are acidic and encourage acetic bacteria in the soil. Drip-coffee grounds are the richest, and contain about 2 percent nitrogen and traces of other nutrients. Add this to the compost pile or scatter and cultivate it in. Use it as topdressing, but in moderation, because it is very acidic.

Compost tea is used by many organic gardeners as the only source of fertilizer. Comfrey is packed with nutrients, and many gardeners grow it just to make compost tea.

Cow manure is sold as steer manure, but it is often collected from dairy herds. Gardeners have used cow manure for centuries, and this has led to the belief that it is a good fertilizer as well as a soil amendment. Steer manure is most valuable as mulch and a soil amendment. It holds water well and maintains fertility for a long time. The nutrient value is low, and it should not be relied upon for the main source of nitrogen. The average nutrient content of cow manure is N – 0.6%, P – 0.3%, K – 0.3%, and a full range of trace elements. Apply at the rate of 25 to 30 pounds per square yard.

Diatomaceous earth, the fossilized skeletal remains of fresh and saltwater diatoms, contains a full range of trace elements, and it is a good insecticide. Apply it to the soil when cultivating or as a topdressing.

Dolomite lime adjusts and balances the pH and makes phosphates more available. Generally applied to sweeten or deacidify the soil. It consists of calcium and magnesium, and is sometimes listed as a primary nutrient, though it is generally referred to as a secondary nutrient.

Feathers and feather meal contain from 12 to 15 percent nitrogen that is released slowly. Feathers included in barnyard chicken manure or obtained from slaughterhouses are an excellent addition to the compost pile or as a fertilizer. Feathers are steamed under pressure, dried, and ground into a powdery feather meal. Feather meal contains slow-release nitrogen of about 12.5 percent.

Fish meal is made from dried fish ground into a meal. It is rich in nitrogen (about 8 percent) and contains around 7 percent phosphoric acid and many trace elements.

It has an unpleasant odor, causing it to be avoided by indoor growers. It is a great compost activator. Apply it to the soil as a fast-acting topdressing. To help control odor, cultivate it into the soil or cover it with mulch after applying. Always store it in an airtight container, so it will not attract cats, dogs, or flies. Fish meal and fish emulsion can contain up to 10 percent nitrogen. The liquid generally contains less nitrogen than the meal. Even when deodorized, the liquid form has an unpleasant odor.

Fish emulsion, an inexpensive soluble liquid, is high in organic nitrogen, trace elements, and some phosphorus and potassium. This natural fertilizer is difficult to over-apply, and it is immediately available to the plants. Even deodorized fish emulsion smells like dead fish. Inorganic potash is added to the fish emulsion by some manufacturers and is semi-organic.

Goat manure is much like horse manure but more potent. Compost this manure and treat it as you would horse manure.

Granite dust or granite stone meal contains up to 5 percent potash and several trace elements. Releasing nutrients slowly over several years, granite dust is an inexpensive source of potash and does not affect soil pH. Not recommended indoors because it is too slow acting.

Greensand (glaucomite) is an iron-potassium silicate that gives the minerals in which it occurs a green tint. It is mined from ancient New Jersey-seabed deposits of shells and organic material rich in iron, phosphorus, potash (5 to 7 percent), and numerous micronutrients. Some organic gardeners do not use Greensand because it is such a limited resource. Greensand slowly releases its treasures in about four years. This is too slow acting for indoor gardens.

Guano (bat) consists of the droppings and remains of bats. It is rich in soluble nitrogen, phosphorus, and trace elements. The limited supply of this fertilizer–known as the soluble organic super bloom–makes it somewhat expensive. Mined in sheltered caves, guano dries with minimal decomposition. Bat guano can be thousands of years old. Newer deposits contain high levels of nitrogen and can burn foliage if applied too heavily. Older deposits are high in phosphorus and make an excellent flowering fertilizer. Bat guano is usually

Bat guano has transformed into the organic super bloom fertilizer.

powdery and is used any time of year as topdressing or diluted in a tea. Do not breathe the dust when handling it, because it can cause nausea and irritation.

Guano (sea bird) is high in nitrogen and other nutrients. The Humboldt Current, along the coast of Peru and northern Chile, keeps the rain from falling, and decomposition of the guano is minimal. South American guano is the world's best guano. The guano is scraped off rocks of arid sea islands. Guano is also collected from many coastlines around the world, so its nutrient content varies.

Gypsum (hydrated calcium sulfate) is used to lower the soil pH, and it improves drainage and aeration. It is also used to hold or slow the rapid decomposition of nitrogen. This is seldom used indoors.

Hoof and horn meal is an excellent source of slow-release nitrogen. Fine-ground horn meal makes nitrogen available quicker and has few problems with fly maggots. Soil bacteria must break it down before it is available to the roots. Apply it two to three weeks before planting. It remains in the soil for six months or longer. Hoof and horn meal contains from 6 to 15 percent nitrogen and about 2 percent phosphoric acid. We advise avoiding use of any dried blood or bone meal that could carry Mad Cow Disease.

Horse manure is readily available from horse stables and racetracks. Use horse manure that has straw or peat for bedding, since wood shavings could be a source of plant disease. Compost horse manure for two months or longer before adding it to the garden. The composting process kills weed seeds, and it will make better use of the nutrients. Straw bedding often uses up much of the available nitrogen. Nutrient content of horse manure is N – 0.6%, P – 0.6%, K – 0.4%, and a full range of trace elements.

Kelp is the *Cedilla* of trace minerals. Kelp should be deep-green, fresh, and smell like the ocean. Seaweed contains 60 to 70 trace minerals that are already chelated (existing in a form that's water soluble and mobile in the soil). Check the label to ensure all elements are not cooked out. See Seaweed on this page.

Oyster shells are ground and normally used as a calcium source for poultry. They contain up to 55 percent calcium and traces of many other nutrients that release slowly. Not practical to use indoors because they breakdown too slowly.

Paper ash contains about 5 percent phosphorus and over 2 percent potash. It is an excellent water-soluble fertilizer, but do not apply in large doses, because the pH is quite high. Paper ash is also full of toxic inks.

Pigeon manure has a very high concentration of nitrogen but is difficult to find. It can be used in the same fashion as chicken manure.

Rabbit manure is also excellent fertilizer but can be difficult to find in large quantities. Use rabbit manure as you would chicken or pigeon manure. According to John McPartland, rabbit poop is the best. Bunnies rule!

Potash rock supplies up to 8 percent potassium and may contain many trace elements. It releases too slowly to be practical indoors.

Rock phosphate (hard) is a calcium or lime-based phosphate rock that is finely ground to the consistency of talcum powder. The rock powder contains over 30 percent phosphate and a menagerie of trace elements, but it is available very, very slowly.

Colloidal phosphate (powdered or soft phosphate) is a natural clay phosphate deposit that contains just over 20 percent phosphorus (P_2O_5), calcium, and many trace elements. It yields only 2 percent phosphate by weight the first few months.

Seaweed meal and/or kelp meal is harvested from the ocean or picked up along the beaches, cleansed of salty water, dried, and ground into a powdery meal. It is packed with potassium (potash), numerous trace elements, vitamins, amino acids, and plant hormones. The nutrient content varies according to the type of kelp and growing conditions. Seaweed meal is easily assimilated by the plants, and contributes to soil life, structure, and nitrogen fixation. It may also help the plants resist many diseases and withstand light frosts. Kelp meal also eases transplant shock.

Seaweed (liquid) contains nitrogen, phosphorus, potash, all necessary trace elements in a chelated form, as well as plant hormones. Apply diluted solution to the soil for a quick cure of nutrient deficiencies. Liquid seaweed is also great for soaking seeds and, dipping cuttings and bare roots before planting.

Sheep manure is high in nutrients and makes a wonderful tea. The average nutrient content is: N – 0.8%, P – 0.5%, K – 0.4%, and a full range of trace elements. Sheep manures contain little water and lots of air. They heat up readily in a compost pile. Cow and pig manures are cold because they hold a lot of water and can be compacted easily, squeezing out the air.

Shrimp & crab wastes contain relatively high levels of phosphorus.

Sulfate of potash is normally produced chemically by treating rock powders with sulfuric acid, but one company, Great Salt Lake Minerals and Chemicals Company, produces a concentrated natural form. The sulfate of potash is extracted from the Great Salt Lake.

Swine manure has a high nutrient content but is slower acting and wetter (more anaerobic) than cow and horse manure. The average nutrient content of pig manure is: N – 0.6%, P – 0.6%, K – 0.4%, and a full range of trace elements.

Wood ashes (hardwood) supply up to 10 percent potash, and softwood ashes contain about 5 percent. Potash leaches rapidly. Collect the ash soon after burning, and store in a dry place. Apply in a mix with other fertilizers at the rate of one-quarter cup per 3-gallon pot (25 cl per 11 L). The potash washes out of the wood ash quickly and can cause compacted, sticky soil. Avoid using alkaline wood ashes in soil with a pH above 6.5.

Worm castings are excreted, digested humus and other (decomposing) organic matter that contain varying amounts of nitrogen as well as many other elements. They are an excellent source of non-burning soluble nitrogen and an excellent soil amendment that promotes fertility and structure. Mix with the potting soil to form a rich, fertile blend. Pure worm castings look like coarse graphite powder and are heavy and dense. Do not add more than 20 percent worm castings to any mix. They are so heavy that root growth can be impaired. Worm castings are very popular and easier to obtain at commercial nurseries.

Note: The nutrients in organic fertilizers may vary greatly depending upon source, age, erosion, climate, etc. For exact nutrient content, consult the vendor's specifications.

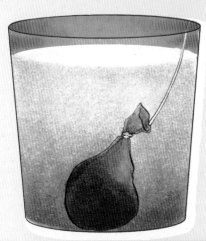

Fill a nylon stocking with sifted, well-rotted compost and soak in a bucket for a few days to make a potent fertilizer and plant elixir.

gal, and high-mycorrhizal teas. Take a look at the super-compost tea makers at www.soil soup.com.

Mixing Fertilizers

Always read the entire label, and follow the directions. To mix, dissolve the powder and the crystals into a little warm water, and make sure it is totally dissolved before adding the balance of the tepid water. This will ensure that the fertilizer and the water mix evenly. Liquid fertilizers can be mixed directly with water.

Containers have very little growing medium in which to hold the nutrients, and toxic salt buildup may become a problem. Follow dosage instructions to the letter. Adding too much fertilizer will not make the plants grow faster. It could change the chemical balance of the soil, supply too much of a nutrient, or lock in other nutrients making them unavailable to the plant.

Fertilizer Application

Some varieties can take high doses of nutrients, and other strains grow best with a minimum of supplemental fertilizer. See the chart at left for recommendations on fertilizing a few varieties. Many fertilizer programs are augmented with different additives that expedite nutrient uptake.

Make super tea by gently agitating and oxygenating the soup. This will supercharge the tea and add 10 to 100 times more microbes than regular compost tea. *The Compost Tea Brewing Manual* by Dr. Elaine R. Ingham of Soil Foodweb, Inc., compares some commercial tea makers, including a bio-blender used in a 5-gallon bucket (19 L), 100- (380 L), and 500-gallon (1900 L) brewers. The book includes recipes for high-bacteria, high-fun-

This ambitious guerrilla grower uses an electric pump to water their plants in Northern California. The pump is wired to the battery in the all-terrain vehicle required to access this remote grow.

Water and fertilize properly and you will be surprised with your results!

To get an idea of which strains need a little or a lot of fertilizer, I asked Alan from Sensi Seeds and Henk from Dutch Passion for their thoughts. To learn the exact best way to fertilize specific strains, you may need to contact the company that sold you the seeds.

Start with an EC of 1.6 and build it up as needed. The absolute maximum EC is 2.3.

Strains which require high doses of fertilizer:

All the *Indicas,* with the possible exception of 'Hindu Kush' (a landrace, with less vigor and not as nutrient-hungry as hybrid Indicas). In this case, 'more fertilizer means using the high end of the recommended dosage, not exceeding it.

'Twilight', 'Green Spirit', 'Khola', 'Hollands Hope', 'Passion#1', 'Shaman' within an EC range of 1.6-2.3

Strains which require medium doses of fertilizer:

'Skunk#1', 'Trance', 'Voodoo', 'Sacra Frasca', 'Cal. Orange', 'Delta 9', 'Skunk Passion', 'Blueberry', 'Durban Poison', 'Purple#1', 'Purple Star', 'Skunk#1', 'Super Haze', 'Ultra Skunk', 'Orange Bud', 'White Widow', 'Power 'Plant', and 'Euforia' within an EC range of 1.6-2.3

Strains which require low doses of fertilizer:

All the *Sativa* hybrids, with the exceptions of 'Silver Pearl', 'Marley's Collie' and 'Fruity Juice' (*Sativa* hybrids, but with a heavy, *Indica*-dominant bud pattern). In this case, less fertilizer means using the low end of the recommended dosage. 'Northern Lights #5 x Haze' has more open buds in growth pattern, but a lot of floral bulk by weight, so may need normal to slightly higher levels of nutrient.

'Isis', 'Flo', 'Dolce Vita', 'Dreamweaver', 'Masterkush', 'Oasis', 'Skywalker' and 'Hempstar' within an EC range of 1.6-2.3. Mazar needs a higher EC during weeks 3 to 5 to prevent early yellowing of the leaves.

Determine if the plants need to be fertilized: make a visual inspection, take an N-P-K soil test, or experiment on test plants. No matter which method is used, remember, plants in small containers use available nutrients quickly and need frequent fertilizing, while plants in large planters have more soil, supply more nutrients, and can go longer between fertilizing.

Visual Inspection - If the plants are growing well and have deep-green, healthy leaves, they are probably getting all necessary nutrients. The moment growth slows or the leaves begin to turn pale green, it is time to fertilize. Do not confuse yellow leaves caused by a lack of light with yellow leaves caused by a nutrient deficiency.

Always use an accurate measuring container.

Pale green leaves signify this plant is low on nitrogen and needs to be fed with an all purpose fertilizer.

GHE
www.eurohydro.com

APPLICATION CHART FLORA-SERIES
For all growing methods : hydroponics and soil
In soil use 1/2 strength and apply every other watering

	18 hours of light			12 hours of light							
Week	1	2	3	4	5	6	7	8	9	10	...
	Cuttings		Veg.	Flowering							
FloraGro*	0,25	0,25	0,5	1,5	1,5	0,5	0,5	0,5	0,5		
FloraMicro*	0,25	0,5	0,5	1	1	1	1	1	1		
FloraBloom*	0,25	0,25	0,5	0,5	0,5	1,5	1,5	1,5	1,5		
Bio Roots	2 ml / 10 l			Roots activator							
Bio Protect*		5			5			5	Immune system activator (Foliar spray, once a week)		
Bio Bloom						2 ml / 10 l			Flowering activator		
Diamond Nectar*			2		Strengthens the root system Improves the plant's general health						
Mineral Magic			Increases the resistance to insects and disease (dosage : see label)								
Ripen						10 last days for faster flowering			4 - 5		

*Dosage in ml/l   Note : week 10 and more : depends on the plant's variety
Adjust your water's pH level regularly.   You will find more details on your labels

General Hydroponics gives growers specific fertilizer and additive instructions for their products.

Taking an N-P-K soil test will reveal exactly how much of each major nutrient is available to the plant. The test kits mix a soil sample with a chemical. After the soil settles, a color reading is taken from the liquid and matched to a color chart. The appropriate percent of fertilizer is then added. This method is exact but more trouble than it is worth.

Experimenting on two or three test plants is the best way to gain experience and develop horticultural skills. Clones are perfect for this type of experiment. Give the test plants some fertilizer, and see if they green up and grow faster. You should notice a change within three to four days. If it is good for one, it should be good for all.

Now, it has been determined that the plants need fertilizer. How much? The answer is simple. Mix the fertilizer as per the instructions and water as normal, or dilute the fertilizer and apply it more often. Many liquid fertilizers are very diluted already. Consider using more concentrated fertilizers whenever possible. Remember,

small plants use much less fertilizer than large ones. Fertilize early in the day, so plants have all day to absorb and process the fertilizer.

It is difficult to explain how often to apply all fertilizers in a few sentences. We know that large plants use more nutrients than small plants. The more often the fertilizer is applied, the less concentrated it should be. Frequency of fertilization and dosage are two of the most widely disagreed upon subjects among growers. Indoor containerized marijuana can be pushed to incredible lengths. Some strains will absorb amazing amounts of fertilizer and grow well. Lots of growers add as much as one tablespoon per gallon (15 ml per 4 L) of Peters™ (20-20-20) with each watering. This works best with growing mediums that drain readily and are easy to leach. Other growers use only rich, organic potting soil. No supplemental fertilizer is applied until a super bloom formula is needed for flowering.

Fertilizing plants in the ground is much easier than fertilizing containerized plants. In the soil

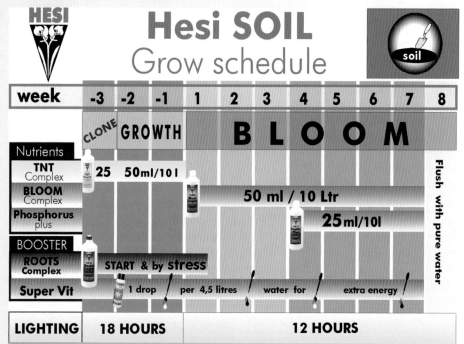

Hesi SOIL
Grow schedule

soil

week	-3	-2	-1	1	2	3	4	5	6	7	8
		CLONE	GROWTH		B	L	O	O	M		

Nutrients

TNT Complex	25	50ml/10 l									
BLOOM Complex					50 ml / 10 Ltr						
Phosphorus plus							25 ml/10l				

Flush with pure water

BOOSTER

| ROOTS Complex | START & by stress | | | | | | | |
| Super Vit | 1 drop | per 4,5 litres | water for | extra energy | | | |

| LIGHTING | 18 HOURS | 12 HOURS |

This Grow Schedule by Hesi details the exact feeding schedule for a super successful crop.

outdoors, roots can find many nutrients, and fertilization is not as critical. There are several ways to apply chemical fertilizer. You can top-dress a garden bed by applying the fertilizer evenly over the entire area. You can side-dress plants by applying the fertilizer around the bases of the plants. You can foliar-feed plants by spray-

This 'Haze' plant is hypersensitive to fertilizer. Leaves curl when given slight overdose.

All leaves in this photo came from the same plant. All leaves show signs of overfertilization.

ing a liquid fertilizer solution on the foliage. The method you choose will depend upon the kind of fertilizer, the needs of the plants, and the convenience of a chosen method.

When using synthetic fertilizers, it is extremely important to read the label carefully, and follow the directions. The initials "WSN" and "WIN" that you may see on the label stand for *water-soluble nitrogen* and *water-insoluble nitrogen*. WSN dissolves readily, and it is considered a fast-release nitrogen source. WIN does not dissolve easily. It is often an organic form of nitrogen and is considered a slow-release nitrogen source.

Use a siphon applicator–found at most nurseries–to mix soluble fertilizers with water. The applicator is simply attached to the faucet with the siphon submerged in the concentrated fertilizer solution with the hose attached to the other end. Often, applicators are set at a ratio of 1 to15. This means that for every 1 unit of liquid concentrate fertilizer, 15 units of water will be mixed with it. Sufficient water flow is necessary for the suction to work properly. Misting nozzles restrict this flow. When the water is turned on, the fertilizer is siphoned into the system and flows out the hose. The fertilizer is generally applied with each watering, since a small percentage of fertilizer is metered in.

A garbage can with a garden-hose fitting attached at the bottom that is set 3-4 feet (90-120 cm) off the floor will act as a gravity-flow source for the fertilizer solution. The container is filled with water and fertilizer.

When it comes to fertilization, experience with specific varieties and growing systems will tell growers more than anything else. There are hundreds of N-P-K mixes, and they all work! When choosing a fertilizer, make sure to read the entire label, and know what the fertilizer claims it can do. Do not be afraid to ask the retail clerk questions or to contact the manufacturer with questions.

Once you have an idea of how often to fertilize, put the garden on a regular feeding schedule. A schedule usually works very well, but it must be combined with a vigilant, caring eye that looks for over-fertilization and signs of nutrient deficiency.

Leach soil with 1-2 gallons (4-8 liters) of mild nutrient solution per gallon of soil every

Spray foliage from underneath so the spray is able to penetrate the stomata located on the leaf's underside.

Leaves and stalks have waxy, cystolith hairs that act like feathers on a duck and shed water.

Stomata close when there is:
Too much CO_2
Low humidity
A dry root system

Stomata open when there is:
High light
Low CO_2
High Humidity

Earth Juice Wetting Agent

month. This is the best form of preventive maintenance against toxic salt buildup in the soil.

Foliar Feeding

Foliar feeding means to spray the nutrients or bio-stimulants onto the foliage to augment available nutrients, vitamins, hormones, etc. Timing is key to achieving the best coverage and absorption. The waxy (cuticle) surface coating (cystolith hairs and resin) on cannabis foliage makes them very poor water absorbers. This barrier wards off pest and disease attacks, but it also slows the penetration of sprays.

Young leaves are more permeable than older leaves. Nutrients and additives penetrate immature leaves faster than tougher, older leaves, and they are easier to damage with strong sprays.

Foliar feed the cannabis plants only when specific deficiency symptoms manifest. Foliar feeding is a quick fix only and is easy to overdo. High levels of nutrients in the foliage stop the roots from taking in more; this is confusing for the plant. Foliar sprays can accumulate and build up in the foliage. Never spray more than once every 10 days, and keep the spray concentration to less than 500 ppm or with an EC of less than 1.0.

Spreader-Stickers

Smart growers use a surfactant, surface-active substance (adjuvant), which enhances the effectiveness of foliar fertilization.

Spreaders (wetting agents) reduce the surface tension of sprays and keep them from beading up and rolling off the foliage. Big, bulbous drops on the leaves mean you need to use a spreader. Flat drops that slide off the foliage mean there is too much spreader. There are nonionic, antionic, and cationic spreaders. The nonionic spreaders that do not ionize in water are the most common, and they do not react with most pesticides. Antionic and cationic spreaders are not used often.

Stickers help the spray adhere to the leaf after spraying, so it does not wash off when it rains or when dew forms. Stickers not only increase adhesion, they slow evaporation, and impart a waterproof coating. Some stickers are spreaders, too. Spreader-stickers allow the stomata on the leaves to be penetrated.

Extender (stabilizing agents) protects applied sprays against the UV radiation and heat that degrade the sprays.

Liquid and powder soaps and detergents act as surfactants, too. But, they are not nearly as effective as horticultural surfactants. Biodegradable surfactants disappear the fastest. Silicone surfactants are also mild insecticides that work to impair pest functions.

Foliar spray concentration is cumulative. Nutrients delivered via the foliage can cause a buildup of salts in and around the leaves. This is similar to the way the salts accumulate in the soil.

Overfertilizing can become one of the biggest problems for indoor growers. Too much fertilizer causes a buildup of the nutrients (salts) to toxic levels, and it changes the soil chemistry. When overfertilized, growth is rapid and lush until the toxic levels are reached. At this point, things become complicated.

Chance of overfertilization is greater in a small amount of soil that can hold only a small amount of nutrients. A large pot or planter can safely hold much more soil and nutrients, but it will take longer to flush if overdone. It is very easy to add too much fertilizer to a small container. Large containers have good nutrient-holding ability.

To treat severely overfertilized plants, leach the soil with two gallons (8 L) of diluted nutrient solution per gallon (4 L) of soil to wash out all excess nutrients. The plant should start new growth and look better in one week. If the problem is severe and the leaves are curled, the soil may need to be leached several times. After the plant appears to have leveled off to normal growth, apply the diluted fertilizer solution.

Additives

Numerous additives or growth supplements have hit the market over the last few years. Generally, additives contain a cocktail of some of the elements listed below. Most of the addi-

tives came from the greenhouse industry or were developed for organic growers. Many of these additives do what they say they will do and work quickly; however, when growing a short eight- to ten-week crop, some of these additives do not have time to work properly if added near the end of the flowering cycle.

The following list will give you an idea of what specific additives are and how they are used.

Abscisic acid (ABA)

Abscisic acid is a naturally occurring hormone that assists plants in adapting to environmental stresses like drought or cold temperatures. During winter, ABA converts leaves into stiff bud

---

How to get the most out of your spray

1) Spray the bottom of the leaves. Spray with a fine mist, and do not create droplets on the leaves. Fine mist is electrically attracted by the foliage. Even young marijuana plants have waxy hairs that impair liquid penetration.

2) Do not spray plants that are hot or when the atmosphere is too dry. Spray in low light, either before the lights go off or just as they are coming on. If spraying in hot conditions, first spray everything with plain water until the temperatures of the room and foliage drop, before applying the real spray. Spraying when the plant foliage is hot causes the spray to crystallize on the surface, and it stops the penetration. Spraying with water 10 minutes afterward often increases the penetration. Mobile nutrients move freely within a plant. Immobile nutrients move slowly, but once deposited, they stay.

3) Apply mobile nutrients sparingly. Immobile nutrients–sulfur, boron, copper, iron, manganese, molybdenum, sulfur, and zinc–often require two or three applications. Calcium and boron are poor candidates for foliar feeding because they translocate poorly. But urea nitrogen applied as a spray in high humidity penetrates almost instantly into leaves. Be careful when spraying urea-based fertilizers, and keep them diluted. Urea also carries other nutrients into the plant and works well for a base to the mix. Foliar feeding should turn the

plant around in less than a week. A second spray could be necessary at week's end to ensure the cure sticks.

4) Boron, calcium, and iron move slowly during flowering. A supplemental foliar dose often speeds the growth when it slows. A foliar spray of potassium can also help flowering, especially if the temperatures dip below 50°F (10°C) or above 80°F (25°C).

5) Always spray new growth. The thin, waxy layer and a few trichomes allow for good penetration.

6) Measure the pH of the spray, and keep it between 7 and 8.5. Potassium phosphate (K_2HPO_4) becomes phytotoxic below pH 4 and above 8.5. Stomata are signaled to close within these pH ranges.

7) Use a surfactant with all sprays, and apply these as per the instructions on the label.

8) Add the proper amount of surfactant so droplets do not form on the leaves. Once formed, the droplets roll off the foliage, rendering it ineffective.

9) Stop the application before the droplets form on the leaves. Make a test spray on a mirror to ensure the spray is even and does not form droplets that roll off the mirror.

10) Spray with as fine a mist as possible to minimize the size of the drop.

Use a spreader/sticker to keep spray droplets from bouncing off foliage.

scales which cover the meristem, protecting it from cold damage or dehydration. In case of an early spring, ABA will also prolong dormancy, preventing premature sprouts which could be damaged by frost.

Used in the garden, ABA may help plants resist drought and unseasonable conditions and improve productivity, strength, and performance.

Ascorbic acid (Vitamin C)

Vitamin C is thought to build tighter, heavier buds and act as an antioxidant. It is often combined with fructose, molasses, or sugar and added to the nutrient solution during the last two weeks before harvest. However, some botanists believe that although vitamin C is very important in fighting the free radical byproducts of photosynthesis, plants make their own vitamin C and are unlikely to recognize any benefit from its addition to the nutrient mix.

Aspirin

Salicylic acid is a naturally occurring plant hormone associated with the Willow. It is effective in preventing pathogens by speeding up the natural "systemic acquired resistance (SAR)" thereby reducing the need for pesticides. Salicylic acid (SA) will block abscisic acid (ABA) allowing the plant to return to normal after a period of stress–something to consider if ABA is being used to strengthen plants.

Aspirin can be used as a spray, a soak, or added to compost and rooting compounds. A 1:10,000 solution used as a spray will stimulate

the SAR response, and the effects will last weeks to months. "Willow water" also makes a popular rooting bath.

Auxins

Auxins represent a group of plant hormones that regulate growth and phototropism. They are associated with elongation of plant cells causing the branches to grow vertically while inhibiting lateral buds. "Pinching off" branch tips will reduce the auxin level and encourage bushy lateral growth as well as inducing new root formation.

Synthetic auxins are more stable and last longer than the natural solutions. They can be used as an herbicide against broadleaf weeds like dandelions, but are most often used to encourage root growth and promote flowering.

Bacteria

Bacteria such as mycorrhizal fungi and rhizobacteria are extremely beneficial in organic gardening. The presence of these organisms in the growing medium produces stronger, healthier plants that require less chemical intervention.

Actino-Iron is a commercial soil additive that contains the Streptomyces *lydicus* microbe. Applied to the soil, the bacterium grows around the root system, protecting it from harmful pathogens while producing anti-fungals. Actino-Iron also contains fulvic acid and iron which feed the plant. For perennials, the effects last one growing season. For annuals, the life of the plant.

B-9 folic acid

There is little literature on the effects of B-9 on plants. It appears to serve in energy transfer within the plant and inhibits the enzyme that makes gibberellic acid resulting in a bushier dwarf-type plant without pruning.

B-9 can be applied as a spray or as a soil drench.

Cellulase

Cellulase is a group of enzymes that act in the root zone to break down organic material which may rot and cause disease. Dead materials are converted into glucose and returned to the substrate to be absorbed by the plant.

It can be used in water gardens to clean up

organic sludge.

Colchicine

Colchicine, an alkaloid, is prepared from the dried corns and seeds of *Colchicum autumnale,* the autumn crocus that also produces saffron. The pale, yellow powder is water soluble.

Colchicine is a *very dangerous, poisonous* compound that can be used to induce polyploid mutations in cannabis. Clandestine breeders started polyploid strains with colchicines, but none of the strains showed any outstanding characteristics, and cannabinoid levels were unaffected.

Rather than explain how to use colchicine, I will advise not to use it. It is very toxic and produces no change in potency. I do not know any seed breeders that use it today.

Cytokinins

Cytokinins are plant hormones derivative of the purine adenine, the most common cytokinin being Zeatin. They are synthesized in the roots promoting cell division, chloroplast development, leaf development, and leaf senescence. As an additive, cytokinins are most often derived from the Seaweed *Ascophyllum nodosum.*

Added to the soil or sprayed on the plants, cytokinins help the plant make more efficient use of existing nutrients and water even in drought conditions. The result is a healthier plant and increased crop. Care must be given to application of cytokinins along with other plant hormones. Many commercial formulas contain a hormone cocktail which includes hormones like auxins and cytokinins that work against one another.

Enzymes

Enzymes are biological protein catalysts that were first crystallized and isolated in 1926. Enzymes accelerate the rates of reactions but do not change themselves as a result of this action. Enzymes are added to fertilizers and growth additives to accelerate biological activity and speed nutrient uptake by roots.

Most enzymatic reactions happen within a temperature range of 85-105°F (30-40°C) and each enzyme has an optimal range of pH for

Without a spreader-sticker, the surfactant sprays often bead up and roll off the foliage which makes them ineffective.

activity. Most enzymes react with only a small group of chemical compounds that are closely related.

More than 1500 different enzymes have been identified. Enzymes are grouped into six main classes and many subclasses.

Ethylene gas

Ethylene gas is a growth regulator hormone that activates the aging and ripening of flowers as well as preventing the development of buds and retarding plant growth. It is most often used by vegetable growers who force ripening of produce heading to market. In gardening, it may be used to trigger flowering in plants.

Flower saver plus

Flower Saver Plus is a commercial product that contains the Mycorrhizae fungus which enters into a symbiotic relationship with the plant by attaching itself to the root system. Mycorrhizal threads enter into root tissue then grow out into the substrate reaching more water and nutrients than the plant could find on its own. In return, the Mycorrhizae receive a protected environment and the sugars they need to thrive.

Use of Mycorrhizae improves root depth, speeds maturation, and helps create resistance to drought and disease. Larger more robust root systems also improve the soil structure promoting better air and water movement.

Flower Saver Plus should be used at planting

time either as a root bath or worked into the top two to four inches of soil. Look for a product that has at least 50 to 100 spores per square foot.

Seek medical attention if ingested. Avoid breathing the dust or spray, and keep out of reach of children.

Fulvic acid

Fulvic acid is a naturally occurring organic substance resulting from the microbial action on decomposing plants. Absorbed into a plant, fulvic acid will remain in the tissues and serve as a powerful antioxidant as well as providing nutrients and acting as a bio-stimulant. Fulvic acid is an excellent source of nutrition for Mycorrhizae.

Growers can create fulvic acid by composting or purchase the product from a retailer. It is available in forms suitable for hydroponics or soil mediums.

Gibberellins

Gibberellic Acid (GA) is a natural plant growth hormone which acts with auxins to break dormancy, stimulate seed germination, and grow long stems.

Gibberellic Acid can be purchased as a commercial product like Mega-Grow and is used to extend the grow season and force larger blooms. For best effect, use GA in complement with fertilizer and mixed into the water supply. Results can be seen in as little as a few weeks.

According to the Material Safety Data Sheet (MSDS), GA is very hazardous to humans, and I do not advise using it; however, the retail advertisements claim the product is safe.

Humic acid

Humic acids are carbons formed by the decomposition of organic substances, primarily that of vegetation. Applied to substrate, it encourages the creation of strong tissue growth and helps in nutrient transport. Plants grow thicker foliage and are more resistant to drought and disease.

Poor soils can be improved by humic acid which enhances the water-holding capability and aeration in sandy soils and frees up nutrients bound in clay. It can be used as a root dip or sprayed directly onto the soil.

Humic acids are extracted from humic substances found in soil. Colors range from yellow (fulvic acid) to brown (humic acid) and black (humin).

Fulvic acid is the fraction of humic substances that is water soluble under all pH conditions. Fulvic acid stays in solution after humic acid dissipates due to acidification.

Humin is the fraction of the soil organic matter that is not dissolved when the soil is treated with dilute alkali.

Hydrogen peroxide

Hydrogen peroxide (H_2O_2) is similar to water but carries an extra, unstable, oxygen molecule which can break down into a reactive atom and either attach itself to another oxygen atom or attack an organic molecule.

Used in horticulture, hydrogen peroxide provides a host of benefits by cleansing water of harmful substances such as spores, dead organic material, and disease-causing organisms while preventing new infections from occurring. It removes the methane and organic sulfates often found in well water as well as removing chlorine from tap water.

Hydrogen peroxide is especially useful in hydroponics, where overwatering can be a problem. It prevents oxygen depletion in the water around the roots, leading to better root growth. A solution of hydrogen peroxide can be used to sterilize seeds resulting in better germination rates.

Hydrogen peroxide is dangerous at high concentrations (35%) and will damage skin, clothing, and most anything it contacts. Lower concentrations like those found at the drug store (3%) will still need to be diluted before use, though they are not as toxic to the gardener.

Indole 3 butyric acid (IBA)

Indole 3 butyric acid is one of the auxin growth hormones. It is most often used as an effective rooting hormone. Application of IBA helps generate roots, build a larger root mass, and improve plant growth and yield.

Many commercial formulas are available in the form of water-soluble salts. Cuttings can be dipped or immersed before planting. Roots can be dipped or sprayed or the soil drenched during transplanting. Once established, plants should be treated at three- to five-week intervals during the growing season. After harvest, IBA can be used to encourage regeneration of flowers.

IBA is hazardous to humans and animals. It can cause moderate eye injury and is harmful if inhaled or absorbed through the skin.

Isopentyl adenine (IPA)

Isopentyl adenine is a naturally occurring cytokinin which is synthetically manufactured as benzylaminopurine (BAP) for use in commercial bio-stimulants such as Rush Foliar XCell Veg and Xcell Bloom.

Xcell Veg acts in the growth stage of the plant by improving the transport of nutrients. Glycine betaine in the solution provides a barrier to environmental stress. The product is used as part of an established feeding program. It can be sprayed on, just before turning off the lights, or used as a soak in the growing medium.

Xcell Bloom also has anti-stress properties and improves nutrient transport. It stimulates flowering, reduces plant growth time, and increases cell division and lateral root growth. Flowers are larger, heavier, and have enhanced color.

Both products can be used in hydroponic or soil mediums.

Rhizobium

Rhizobium is the name given to a group of bacteria which infect the roots of legumes and create nodules that act in symbiosis with the plant. Rhizobia are host-specific and will not work with all crops. With the proper host, however, Rhizobia improve nitrogen fixation while simultaneously providing an additional source of nitrogen.

Rhizobium is most effective when added to irrigation, but it can be added to a drip or directly to the soil. Benefits will depend on proper crop/Rhizobium match. Re-inoculation is recommended every three to five years.

Spray-n-grow

Spray-N-Grow is a brand name vitamin and nutrient solution that includes barium and zinc. It is sprayed on plants to provide micronutrients through the foliage, a technique said to be more effective than root nutrition. Plants will grow faster, bloom earlier and more prolifically, have larger roots, and have a higher vitamin, mineral, and sugar content.

Because it is absorbed through the leaves, Spray-N-Grow works quickly, in as little as seven to thirty days. Tender plants will realize benefits faster than woody plants. Spray-N-Grow can be used in any type of growing medium as a complement to the established feeding regimen. It is non-chemical and safe for people and pets.

Sugar

Molasses, honey, and other sugars are said to increase soil microbials, enhance regrowth, and make the plant's use of nitrogen more effective. Molasses will raise the energy level of the plant and acts as a mild natural fungicide. Molasses is the "secret ingredient" in many organic fertilizers.

Trichoderma (002/003)

Trichoderma are fungi that colonize in the root zone, crowding out negative fungi and microorganisms while stimulating root development and resistance to environmental stress. The result is a more vibrant, stronger plant.

Canna was the first company in the indoor grow industry to sell a commercial product as a growth-promoter which contains Trichoderma fungi. Colorado State University studies indicate that Promot Plus, a product containing Trichoderma, is effective in suppressing pathogenic fungi that cause rot in the seeds, roots, and stems.

The product can be applied to seeds, used during transplanting, mixed with liquid fertilizer or via drip irrigation and/or watered in. Canna's Trichoderma contains living organisms that will reproduce after application, so a small amount will do a lot. It is nontoxic and environmentally safe.

Zeatin

Zeatin is one of the cytokinin growth hormones. Upon germination, zeatin moves from the endosperm to the root tip where it stimulates mitosis.

Adding sugar during the last 6 weeks augmented harvest weight of the bud on the right by 20 percent.

This Swiss hydroponic setup is simple, efficient, and economica.

Introduction

Hydroponics is the science of growing plants without soil, most often in a soilless mix. In fact, many growers are already cultivating hydroponically. Cultivating clones in rockwool, peat moss, and coconut fiber is growing hydroponically. Growing mature plants in soilless Sunshine Mix or Terra-Lite, even when watered by hand, is hydroponic gardening. With hydroponics, nutrient uptake and grow medium oxygen content can be controlled easily. Manage these two factors, along with a few other requirements, to grow a bumper crop of buds with every harvest.

The inert soilless hydroponic medium contains essentially no nutrients. All the nutrients are supplied via the nutrient solution–fertilizer diluted in water. This solution passes over or floods around roots at regular intervals, later draining off. The extra oxygen trapped in the soilless medium and around the roots speeds nutrient uptake by tiny root hairs. Cannabis grows fast hydroponically, because it is able to take in food as fast as it can be used. In soil, as in hydroponics, the roots absorb nutrients and water. Even the best soil rarely has as much oxygen in it as a soilless hydroponic medium.

Contrary to popular belief, hydroponic gardens often require more care than soil gardens. If growing hydroponically, expect to spend more time in the garden. Extra maintenance is necessary because plants grow faster, there are more things to check, and more can go wrong. In fact, some growers do not like hydroponic gardening, because it requires too much additional care.

Hydroponic gardening is productive, but exacting–not as forgiving as soil gardening. Soil works as a buffer for nutrients and holds them longer than inert hydroponic growing mediums. In fact, advanced aeroponic systems do not use a soilless mix; they use nothing at all!

In hydroponics, the nutrient solution can be controlled, so plants grow less leafy foliage and more dense flower buds. The stepped-up nutrient control makes plants flower faster and be ready for harvest a few days earlier than soil-grown cannabis.

Small flowering plants grow well in small hydroponic containers and horizontal tubes. Mother plants grow longer and are best suited to a large bucket system, which allows room for root development. The mother plant's root system is easily contained in the bucket, and she is able to produce

Good looking buds are grown hydroponically in expanded clay pellets, an inert soilless medium. Plants can take in all the nutrients they need.

thousands of clones during her lifetime. Mother plants must have a huge root system to take in lots of nutrients to keep up with the heavy growth and clone production schedule.

Most grow rooms have two limiting factors: the number of plants in the garden and the electrical consumption expressed in watts. For example, if growing 12 large plants in a five-gallon (19 L) bucket hydroponic system, you will need about ten clones and one mother plant. The flowering room could be illuminated with two 600-watt HP sodium lamps. A 40-watt fluorescent fixture could be used to root clones, and a 175-watt metal halide will keep the mother and vegetative plants growing. This is a total of 1415 watts that cost about $35 to $60 monthly. That's a bargain, considering the garden will yield at least a pound (450 gm) of beautiful hydroponic buds every month!

If flowering is induced when clones are six to eight inches (15-20 cm) tall, they will be two to three feet (60-80 cm) tall when they finish flowering. You can pack short plants tightly together in a "sea of green" (SOG) or a "screen of green" (SCROG) to maximize yield. It is easy to grow 60,

four-inch (10 cm) rockwool cubes on a flood and drain table or in three-gallon (11 L) grow bags full of soilless medium. To get the maximum yield, a plant or two is harvested every day or two. When a ripe plant is harvested, two small clones take its place. The weaker clone is culled out after two weeks.

Hydroponic Systems

Hydroponic systems are distinguished by the way the nutrient solution is applied. The first distinction is whether the nutrient solution is applied in an "active" or "passive" manner.

Passive systems rely on capillary action to transfer the nutrient solution from the reservoir to the growing medium. Nutrient solution is passively absorbed by a wick or growing medium and transported to the roots. Absorbent growing mediums such as vermiculite, sawdust, peat moss, etc., are ideal for passive systems. The growing medium can stay very wet in passive systems, and substrate selection is important. Soggy substrates hold less air and deprive roots of rapid nutrient uptake. Although passive gardens are not considered "high

This flood hydroponic garden, fertilized with Bio-Green, uses a soilless mix heavy in coco peat. All nutrients are supplied by the nutrient solution.

Classic wick gardens use cloth wicks that absorb nutrient solution and transport it to the growing medium.

This passive wick system uses a soilless mix heavy in coco peat to wick up the nutrient solution. Such low-tech gardens are very productive.

performance," the Dutch have managed to perfect them and achieve amazing results. Wick systems have no moving parts. Seldom does anything break or malfunction. Low initial cost and low mainte-nance enhance wick systems' popularity.

Dutch growers line the floor of a room with heavy plastic or pond liner. They fill three-gallon (3 L) pots with an absorbent soilless mix that holds plenty of air. They flood the garden with two to three inches (6-9 cm) of nutrient solution. Roots absorb the nutrient solution in two to five days. No nutrient solution is drained off; it is all absorbed by plants!

One Spanish grower uses passive irrigation to water his garden. He drives a delivery truck and is away from home five days a week. He keeps his indoor garden under a 400-watt HPS lamp. The plants are in a rich potting soil, and the pots are in a large tray with four-inch (12 cm) sides. Every Monday morning he fills the tray with mild nutrient solution. When he returns on Friday, the plants are strong and happy!

Active hydroponic systems "actively" move the nutrient solution. Examples of active systems are: flood and drain, and top feed. Cannabis is a fast-growing plant and very well suited to active hydro-ponic systems.

Active hydroponic gardens are considered a "recovery" system if the nutrient solution is recov-ered and reused after irrigation. A "non-recovery" system applies the nutrient solution once, then it runs to waste. The solution is not reused. Non-recovery systems have few complications but are not practical for most cannabis hydroponic gardens. The commercial growers "run-to-waste" systems are avoided, because they pollute ground water with high levels of nitrates, phosphates, and other elements. Indoor growers seldom use non-recovery systems, because they require disposing of so much nutrient solution into the local sewer system.

Active recovery hydroponic systems such as the flood and drain (ebb and flow), top feed, and nutrient film technique (NFT) are the most popular and productive available today. All three systems cycle reused nutrient solution into contact with roots. Recovering and reusing the nutrient solution makes management more complex, but with the proper nutrient solution, schedule, and a little experience, it is easy to manage. Active recovery systems use growing mediums that drain rapidly and hold plenty of air, including: expanded clay, pea gravel, pumice rock, crushed brick, rockwool, and coconut coir.

Ebb and Flow Gardens

Ebb and flow (flood and drain) hydroponic systems are popular because they have proven track records as low maintenance, easy-to-use gardens. Ebb and flow systems are versatile, simple by design, and very efficient. Individual plants in pots or rockwool cubes are set on a special table. The table is a growing bed that can hold one to four inches (3-10 cm) of nutrient solution. Nutrient solution is pumped into the table or growing bed. The rockwool blocks or containers are flooded from the bottom, which pushes the oxygen-poor air out. Once the nutrient solution reaches a set level, an overflow pipe drains the excess to the reservoir. When the pump is turned off and the growing medium drains, it draws new oxygen-rich air into contact with the roots. A maze of drainage gullies in the bottom of the table directs runoff solution back to the catchment tank or reservoir. This cycle is repeated several times a day. Ebb and flow systems are ideal for growing many short plants in a Sea of Green garden.

Nutrient solution is pumped up into the bed via the short flood fixture on the left. The overflow fitting on the right guarantees the nutrient solution will not spill over the top of the table.

Nutrient solution floods the growing bed and drains back into a reservoir in an ebb and flow garden.

Self-leveling legs, similar to those of a washing machine, support this ebb and flow garden bed and ensure all plants receive a level dose of nutrient solution and that it all drains back into the reservoir below.

Flood the table to half to three-quarters the height of the container to ensure even nutrient solution distribution. Avoid lightweight mediums such as perlite that may cause containers to float and fall over.

A large volume of water is necessary to fill the entire table. Make sure the reservoir has enough solution to flood the reservoir and still retain a minimum of 25 percent extra to allow for daily evaporation. Replenish reservoir daily if necessary. Do not let nutrient solution stand in the table for more than a half hour. Submerged roots drown in the depleted oxygen environment.

Flood the table when the medium is about half-full of moisture. Remember, rockwool holds a lot of moisture. Irrigation regimens will need to change substantially when temperatures cool and light is lacking.

Ebb and flow tables or growing beds are designed to let excess water flow freely away from the growing medium and roots. When flooded with an inch (3 cm) or more of nutrient solution, the growing medium wicks up the solution into the freshly aerated medium.

Air Table

Air tables are simple, easy-to-use hydroponic gardens. Seasoned growers and novices love their simplicity and low maintenance. The unique oper-

Nutrient solution can be applied from above and the table serves as a drain.

The grow room is lined with white Visqueen. The grower takes off his shoes to avoid damaging the plastic and to keep the grow show clean.

Growing is easy and efficient in this beautiful Visqueen-lined room.

ating principle is simple, effective, and nearly fail-safe. The nutrient solution is forced up to the growing bed with air pressure generated by an external air pump. The pump can run on ordinary household electrical current or a solar-powered 12-volt system. Once flooded, the nutrient solution stays in the growing bed for a few minutes before it drains back to the reservoir. Constant air pressure during flooding also aerates the growing medium. The sealed, airtight reservoir limits evaporation, which in turn prevents algae growth and keeps the nutrient fresh. The external pump reduces the overall cost of the system and helps prevent electrical accidents. You can use rockwool, coco coir, peat, or a composite growing medium with excellent results. Check out the Terraponic air table at www.fearless gardener.com.

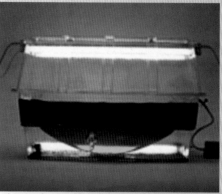

The simple air table design makes them low maintenance. Air is pumped into a reservoir filled with nutrient solution. The air pressure forces the solution up into the growing bed.

Deep Water Culture (DWC)

Growing in deep water culture (DWC) is simple, easy, and productive.

If growing outdoors in a DWC garden, a simple overflow drainage hole can be cut in the side of the reservoir to prevent rainwater from causing it to overflow.

Seedlings and clones are held in net pots full of expanded clay pellets, rockwool or other growing medium. The net pots are nestled in holes in a lid that covers the reservoir. The roots of seedlings and cuttings dangle down into the nutrient solution. A submersible pump lifts nutrient solution to the top of a discharge tube where it splashes into the access lid. Nutrient solution cascades down, wetting roots and splashing into the self-contained reservoir below, which in turn increases dissolved oxygen in the solution. Roots easily absorb nutrients and water from the solution in the oxygenated environment. Many gardens also keep an air stone bubbling new air into the reservoir to supply more oxygen.

These gardens are simple by design and require no timer, because the pumps are on 24 hours a day. This low-maintenance garden is perfect for casual gardeners as well as hydroponic enthusiasts.

This ingenious DWC garden uses an air pump to aerate and agitate the nutrient solution.

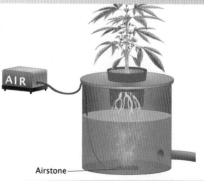

Airstone

Cutaway of the inside of a DWC garden

Various emitters are available to apply nutrient solution. A single application point is common when growing in absorbent growing mediums such as rockwool and coco coir. Expanded clay works best when nutrient solution is applied via a large round emitter, several single emitters, or a spray emitter.

Always use a filter when using emitters. The filter will remove foreign objects that plug emitters.

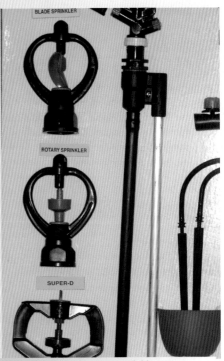

BLADE SPRINKLER

ROTARY SPRINKLER

SUPER-D

Circular emitters apply nutrient solution all the way around the plant, so all roots receive adequate moisture.

Pressure regulated drip emitters control solution flow.

This emitter sprays nutrient solution over the top of the growing medium to aerate and disperse it evenly.

Mini sprinkler emitters are available in many sizes and outputs.

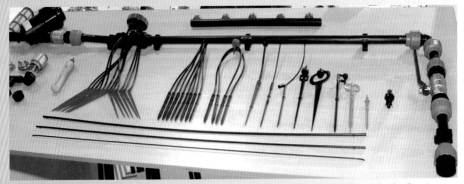

An array of different emitters connected to a main manifold shows the many different kinds of emitters available to hydroponic gardeners. Across the bottom are three different diameters of spaghetti tubes that dispense three different volumes of nutrient solution to plants.

Top-Feed Systems

Top-feed hydroponic systems are very productive, easy to control, precise, easy to maintain, and efficient. The nutrient solution is metered out in specific doses and delivered via spaghetti tubing or an emitter placed at the base of individual plants. Aerated nutrient solution flows into the growing medium and is taken up by roots. The runoff nutrient solution is directed back to the reservoir as soon as it drains from the growing medium. Rockwool, gravel, coconut coir, and expanded clay are the most common growing mediums found in top-feed systems. Versatile top-feed systems can be used with individual containers or slabs in individual beds or lined up on tables.

These top feed buckets filled with hydroclay are all set up and ready to be planted. More hydroclay will be added when clones are transplanted.

Top-feed systems come in many configurations. Systems with several gallons of growing medium are best for growing large plants that may require support. Small containers are perfect for smaller plants.

The grower plants three well-rooted cuttings in each container.

Top-Feed Buckets

Self-contained top-feed buckets consist of a growing container nested inside a reservoir containing a pump. Individual buckets make culling out and replacing a sick plant quick and easy. Self-contained top-feed bucket systems are also perfect for growing large mother plants. The container can be moved anywhere easily. Some containers have a net pot suspended in the lid of a five-gallon (19 L) bucket/reservoir. The roots hang down into the reservoir. An air stone in the bottom of the reservoir aerates the nutrient solution. A separate pump cycles the irrigation to the container. Other self-contained top-feed buckets use a large growing container filled with expanded clay pellets. A pump constantly cycles nutrient solution in the system, aerating the solution and irrigating the plant. Roots grow down into the nutrient solution to form a mass on the bottom. Irrigation from the top circulates aerated nutrient solution and flushes out old oxygen-poor solution. Some systems contain a one-inch (3 cm) pipe to draw air directly down to the root zone. There are many different variations of this system, and they all work!

Other top-feed bucket systems employ **multiple buckets** that are connected to a main reservoir. A flexible drain hose is attached near the bottom of the bucket/reservoir. The hose is connected to a drainage manifold that shuttles runoff nutrient solution back to a central reservoir.

Each reservoir below the growing container holds an inch or two of water. It is important to regularly cycle irrigation in these gardens, so the solution in the bottom of the buckets does not stagnate.

Top-feed buckets can also be lined up on a drainage table. Square containers make most efficient use of space. Plants are fed with irrigation tubing attached to a manifold. Once delivered, the nutrient solution flows and percolates through the growing medium. Roots take in the aerated nutrient solution before it drains onto the tray and back to the reservoir.

Containers are irrigated with spaghetti tubes attached to a manifold that runs between the rows. Excess nutrient solution drains out the bottom and is directed back to the reservoir via a drain tube.

This cutaway of a top-feed bucket system shows how roots dangle in a 100 percent humid environment before growing into the nutrient solution. Remember to screen the drain in the reservoir so roots do not block it.

Individual containers in top-feed bucket systems are easy to arrange to fit into the allotted garden space. Plants can also be transplanted or removed from pots and cared for individually.

Top-Feed Slabs

Top-feed slab systems are popular among small and large indoor and greenhouse growers. Rockwool or coco slabs covered in plastic serve as growing containers. The nutrient solution is delivered via spaghetti tubes from the top of the slab. An emitter attached to the spaghetti tube doses a specific measure of nutrient solution to each plant. The nutrient solution is aerated as it is applied, before being absorbed by the growing medium and draining back to the reservoir.

A simple nutrient solution delivery manifold consists of emitters connected to spaghetti delivery tubes. The tubes are attached to a short manifold that is fed by a pump submerged in a reservoir.

Emitters are designed to be anchored in growing medium and to emit a measured dose of nutrient solution.

Some systems use individual trays to contain slabs. Nutrient solution is pumped from the reservoir and delivered to plants via spaghetti tubes attached to emitters. Individual trays are easy to configure for different sized gardens.

Tables of Slabs

You can also set up a drainage table and place slabs on top. The nutrient solution is pumped from the reservoir below the table and delivered to individual plants via spaghetti tubes attached to emitters. The solution flows into the growing medium where it comes into contact with roots. Excess nutrient solution drains from pots onto the table and is carried back to the reservoir. Make sure the table is set up on an incline so it drains evenly. Pockets of standing water on the table contain less oxygen and promote rot.

Individual Blocks

Individual blocks in this rockwool system allow gardeners the possibility of removing or changing plants if necessary. Nutrient solution is pumped via spaghetti tubes from the reservoir below and distributed via emitters pressed into rockwool cubes.

Vertical Top-Feed Systems

Vertical gardens can increase overall yield more than ten-fold over a flat garden. Substrate bags, tubes, or slabs are positioned vertically around an HID. Short plants are placed in the medium and fed individually with a drip emitter. The runoff drains through the growing medium and back to the reservoir. The solution is re-circulated once it returns to the reservoir.

Use rockwool or coco mixed with lightweight vermiculite as a growing medium to lessen weight when substrate is wet. Irrigate constantly to keep

Nutrient solution from this bat of Canna coco drains into an open trough and is carried back to the reservoir. Salt buildup from the nutrient solution is easy to scrub out of the open trough.

Top-feed slabs of rockwool fit in individual containers. Spaghetti tubes irrigate plants from the top.

This cutaway drawing shows how nutrient delivery is simple and easy with a top-feed bat system. Aerated nutrient solution is metered via emitter onto a grow cube. Aerated solution percolates down through the medium. Channels in the bottom of the tray speed drainage back to the reservoir.

Ebb and flow tables catch nutrient solution runoff and direct it back to the reservoir.

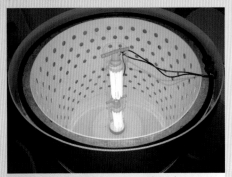

This new vertical garden uses rockwool as a growing medium and compact fluorescent lamps.

roots supplied with water and nutrients from a well-aerated solution.

Vertical hydroponic systems save space, but require more maintenance. These systems can also be tricky to fine-tune so they operate at peak capacity.

Nutrient Film Technique (NFT)

Nutrient Film Technique (NFT) hydroponic systems are high performance gardens that perform well when fine-tuned. This relatively new form of hydroponics supplies aerated nutrient solution to roots located in gullies. Seedlings or cuttings with a strong root system are placed on capillary matting located on the bottom in a covered channel. The capillary matting stabilizes nutrient solution flow and holds roots in place. Constantly aerated nutrient solution flows down the channel, or gully, over and around the roots, and back to the reservoir. Irrigation is most often constant, 24 hours a day. Roots receive plenty of oxygen and are able to absorb a maximum of nutrient solution. Proper gully incline, volume, and flow of nutrient solution are key elements in NFT gardens.

Gullies or channels are covered to keep humidity high in the root zone and light from shining on roots. Root hairs responsible for most water and nutrient uptake cover the growing tips of advancing roots. These roots are submerged in turbulently flowing nutrient solution and the tops are intermittently in humid air. The nutrient solution is constantly aerated as it flows down the inclined gulley.

The slope of the gulley is adequate to prevent water from stagnating. Often a filter is necessary to prevent debris from blocking gullies and pump.

Although high performance, NFT systems offer practically no buffering ability. In the absence of a growing medium, roots must be kept perfectly moist by the nutrient solution at all times. If a pump fails, roots dry and die. If the system dries out for a day or longer, small feeder roots will die and grave consequences will result. The system is very easy to clean and lay out after each crop. Only growers with several years experience should try an NFT system if working alone. With help, they are easier to master.

Double reinforced bottom makes gullies durable and rigid when supporting large plants, root systems, and large volumes of nutrient solution. Some NFT gullies have ribs below to provide support and prevent warping and movement. The ribs also function as drainage channels and direct nutrient solution evenly along the bottom of the gully.

Many NFT systems are hybrids. For example, the nutrient solution in some hybrid NFT systems is delivered via spaghetti tubing to each plant. More irrigation sites help each plant receive proper irrigation. The nutrient solution flows through a small basket of growing medium before it runs down the gulley, over the roots, and back to the reservoir. Yet another hybrid NFT system employs spray nozzles inside the gulley. The nozzles spray nutrient solution on and around roots to keep the root zone environment at 100 percent humidity. The nutrient solution flows down a PVC pipe, over roots, and back to the reservoir.

Too often, these hybrid systems are poorly planned and designed. Many times they are constructed from white four-inch PVC pipe. The thin white walls of the PVC pipe allow enough light to illuminate roots that they turn green or rot more easily. I have also seen systems with nozzles inside the PVC pipe. If a nozzle plugged inside the pipe, there was no easy way to access the nozzle for maintenance.

Nutrient solution is pumped from the reservoir into gullys via a manifold and tubing at the upper end. The table is set up on an incline so the nutrient solution flows quickly over roots to create an environment packed with air and available nutrients. A catchment drain directs the nutrient back into the nutrient reservoir.

Aeroponics

Aeroponic systems use no growing medium and offer the highest performance possible. Roots are suspended in a dark growth chamber without growing medium where they are misted with oxygen-rich nutrient solution at regular intervals. The humidity in the chamber remains at or near 100 percent 24 hours a day. Roots have the maximum potential to absorb nutrient in the presence of air. Humid air and nutrient solution are all that fill the growth chamber. Plants are most often grown in net pots full of growing medium and suspended

Small net pots are preferred for most NFT systems. Larger net pots are used in NFT systems as well as top-feed hydroponic systems.

Nutrient solution in this hybrid NFT system is delivered via nozzles attached to a PVC pipe inside the main growing tubes.

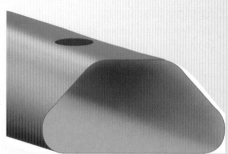

Gullies with rounded corners are very popular in Australia. Growers who use them say the nutrient solution flows more smoothly.

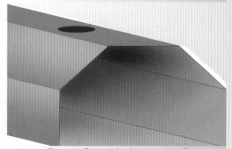

Many gullies are flat on the bottom. Capillary matting is placed on the bottom under the growing cubes. The capillary matting anchors roots and helps direct nutrient solution evenly over roots.

Stagnant nutrient solution and salt buildup stifle root development. Soon roots turn dark and rot. Note burned and discolored leaves that signify salt buildup.

Roots in this NFT system are strong and healthy. This system produced a heavy harvest of buds on robust plants.

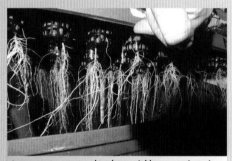

Long root systems develop quickly on cuttings in this Rain Forest aeroponic system.

Rooted clones and seedlings grown in aeroponic systems develop exceptionally fast. To grow clones, simply insert clone stems into the growth chamber and turn it on. The roots will grow in a perfect environment to develop roots.

from the top of the system.

Aeroponic systems require greater attention to detail. There is no growing medium to act as a water/nutrient bank, which makes the system delicate and touchy to use. If the pump fails, roots soon dry, and plants suffer. Systems that use delicate spray nozzles must be kept free of debris. Imbalanced nutrient solution and pH can also cause problems quickly. This is why it is important to purchase quality components or a ready-made system from a qualified supplier.

The RainForest (www.generalhydroponics.com) is very popular. Nutrient solution is actually atomized into the air creating 100 percent humidity. Nutrient solution is dripped onto a spinning plate. The solution atomizes, mixing with the air as it spins off the plate. The spinning plate is located above the water in the reservoir.

Growing Mediums

Soilless growing mediums provide support for the root system, as well as hold and make available oxygen, water, and nutrients. Three factors contribute to cannabis roots' ability to grow in a substrate: texture, pH, and nutrient content, which is measured in EC, electrical conductivity.

The texture of any substrate is governed by the size and physical structure of the particles that constitute it. Proper texture promotes strong root penetration, oxygen retention, nutrient uptake, and drainage. Growing mediums that consist of large particles permit good aeration and drainage. Increased irrigation frequency is necessary to compensate for low water retention. Water- and air-holding ability and root penetration are a function of texture. The smaller the particles, the closer they pack together and the slower they drain. Larger particles drain faster and retain more air.

Irregular shaped substrates such as perlite and some expanded clays have more surface area and hold more water than round soilless mediums. Avoid crushed gravel with sharp edges that cut into roots if the plant falls or is jostled around. Round pea gravel; smooth, washed gravel; and lava rocks are excellent mediums to grow marijuana in an active recovery system. Thoroughly wash clay and rock growing mediums to get out all the dust that will turn to sediment in your system.

Fibrous materials like vermiculite, peat moss, rockwool, and coconut coir retain large amounts of moisture within their cells. Such substrates are ideal for passive hydroponic systems that operate via capillary action.

Mineral growing mediums are inert and do not react with living organisms or chemicals to change the integrity of the nutrient solution. Coconut coir and peat mosses are also inert.

Non-inert growing mediums cause unforeseen problems. For example, gravel from a limestone quarry is full of calcium carbonate, and old concrete is full of lime. When mixed with water, calcium carbonate will raise the pH, and it is very difficult to make it go down. Growing mediums made from reconstituted concrete bleed out so much lime, they soon kill the garden.

Avoid substrates found within a few miles of the ocean or large bodies of salt water. Most likely, such mediums are packed with toxic salts. Rather than washing and leaching salts from the medium, it is easier and more economical to find another source of substrate.

Air is a great medium when it is filled with 100 percent humidity 24 hours a day.

Coconut fiber is an excellent hydroponic medium. See "Coconut Fiber" under soil amendments. Hit the site www.canna.com for detailed information about growing marijuana in coconut fiber.

Expanded clay, also called hydroclay, or hydrocorn, is made by many different manufacturers. The clay pellets are cooked at high temperatures in a kiln until they expand. Many little catacomblike pockets form inside each pellet that holds air and nutrient solution. It is an excellent medium to mix with Peat-Lite and to grow mothers in large containers. I like the way it drains so well and still retains nutrient solution while holding lots of oxygen. Examples of expanded clay include commercially available Hydroton, Leca, Grorox, Geolite.

Some clay pellets will float.

Expanded clay can be reused again and again. Once used, pour expanded clay pellets into a

Coco is compressed into slabs and packaged in plastic. Add water to expand coco to full size.

Coconut fiber is also available in bags.

Expanded clay holds moisture and nutrients along with lots of oxygen.

Artificial foam slabs are used by some growers. To date they are still gaining popularity.

Pumice is a good growing medium. It can also be used as mulch or as an inert soil amendment.

Peat moss mixed with perlite is one of the all-time favorite growing mediums. It is also an excellent soil amendment.

Perlite is sand or volcanic glass expanded by heat. See Chapter Ten for more information.

container and soak in a sterilizing solution of ten milliliters hydrogen peroxide per four liters of water. Soak for 20-30 minutes. Remove expanded clay and place on a screen of hardware cloth. Wash and separate clay pellets from dead roots and dust. Let dry and reuse.

Expanded mica is similar to expanded clay. For lots of exacting information on how and why this stuff works so well, check out www.hydroponics.com.

Foam is somewhat popular. It lasts a long time, lends itself to easy sterilization, and holds a lot of water and air.

Gravel is one of the original hydroponic mediums. Although heavy, gravel is inert, holds plenty of air, drains well, and is inexpensive. Still popular today, gravel is difficult to over-water. It holds moisture, nutrient, and oxygen on its outer surfaces. Use pea gravel or washed river gravel with round edges that do not cut roots when jostled about. Gravel should be 0.125-0.375-inches (3-10 mm) in diameter, with more than half of the medium about 0.25-inch (6 mm) across. Crushed rock can be packed with many salts. Pre-soak and adjust its pH before use. Gravel has low water retention and low buffering ability.

Pumice is a naturally occurring, porous, lightweight, volcanic rock that holds moisture and air in catacomb-like surfaces. Light and easy to work with, some lava rock is so light it floats. Be careful that sharp edges on the rocks do not damage roots. Lava rock is still a good medium and acts similarly to expanded clay. See "Pumice" under "Soil Amendments."

Peat moss is partially decomposed vegetation. Decomposition has been slow in the northern regions where it is found in bogs. There are three common kinds of peat moss–Sphagnum, Hypnum, and Reed/Sedge. Sphagnum peat is about 75 percent fiber with a pH of 3 to 4. Hypnum peat is about 50 percent fiber with a pH of about 6. Reed/sedge peat is about 35 percent fiber with a pH of six or more. For more information see "Soil Amendments" in Chapter Ten.

Perlite drains fast, but it's very light and tends to float when flooded with water. Perlite has no buffering capacity and is best used to aerate soil or soilless mix. See "Soil Amendments" in Chapter Ten.

Rockwool is an exceptional growing medium and a favorite of many growers. It is an inert, sterile, porous, non-degradable growing medium that provides firm root support. Rockwool has the ability to hold water and air for the roots. The roots are able to draw in most of the water stored in the rockwool, but it has no buffering capacity and a high pH. Rockwool is probably the most popular hydroponic growing medium in the world. Popular brand names include Grodan, HydroGro and Vacrok.

Sand is heavy and has no buffering ability. Some sand has a high pH. Make sure to use sharp river sand. Do not use ocean or salty beach sand. Sand drains quickly but still retains moisture. Sand is best used as a soil amendment in volumes of less than ten percent.

Sawdust holds too much water for marijuana growth and is usually too acidic. Be wary of soils with too much wood matter. Such mediums use available nitrogen to decompose the leglin in the wood.

Vermiculite holds a lot of water and is best suited for rooting cuttings when it is mixed with sand or perlite. With excellent buffering qualities, vermiculite holds lots of water and has traces of magnesium (Mg), phosphorus (P), aluminum (Al), and Silicon (Si). Do not use construction grade vermiculite which is treated with phytotoxic chemicals. See "Soil Amendments" in Chapter Ten for more information.

Water alone is a poor medium, because it cannot hold enough oxygen to support plant life. When aerated, water becomes a good growing medium.

Sterilizing

To reuse a growing medium, it must be sterilized to remove destructive pests and diseases. Sterilizing is less expensive and often easier than replacing the growing medium. Sterilizing works best on rigid growing mediums that do not lose their shape such as gravel, expanded clay, and mica. Avoid sterilizing and reusing substrates that compact and lose structure such as rockwool, coconut coir, peat moss, perlite, and vermiculite. Avoid problems caused by compaction and dead roots by replacing used growing mediums. Once sterilized, the medium is free of harmful microorganisms including bacteria and fungi, plus pests and their eggs.

Remove roots from the growing medium before sterilizing. A three- to four-month-old marijuana plant has a root mass about the size of an old desk telephone. Separate the medium by shaking and pulling roots away. Bounce the medium on

Rockwool cubes hold plenty of air and nutrient solution within their fiber; plus, they are clean and easy to use.

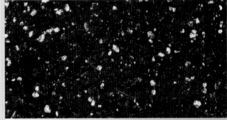
Soilless grow medium.

Vermiculite holds a lot of nutrient solution.

This chart shows the porosity and air space available in different substrates.		
	Substrate Porosity	Air Space
Coconut fiber	90%	10%
Peat/Vermiculite	88%	9%
Peat/Perlite	78%	15%
Peat/Rockwool	88%	14%
Peat moss	90%	15%
Perlite	68%	30%
Rockwool	90%	20%
Sand	38%	3%
Vermiculite	80%	10%

Remove harvested plant root balls from the growing medium, and remove roots and stems.

Wash substrate with plenty of fresh water to remove built-up salts and dead roots.

a screen so roots come to the top. Scoop up and remove roots by hand. Fewer decaying roots cause fewer pest and disease problems, and decrease incidence of clogged feeder tubes.

Substrate can also be washed in a large container such as a barrel or bathtub. Washing works best with lighter substrates such as expanded clay or mica. Roots float to the top and are readily skimmed off with a screen or by hand.

Once roots are removed, soak the substrate in a sterilant such as a five percent laundry bleach (calcium or sodium hypochlorite) solution for at least an hour. Or mix hydrochloric acid, the kind used in hot tubs and swimming pools. Pour, drain, or pump off the sterilant, and flush the medium with plenty of fresh water. A bathtub and a shower nozzle on a hose are perfect for washing substrate. Place the substrate in the bathtub, set a screen over the drain, and use the showerhead or a hose to wash down the medium. It may be necessary to fill the tub with fresh water and drain it a couple of times to rinse any residual sterilants from the substrate.

If you decide to use rockwool or coco a second time, you may have problems with pests and diseases. In general, I recommend reusing a medium only if it does not deteriorate or compact. Examples include: pea gravel, expanded clay, lava rock, sand, etc. Once used indoors, reuse rockwool and biodegradable coco in the outdoor garden.

To sterilize a hydroponic garden, remove the nutrient solution from the reservoir. Pump the solution into the outdoor garden. Avoid pumping it down household drains, and definitely do not pump it into a septic tank. The nutrients will disrupt the chemistry!

Flood the growing medium with the sterilizing solution for at least one-half hour, let drain, and flush again. Pump the bleach solution out of the system and down the drain. Do not dump sterilants outdoors; they will defoliate plants where they are dumped. Use lots of fresh water to leach and flush the entire system including beds, connecting hoses, drains, and reservoir. Make sure all residues are gone by flushing entire system twice for a half-hour. Remove all solution from the tank, and scrub

Buy pH Up and pH Down rather than making your own from concentrated acids. Commercial mixes are buffered and safe to use.

Adjust nutrient
solution
pH level up
with:

pH Up
Potassium hydroxide
Do not use
dangerous and
caustic
sodium hydroxide
to raise pH.

Adjust nutrient
solution
pH level down
with:

pH Down
Nitric acid
Phosphoric
acid
Citric acid
Vinegar

rockwool outside on a sheet of black plastic, and cover with black plastic. Let the sun bake the layer of slabs, or flock, for several days. The temperatures in the rockwool will climb to 140°F (60°C) or more, enough to sterilize for most all harmful diseases and pests.

pH

The pH of the nutrient solution controls the availability of ions that cannabis needs to assimilate. Marijuana grows well hydroponically within a pH range of 5.5-6.5, with 5.8-6.0 being ideal. The pH in hydroponic gardens requires a somewhat vigilant eye. In hydroponics, the nutrients are in solution and more available than when in soil. The pH of the solution can fluctuate a half point and not cause any problems.

Roots take in nutrients at different rates, which causes the ratios of nutrients in solution to change the pH. When the pH is above 7 or below 5.5, some nutrients are not absorbed as fast as possible. Check the pH every day or two to make sure it is at or near the perfect level.

Deviations in pH levels often affect element solubility. Values change slightly with different plants, grow mediums, and hydro-

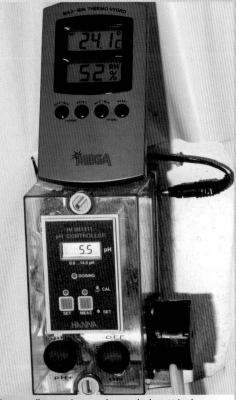

This controller monitors and controls the pH in the reservoir by dispersing pH Up or pH Down. The separate thermometer/hygrometer on top of the controller in the photo monitors ambient temperature and humidity.

Follow manufacturer's guidelines for pH level, and correct the pH using the manufacturer's suggested chemicals, because they will react best with their fertilizer.

The pH can easily fluctuate up and down one full point in hydroponic systems and cause little or no problem with nutrient uptake.

Follow the directions on the container, and remember to mix adjusters into the reservoir slowly and completely. Fertilizers are normally acidic and lower the pH of the nutrient solution. But nutrient solution is still taken in by plants, and water transpires and evaporates into the air, which causes the pH to climb.

Stabilize the pH of the water before adding fertilizer.

Make a correction if readings vary ± one-half point.

ABOVE LEFT: The probe of this meter is submerged in the nutrient solution to monitor pH 24 hours a day.

ABOVE RIGHT: Constant readout, temperature-compensated EC/ppm meters with a probe immersed in the nutrient tank provide round-the-clock intelligence.

RIGHT: This quick-dip Thruegeon measures EC quickly and efficiently. It was one of the first accurate, economical EC meters that was easy to use.

EC = Electrical Conductivity
CF = Conductivity Factor
PPM = Parts Per Million
TDS = Total Dissolved Solids
DS = Dissolved Solids

EC, TDS, DS, CF, PPM
EC METERS

Pure distilled water has no resistance and conducts little electrical current. When impurities are added to pure distilled water in the form of fertilizer salts, it conducts more electricity. A water analysis will indicate the impurities or dissolved solids found in household tap water. These impurities conduct electricity.

Nutrient (salt) concentrations are measured by their ability to conduct electricity through a solution. Dissolved ionic salts create electrical current in solution. The main constituent of hydroponic solutions is ionic salts. Several scales are currently used to measure how much electricity is conducted by nutrients including: Electrical Conductivity (EC), Conductivity Factor (CF), Parts Per Million (ppm), Total Dissolved Solids (TDS), and Dissolved Solids (DS). Most American growers use ppm to measure overall fertilizer concentration. European, Australian, and New Zealand growers use EC, however they still use CF in parts of Australia and New Zealand. Parts per million is not as accurate or consistent as EC to measure nutrient solution strength.

The difference between EC, CF, ppm, TDS, and DS is more complex than originally meets the eye.

Different measurement systems all use the same base, but interpret the information differently. Let's start with EC, the most accurate and consistent scale.

Electrical conductivity is measured in milliSiemens per centimeter (mS/cm) or microSiemens per centimeter (µS/cm). One microSiemen/cm = 1000 milliSiemens/cm.

Parts per million testers actually measure in EC and convert to ppm. Unfortunately, the two scales (EC and ppm) are not directly related. Each nutrient or salt gives a different electronic discharge reading. To overcome this obstacle, an arbitrary standard was implemented which assumes "a specific EC equates to a specific amount of nutrient solution." Consequently, the ppm reading is not precise; it is only an approximation, a ball park figure! It gets more complex! Nutrient tester manufacturers use different standards to convert from EC to the ppm reading.

Every salt in a multi-element solution has a different conductivity factor. Pure water will not conduct electrical current, but when elemental salts/metals are added, electrical conductivity increases proportionately. Simple electronic meters measure this value and interpret it as total dissolved solids (TDS). Nutrient solutions used to grow marijuana generally range between 500 and 2000 ppm. If the solution concentration is too high, the internal osmotic systems can reverse and actually dehydrate the plant. In general, try to maintain a moderate value of approximately 800 to 1200 ppm.

Nutrient solution concentration levels are affected by nutrient absorption by roots and by water evaporation. The solution weakens as plants use nutrients, but water also evaporates from the solution, which increases the nutrient concentration. Adjust the concentration of the solution by adding fertilizer or diluting with more water.

Many factors can alter the EC balance of a solution. For example, if under-watered or allowed to dry completely, the EC reading will rise. In fact, the EC may increase to two- or three-times as high as the input solution when too little water is applied to rockwool. This increase in slab EC causes some nutrients to build up faster than others. When the EC doubles, the amount of sodium can increase

as much as four- to six-fold under the right conditions! There should not be any sodium present in your garden unless it is in the water supply, and it should not be in excess of 50 ppm.

Let 10-20 percent of the nutrient solution drain from the growing medium after each irrigation cycle to help maintain EC stability. The runoff carries away any excess fertilizer salt buildup in the growing medium.

If the EC level of a solution is too high, increase the amount of runoff you create with each flush. Instead of a 10-20 percent runoff, flush so 20-30 percent of the solution runs off. To raise the EC, add more fertilizer to the solution, or change the nutrient solution.

A dissolved solids (DS) measurement indicates how many parts per million (ppm) of dissolved solids exist in a solution. A reading of 1800 ppm means there are 1800 parts of nutrient in one million parts solution, or 1800/1,000,000.

An EC meter measures the overall volume or strength of elements in water or solution. A digital LCD screen displays the reading or the EC of the electrical current flowing between the two elec-

---

Parts per million meters measure the overall level of dissolved solids or fertilizer salts. Each fertilizer salt conducts different quantities of electricity. Use a calibrating solution that imitates the fertilizer in the nutrient solution to calibrate ppm or EC meters. Using such a solution ensures the meter readings will be as accurate as possible. For example, 90 percent of ammonium nitrate dissolved in water is measured, and a mere 40 percent of the magnesium is measured! Do not use sodium-based calibration solutions. They are intended for other applications than gardening. Purchase calibrating solution from the manufacturer or retailer when you buy the meter. Ask for a stable calibrating solution that mimics your fertilizer. Calibrate EC and ppm meters regularly. A good combination ppm, EC, pH meter that compensates for temperature costs about $200 and is well worth the money. Batteries last a long time, too.

1. Hanna   1 mS/cm = 500 ppm
2. Eutech   1 mS/cm = 640 ppm
3. New Zealand Hydro. 1 mS/cm = 700 ppm

Parts per million recommendations are inaccurate and confusing. To help you through this confusion, an Australian friend compiled the following easy reference conversion chart.

1 mS/cm = 10 CF e.g. 0.7 EC = 7 CF

Conversion scale from ppm to CF and EC.

EC mS/cm	Hanna 0.5ppm	Eutech 0.64ppm	Truncheon 0.70ppm	CF 0
0.1	50	64	70	01
0.2	100	128	140	02
0.3	150	192	210	03
0.4	200	56	280	04
0.5	250	320	350	05
0.6	300	384	420	06
0.7	350	448	490	07
0.8	400	512	560	08
0.9	450	576	630	09
1.0	500	640	700	10
1.1	550	704	770	11
1.2	600	768	840	12
1.3	650	832	910	13
1.4	700	896	980	14
1.5	750	960	1050	15
1.6	800	1024	1120	16
1.7	850	1088	1190	17
1.8	900	1152	1260	18
1.9	950	1260	1330	19
2.0	1000	1280	1400	20
2.1	1050	1344	1470	21
2.2	1100	1408	1540	22
2.3	1150	1472	1610	23
2.4	1200	1536	1680	24
2.5	1250	1600	1750	25
2.6	1300	1664	1820	26
2.7	1350	1728	1890	27
2.8	1400	1792	1960	28
2.9	1450	1856	2030	29
3.0	1500	1920	2100	30
3.1	1550	1984	2170	31
3.2	1600	2048	2240	32

trodes. Pure rainwater has an EC close to zero. Check the pH and EC of rainwater to find out if it is acidic (acid rain) before using it.

Distilled bottled water from the grocery store often registers a small amount of electrical resistance, because it is not perfectly pure. Pure water with no resistance is very difficult to obtain and not necessary for a hydroponic nutrient solution.

Electrical conductivity measurement is temperature-sensitive and must be factored into the EC reading to retain accuracy. High-quality meters have automatic and manual temperature adjustments. Calibrating an EC meter is similar to calibrating a pH meter. Simply follow manufacturer's instructions. For an accurate reading, make sure your nutrient solution and stock solution are the same temperature.

Inexpensive meters last for about a year, and expensive meters can last for many years. However, the life of most EC meters, regardless of cost, is contingent upon regular maintenance. The probes must be kept moist and clean at all times. This is the most important part of keeping the meter in good repair. Read instructions on care and maintenance. Watch for corrosion buildup on the probes of your meter. When the probes are corroded, readings will not be accurate.

To check the EC of the nutrient solution, collect samples from both the reservoir and the growing medium. Save time and effort; collect EC and pH samples simultaneously. Collect samples with a syringe or baster at least two inches deep into the rockwool and coco. Collect separate sample from the reservoir. Place each sample in a clean jar. Use calibrated EC meter to measure the samples. Under normal conditions, the EC in the slab should be a little higher than the nutrient solution in the reservoir. If the EC of the solution drawn from the growing medium is substantially higher than the one from the reservoir, there is a salt buildup in the substrate. Correct the imbalance by flushing substrate thoroughly with diluted nutrient solution, and replace with new solution. Regularly check the EC of your water, slab, and runoff.

Hydroponic Nutrients

High quality hydroponic formulations are soluble, contain all the necessary nutrients, and leave no impure residues in the bottom of the reservoir. Always use the best hydroponic fertilizer you can find. There are many excellent commercial hydroponic fertilizers that contain all the nutrients in a balanced form to grow great cannabis. Quality hydroponic fertilizers packed in one, two, or three-part formulas have all the necessary macro- and micronutrients for rapid nutrient assimilation and growth. Cheap fertilizers contain low-quality, impure components that leave residue and sediments. These impurities build up readily and cause extra maintenance. High-quality, soluble hydroponic nutrients properly applied are immediately available for uptake. Exact control is much easier when using pure high-grade nutrients. Many companies use food-grade nutrients to manufacture their fertilizer formulations.

Nutrients are necessary for marijuana to grow and flourish. These nutrients must be broken down chemically within the plant, regardless of origin. The nutrients could be derived from a natural organic base which was not heated or processed to change form, or they could be simple chemical elements and compounds. When properly applied, each type of fertilizer, organic or chemical, theoretically produces the same results.

For a complete background on nutrients and fertilizers, see Chapter Eleven, "Water and Nutrients." Many of the same principles that apply to soil apply to the hydroponic medium.

To remove roots and sterilize the growing medium:

1. Manually remove the mat of roots that are entwined near the bottom of the bed, and shake loose any attached growing medium. It may be easier to add more medium than to pick it from between the matted roots

2. Pour growing mediums such as expanded clay and gravel through a screen placed over a large bucket. Most of the roots will stay on the screen.

3. Lay growing medium out on the floor, and train an oscillating fan on it to dry out remaining roots.

Nutrient Solutions

To avoid nutrient problems, change the nutrient solution in the reservoir every week. Change nutrient solution every two weeks in systems with a large reservoir. Change the nutrient solution more often when plants are in the last stages of flowering, because they use more nutrients. You can wait to change the nutrient solution, but imbalances are more common. Plants absorb nutrients at different rates, and some of them run out before others, which can cause more complex problems. The best form of preventive maintenance is to change the solution often. Skimping on fertilizer can cause stunted growth. Nutrient imbalances also cause the pH to fluctuate, usually to drop. Nutrients used at different rates create an imbalanced formulation. Avert problems by using pure nutrients and thoroughly flushing the soilless medium with fresh tepid water between nutrient solutions.

Hydroponics gives the means to supply the maximum amount of nutrients a plant needs, but it can also starve them to death or rapidly over-fertilize them. Remember, hydroponic systems are designed for high performance. If one thing malfunctions, say the electricity goes off, the pump breaks, the drain gets clogged with roots, or there is a rapid fluctuation in the pH, major problems could result in the garden. A mistake could kill or stunt plants so badly that they do not have time to recover before harvest.

Here is one of the many popular brands of liquid hydroponic fertilizer.

Solution Maintenance

Plants use so much water that nutrient solutions need to be replenished regularly. Water is used at a much faster rate than nutrients. Casually "topping off" the reservoir with pH-balanced water will keep the solution relatively balanced for a week or two. Some growers top off the nutrient solution with 500-700 ppm-strength nutrient solution every two to three days. Never let the nutrient solution go for more than four weeks before draining it and adding fresh solution. Smart growers leach the entire system with weak nutrient solution for an hour or more between changing the reservoir. Wipe down the entire system with the solution.

Do not flush with plain water. Flushing with mild (quarter-strength) nutrient solution will actually remove more excess fertilizer than plain water.

Check EC of reservoir, growing medium, and run-off nutrient solution at the same time every day.

Use an electronic EC pen to monitor the level of dissolved solids in the solution. Occasionally you will need to add more fertilizer concentrate to maintain the EC level in the reservoir during the "topping off" times. Keep the reservoir full at all times. The smaller the reservoir, the more rapid the depletion and the more critical it is to keep it full. Smaller reservoirs should be refilled daily.

Nutrient Solution Composition
The chart is a guideline of satisfactory nutrient limits expressed in ppm. Do not deviate too far from these ranges to avert nutrient deficiencies and excesses.

ELEMENT	Limits	Average
Nitrogen	150-1000	250
Calcium	100-500	200
Magnesium	50-100	75
Phosphorus	50-100	80
Potassium	100-400	300
Sulfur	200-1000	400
Copper	0.1-0.5	0.05
Boron	0.5-5.0	1.0
Iron	2.0-10	5.0
Manganese	0.5-5.0	2.0
Molybdenum	0.01-0.05	0.02
Zinc	0.5-1.0	0.5

Hydro-Organic

Hydro-Organic is a means of growing cannabis in an inert soilless medium and feeding with a soluble organic nutrient solution. Organic fertilizers are most often defined as containing substances with a carbon molecule or a natural unaltered substance such as ground-up rocks.

Dedicated growers spend the time and trouble it takes to grow hydro-organically, because the natural nutrients bring out a sweet organic taste in buds. Indoor and outdoor crops grown in less than 90 days do not have time to wait for organic nutrients to be broken down. Organic nutrients must be soluble and readily available for short cannabis crops to benefit.

An exact balance of organic nutrients can be achieved with constant experimentation and attention to details. Even when you buy ready-mixed commercial fertilizers like BioCanna, Earth Juice, or Fox Farm, you will need to try different feeding amounts and schedules to get the exact combination to grow top-quality bud.

Taking an accurate EC reading or mixing the exact amount of a specific nutrient is very difficult in organic hydroponics. Chemical fertilizers are easy to measure out and apply. It is easy to give plants the specific amount of fertilizer they need in each stage of growth.

Organic nutrients have a complex structure, and measuring content is difficult. Organics are difficult to keep stable, too. Some manufacturers, including BioCanna, Earth Juice, and Fox Farm, have managed to stabilize their fertilizers. When buying organic nutrients, always buy from the same supplier, and find out as much as possible about the source from which the fertilizers were derived.

Combine premixed soluble organic fertilizers with other organic ingredients to make your own blend. Growers experiment to find the perfect mix for their system and the varieties they are growing. Adding too much fertilizer can toxify soil and bind up nutrients, making them unavailable. Foliage and roots burn when the condition is severe.

Soluble organic fertilizers are fairly easy to flush from the growing medium. Like chemical fertilizers, organic fertilizers build to toxic levels easily. Look for the same symptoms as in soil–burned leaf tips, discolored misshapen leaves, brittle leaves, etc. Organic nutrients require heavier flushing. Rinse medium with three gallons of water for every gallon of medium. Some growers flush with plain water the last two weeks of flowering to get all fertilizer taste out of buds.

Mix seaweed with macronutrients and secondary nutrients to make a hydro-organic fertilizer. The amount of primary and secondary nutrients is not as important as the menagerie of trace elements that are in an available form in the seaweed. Major nutrients can be applied via soluble fish emulsion for nitrogen; phosphorous and potassium are supplied by bat guano, bone meal, and manures. More and more organic growers are adding growth stimulators such as humic acid, trichoderma bacteria, and hormones.

Reservoirs

Nutrient solution reservoirs should be as big as possible and have a lid to lessen evaporation. Gardens use from 5-25 percent of the nutrient solution every day. A big volume of nutrient solution will minimize nutrient imbalances. When the water is used, the concentration of elements in the solution increases; there is less water in the solution and nearly the same amount of nutrients. Add water as soon as the solution level drops. The reservoir should contain at least 25 percent more nutrient solution than it takes to fill the beds to compensate for daily use and evaporation. The greater the volume of nutrient solution, the more forgiving the system and the easier it is to control. Forgetting to replenish the water supply and/or nutrient solution could result in crop failure.

Check the level of the reservoir daily, and replenish if necessary. A reservoir that loses more than 20 percent of its volume daily can be topped off with pure or low (500 ppm) EC water. Sophisticated systems have a float valve that controls the level of water in the reservoir.

If your reservoir does not have graduated measurements to denote liquid volume, use an indelible marker to make a full line and the number of gallons or liters contained at that point on the inside of the reservoir tank. Use this volume measure when mixing nutrients.

The pump should be set up to lift the solution out of the reservoir. Set reservoirs high enough so spent nutrient solution can be siphoned or gravity-flow into a drain or the outdoor garden.

Reservoir Temperature

The temperature of the nutrient solution should stay between 60-75°F (15-24°C). However, nutri-

Soluble Salts Range Chart

Electrical conductivity (EC) as milliSiemen (mS) and total dissolved solids (TDS) as parts per million (ppm)

RANGE

DESIRABLE	PERMISSIBLE	PROBABLE SALT DAMAGE
(but potential for concern)		
EC as mS		
0.75 to 2.0	2.0 to 3.0	3.0 and up TDS as ppm
500 to 1300	1300 to 2000	2000 and up

For nutrient solution determinations, one (1) mS (milliSiemen) or one mMho/cm^2 is equivalent to approximately 650 ppm total dissolved solids.

This innovative reservoir was made by lining a large galvanized pipe with heavy-duty plastic.

Cover reservoirs to avoid extra evaporation, and to prevent contamination and algae growth.

A float valve will turn water on to fill the reservoir when the level drops.

Nutrient solution is aerated by falling through the air when it returns to the reservoir.

A two-part nutrient solution is mixed before application. Each reservoir holds one part of the solution.

Attach a recirculating pipe with an on/off valve to the pump outlet pipe. This is a convenient and easy-to-control method of aerating the nutrient solution.

ent solution will hold much more oxygen at 60°F (15°C) than it will at 75°F (24°C). Never let the nutrient solution temperature climb above 85°F (29°C). Above 85°F (29°C), the solution holds little oxygen. Roots are easily damaged by temperatures 85°F (29°C) and above. Heat-damaged roots are very susceptible to rot, wilts, and fungus gnat attacks.

To save energy and money, heat the nutrient solution instead of the air in a room. Heat the nutrient solution with a submersible aquarium heater or grounded propagation heating cables. The heaters might take a day or longer to raise the temperature of a large volume of solution. Do not leave heaters in an empty reservoir. They will soon overheat and burn out. Aquarium heaters seldom have ground wires, a seemingly obvious oversight. But I have yet to learn of an electrocution by aquarium heater. Avoid submersible heaters that give off harmful residues.

Large non-submersible pumps quickly and efficiently move considerable volumes of nutrient solution.

When air is cooler than water, moisture rapidly evaporates into the air; the greater the temperature differential, the higher the relative humidity. Maintaining the nutrient solution temperature around 60°F (15°C) will help control transpiration and humidity. It will also promote the uptake of nutrients.

An air pump submerged in the reservoir not only aerates the solution, it will help level out the temperature differential between ambient air and reservoir.

A removable foam filter on the intake of this submersible pump removes particles that could clog the impeller and feeder tubes.

Irrigation

Irrigation is a science unto itself. Irrigation cycles depend on plant size, climate conditions, and the type of medium used. Large, round, smooth particles of substrate drain rapidly and need to be irrigated more often–four to twelve times daily for five- to thirty-minute cycles. Fibrous mediums with irregular surfaces, such as vermiculite, drain slowly and require less frequent watering, often just once per day. The water comes to within one-half inch (1.5 cm) of the top of the gravel and should completely drain out of the medium after each watering. Top-feed systems cycle for about five minutes

A handle and stand on this pump make it easy to move and mount into a fixed position.

or longer and should be irrigated at least three times daily. Often growers cycle the nutrient solution 24 hours a day, especially when growing in fast-draining expanded clay or similar mediums.

In fast-draining mediums, overhead irrigation

Reservoir

Reservoir temperature range

Use an aquarium heater to warm cold reservoirs. Do not let the reservoir dry out when the heater is on or it will burn out.

is continual. Drip irrigation in coco coir is four or five times daily. Flood and drain irrigation cycles are five to ten times daily.

During and soon after irrigation, the nutrient content of the bed and the reservoir are the same concentration. As time passes between irrigations, the EC and the pH gradually change. If enough time passes between irrigations, the nutrient concentration might change so much that the plant is not able to draw it in.

There are many variations on how often to water. Experimentation will tell you more than anything else.

Nutrient Disorders

When the hydroponic garden is on a regular maintenance schedule, and the grower knows the crop well, nutrient problems are usually averted. If nutrient deficiency or excess affects more than a few plants, check the irrigation fittings to ensure nutrient-challenged plants are receiving a full dose of nutrient solution. Next, check the substrate around affected plants to ensure nutrient solution is penetrating entire medium and all roots are wet. Check the root zone to ensure roots have not plugged drainage conduits and are not standing in stagnant solution.

Change the nutrient solution if there is a good flow of nutrient solution through the root zone, but plants still appear sickly. Make sure the pH of the water is within the acceptable 5.5-6.5 range before adding new nutrients.

If changing solution does not solve the problem, changing to a new brand of fertilizer may do the trick. Check out the color drawings of specific nutrient deficiencies and excesses in Chapter Eleven to determine the exact problem, and add 10 to 20 percent more of the deficient nutrient in a chelated form until the disorder has disappeared. Leach growing medium with dilute nutrient solution to solve simple overdose nutrient problems.

Hydroponic gardens have no soil to buffer the uptake of nutrients. This causes nutrient disorders to manifest as discolored foliage, slow growth, spotting, etc., at a rapid rate. Novice gardeners must learn how to recognize nutrient problems in their early stages to avoid serious problems that cost valuable time for plants to recoup. Treatment for a nutrient deficiency or excess must be rapid and certain. But once treated, plants take several days to respond to the remedy. For a fast fix, foliar feed plants. See "Foliar Feeding" in Chapter Eleven.

Nutrient deficiency or excess diagnosis becomes difficult when two or more elements are deficient or in excess at the same time. Symptoms might not point directly at the cause. Solve mind-bending unknown nutrient deficiency syndromes by changing the nutrient solution. Plants do not always need an accurate diagnosis when the nutrient solution is changed.

Over-fertilization, once diagnosed, is easy to remedy. Drain the nutrient solution. Flush the system at least twice with fresh dilute (5-10 percent) nutrient solution to remove any lingering sediment and salt buildup in the reservoir. Replace with properly mixed solution.

Nutrient disorders most often affect a strain at the same time when it is receiving the same

A handle and stand on this pump make it easy to move and mount into a fixed position.

nutrient solution. Different varieties often react differently to the same nutrient solution. Do not confuse other problems–wind burn, lack of light, temperature stress, fungi and pest damage–with nutrient deficiencies. Such problems usually appear on individual plants that are most affected. For example, foliage next to a heat vent might show signs of heat scorch, while the rest of the garden looks healthy. Or a plant on the edge of the garden would be small and leggy because it receives less light.

Here are some guidelines:

1. Water when plants are half-empty of water; weigh pots to tell.
2. Water soil gardens when soil is dry one-half inch (1.5 cm) below the surface.
3. Water soil gardens with a mild nutrient solution and let 10-20 percent drain off at each watering.
4. Do not let soil dry out to the point that plants wilt.

Top feed buckets.

Ebb and flow tables can be the length of a greenhouse. Long tables take a long time to flood and require a huge reservoir of nutrient solution.

Big beautiful buds grow super dense on tables.

Chapter THIRTEEN

A carbon filter and ozone exchange box dominate the landscape in this Dutch grow room.

Introduction

Fresh air is essential in all gardens. Indoors, it could be the difference between success and failure. Outdoor air is abundant and packed with carbon dioxide (CO_2) necessary for plant

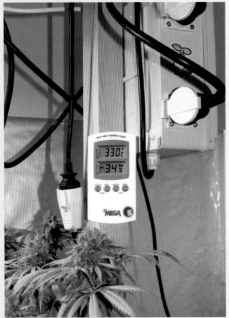

Monitor temperature and humidity regularly. The 86°F (33°C) 34 percent relative humidity conditions make plants use more water and less fertilizer. Adjust irrigation schedule to meet needs.

Smoke is immediately sucked out of the room when using this inline fan. The fan demonstration took place at the 2000 CannaBusiness trade show in Germany.

life. For example, the level of CO_2 in the air over a field of rapidly growing cannabis could be only a third of normal on a very still day. Wind blows in fresh CO_2-rich air. Rain washes air and plants of dust and pollutants. The outdoor environment is often harsh and unpredictable, but there is always fresh air. Indoor gardens must be meticulously controlled to replicate the outdoor atmosphere.

Carbon dioxide and oxygen provide basic building blocks for plant life. Oxygen is used for respiration—burning carbohydrates and other foods to provide energy. Carbon dioxide must be present during photosynthesis. Without CO_2 a plant will die. Carbon dioxide combines light energy with water to produce sugars. These sugars fuel the growth and metabolism of the plant. With reduced levels of CO_2, growth slows to a crawl. Except during darkness, a plant releases more oxygen than is used and uses much more carbon dioxide than it releases.

Roots use air, too. Oxygen must be present along with water and nutrients for the roots to be able to absorb nutrients. Compacted, water-saturated soil leaves roots little or no air, and nutrient uptake stalls.

Air Movement

Air ventilation and circulation are essential to a healthy indoor harvest. Indoors, fresh air is one of the most overlooked factors contributing to

At least one good circulation fan and an extraction fan are necessary in grow rooms. The extraction fan in this grow room is attached to a carbon filter.

a healthy garden and a bountiful harvest. Fresh air is the least expensive essential component required to produce a bumper crop. Experienced growers understand the importance of fresh air and take the time to set up an adequate ventilation system. Three factors affect air movement: stomata, ventilation, and circulation.

Stomata

Stomata are microscopic pores on leaf undersides that are similar to an animal's nostrils. Animals regulate the amount of oxygen inhaled and carbon dioxide and other elements exhaled through the nostrils via the lungs. In cannabis, oxygen and carbon dioxide flows are regulated by the stomata. The larger the plant, the more stomata it has to take in carbon dioxide and release oxygen. The greater the volume of plants, the more fresh CO_2-rich air they will need to grow quickly. Dirty, clogged stomata do not work properly and restrict airflow. Stomata are easily clogged by dirt from polluted air and sprays that leave filmy residues. Keep foliage clean. To avoid clogging stomata, spray foliage with tepid water a day or two after spraying with pesticides, fungicides, or nutrient solution.

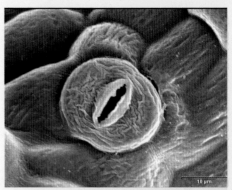

This photo of a half-opened stomata, the mouthlike opening on leaf underside, was magnified 2500 times.

circulation breaks up these air masses, mixing them together. Avoid these would-be problems by opening a door or window and/or installing an oscillating circulation fan. Air circulation also helps prevent harmful pest and fungus attacks. Omnipresent mold spores do not land and grow as readily when air is stirred by a fan. Insects and spider mites find it difficult to live in an environment that is constantly bombarded by air currents.

Circulation

Plants use all CO_2 around the leaf within a few minutes. When no new CO_2-rich air replaces the used CO_2-depleted air, a dead air zone forms around the leaf. This stifles stomata and virtually stops growth. If it is not actively moved, the air around leaves stratifies. Warm air stays near the ceiling, and cool air settles near the floor. Air

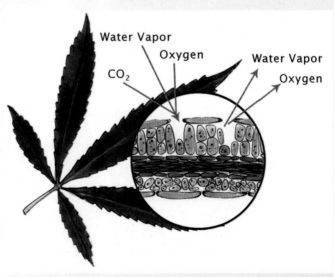

Water Vapor

Oxygen

Water Vapor

CO_2

Oxygen

Microscopic stomata located on leaf undersides must remain clean and un-stifled by humidity to promote rapid growth.

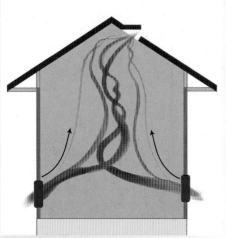

This garden has several circulation fans to move air between dense, resinous buds.

Hot air flows upward naturally. Always design grow rooms and greenhouses to take advantage of this principle.

Floor-mounted oscillating fans stir the air in this room 24 hours a day.

CO_2 around leaves is used quickly and must be replaced every few minutes.

Place circulation fans far enough away from plants to prevent too much airflow on any one portion of the garden.

Here is an example of a heavy-duty extractor fan from a Dutch grow room.

Ballasts are kept in the box which contains the extra heat. Separate ducting carries out the hot air.

A booster fan in the gray box pushes intake air down the duct to the bottom of the garden.

This blower is at the end of intake air ducting. The main fan is at the other end.

Avoid long, unnecessary ducting such as shown above. Keep ducting as short as possible.

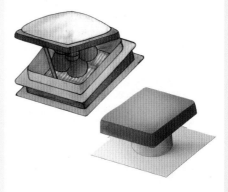

Roof fans and vents make grow room ventilation easy and inconspicuous.

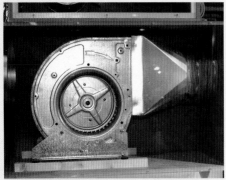

Squirrel cage blower moves a lot of air, but it is noisy! This blower has been necked down to force more air through the ducting.

This fan is suspended by bungee cords to shunt noisy vibrations. Always keep your fans well lubricated so they run smoothly and quietly.

Ventilation

Fresh air is easy to obtain and inexpensive to maintain—it is as simple as hooking up and placing the proper-sized exhaust fan in the most efficient location. An intake vent may be necessary to create a flow of fresh air in the room.

A 10-foot square (0.92 m²) garden will use from 10 to 50 gallons (38 to 190L) or more of water every week. Plants transpire (similar to evaporation) most of this water into the air. Every day and night, rapidly growing plants transpire more moisture into the air. If this moisture is left in the grow room, humidity increases to 100 percent, which stifles stomata and causes growth to screech to a halt. It also opens the door for pest and disease attacks. Replace moist air with fresh, dry air, and tran-

spiration increases, stomata function properly, and growth rebounds. A vent fan that extracts air from the grow room is the perfect solution to remove this humid, stale air. Fresh air flows in through an intake vent or with the help of an intake fan.

Ventilation is as important as water, light, heat, and fertilizer. In many cases, fresh air is even more important. Greenhouses use large ventilation fans. Grow rooms are very similar to greenhouses and should follow their example. Most grow rooms have an easy-to-use opening, such as a window in which to mount a fan, but security or room location may render it unusable. If no vent opening is available, one will have to be created.

All grow rooms require ventilation. This system could be as simple as an open door or window that supplies and circulates fresh air throughout the room, but open doors and windows can be inconvenient and problematic. Most growers

For indoor rooms, inline fans are one of growers' favorites. These fans are quiet and efficiently move large volumes of air.

elect to install a vent fan. Some growers need to install an entire ventilation system including ductwork and several fans.

A vent fan *pulls* air out of a room four times more efficiently than a fan is able to push it out. Vent fans are rated by the amount of air, measured in cubic feet per minute (CFM) or (cubic meters per hour [m3/h]) they can move. The fan should be able to replace the air volume (length × width × height = total volume in cubic feet or meters) of the grow room in less than 5 minutes. Once evacuated, new air is immediately drawn in through an intake vent or an intake fan. (Covering the intake vent with fine mesh silkscreen will help exclude pests.) An intake fan might be necessary to bring an adequate volume of fresh air into the room quickly. Some rooms have so many little cracks for air to drift in that they do not need an intake vent.

Do not set up a circulation fan in the room and expect it to vent the area by pushing air out a distant vent. The circulation fan must be very large to adequately increase air pressure and push enough air out a vent to create an exchange of air. A vent fan, on the other hand, is able to change the pressure and exchange the air quickly and efficiently.

Squirrel cage blowers are efficient at moving air but are very loud. Blowers with a balanced, well-oiled wheel run most quietly. Felt or rubber grommets below each foot of the fan will reduce noise caused by vibrations. Run motor at a low RPM to lessen noise.

Inline fans are designed to fit into a duct pipe. The propellers are mounted to increase the airflow quickly, effortlessly, and as quietly as possible. Inline fans are available in quiet, high-quality models that run smoothly.

Propeller or muffin fans with large fan blades expel air through a large opening, and are most efficient and quiet when operated at low RPM. A slow-moving propeller fan on the ceiling of a grow room will quietly and efficiently move the air.

Hot air rises. Adept growers locate air exit vents in the hottest peak of the room for passive, silent air venting. The larger the diameter of the exhaust ducts, the more air that can travel

Straight with no bend is the most efficient

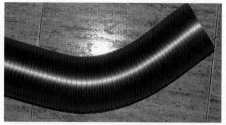

Thirty degree curve cuts up to 20 percent of air transmission.

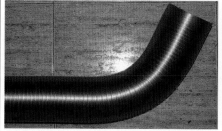

Forty-five degree curve cuts up to 40 percent of air transmission.

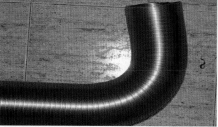

Ninety degree curve cuts up to 60 percent of air transmission.

Intake air ducting has holes covered with duct tape. Air flow is directed by removing pieces of tape.

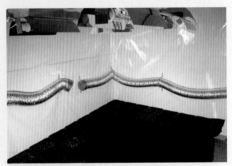

Fresh air in this room is piped in directly where plants need it.

To control the air temperature, hang the thermostat near the canopy of the garden.

through them. By installing a big, slow-moving vent fan in this vent, hot stale air is quietly and efficiently evacuated. A fan running at 50 RPM is quieter than one running at 200 RPM. Smart growers install 12-inch ducting and inline fans.

Most often, the vent fan is attached to ducting that directs air out of the grow room. Flexible ducting is easier to use than rigid ducting. To install, run the duct the shortest possible distance, and keep curves to a minimum. When turned at more than 30°, much of the air that enters a duct will not exit the other end. Keep the ducting straight and short.

Intake Air

Many rooms have enough fresh air coming in via cracks and holes. But other grow rooms are tightly sealed and require fresh air to be ushered in with the help of an intake fan. An intake fan is the same as an exhaust fan, except it blows fresh air into the room. The ratio of 1 to 4 (100 CFM [m³/h] incoming and 400 CFM [m³/h] outgoing) should give the room a little negative pressure. Delivering fresh air to plants ensures they will have adequate CO_2 to continue rapid growth. One of the best ways to deliver air directly to plants is to pipe it in via flexible ducting. Ingenious growers cut holes in the intake ducting to direct air where it is needed. The air is dispersed evenly throughout the room.

Always make sure fresh air is neither too hot nor too cold. For example, one friend that lives in a hot, arid climate brings cool fresh air in from under the house, where the air is a few degrees cooler than ambient air.

Security

When installing a vent fan, security concerns dictate that no light or odor escape from the exterior vent while allowing ample air release. This can be accomplished in several ways. Baffle or turn the light around a corner to subdue brilliance. Many chimneys in British Columbia, Canada, shoot light out like a spotlight against the low cloud cover. You can walk down city streets where half the chimneys in the neighborhood are beacons of bright light. A 4-inch (10.16 cm) flexible dryer hose will subdue light in smaller grow rooms. Larger 8, 10, and 12-inch (20, 25, 30 cm) heat duct pipe is ideal for moving larger volumes of air.

Place one end of the duct outdoors. It should be high enough, preferably over 12 feet (3.6 m), so the odor disperses above most people's heads. One of the best vents is the chimney. The outlet may be camouflaged by using a dryer hose wall outlet attached to a vent fan. The vent fan is then placed near the ceiling so it vents hot, humid air. Check for light and air leaks. Set up the fan and go outdoors after dark to inspect for light leaks. See "Setting Up the Vent Fan" and "Odor" in this chapter.

Greenhouse fans are equipped with louvers (flaps or baffles) to prevent backdrafts. During cold and hot weather, undesirable backdrafts could alter the climate in the room and usher in a menagerie of pests and diseases. Installing a vent fan with louvers eliminates backdrafts, but may present a security risk if it attracts the attention of the wrong crowd.

Temperature

An accurate thermometer is essential to measure temperature in *all* grow rooms. Mercury or liquid thermometers are typically more accurate than spring or dial types, but ecologically unsound. An inexpensive thermometer will collect basic information, but the ideal thermometer is a day-night or maximum/minimum type that measures how low the temperature drops at night and how high it reaches during the day. The maximum and minimum temperatures in a grow room are important for the reasons explained below.

Under normal conditions, the ideal temperature range for indoor growth is 72-76°F (22-24°C). At night, the temperature can drop 5-10°F (2-5°C) with little noticeable effect on growth rate. The temperature should not drop more than 15°F (8°C), or excessive humidity and mold might become problems. Daytime temperatures above 85°F (29°C) or below 55°F (13°C) will slow/stop growth. Maintaining the

Check the temperature and humidity in several places in the grow room. Lights really heat a room!

A thermometer that measures in Fahrenheit and Celsius will come in very handy.

Thermometer Hygrometer

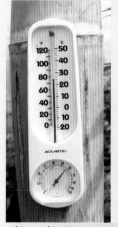

This combination thermometer/hygrometer is fairly accurate and easy to mount.

Day/Night

F __ C

75° ___ 24°
72° __ Day __ 22°
67° ___ 19°
62° __ Night __ 16°

Knowing Celsius and Fahrenheit equivalents makes grow room calculations more precise.

Fill barrels with water and let the sun heat them several days. Water stays warm all night to heat the greenhouse!

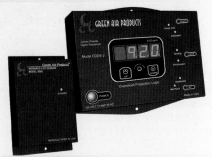

This simple humidistat/thermostat controller is just one of many different time/controllers found at www. greenair.com. It is very easy to use and foolproof.

proper, constant temperature in the grow room promotes strong, even, healthy growth. Make sure plants are not too close to a heat source, like a ballast or heat vent, or they may dry out, maybe even get heat scorch. Cold intake air will also stunt plant growth.

Cannabis regulates its oxygen uptake in relation to the ambient air temperature rather than the amount of available oxygen. Plants use a lot of oxygen; in fact, a plant cell uses as much oxygen as a human cell. The air must contain at least 20 percent oxygen for plants to thrive. Leaves are not able to make oxygen at night, but roots still need oxygen to grow. A plant's respiration rate approximately doubles every 20°F

(10°C). Root respiration increases as the roots warm up, which is why fresh air is important both day and night.

Temperatures above 85°F (29°C) are not recommended even when using CO_2 enrichment. Under the proper conditions, which are very demanding to maintain, higher temperatures step up metabolic activity and speed growth. The warmer it is, the more water the air is able to hold. This moist air often restrains plant functions and decelerates growth rather than speeding it. Other complications and problems result from excess humidity and moisture condensation when the temperature drops at night.

Heat buildup during warm weather can catch growers off guard and cause serious problems. Ideal grow rooms are located underground, in a basement, taking advantage of the insulating qualities of Mother Earth. With the added heat of the HID and hot, humid weather outdoors, a room can heat up rapidly. More than a few American growers have lost their crops to heat stroke during the Fourth of July weekend, since it is the first big holiday of the summer, and everybody in the city wants to get away to enjoy it. There are always some gardeners that forget or are too paranoid to maintain good ventilation in the grow room while on vacation. Temperatures can easily climb to 100°F (38°C) or more in grow rooms that are poorly insulated and vented. The hotter it is, the more ventilation and water that are necessary.

The cold of winter is the other temperature extreme. Montreal, Quebec, Canada, growers will remember the year of the big ice storm. Electricity went out all over the city and surrounding areas. Water pipes froze, and heating systems failed. Residents were driven from their homes until electricity was restored some days later. Many growers returned to find their beautiful gardens wilted, stricken with the deepest, most disgusting green only a freeze can bring. Broken water pipes, ice everywhere! It is difficult to combat such acts of God, but if possible, always keep the grow room above 50°F (10°C) and definitely above freezing, 32°F (0°C). If the temperature dips below this mark, the freeze will rupture plant cells, and foliage will die back or, at best, grow slowly. Growth slows/stops when the temperature dips below 55°F (13°C). Stressing plants with cold weather conditions is not recommended; it may yield a proportionately higher THC content, but will reduce plants' overall productivity.

A thermostat measures the temperature, then controls it by turning on or off a device that regulates heating or cooling, keeping the temperature within a predetermined range. A thermostat can be attached to an electric or combustion heater. In fact, many homes are already set up with electric baseboard heat and a thermostat in each room.

A thermostat can be used to control cooling vent fans in all but the coldest grow rooms. When it gets too hot in a room, the thermostat turns on the vent fan, which evacuates the hot stale air. The vent fan remains on until the desired temperature is reached, then the thermostat turns off the fan. A thermostat-controlled vent fan offers adequate temperature and humidity control for many grow rooms. A refrigerated air conditioner can be installed if heat and humidity are a major problem. Just remember, air conditioners draw a lot of electricity. If excessive heat is a problem, but humidity is not a concern, use a swamp cooler. These evaporative coolers are inexpensive to operate and keep rooms cool in arid climates.

Common thermostats include single-stage and two-stage. The single-stage thermostat controls a device that keeps the temperature the same both day and night. A two-stage thermostat is more expensive but can be set to maintain different daytime and nighttime temperatures. This convenience can save money on heating, since room temperature can drop 5-10°F (2-5°C) at night with little effect on growth.

Many new grow room controllers have been developed in the last ten years. These controllers can operate and integrate every appliance in the grow room. More sophisticated controllers integrate the operation of CO_2 equipment,

This air conditioner lowers grow room temperature and humidity. The hot radiator is outside, about 10 feet (3 m) away.

A simple electric heater may be necessary to warm the room after lights go out.

vent, and intake fans. Relatively inexpensive computerized controllers are also available for grow rooms. If temperature and humidity regulation are causing cultural problems in the grow room, consider purchasing a controller.

Uninsulated grow rooms or grow rooms that experience significant temperature fluctuations require special consideration and care. Before growing in such a location, make sure it is the only choice. If forced to use a sun-baked attic that cools at night, make sure maximum insulation is in place to help balance temperature instability. Enclose the room to control heating and cooling.

When CO_2 is enriched to 0.12-0.15 percent (1200–1500 ppm), a temperature of 80°F (27°C) promotes more rapid exchange of gases. Photosynthesis and chlorophyll synthesis are able to take place at a more rapid rate causing plants to grow faster. Remember, this higher temperature increases water, nutrient, and space consumption, so be prepared! Carbon dioxide-enriched plants still need ventilation to remove stale, humid air and promote plant health.

The temperature in the grow room tends to stay the same, top to bottom, when the air is circulated with an oscillating fan(s). In an enclosed grow room, HID lamps and ballasts keep the area warm. A remote ballast placed near the floor on a shelf or a stand also helps break up air stratification by radiating heat upward. Grow rooms in cool climates stay warm during the day when the outdoor temperature peaks, but often cool off too much at night when cold temperatures set in. To compensate, growers turn on the lamp at night to help heat the room, but leave it off during the day.

Sometimes it is too cold for the lamp and ballast to maintain satisfactory room temperatures. Grow rooms located in homes are usually equipped with a central heating and/or air conditioning vent. The vent is usually controlled by a central thermostat that regulates the temperature of the home. By adjusting the thermostat to 72°F (22°C) and opening the door to the grow room, it can stay a cozy 72°F (22°C). However, using so much power is expensive, and could cause a security quandary. Keeping the thermostat between 60 and 65°F (15-18°C), coupled with the heat from the HID system, should be enough to sustain 75°F (24°C) temperatures. Other supplemental heat sources such as inefficient incandescent lightbulbs and electric heaters are expensive and draw extra electricity, but they provide instant heat that is easy to regulate. Propane and natural gas heaters increase temperatures and burn oxygen from the air, creating

CO_2 and water vapor as by-products. This dual advantage makes using a CO_2 generator economical and practical.

Kerosene heaters also work to generate heat and CO_2. Look for a heater that burns its fuel efficiently and completely with no tell-tale odor of the fuel in the room. Do not use old kerosene heaters or fuel-oil heaters if they burn fuel inefficiently. A blue flame is burning all the fuel cleanly. A red flame indicates only part of the fuel is being burned. I'm not a big fan of kerosene heaters and do not recommend using them. The room must be vented regularly to avoid buildup of toxic carbon monoxide, also a by-product of combustion.

Diesel oil is a common source of indoor heat. Many furnaces use this dirty, polluting fuel. Wood heat is not the cleanest either, but works well as a heat source. A vent fan is extremely important to exhaust polluted air and draw fresh air into a room heated by an oil furnace or woodstove.

Insect populations and fungi are also affected by temperature. In general, the cooler it is, the slower the insects and fungi reproduce and develop. Temperature control is effectively integrated into many insect and fungus control programs. Check recommendations in Chapter 14, "Pests, Fungi and Diseases."

Humidity

Humidity is relative; that is, air holds different quantities of water at different temperatures. Relative humidity is the ratio between the amount of moisture in the air and the greatest amount of moisture the air could hold at the same temperature. In other words, the hotter it is, the more moisture air can hold; the cooler it is, the less moisture air can hold. When the temperature in a grow room drops, the humidity climbs, and moisture condenses. For example, an 800 cubic foot (10 × 10 × 8 feet) (21.5 m²) grow room will hold about 14 ounces (414 ml) of water when the temperature is 70°F (21°C) and relative humidity is at 100 percent. When the temperature is increased to 100°F (38°C), the same room will hold 56 ounces (1.65 L) of moisture at 100 percent relative humidity. That is four times more moisture! Where does this water go when the temperature drops? It condenses, onto the surface of plants and grow-room walls, just as dew condenses outdoors.

Relative humidity increases when the temperature drops at night. The greater the temperature variation, the greater the relative humidity variation will be. Supplemental heat or extra ventilation is often necessary at night if temperatures fluctuate more than 15°F (8°C).

Seedlings and vegetative plants grow best when the relative humidity is from 60 to 70 percent. Flowering plants grow best in a relative humidity range from 40 to 60 percent. The lower humidity discourages diseases and pests. As with temperature, consistent humidity promotes healthy, even growth. Relative humidity level affects the transpiration rate of the stomata. When humidity is high, water evaporates slowly. The stomata close, transpiration slows, and so does plant growth. Water evaporates quickly into drier air causing stomata to open, increasing transpiration, fluid flow, and growth. Transpiration in arid conditions will be rapid only if there is enough water available for roots to draw in. If water is inadequate, stomata will close to protect the plant from dehydration, causing growth to slow.

When the relative humidity climbs beyond 70 percent, the pressure outside the leaf is too high and inside too low. This causes the stomata to close, which slows growth. For example, a 40-inch (1 m) tall plant can easily transpire a gallon (4 L) per day when the humidity is below 50 percent. However, the same plant will transpire about a half-pint (0.5 L) on a cool humid day.

A 10 × 10 × 8 foot (800 cubic feet) (21.5 m³) grow room can hold:

4 oz (118 ml) of water at 32°F (0°C).
7 oz (207 ml) of water at 50°F (10°C).
14 oz (414 ml) of water at 70°F (21°C).
18 oz (532 ml) of water at 80°F (26°C).
28 oz (828 ml) of water at 90°F (32°C).
56 oz (1.65 L) of water at 100°F (38°C).

The moisture holding capacity of air doubles with every 20°F (10°C) increase in temperature.

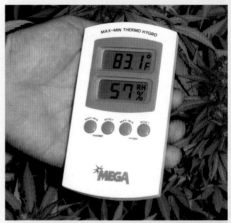

A maximum/minimum digital hygrometer registers the high and low humidity as well as current humidity.

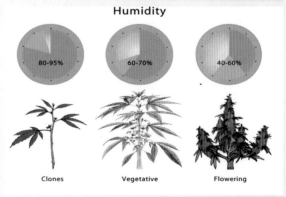

This is the best relative humidity range for clones, as well as vegetative and flowering plants.

Air conditioners cool and dehumidify grow rooms. Growers must weigh the benefits against the extra electricity they use.

Measuring Relative Humidity

Relative humidity control is an integral part of insect and fungus prevention and control. Humidity above 80 percent discourages spider mites but promotes fungus as well as root and stem rot. Humidity levels below 60 percent reduce the chances of fungus and rot.

Measure relative humidity with a hygrometer. This extremely important instrument will save you and your garden much frustration and fungi. By knowing the exact moisture content in the air, humidity may be adjusted to a safe 40 to 60 percent level that encourages transpiration and discourages fungus growth.

There are two common types of hygrometers. The spring type is accurate within 5 to 10 percent. This hygrometer is inexpensive and adequate for most hobby growers whose main concern is to keep the humidity near 55 to 60 percent. The second type, a psychrometer, is more expensive but very accurate. A psychrometer that measures relative humidity with a wet and dry bulb is an excellent way to keep an accurate vigil on relative humidity. Today there are many exceptionally accurate high-tech gadgets, plus they are equipped with memory!

A humidistat is similar to a thermostat, but regulates humidity instead of temperature. Humidistats are wonderful and make controlling the environment very easy. Humidistats cost less than $100 and are worth their weight in resin glands. A humidistat and thermostat can be wired "in line" to control a vent fan. Each can operate the fan independently. As soon as the humidity (or temperature) exceeds the acceptable range, the fan turns on to vent the humid (or hot) air outdoors.

The HID lamp and ballast radiate heat, which lowers humidity. Heat from the HID system and a vent fan on a thermostat/humidistat are all the humidity control necessary for most grow rooms. Other dry heat sources, such as hot air vented from a furnace or wood stove, dry the air and lower the humidity. Be careful. Do not let piped-in, warm, dry air blow directly on foliage. It will rapidly dehydrate plants.

Increase humidity by misting the air with water or setting out a bucket of water to evaporate into the air. A humidifier is convenient and relatively inexpensive. Humidifiers evaporate water into the air to increase humidity. Just set the dial to a specific humidity, and presto! The humidity changes to the desired level as soon as the humidifier is able to evaporate enough water into the air. A humidifier is not necessary unless there is an extreme problem with the grow room drying out. Problems seldom occur that can be remedied by a humidifier. All too often, there is too much humidity in the air as a result of irrigation and transpiration. If a ventilation system is unable to remove enough air to lower humidity, a dehumidifier could be just the ticket!

A dehumidifier removes moisture in a room by condensing it from the air. Once the water is separated from the air, it is captured in a removable container. This container should be emptied daily. It is easy to remove and catch 10 ounces (0.3 L) of water in a 10 × 10 × 8-foot (21.5 m²) room when the temperature drops just 10°F (5°C).

A dehumidifier can be used anytime to help guard against fungus. Just set the dial at the desired percent humidity and presto, perfect humidity. Dehumidifiers are more complex, use more electricity than humidifiers, and cost more, but to growers with extreme humidity problems not yet cured by a vent fan, they are worth the added expense. The best prices on dehumidifiers have been found at Home Depot, Home Base, and other discount stores. Check the rental companies in the Yellow Pages for large dehumidifiers if only needed for a short time. Air conditioners also function as dehumidifiers but use a lot of electricity. The water collected from a dehumidifier or air conditioner has a very low EC and can be used to water plants.

Note: Air conditioners draw moisture from the air and lower the humidity. The moisture condenses into water that is collected in a container or expelled through a tube outdoors. The condensed water carries the fragrance of cannabis. Sniffer dogs can easily smell the fragrance of cannabis in the "tainted" water expelled outdoors.

Rooting clones thrive when the humidity is from 70 to 100 percent. Under arid conditions, the undeveloped root system is not able to supply water fast enough to keep clones alive. See "Clones and Cloning" for more specific information on humidity levels during different stages of cloning.

CO$_2$ Enrichment

Carbon dioxide (CO$_2$) is a colorless, odorless, nonflammable gas that is around us all the time. The air we breathe contains 0.03-0.04 percent CO$_2$. Rapidly growing cannabis can use all of the available CO$_2$ in an enclosed grow room within a few hours. Photosynthesis and growth slow to a crawl when the CO$_2$ level falls below 0.02 percent.

Carbon dioxide enrichment has been used in commercial greenhouses for more than 35 years. Adding more CO$_2$ to grow room air stimulates growth. Indoor cannabis cultivation is similar to conditions in a greenhouse, and indoor growers apply the same principles. Cannabis can use more CO$_2$ than the 0.03-0.04 percent (300-400 ppm) that naturally occurs in the air. By increasing the amount of CO$_2$ to 0.12–0.15 percent (1200-1500 ppm)—the optimum amount widely agreed upon by professional growers—plants can grow up to 30 percent faster, providing that light, water, and nutrients are not limiting. Carbon dioxide enrichment has little or no affect on plants grown under fluorescent lights. Fluorescent tubes do not supply enough light for the plant to process the extra available CO$_2$.

*Carbon dioxide can make people woozy when it rises above 5000 ppm and can become toxic at super high levels. When CO$_2$ rises to such high levels, there is always a lack of oxygen!

Carbon dioxide enrichment does not make plants produce more potent THC; it causes more foliage to grow in less time. The larger the volume of THC-potent cannabis, the larger the volume of THC produced.

Carbon dioxide-enriched cannabis demands a higher level of maintenance than normal plants. Carbon dioxide-enriched plants use nutrients, water, and space faster than non-enriched plants. A higher temperature, from 75 to 80°F (24 to 26°C) will help stimulate more rapid metabolism within the super-enriched plants. When temperatures climb beyond 85°F (29°C), CO$_2$ enrichment becomes ineffective, and at 90°F (32°C) growth stops.

Carbon dioxide-enriched plants use more water. Water rises from plant roots and is released into the air by the same stomata the plant uses to absorb CO$_2$ during transpiration. Carbon dioxide enrichment affects transpiration by causing the plants' stomata to partially close. This slows down the loss of water vapor into the air. Foliage on CO$_2$-enriched plants is measurably thicker, more turgid, and slower to wilt than leaves on non-enriched plants.

Carbon dioxide affects plant morphology. In an enriched growing environment, stems and branches grow faster, and the cells of these plant parts are more densely packed. Flower stems carry more weight without bending. Because of the increased rate of branching, cannabis has more flower initiation sites. Plants that sometimes do not bear from the first flower set are more likely to set flowers early if CO$_2$ enrichment is used.

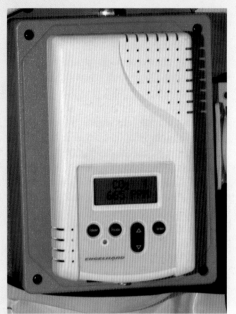

Inexpensive electronic components have made it possible for manufacturers to lower the price on CO_2 monitors.

With CO_2-enriched air, plants that do not have the support of the other critical elements for life will not benefit at all, and the CO_2 is wasted. The plant can be limited by just one of the critical factors. For example, the plants use water and nutrients a lot faster, and if they are not supplied, the plants will not grow. They might even be stunted.

To be most effective, the CO_2 level must be maintained at 1000 to 1500 ppm everywhere in the room. To accomplish this, the grow room must be completely enclosed. Cracks in and around the walls should be sealed off to prevent CO_2 from escaping. Enclosing the room makes it easier to control the CO_2 content of the air within. The room must also have a vent fan with flaps or a baffle. The vent fan will remove the stale air that will be replaced with CO_2-enriched air. The flaps or baffle will help contain the CO_2 in the enclosed grow room. Venting requirements will change with each type of CO_2-enrichment system and are discussed below.

Measuring CO_2

Measuring and monitoring CO_2 levels in the air is rather expensive and often unnecessary for small growers. Monitoring CO_2 levels in grow rooms with ten or more lights really helps keep the levels consistent.

Disposable comparative colorimetry CO_2 test kits are easy to use, accurate, and inexpensive. The test kits contain a syringe and test tubes and sell for about $30. To use the kit, break off each end tip of the test tube, and insert one end into the closed syringe. Pull 100 cubic centimeters into the syringe, and note the blue color change in the cylinder where the active ingredient reacts with the CO_2 in the air drawn through the cylinder. These kits are reliable to within 40 ppm.

Electrochemical sensing systems measure electrical conductivity of an air sample in either an alkali solution or distilled or deionized water. These systems are relatively inexpensive, but they have drawbacks: limited accuracy and sensitivity to temperature and air pollutants.

Infrared monitoring systems are more accurate and versatile. They correctly measure CO_2 and can be synchronized with controllers that operate heat, ventilation, and CO_2 generators. Even though the initial cost for a monitor is high, they can solve many CO_2 problems before they occur and can ensure optimum growing conditions. Specialty indoor garden stores sell the monitors for less than $1000.

Growers who do not want to spend the time and energy required to monitor CO_2 can use a set of scales and simple mathematics to determine the approximate amount of CO_2 in the air, but this calculation does not account for ventilation, air leaks, and other things that could skew the measurement. It is easier to measure the amount of CO_2 produced rather than to measure the amount of CO_2 in the grow room's atmosphere.

To measure the amount of fuel used, simply weigh the tank before it is turned on, use it for an hour, and then weigh it again. The difference in weight is the amount of gas or fuel used. See the calculations (page 340) for more information on calculating the amount of CO_2 in the room.

Producing CO_2

There are many ways to raise the CO_2 content of an enclosed grow room. The two most popular ways are to disperse it from a tank or burn a fuel to manufacture it. Carbon dioxide is one of the byproducts of combustion. Growers can burn any fossil (carbon-based) fuel to produce CO_2 except for those containing sulfur dioxide and ethylene, which are harmful to plants. Carbon dioxide gas is a by-product of fermentation and organic decomposition. The CO_2 level near the ground of a rain forest covered with decaying organic matter could be two to three times as high as normal, but bringing a compost pile inside to cook down is not practical. Dry ice is made from frozen CO_2. The CO_2 is released when dry ice comes in contact with the atmosphere. It can get expensive and be a lot of trouble to keep a large room constantly supplied with dry ice. It is difficult to calculate how much CO_2 is released into the air by fermentation, decomposition, or dry ice without purchasing expensive equipment.

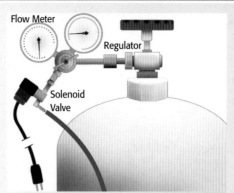

When open, the red on/off valve on top supplies compressed CO_2 via the regulator and flow meter. An electric solenoid valve controls the timed bursts of CO_2 gas.

CO_2 Emitter Systems

Compressed CO_2 systems are virtually risk-free, producing no toxic gases, heat, or water. These systems are also precise, metering an exact amount of CO_2 into the room. Carbon dioxide is metered out of a cylinder of the compressed gas using a regulator, flow meter, a solenoid valve, and a short-range timer. Two types of systems are: continuous flow and short range. Metal carbon dioxide cylinders which hold the gas under 1000 to 2200 pounds of pressure per square inch (psi) (depending upon temperature) can be purchased from welding or beverage supply stores. The cylinders are often available at hydroponic stores. In North America, cylinders come in three sizes: 20, 35, and 50 pounds (9, 16, and 23 kg), and average between $100 and $200 (with refills costing about $30). Tanks must be inspected annually and registered with a nationwide safety agency. Welding suppliers and beverage suppliers often require identification such as a driver's license.

Most suppliers exchange tanks and refill them. Fire extinguisher companies and beverage supply companies normally fill CO_2 tanks on the spot. If you purchase a lighter and stronger aluminum tank, make sure to request an aluminum tank exchange. Remember, the tank you buy is not necessarily the one you keep. To experiment before purchasing equipment, rent a 50-pound (23 kg) tank. A large 50-pound (23 kg) cylinder is heavier but saves you the time of returning to the store to have it refilled. When full, a 50-pound steel tank weighs 170 pounds (77 kg). A full 20-pound (9 kg) steel tank weighs 70 pounds (32 kg) and might be too heavy to carry up and down stairs. A full 20-pound (9 kg) aluminum tank weighs about 50 pounds (23 kg), and a full 35-pound (16 kg) tank weights 75 pounds (34 kg). Make sure CO_2 tanks have a protective collar on top to shield the valve. If the valve is knocked off by an accidental fall, there is enough pressure to send the top (regulator, flow meter, valve, etc.) straight through a parked car.

Buying a complete CO_2 emitter system at a hydroponic store is the best option for most closet growers. These systems offer a good value for small indoor growers. You can make your own system as described below, but these systems often cost more than the pre-manufactured models.

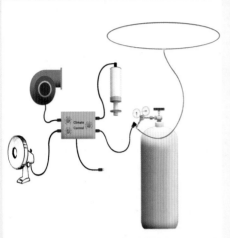

A setup consists of a tank of CO_2 gas, regulator, solenoid valve, and a flow meter.

Welding suppliers also carry regulators, and flow meters. Flow meters reduce and control the cubic feet per hour (cfh). The regulator controls the psi. Models with smaller flow rates, 10 to 60 cfh, are preferable for gardening purposes. Buy a quality regulator-flow meter. Buy all components at the same time, and make sure they are compatible.

Carbon dioxide is very cold when released from a bottle where it has been kept under pressure. Even a quick blast can do damage to skin or eyes. If the flow rate is above 20 cfh, your regulator might freeze.

A regulator and flow valve are essential, but the solenoid valve and the timer are optional. However, growers who do not use a solenoid valve and timer waste CO_2. The solenoid valve and timer regulate the flow of CO_2. A solenoid valve is electrically operated and is used to start and stop the gas flow from the regulator and flow meter. The least expensive timer is plastic and is commonly used for automatic sprinkler systems, but 240-, 115-, 24- and 12-volt systems are available. They cost about the same, but the lower voltages offer added safety from electrical shock.

To automate the system, you need a "short range" digital timer to open the solenoid valve for brief periods several times a day.

Control the exact amount of CO_2 released into the garden room by altering the flow and duration of CO_2. To determine how long the valve should remain open, divide the number of cubic feet of gas required by the flow rate. If the flow meter is set at 10 cfh, the valve will need to be open for 0.1 hours (1 divided by 10) or 6 minutes (0.1 hour × 60 minutes) to bring the room up to 1500 ppm. Remember, CO_2 leaks out of the grow room. On average, the CO_2 level of the room returns to 300 ppm in about three hours due to plant usage and room leakage. To maintain a steady level of CO_2, split the amount of CO_2 released per hour into two or four smaller increments dispersed more frequently.

Distribute the CO_2 from the tank to the grow room by using a tube or fan. Suspend lightweight perforated plastic from the ceiling to disperse the CO_2. The tubing carries CO_2 from the supply tank to the center of the grow room. The main supply line is attached to several smaller branches that extend throughout the garden. CO_2 is heavier and cooler than air and cascades onto the plants below.

To make sure the CO_2 is dispersed from the tubing evenly, submerge the lightweight plastic tubing in water and punch the emission holes under water while the CO_2 is being piped into the line. This way you know the proper diameter holes to punch and where to punch them to create the ideal CO_2 flow over the garden.

Overhead fans help distribute CO_2 evenly throughout the room. The CO_2 is released directly below the fan into its airflow. This evenly mixes the CO_2 throughout the air and keeps it recirculating across the plants.

Compressed CO_2 is expensive, especially in large grow shows. At roughly $0.50 per pound (450 gm), compressed gas is much more expensive than fuels used in generators. Cost of equipment and fuel make compressed CO_2 enrichment systems less economical than generators.

CO₂ Generator Systems

CO$_2$ generators are used by commercial flower, vegetable, and marijuana growers. Green Air Products has introduced a complete line of reasonably priced CO$_2$ generators that burn natural gas or LP (propane) to produce CO$_2$. However, heat and water are by-products of the combustion process. Generators use a pilot light with a flow meter and burner. The inside of the generator is similar to a gas stove burner with a pilot light enclosed in a protective housing. The generator must have a cover over the open flame. You can operate the generators manually or synchronize them with a timer to operate with other grow room equipment such as ventilation fans.

CO$_2$ generators produce hot exhaust gasses (CO$_2$ + H$_2$O). Even though CO$_2$ is heavier than air, it is hotter and therefore less dense and rises in a garden room. You must have good air circulation for even distribution of CO$_2$.

Carbon Dioxide generators can burn any fossil fuel—kerosene, propane, or natural gas. Low grades of kerosene can have sulfur content as high as 0.01 of 1 percent, enough to cause sulfur dioxide pollution. Use only high-quality kerosene even though it is expensive. Always use grade "1-K" kerosene. Maintenance costs for kerosene generators are high, because they use electrodes, pumps, and fuel filters. For most grow rooms, propane and natural gas burners are the best choice.

When filling a new propane tank, first empty it of the inert gas which is used to protect it from rust. Never completely fill a propane tank. Propane expands and contracts with temperature change and could release flammable gas from the pressure vent if too full.

Generators burn either propane or natural gas, but must be set up for one or the other. They are inexpensive to maintain and do not use filters or pumps. Hobby CO$_2$ generators range from $300 to $500, depending on size. The initial cost of a generator is slightly higher than a CO$_2$ emitter system that uses small, compressed-gas cylinders. Nonetheless, growers prefer propane

CO$_2$ generators produce carbon dioxide by burning LP or propane gas. They also generate heat and water vapor as by-products.

Spray soapy water around all propane gas connections to check for bubbles (leaks).

and natural gas generators, because they are about four times less expensive to operate than bottled CO$_2$ generators. One gallon of propane, which costs about $2, contains 36 cubic feet of gas and over 100 cubic feet of CO$_2$ (every cubic foot of propane gas produces 3 cubic feet of CO$_2$). For example, if a garden used one gallon of propane every day, the cost would be about $60 per month. In contrast, bottled CO$_2$ for the same room would cost more than $200 per month!

CO$_2$ generators are less expensive to maintain and less cumbersome, but they have some disadvantages, too. One pound of fuel produces 1.5 pounds of water and 21,800 Btu of heat. For grow rooms less than 400 cubic feet, this makes generators unusable. Even for larger gar-

1 pound of CO_2 displaces 8.7 cubic feet (246 cm^3) of CO_2.
0.3 pound (0.135 kg) of fuel produces 1 pound (454 gm) of CO_2.

Divide the total amount of CO_2 needed by 8.7 and multiply by 0.33 to determine the amount of fuel needed. In our example we found we need 1 cubic foot of CO_2 for an 800 cubic foot garden room.

L × W × H = room volume (cubic feet)
12 × 14 × 8 = 1344 cubic feet (38 m^3)

Desired CO_2 level is 1200 ppm (0.0012 ppm)*
Multiply room volume by 0.0012 = desired CO_2 level
1344 cubic feet (38 m^3) × 0.0012 = 1.613 cubic feet (46 cm^3) CO_2

1 pound (0.45 kg) of fuel burned = three pounds (1.35 kg) of CO_2 gas
0.33 pound (0.148 kg) fuel burned = one pound CO_2 gas

0.33 × 1.613 = 0.56 pounds of CO_2 fuel to burn to bring the CO_2 level to 1200 ppm.

Three times this amount (0.53 × 3 = 1.59 pounds) of fuel will create enough CO_2 for the room for 12-18 hours.

Convert this into ounces by multiplying by 16 (there are 16 ounces in a pound). .037 × 16 = 0.59 ounces of fuel are needed for every injection.

**Check out www.onlineconversion.com to convert
to or from the English and Metric Systems.**

den rooms, the added heat and humidity must be carefully monitored and controlled so as not to affect plants. Growers in warm climates do not use generators, because they produce too much heat and humidity.

If fuel does not burn completely or cleanly, CO_2 generators can release toxic gases—including carbon monoxide—into the grow room. Nitrous oxide, also a byproduct of burning propane, can grow to toxic levels, too. Well-made CO_2 generators have a pilot and timer. If leaks or problems are detected, the pilot and timer will turn off.

A CO_2 monitor is necessary if you are sensitive to high levels of the gas. Digital alarm units or color change plates (used in aircraft) are an economical alternative. Carbon monoxide is a deadly gas and can be detected with a carbon monoxide alarm available at most hardware and building supply stores.

Check homemade generators frequently, including kerosene or gas heaters. Propane and natural gas produce a blue flame when burning efficiently. A yellow flame means unburned gas (which creates carbon monoxide) and needs more oxygen to burn cleanly. Leaks in a system can be detected by applying a solution of equal parts water and concentrated dish soap to all connections. If bubbles appear, gas is leaking. Never use a leaky system.

Oxygen is also burned. As it becomes deficient in the room, the oxygen/fuel mixture changes. The flame burns too rich and yellows. This is why fresh air is essential.

Turn off CO_2 generators at night. They create excess heat and humidity in the grow room, and they need oxygen to operate. At night, roots need the extra oxygen in the room for continued growth.

If you are using CO_2 and the yield does not increase, check to make sure the entire grow room is running properly and that plants have the proper light and nutrient levels, as well as the correct temperature, humidity, grow-medium moisture, and pH. Make sure roots receive enough oxygen both day and night.

Other Ways to Make CO_2

There are many ways to make CO_2. You can enrich small areas by burning ethyl or methyl alcohol in a kerosene lamp. Norwegians are studying charcoal burners as a source of CO_2. When refined, the system will combine the advantages of generators and compressed gas. Charcoal is much less expensive than bottled CO_2 and is less risky than generators in terms of toxic by-products. Others are studying the use of new technology to extract or filter CO_2 from the air.

This little inexpensive puck called Excellofizz (www.fearlessgardener.com) releases CO_2 into the atmosphere. It is simple to use; just add a few ounces of water and a puck or two to cause a chemical reaction that will disperse enough CO_2 to augment the air in a 10-foot-square (9 m^2) room to about 1000 ppm all day. It also releases a eucalyptus fragrance to help mask odors. Make sure to keep the fizz contained, and if using an ozone generator, keep the lamp clean.

Compost and Organic Growing Mediums

Decomposing organic materials like wood chips, hay, leaves, and manures release large amounts of CO_2. Although you can capture CO_2 from this decomposition, it is most often impractical for indoor growers. Piping indoors the CO_2 and fumes from a compost pile is complicated, expensive, and more work than it is worth.

The Excellofizz puck is a low-cost product that releases CO_2 when it is bathed in water.

Fermentation

Small-scale growers use fermentation to produce CO_2. Combine water, sugar, and yeast to produce CO_2. The yeast eats the sugar and releases CO_2 and alcohol as by-products. Growers who brew beer at home can use a small-scale system to increase the CO_2 levels in a room. Non-brewers can mix one cup of sugar, a packet of brewer's yeast, and three quarts of warm water in a gallon jug to make CO_2. You will have to experiment a little with the water temperature to get it right. Yeast dies in hot water and does not activate in cold water. Once the yeast is activated, CO_2 is released into the air in bursts. Punch a small hole in the cap of the jug, and place it in a warm spot (80 to 95°F [26 to 34°C]) in your grow room. Many gardeners buy a fermentation lock (available for under $10 at beer-brewing stores). Such locks prevent contaminants from entering the jug, and they bubble CO_2 through water so the rate of production can be observed. The hitch is that you must change the concoction up to three times a day. Pour out half the solution, and add 1.5 quarts (1.4 L) of water and another cup (24 cl) of sugar. As long as the yeast continues to grow and bubble, the mixture can last indefinitely. When the yeast starts to die, add another packet. This basic formula can be adapted to

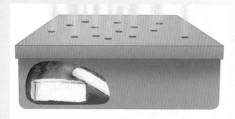

Put dry ice in a plastic container with holes to slow evaporation of CO_2 gas.

make smaller or larger-scale fermenters. Several jugs scattered around the garden room have a significant impact on CO_2 levels.

Fermentation is an inexpensive alternative to produce CO_2. It releases no heat, toxic gases, or water and uses no electricity. But because it stinks, it is unlikely that a gardener could tolerate a large-scale fermentation process. In addition, it is difficult to measure CO_2 production from this system, making it difficult to maintain uniform levels throughout the day.

Dry Ice

Dry ice gets very expensive with prolonged use. Two pounds of dry ice will raise the CO_2 level in a 10 × 10-foot (3 m²) grow room to about 2000 ppm for a 24-hour period. One chagrined grower remarked, "I can't believe that stuff melts so fast."

Growers have long used large, insulated tanks filled with dry ice to add CO_2. Dry ice is carbon dioxide that has been chilled and compressed. As it melts, it changes from solid to gas. Gaseous CO_2 can be mixed into the air with fans that circulate it among the plants. Dry ice works well on a smaller scale without a tank and converter. It is readily available (check out the Yellow Pages) and inexpensive. Because CO_2 has no liquid stage, the transformation from solid to gas as the ice melts is clean and tidy. It's also easy to approximate the amount of CO_2 being released. A pound of dry ice is equal to a pound of liquid CO_2. Determining the thawing period for a particular size of dry ice will allow you to estimate how much CO_2 is released during a particular time period. To prolong the thawing process,

put dry ice in insulating containers such as foam ice coolers, and cut holes in the top and sides to release the CO_2. The size and number of holes allow you to control the rate at which the block melts and releases CO_2.

Dry ice is economical and risk free; it releases no toxic gases, heat, or water. Although dry ice is easier to handle than compressed CO_2 tanks, it is difficult to store. The melting can be slowed through insulation, but it cannot be stopped. Because it is extremely cold, dry ice can also cause tissue damage or burn the skin after prolonged contact.

Baking Soda and Vinegar

Consider using vinegar and baking soda to produce CO_2 in a small grow room. This method eliminates excess heat and water vapor production and requires only household items. Create a system that drips vinegar (acetic acid) into a bed of baking soda. The main disadvantage of this system is the erratic level of CO_2 produced. It takes a considerable amount of time for the CO_2 to build up to a level where it helps plants. However, once it reaches an optimum level, it can continue to rise until it reaches levels detrimental to plants. If you have time to experiment, it is possible to set up a drip system operated by a solenoid valve and a short-term timer. With such a system, CO_2 could be released periodically in small increments and coordinated with ventilation schedules.

Note: Some recipes replace vinegar with muriatic (hydrochloric) acid. I advise using vinegar, because hydrochloric acid is very dangerous. It can burn flesh, eyes, and respiratory system; it can even burn through concrete.

Odor

A good exhaust fan, vented outdoors, is the first step in cannabis odor control and the easiest way to keep the house from reeking of fresh marijuana. If the odor is strong and venting is a problem, a negative ion generator (deionizer); deodorizing liquid, gel, puck, or spray; ozone generator; activated charcoal filter; or a combination of two or more of these will solve fragrance problems.

Deodorizers

Kill odors by changing their structure at the molecular level. Products such as Odor Killer™, Ona™, VaporTek™, and Ozium™, are made from essential oils that kill odors by creating a neutral atmosphere at the atomic level. Such products are usually available in gel and spray. Many growers prefer to use the gel over the long term and spray for emergency situations, such as when unexpected guests stop by during harvest.

The deodorizers can be set out in the room, around the house, and near doorways. Several companies offer products that stick to the wall. One ingenious grower I interviewed stuck one such deodorizing puck to the inside of the front door, just below the mail slot to keep the house fresh. Other products are designed to be attached to the ventilation ductwork system. Often these products are used not only to alter the odor of marijuana, but also to alter the telltale odor produced by an ozone generator. Other companies offer aerosol spray cans with a dispenser that periodically meters out a burst of spray.

Although a bit of a trick to keep going all the time, pouring vinegar on baking soda is a fair source of CO_2.

Negative Ion Generators

Negative ion generators are small and somewhat efficient to control odors, smoke, airborne pollen, mold, dust, and static electricity. They pump negative ions into the atmosphere. The negative ions are attracted to positive ions containing odors and other airborne pollutants. The negative ions attach to positive ions, and the odor becomes neutralized. The particles fall to the floor and create a fine covering of dust on the ground, walls, and objects in the room. These devices work fairly well for small grow rooms with minimal odor problems. The generator uses very little electricity and plugs into a regular 115-volt current. Visually check the filter every few days, and make sure to keep it clean.

Ozone Generators

Ozone has many applications including food and water sterilization and removing odors from

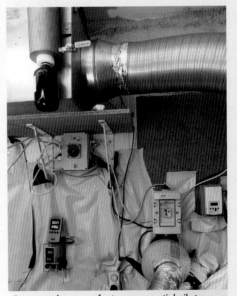

Some gardeners prefer to use essential oils to overpower fragrance. Such products are available in liquid, gel, and spray forms.

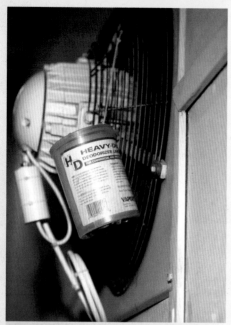

Fan with deodorizer

This grower treats the air with ozone and deodorizes air again just before it is expelled.

the air at the molecular level. Some growers even use high levels of ozone to exterminate grow room pests.

Ozone generators neutralize odors by converting oxygen (O_2) into ozone (O_3) by exposing the stinky air to ultraviolet (UV) light. The extra molecule is always a positively charged ion that is predisposed to attach to a negatively charged ion (cation). Odors are negatively charged cations. When the extra oxygen ion attaches to the cation, they neutralize one another and the odor, too. Once the extra molecule is shed, O_3 is converted back into O_2. The chemistry takes a minute or longer to occur, so treated air must be held in a chamber to be converted effectively.

Ozone has an unusual odor similar to the smell of the air after a good rain. Anybody who has ever smelled the air in a room recently treated with ozone knows the smell and will never forget it. Make sure not to produce too much ozone, and give it enough time to mix with smelly air to neutralize odors. The distinctive odor of excess ozone exiting a building will tip off narcs and thieves. For this reason, many growers also use a carbon filter to further scrub the air.

There are many ozone generators available. When shopping for an ozone generator, look for one that has been on the market for a few years and has an established track record. Watch

Ozone generators are rated by the number of cubic feet (m^3) they are able to treat.

for important features such as self-cleaning (or easy to clean) and easy, safe bulb replacement. When UV light encounters moisture in the air, nitric acid is produced as a by-product. This white, powdery nitric acid collects around the lamps at connection points. This is an unpleasant, very corrosive acid that will severely burn skin and eyes. Verify that the ozone generator has proper safety features built in, such as a switch that turns off the lamp for maintenance, making it impossible to look at the retina-searing UV rays. Legal exposure for humans is about 0.1 ppm for a maximum of 8 hours. Most grow room ozone generators produce about 0.05 ppm at timed intervals. See (page 348) for plant symptoms of ozone overdose.

The Air Tiger is a very popular ozone generator that is designed to fit inside ductwork.

UV light is very dangerous. In a flash, intense UV light can burn your skin and the retinas in your eyes beyond repair. Never, under any circumstances, look at the UV lamp in an ozone generator. Sneaking a peek at a UV lamp in an ozone generator has cost more than one aspiring grower their eyesight! Ozone is also capable of burning your lungs. At low levels, there is no damage, but at higher levels, danger is imminent. Never, never use too much!

The Air Tiger™, manufactured by Rambridge, www.rambridge.com, is an excellent value for growers. It is one of the safest available and easy to maintain. A deadman's switch makes direct eye contact with the 10-inch-long UV light tube impossible. Highly corrosive ozone stays away from interior wiring, and little moisture can penetrate the outer shell to combine with O_3 to form powdery nitric acid.

Ozone generators are rated by the number of cubic feet (m^3) they are able to treat. (To figure cubic feet or meters, multiply the length × width × height of the room). Some growers set up the ozone generator in the grow room and let it treat all the air in the room. They add a timer so the ozone generator intermittently disperses ozone into the room to maintain a relatively constant level. This practice can diminish the fragrance of the bud. Smart growers set up an ozone generator in a spare closet or build an ozone exchange

Mixing ozone-treated air for a minute or more allows O_3 to shed a molecule and become O_2.

chamber and route fragrant grow room air through the closet for ozone treatment before being evacuated outdoors. Other growers set up the ozone generator in ventilation ductwork to treat air before it exits. Once generated, ozone has a life of about 30 minutes. It takes a minute or two for the O_3 molecules to combine with oxygen to neutralize odors.

Ozone Damage

For best results, keep the ozone generator in another room or isolated from the growing plants. Ozone causes chlorotic spots on leaves. The mottled spots that appear at first to be a Mg deficiency, increase in size and turn dark in the process. Most often, the symptoms are

A vent-fan duct hooks to each tube, and the air-cleansing agent is imparted before air is evacuated.

Ozone generators are located inside ducting. Grow room air mixes with ozone in ducting and big metal box. Air smells fresh and clean once treated properly with ozone.

found on foliage near the generator. Leaves wither and drop, and overall plant growth slows to a crawl.

Activated Carbon Filters

Activated charcoal filters are fantastic, and they work! The charcoal is "activated" with oxygen, which opens millions of pores in the carbon. The activated charcoal absorbs odor molecules and other pollutants in the air. The mechanics are simple, and there are three important things to remember when using a charcoal filter. First, keep room humidity below 55 percent. At about 65 to 70 percent relative humidity, the charcoal absorbs moisture and clogs. At 80 percent humidity, it stops removing odors. Second, air must move slowly through charcoal filters to extract odors. The fan on professional units lets just enough air through the filter so the odors have enough (dwell) time to be absorbed by the carbon filter. Third, use a pre-filter. The pre-filter catches most of the dust and airborne pollutants before they foul the carbon filter. Change the pre-filter regularly—every 60 days, or more often if the room is dusty. Carbon lasts about a year. Many growers prefer activated carbon made from coco. Do not use activated carbon that is "crushed," because it is less efficient than charcoal pellets.

Install an intake screen that filters out large particles of dust to prolong the life of the activated charcoal filter. Whether the intake is passive or brought in by a fan, use a filter for incoming air to minimize pollutants in the grow room.

Ozone can severely damage foliage. This is what it does to foliage.

Charcoal filters remove fragrance and pollen from the air. The model shown above has a half-inch outer filter that encases porous ducting surrounded by activated charcoal. These filters are efficient until humidity climbs beyond 60 percent, at which point moisture-filled charcoal fails to absorb.

Check with filter manufacturers or retailers about venting specifications for your grow area. A more powerful exhaust fan will be necessary to draw an adequate volume of air through the activated charcoal filter. An adequate airflow is imperative to keep a high CO_2 content in the grow room air.

Setting Up the Vent Fan - Step-by-Step

Step One: Figure the total volume of the grow room. Length × width × height = total volume. For example, a grow room that is 10 × 10 × 8 feet (21.5 m²) has a total volume of 800 cubic feet (10 × 10 × 8 feet = 800 cubic feet) (21.5 m²). A room measuring 4 × 5 × 2 meters has a total volume of 40 cubic meters.

Step Two: Use a vent fan that will remove the total volume of air in the room in less than five minutes. Buy a fan that can easily be mounted on the wall or inline in a duct pipe. Quality inline fans move much air and make very little noise.

It's worth spending the extra money on an "in line" fan. Small rooms can use a fan that can be attached to a flexible 4-inch (12 cm) dryer hose. Many stores sell special ducting to connect high-speed squirrel cage fans with the 4-inch (12 cm) ducting.

Step Three: Place the fan high on a wall or near the ceiling of the grow room so it vents off hot, humid air.

Step Four: If possible, cut a hole in the wall, and secure the fan in place over the hole. Most locations require special installation. See: Steps 5-9 below.

Step Five: To place a fan in a window, cut a 0.5-inch (1.5 mm) piece of plywood to fit the windowsill. Cover window with a lightproof dark-colored paint or similar covering. Mount the fan near the top of the plywood so it vents air out of the grow room. Secure the plywood and fan in the windowsill with sheet rock screws. Open the window from the bottom.

Step Six: Another option to make a lightproof vent is to use 4-inch (12 cm) flexible dryer duct-

An activated charcoal filter is attached to a vent fan. The air is cleaned before leaving the grow room.

ing. Vent the hose outdoors, and attach a small squirrel cage fan to the other end of the ducting. Make sure there is an airtight connection between the fan and hose by using a large hose clamp or duct tape. Stretch the flexible ducting so it is as smooth as possible inside. Irregular interior surfaces cause air turbulence and seriously diminish airflow.

Step Seven: Another option is to vent the air up the chimney or into the attic where light leakage and odor are seldom a problem. If using the chimney for a vent, first clean out the excess ash and creosote. Tie a chain to a rope. Lower the chain down the chimney, banging and knocking all debris inside to the bottom. There should be a door at the bottom to remove the debris. This door is also used as the exhaust vent.

Step Eight: Attach the fan to a thermostat/humidistat or other temperature/humidity monitor/control device to vent hot, humid air outside. Set the temperature on 75°F (24°C) and the humidity on 55 percent in flowering rooms and 60 to 65 percent in

Can carbon filters are available in many sizes and are a popular brand.

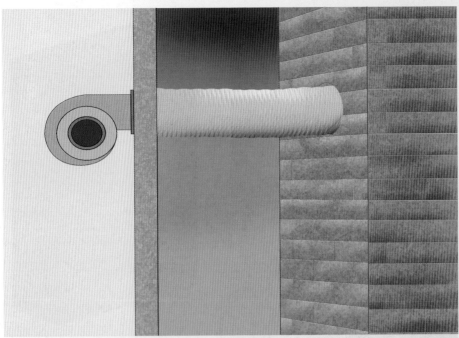

Air is deodorized by an ozone generator that is inside this ducting.

vegetative rooms. Most control devices have wiring instructions. More sophisticated controllers have built-in electrical outlets, and the peripherals are simply plugged into them.

Step Nine: Or attach the vent fan to a timer and run it for a specific length of time. This is the method used with CO_2 enrichment. Set the fan to turn on and vent out used CO_2-depleted air just before new CO_2-rich air is injected.

Air flow and volume are diminished when they turn corners.

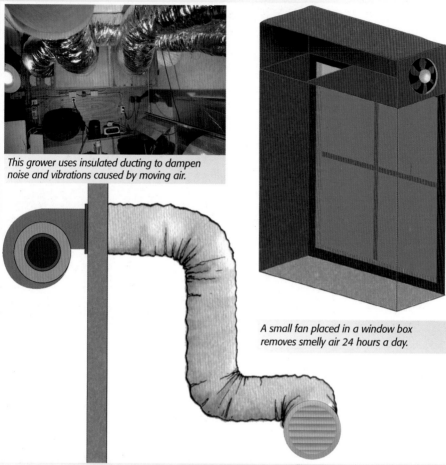

This grower uses insulated ducting to dampen noise and vibrations caused by moving air.

A small fan placed in a window box removes smelly air 24 hours a day.

Turning air around a corner keeps grow room light from signaling passersby.

Here is a charcoal filter without the outer dust filter. The inline fan adds extra suction to pull and push air through flexible ducting before it meets the extraction fan at the end of the duct.

PESTS, FUNGI & DISEASES

This beautiful greenhouse crop was destroyed by Botrytis

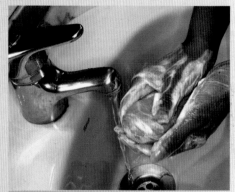

Simple hygiene in the grow room keeps pests and diseases in check.

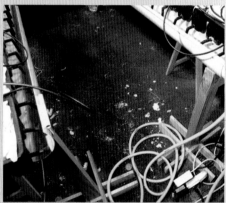

Dirty grow rooms help cause pest and disease problems.

Sweep the grow room floor every few days to avoid problems with pests and diseases.

Introduction

Insects, mites, and maggots slither into grow rooms eating, reproducing, and wasting weed. Outdoors, they live everywhere they can. Indoors, they live anywhere you let them. Fungi are present in the air at all times. They may be introduced by an infected plant or from air containing fungus spores. Fungi will settle down and grow if climatic conditions are right. Pests, fungi, and diseases can be prevented, but if allowed to grow unchecked, extreme control measures are often necessary to eradicate them.

Prevention

Cleanliness is the key to insect and fungus prevention. The grow room should be totally enclosed so the environment can be controlled easily. Keep the floor clean. Keep all debris off soil surface. Do not use mulch. Insects and fungi like nice hideaway homes found in dirty, dank corners, and under dead decaying leaves or rotting mulch. Growers and their tools often transport many microscopic pests, diseases, and fungi that could ultimately destroy the garden. This does not mean growers and their tools have to be hospital clean every time they enter a grow room, even though that would be nice. It does mean normal and regular sanitary precautions must be taken. Growers who wear clean clothes and use clean tools reduce problems considerably. A separate set of indoor tools is easy to keep clean. Pests, diseases, and fungi habitually ride from plant to plant on dirty tools. Disinfect tools by dipping in rubbing alcohol or washing with soap and hot water after using them on each diseased plant. Another quick way to sterilize pruners is with a hand-held torch. A quick heating with the torch will sterilize metal tools immediately.

Personal cleanliness is fundamental to preventing pests and diseases. Wash your hands before touching foliage and after handling diseased plants. Smart growers do not walk around the buggy outdoor garden and then visit the indoor garden. They do it vice versa. Think before entering the indoor garden and possibly contaminating it. Did you walk across a lawn covered with rust fungi or pet the dog that just came in from the garden outside? Did you just fondle your spider mite-infested split-leaf philodendron in the living room? Avoid such problems by washing your hands, and changing shirt, pants, and shoes before entering an indoor garden.

Once a crop has been grown in potting soil or soilless mix, throw out the grow medium. Some growers brag about using the same old potting soil over and over, unaware that this savings is repaid with a diminished harvest. Used soil may harbor harmful pests and diseases that have developed immunity to sprays. Starting a new crop in new potting soil will cost more up front but will eliminate many potential problems. Used soil makes excellent outdoor garden soil.

Be careful when discarding used soil! Growers in Eugene, Oregon, tossed their outdoor soil out in the backyard for many years. The soil was about 50 percent white perlite and had a distinctive color. This oversight eventually led to the growers' arrest.

Once potting soil is used, it loses much of the fluff in the texture, and compaction becomes a problem. Roots penetrate compacted soil slowly, and there is little room for oxygen, which restricts nutrient uptake. Used potting soil is depleted of nutrients. A plant with a slow start is a perfect target for disease, and worst of all, it will yield less!

Companion planting helps discourage insects outdoors. Pests have nowhere to go indoors, so companion planting is not viable in the grow rooms.

Plant insect- and fungus-resistant strains of marijuana. If buying seeds from one of the many seed companies, always check for disease resistance. In general, *Cannabis indica* is the most resistant to pests, and *sativa* is more resistant to fungal attacks. Choose mother plants that you know are resistant to pests and diseases.

Keep plants healthy and growing fast at all times. Disease attacks sick plants first. Strong plants tend to grow faster than pests and diseases can spread.

Forced air circulation makes life miserable for pests and diseases. Pests hate wind because holding on to plants is difficult, and flight paths are haphazard. Fungal spores have little time to settle in a breeze and grow poorly on wind-dried soil, stems, and leaves.

Ventilation changes the humidity of a room quickly. In fact, a vent fan attached to a humidistat is often the most effective form of humidity control. Mold was a big problem in one of the grow rooms that I visited. The room did not have a vent fan. Upon entering the enclosed room, the humid air was overpowering. It was terrible! The environment was so humid that roots grew from

Healthy plants are easy to keep strong and are able to fight off pests and diseases.

plant stems. The grower installed a vent fan to suck out moist, stale air. The humidity dropped from nearly 100 percent to around 50 percent. The mold problem disappeared, and harvest volume increased.

Indoor horticulturists who practice all the preventative measures have fewer problems with pests and diseases. It is much easier to prevent the start of a disease than it is to wipe out an infestation. If pests and diseases are left unchecked, they can devastate the garden in a few short weeks.

Control

Sometimes, even when all preventative measures are taken, pests and diseases still slink in and set up housekeeping. First, they establish a base on a weak, susceptible plant. Once set up, they launch an all-out assault on the rest of the garden. They move out in all directions from the infested base, taking over more and more space, until they have conquered the entire garden. An infestation can happen in a matter of days. Most insects lay thousands of eggs in short periods of time. These eggs hatch and grow into mature adults within a few weeks. For example, if 100 microscopic munchers each laid 1000 eggs during their two weeks of life and these eggs grew into adults, two weeks later 100,000 young adults would lay 100 eggs each. By the end of the month, there would be 100,000,000 pests attacking the infested garden. Imagine how many there would be in another two weeks!

Logical Progression of Insect Control

1. Prevention	2. Manual Removal
a. Cleanliness	a. Fingers
b. Use new soil	b. Sponge
c. One indoor	
set of tools	
d. Disease-resistant	3. Organic Sprays
plants	
e. Healthy plants	
f. Climate control	4. Natural Predators
g. No animals	
h. Companion	5. Chemicals
planting	

Manually remove small populations of pests by smashing pests and eggs between your fingers. Make sure to wash your hands afterward.

Sprays often kill adults only. In general, sprays should be applied soon after eggs hatch so young adults are caught in their weakest stage of life. Very lightweight (low viscosity) horticultural oil spray works well alone or as an additive to help kill larvae and eggs.

The availability of some sprays can be seasonal, especially in more rural areas. Garden sections of stores are changed for the winter, but extra stock is sometimes kept in a storage room. Look for bargains on sprays at season-end sales. Today, there are many indoor grow stores that carry pest and disease controls all year round.

Insect Control

Indoor gardeners have many options to control insects and fungi. Prevention and cleanliness are at the top of the control list. A logical progression to pest and disease control is outlined in the chart on this page. (Note that it begins with cleanliness!)

Manual removal is just what the name implies –smashing all pests and their eggs in sight between the thumb and forefinger or between two sponges.

I like natural-organic sprays such as pyrethrum and neem and use harsh chemicals only as a last resort. Any spray, no matter how benign, always seems to slow plant growth a little. Stomata become clogged when foliage is sprayed

Yellow sticky traps are used to monitor pest populations as well as to control small flying insects.

A 30X battery-powered magnifying scope makes insects and diseases easier to identify.

Common chemicals with their trade names and the insects they control:
Note: Do not apply these substances to edible plants

Generic Name	Purpose	Enter System
Griseofulvin	fungicide	systemic
Streptomycin	bactericide	systemic
Carbaryl	fungicide	systemic
Tetracycline	bactericide	semisynthetic (Terramycin®)
Nitrates	foliar fertilizers	systemic
Avid	insecticide	not truly systemic, actually translaminar
Pentac	miticide	systemic
Temik	insecticide	systemic
Neem	insecticide	systemic
Funginex	fungicide	systemic
Vitavax	fungicide	systemic
Orthene	insecticide	systemic

NOTE: This list is not all-inclusive. The basic rule is to not use systemic products.

and covered with a filmy residue. Stomata stay plugged up until the spray wears off or is washed off. Stronger sprays are often more phytotoxic, burning foliage. Spray plants as little as possible and avoid spraying for two weeks before harvest. Read all labels thoroughly before use.

Use only contact sprays that are approved for edible plants. Avoid spraying seedlings and tender unrooted cuttings. Wait until cuttings are rooted and seedlings are at least a month old before spraying.

Sprays and Traps

I do not recommend using chemical fungicides, fungistats, insecticides, or miticides on plants that are destined for human consumption. Most contact sprays that do not enter the plant system are approved for edible fruits and vegetables. However, there are numerous ways to control fungi, diseases, and pests without resorting to chemicals. On the previous page is a chart of common chemicals with their trade names and the insects they control.

EPA pesticide acute toxicity classification:

Class	LD50 to kill Rat Oral (mg kg-1)	LD50 to kill Rat Dermal (mg kg-1)	LD50 to kill Rat Inhaled (mg kg-1)	Eye Effects	Skin Effects
I	50 or less	200 or less	0.2 or less	corrosive opacity not reversible	corrosive
II	50-500	200-2000	0.2-2.0	corneal opacity reversible within 7 days, irritation persists for 7 days	severe irritation at 72 hours
III	500-5000	2000-20,000	2.0-20	no corneal opacity, irritation reversible within 7 days	moderate irritation at 72 hours
IV	> 5000	> 20, 000	> 20	no irritation	mild irritation

Natural Remedy Chart

Generic name Active ingredient	Form	Trade name	Toxicity precautions EPA Class
Bacillus species	G, D, WP	Bt, DiPel, M-Trak, Mattch, Javelin, etc.	IV
Copper sulfate	D, WP	Brsicop	III
Copper sulfate/lime	D, WP	Bordeaux mixture	III
Diatomaceous earth	D	Celite	IV
Neem	O, EL	Neem, Bioneem	IV
Nicotine sulfate	L, D	Black Leaf 40	II
Oil, dormant horticultural	O	Sunspray	IV
Pyrethrins	A, L, WP	Many trade names	III, IV
Quassia	WP	Bitterwood	IV
Rotenone	D, WP, EC	Derris, Cubé	II, III
Ryania	D, WP	Dyan 50	IV
Sabadilla	D	Red Devil	IV
Soap, insecticidal	L	M-Pede, Safer's	IV
Sodium bicarbonate	P	Baking soda	IV
Sodium hypochlorite	L	Bleach	II, III
Sulfur	D, WP	Cosan	V

Legend
A - Aerosol
D - Dust
EL - Emulsifiable Liquid
L - Liquid
WP - Wettable Powder
O - Oil
G - Glandular

Spreader-Sticker for Pesticides

Spreader-stickers improve and promote wetting and increase sticking and absorption through foliage. Spreader-sticker products increase effectiveness of fertilizers, fungicides, insecticides, etc. They are especially important to use when plants develop a waxy coating of resin. Spreader-stickers also impair insects' respiration mechanisms and function as pesticides. One of my favorite spreader-stickers is Coco-Wet from Spray-N-Grow.

Abamectin

Ingredients: Abamectin derivatives include emamectin and milbemectin. Does not bioaccumulate. Used extensively on hops; abamectin is not truly systemic. It is absorbed from the exterior of foliage to other leaf parts, especially young leaves, in the process of translaminar activity.

Controls: Russet and spider mites, fire ants, leafminers, and nematodes.

Mixing: Dilute in water. Mix 0.25 teaspoon (0.125 cl) per gallon (3.8 L). Use a wetting agent.

Application: Spray. Works best when temperature is above 70°F (21°C). Repeat applications every seven to ten days.

Persistence: One day.

Forms: Liquid.

Toxicity: Toxic to mammals, fish, and honeybees in high concentrations. Sucking insects are subject to control while beneficials are not hurt.

Safety: Wear gloves, mask, and safety glasses.

Bacillus thuringiensis (Bt) and Bacillus species

Ingredients: *Bacillus thuringiensis (Bt)* is the best known of several bacteria that are fatal to caterpillars, larvae, and maggots.

Caterpillars, larvae, and maggots all eat *Bt* bacteria, which can be applied as a spray, dust, or granules. Inject liquid *Bt* into stalks to kill borers. Shortly after they ingest it, their appetite is ruined, and they stop eating. Within a few days they shrivel up and die; cabbage loopers, cabbageworms, corn earworms, cutworms, gypsy moth larvae, and hornworms are controlled. Commercial *Bt* products do not reproduce within insect bodies, so several applications may be necessary to control an infestation. Microbial *Bt* bacteria are nontoxic to animals (humans), beneficial insects, and plants; however, some people do develop an allergic reaction. Commercial *Bt* products do not contain living *Bt* bacteria, but the *Bt* toxin is extremely perishable. Keep within prescribed temperature range, and apply according to the directions. Most effective on young caterpillars, larvae, and maggots, so apply as soon as they are spotted.

Get the most out of *Bt* applications by adding a UV inhibitor, spreader-sticker, and a feeding stimulant such as Entice®, Konsume® or Pheast®. *Bt* is completely broken down by UV light in one to three days.

B. thuringiensis var. *kurstaki* (Btk)–introduced on the market in the early 1960s–is the most popular *Bt*. Toxic to many moth and caterpillar larvae including most of the species that feed on flowers and vegetables. Sold under many trade names *DiPel®*, *BioBit®*, *Javelin®*, etc., Btk is also available in a microencapsulated form, M-Trak®, Mattch®, etc. The encapsulation extends the effective life on foliage to more than a week.

B. thuringiensis var. *aizawai* (Bta) is effective against hard-to-kill budworms, borers, armyworms and pests that have built up a resistance to *Btk*.

B. thuringiensis var. *israelensis* (Bt-i) is effective against the larvae of mosquitoes, black flies, and fungus gnats. Look for Gnatrol®, Vectobac®, and Bacrimos®. All are lethal to larvae. Adults do not feed on plants and are not affected. Fungus gnats can cause root problems including rot. Use *Bti* to get rid of them as soon as they are identified.

B. thuringiensis var. *morrisoni* is a new strain of *Bt* under development for insect larvae with a high pH in their guts.

B. thuringiensis var. *san diego* (Btsd) targets the larvae of Colorado potato beetles and elm beetle adults and other leaf beetles.

B. thuringiensis var. *tenebrionis* (Btt) is lethal to Colorado potato beetle larvae.

B. cereus helps control damping-off and root-knot fungus. It flourishes in water-saturated mediums and promotes beneficial fungus that attacks the diseases.

B. subtilis is a soil-dwelling bacterium that curbs *Fusarium*, *Pythium*, and *Rhizoctonia* that cause damping-off. It is commercially available under the brand names Epic®, Kodiac®, Rhizo-Plus®, Serenade®, etc. Soak seeds and apply as a soil-drench.

B. popilliae colonize larvae and grub bodies that consume it, causing them to turn milky-white before dying. It is often called *milky spore* disease. It is most effective against Japanese beetle grubs.

Baking Soda

Ingredients: Sodium bicarbonate.

Controls: Powdery mildew.

Caution: Baking soda kills fungus by changing the pH of foliage surface. It functions as a fungistat, not as a fungicide, that eradicates the organisms.

Mixing: Saturate in water.

Application: Spray or dust foliage.

Persistence: One to three days.

Forms: Powder.

Toxicity: None to mammals, fish, beneficials.

Safety: Wear a mask to avoid inhaling dust.

Bleach, Laundry

Ingredients: Sodium hypochlorite.

Controls: Numerous bacteria and fungi.

Caution: Avoid skin contact and inhalation. Concentrate burns skin and stains clothes.

Mixing: Dilute 5 or 10 percent solution with water.

Application: Use as a disinfectant on containers, walls, tools, etc.

Persistence: Evaporates with little residual in a couple of days.

Forms: Liquid.

Toxicity: Toxic to fish, beneficials, and humans if swallowed or gets in eyes.

Safety: Wear a mask and gloves when handling concentrate. Avoid skin contact and respiration.

Bordeaux Mixture

Ingredients: Water, sulfur, copper (copper sulfate) and lime (calcium hydroxide).

Controls: Most often used as a foliar fungicide. Also, controls bacteria and fends off other insects.

Caution: Phytotoxic when applied to tender seedlings or foliage in cool and humid conditions.

Mixing: Apply immediately after preparing.
Application: Agitate the mixture often while spraying so ingredients do not settle out.
Persistence: Until it is washed from foliage.
Forms: Powder and liquid.
Toxicity: Not toxic to humans and animals, but somewhat toxic to honeybees and very toxic to fish.
Safety: Wear a mask, gloves, and long sleeves.

Boric Acid

Ingredients: Available in the form of borax hand soap and dust.
Controls: Lethal as a contact or stomach poison. Kills earwigs, roaches, crickets, and ants.
Caution: Phytotoxic when applied to foliage.
Mixing: Mix borax soap in equal parts with powdered sugar to make toxic bait.
Application: Set bait out on soil near base of plants.
Persistence: Avoid getting bait wet as it disperses rapidly.
Forms: Powder.
Toxicity: Not toxic to honeybees and birds.
Safety: Avoid breathing dust.

Bug Bombs

Ingredients: Often bug bombs are packed with very strong insecticides and miticides, including synthetic pyrethrins that exterminate every pest in the room. They were developed to kill fleas, roaches, and their eggs that hide in furniture and in carpets.
Controls: According to most bug bomb labels, they kill everything in the room!
Caution: Use only as a last resort and follow the label's instructions to the letter.
Mixing: None.
Application: Place the bug bomb in the empty room. Turn it on and then leave the room.
Persistence: Low residual. Persistence is limited to a day or two.
Forms: Aerosol.
Toxicity: Read label for details.
Safety: Wear a mask, gloves, and cover exposed skin and hair.

Copper

Ingredients: The compounds–copper sulfate, copper oxychloride, cupric hydroxide and cuprous oxide –are common forms of fixed copper used as a fungicide and are less phytotoxic than unfixed (pure) copper.
Controls: Gray mold, foliar fungus, anthracnose, blights, mildews, and a number of bacterial diseases.
Caution: Easy to overapply and burn foliage or create a copper excess in plant.
Mixing: Apply immediately after preparing.
Application: Agitate the mixture often while spraying, so ingredients do not settle out. Preferred temperature range for application is 65-85°F (18-29°C).
Persistence: Lasts two weeks or longer indoors, if not washed off.
Forms: Powder and liquid.
Toxicity: Toxic to fish. Not toxic to birds, bees, mammals.
Safety: Wear a mask and gloves, cover exposed skin and hair.

Diatomaceous Earth (DE)

Ingredients: Naturally occurring DE includes fossilized-silica-shell, remains of the tiny one-celled or colonial creatures called diatoms. It also contains 14 trace minerals in a chelated (available) form.
Controls: Although not registered as a pesticide or fungicide, DE abrades the waxy coating on pest shells and skin, including aphids and slugs, causing body fluids to leak out. Once ingested, the razor-sharp particles in DE rip tiny holes in the pest's guts, causing death.
Caution: Do not use swimming pool diatomaceous earth. Chemically treated and heated, it contains crystalline silica that is very hazardous if inhaled. The body is unable to dissolve the crystalline form of silica that causes chronic irritation.

Mixing: No mixing required when used as a dust. Mixing required when used as spray. Apply as a powder or encircle slug-damaged plants and use as a barrier.

Application: Apply this spray to infestations caused by pest insects.

Persistence: Stays on foliage for a few days or until washed off.

Forms: Powder.

Toxicity: Earthworms, animals, humans, and birds can digest diatomaceous earth with no ill-effects. Avoid contact with skin and eyes.

Safety: Wear a protective mask and goggles when handling this fine powder to guard against respiratory and eye irritations.

Homemade Pest and Disease Sprays

Ingredients: A strong, hot taste, smelly odor, and a desiccating powder or liquid are the main ingredients in home-brewed pesticide and fungicide potions. See below.

Controls: Homemade sprays discourage and control pests including aphids, thrips, spider mites, scale, and many others.

Caution: Be careful when testing a new spray. Apply it to a single plant and wait for a few days to learn the outcome before applying to all plants.

Mixing: Make spray concentrates by mixing repellent substances with a little water in a blender. Strain the resulting slurry concentrate through a nylon stocking or fine cheesecloth before being diluted with water for application.

Application: Spray foliage until it drips from both sides of leaves.

Persistence: A few days.

Forms: Liquid.

Toxicity: Usually not toxic to humans in dosages lethal to pests.

Safety: Wear a mask and gloves, and cover skin and hair. Avoid contact with eyes, nose, lips, and ears.

Neem

Ingredients: Relatively new in the USA, neem has been used for medicine and pest control for more than four centuries in India and Southeast Asia. Extracted from the Indian neem tree, *Azadirachta indica*, or the chinaberry tree, *Melia azedarach*, neem is an antifeedant and disrupts insect life cycles. The trees are known as the village pharmacy because they supply cures

Homemade sprays can be made by blending water, lemon, vegetable oil, and garlic.

for humans and animals as well as safely control countless pests and fungi. Neem powder is made from leaves. The active ingredient, azadirachtin, confuses growth hormones and pests never mature into adults to produce more young. It is most effective against young insects and is available in various concentrations. It also contains N-P-K and trace elements.

Controls: Most effective against caterpillars and other immature insects including larvae of whiteflies, fungus gnats, mealybugs, and leafminers.

Caution: Neem is not as effective against spider mites as neem oil.

Mixing: Often mixed with vegetable (canola) oil. Mix just before using in water with a pH below 7 and use a spreader-sticker. Agitate constantly while using to keep emulsified, throw out excess.

Application: Use as a soil-drench or add to the nutrient solution. This allows neem to enter into the plant's tissue and become systemic. Used as a spray, neem becomes a contact spray and an

Recipes and Controls Chart

Ingredients:

Alcohol: Use isopropyl (rubbing). Add to sprays to dry out pests.

Bleach: Use a 5 percent solution as a general disinfectant.

Cinnamon: Dilute cinnamon oil with water. Use just a few drops per pint as pesticide.

Citrus: Citrus oils make great ingredients that kill insects dead.

Garlic: Use a garlic press to squeeze garlic juice into mix. Use liberal amounts.

Horseradish: Stinky stuff! Add as you would garlic. Best to use fresh root.

Hot pepper: Dilute Tabasco® or any store-bought concentrate in water.

Hydrated lime: Saturate in water to form a fungicide.

Mint: Mint oil drives insects away. Dilute in water, measure several drops per pint.

Oil, vegetable is comprised mainly of fatty acids and glycerides. Mix with rubbing alcohol to emulsify in water. Great stuff!

Oregano: Grind up fresh herb and use as a repellent. Mix with water.

Soap: I like Ivory® or Castille® soap. Use as an insecticide and wetting agent. Mix with water.

Tobacco: Mix tobacco with hot water to extract the poisonous alkaloid. Do not boil. Dilute concentrate with water.

Precautions:

Cooking or heating preparations can destroy active ingredients. To draw out (extract) ingredients, mince plant and soak in mineral oil for a couple of days. Add this oil to the water including a little detergent or soap to emulsify the oil droplets in water. Biodegradable detergents and soaps are good wetting-sticking agents for these preparations. Soap dissolves best if a teaspoon (0.75 cl) of alcohol is also added to each quart (0.9 L) of mix.

Chrysanthemum, marigold, and nasturtium blossoms; pennyroyal; garlic; chive; onion; hot pepper; insect juice (target insects mixed in a blender); horseradish; mint; oregano; tomato; and tobacco residues all will repel many insects including aphids, caterpillars, mites, and whiteflies.

Spray made from pests ground up in a blender and emulsified in water will reputedly repel related pests. Best used on large pests! The insecticidal qualities in the dead bug parts will degrade quickly if combined with other things; do not include insects mixed in a blender with other ingredients besides water. Mixes that include tobacco may kill these pests if it is strong enough. These mixes can vary in proportions, but always filter the blended slurry before mixing with water for the final spray. Straining avoids clogging spray nozzles and plumbing.

Recipe 1. Mix three tablespoons (4.5 cl) each of isopropyl alcohol, lemon juice, garlic juice, horseradish juice, Ivory liquid, and a few drops of Tabasco®, mint, and cinnamon oil. Mix all of the ingredients in a small bowl into a slurry. Dilute the slurry at the rate of one teaspoon (0.5 cl per 47 cl) per pint of water and mix in a blender. Potent mix!

Recipe 2. Place one teaspoon (0.5 cl) of hot pepper or Tabasco® sauce and four cloves of garlic in a blender with a pint of water and liquefy, then strain through a nylon stocking or cheesecloth before using in the sprayer.

Recipe 3. A mix of one-eighth to one-quarter cup (3-6 cl) of hydrated lime combined with a quart (0.9 L) of water makes an effective insect and mite spray. Mix a non-detergent soap with lime. The soap acts as both a sticking agent and insecticide. Lime can be phytotoxic to plants in large doses. Always try the spray on a test plant and wait a few days to check for adverse effects to the plant before applying to similar plants.

Recipe 4. Liquid laundry bleach–sodium hypochlorite–is a good fungicide for non-plant surfaces. Mix as a five or ten percent solution. It is an eye and skin irritant, so wear gloves and goggles when using it. Mix 1 part bleach to 9 parts water for a 5 percent solution. Mix one part to four parts water for a 10 percent solution. Use this solution as a general disinfectant for grow room equipment, tools, and plant wounds. The bleach solution breaks down rapidly and has little, if any, residual effect.

antifeedant when eaten by pests. Performs best in rooms with 60 percent plus humidity.

Persistence: Contact neem stays on foliage for up to a month or until it is washed off. Stays in plant system up to a month when absorbed via roots.

Forms: Emulsifiable concentrate.

Toxicity: Not toxic to honeybees, fish, and earthworms. Not toxic to beneficial insects in normal concentrations that kill target insects.

Safety: Irritates eyes; wear a mask and gloves.

Neem Oil

Ingredients: Purified extract from neem seeds. Buy only cold-pressed oil that is stronger and contains all the natural ingredients. Do not use heat-processed neem oil. Cold-pressed oil also contains azadirachtin, the active ingredient in neem. Brand names include Neemguard®, Triact®, and Einstein Oil®. NOTE: Einstein Oil works the best of all brands tested.

Einstein Oil

Controls: Effective against spider mites, fungus gnats, and aphids. It is also a fungistat against powdery mildew and rust.

Neem Oil

Caution: Neem oil is very effective against spider mites.

Mixing: Mix just before using in water with a pH below 7 and use a spreader-sticker. Agitate constantly while using to keep emulsified. Throw out excess.

Application: Spray on foliage, especially under leaves, where mites live. Apply every few days so hatching larvae will eat it immediately. Spray heavily so mites have little choice but to eat it. Avoid spraying the last few days before harvest. Some growers report a foul taste when applied just before harvest.

Persistence: Contact neem stays on foliage for up to a month or until it is washed off. Stays in plant system up to a month when absorbed via roots.

Forms: Emulsifiable concentrate.

Toxicity: Toxicity to beneficial insects has been reported. Not toxic to humans.

Safety: Irritates eyes, wear a mask and gloves.

Neem products have numerous other applications. For more information check out the Neem Foundation, http://www.neemfoundation.org, and the Neem Association, hometown.aol.com/neemassoc, and www.einsteinoil.com, or the book, *Neem: India's Miraculous Healing Plant*, by Ellen Norten, ISBN: 0-89281-837-9.

Nicotine and Tobacco Sprays

Ingredients: Nicotine is a nonpersistent pesticide derived from tobacco, *Nicotiana tabacum*. It is a stomach poison, contact poison, and respiratory poison. This very poisonous compound affects the neuromuscular system, causing pests to go into convulsions and die. Nicotine sulfate is the most common form.

Caution: Do not swallow any of this vile poison, and avoid skin contact. Do not use around nightshade family–eggplants, tomatoes, peppers and potatoes–because they may contract Tobacco Mosaic Virus (TMV) from exposure to tobacco-based substances.

Controls: Sucking and chewing insects.

Mixing: Use a spreader-sticker.

Application: Seldom phytotoxic when used as directed. Combine with insecticidal soap to increase killing ability.

Persistence: One week to ten days.

Forms: Liquid.

Toxicity: Although naturally derived, nicotine is very toxic to most insects (including beneficials), honeybees, fish, and humans. If concentrate is ingested or built up over years, humans may develop lung cancer and other cancers.

Safety: Wear a mask and gloves; avoid skin and eye contact.

Oil, Horticultural

Ingredients: Often underrated and overlooked as an insecticide and miticide, horticultural oil is very popular in greenhouses and is regaining popularity among indoor growers. Similar to medicinal mineral oil, horticultural oils are made from animal (fish) oils, plant seed oils, and petroleum oils refined by removing most of the portion that is toxic to plants. Lighter weight oil (viscosity 60-70) is less phytotoxic. Vegetable oil is also horticultural oil.

Controls: Virtually invisible, horticultural oil kills slow moving and immobile sucking insects, spider mites and their eggs by smothering, as well as generally impairing their life cycle.

Caution: Do not use lubricating oils such as 3-in-1 or motor oil!

Mixing: Mix ¾ teaspoon (0.75 cl) of oil spray–no more than a one percent solution–per quart (0.9 L) of water. More than a few drops could burn tender, growing shoots.

Application: Spray foliage entirely, including under the suface of the leaves. Apply oil sprays up until two weeks before harvest. Repeat applications as needed. Usually three applications, one every five to ten days, will put insects and mites in check. Lightweight-oil residue evaporates into the air in a short time.

Persistence: Disappears in one to three days, under normal growing conditions.

Forms: Liquid

Toxicity: Safe, nonpoisonous, and nonpolluting insecticide. Can become phytotoxic if too heavy (viscosity), if applied too heavily, or when temperatures are below 70°F (21°C), or very humid; this slows evaporation, increasing phytotoxicity.

Safety: Wear a mask and gloves.

Oil, Vegetable

Ingredients: Fatty acids and glycerides.

Controls: Lightweight vegetable oil kills slow-moving and immobile sucking insects, spider mites, and their eggs by smothering as well as generally interrupting their life cycles.

Caution: Vegetable oil does not kill as well as horticultural oil.

Mixing: Mix two drops of oil spray–no more than a one percent solution–per quart of water.

Application: Spray foliage entirely, including under surface of leaves. Stop spraying two weeks before harvest.

Persistence: Several days.

Forms: Liquid.

Toxicity: Not toxic to mammals or fish.

Safety: Wear a mask and gloves.

Pyrethrum

Ingredients: Pyrethrum, the best-known botanical pesticide, is extracted from the flowers of the pyrethrum chrysanthemum, *Chrysanth-emum*

coccineum and *C. cinerariifoliu*. Pyrethrins– pyrethrins, cinerins, and jasmolins–are the active ingredients in natural pyrethrum and kills insects on contact. Pyrethrum is often combined with rotenone or ryania to ensure effectiveness. Aerosol forms contain synergists. (See "Application" below.)

Pyrethrum

Controls: A broad-spectrum contact pesticide, pyrethrum kills aphids, whiteflies, spider mites, and insects including beneficials. It is very effective to control flying insects, but they must receive a killing knockdown dose, or they may revive and buzz off.

Caution: Do not mix with sulfur, lime, copper, or soaps. The high pH of these substances render it ineffective. Wash these substances off foliage with plain water (pH below 7) before applying pyrethrum.

Mixing: Mix in water with a pH below 7 and use a spreader-sticker.

Application: Spot spray infested plants. Aerosol sprays are most effective especially on spider mites. This can burn foliage–spray is ice-cold when it exits the nozzle–if applied closer than one foot. Aerosol spray contains a synergist, piperonyl butoxide (PBO) or MGK 264. Both are toxic to people. Pyrethrum dissipates within a few hours in the presence of air, HID light, and sunlight. Overcome this limitation by applying just before turning off the lights, the circulation, and vent fans for the night. One manufacturer, Whidmere®, offers encapsulated pyrethrum in aerosol form called Exclude®. As the spray fogs out of the nozzle, a bubble forms around each droplet of pyrethrum mist. The outside coating keeps the pyrethrum intact and extends its life for several days. When a pest prances by touching the bubble, it bursts, releasing the pyrethrum. Liquid and wettable pyrethrum applied with a pump-type sprayer is difficult to apply under leaves where spider mites live.

Persistence: Effective several hours after application when the lights are on, longer when applied after lights-out and the fan is turned off.

Forms: Wettable powder, dust, liquid, granular bait, and aerosol.

Toxicity: Not toxic to animals and humans when eaten, but becomes toxic to people when inhaled. It is toxic to fish and beneficials.

Safety: Wear a mask and protective clothing when applying sprays or breathing in any form of pyrethrum, especially aerosols. Aerosols contain toxic PBO and MGK 464–possible carcinogens –which are easily inhaled.

Synthetic Pyrethroids

Ingredients: Synthetic pyrethroids such as permethrin and cypermethrin act as broad-spectrum, Nonselective contact insecticides and miticides. There are more than 30 synthetic pyrethroids available in different formulations. Deltamethrin is available as a sticky paint that is used as a trap when applied to stems and colored objects. Other pyrethroids include Allethrin, cyflutrin, fenpropathin, phenothrin, sumithrin, resmitherin, and tefluthrin.

Controls: Aphids, whiteflies, thrips, beetles, cockroaches, caterpillars, and spider mites. NOTE: Many insects and mites are resistant to pyrethroids.

Caution: Nonselective pyrethroids kill all insects and mites including beneficials and bees.

Mixing: Follow directions on container.

Application: Follow directions on container. (See "Application" under "Pyrethrum.")

Persistence: Breaks down in one to three days. Newer pyrethroids, such as Permethrin, stay active the longest.

Forms: Powder, liquid, aerosol.

Toxicity: Toxic to all insects. It is somewhat toxic to mammals.

Safety: Wear a mask and protective clothing when applying sprays or breathing in any form of pyrethrum, especially aerosols. Aerosols contain toxic PBO and MGK 464–possible carcinogens– which are easily inhaled.

Quassia

Ingredients: Quassia is made from a subtropical South American tree, *Quassia amara*, and the tree-of-heaven, *Ailanthus altissima*.

Controls: Soft-bodied insects including aphids, leafminers, and some caterpillars.

Mixing: Available in the form of bark, wood chips, and shavings. Soak 6 ounces (18 cl) of chips per gallon (0.9 L) of water for 24 hours. Afterward, boil for two hours. Add a potassium-based soap to increase effectiveness. Strain and cool before spraying.

Application: Spray on foliage until saturated.

Persistence: Two to five days on the surface of plants.

Forms: Bark, wood chips, and shavings.

Toxicity: Safe for mammals and (possibly) beneficials.

Safety: Wear a mask and gloves.

Rotenone

Ingredients: Rotenone is an extract of roots of several plants including *Derris* species, *Lonchocarpus* species, and *Tephrosia* species. This poison is a Nonselective contact insecticide, stomach poison, and slow-acting nerve poison.

Controls: Nonselective control of beetles, caterpillars, flies, mosquitos, thrips, weevils, and beneficial insects, but death is slow. According to *Hemp Diseases and Pests*, target insects can consume up to 30 times their lethal dose before dying!

Caution: Kills beneficials. New evidence indicates rotenone may be toxic to people and may cause Parkinson's disease. Use only as a last resort!

Mixing: Follow directions on the package.

Application: Follow directions on the package.

Persistence: Breaks down in three to ten days.

Forms: Powder, wettable powder, liquid.

Toxicity: The effect on mammals is undetermined. Chronic exposure may cause Parkinson's. It is toxic to birds, fish, and beneficials.

Safety: Wear a mask and gloves; cover exposed skin and hair. Avoid skin contact.

Ryania

Ingredients: This contact-alkaloid stomach poison is made from stems and roots of the tropical shrub, *Ryania speciosa*.

Controls: Toxic to aphids, thrips, European corn borers, hemp borers, flea beetles, leaf rollers, and many caterpillars. Once pests consume ryania, they stop feeding immediately and die within 24 hours.

Caution: Somewhat toxic to beneficials and mammals!

Mixing: Follow directions on package.

Application: Follow directions on package. Apply as dust.

Persistence: Two weeks or longer.

Forms: Powder, wettable powder.

Toxicity: Toxic to mammals, birds, fish, and beneficials.

Safety: Wear a mask, gloves, and safety glasses, and cover exposed skin and hair. Avoid skin contact.

Sabadilla

Ingredients: This alkaloid pesticide is made from the seeds of a tropical lily, *Schoenocaulon officinale*, native to Central and South America, and a European hellebore, *Veratrum album*.

Controls: A contact and stomach poison, this centuries-old poison controls aphids, beetles, cabbage loopers, chinch bugs, grasshoppers, and squash bugs.

Caution: Very toxic to honeybees and moderately toxic to mammals!

Mixing: Follow directions on package.

Application: Most potent when applied at 75-80°F. Follow directions on package.

Persistence: Two or three days.

Forms: Powder, liquid.

Toxicity: Somewhat toxic to mammals, toxic to honeybees.

Safety: Wear a mask, gloves, and safety glasses, and cover exposed skin and hair. Avoid skin, eye, ear, and nose contact. Irritates eyes and nose.

Seaweed

Ingredients: Numerous elements including nutrients, bacteria, and hormones.

Controls: Suspended particles in seaweed impair, and even kill, insects and spider mites by causing lesions. The particles cut and penetrate the soft-bodied pest insects and mites causing their body fluids to leak out.

Mixing: Dilute as per instructions for soil application.

Application: Spray on foliage, especially under leaves where mites live.

Persistence: Up to two weeks when spreader-sticker is used.

Forms: Powder and liquid.

Toxicity: Not toxic to mammals, birds, and fish. Nonselective, kills beneficials.

Safety: Wear a mask and gloves.

Soap, Insecticidal

Ingredients: Mild contact insecticides made from fatty acids of animals and plants. A variety of soaps are available in potassium-salt based liquid concentrates. Soft soaps such as Ivory liquid dish soap, Castille soap, and Murphy's Oil soap are biodegradable and kill insects in a similar

manner to commercial insecticidal soaps, but they are not as potent or effective.

Controls: Controls soft-bodied insects such as aphids and mealy bugs, spider mites, thrips, and whiteflies by penetrating and clogging body membranes.

Caution: Do not use detergent soaps because they may be caustic.

Mixing: Add a few capfuls of soap to a quart of water to make a spray. Ivory or Castille soap can also be used as a spreader-sticker to mix with other sprays. The soaps help the spray stick to the foliage better.

Application: Spray at the first appearance of insect pests. Follow directions on commercial preparations. Spray homemade mixes every four to five days.

Persistence: Soft soaps will last only for about a day before dissipating.

Forms: Liquid.

Toxicity: These soaps are safe for bees, animals, and humans.

Safety: Wear a mask and gloves.

Safer Insecticidal Soap

Sulfur

Ingredients: Sulfur. Mixed with lime, sulfur is more toxic to insects but more phytotoxic to plants.

Controls: Centuries-old fungicide is effective against rusts and powdery mildew.

Caution: Do not apply in temperatures above 90°F (32°C) and less than 50 percent humidity. It will burn foliage.

Mixing: Follow directions on package.

Application: Apply in light concentration. It is phytotoxic during hot, 90°F, arid weather.

Persistence: It stays on foliage until washed off.

Forms: Powder.

Toxicity: Not toxic to honeybees, birds, and fish.

Safety: Wear a mask, gloves, and safety goggles; cover exposed skin and hair. Avoid skin, eye, ear, and nose contact. Irritates eyes, lungs, and skin.

Sulfur Fungicide

Traps

Ingredients: Sticky traps, such as Tanglefoot™ resins, can be smeared on attractive yellow or red cards to simulate ripe fruit. When the pests land on the fruit, they are stuck forever!

Controls: Helps contain spider mites and non-flying insects within the bounds of the barriers. Monitors fungus gnat populations and helps control thrips. Other insects get stuck haphazardly to the sticky stuff.

Tanglefoot

Black-light traps catch egg-laying moths and other flying insects most of which are not plant pests. Light and fan traps attract many insects including beneficials, and their use may do more harm than good.

Sex-lure traps exude specific insect pheromones, sexual scents, of females that are ready to mate. These traps are most effective to monitor insect populations for large farms.

Caution: Do not touch sticky substance. It is difficult to remove!

Mixing: Follow directions on container. Smear on desired objects.

Application: Smear Tanglefoot™ around the edges of pots, base of stems, and at the end of drying lines to form an impenetrable barrier-trap against mites and insects. This simple precaution helps keep mites isolated. However, resourceful spider mites can spin a web above the barrier. The marauding mites also ride the air currents created by fans from plant to plant!

Persistence: It is persistent until it is wiped off or completely fouled with insect bodies.

Forms: Sticky, thick paint.

Toxicity: Not toxic to mammals or insects. Trapped insects and mites starve to death.

Safety: Wear gloves.

Water

Ingredients: A cold jet of water–preferably with a pH between 6 and 7–blasts insects, spider mites, and their eggs off leaves and often kills them. Hot water vapor and steam also work as a sterilant.

Controls: A cold jet of water is an excellent first wave of attack against spider mites, aphids, and other sucking insects. Steam controls spider mites, insects, and diseases on pots, growing medium, and other grow-room surfaces.

Caution: Avoid spraying fully formed buds with water. Standing water in or on buds promotes gray mold. Do not apply hot steam to foliage.

Mixing: None.

Application: Spray leaf undersides with a jet of cold water to knock off sucking spider mites and aphids. Apply water as a mist or spray when predatory mites are present. The extra humid conditions impair the pest mite lifecycles and promote predatory mite health. Rent a wallpaper steamer. Get it cooking, and direct a jet of steam at all grow-room cracks and surfaces.

Persistence: None.

Forms: Liquid, steam vapor.

Toxicity: Not toxic to mammals, fish, and beneficials.

Safety: Do not spray strong jet of water in eyes, up nose, or into other body orifices.

Biological Controls
Predators and Parasites

Predator and parasite availability and supply have changed substantially over the last 10 years. Today, many more predators and parasites are available to home growers than ever before. Shipping, care, cost, and application of each predator or parasite is very specific and should be provided in detail by the supplier. Make sure the supplier answers the following questions:

1) Latin name of the predator so there is no confusion as to identity.
2) Specific pests attacked.
3) Life cycle.
4) Preferred climate including temperature and humidity range.
5) Application rate and mode of application.

For more information about predators check out the following web pages:
www.naturescontrol.com
www.koppert.nl/english
www.entomology.wisc.edu/mbcn/mbcn.html

By definition, a predator must eat more than one victim before adulthood. Predators, such as ladybugs (ladybird beetles) and praying mantises, have chewing mouthparts. Other predators, such as lacewing larvae, have piercing-sucking mouthparts. Chewing predators eat their prey whole. The piercing, sucking-type, suck the fluids from their prey's body.

Parasites consume a single individual host before adulthood. Adult parasitoids typically place a single egg into many hosts. The egg hatches into larvae that eat the host insect from the inside out. They save the vital organs for dessert! Most often, the larvae pupate inside the host's body and emerge as adults.

Spiders are predatory and eat other insects. If you see a spider in the garden, let it help you!

Young spider mites, adults, and eggs are visible in this photo.

Parasites, unlike predators, hunt until the prey is almost eliminated. Predators choose to be surrounded by prey. When prey population starts to diminish a little, predators move on to find a nice, fat infestation. They never truly eradicate the pests. This is why predators work best for preventative control, but are slow to stop an infestation.

The rate at which the predators and parasites keep the infestation in check is directly proportionate to the amount of predators. The more predators and parasites, the sooner they will get infestations into check. Predators and parasites outbreed their victims, reproducing faster than pests are able to keep up with.

One of the best places in the country to buy predatory and parasitoid insects is from Nature's Control, Medford, Oregon. Check out their very informative web site at www.naturescontrol.com. This supplier gives advice and supplies specific care and release instructions. Nature's Control has a good predator and parasite supply and can ship year round. Predators and parasites are shipped special delivery and may arrive after the daily-mail delivery. Make sure to pick them up as soon as they arrive. Do not let predators sit inside a mailbox in the hot sun. It could easily reach 120°F (49°C) or more!

When predators and parasites are introduced into a garden, special precautions must be taken to ensure their well-being. Stop spraying all-toxic chemicals at least two weeks before introducing the predators. Pyrethrum and insecticidal soaps can be applied up to a few days before, providing any residue is washed off with fresh water. Do not spray after releasing predators and parasites.

Predators and parasites survive best in gardens that are not sterilized between crops. Gardens with perpetual harvests are ideal for predators.

Most of the predators and parasites that do well in an indoor HID garden cannot fly. Insects that can fly often head straight for the lamp. Ladybugs are the best example. If 500 ladybugs are released on Monday, by Friday, only a few die-hards will be left. The rest will have popped off the lamp. If using flying predators or parasitoids, release when it is dark. They will live longer.

Predators are most often very small and must be introduced to each plant separately. Introducing predators to a garden and plants takes a little time and patience. Predators also have very specific climatic requirements. Pay attention to the predators' needs and maintain them for best results.

Spider Mites and Insects

Here is one of the best web sites I have found that describes insects. They have excellent photos of all pests and predators that attack marijuana: http://vegipm.tamu.edu/imageindex.html

Spider Mites

Identify: The spider mite is the most common pest found on indoor plants and causes the most problems. Spider mites have eight legs and are classified as spiders rather than insects, which have six legs. Find microscopic spider mites on leaf undersides sucking away life-giving fluids. To an untrained naked eye, they are hard to spot. Spider mites appear as tiny specks on leaf undersides; however, their telltale signs of feeding–yellowish-white spots, stippling–on the tops of leaves are easy to see. Careful inspection reveals tiny spider webs–easily seen when misted with water–on stems and under leaves as infestations progress. A magnifying glass or low-power microscope (10-30X) helps to identify the yellow-white, two-spotted brown or red mites and their translucent eggs. Indoors, the most common is the two-spotted spider mite. After a single mating, females are fertilized for life and reproduce about 75 percent female and 25 percent male eggs. Females lay about 100 eggs.

Damage: Mites suck life-giving sap from plants, causing overall vigor loss and stunting. Leaves are pocked with suck-hole marks and yellow from failure to produce chlorophyll. They lose partial

Spider mites cause stippling, small spots, on the top of leaves.

This is the worst spider mite infestation I have seen!

| 0% | 10% | 20% | 50% |

Remove leaves with 50 percent or more damage.

to full function, and leaves turn yellow and drop. Once a plant is overrun with spider mites, the infestation progresses rapidly. Severe cases cause plant death.

Controls: Cleanliness! This is the most important first step to spider mite control. Keep the grow room and tools spotless and disinfected. Mother plants often have spider mites. Spray mothers regularly with miticides, including once three days before taking cuttings. Once mite infestations get out of control and miticides work poorly, the entire grow room will have to be cleaned out and disinfected with a pesticide and 5 percent bleach solution. Steam disinfection is also possible but too difficult in most situations.

Cultural and physical control: Spider mites thrive in a dry, 70-80°F (21-27° C) climate, and reproduce every five days in temperatures above 80°F (27° C). Create a hostile environment by lowering the temperature to 60°F (16°C) and spray foliage, especially under leaves, with a jet of cold water. Spraying literally blasts them off the leaves as well as increases humidity. Their reproductive cycle will be slowed, and you will have a chance to kill them before they do much damage. Manual removal works for small populations. Smash all mites in sight between the thumb and index finger, or wash leaves individually in between two sponges. Avoid infecting other plants with contaminated hands or sponges.

Remove leaves with more than 50 percent damage and throw away, making sure insects and eggs do not reenter the garden. If mites have attacked only one or two plants, isolate the infected plants and treat them separately. Take care when removing foliage not to spread mites to other plants. Severely damaged plants should be carefully removed from the garden and destroyed.

Smear a layer of Tanglefoot™ around the lips of containers and at the base of stems to create barriers spider mites cannot cross. This will help isolate them to specific plants. Note: smear a layer of Tanglefoot™ at each end of drying lines when hanging buds to contain spider mites. Once foliage is dead, mites try to migrate down drying lines to find live foliage with fresh, flowing sap.

Biological: *Neoseiulus (Amblyseius) californicus* and *Mesoseiulus (phytoseiulus) longipes*, are the two most common and effective predators. *Phytoseiulus persimilis, Neoseiulus (Amblyseius) fallacius, Galendromus (Metaseiulus) occidentalis,* and *Galendromus (Typhlodromus) pyri* predators are also available commercially.

When properly applied and reared, predatory spider mites work very well. There are many

Progressive Control Measures for Spider Mites

Cleanliness - Clean room daily, disinfect tools, do not introduce new pests into the garden on clothes, no animal visits, etc.

Create hostile environment - Humidity, temperature, water spray.

Create barriers - Smear Tanglefoot™ around pot lips, stems, drying lines.

Dip cuttings and vegetative plants - Dip small plants in pyrethrum, horticultural oil, neem oil.

Remove damaged foliage - Remove foliage more than 50 percent damaged.

Introduce predatory mites - Release predators before infestations grow out of hand.

Spray - Apply pyrethrum or neem oil; use strong miticides only if necessary. Rotate sprays so mites do not develop immunity.

50%
Humidity

F   C

70° - - 21°
60° - - 15°

Keep relative humidity below 50 percent to discourage bud mold.

If plants are infested with spider mites, lower the temperature to 60-70°F (10-21°C). This temperature range will slow their reproduction.

things to consider when using the predators. First, predators can eat only a limited number of mites a day; the average predator can eat 20 eggs or 5 adults daily. As soon as the predators' source of food is gone, some mites die of starvation while others survive on other insects or pollen. Check with suppliers for release instructions of specific species. A general dosage of 20 predators per plant is a good place to start. Predatory mites have a difficult time traveling from plant to plant, so setting them out on each plant is necessary. Temperature and humidity levels must be at the proper levels to give the predators the best possible chance to thrive. When spider mites have infested a garden, the predatory mites cannot eat them fast enough to solve the problem. Predatory mites work best when there are only a few spider mites. Introduce predators as soon as spider mites are seen on vegetative growth, and release them every month thereafter. This gives predators a chance to keep up with mites. Before releasing predators, rinse all plants thoroughly to ensure all toxic-spray residues from insecticides and fungicides are gone.

The fungus, *Hirsutella thompsonii*, trade name Mycar®, kills spider mites.

Sprays: Homemade sprays often lack the strength to kill infestations but work as a deterrent by repelling mites. Popular homemade sprays include Dr. Bonner's Soap, garlic, hot pepper, citrus oil, and liquid seaweed combinations. If these sprays do not deter spider mites after four to five applications, switch to a stronger spray: neem oil, pyrethrum, horticultural oil, or nicotine sulfate, cinnamaldehyde.

Insecticidal soap does a fair job of controlling mites. Usually two or three applications at five- to ten-day intervals will do the trick.

Horticultural oil smothers eggs and can be mixed with pyrethrum and homemade sprays to improve extermination.

Pyrethrum (aerosol) is the best natural miticide! Apply two to three applications at five- to ten-day intervals. Pyrethrum is the best control for spider mites. Spider mites should be gone after two or three applications at five- to ten-day intervals, providing sanitary preventative conditions are maintained. Eggs hatch in five to ten days. The second spraying will kill the newly hatched eggs and the remaining adults. The third and subsequent applications will kill any new spider mites, but mites soon develop a resistance to synthetic pyrethrum.

Neem oil works great!

Heavy-duty chemical miticides are available but are not recommended on plants that will be consumed by humans. If using any chemical miticide, be sure it is a contact poison and not systemic. Use StirrupM®, described below, to improve the spider mite kill rate. Cinnamaldehyde extracted from *Cinnamonum zeylanicum* kills mites. The synthetic hormone–sold under the brand name StirrupM®–attracts spider mites, and is used very successfully to enhance miticides.

Aphids
Identify: Aphids, also called *plant lice*, are about the size of a pinhead. They are easy to spot with the naked eye, but use a 10X magnifying glass for positive identification. Aphids are found

Chemical Insecticides and Miticides

Chemical	Trade Name*	Notes
abamectin	Avid®	Produced by soil fungi, Streptomyces species
dienochlor	Pentac®	Slow-acting but selective against mites
aldicarb	Temik®	Systemic miticide DO NOT USE
methomyl	Subdue®	Systemic insecticide DO NOT USE
dicofol	Kelthane®	Selective miticide, DDT relative, DO NOT USE
acephate	Orthene®	Systemic miticide/ insecticide, DO NOT USE

*All trade names are not included. Check insecticides and miticides for chemical name.

Ants farm aphids. They move aphids to uninfected plants.

in all climates. Normally grayish to black, aphids can be green to pink–in any color, aphids attack plants. Most aphids have no wings, but those that do have wings that are about four times the size of their bodies. Aphids give birth to mainly live female larvae, without mating, and can pump out 3 to 100 hungry larvae every day. Each female reproduces between 40 and 100 offspring that start reproducing soon after birth. Aphids are most common indoors when they are plentiful outdoors. Install yellow sticky traps near base of several plants and near the tops of other plants to monitor invasions of winged aphids, often the first to enter the garden. As they feed, aphids exude sticky honeydew that attracts ants that feed on it. Ants like honeydew so much that they take the aphids hostage and make them produce honeydew. Look for columns of ants marching around plants, and you will find aphids.

Damage: Aphids suck the life-giving sap from foliage causing leaves to wilt and yellow. When infestation mounts, you may notice sticky honeydew excreted by aphids. They prefer to attack weak, stressed plants. Some species prefer succulent, new growth, and other aphids like older foliage or even flower buds. Look for them under leaves, huddled around branch nodes, and growing tips. This pest transports (vectors) bacterium, fungi, and viruses. Aphids vector more viruses than any other source. Destructive sooty mold also grows on honeydew. Any aphid control must also control ants, if they are present.

Controls: Manually remove small numbers. Spot-spray small infestations, and control ants. Introduce predators if problem is persistent.

Cultural and physical control: Manual removal is easy and works well to kill them. When affixed to foliage–sucking out fluid–aphids are unable to move and easy to crush with fingers or sponges dipped in an insecticidal solution.

Biological: Lacewings, *Chrysoperla* species, are the most effective and available predators for aphids. Release one to 20 lacewings per plant, depending on infestation level, as soon as aphids appear. Repeat every month. Eggs take a few days to hatch into larvae that exterminate aphids. Gall-midge, *Aphidoletes aphidimyz*, is available under the trade name Aphidend; parasitic wasp, *Aphidius matricaria*, is available commercially as Aphidpar.

Ladybugs also work well to exterminate aphids. Adults are easily obtained at many retail nurseries during the summer months. The only drawback to ladybugs is their attraction to the HID lamp–release about 50 ladybugs per plant, at least half of them will fly directly into the HID, hit the hot bulb, and buzz to their death. Within one or two weeks all the ladybugs will fall victim to the lamp, requiring frequent replenishment.

Verticillium lecanii (fungus)–available under the trade name of *Vertalec®*–is very aphid specific and effective.

Control ants by mixing borax hand soap or borax powder with powdered sugar. Ants eat the sweet mix and borax kills them. They excrete sweet borax mix in the nest where other ants eat the feces and die.

Sprays: Homemade and insecticidal soap sprays are very effective. Apply two or three times at five- to ten-day intervals. Pyrethrum (aerosol) applied two to three times at five- to ten-day intervals.

Bees and Wasps

Identify: Bees and wasps that sting are usually from a half inch (1.5 cm) to more than an inch (3 cm) long. Most have yellow stripes around their bodies and others have none. They are especially attracted to indoor gardens when weather cools outdoors– they move right in.

Wasp Trap

Damage: They cause no damage to plants but can become a nuisance in grow rooms and hurt like hell when they sting.

Controls: Occasionally a problem indoors, bees and wasps are most efficiently controlled with sprays.

Cultural and physical control: They enter grow rooms through vents and cracks, attracted by the growing plants, a valuable commodity in the middle of a cold winter! Screen all entrances to the room. Install more circulation fans to make flying difficult. Wasp traps, sweet flypaper, and Tanglefoot™ impair these pests. Bees and wasps are also attracted to the hot HID and fly into it and die.

Biological: Unnecessary.

Sprays: Pyrethrum is recommended. Stuff small nests into a wide-mouthed jar–do it at night when the wasps are quiet–and place the jar in a freezer for a few hours. Use Sevin, *Carbaryl*, only if there is a problem with a wasp nest.

Beetle Borers

Identify: Larvae from several boring beetles tunnel or bore into stems and roots. Look for their entry hole and dead growth on either side of the entry hole along the main stem, often discolored and accompanied by sawdust. Borers are more common outdoors than indoors.

Damage: Tunnels inside the stem and roots; curtails fluid flow, and causes plant parts to wilt. If

Beetle Borer.

borer damages the main stem severely, fluid flow to the entire plant could stop, causing death.

Controls: Seldom a problem indoors. Borers often cause so much damage on a particular stem that it has to be removed and destroyed.

Cultural and physical control: Handpick all beetle grubs.

Biological: Several mixes of beneficial nematodes control these borers in soil.

Sprays: *Bacillus popilliae* is specific to beetles or rotenone individually injected into stems.

Caterpillars and Loopers

Caterpillars and loopers leave plenty of droppings on the plant. The droppings accumulate in between buds. Droppings fall out when the buds are hung to dry; inspect below the hung buds to find the poop droppings.

Identify: From half inch to four inches (1.5-10 cm), caterpillars and loopers are cylindrical with feet, often green, but can be virtually any color

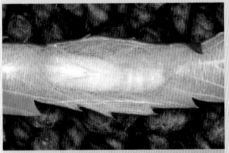

This cocoon is attached to the bottom of a leaf.

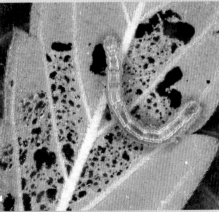

Caterpillars can cause major damage to foliage.

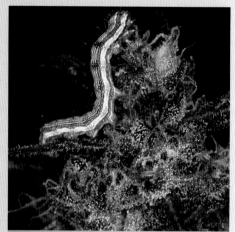

This caterpillar burrows into buds, leaving a wake of poop. The wound and feces both attract more diseases.

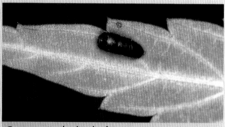

Cocoon attached to leaf.

Loopers arch their body upward to move forward.

from white to black. Caterpillars have sets of feet the entire length of the body, while loopers have two sets of feet at either end of the body. Loopers place their front feet forward, arch their body upward in the middle, and pull their rear sets of legs forward. Some have stripes, spots, and other designs that provide camouflage. Seldom a problem indoors, caterpillars and loopers are in a life stage–between a larva and a flying moth or

butterfly–and are most common when prevalent outdoors. One way to check for caterpillars and loopers is to spray one plant with pyrethrum aerosol spray and shake the plant afterward. The spray has a quick knockout effect, and most caterpillars will fall from the plant.

Damage: These munching critters chew and eat pieces of foliage and leave telltale bites in leaves. Some caterpillars will roll themselves inside leaves. An infestation of caterpillars or leafhoppers will damage foliage and slow growth, eventually defoliating, stunting, and killing a plant.

Cultural and physical control: Manually remove.

Biological: *Trichogramma* wasps, spined soldier bug (*Podisus maculiventris* Podibug®).

Sprays: Homemade spray/repellent, hot pepper and garlic. *Bt*, pyrethrum, and rotenone

Leafhoppers

Identify: Leafhoppers include many small, 0.125 inch (3 mm) long, wedge-shaped insects that are usually green, white, or yellow. Many species have minute stripes on wings and bodies. Their wings peak like roof rafters when not in use. Leafhoppers suck plant sap for food and exude sticky honeydew as a by-product. Spittlebug and leafhopper larvae wrap themselves in foliage and envelop themselves in a saliva-like liquid, plant sap.

Damage: Stippling (spotting) similar to that caused by spider mites and thrips on foliage. Leaves and plant lose vigor, and in severe cases death could result.

Cultural and physical Control: Cleanliness! Black light traps are attractive to potato beetles.

Biological: The fungus, *Metarhizium anisopliae*, is commercially available under the trade name *Metaquino®*.

Sprays: Pyrethrum, rotenone, sabadilla.

Leaf Miner

Identify: Adult leaf miner flies lay eggs that hatch into one-eighth-inch (0.25 mm) long (green or black) maggots. You seldom see the maggots before you see the leaf damage they create when they tunnel through leaf tissue. Leaf miners are more common in greenhouses and outdoors than indoors.

Damage: The tiny maggots burrow between leaf surfaces, leaving a telltale whitish-tunnel outline. The damage usually occurs on or in young supple growth. It is seldom fatal, unless left unchecked. Damage causes plant growth to slow, and if left unchecked, flowering is prolonged and buds are small. In rare cases the damage is fatal. Wound damage encourages disease.

Controls: These pests cause little problem to indoor crops. The most efficient and effective control is to remove and dispose of damaged foliage, which includes the rogue maggot, or to use the cultural and physical control listed below.

Cultural and physical control: Smash the little maggot trapped within the leaf with your fingers. If the infestation is severe, smash all larvae possible and remove severely infested leaves. Compost or burn infested leaves. Install yellow sticky traps to capture adults.

Biological: Branchid Wasp (*Dacnusa sibirica*), chalcid wasp (*Diglyphus isaea*), parasitic wasp (*Opius pallipes*).

Sprays: Repel with neem oil and pyrethrum sprays. Maggots are protected within tunnels, and sprays are often ineffective. *Hemp Diseases and Pests* suggests to water plants with a 0.5 percent solution of neem. This solution works fast and stays on plants for four weeks after application.

Fungus Gnat

Identify: Maggots, larvae, grow to 4-5 mm long and have translucent bodies with black heads. Winged adult gnats are gray to black, 2-4 mm long, with long legs. Look for them around the base of plants in soil and soilless gardens. They love the moist, dank environments in rockwool and the environment created in NFT-type hydroponic gardens. Adult females lay about 200 eggs every week to ten days.

Damage: Infests growing medium and roots near the surface. They eat fine root hairs and scar larger roots, causing plants to lose vigor and foliage to pale. Root wounds invite wilt fungi like *Fusarium* or *Pythium* especially if plants are nutrient-stressed and growing in soggy conditions. Maggots prefer to consume dead or decaying, soggy plant material; they also eat green algae growing in soggy conditions. Adults and larvae can get out of control quickly, especially in hydroponic systems with very moist growing mediums. The adult gnats stick to resinous buds like *flypaper*! The gnats are very difficult to clean from the buds.

Leaf miner larvae burrow in the leaf. They cause few problems indoors and are most common outdoors in spring and early summer. Kill them by smashing them between your fingers.

Microscopic fungus gnats are difficult to see with the naked eye.

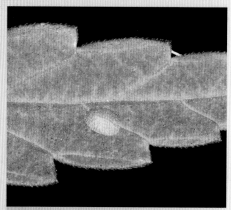

Scale affix themselves to stems and foliage. They are a minor problem indoors and outdoors.

This nematode attacked the stem. Most often nematodes attack roots. Large knots grow where nematodes damage both roots and stems.

Controls: The easiest way to control these pests is with Vectobac®, Gnatrol®, and Bactimos®, all contain *Bacillus thuringiensis* var. *israelensis* (*Bt-i*). This strain of *Bt* controls the maggots; unfortunately, it is available only in large one-gallon (3.8 L) containers. Difficult to find at garden centers, check hydroponic stores.

Cultural and physical control: Do not overwater, and keep ambient humidity low. Do not let growing medium remain soggy. Cover growing medium so green algae won't grow. Yellow sticky traps placed horizontally 1-2 inches (3-6 cm) over growing medium catches adults.

Biological: The aforementioned *Bt-i* works best. Alternatives include the predatory soil mite (*Hypoaspis* (Geolaelapumites) and the nematode (*Steinernema feltiae*).

Sprays: Apply neem or insecticidal soap as a soil-drench.

Mealybugs and Scales
Mealybugs:
Identify: Somewhat common indoors, these 0.08-0.2 inch (2-7 mm) oblong, waxy-white insects move very little, mature slowly, and live in colonies that are usually located at stem joints. Like aphids, mealybugs excrete sticky honeydew.
Scales:
As uncommon indoors as mealybugs, scale looks and acts similar to mealybugs but is usually more round than oblong. Scales may be white, yellow, brown, gray, or black. Their hard protective shell is 0.08-0.15 inch (2-4 mm) across. Mealybugs rarely or never move. Check for them around stem joints where they live in colonies. Scales sometimes excrete sticky honeydew.

Damage: These pests suck sap from plants which causes growth to slow. They also exude sticky honeydew as a by-product of their diet of plant sap which encourages sooty mold and draws ants that eat the honeydew.

Controls: These pests present little problem to indoor growers. The easiest and most efficient control is listed under *Cultural and physical* below.

Cultural and physical control: Manual removal is somewhat tedious but very effective. Wet a Q-Tip in rubbing alcohol and wash scale away. A small knife, fingernails, or tweezers may also be necessary to scrape and pluck the tightly affixed mealybugs and scales after they are Q-Tipped with alcohol.

Biological: There are numerous species of mealybugs and scales. Each has natural predators including species of ladybeetles (ladybugs) and parasitic and predatory wasps. There are so many species of each that it would be exhaustive to list them here. For more specific information see *Hemp Diseases and Pests.*

Sprays: Homemade sprays that contain rubbing alcohol, nicotine, and soaps all kill these pests. Insecticidal soap, pyrethrum, and neem oil are all recommended.

Nematodes
Identify: Of the hundreds and thousands of species of microscopic nematodes–sometimes, big ones are called *eelworms*–a few are destructive to plants. Most often nematodes attack roots

and are found in the soil; however, a few nematodes attack stems and foliage. Root nematodes can often be seen in and around roots with the help of a 30X microscope. Often growers just diagnose the damage caused by destructive nematodes rather than actually seeing them.

Damage: Slow growth, leaf chlorosis, wilting several hours during daylight hours from lack of fluid flow–symptoms can be difficult to discern from nitrogen deficiency. Root damage is often severe by the time they are examined. Root knot nematodes are some of the worst. They cause roots to swell with galls. Other nematodes scrape and cut roots, compounded by fungal attacks. Roots turn soft and mushy.

Cultural and physical control: Cleanliness! Use new, sterilized potting soil or soilless mix to exclude nematodes' entrance. Nematodes rarely cause problems indoors in clean grow rooms.

Biological: French marigolds, *Tagetes patula,* repels soil nematodes, fungus (*Myrothecium verrucaria,* trade name DeTera ES®)

Sprays: Neem used as a soil-drench.

Root Maggot

Identify: Both the seed corn maggot and the cabbage maggot attack cannabis roots. The seed corn maggot is 1.5 to 2 inches (5-6 cm) long. The seed corn maggot converts into a fly and is a bit smaller than a common housefly. Cabbage maggots are 0.3 inch (1 cm) long, and the adult fly is bigger than a housefly. These pests winter over in the soil and live in unclean soil. In the spring, they emerge as adult flies and soon lay eggs in the soil at the base of young plants. The squirmy, whitish larvae hatch several days later with a ravenous appetite.

Damage: Root maggots chew and burrow into stems and roots. The seed corn maggot attacks seeds and seedling roots. Cabbage maggots attack roots, leaving hollowed out channels and holes in larger roots. Both maggots destroy small hairlike feeder roots. Wounds made by the root maggots also foster soft rot and fungal diseases.

Cultural and physical control: Cleanliness! Use fresh, new store-bought soil when planting in containers. Cover seedlings with Agronet® to exclude flies, and plant late in the year to avoid most adult flies. Place a collar 18-inch (45 cm) of foam rubber around the base of the plant to exclude flies.

Root knot nematodes cause roots to develop lumps. Fluid flow from roots causes impaired growth.

Biological: Control with parasitic nematodes, *Steinernema feltiae* or *Heterorhabditis bacteriophora.*

Sprays: Kill root maggots with neem and horticultural oil used as a soil-drench.

Slugs and Snails

Identify: Slugs and snails are soft, slimy white, dark, or yellow, and occasionally striped. They are 0.25-3 inches (1-9 cm) long. Snails live in a circular shell, slugs do not. They hide by day and feed at night. Slugs and snails leave a slimy, silvery trail of mucus in their wake. They lay translucent eggs that hatch in about a month. They reproduce prolifically, and the young mollusks often eat relatively more than adults.

Damage: They make holes in leaves often with a weblike appearance. They will eat almost any vegetation, roots included. These creatures winter over in warm, damp locations in most climates. Slugs and snails especially like tender seedlings. They will migrate to adjacent gardens in quest of food.

Cultural and physical control: A clean, dry perimeter around the garden will make it difficult for them to pass. Spotlight and handpick at night. A thin layer of lime, diatomaceous earth, or salty beach sand two to six (6-15 cm) inches wide around individual plants, beds, or the entire garden will present an impassable barrier. The lime is not thick enough to alter the pH and will repel or dissolve pests. To trap, attach short one-inch (3 cm) feet on a wide board and leave it in the garden. The pests will seek refuge under the board. Pick up the board every day or two, and

Root maggots are found in contaminated soil. They gnaw off root hairs and hollow out larger roots.

Slugs and snails cause most damage to seedlings outdoors. Look for slime trails and holes in leaves to help identify the pests.

Thrips make light abrasions on leaf surfaces.

shake the slugs off and step on them.

Poisonous baits usually have metaldahyde as a base. Confine the bait to a slug hotel. Cut a 1 x 2-inch (3-6 cm) slot in a covered plastic container to make a slug and snail hotel. Place slug and snail bait inside the hotel. The hotel must keep the bait dry and off the soil. In a slug hotel, none of the poison bait touches the soil, and the bait is inaccessible to children, pets, and birds. Place slug and snail hotels in out of the way places. Natural baits include a mix of jam and water and beer. If using beer, it must be deep enough to drown mollusks.

Biological: The predatory snail, *Ruminia decollata*–available commercially–is yet another way to combat plant-eating slugs and snails.

Sprays: Young slugs and snails are not attracted to bait. Spray for young at night or early morning with a 50 percent ammonia-water solution.

Thrips

Identify: More common in greenhouses than indoors. These tiny, winged, fast moving little critters are hard to see but not hard to spot. From 0.04-0.05 inch (1-1.5 mm) long, thrips can be different colors, including white, gray, and dark colors, often with petite stripes. Check for them under leaves by shaking parts of the plant. If there are many thrips present, they choose to jump and run rather than fly to safety. But often you will see them as a herd of specks thundering across foliage. Females make holes in soft plant tissue where they deposit eggs that are virtually invisible to the naked eye. Winged thrips easily migrate from infested plants to the entire garden.

Damage: Thrips scrape tissue from leaves and buds, afterward sucking out the plant juices for food. Stipples–whitish-yellowish specks–appear on top of leaves; chlorophyll production diminishes and leaves become brittle. You will also see black specks of thrip feces and little thrips. Many times thrips feed inside flower buds or wrap-up and distort leaves.

Cultural and physical control: Cleanliness! Blue or pink sticky traps, misting plants with water impairs travel. Manual removal works okay if only a few thrips are present, but they are hard to catch. Thrips can be very vexing to control once they get established.

Biological: Predatory mites (*Amblyseius cucumeris* and *Amblyseius barkeri*, *Neoseiulus cucumeris*, *Iphiseius degenerans*, *Neoseiulus barkeri*,

Euseius hibisci), parasitic wasps (*Thripobis semi-luteus, Ceranisus menes, Goetheana shake-spearei*), pirate bugs (*Orius* species), fungus, *Verticillium lecani,* is effective.

Sprays: Homemade sprays such as tobacco-nicotine base; commercial pyrethrum, synthetic pyrethrum, insecticidal soap. Apply two to four times at five- to ten-day intervals.

Whiteflies

Identify: The easiest way to check for the little buggers is to grab a limb and shake it. If there are any whiteflies, they will fly from under leaves. Whiteflies look like a small, white moth about 0.04-inch (1 mm) long. Adult whiteflies have wings. They usually appear near the top of the weakest plant first. They will move downward on the plant or fly off to infest another plant. Eggs are also found on leaf underside, where they are connected with a small hook.

Damage: Whiteflies, like mites, may cause white speckles, stipples, on the tops of leaves. Loss of chlorophyll production and plant vigor diminishes as infestation progresses.

Cultural and physical control: Mites are difficult to remove manually because they fly. Adults are attracted to the color yellow. To build a white-fly trap similar to flypaper, cover a bright, yellow object with a sticky substance like Tanglefoot™. Place the traps on the tops of the pots among the plants. Traps work very well. When they are full of insects, toss them out.

Biological: The wasp, *Encarisa formosa,* is the most effective whitefly parasite. The small wasps only attack whiteflies, they do not sting people! All toxic sprays must be washed completely off before introducing parasites and predators. Since the *Encarsia formosa* is a parasite, about 0.125 inch (3 mm) long, smaller than the whitefly, it takes them much longer to control or even keep the whitefly population in check. The parasitic wasp lays an egg in the whitefly larva that later hatches and eats the larva alive, from the inside out–death is slow. If you use them, set them out at the rate of two or more parasites per plant as soon as the first whitefly is detected. Repeat every two to four weeks throughout the life of the plants.

The fungus *Verticillium lecanii* AKA *Cephalosporium lecanii,* trade name Mycatal®, is also very effective in whitefly control.

Sprays: Easily eradicated with natural sprays.

Whiteflies can be seen in between yellowish aphids. Dark spots are honeydew that has started to mold.

Before spraying, remove any leaves that have been over 50 percent damaged and cure with heat or burn infested foliage. Homemade sprays applied at five- to ten-day intervals work well. Insecticidal soap applied at five- to ten-day intervals. Pyrethrum (aerosol) applied at five- to ten-day intervals.

Fungi and Diseases

Fungi are very primitive plants and do not produce chlorophyll, the substance that gives higher plants their green color. Fungi reproduce by spreading tiny microscopic spores rather than seeds. Countless fungal spores are present in the air at all times. When these microscopic-airborne spores find the proper conditions, they will settle, take hold, and start growing. Some fungi, such as bud-rotting gray mold (*Botrytis*) are so prolific that they can spread through an entire crop in a matter of days! In fact, one grow room was located near a swamp and *Botrytis* spores were omnipresent in the environment. Buds and stems contracted gray mold quickly and were often reduced to a wisp-of-powdery-foliage in short order. The grower lost four consecutive crops. Finally, the grower moved to greener pastures and had no trouble with mold. Unsterile, soggy

A good vent fan is essential to control humidity indoors.

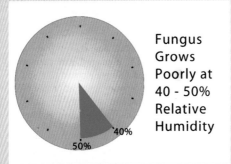

Fungus Grows Poorly at 40 - 50% Relative Humidity

In general, most fungus does not grow or grows poorly when relative humidity stays between 40 and 50 percent.

soil, coupled with humid, stagnant air, provides the environment most fungi need to thrive. Although there are many different types of fungi, they are usually prevented with similar methods.

Prevention

Prevention is the first step and the true key to fungi control. The section "Setting up the Grow Room" instructs growers to remove anything–cloth curtains, clothes, and other debris–that might attract, harbor, and spread fungi. Cover the carpet with white Visqueen® plastic. If mold should surface on the walls, spray with fungicide.

Wash walls with a five percent bleach solution or Pinesol® (made from natural pine oil) and apply paint that contains a fungus-inhibiting agent. Specially designed paints for damp conditions contain a fungicide and are attracted by moisture. When applied to a damp, cracked basement wall, the paint is drawn into the moist crack. Remove all mold from the walls by washing it a with bleach solution before painting with fungus-resistant paint. Cleanliness and climate control are the keys to preventing fungi. Few clean, well ventilated grow rooms have problems with fungi. In contrast, every dingy, dank, ill-kept indoor garden I have seen had fungal problems and yielded a substandard harvest.

Install a vent fan(s) large enough to remove moist air quickly and keep humidity at 50 percent or less. A vent fan is the easiest and least expensive humidity control device available. CO_2 generators produce humidity-increasing water vapor as a by-product. Dehumidifiers are relatively inexpensive, readily available at discount stores, and do a good job of keeping humidity under control in enclosed grow rooms. Dehumidifiers draw extra electricity, and the condensed water must be removed daily. Wood, coal, and electric heat all dry and dehumidify the air. Most air conditioners can be set to a specific humidity level. If the grow room(s) have a central heating/air-conditioning vent, the vent can be opened to control temperature and lower humidity.

Control

Prevent fungus by controlling all the factors contributing to its growth: remove hiding places, keep room clean, lower humidity to 50 percent, and keep the air well-circulated. If prevention proves inadequate and fungi appear, advanced control measures are necessary. Carefully remove and destroy dead leaves. Wash your hands after handling diseased foliage. If the problem attacks one or a few plants, isolate and treat them separately. Remember, fungi can spread like wildfire if the conditions are right. If they get a good start even after all preventive measures are taken, do not hesitate to take extreme control methods including spraying the entire garden with the proper fungicide.

Gray Mold (*Botrytis*), a.k.a. Bud Mold

Identify: Gray mold is the most common fun-

Logical Progression of Fungus Control

Prevention
Cleanliness
Low humidity
Ventilation
Removal
Copper, lime sulfur sprays
Specific fungicide

gus that attacks indoor plants and flourishes in moist temperate climates common to many grow rooms. *Botrytis* damage is compounded by humid (above 50 percent) climates. It starts within the bud and is difficult to see at the onset–grayish-whitish to bluish-green in color–*Botrytis* appears hairlike and similar to laundry lint in moist climates. As the disease progresses, the foliage turns somewhat slimy. Damage can also appear as dark, brownish spots on buds in less humid environments. Dry to the touch, *Botrytis*-affected area often crumbles if rubbed. Gray mold attacks countless other crops, and airborne spores are present virtually everywhere. While most commonly found attacking dense and swelling flower buds, it also attacks stems, leaves, and seeds, causes damping-off, and decomposes dry, stored bud. It is also transmitted via seeds.

Damage: Watch for single leaves that mysteriously dry out on the buds. They could be the telltale signs of a *Botrytis* attack inside the bud. Constant observation, especially during the last two weeks before harvest, is necessary to keep this disease out of the garden. Flower buds are quickly reduced to slime in cool, humid conditions or unsmokable powder in warm, dry rooms. *Botrytis* can destroy an entire crop in seven to ten days if left unchecked. Stem damage–*Botrytis* starts on stems and not buds–is less common indoors. First, stems turn yellow and cankerous growths develop. The damage causes growth above the wound to wilt and can cause stems to fold over. Transported by air, contaminated hands, and tools, gray mold spreads very quickly indoors, infecting an entire grow room in less than a week when conditions are right.

Control: Minimize *Botrytis* attack incidence with low humidity (50 percent or less), ample air circulation, and ventilation. Grow varieties that do not produce heavy, tightly packed buds that provide

Botrytis, *also known as bud mold, attacks both buds and stems of plants.*

Botrytis *on this plant progressed from the bud down the stem.*

This bud is covered with Botrytis. *It was removed from the garden and destroyed.*

Evaporated sulfur in a grow room or greenhouse stops Botrytis *from contaminating plants.*

Damping-off attacked this stem at the soil line, rotting the buried end of the stem.

a perfect place for this fungus to flourish. Cool (below 70°F [21°C]), moist climates with humidity above 50 percent are perfect for rampant gray mold growth. Remove dead leaf stems, petioles, from stalks when removing damaged leaves to avoid *Botrytis* outbreaks, which is often harbored by dead, rotting foliage. Increase ventilation and keep humidity below 60 percent, and keep the grow room clean! Use fresh, sterile growing medium for each crop.

Cultural and physical control: As soon as *Botrytis* symptoms appear, use alcohol-sterilized pruners to remove *Botrytis*-infected buds at least one inch (3 cm) below the infected area. Some growers amputate two to four inches (5-10 cm) below damage to ensure removal. Do not let the bud or anything that touches it contaminate other buds and foliage. Remove from the garden and destroy. Wash your hands and tools after removing. Increase temperature to 80°F (26°C) and lower humidity to below 50 percent. Excessive nitrogen and phosphorus levels make foliage tender, so *Botrytis* can get a foothold. Make sure pH is around 6 to facilitate calcium uptake. Low light levels also encourage weak growth and gray mold attack. Avoid heavy crowding of plants and keep the light levels bright. *Botrytis* needs UV light to complete its life cycle; without UV light it cannot live. Some varieties seldom fall victim to gray mold. Many crosses are more resistant to gray mold than pure *indica* varieties. Harvest when resin glands are still translucent. Once glands turn amber, threat of gray mold increases substantially.

Biological: Spray plants with *Gliocladium roseum* and *Trichoderma* species. Prevent damping-off with a soil application of *Gliocladium* and *Trichoderma* species. *Hemp Diseases and Pests* suggests to experiment with the yeasts *Pichia guilliermondii* and *Candida oleophila* or the bacterium *Pseudomonas syringae*.

Sprays: Bordeaux mixture keeps early stages of *Botrytis* in check as long as it is present on the foliage. Preventive spraying is advised if in a high-risk area, but spraying buds near harvesttime is not advised. Seeds are protected from *Botrytis* with a coating of Captan. Check with your local nursery for product recommendations.

Damping-off
Identify: This fungal condition, sometimes called *Pythium* wilt, is often found in soil and growing mediums. It prevents newly sprouted seeds from emerging, and attacks seedlings causing them to rot at the soil line, yellows foliage and rots older plants at soil line. It occassionally attacks rooting cuttings at the soil line, too. It is caused by different fungal species, including *Botrytis*, *Pythium*, and *Fusarium*. Once initiated, damping-off is fatal. At the onset of damping-off, the stem looses girth at the soil line, weakens, then grows dark, and finally fluid circulation is cut, killing the seedling or cutting.

Control: Damping-off is caused by a combination of the following: (1) Fungi are already present in an unsterile rooting medium; (2) Overwatering and maintaining a soggy growing medium; (3) Excessive humidity. The disease can be avoided by controlling soil moisture. Overwatering is the biggest cause of damping-off and the key to prevention. Careful daily scrutiny of soil will ensure the proper amount of moisture is available to seeds or cuttings. Start seeds and root cuttings in a fast-draining, sterile coarse sand, rockwool, Oasis™, or Jiffy™ cubes, which are difficult to overwater. Do not place a humidity tent over sprouted seedlings–a tent can lead to excessive humidity and damping-off. Cuttings are less susceptible to damping-off and love a humidity tent to promote rooting. Keep germination temperatures between 70-85°F (21-29°C). Damping-off is inhibited by bright light; grow seedlings under the HID rather than fluorescent bulbs. Keep fertilization to a minimum during the first couple weeks of growth. Germinate seeds between clean, fresh paper towels and move seeds to soil once sprouted. Do not plant seeds too deeply, cover with soil the depth of the seed. Use fresh, sterile growing medium and clean pots to guard against harmful fungus in the soil.

Biological: Apply Polygangron® (Pythium oligandrum) granules to soil and seed. Bak Pak® or Intercept® are applied to the soil and Deny® or Dagger®–forms of the bacterium Burkholderia cepacia–are put on the seeds. Epic®, Kodiac®, Quantum 4000®, Rhizo-Plus®, System 3®, and Seranade® also suppress many causes of damping-off.

Chemical: Dust the seeds with Captan®. Avoid benomyl fungicide soil drench because it kills beneficial organisms.

Downy Mildew

Identify: Sometimes called *false mildew*, downy mildew affects vegetative and flowering plants. Young, succulent foliage is a favorite starting place. Powdery mildew develops in temperatures below 76°F (26°C).

It appears as whitish-yellow spots on top of leaves creating pale patches. Grayish mycelium spawn is on leaf undersides, opposite the pale patches. Downy mildew can spread very quickly, causing a lack of vigor and slow growth; leaves yellow, die back, and drop. The disease is in the plant system and grows outward. It is often fatal,

A small, white spot and the beginning of rot at the soil line are the first visual signs of damping-off.

Lack of oxygen caused by overwatering impairs root development along the stem and contributes to damping-off.

Powdery mildew, fuzzy white spots signify the disease already permeates the entire plant. Climate control will prevent powdery mildew.

Foliar spots started on this leaf after it became severely nitrogen-deficient.

spreads quickly, and can wipeout a crop. Avoid promoting this disease by not crowding plants. Keep temperatures above 76°F (26°C) and the humidity below 50 percent.

Control: Cleanliness! Use sterile growing medium. Remove and destroy affected plants, not just foliage.

Biological: Apply Serenade® (*Bacillus subtilis*). Bordeaux mixture is also somewhat effective.

Blight

Identify: Blight is a general term that describes many plant diseases which are caused by fungus, most often a few weeks before harvest. Signs of blight include dark, blotchy spots on foliage, slow growth, sudden yellowing, wilting, and plant death. Most blights spread quickly through large areas of plants.

Control: Cleanliness! Use fresh, sterile growing medium. Avoid excess nitrogen fertilization. Avoid blights by keeping plants healthy with the proper nutrient balance and good drainage to prevent nutrient buildup.

Biological: Use Serenade® (*Bacillus subtilis*) against Brown Blight. Use Binab®, Bio-Fungus®, RootShield®, Supresivit®, Trichopel®, (*Trichoderma harzianum*) or SoilGuard® (*Trichoderma virens*). Use a Bordeaux mixture to stop fungal blights. Stopping blights in advanced stages is difficult; the best solution is to remove diseased plants and destroy them.

Foliar Spots and Fungi

Identify: Leaf and stem fungi, including leaf spot, attack foliage. Brown, gray, black, or yellow to white spots or blotches develop on leaves and stems. Leaves and stems discolor and develop

spots that impair plant fluid flow and other life processes. Spots expand over leaves causing them to yellow and drop. Growth is slowed, harvest prolonged, and in severe cases, death results. Leaf spot is the symptomatic name given to many diseases. These diseases may be caused by bacteria, fungus, and nematodes. Spots or lesions caused by fungi often develop different colors as fruiting bodies grow. Leaf spots are often caused by cold water that was sprayed on plants under a hot HID. Temperature stress causes the spots that often develop into a disease.

Control: Cleanliness! Use fresh, sterile growing medium with each crop. Move HIDs away from the garden canopy about 30 minutes before spraying so plants won't be too hot. Do not spray within four hours of turning the lights off as excess moisture sits on the foliage and fosters fungal growth. Do not wet foliage when watering, avoid overwatering., and lower grow room humidity to 50 percent or less. Check the humidity both day and night. Employ dry heat to raise the nighttime temperature to 5-10°F (3-6°C) below the daytime levels, and keep humidity more constant. Allow adequate spacing between plants to provide air circulation. Remove damaged foliage. Avoid excessive nitrogen application.

Biological: Bordeaux mixture may help keep leaf spots in check, but it is often phytotoxic when applied regularly indoors.

Sprays: Bordeaux mixture.

Fusarium Wilt

Identify: *Fusarium* wilt is most common in warm grow rooms and greenhouses. Recirculating nutrient solutions above 75°F (24°C) creates perfect conditions for *Fusarium*. The water and nutrient solution carries this disease with it when contaminated. Fusarium starts as small spots on older, lower leaves. Interveinal leaf chlorosis appears swiftly. Leaf tips may curl before wilting and suddenly drying to a crisp. Portions of the plant or the entire plant will wilt. The entire process happens so fast that yellow, dead leaves dangle from branches. This disease starts in the plant's xylem, the base of the fluid transport system. Plants wilt when fungi plug the fluid flow in plant tissue. Cut one of the main stems in two, and look for the telltale reddish-brown color.

Control: Cleanliness! Use fresh, clean growing medium. Avoid nitrogen overfertilization.

Preventive action is necessary. Keep nutrient solution below 75°F (24°C). Hydrogen peroxide infusions will also arrest Fusarium. Always remove infested plants and destroy.

Biological: Mycostop® (*Streptomyces griseoviridis*), or Deny®, or Dagger® (*Burkholderia cepacia*) and *Trichoderma*.

Sprays: Treat seeds with chemical fungicides to eradicate the seed-borne infection. Chemical fungicides are not effective on foliage.

Green Algae

Identify: Slimy green algae need nutrients, light, and a moist surface on which to grow. These algae are found growing on moist rockwool and other growing mediums exposed to light. They cause little damage but attract fungus gnats and other critters that damage roots. Once roots have lesions and abrasions, diseases enter easily.

Control: Cover the moist rockwool and growing mediums to exclude light. Run an algaecide in the nutrient solution or water with an algaecide.

Powdery Mildew

Identify: First indication of infection is small spots on the tops of leaves. At this point the disease has been inside the plant a week or more. Spots progress to a fine, pale, gray-white powdery coating on growing shoots, leaves, and stems. Powdery mildew is not always limited to the upper surface of foliage. Growth slows, leaves yellow, and plants die as the disease advances. Occasionally fatal indoors, this disease is at its worst when roots dry out and foliage is moist. Plants are infected for weeks before they show the first symptoms.

Fusarium wilt causes the center of the stem to turn reddish-brown in color.

Control: Cleanliness! Prevent this mildew by avoiding cool, damp, humid, dim grow room conditions, as well as fluctuating temperatures and humidity. Low light levels and stale air affect this disease. Increase air circulation and ventilation, and make sure light intensity is high. Space containers far enough apart so air freely flows between plants. Allow foliage to dry before turning off lights. Remove and destroy foliage more than 50 percent infected. Avoid excess nitrogen. Copper and sulfur-lime sprays are a good prophylactic.

Biological Control: Apply Serenade® (*Bacillus subtilis*) or spray with a saturation mix of baking soda and water.

Sprays: Bordeaux mixture may keep this mold in check. A saturation of baking soda spray dries to a fine powder on the leaf; the baking soda changes the surface pH of the leaf to 7, and powdery mildew cannot grow.

Root Rot

Identify: Root rot fungi cause roots to turn from a healthy white to light brown. As the rot progresses, roots turn darker and darker brown. Leaf chlorosis is followed by wilting of the older leaves on the entire plant, and its growth slows. When severe, rot progresses up to the base of the plant stock, turning it dark. Root rot is most common when roots are deprived of oxygen and stand in un-aerated water. Soil pests that cut, suck, and chew roots create openings for rotting diseases to enter. Inspect roots with a 10X magnifying glass for signs of pest damage.

Control: Cleanliness! Use fresh, sterile growing medium. Make sure calcium levels are adequate, and do not overfertilize with nitrogen. Keep pH above 6.5 in soil and about 6.0 in hydroponic mediums to lower disease occurrence. Control any insects, fungi, bacteria, etc., that eat roots.

Biological: Binab®, Bio-Fungus®, RootShield®, Supresivit®, Trichopel® (*Trichoderma harzianum*), or SoilGuard® (*Trichoderma virens*).

Sprays: Sprays are not effective.

Pythium Wilt/Rot

Identify: (See "Damping Off.")

Sooty Mold

Identify: Black sooty mold is a surface fungus

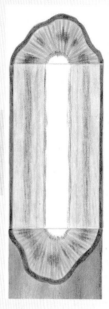

Right: Verticillium *wilt is less common than* Fusarium *wilt, but the symptoms are similar. Cut a stem and look for discolored xylem.*

Rotten roots have been soaking in stagnant nutrient solution. Foliage is very slow to grow when roots are rotten!

that grows on sticky honeydew excreted by aphids, mealybugs, scale, whiteflies, etc. Sooty mold is only a problem on indoor plants when honeydew is present. Sooty mold restricts plant development, slows growth, and diminishes harvest.

Control: Remove insects that excrete honeydew. Once honeydew is controlled, mold dies. Wash away honeydew and mold with a biodegradable soapy solution. Rinse away soapy water a few hours after applying.

Verticillium Wilt

Identify: Lower leaves develop chlorotic yellowing on margins and between veins before turning dingy brown. Plants wilt during the day and recoup when the light goes off. Wilt soon overcomes parts of the plant or the entire plant. Cut the stem in two and look for the telltale brownish xylem tissue. The fungus blocks the flow of plant fluids, causing wilting.

Control: Cleanliness! Use fresh, sterile soil. Good drainage. Use amonical nitrogen as a source of nitrogen. Do not overfertilize.

Biological: Bio-Fungus® (*Trichoderma* species), Rhizo-Plus® (*Bacillus subtilis*).

Sprays: No chemical spray is effective.

Viruses

Identify: Viruses are still a mystery. They act like living organisms in some instances and nonliving chemicals in other cases. They must enter plants via wounds. Once a virus takes over plant cells, it is able to multiply. Viruses are spread by insects, mites, plants, animals, and human vectors. Aphids and whiteflies are the worst. Infected tools also transport viruses from one plant to another. Typical symptoms of viral infection are: sickly growth, leaf and stem spots, yellowing, and low yields. Viral diseases move into the plant's fluid distribution system and destroy it, which often causes leaf spots and mottling. A virus can completely take over a plant in a few days. Once a plant gets a virus, there's little you can do.

Control: Cleanliness! Always use fresh, sterile growing medium. Disinfect tools before cutting foliage on different plants. Destroy all plants infected with virus.

Biological: None.

Sprays: No chemical sprays are effective against viruses.

Troubleshooting

This simple troubleshooting chart will solve 90 percent of the grow problems encountered when growing cannabis. This chart started with an article in *High Times* magazine and borrowed from the "Problem Identification Keys" presented in *Hemp Diseases and Pests: Management and Biological Control*, by J. M. McPartland, R. C. Clarke, D. P. Watson. Please see that book for much, much more information. One word of caution–this troubleshooting chart assumes the grow room is clean.

Clones are relatively easy to root. Success rate depends on the proper combination of heat, humidity, light, rooting hormone, and growing medium aeration/moisture. The more precise the combination, the faster and stronger roots grow.

The vegetative growth stage is when problems begin to show. Often, these problems continue through flowering. Remedy problems before they progress. If allowed to persist through flowering, yield will be substantially diminished.

Flowering is the last stage in life and only six to ten weeks long. Problems must be solved within the first two weeks (at the absolute latest, three weeks) of flowering, or yields decrease in relation to the severity of the problems.

Note: Keep growing area super clean to help prevent problems. If you notice insects or fungus on foliage, remove them and check them against color photos and drawings in this book and the troubleshooting chart below.

Troubleshooting Chart

Growth Stage	Cause	Quick Fix
Seeds and Seedlings Seeds do not germinate	Damping-off Bad seed	Buy new seed, start over Get your money back!
	Root maggots	Drench soil with neem or horticultural oil
Seed germinates, seedling has signs of pests eating/sucking foliage	Spider mites (stippled leaves) Aphids (exude honeydew)	Spray neem oil pyrethrum Spray pyrethrum, insecticidal soap, or nicotine sulfate
Seedling stem at base has dark or sickly growth, suddenly falls over, or suddenly wilts	Damping off Damping off or a wilt disease Too much or too little moisture	Drench soil with metalaxyl or buy new seeds Uncommon in clones Correct accordingly
Seedling leaves have yellow, gray, black, and/or dark green (fungus-like) spots	Blight or anthracnose	Remove growing plants and growing medium

Continued on next page:

Clones

Wilt and die	Lack of moisture	Add humidity dome, mist 4-6 times daily
Wilt and die	Medium too wet	Drain medium, do not water, no standing water in tray
Won't root	Medium too dry or too wet	See "Wilt and die" see above
	Inconsistent rooting hormone	Change to liquid or gel rooting hormone

Vegetative stage

Leggy, weak plants	Lack of light	Add lamp, change reflector, move lamp closer to plants
Leggy, weak plants	Lack of ventilation, Soil too wet Soil too dry Toxic nutrient buildup	Add vent fan Irrigate less Irrigate more Leach grow medium* change nutrient solution
Stunted, stubby plants	Insect damage Rotten roots Toxic nutrient buildup	Spray pyrethrum** Irrigate less Leach grow medium*
Burned leaf tips Purple stems & burned leaf spots	Toxic nutrient buildup- Could be one of many different nutrients	Leach medium* weekly Lower nutrient dose & leach medium* weekly
Leaf spots, margins burned, discolored leaves, pale leaves	Nutrient toxicity	Leach medium*, change nutrient solution, change fertilizer, refer to specific nutrient problems
Small, whitish spots on leaves	Spider mite damage	Spray pyrethrum**, neem oil
Insect damage-chewed leaves, insects/eggs visible on plants- check under leaves with 20X loop.	Whiteflies, aphids, scale, caterpillars, larva, etc.	Spray pyrethrum** or neem oil
Fungus or mold on foliage or soil	High humidity (above 60%) High temperature (above 80°F)	Add vent fan Add vent fan Spray soil with 5% bleach solution and wash off next day. Spray foliage with 10% baking soda solution

Severe, sudden wilting of plant	*Fusarium* or *Verticillium* wilt	Remove plant & growing medium and destroy
	Lack of water	Irrigate plant, submerge roots in water

Flowering

Slow growth and small buds cooked or rotten roots	Overfertilized, water/light/air-stressed,	Leach* grow medium Add big/more vent fans Keep grow medium evenly moist. The closer to harvest, the less that can be done. Must remedy three to six weeks before harvest for results.
Older leaf discoloration and dieback	Nitrogen, potassium, phosphorus, or zinc deficiency	See specific nutrient for solution
New leaf discoloration and dieback	One of the secondary or trace elements	See specific nutrient for solution
Dead grayish spots in buds	Bud mold (*Botrytis*)	Remove entire bud one inch below damage. Drop the humidity
Pungent odors from grow room	Ripening bud smells much more than early bud	Install ozone generator in large rooms. Use "Ona" or "Odor Killer" in small rooms

*Leach or flush growing medium with mild (quarter-strength) nutrient solution. Flush with at least three times the volume of nutrient solution per gallon of medium.
**Spray at five-day intervals for 15 days. Use aerosol pyrethrum, and spray under leaves. If problem persists, switch to neem oil and alternate with pyrethrum.

Drying & Post-Harvest

Buds smoke harsh	Dried too fast	Move buds into room with 80% humidity
Buds full of mold	Lack of air circulation	Increase air circulation
Spider mites on buds & drying lines	Sloppy growing	Mites escape to ends of lines and subdue them with Tanglefoot™
Buds crackle when smoked	Too much fertilizer at harvest	Too late! Next time flush plants with water ten days before harvest

Spraying

Use only contact sprays approved for edible fruits and vegetables.

Warning: Do not use TOXIC SYSTEMIC CHEMICALS! Read the entire label on all sprays. The toxic or active life of the spray is listed on the label. Wait twice as long as the label recommends, and thoroughly wash any foliage before ingesting it. Toxic life is many times longer indoors, because sunlight and other natural forces are not able to break down chemicals.

Sprays are beneficial if not overdone. Every time a plant is sprayed, the stomata are clogged and growth slows. At 24-28 hours after spraying, rinse leaves on both sides with plain water until it drips from leaves. Avoid sprays that leave a residual during the weeks before harvest. Spraying increases chances of gray (bud) mold once dense buds form.

Phytotoxicity is the injury to plants caused by sprays. Symptoms include burned leaves, slow growth, or sudden wilt. Spray a test plant and wait a few days to see if spray is phytotoxic. Water plants before spraying. Phytotoxicity is diminished when more liquid is in foliage.

Temperatures above 68°F (20°C) make virtually all sprays, even organic ones, phytotoxic and damaging to foliage.

Intense light causes leaves to take in the chemicals too quickly and will often cause leaf damage.

Spray early in the day so ingredients are absorbed and foliage dries. Spraying two hours or less before lights-out can cause foliar fungus when water sits on leaves too long.

Do not mix two products. It could change the characteristics of both.

Warm temperatures mean spraying twice as often, because the bugs breed twice as fast.

Use a clean, accurate measuring cup or spoon. Measure quantities carefully!

Mix pesticides and fungicides just before using them, and safely dispose of unused

A pump-up sprayer with a spray wand allows you to deliver spray under leaves where most pests live.

Curled leaves are the result of mixing and applying sprays that are too strong. The natural spray applied to this plant was mixed double-strength.

Powder fungicides are easiest to apply with an applicator that disperses the powder evenly on foliage.

This grower is taking no chances. He suited up to avoid any contact with sprays.

Hold foliage back so you can spray under the leaves where most pests reside.

Too strong a spray caused brown burn spots and made this leaf curl downward.

spray. Mix fertilizer and use for several weeks.

Mix wettable powders and soluble crystals in a little hot water to make sure they dissolve before adding the balance of the tepid water.

Use chemical sprays with extreme care, if at all, in enclosed areas; they are more concentrated indoors than outdoors in the open air.

Use a facemask when spraying, especially if using an aerosol fogger.

Spray entire plants, both sides of the leaves, stems, soil, and pot. Be careful with new, tender-growing shoots; they are easily burned by harsh sprays.

A one quart (0.9-1.8 L) or two quart pump-up spray bottle with a removable nozzle that is easy to clean is ideal. Keep a paper clip handy to ream out clogged debris in nozzle.

A 1-2 gallon (3.8-7.6 L) sprayer costs less than $50 and works well for large gardens. An application wand and nozzle attached to a flexible hose makes spraying under leaves where insects live easy. Plastic is recommended; it does not corrode or rust.

Electric foggers work well for large jobs. The spray is metered out a nozzle under high pressure, which creates a fine penetrating fog.

Wash the sprayer and the nozzle thoroughly after each use. Using the same bottle for fertilizers and insecticides is okay. Do not mix insecticides and fungicides together or with anything else. Mixing chemicals could cause a reaction that lessens their effectiveness.

Raise HID lamp out of the way so mist from spray will not touch the bulb; temperature stress, resulting from the relatively cold water hitting the hot bulb, may cause it to shatter. This could not only scare the hell out of you, it could burn eyes and skin. If the bulb breaks, turn off the system immediately and unplug!

∎

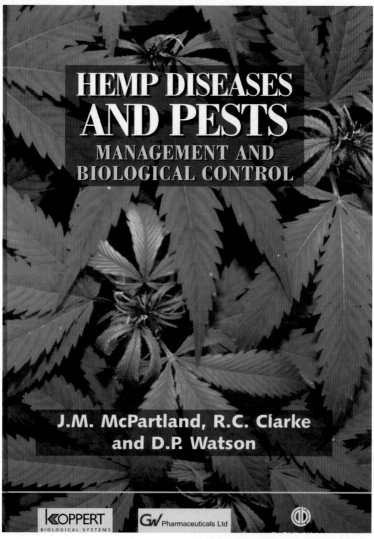

HEMP DISEASES AND PESTS

MANAGEMENT AND BIOLOGICAL CONTROL

J.M. McPartland, R.C. Clarke and D.P. Watson

Hemp Diseases and Pests is a detailed troubleshooting guide focusing on diseases and pests of cannabis that arise in greenhouse, growroom, and outdoor crops. Pests and diseases can be identified by written descriptions, plant symptom keys, detailed line drawings, and photographs. Organic methods are emphasized, with explicit instructions for biodynamic techniques and biological pest control.

Stats: oversized hardcover (British A4-paper), 251 pp.

Profusely illustrated: 111 black & white photos and drawings, 86 color photos, 36 tables and charts.

More info and ordering: Jorge's site: www.marijuanagrowing.com

Oxford University Press: www.oup-usa.com; in Europe: www.cabi-publishing.org/Bookshop

Copies also available at Ebay and Amazon.com

This piece of Swiss hash was collected and pressed shortly after harvest

Resin glands generally break off near the bottom of the stalk and just under the round head.

premature use of the end-product before all solvents and residuals have been extracted. You can find much information on these subjects at www.marijuana-growing.com.

Introduction

Hashish is the connoisseur's smoke. Hashish, also called hash, is the resin heads of glandular trichomes that are collected, pressed together, and shaped. The more resin on the input material, the better the *hash*. Here we will touch on the basics of making hashish using safe extraction methods. I have omitted detailed information on chemical extraction methods using butane, acetate, different alcohols, etc., because of possible health risks from explosion, fire, and fumes. Chemical damage may result from

Resin can be collected by scraping it from your hands after handling resinous plants or buds. It can be scraped from tools, too. Resin can be collected by separating it from foliage and letting it fall through a sieve. Or it can be separated from foliage using cold water and sieves.

Before Making Hash

Make sure your plants are as clean as possible. Any oil-based residues on leaves will show up in the hash. For example, if extracting resin with water, you can see impurity residues as a sheen of oil in the water. During the month before harvest, do not use any harmful chemicals that leave residues. I prefer to use only water-based organic products to avoid potential health risks to the consumer.

Flush plants with water for seven to ten days prior to harvest, to remove built-up fertilizers in the soil

Capture resin glands with small heads with a smaller mesh sieve. Courtesy of the Greenhouse.

> **Pollen** - In Europe and other parts of the world, sieved resin powder is called pollen. The term is used because the two look similar, but resin powder is not pollen. When you hear somebody talking about "pollen," you know they are referring to resin powder.

and foliage. This will help ensure clean, sweet-tasting hash.

Freeze First - Once dry, freeze leaf trim immediately to prepare for making hash. Place leaves in freezer for an hour or longer. Remove them from the freezer, and use a dry or wet sieve to separate gland heads from foliage. Collect more resin by making foliage and resin glands brittle. Cold, brittle resin gland heads snap off and separate easily.

Your tools and hands are a great source of "finger hash." Scrape the resin from tools and manicuring gloves.

Yield per gram of leaf and small buds		
Quantity	Dry Sieve	Water Extraction
100 gm leaf	4-6 gm	6-10 gm

> **Keep the entire operation clean.** This is the key to keeping everything separated properly and having minimal contamination.

The yield from 7 ounces (200 gm) of leaves and small buds is around 0.2-0.7 ounces (6-20 gm) with the average around 0.36 ounce (10 gm). The quantity of hash produced depends in large part upon the quality of your original material.

Clean stems, dead material, large leaves with no visible resin, and other debris leaf and bud before making hash with it.

Male plants contain resin with THC but much less overall than female plants.

Outdoor plants are subject to wind, rain, dust, etc., which may prevent resin growth or cause much of the resin to be knocked off the plant. Because they live in a protected environment, indoor plants are able to exude as much resin as possible. Such plants with heavy resin make the best hash. Great hash comes from the close trim around the buds.

This piece of "finger hash" was scraped from fingers and trimming tools in a single day of trimming!

This beautiful brick of Moroccan hash was pressed a month before the photo was taken. The resin crystals glisten in the sunlight. Now European and North American aficionados are learning to make better hash!

Sativa-dominant strains have smaller trichome heads than *indica*-dominant strains. Smaller mesh sieves do a good job of separating smaller resin heads.

Hand Rub Hash

Hand rubbing hash is simple and easy, but horridly inefficient and wasteful. All you need to hand rub are a good pair of hands, adequate cannabis buds, and desire. Much of the resin falls to the ground or becomes "lost" deep within buds or sticks to other foliage. Overall hand rubbed hash is lower quality and contains more debris than sieved or water-extracted hash.

Hand rubbing is most common in the Himalayan Foothill regions of Nepal, India, and Kashmir where "charas" (the Indian word for [hand rubbed] hash) are fairly common. Most small-scale and commercial growers collect the little bit of hash from their hands and tools during manicuring. This is the closest thing to hand rubbed hash most growers experience.

Plants that are best suited to hand rubbing have sticky resin that adheres to hands much better than it sticks to other foliage. At the same time, the resin must be relatively easy to roll into little balls to remove from hands.

Collect hand rub from healthy, strong, mature plants with green leaves. However, some large leaves may already have started to turn yellow. Remove brown, crisp, and dead foliage before rubbing. Remember, cannabis plants are generally pretty tough and can take vigorous but not abusive rubbing.

Once collected on hands, resin must not be allowed to collect other debris or foliage. Any foreign matter that sticks to resin-laden hands should be able to be brushed off easily.

Gather resin by rubbing individual flowering branches firmly between hands. Slowly move hands up from the bud, continually rubbing back and forth. Rub palms and fingers in between resin-covered flower clusters so they come in contact with as much resin as possible. Each branch should be rubbed 20-30 seconds or more. After rubbing a few branches, you settle into the intoxicating, hypnotic rhythm. Aromatic fragrances are released as you rub the buds.

The resin sticks to hands slowly at first, but once they are covered with a light sheen of resin, the accumulation process speeds. Brush off any foliage or debris from hands as soon as it sticks so the resin remains reasonably pure.

To remove the resin from hands, rub your palms together so resin clusters together into sticky little balls. At first the resin will ball up relatively quickly. Lump the balls together to form a single piece. Use this piece to rub on resin that is still on your hand to help remove it. If hands are moist or sweaty, soak up moisture with a paper towel before removing hash.

Once collected, knead it in your hand until it reaches your desired consistency. Hand rubbed hash is best enjoyed within a few weeks of collection. Collecting hand rubbed resin is time consuming. An average collector can rub all day and collect a mere five to ten grams!

Sieves

The first time I saw sieved cannabis resin was in 1983 at the Cannabis Castle in Holland. Neville, owner of the Seed Bank, had a large silkscreen stretched across a frame that was set on top of a large desk with a glass top. We would toss a handful or two of buds on the screen and bounce them around a few seconds. After two or three rounds of tossing and bouncing, a thin sheen of resin could be found on the top of the glass below the silkscreen. I had never smoked anything so potent in my life!

Resin heads are different sizes. With the help of sieves, you can use the differences in resin head sizes to separate them from other plant matter. Typically, a minimum of two sieves are used to make hash. The first one filters out the large plant matter and larger debris, letting the resin glands and small debris pass through to the second sieve. The first sieve should have 135-150-micron pores. The second sieve allows small resin glands to pass, while it holds back large, mature resin glands. The pores on the second sieve should be from 50-60 microns. You can find silkscreens at your local hobby and art supply store. Printing supply stores also sell framed screens.

To sieve, plants should be as dry as possible and cold (about 41°F [5°C]) so resin glands break off easily. Be careful not to force the plant material through the sieve. Forcing will break more resin glands and smear their contents on the sieve and other plant material. The contents of these ruptured glands cannot be recovered.

Normally, the largest mature resin glands fall first. They are followed by less mature glands and debris including pistillate hairs and plant debris. If you abuse sieving and force too much through the sieve, the hash will be green and of low quality. At best, sieving removes only half of the THC-rich resin in cannabis.

Atmospheric relative humidity can slow the sieving process to a halt because it causes the pores of the sieve to clog. High humidity also remoistens dry plants, thus making it more difficult for resin to fall free.

Resin glands come in three basic sizes:

60-70 microns includes Moroccan cannabis and some other sativas.

80-110 microns is the most common size range for many quality cannabis strains

135-150 micron sieves are necessary to capture the mature resin glands of many well-grown, very resinous strains.

Remember, there are several sizes of resin glands. Use the appropriate screen size to collect the most resin powder for the strains you are processing.

A micron is one millionth of a meter (1/1,000,000 m) or one-thousandth of a millimeter (1/1000 mm). This length is also referred to as a micrometer, and the symbol used to denote a micron is "μ".

	Microns (μ)	Thousandths of an inch
1.	220μ	8.66
2.	190μ	7.48
3.	160μ	6.30
4.	150μ	5.91
5.	120μ	4.72
6.	104μ	4.09
7.	73μ	2.87
8.	66μ	2.60
9.	45μ	1.77
10.	43μ	1.69
11.	25μ	0.98

Make sure the micron size is labeled on sieves. Color coding helps, but there is nothing as good as the micron size of the screen.

Once prepared, break up buds and foliage over a sieve, and tap the sieve lightly to jostle resin heads through the pores. You can also rub the leaves lightly on the sieve, but this will force through more green foliage. Resin powder

The Resin Heaven from Portland, Oregon, USA, was the first rolling tray equipped with a screen to collect resin.

Sieving low-quality leaves is just about as much trouble as it is worth. The leaf is unsmokable, but still harbors a little bit of resin.

I sifted the 150μ screen for about a minute and collected enough hash for a flying hit!

This tool box was loaded by an ambitious Swiss grower. He made hash from each crop he grew during the last two years.

will sift through the screen. The more resin on the plant material, the more resin that will fall through the sieve. Use a credit card to move the cannabis back and forth across the sieve. Exert minimal pressure on the cannabis to coax the highest quality resin through the sieve. The first layer of powder will be the purest. Sieved hash contains more debris than most other methods, but sieving is a simple and inexpensive method to make hash.

Collect the powder below the sieve. Now the resin powder is ready to press into a piece of hash. Pressing generates a little heat which also helps congeal the resin glands and debris together.

The Pollinator

Mila is a good friend, and she has carried the hash torch for countless connoisseurs. She has spent much of her life learning and teaching how to extract more resin from cannabis. She invented and popularized the Pollinator, a motorized cylindrical-shaped sieve to separate resin powder from leaf and buds. Mila has many ongoing experiments with hash and cannabis, one of which includes teaching the doctors in

This container holds all the different hashes Mila made in Kazakhstan, Central Europe. Every time she found some likely wild cannabis, she would sieve it to extract the hash. Mila used a Global Positioning System (GPS) to pinpoint plant locations for future trips.

Kazakhstan to grow medicinal cannabis.

The Pollinator consists of a drum that turns inside a box. Cold, dried cannabis is placed inside the drum that is made from 150-micron screen. A motor turns the drum, and resin glands fall through the 150-micron screen as the cannabis tumbles inside. Resin is collected below the drum.

Highest quality resin falls through the screen first. Progressively lower quality resin falls through the mesh the longer the drum turns. More green matter and other adulterants fall through the screen when the Pollinator turns for longer periods of time.

First you must prepare the dry cannabis. Put it in an airtight bag, and place the bag in the freezer for two hours. This will make the cannabis hard and brittle, which makes the sieving process much more efficient and productive.

Let the drum turn for two to five minutes. Use a short-range kitchen timer to make sure not to let the drum run too long. As the drum turns, the purest resin falls through the screen first. The THC-rich resin falls onto the bottom of the box underneath the drum.

Remove the magnetic lid from the drum, and add small leaves and buds. Do not put any sharp sticks or objects into the drum, because they could damage it.

Fill the drum about half full of dry leaf material so the cannabis will have enough room to tumble inside. This action is important to facilitate resin gland separation from foliage.

Open the lid of the Pollinator, and lift out the silkscreen drum. Pick up the drum and remove it from the containing box.

Put the lid back on the drum, and set it back in the Pollinator. Close the top of the Pollinator, and turn it on for the first turning period.

Remove the drum, and scrape the resin from the bottom of the box. Collect the dry resin, and press it into hash.

An inexpensive microscope enables a magnified view of the resin. To grade the resin, make several batches. The first batch should turn for two to five minutes, second batch five to six minutes, and the third more than six minutes. Inspect each batch of resin with the microscope. You will see progressively more debris in the batches that turned longer.

Water Extracted Hash

Hash extracted using cold water is known as water hash, Ice-O-Lator hash, ice hash, THC crystal, etc. When very pure, hash will bubble releasing volatile resins when exposed to a flame, hence the name Bubble Hash. This boiling effect is called "full-melt bubble" hash.

Modern water hash extraction started with "Sadu Sam's Secret" that was published in HASHISH! by Robert Connell Clarke. Sadu Sam's Secret is simple physics: resin is oil-based and cannabis foliage is water-based. This difference makes separating the two in aqueous solution easy. Heavy, oil-soluble resin glands will not dissolve in water; they are heavier than water so they will sink. Water-soluble material dissolves in liquid, and foliage is lighter than water, which makes it float!

A passage from HASHISH! states:

"Sadu Sam's Secret involves stirring a few grams of pulverized flowers or freshly sieved resin powder into a tall container of cool water containing ten to twenty times the volume of water to dry powder. Cool or cold water is essential because warm water softens the resin, which tends to stick together forming an unmanageable lump. The mixture must be stirred vigorously for several minutes until the lumps of the powder disperse. Once stirring ceases, the differing particles in the suspension begin to separate. Plant particles and other light debris (such as plant "hairs") float to the surface. Small, immature resin glands also tend to float. Mature resin glands and any dense debris such as sand and mineral dust sink, settling to the bottom."

Sadu Sam and Mila (the Pollinator) are old friends, and both live in Amsterdam, Holland. Mila continued to play with the separation method and refined it. Within a short time, she combined the dry sieving process with ice-cold water–the outcome was Ice-O-Lator bags. They are three waterproof nylon bags with progressively smaller micron silk screens sewn into the bottom of each. Clean cannabis is chopped and placed in ice-cold water in the bags. The water is mixed. When the slurry settles, the resin glands pass through the screens, and the foliage and debris are retained in bags. The water is drained, and a few nice clumps of high-quality hash remain.

Bubble Man refined the process by adding more bags with progressively smaller mesh. He has been adding screens, and at the time of publication, he uses seven different screens. He found that each screen separates unique sediments, some of which contain exceptionally pure THC. This hash is so pure that it bubbles when heated. Bubble Man popularized this saying, "If it don't bubble, it ain't worth the trouble."

Water-soluble terpinoids found in cannabis resin contribute to fragrance and taste. The majority of these soluble terpinoids dissolve and are washed out when extracting resin with water. The result is often hash with little flavor and aroma.

Now the hash is out of the bag! Many manufacturers have jumped on the bandwagon. Your time and budget will dictate how many bags you want to use for making water hash.

Use three bags and process the mix twice to extract virtually all of the THC-rich resin. Keep the wet plant material from the first water hash extraction. Freeze it and process again to make more resin. Or you can use five or more bags in a single run and harvest different qualities, some of which are very pure.

Ice-cold water makes trichomes brittle, and agitation knocks the heads off. Strain the mix through filters for increased purity.

Use leaves that have visible resin. Using large fan leaves or immature leaves will result in disappointing hash.

Use a mixer with paddles. If you can, find one with long shanks on the paddles for easy, deep mixing in a five-gallon (20 L) bucket. You can cover the bucket when mixing to help contain splashes. However, moving the mixer around the perimeter of the slurry helps mix up any dry or stagnant places.

Ice-O-Lator Step-by-Step

The Ice-o-Lator was popularized by Mila, owner

Water Extracted Resin
- Resin glands are oil soluble and heavier than water.
- Bathed in cold water, resin glands separate from foliage easily.
- Agitate the mix, and let resin glands settle through a sieve.
- Resin glands, as well as other small heavy particles, will fall through the sieve.
- Make some practice runs using large leaf trimmings before you delve into your best trimmings!

DO NOT use the mixer with a small cutting blade to mix the bucket full of leaf, ice and cold water. This mixer will cut foliage and bruise resin glands.

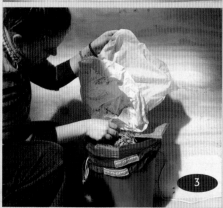

of the Pollinator, in Amsterdam, Holland. This water extraction process is a simple, efficient method of extracting THC-packed resin crystals from cannabis plants. Using the Ice-O-Later is very easy. Here is a brief recap of the process. The instructions below are adapted from Mila's site, www.pollinator.nl where there is much more information on making hash.

You will need:

Ice-O-Lator set

20-25-liter (5-gallon) bucket with lid

Kitchen mixer - Use the kind with paddles for mixing. Do not use the kind with a short chopping blade.

Paper towels

Dinner plate

Plastic card

Large mixing spoon

± 4.5-11 pounds (2-5 kg) of ice cubes, enough to keep the temperature down to 41°F (5°C)

Keep the temperature of the water just above freezing at 41°F (5°C)

Put in the most resinous leaf trim available. Make sure the chopped cannabis does not contain stems or other sharp plant parts that would damage the precision screen. Prepare buds by pulling apart or cutting into bits before introducing to the mix.

Fill the bucket with ice-cold water to six inches (15 cm) below the rim. Put the bags into the bucket in the proper order. Make sure there are no air bubbles trapped between the bags or the bucket. The bags will hang straight down, nested inside one another and the bucket. Pull the top edge of each bag over the rim of the bucket, hold it down and lock it in place with the drawstring and sliding lock.

Now you are ready to throw in the frozen cannabis.

Put up to seven ounces (200 gm) into the water. Do not put too much plant material into the water because it needs space to mix and

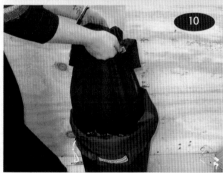

for the resin to separate and fall through the sieves below. When there is too much plant material in the water, many resin glands adhere to the foliage.

Add more ice on top of the plant material. This helps ensure the leaves get wet.

Fill the bucket with more water to within two inches (5 cm) of the top of the bucket. Let the mix soak for 15 minutes. Time is needed for the mass of foliage to become as cold as the water. The temperature should be about 41°F (5°C).

Cut two holes in the lid of the bucket–a little bigger than the shafts of the mixer. Attach the paddles of the mixer with the top of the lid in between. Put the lid on the bucket, and turn the mixer on at a low speed. The mixer will stir the concoction. Keep the mixer on and let it mix for 15 minutes.

Remove the lid. Use a spoon to move the plant material on the perimeter to the center. The goal here is to make sure everything mixes evenly. Let the mix soak for five minutes longer. Replace the lid and turn the mixer on again.

Repeat the process until all leaves have been stirred with cold water. Mila likes to mix it for about an hour so all the wet trim and leaves are floating on top of the water.

Turn off the mixer and let the resin settle one more time for about 15 minutes. Remove the first bag that contains all the raw material. Close the top and hang in a place where it can easily drain. Remove the debris in the bag and turn it inside out. Run water though the screen to wash out any latent resin that may have gotten caught in it.

Cleanliness is of paramount importance from beginning to end!

Everything that falls in the second bag will end up in the end product. When cleaning out the first bag, make sure the crystals do not stick on the outside of the second bag. Ample water here is important. Remember, it is a rinsing and separating operation.

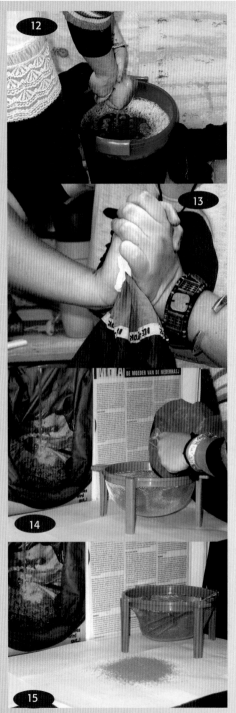

Remove the last bag having the finest screen. The water will drip out slower than from any other bag. You may have to hold the bag between your hands and sift the water back and forth across the sieve in the bottom to evacuate all the water because the accumulated hash slurry in the bottom tends to block the sieve. This part is fun! You can watch the slurry of hash congeal as the water drips through the sieve in the bottom of the bag.

Once the water is gone, the ever-changing slurry of hash remains, seemingly floating on the sieve in the bottom of the bag. If the slurry is green and full of contaminating debris, rinse carefully in cold water. The rinse will carry some of the green matter through the sieve.

Concentrate the wet hash in the bottom of the sieve. Fold the sieve and squeeze out more water. Place a couple of paper towels on the

bottom of the screen to absorb more moisture. Dance around the room with the hash in your hands high above your head. You have made your first Ice-O-Lator hash!

Do not waste the cold water; start another load! You can make up to five batches with the same cold water!

When you are done with the water, pour it on your plants. They love the nutrients!

Remove the semi-dry caked resin from the screen. Scrape it out with a plastic credit card or a small thin teaspoon.

Thoroughly rinse out all the bags to remove resin and debris. Clean screens with 96 percent pure alcohol so no oil-based resin remains. Hang to dry.

Moisture must quickly be removed from the resin powder to prevent mold. Crumble it up and spread it out on a screen or hard surface. I like a screen because you can sop up moisture by pressing a paper towel under the screen.

Another option is to hand press all the water out of the ball. Continue working the wet powder until it transforms into a cohesive ball of oily hash.

Or you can hand press until you have a solid ball. Keep squeezing and pressing, water will become visible on your hands.

Remove the last bit of moisture by flattening out the ball and putting it in the freezer. Freezing expands the volume of water, which will appear on the surface of the hash. Simply wipe off the ice when you remove the hash from the freezer.

When you press powder, the resin crystals will break and the oil will be released. The mix will darken as it oxidizes. The resin crystals from very fresh leaf will remain white, a very high quality.

For more information see: www.pollinator.nl

Water Hash with 15 Bags

The guys at THSeeds in Amsterdam, Holland, are expert hash makers. They taught and

Get all your supplies ready before starting a water extraction run. A bathtub and a clean bathroom make an excellent water hash-making environment.

inspired my good friend Moño to strive to make the absolute best possible hash. Moño uses bags from several manufacturers to separate more and different grades of hash. Moño uses 15 different bags and extracts more resin than anybody else! Moño's work is so impressive that we decided to profile his extraction process here.

More wet sieves separate more and different qualities of cannabis resin. Resin heads are different sizes. They fall through different size pores in a sieve. You can separate different sizes of resin glands with different size wet or dry sieves.

Separate hash with progressively smaller sieves so smaller screens do not clog with wet hash.

Moño has a full array of separating bags from several manufacturers. His laboratory is set up in the bathroom, with the tub the center of attention. He keeps the "laboratory" clean with a shower head attached to a flexible hose. Here is the array of bags he uses to separate the trash from the hash.

The "work bag" is the one that contains the bulk of the processed resin-less leaf. The work bag is usually drained and set aside so the debris inside can be discarded at will.

Moño likes bags with rigid sides. They perform better because they retain their shape inside the bucket and are easier to use when only one person is making water hash.

The process is done in two steps. First, he washes and separates the resin glands from the marijuana foliage using six screens. This process washes out virtually all of the foliage and contaminants.

The hash-laden water that is left over after passing through six bags is separated again by running it through eight more bags. The resulting hash is very clean.

Instructions for a 15-bag kit. The basic process is the same for each bag. You can add more or use fewer bags. Make sure to have everything ready before you start. You will not have time to look for supplies once you start this process.

You will need:

Bags with silkscreens

5-gallon (20-25 L) bucket with lid

Kitchen mixer - Use the kind with paddles for mixing. Do not use the kind with a short chopping blade.

Paper towels

Dinner plate

Plastic card

Large mixing spoon

± 4.5-11 pounds (2-5 kg) of ice cubes, enough to keep the temperature down to 41°F (5°C).

Make sure to have plenty of ice, and do not add too much cold water before adding ample ice. Keep the ice mixed with ice-cold water to make it last longer.

Start First Run

Before you start, remember to clean out each bag and rinse thoroughly with plenty of water. This little bit of timely cleanup will keep gooey resin and debris from clogging sieves and will avoid laborious scrubbing (with alcohol) later. Set bags out to dry. To avoid fungus, make sure the bags are completely dry before storing.

End first run

Use fresh-frozen bud trim. You can use large leaves, but they have little resin.

Fill the bags at least halfway and above the level of the screens. The screens must be covered with water before introducing plant matter.

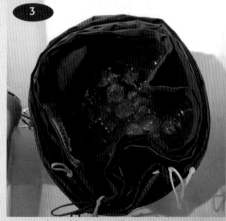

Pour in the cold water and ice.

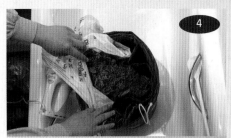

Add the plant matter.

Rub wet, cold leaves between hands to knock off resin glands into water.

The cannabis will float and take a little while to absorb the water.

Mix with mixer for 15-20 minutes. Do not let the mixer's motor or electrical wiring touch water. It could give you the shock of your life!

Add ice and a bit more cold water to bring the temperature to about 41°F (5°C).

Periodically rinse the paddles with cold water.

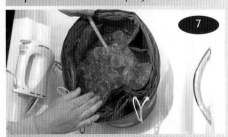

Use a large spoon or flat stick to stir and to sink the cannabis until it becomes wet. Continue to stir the mix by hand until completely soaked with water.

Let the mixed-up slurry sit for 15-20 minutes to allow resin to settle through screens.

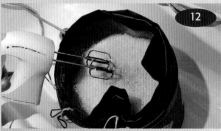

If foam develops, spray and wash away so you can see what you are doing and prevent foam from depositing resin and debris on bags.

Spray water on the foam to burst the bubbles.

Keep the wet leaf. Put it in a bag and freeze. If the material is good, you can make another extraction!

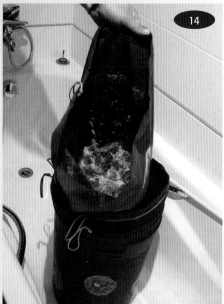

Pull up the top "work bag," taking care to prevent unscreened material from falling into the next bag.

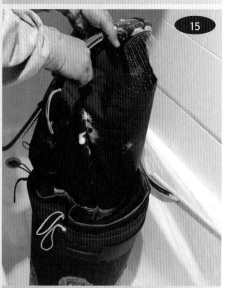

Remove the first bag; we call it the "work bag" because it contains the bulk of the leaf material. You can compost the contents or freeze the material to separate again.

Spray and rinse away foam and debris from the wet hash.

Once drained, set sieve on top of absorbent paper towels and rags before removing wet hash with a spoon or plastic card.

Start Second Run

Mix and separate again

Now it is time for the second run. The second run is done just like the first, except there is no foliage to deal with!

Here are the results. We started with 100 grams of pretty good leaf from a 'White Widow' strain. We used water extraction with 15 sieves to separate the resin and plant matter. Below are photos of the wet resin extracted from 150μ, 120μ, 104μ, 73μ, 66μ, 45μ, 43μ, and

You can see the greenish water filled with golden-colored resin glands.

The last of the water in the bucket is loaded with pure resin! The resin in this water will be separated in the second run.

25µ bags and the dry resin along with the dry weight of each. We found that all hashes were of fair quality but smokable. The bags with a mesh of 45, 43, and 25 were also good to smoke, but still not the best. The hashes that were separated with the 120µ, 104µ, 73µ, and 66µ sieves were the best, both in quantity and quality.

First Run

1.	220µ	Work Bag
2.	220µ	0.1 gm
3.	190µ	0.1 gm
4.	190µ	0.0 gm
5.	160µ	0.4 gm
6.	160µ	0.1 gm

Second Run

7.	160µ	0.4 gm
8.	150µ	0.7 gm
9.	120µ	1.9 gm
10.	104µ	3.1 gm
11.	73µ	1.9 gm
12.	66µ	1.5 gm
13.	45µ	0.3 gm
14.	43µ	0.7 gm
15.	25µ	0.4 gm
Total		11.6 gm

Toss the separated hash on a silkscreen. Lightly press it from the top while holding a paper towel under the silkscreen to absorb the excess moisture.

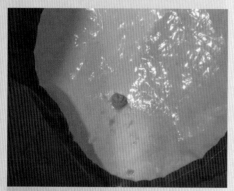

150µ bag = 0.7 gm

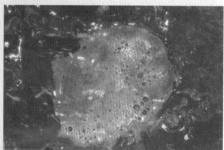

120µ bag = 1.9 gm

150µ bag = 0.7 gm

120µ bag = 1.9 gm

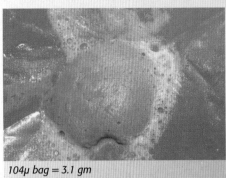

104μ bag = 3.1 gm

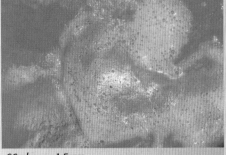

66μ bag = 1.5 gm

104μ bag = 3.1 gm

66μ bag = 1.5 gm

73μ bag = 1.9 gm

45μ bag = 0.3 gm

73μ bag = 1.9 gm

45μ bag = 0.3 gm

43µ bag = 0.7 gm

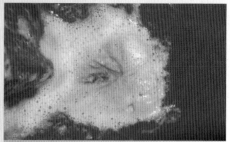

25µ bag = 0.4 gm

43µ bag = 0.7 gm

25µ bag = 0.4 gm

Look at the water line inside the bucket. You will see a fine sheen of oil or contaminant here or floating on top of the water if foliage contains any residues.

Do not squeeze wet hash in sieve bags. It is too early. Wait until the hash is dry to press, so resin heads will not be bruised or damaged.

This synopsis was adapted from Bubble Man's postings on www.overgrow.com (now closed).

1. 25µ bag - most often full of *sativa* full melt and physically the smallest bag
2. 45µ bag - nice head hash - most often consistent and yellowish to white in color
3. 73µ bag - full melt all the way
4. 120µ bag - good bubble
5. 160µ bag - best for big headed *indica* glands. Debris can also settle here
6. 190µ bag - removes the majority of the big debris out of the settling process
7. 220µ bag - is the first filter where all the big stuff stays

The color of water should be light green, which signifies all the hash and impurities have been cleaned out. Dirty water contains more contaminants.

Here are the different grades of hash from two runs using 14 bags.
The hash labeled with black letters is first run. Red numbers signify second run.

We loaded up the first run into separate vials; each is labeled with the micron (µ) size used to make the water extraction.

Once pressed quickly by hand, the hash is ready to smoke. We tossed it into a bong on top of a stainless steel screen.

Let's see what happens to this wafer of fresh hash when we apply a little flame.

Voilà! It bubbles, which means it is very pure.

The second test of purity is the amount and color of ash after the burn. White and clean–pure!

Washing Machine Hash

On a recent trip to the tropical region of Colombia, I was able to record how expert grower friends made hash in volume. They learned this technology from Mila. This information is very useful to process the leaf that is left over after the harvest. Using an everyday washing machine will save hours of labor. Following all the steps and paying attention to the water temperature in this simple process will extract all remaining cannabinoids from the leaves.

The best bet is to purchase the proper bags that have been tested. Mila and other manufacturers make different bags for outdoor and indoor crops. Plants grown outdoors have smaller resin heads than plants grown indoors and require a smaller mesh bag to collect the resin.

Use an everyday heavy-duty washing machine.

Fill the "zipped" Ice-O-Lator bag with leaf and place in the washing machine filled with cold water and ice.

Stuffing bags of cold leaves into the washing machine takes a little patience.

Make sure to include plenty of ice so the mix stays below 41°F (5°C).

Turn the machine on and let it agitate for 12 minutes to knock loose and separate resin glands from foliage.

Drain the hash-laden water and strain through an Ice-O-Lator bag.

Remove large Ice-O-Lator bag from the container.

Squeeze excess water from the large Ice-O-Lator bag.

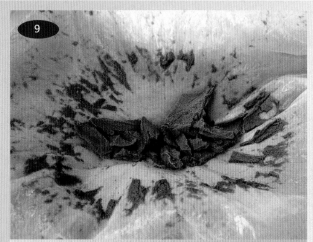

Dry the wet resin.

The dried resin.

Once dry, Colombian hash makers rolled and pressed the hash into a beautiful ball.

A washing machine filled with cold water is used to agitate the leaf and glands that are located inside of a zipped silkscreen Ice-O-Lator bag. This process separates the resin glands from the green leafy material. Once separated, resin glands fall through the sieve into the washing machine water. The leafy material stays inside the bag. The hash-laden water is evacuated out the washing machine's drain hose and separated from the water in a simple filtering process.

The machine is filled with ice and ice-cold water. Cold water is used to keep the resin glands intact and facilitate separation from the leaf. The principle is simple. Resin is oil-based and leaf is water-based.

First, the Colombians place paper bags of 500 grams of leaf in the freezer for one and a half hours. Cold temperatures make the leaves brittle, which allows them to easily separate from the resin glands.

Next, the two, one-pound (450 gm) bags of the cold leaves are loaded into a zipped Ice-O-Lator bag. The drum of the washing machine is filled with very cold water. Chunks of ice the size of your fist are added to the water until the desired temperature of 41°F (5°C) is achieved.

Two zipped Ice-O-Lator bags are loaded into the drum and the machine turned on to agitate for 10-12 minutes. Two bags are used to keep the machine in balance. As the machine agitates the bags, resin glands slip out through the mesh of the bags into the water.

The next step is to evacuate the resin-laden water out the drain. The drain water is sifted through an Ice-O-Lator bag to remove any remaining leaf. The water is collected in a larger bag placed in a large container. Once all the water is evacuated, they lift the large bag from the container. The "clean" water flowed out the sieve in the bottom of the big bag, and the wet resin stayed in the big bag. They squeeze the last of the water by hand out of the big Ice-O-Lator bag and the resulting unpressed hash is set out to dry. Every one-kilo bag of leaves yields 30-40 grams of dried resin. In a single 14-hour day they can process 100 kilos of leaf and transform it into three kilos of quality resin that is later pressed into hash.

Resin Extraction for Cooking

Cannabis butter and oil are simple to make. Each takes a little time to make, but large batches can be processed and stored in the refrigerator or freezer.

The psychoactive cannabinoids dissolve in butter, cooking oil, or alcohol (see "Tinctures" below). Dissolving the resin in the butter, oil, or alcohol makes it available for absorption by the body. Cannabis butter contains about 80 percent of the cannabinoids that were in the original foliage used to make it.

Heat 1.6 quarts (1.5 L) of water in a large pan on the stove. Add 4 ounces (112 gm) of marijuana leaf, one pound of butter (or margarine) and stir.

Bring the liquid to a boil. Put the lid on the pot and simmer two hours on low heat, stirring occasionally.

Strain the mix through a colander, catching the liquid below. Press the wet foliage to get all the liquid out.

Pour 0.5 quart (0.5 L) of boiling water over the wet leaf to wash out remaining butter. Press the leaves to squeeze out all the liquid possible.

Let the mix stand and cool. Within an hour or two, the mix will separate—water on the bottom and cannabis butter on top. You can speed the process by placing the hot mix into the refrigerator.

Pour off and discard the water, and retain the cannabis butter.

Use the butter in any recipe that calls for butter. Use small portions until you are familiar with dosage and effects. Be careful when consuming; the butter is quite potent!

Cannabis vegetable oil is made very much like cannabis butter.

First, you substitute one quart (1 L) of vegetable oil instead of butter.

Heat 1.6 quarts (1.5 L) of water in a large pan on the stove. Add 4 ounces (112 gm) of marijuana leaf, one quart (1 L) of vegetable oil, and stir.

Bring the liquid to a boil. Put the lid on the pot, and simmer two hours on low heat, stirring occasionally.

Strain the mix through a colander, catching the liquid below. Press the wet foliage to get all the liquid out.

Pour 0.5 quart (0.5 L) of boiling water over the wet leaf to wash out remaining oil. Press the leaves to squeeze out all the liquid possible.

Let the mix stand and cool. Within an hour or two, the mix will separate. Once completely separated, put the mix into the freezer. The water will freeze in 4-6 hours. Pour off the cannabis oil. If you are using olive or peanut oil, they will coagulate in the freezer and cannot be poured off. Use a spatula to scrape the oil from the water.

The oil will liquefy at room temperature. It will keep for about a month at room temperature. Keep in the freezer for longer term storage.

Use cannabis oil in recipes as you would any vegetable oil.

Cannabis Tinctures

Use liquor as a solvent to dissolve resin glands into a potent cannabis potion. You can use any

Well-made cannabis oil is extremely potent, often registering more than 70 percent THC!

liquor, but the higher the percentage of alcohol, or proof, the quicker and more efficient the process. You can let the spirits evaporate so the tincture contains virtually no alcohol.

If you prefer a flavored drink with alcohol, use Kahlua, Cointreau, Galliano, etc. Just remember, liqueurs contain a lower percentage of alcohol, and the extraction process will take longer.

Clean 4 ounces (112 gm) of clean cannabis leaf in two quarts (about 2 liters) of lukewarm (90°F [32°C]) water. Stir the leaf and water so they are well-mixed and the leaf is wet. Keeping the leaves whole makes them easier to work with. Strain out the leaves with a colander, letting the greenish water drain into a receptacle. This step will wash out much of the green chlorophyll.

Place the wet foliage in a bowl and cover with one quart (0.95 L) of 80 proof alcohol of your choice. Stir the blend until the alcohol and foliage are well-mixed. Make sure all foliage is covered with alcohol. Put a lid on the bowl so the alcohol cannot evaporate, and let it sit for 48 hours.

Take the lid off the bowl, and let the mix sit uncovered for 12 hours, until about half the alcohol evaporates.

Stir the brew again so it is well-mixed, and pour it through a coffee filter into a receptacle. Use the coffee filter to wring all liquid out of leaves.

Pour the alcohol through the leaves again, and wring out the liquid.

You will have about two cups of cannabis tincture concentrate that is ready to use. Or you can boil the mixture down to concentrate it more. The tincture will have 60 percent or more of the THC contained in the entire four ounces (112 gm) of raw material.

The tincture can be added to recipes in lieu of other liquids such as water, wine, etc.

Store concentrated tinctures in a cool, dark place to avoid early degradation. Heat and light degrade tinctures quickly. Use the tincture in one to three months.

Be very careful when you drink the tincture; it is potent! The buzz is similar to the one you get when eating cannabis, but it comes on in less time.

This is a shorthand version of cannabis extraction using butter, oil, and alcohol. For more complete information see the *Marijuana Herbal Cookbook*, by Tom Flowers, Flowers Publishing, 1995.

Hash or Cannabis Oil

Hash oil is a concentrate of hash or marijuana (cannabis oil) that has been dissolved in nasty hydrocarbon solvents such as ether and alcohol to extract the THC. Hash and cannabis oil frequently retain residues from solvents used to extract the THC. These residues are a health risk. The oils can be very concentrated and potent.

Honey oil was somewhat popular in America in the early 1970s. The oil was a translucent golden-amber color. The oil transformed from stiff, toffee-like consistency to runny oil when warmed. Cannabis oils are normally dark in color because they contain chlorophyll and other contaminants. Filtering the oil through charcoal will remove virtually all of the impurities.

Hash oil never became super popular because it is inconvenient to smoke and many users do not want to be exposed to the health risks associated with the solvents used for processing. There are many safe ways to separate the THC-potent glands from the foliage.

The oil can be wiped on joint papers, cigarettes, pipe screens, hot knives, etc. A popular smoking method is to smoke it in an oil pipe, a stem with a glass bubble on one end. A little oil is placed inside the glass bubble. When heat is applied, the THC vaporizes and is inhaled through the stem.

We do not recommend volatile solvent extraction because it requires the use of dangerous chemical solvents such as isopropyl alcohol, ethyl alcohol, and white gas.

Cannabis is soaked in the solvent, and the solvent is removed by evaporation. The resulting residual is a sludge that contains chlorophyll, plant waxes, other debris, and cannabinoids.

Isomerization is a chemical resin extraction process that was very popular in the 1970s and early 1980s. The process has fallen out of favor because of the harsh and dangerous chemical solvents–white gas, sulfuric acid, hydrochloric acid, etc.–used in the process.

Butane cannabis oil is made by passing butane gas through chopped cannabis. The butane dissolves the THC and transports it out a drain where it is collected. The captured butane contains THC. The butane is evaporated away by setting the collection container in a pan of warm water. Once the butane has dissipated completely, the residual honey-colored oil is scraped from the bottom of the collection pan.

Butane hash oil is dangerous to make because the process involves using a quantity of butane in an open container. The fumes are toxic and a small flame or spark could cause the butane to explode. People who make butane hash should make it in a well-ventilated or outdoor location.

Jelly hash is a combination of high quality hash and cannabis oil made from butane extraction. The typical recipe contains eight parts hash and one part cannabis oil (AKA hash oil) usually extracted with butane. Although very strong, the dark jelly hash has a characteristic sticky, oily consistency which makes it difficult to handle.

You can find out more about these processes in *Marijuana Chemistry: Genetics, Processing & Potency*, by Michael Starks, Ronin Press, and *Cannabis Alchemy: The Art of Modern Hashmaking: Methods for Preparation of Extremely Potent Cannabis Products*, by D. Gold, Ronin Press.

Pressing Hash

Once collected, resin powder is often pressed to facilitate handling and storage. Bulky resin powder is awkward to handle. It is easily spilled, blown away, and contaminated by dust and dirt. Resin powder is also more difficult to smoke, especially if no screen is available. Once pressed into a piece of hash, the resin is easy to handle, store, transport, and consume. Proper pressing is essential for storage and to slow decomposition.

Pressing ruptures resin glands and warms the resin, causing many volatile aromatic terpenoids to release their aromas and flavors.

You can press the resin powder by hand or with a mechanical device. You can elect to add heat, a drop or two of water, or alcohol while pressing to make less-pure hash stick together in a block.

Mechanical presses must be precise and align well so pressed hash does not ooze out seams. When pressed, heat and friction cause the outer layer of pressed hash to oxidize and turn darker than the interior. In fact, hash can have a dark exterior and a blonde interior packed with creamy resin glands.

Make sure to pre-press water-extracted hash in a piece of cellophane to contain it and help get rid of the water. The cellophane will give the pressed hash a shiny skin.

Remove a few clumps of water-extracted hash from the glass cone.

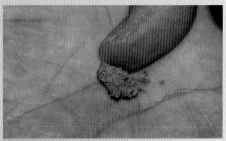

Ball up the clumps of resin and work it in the palm of your hand, pressing it together with your

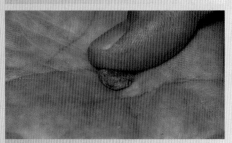

Continue to knead the resin in your hands until it forms into a solid shape.

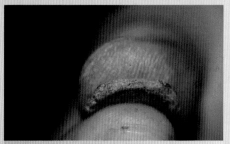

Press the resin into a wafer. Check out this compressed resin powder. You can see the resin glisten!

Pressing Small Amounts of Hash

By hand pressing, you experience the transformation of the resin powder into your very own piece of fragrant, dense hash.

To hand press, collect one to four grams of resin powder in the palm of your hand and apply pressure to the powder, working it between the palms of your hands. Also push your thumb into your palm full of resin powder to work it into a piece of hash. Continue this process for 10-30 minutes until the piece of hash is completely pliable and whole. Heat will be generated and help rupture and meld the resin glands together. Relatively pure resin powder will congeal faster than less-potent powders that contain impurities. But a little vegetable matter and debris gives hash different flavors and more body.

Potent resin powder is a creamy white to gold in color. Pressing the powder together and working it in your hands ruptures and oxidizes resin glands, which makes the mass turn ever darker.

Bottle Pressing

Press small amounts of resin powder between cellophane to form a pancake. Fill a long cylindrical bottle with warm water and use it as a "rolling pin" to press the pancake of hash.

Shoe Hash

Press small amounts of hash by putting resin powder in cellophane and putting it under your

Now pressed into a wafer, the piece of hash will be easy to smoke and will burn evenly.

heel inside your shoe. Walk around for an hour or so, doing what you would normally. Take your shoe off and voilà, fresh hash!

You can use a laminator–the kind that laminates photos and documents between two sheets of plastic–to press your hash! Simply sprinkle out the best resin powder you can make onto a piece of cellophane. Lay another piece of cellophane on top. Roll it with a bottle full of hot water to get it into preliminary shape and make it easy to work with. Remove the piece of hash from the cellophane; treat it like you would a document and laminate it. If your laminator can control the level of heat, wonderful! You are now ready to pack hash for a rainy day!

Mechanical Pressing

Place resin powder in a plastic bag or cellophane wrapper to contain it while pressing. All the powder will be pressed within the wrapper into a brick or plaque of hash. Poke a few small holes in the bag before pressing to allow trapped air to escape. The bag is placed into a heavy-duty steel mold, and pressure is applied with a hydraulic jack. Hydraulic jacks have a capacity from 10-20 tons and are mounted to heavy-duty steel frames that normally contain a 100-gram mold.

The pressure exerted to form a cohesive block is contingent upon the volume of contaminants in the powder. The more pure the resin powder, the less pressure it takes to form it into a block.

If your hash was made with water, make sure it is totally dry before pressing to avoid mold.

Water hash does not react like dry-sieved hash when pressed. Resin has been melded together in a different way than dry powder.

Pressing the resin when it is wet will trap moisture inside the hash. The hash will not dry completely, and it will not properly gel together later. It will retain a powdery consistency.

Dry-sieved resin powder will press easily and stay together under lower pressure when it is relatively pure. If it is adulterated with impuri-

Three grams of dry-sieved resin powder that is ready to press.

Cover resin with cellophane and fill a wine bottle with hot water.

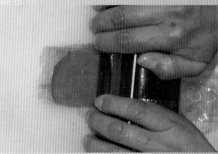

Roll the wine bottle over the dry resin powder that is wrapped in cellophane.

This small wafer of pressed "pollen" can be broken off and vaporized or smoked in a pipe.

ties, more pressure and heat will be necessary to press it into a block.

Add a little heat to hard-to-press hash that contains impurities. The heat will help the mass congeal so bricks do not need excessive pres-

Wrap a gram or two of resin in a bit of cellophane. Place it in the heel of your shoe to press into "shoe hash."

sure to stay together. But do not heat the resin too much or it will be damaged. Do not forget that pressing also increases heat.

You can also add a drop of alcohol in the form of brandy, whisky, bourbon, rum, etc. Higher alcohol content spirits are favored. The alcohol melds the glands together. Add only a drop at a time; alcohol takes a few minutes to completely penetrate and act. Be careful, add only a little!

Hammering

Hammering hash is a popular method of pressing in Morocco but uncommon in Australia, New Zealand, Europe, and North America. Hammering bursts and blends resin glands together into a cohesive mass. Often resin glands are hammered before being hydraulically pressed into plaques.

To hammer hash, place resin powder into an extra heavy-duty plastic bag. Place the bag on a wooden bench, tree stump, board, etc. Place a piece of plywood over the bag. Whack the plywood with a hammer until the resin powder forms a cohesive pancake. Remove the hash from the bag and fold once or twice to make it smaller and thicker. Repeat the hammering and folding process until the resin glands transform into a sticky piece of hash. Apply a little heat if the hash is slow to form.

Storing Hash

Make sure hash is dry before storing. Moist hash contracts fungus easily and decomposes quickly. Decomposition decreases THC levels. If you make hash using ice and water, make

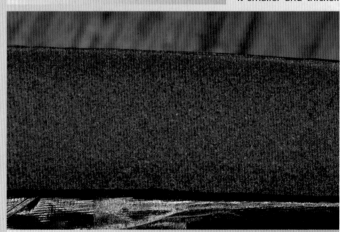

This 100-gram brick of pressed hash shows oxidation on and near the surface.

sure to dry it well. Dry by pressing the water hash into a flat pancake that has much surface area. Leave the pancake out in an arid room for a few days to dry completely. Cover the hash with a paper towel so dust does not contaminate it. If you made hash with a dry method such as sieving, you should not have to take any extra precautions before storing, unless working in a humid climate.

Small hand press makes nice little hash wafers.

My favorite way to store high quality water hash is to put it in a glass tube. This way all the resin stays intact until it is consumed. Upon smoking, you should press it a little so it will burn evenly.

Store hash in a cool, dark, dry place. Keep in an airtight container with a packet of silica crystals. You can also put the hash in the freezer for long-term storage.

For a complete account of the history and detailed methods of production see *HASHISH!* by Robert Connell Clarke, Redeye Press, 1998, www.fsbookco.com. If you want to make the best hash and have a springboard to launch into advanced processes, this is the book!

For current methods of hash making as well as stimulating discussion and interaction, check out the Hashish forums at www.cannabisculture.com.

This fashionable 9-pound hash necklace is the result of a long day slaving over a gyrating washing machine!

Beautiful blond Moroccan hash is a mass of creamy, golden resin glands.

The dark gloss on this piece of Moroccan hash is the result of oxidation and being placed in cellophane.

HASHISH!

History • Cultures • Ingredients • Recreation • Medicine
Hashish-making — Traditional, High-tech, Home-made

Robert Connell Clarke

HASHISH! is the absolute best book written on the subject!

Kilos of ooozy slabs of ice hash like this are extracted at the rate of 10 grams (0.35 oz) of hash for 100 grams (3.5 oz) of good trim leaf.

Ninety different strains from Holland were grown out in a Colombian breeding program.

Chimera, owner of Chimera Seeds.

Cuttings, or clones, taken from the same parent and grown under the same conditions are identical.

Male plants grow flowers that consist of pollen sacks.

Introduction

Chimera is without a doubt one of the most dedicated and knowledgeable people working with cannabis today; he brings a passion to cannabis breeding and research not often seen in the industry. Founder of Chimera Seeds, he has produced some excellent varieties of cannabis including `C4', `Frostbite', `Calizahr' and `Schnazzleberry'.

Chimera is a well-educated individual, who for years has tried to understand cannabis and how it functions in the brain. This path has seen him through a B Sc. Neuroscience, and post graduate research in the field of Biotechnology and Plant Sciences. He works on the cutting edge of cannabis research, and will certainly bring many new ideas and technologies to cannabis, over the years to come.

I am very pleased to present Chimera's contribution to this book in the form of this breeding chapter, as he takes the mystery out of breeding and does a great job of simplifying a very complex subject. Thanks, Chimera, for your contributions!

- Jorge Cervantes
Check out www.chimeraseeds.co.uk.

This chapter explains the basic biological processes of sexual propagation in cannabis and the formation of a new generation of seed. Armed with the information in this chapter, any grower will be able to design and begin a rudimentary breeding program and create new generations of seed for future use. These new populations make up a pool of genetic material from which superior individual plants can be selected for production (cloning stock) or for use in breeding programs. It is difficult for small growers to breed better varieties than are available from premium seed companies; however, for the many seed-starved growers who reside in prohibitive societies, making seeds for future use is often a necessity.

Cannabis can be reproduced asexually or sexually. Asexual propagation is more commonly referred to as taking cuttings, or cloning. Branches or growth shoots are removed from chosen donor plants and induced to form roots in a separate medium; these rooted cuttings are then used to plant a uniform crop of genetically identical individuals. Most commercial and many hobby growers propagate their crops asexually to ensure uniformity in growth, yield, and consistency of product in their crops. By planting gardens of genetically identical cuttings from their favorite preselected mother plants, growers are able to maintain an even garden profile, produce a consistent, known quality and quantity from each plant, and expect that all plants will mature at the same time. This ensures the same consistent, quality product from consecutive crops, as long as the same high-quality clones are used for each planting. Gardens propagated solely from clones are the most productive and consistent.

Sexual propagation is the process in which male and female sex cells (gametes) from separate parents unite in the female plant to form what will eventually mature into a new, genetically distinct individual. This process occurs when pollen from a male (staminate) parent unites with an ovule within the ovary of a female flower to create an embryo. This embryo, when mature and fully developed, will become a seed.

Each seed is genetically unique and contains some genes from each of its parent plants. Offspring grown from seed are most often different in some way from each other, just as brothers and sisters share some physical qualities of each of their parents, but are rarely identical to their parents or siblings. Because of this variation in plant traits and characters, breeders are able to use sexual reproduction to their advantage by crossing different individuals within a population or family, or hybridizing unrelated lines and subsequently inbreeding the progeny. This results in a phenomenon known as recombination of traits, and it allows breeders the possibility to recover individuals with a combination of the positive traits of both parental lines, all the while selecting plants that do not express the negative aspects. These selected plant stocks are then used as a basis to develop new and improved varieties.

A single male flower on a predominately female plant will release much pollen.

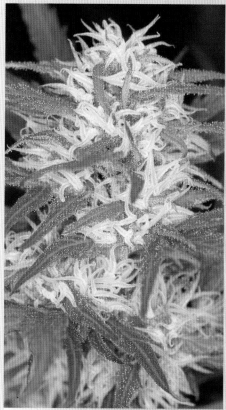

Female plants grow (white) pistils to attract male pollen.

Distinguishing between male (staminate) and female (pistillate) plants is easy. Male plants are distinguished by the appearance of "pollen sacks," or anthers, that grow from branch unions. Anthers look similar to a cluster of grapes or a collection of miniature lobster claws growing upwards and inverted from the branch union. Males typically begin to produce these flowers one to four weeks before the females of the same variety, and often bolt, or stretch, when they enter their floral development stage. Females can be distinguished by the development of two whitish hairs, or stigmas, which develop as part of the pistil–the female flower that appears in branch unions or "nodes."

Cannabis is an interesting species, in that it is one of the only annual plants that produces each of the male and female sexual organs on different individuals. This is a condition known as dioecy; dioecious plant groups contain individual plants that are either male (staminate; stamen bearing) or female (pistillate; pistil bearing). Dioecy is a hallmark of a cross-pollinating species; under normal conditions, cross-pollinated plants (outcrossers) are only able to fertilize other individuals, which has implications we will discuss later.

Although dioecy is most common in cannabis, monoecious varieties do exist. Monoecious varieties produce both staminate and pistillate flowers on the same individual.

These monoecious varieties are mainly used for hemp seed production, as they generate the highest yield of seed per acre. Monoecy is not a desirable trait for drug cultivation, where seedless cannabis, or sinsemilla, is sought.

Plants exhibiting both staminate and pistillate flowers are most often referred to as "hermaphrodites" by drug cannabis cultivators but are more correctly referred to as intersex plants. Intersex plants are a problem for growers who wish to produce seedless cannabis for consumption; just as seedless grapes or oranges are more desirable to consume, the same is true for cannabis. Having to remove the seeds from cannabis flowers prior to consumption is an inconvenience, and burning seeds taste bad and can ruin the smoking or vaporizing experience. We will discuss intersex plants in more detail later in the chapter.

The Creation of a Seed

Cannabis is an anemophilous species; this is a fancy way of saying that it is wind-pollinated. Under natural, or wild conditions, male plants undergo dehiscence (shedding of pollen) and disperse vast quantities of pollen into the wind. The pollen travels on air currents and, by chance, lands on the stigma or style of a nearby, or not so nearby, pistillate individual. This is the pollination event. Because pollen from many species floats in the air, and there is a significant chance that pollen from other species will land on a fertile stigma of

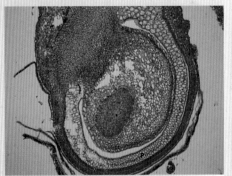

Scanning electron microscope photo of the inside of a seed.

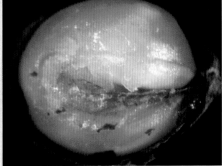

The inside of a seed with half the outer shell removed.

a waiting female plant, cannabis has evolved recognition systems that insure only species-specific pollen is able to germinate on the style and thus fertilize the female's ovules. There is physical and biochemical recognition between the pollen grain and the stigmatic surface; together, these insure species identity.

If the biochemical signal is correct and the stigma recognizes the pollen grain as cannabis, the pollen grain is hydrated by a flow of water from the pistil, and it germinates. Just as a seed germinates and sends a taproot into the soil, the pollen grain germinates and sends a pollen tube into the stigma and burrows toward the ovule. Once the tube reaches the ovary, the genetic material carried within pollen is delivered to the ovule, where it is united with the genetic material from the pistillate plant. This fertilization event occurs and creates what is to become an embryo. This embryo grows within a seed coat, and when fully mature in four to five weeks, can be planted and will blossom into a new generation of life.

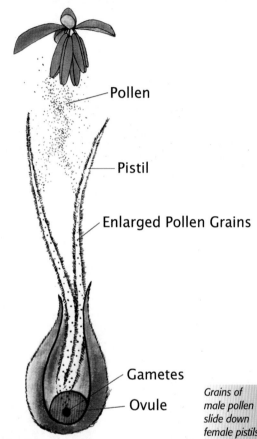

Staminate Flowers

Pollen

Pistil

Enlarged Pollen Grains

Gametes

Ovule

Pistillate Calyx

Grains of male pollen slide down female pistils to fertilize the ovule located within the seed

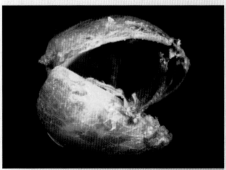

Protective outer shell of a seed.

This germinated seed is the result of much selective breeding.

Yellowish clouds of pollen travel many miles to pollinate receptive females.

How to Handle and Use Pollen

1. Collect carefully
2. Move male as far away from females as possible.
3. Limit pollen travel with filters and water.

Making Seeds Step-by-Step

Step One: Choose breeding parents. Selecting female plants for breeding is a much easier task than selecting males, because female plants readily demonstrate all the traits that are essentially important to a grower, or smoker (sometimes these are conflicting interests!). The breeder may want to place an emphasis on selecting for potency, flavor, yield, smell, resistance to pests, color, growth stature, etc. Cannabis for consumption is a group of pistillate flowers; a bud (a bud is a collection of pistillate flowers; a cola is a group of buds). All a grower/breeder/smoker has to do is watch these flowers develop over the life cycle, harvest, smoke a bud sample from each plant, and determine the positive and negative characters of each plant, for its growth as well as its smoking characteristics. Postharvest evaluation allows additional inspection of aromas and flavors, since these can change as the flower dries and cures.

Ben Dronkers, owner of Sensi Seeds, seated in the center in white, collecting seeds in Afghanistan.

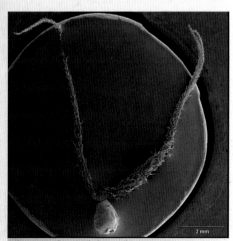

Close-up of a pistil shows the complex structure.

Choosing male plants with desirable characteristics is not so easy. Males obviously don't produce female flowers; thus, judging resin content, floral stature, smells, etc., is more of an inferential task–males just don't demonstrate these characters. Some breeders feel a good method for choosing a potential male is to rub the stem with your finger. The idea is if it exudes a pungent, resinous odor, it may be a good plant. This is really only a crude measure of the odor of the candidate. Although it can be a useful technique, it certainly should not be the major selection criteria.

The best method for determining a potential male's contribution as a breeding parent is the progeny test. Progeny testing is achieved by taking pollen from a potential breeding male and using it to make seeds with the chosen female(s). The resulting seed population is grown out and examined to determine the effect of the male on the progeny. Progeny tests are without doubt the most reliable method for determining the genetic value of the chosen male as a contributor to the next generation–a concept known as combining ability. One drawback of the progeny test is that it takes time to grow and evaluate the progeny, and the potential male plants must be kept alive if they are to be used again. Sometimes breeders choose to not keep these males alive, only keeping the progeny lots that correspond to the better male plants and destroying the rest. Only the best-performing males are allowed to make a genetic contribution to the next generation.

Step Two: Collecting pollen. One branch of male flowers will supply all the pollen necessary for small-scale breeders to produce ample seed for their own use. Strip away other branches to guard against accidental random pollination, and to avoid premature pollination, isolate the male as soon as anthers show. Be considerate of the fact that airborne pollen can travel miles. If you brush up against a plant in dehiscence, pollen will become airborne and travel throughout the area.

Neville, founder of the Seed Bank, traveled the world to find the best cannabis seeds.

One large healthy male top is all you will need when collecting pollen.

Cut a branch of male flowers and place it in a plastic bag to collect pollen.

Male pollen literally covers this large male leaf.

Collect male flowers and separate the pollen with a fine sieve.

Just prior to the anther's opening, place a clean paper or plastic bag over the branch. Secure the bag at the bottom with a piece of string or a wire tie to prevent pollen from escaping. Keep the bag over the branch for several days to collect pollen. When enough pollen seems to have been collected, tap the branch and shake remaining pollen off into the bag. Carefully remove spent branch and bag so the pollen does not escape.

Step Three: Store and protect pollen (optional). Pollen does not have a long shelf life under natural conditions; it is easily destroyed by high temperatures and moisture. Pollen can, however, be stored in the freezer for several months, if needed. This is accomplished by carefully removing the pollen from the collection bag and subsequently passing it through a screen. This removes any leaf matter from the anthers that may have fallen into the bag and contaminated the pollen, causing it to spoil. Wax paper is placed under the screen, and used to catch the pollen. The pollen can then be collected with a sterile scraper, placed in a small coin envelope or sterile test tube, and placed in the freezer. Cleanliness counts! Pollen should not be repeatedly frozen and thawed, which will decrease its viability.

Step Four: Pollination. Pollination occurs when pollen comes into contact with the pistil.

Pollen
F   C

32°   0°
20°   -7°

Store viable pollen at temperatures below freezing.

FREEZER

Store pollen in an airtight vial in the freezer.

Depending on variety, fresh pistils are ready to pollinate from two to twelve weeks after flowering is induced. The more pistils on the bud at the time of pollination, the more seed will be produced. Fertile pistils appear turgid and most often are white or off-white in color. Pistils that are withered, rust- or brown-colored are past the point where successful pollination can occur.

To pollinate, cover the female branch with the pollen filled bag, and briefly shake the bag to ensure the pollen comes into contact with as many pistils as possible. Leave the bag for two days and nights to ensure thorough pollination. Be careful not to scatter pollen when removing the bag, as viable pollen can still become airborne and pollinate any nearby plants. If other plants are in the garden and are not intended for pollination, the grower may move target plants from the main grow area into a separate, smaller space for pollination. After a couple days in the pollen chamber with the males, the female plants are thoroughly sprayed with water to destroy any remaining pollen, before they are moved back into the main grow area

where these seeds will mature over the coming weeks. This practice minimizes the possibility of pollen fertilizing the rest of the crop, keeping it seedless as the cultivator requires. To reduce or eliminate pollen contamination of future seed crops, make sure to clean the pollination chamber between each pollen release.

An alternate approach is to use a small paint brush to "paint" pollen onto the pistils. Dip the brush in the pollen container and gently brush the pollen onto the pistils. Again, the breeder must have a steady hand to ensure pollen doesn't become airborne during the process. This technique is perfect if the cultivator only needs to make a few seeds.

Collect male pollen and put a little on a small artist's paint brush.

Store male branch in a glass of water.

Brush a little pollen on female pistils to pollinate.

Male flowers have fallen and stuck to this fertilized seeded female.

This green seed will be mature in a few weeks. 'Rene' courtesy Chimera Seeds.

Cover pollinated female branch with a plastic bag to keep pollen from contaminating other females.

Seeded female.

A bathroom is a good place to isolate and breed plants. The male on the right is pollinating the females in the bath tub.

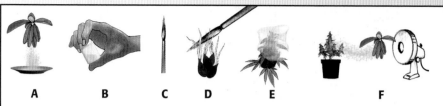

A-collect pollen, B-contain and store pollen, C-put some pollen on a brush, D-brush pollen on female pistils, E-cover to contain or F-set male in front of fan to pollinate all females.

After fertilization, most seeds will be fully ripe in about six weeks, although some may be viable earlier. As the seeds mature, they can split open the calyxes allowing the breeder to see the development of the seed within. Seeds are ripe when they are mostly dark brown or grey, well-mottled (tiger striped), and sitting loosely in the calyx. Green, yellow, or white seeds are almost always immature and not viable. (Sprinkle them on your salad or cereal.) To test the ripeness of the seed crop, you can sample-harvest a few seeds and try to press them between your thumb and index finger to test the firmness. If most of the seeds do not crush with a reasonable amount of pressure, it's time to harvest. If seeds are left on the plant too long, some may fall out of the buds and germinate on the growth medium below. This is more common with *sativa*-dominant varieties. *Indica* varieties typically have more dense flowers, which hold the seeds more tightly. Breeders must remove seeds from *indicas* by crushing and sorting the seeds from the plant matter.

Seeds are ready to plant immediately, but the initial germination rates may be low. Germination rates can be increased by drying seeds out post harvest, leaving them in a cool, dark, well-ventilated area for a few weeks, and then placing them in the refrigerator for one or two months before sprouting.

Please keep in mind this is only a guideline intended for small-scale seed production. Any method where pollen comes into contact with a pistil will result in seeds. Often breeders and seedmakers will place multiple males, or multiple copies of the same male (clones from a father donor plant) in the seed production grow

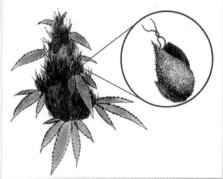

The seed can be seen inside of the seed bract in the circle. The bud on the left contains a mass of seed bracts filled with seeds.

room with their chosen females when creating seeds. Placing these males in a well-ventilated room and allowing full release of pollen ensures the crop will be completely pollinated, and produces a vast amount of seeds per plant. Scale the process to suit the number of seeds you require.

Seed Crop Care

Typically, cannabis growers use a high-phosphorus, low-nitrogen diet during the flowering cycle. My personal philosophy is to give seed production plants a complete balanced diet throughout the seed gestation period, so all nutrients required for proper development of the seeds are available. Because most cannabis-specific flowering fertilizers are low on nitrogen, growers may wish to combine vegetative and flowering fertilizers to ensure a complete diet for their seed mothers. Flowering nutrient formulas often lack certain nutrients, and the gestation

Young seedlings require a complete balanced diet.

Vegetative and flowering plants require the same fertilizer for good seed development.

period is not the time to be starving plants of these needs. Provide a complete diet, and let the developing seeds have all they need.

I've found that complete, balanced, organic-based soil mixes produce the most healthy, viable seeds. Organic soils contain various bacterial populations that break down and digest soil amendments to make them usable by plants. 'Sterile' salt-fertilizer based soils do not support these bacterial populations, and while they do support plant growth, they lack the "alive" quality of an organic soil. Many growers agree that organically grown pot has more flavor and taste than pot grown on a synthetic salt diet. It could well be that these organic bacterial populations provide some benefit to plant health, and thus produce more mature, healthy, viable seeds.

Breeding Terms

In order to have a discussion on breeding, there are some terms we must learn in order to fully understand the concepts. There are more terms defined in the Glossary.

Genetic material is inherited as described above, in the seed making section, from both the pollen donor and mother plant. The genetic material, or deoxyribonucleic acid (DNA) is coiled into long, X-shaped strands called chromosomes and stored in the nucleus of every cell. In cannabis, each individual inherits 10 different chromosomes from the staminate pollen parent, and 10 different chromosomes from the seed mother or pistillate parent. The resulting individual has 20 chromosomes total; 2 copies of each of the 10 chromosomes, or 2 full genomes. This means there are 2 copies of every gene in the plant, one from the mother and one from the father. Each and every cell in the plant has a copy of this unique DNA compliment. The genetic code is written along the length of the chromosome strands, and each gene has a specific location along its length.

Phenotype - We consider phenotype as the observable, qualifiable, or quantifiable representation of a given trait. Anything you can measure, categorize, or otherwise observe in an individual can be considered a phenotype. Every plant has many different phenotypes. For example, plant height might be broken down into three categories or phenotypes: short, medium, and tall stature. There is a short phenotype, a medium phenotype, and a tall phenotype.

Cannabis flowers demonstrate different color phenotypes as well. Most often we see green calyxes, but there are also plants that have purple calyxes. Sometimes there are even green calyxes with purple markings. These are all different calyx-color phenotypes. There are also calyx-size and calyx-shape phenotypes, or leaf size and shape phenotypes. Every trait has different phenotypes that can be selected for or against.

All phenotypes are the observable result of genes acting within the cells of the plant. Sometimes a single gene controls one trait (monogenic traits), and sometimes sets of genes operate together and contribute to make what we see as a phenotype (polygenic traits).

Genotype - The genotype of a plant is a way of describing the actual genetic condition that results in the phenotype. As the genetic constitution or makeup of an individual, genotypes are not always expressed. Some are latent and only express themselves given the proper environmental stimulus. For example, some plants have green leaves, but the leaves will turn purple under cold conditions. Other green-leaved plants will not turn purple even under cold conditions.

This happens because these plants have a different version of the gene(s) that control whether purple pigments are to be produced in the leaves. These different gene versions are called *alleles*.

These plants initially both had the green-leaved phenotype, but one plant developed an altered phenotype (purple leaf) in response

to an environmental condition. This is due to an interaction of the genetics of the particular plant with respect to this trait (genotype) and the environment.

A simplistic way to think of the concept is:

Phenotype = Genotype + Environment

Remember, this isn't 100% true. More accurately, the phenotype(s) seen in a given individual are the result of an interaction of the plant's genotype with the environment.

Let's look at some possible corresponding genotypes in our short, medium, tall phenotype example. Remember, the genotype is our way of describing the genetic condition responsible for the phenotype, therefore we can assign it whatever values we want, it's really just a symbol.

Phenotypes	Genotypes
Short	ss
Medium	Ss
Tall	SS

There are always 2 alleles, or versions of every gene, including the gene responsible for stature. When we have 2 "s" (lower case s) or "small stature" alleles, we see the short phenotype in the plant. Conversely, when the plant has 2 "S" (capital S) or tall alleles, the phenotypic outcome is a plant of tall stature. If the plant happens to inherit a copy of the tall and short allele, the resulting phenotype is a plant of medium stature.

Often, breeders base the symbol for the genotype on the first letter of the recessive expression of a trait. What this means will become clear over the next paragraph or so.

Homozygous / Heterozygous - These are terms used in describing the genotypic condition of a plant, with regard to the similarity of the alleles for a given trait. If a plant is *homozygous* for a given trait, it has two copies of the same allele (homo = same). If a plant is *heterozygous*, it has two *different* alleles for a given trait (hetero = different).

Dominance

Consider two true-breeding varieties; a white pistil variety and a variety showing only pink pistils. Both conditions are true-breeding and therefore homozygous; in each case sexual reproduction of each group separately leads to only pink pistil or white pistil plants respectively. An F1 hybrid, or first generation cross of these two varieties, results in only white pistil plants; no pink pistils are seen regardless of how many F1 seeds are grown.

Upon sib mating of these F1 plants (crossing brothers to sisters, or mating F1 siblings), the resulting F2 generation produces 75% white pistil plants and 25% pink pistil plants. Notice the "disappearance" of the pink pistil plants in the F1 generation, and their subsequent "reappearance" in the F2 generation. In this case, white pistils are said to be *dominant* over pink pistils, and pink pistils are said to be *recessive* to white pistils.

Again, let's consider the phenotypes seen, and provide symbols and deduce the genotypes:

P1 - White pistils × P2 - Pink pistils

F1 generation
(All white-pistil plants)

F1 male × F1 female

F2 generation

25% pink-pistil plants, 75% white-pistil plants

Remember our rule about naming the genotype symbol based on the first letter of the recessive condition, in this case pink.

Phenotypes: Pink (recessive) and White (dominant)

Phenotype	Genotype
P1 - (pink pistils)	pp
P2 - (white pistils)	PP
F1 - (White pistils)	Pp
F2 - (White- and pink-pistil plants)	
25% Pink	pp
75% White	PP or Pp

This 75% can be broken down into 2 genotypic classes, PP and Pp.

When we cross Pp × Pp plants, we get three possible combinations of genotypes. 25% PP, 50% Pp, 25% pp.

	P	p
P	PP	Pp
p	pP	Pp

Therefore we know the 75% white pistil plants are actually 50% Pp + 25% PP, for a total of 75%.

Recessive: An intra-allelic interaction such that an allele of one parent is masked by the presence of an allele from the other parent plant, in the expression of a given trait in the progeny. The recessive trait is not shown in the first generation of progeny (F1) but will reappear if siblings are mated, and the F2 progeny will result in 25% plants showing the recessive condition.

Dominant: An intra-allelic interaction such that the presence of an allele of one parent masks the presence of an allele from another parent plant, in the expression of a given trait in the progeny. Only the dominant trait is shown in the first generation of offspring. Of the F2 generation, 75% will also show the dominant condition.

Primary Components of a Breeding Program

1 - Develop a vision or a breeding goal.

Every breeding program should begin by developing a breeding goal. Why are you trying to make seed? What are you trying to accomplish by mating these sets of parents? You might be trying to make a seed population that represents the traits of an ideal, or mostly ideal plant you have previously selected. In the case of the latter, you might be trying to add new traits to your mostly ideal plant and incorporate these new traits into a new seedline. Some may just want some seeds to plant for next year's crop. Think of your breeding goal as your final destination; the breeding process is the roadmap or route to get to that goal.

2 - Find or Create Variability.

Finding variable seedlots these days is certainly not a difficult task, because very few breeders take the time to stabilize or fix certain traits within a given breeding population prior to release. Your starting seed stock likely represents a range of variation for most traits, depending on the source of your initial starting material. The sad reality is that most of the seed industry today focuses more on creating seed for sale than on developing improved or even uniform plant stock. As a breeder looking for germ plasm to work with, this leaves unstable populations with ample variation for future selection. If searching for variation, this could be considered a good thing. However, since true-breeding stable plants are what breeders look for when choosing stock for their own breeding, this is a hindrance as well. It is much easier to breed with true breeding plants because one can see patterns emerging in a predictable manner in subsequent generations, and thus expect reliable, consistent results when hybrid-

izing known true-breeding parents. This can only be achieved if the breeder is using true-breeding starting parent stock. Due to the lack of commercially available true-breeding stock to work with, serious breeders must stabilize their initial breeding stock before beginning the hybridizing or outcrossing phases of their breeding programs.

3 - Grow and evaluate.

Do just as it says. The more plants you grow, the more variations you will see. I am repeatedly surprised and even amazed to see new expression of traits when growing this fabulous species. Cannabis is an extremely variable and polymorphic species, many traits have numerous possible expressions. Growing varied seed stocks of different heritage (and many of each population) ensures the breeder a wide array of phenotypes and combinations of traits for future selection.

Choosing from as many plants as possible is always preferable; having a wide and diverse starting stock assures the highest chances of finding what you might be looking for. When selecting from just a few seeds, it's not possible to assure all plants will be vigorous or show the traits of interest even if they are seeds of known quality. Breeders must weed through large populations of potential plants, and "rogue out" the undesirable individuals. In any breeding program, off-types which do not suit the goal should be removed from the breeding populations.

Some recessive traits, especially those controlled by multiple genes (polygenic traits), have the potential for phenotypes that are only apparent in 1 in 100 or even 1 in 1000 plants. Unless growing many individuals, the breeder has a very low likelihood of discovering these phenotypes. All other things being equal, the breeder who grows the most plants has the greatest possibility of finding the best breeding candidates. Testing the final product is a crucial part of the evaluation process, so get out that bong or those rolling papers and put all your hard work to the test!

4 - Screen, Select, and Apply Selection

Rogue out weak females.

Pressures.

To paraphrase one of the great breeders of the 20th century, select only plants that closely match your goal, and reject all others. This is an important rule to follow if your future generations are to gradually approach your goal.

Breeders select plants for future breeding on the basis of their desirable characteristics. There is no "right" or "correct" ranking of priority for selecting one trait over another; this is purely based on what traits are most important to the breeder. For indoor cultivation, these include short, squat, bushy growth; large, densely formed buds; discernible taste or particular flavors and aromas; high THC content and quality of high (long-lasting, soaring, sedative); and resistance to specific insects or diseases. It's a good general rule to look for plants with overall vigor and good health.

Sometimes, we find a plant that is almost ideal in every respect, but has some negative trait that is undesirable. For example, the breeder may select a highly potent plant that produces exceptionally aromatic or flavorful flowers but is tall and lanky and difficult to grow indoors under artificial light. Even with this negative trait, the breeder decides the plant is a worthwhile breeding candidate. The breeder must realize and note that when selecting plants that may have some genetic weakness, the unwanted negative

traits must be removed from the population at a later point. The breeder must balance positive and negative aspects of each plant as a possible genetic contributor to future generations.

When planting a large number of seeds, you will generally find that some plants differ greatly in regard to certain traits while being otherwise nearly identical. For example, some plants are more-or-less susceptible to fungal infection such as *botrytis* (grey mold) or powdery mildew. Once suitable plants are selected, they can be exposed to a particular pathogen or environment as a selection pressure; growing potential breeding parents in an environment may expose genetic strengths or weaknesses associated with a particular environment. For mold resistant varieties, select plants for future mating that resist mold in a mold prone environment. For potent varieties, select only the most potent plants, after harvest. If you require your plants finish at less that 6 feet of height, remove or only keep seeds from plants that mature at less than 6 feet. If you require an outdoor acclimated variety, perform your selection outdoors under those particular conditions, and put an emphasis for selection on plants that mature early enough to finish in your particular environment. Selecting the earliest of the most potent plants is a better way to preserve potency, than selecting the most potent of the early plants. It really depends on what traits the breeder ranks in importance to the program, a decision based on the breeding goal.

Usually, varieties that perform well under artificial lights will also perform well outside or in a glass house under natural sunlight after two or three years of acclimation. The converse doesn't hold true nearly as often. Varieties that perform well outside, especially pure *sativa* varieties, often prove disappointing when grown under artificial light.

Post-harvest selection requires either partial seeding of each plant (only seeds from the most potent plants are sown for successive generations) or keeping clone copies of each and every plant, for future seed production use once post harvest evaluations are done.

5 - Commercialize.

This is an optional part of a breeding program. Some people breed to create a variety that suits their specific growing environment and smoking tastes, without ever intending to profit from the sale of their work. They just want reliable seeds for their own planting and future use. Some are of the opposite extreme; they make seeds exclusively to sell. These "breeders" do very little breeding. We refer to them as seed makers.

Because cannabis is a species under attack from various governments and other evil forces around the world, true breeders with goals and intentions other than financial are sorely needed to protect the genetic resources cannabis has left. Years of persecution from governments and greedy seed-making practices without improvement or preservation have led to a genetic bottleneck, a narrowing of the potentially available breeding stock. Now more than ever, ethical breeding should be of utmost concern to cannabis enthusiasts. The species desperately needs breeders who are willing to improve populations in their possession, all the while preserving valuable genetic resources for future generations of breeders.

Sam the Skunkman, a great ally of cannabis, says we all stand on the shoulders of those who have come before us. We can build upon the improvements our ancestors have made to landraces and wild populations, but we can only work with what they have left us. Selections and advancements come at a cost to genetic variability. Breeders often reduce variability by narrowing the gene pool of that particular population as a consequence of fixing traits. The best breeders strive to advance and

Growing out a large number of seedlings is the best way to find a good mother plant.

You can find just about any marijuana seed you can imagine on the market today.

improve a given variety or population while preserving the variation present for the traits not under selection, which may prove valuable for future breeders and growers.

Types of Seed Populations
Inbred Line/Pure Line

Some refer to these as IBLs. An inbred line is a seedlot that has been bred for generations while selecting repeatedly for specific traits, to the point where the population reliably reproduces the traits under selection in each successive generation of breeding. These plants are said to breed true for these characteristics. There is little or no variation for these traits, which are thus considered pure. Pure lines make the best breeding stock as the progeny of crosses using known pure parental lines have a predictable outcome in subsequent generations. Inbred lines are uniform in growth patterns and traits and are stable genetically–each generation of inbred seed results in plants similar in most ways to the previous generation. Pure lines are homozygous at most alleles.

Hybrids

Hybrids are a product of a cross between genetically unlike parents. Hybrids retain their distinctive characters if reproduced asexually but fail to reproduce these characters completely or reliably when reproduced sexually. Hybrid cultivars are developed by using available inbred lines or creating new ones from segregating populations, and then coupling selection with inbreeding for homozygosity, evaluation of inbreds for combining ability in hybrid combinations, and subsequent multiplication of selected inbred lines for hybrid seed production.

There are various types of hybrid varieties:

F1 hybrids ('Northern Lights' × 'Blueberry', 'Northern Lights' × 'Haze', 'Frostbite')

3-way crosses ('Skunk #1' - a cross of (Mexican × Columbian) × Afghani)

Double cross hybrids (a cross of 2 unrelated F1 hybrids 'Haze' (Afghani × Thai) × (Mexican × Columbian).

F1 hybrid varieties -

An F1 hybrid population is obtained by crossing two unrelated, true breeding varieties. F1 hybrids are unique in that they are uniform when grown from seed, but, like all hybrids, are genetically unstable. If reproduced sexually by inbreeding within the F1 population, the subsequent generation will be neither uniform nor similar to the F1 generation.

One of the major benefits of F1 seed to the grower is a condition known as hybrid vigor, or heterosis. Hybrid vigor occurs when the progeny resultant from crossing the two parental inbred lines exceed the performance of the parental lines in some character, or most often in sets of characters (F1 < or > P1 or P2).

F1 hybrids are often bigger and more robust and grow faster than either of the parent populations used in the creation of the F1 population. For example, a ('Skunk#1' × 'Blueberry') F1 hybrid may grow faster and yield more than either the pure 'Skunk #1' or 'Blueberry' parent populations. Often, heterosis is apparent as a tolerance to adverse environmental conditions.

F1 seed production has benefits to the breeder or seed-maker, as well as the grower. True-breeding seed can be easily reproduced by open-pollination. Most seed companies have no interest in selling easily reproduced seed. This is as true of corn as it is of cannabis. Very few companies that do take the time and effort to breed stable parent stock release it in a pure form. Most make and release hybrids, as certain competitor companies' sole mission is to create knockoff versions of lines released by those who have actually taken the time to develop new true-breeding lines. By releasing only hybrids of their pure lines, seed banks ensure the customer comes back to buy more of the F1 seed each time they wish to do a new seed planting of the variety. They also protect the investment of their long-term breeding effort by removing the possibility that a competitor will reproduce their work and sell it as their own.

Unfortunately, breeders of cannabis drug varieties have no recourse to the law when others reproduce and market their years of work. Due to the illegal nature of the plant, drug cannabis varieties are not protected by the various plant breeder's rights legislation around the world.

There is, however, at least one drug type cannabis clone registered for plant protection in Holland. The clone registered as 'Medsins' is owned for use by a pharmaceutical company licensed to grow cannabis for pharmaceutical production.

Variety - A subdivision of a kind, group, or family that is distinct in some characters. Within the variety, all plants exhibit a set of defined morphological, physiological, or other chemical characteristics that differentiate the variety from all other varieties. *The variety must be uniform.* Variations in essential and distinctive characters are described and characterized by the breeder. The variety will remain unchanged to a reasonable degree of reliability in its essential and distinctive characteristics and its uniformity when reproduced.*

Cultivar (abbreviated cv) - A term derived from "cultivated variety," a population of cultivated plants clearly distinguished by any number of morphological, physiological, cytological, or chemical characteristics. When reproduced sexually or asexually the population retains its distinguishing characters.*

New selections derived from a cultivar or variety such that the selection shows sufficient variation from the parent cultivar to render it worthy of a name, are to be regarded as a distinct cultivar.

* Note that the Guidelines for Classifying Cultivated Plant Populations (1978) stipulate that variety and cultivar are considered equivalents.

Strain - Strain is not a scientifically accepted botanical term, although in the cannabis industry many use the term when discussing seedlots for purchase, for lack of a more accurate term. Strain is a term incorrectly applied to selections of cultivars or varieties. In the cannabis seed industry, very few seedlots could be considered true varieties or cultivars, because they are not uniform or do not breed true. All plants within the population do not reproduce the defining characteristics, and, usually the variations in the defining characteristics are not described. Very often, commercially sold seeds are nothing more than hybrids of hybrids with names, and there are no defining characteristics of the "strain." Perhaps "family" or "group" are more appropriate terms.

Open Pollinated Varieties - Non-hybrid populations reproduced by random pollination within the variety. All pistillate individuals have the potential to mate with all staminate individuals as the pollen spreads randomly, ensuring preservation of the genetic diversity within the breeding population. In cannabis, open pollination is carried out by planting the breeding population together in a given plot isolated from other pollen sources and left to the will of the wind. To maintain varietal purity, hemp breeders ensure there is no non-varietal pollen source within four miles upwind, and one mile downwind–which should demonstrate just how far cannabis pollen can travel on the wind.

Heirloom varieties/Heirloom seeds are the product of many years of selective planting and seed saving. The original seeds bore a plant or flower that had particular traits the grower liked–typically flavor, color, or psychoactive effect. The grower then saved the seeds from the desirable plant and repeated the process the next season selecting for similar type plants. The term "heirloom seeds" came about because the selection process for some cultivars has been going on for generations, often passed along within a family and/or shared with friends.

Heirloom varieties are non-hybrid (open-pollinated). This simply means that they breed relatively true. Thus, growers can save seeds from their crops, plant them the following year, and expect to see offspring that are very much like the parent generation. Any off-types in each generation should be rogued out of the breeding population to keep it pure, as they are likely the result of pollen contamination from an external source.

Multi-line - Two or more pure-breeding lines, which are very similar, but differ in a small part of the overall phenotype (i.e., maturation, disease resistance). The varieties are grown and bred separately but are subsequently mixed together and sold in the same seed package. These packs are a benefit to growers if the grower's given environment is inconsistent from year to year, or for growers who are experimenting with growing in a new location. For example, a multi-line may include a slightly earlier-maturing variety with a slightly more mold-resistant variety; most other traits are equivalent in each population. The variations in performance of each variety with regard to mold or earliness of maturity ensure that there will be some harvest even in a year where only the early varieties finish (as a result of early rains), or even if mold is more prevalent during the particular grow season. If a grower is new to an area, multi-lines may be useful for the first few years of planting. It is always a shame to plant a single variety, only to find it is not suitable for the particular climate, thus wasting the year of production. The grower may not reap the highest yield as may be possible from a single hybrid variety particularly suited to the climate, but the degree of variation present in multi-lines helps to ensure at least some plants are harvested.

Synthetic variety - an interbreeding population derived from intermating a group of specific genotypes, each of which were selected for good combining ability in all possible hybrid combinations. Subsequent maintenance of the variety is achieved by open pollination and usually involves rounds of recurrent selection over a series of generations.

Intersexuality Is a trait that can be expressed due to a multitude of causes, both genetic and environmental. There are intersex plants which are strictly genetic; these plants have inherited a gene that triggers the intersex condition, even given a perfect growing environment. They produce both pistillate and staminate flowers on the same individual under typical environmental conditions. Strict negative selection against these plants is required by breeders and growers in order to eliminate the intersex trait from the breeding population. Cultivators and breeders alike have wisely selected against plants that show the slightest degree of intersexuality. They know even a single male flower on an otherwise female plant can result in the majority of the crop being pollinated, and thus seeded.

Indoors, where growers attempt to mimic Mother Nature, plants often undergo stresses which are not present under natural conditions. When plants are stressed by being grown in an inhospitable environment, the typical expression of characteristics can be altered. Intersexuality, for example, can also be induced

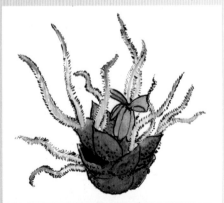

Intersex plants are often mistakenly called hermaphrodites.

Hermaphrodite plant with both female and male flowers together.

in cannabis by a grower's influence as a result of an inconsistent growth environment.

Environmentally stressed female plants have been known to show the occasional male flower. Interrupted dark cycles and other types of stressors can result in the development of staminate flowers on otherwise pistillate individuals. Environmental conditions which may provoke sexual reversal include an inconsistent photoperiod, nutrient toxicities and deficiencies, pH issues, or drastically fluctuating temperatures during the flowering cycle. Females severely stressed, for any reason, are more prone to develop a few male flowers. These stresses cause changes in the levels of a plant hormone called ethylene.

Ethylene is one of only a few known plant hormones, and plays many roles in plant devel-

Applying a hormonal spray is easy.

opment across a range of species. In cannabis, one of ethylene's major roles is its involvement in the determination of sex. It regulates which flowers should be produced–stamen or pistil. We know this because applying high enough concentrations of ethylene to staminate individuals in the flowering cycle results in the formation of pistils. Conversely, applying ethylene-inhibiting agents to pistillate individuals as they enter flowering results in the formation of stamens in place of pistils. This practice can be of use to breeders in the creation of "feminized" seeds, or all-female (gynoecious) seedlots.

All female seeds are produced by obtaining pollen from one female individual, and subsequently fertilizing another female plant.

When we previously discussed chromosomes, we said there were 20 chromsomes in each cell of the plant. The 10th pair of chromosomes, the smallest pair, are the sex chromosomes. Female cannabis plants have two copies of the X chromosome, therefore their genotype is XX. Male plants have only 1 copy of the X chromosome, and a Y chromosome instead of a second X chromosome. The genotype of male plants in terms of the sex chromosomes is XY.

When pollen is created within the plant, one of each of the chromosome pairs is packaged into the cells that develop into pollen. Each pollen grain or ovule contains 10 chromosomes, 1 copy of each pair. When the pollen deposits the genetic material into the ovule, the 10 chromosomes from the pollen and the ovule unite to make a total of 20 chromosomes, a full genetic compliment.

Let's examine a Punnet square from a typical male:female cross -
Male genotype = XY
Female genotype = XX

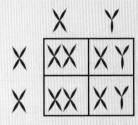

From above we can see that half of the plants are XY (male) and half of the plants are XX (female).

Let's now look at a Punnet square from a female:female cross -

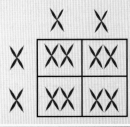

This Punnet square shows us that female: female breeding schemes produce only female (XX) offspring.

Some growers intentionally use the pollen from intersex plants to fertilize females. They have found that the seeds and subsequent offspring produced from this union will be predominately female. The major problem with this technique is that these plants will have intersex tendencies. By selecting parent plants that have intersex tendencies, we ensure that some of the progeny will also have intersex tendencies. Using pollen from an intersex or hermaphrodite plant is an intentional selection for intersexuality–like begets like.

Some seed companies market "feminized seeds," which are produced by collecting pollen from carefully selected, latent, stress-induced hermaphrodites, and use it to pollinate female plants. This process is time consuming and arduous, but yields mostly female plants when grown without stress. However, under the stresses that resulted in the intersexuality for the pollen parent, the progeny will often show some degree of intersexuality as well. Again, like begets like.

So how do we get true females (that do not show any degree of intersexuality under normal conditions) to produce pollen? Can we get pollen from female plants that do not show a degree of intersexuality?

There are hormone treatments, which, when applied to cannabis, result in the formation of staminate flowers on otherwise pistillate plants. To select against the intersex condition, we take our chosen female breeding candidates and grow them under stressful conditions that may lead to the formation of male flowers–irregular light cycle, high heat, etc. Only plants that resist intersexuality under these conditions should be considered as potential breeding parents for the creation of all-female seed lines. We call these intersex-resistant plants "true females." Intentional selection against intersex plants is the only way to ensure intersex-free offspring.

Clone copies of these pistillate intersex-resis-

tant plants are then sprayed with our hormone treatment and placed into the flowering cycle and allowed to develop stamens. It typically takes three to five weeks for the plants to enter dehiscence and shed pollen. True female candidates that also resist intersexuality under typical stresses, are pollinated by pollen obtained by our hormone-treated, gender-reversed, stamen-bearing female plants. The result is a true gynoecious population, consisting entirely of female plants.

An American company, Hybritech, was the first to introduce an effective ready-to-use hormone treatment–eliteXelite. This product is no longer available for public purchase. Another plant research firm, PG-Solutions, has since developed and released a ready-to-use hormone therapy spray, Stamen-It!. Stamen-It! is extremely effective in causing gender reversal of pistillate individuals. Some hormone sprays are able to induce staminate flower formation, but fail to produce viable pollen in any significant quantities. PG-Solutions has developed a formulation that causes significant pollen production, even in the most reversal-resistant genotypes. If you are interested in this technology, check their website, www.pgsolutions.ca.

Breeding Schemes For Cross-Pollinated Crops

There are many types of breeding programs, some more complex than others. Which breeding method to employ depends entirely on the breeder's goal. Ideally, potential breeders understand the benefits and drawbacks of each strategy, so a suitable strategy can be chosen to achieve the desired goal. The breeder's personal preference always comes into play when choosing a breeding program. Previous successes may influence a breeder to use one specific breeding strategy over another. Some breeders rely heavily on science and statistics when analyzing the performance of their hybrids or progeny. Others consider breeding more of an art, and select based on feeling. Over the course of a breeding program, a breeder will often use more than one method to achieve various aspects of the goal.

When breeding cross-pollinators, we discuss hybrid performance in terms of combining ability–the ability of an inbred line to give characteristic performance in hybrid combinations with other lines. The progenies are tested for performance as populations and related back to the parental generation. Some often-used measures of performance are general combining ability (GCA) and specific combining ability (SCA). General combining ability is the average or overall performance of a given line in hybrid combinations open-pollinated with other lines.

Specific combining ability is the performance of a specific line, as compared to other lines, when crossed with the same specific pollen source.

Open pollination is a very low effort type of seed production and involves minimal, if any, selection. Seeds are planted, grown to maturity, and allowed to interbreed. Off-types, or plants that do not represent the defining characteristics of the variety, are rogued from the breeding population, to ensure the variety remains pure and true to type. Inbred lines, and other populations maintained through open pollination, are often bred by one person, and then produced for commercial production and release by others. Some breeders create true-breeding populations, then licence them to other companies who plant them and expand the seed populations by growing out many, many plants and allowing them all to fully seed. This is called a seed-increase.

Inbreeding

Inbreeding is nothing more than crossing a group, family, or variety of plants within themselves with no additions of genetic material from an outside or unrelated population. The most severe form of inbreeding is the self-cross, in which only one individual's genetic material forms the basis of subsequent generations. 1:1 hybrid populations are only slightly less

A male plant is fertilizing a female.

Inbreeding consists of crossing a group, family, or variety of plants with themselves.

narrow, derived from the genetic material of 2 individuals. Such tight or narrow breeding populations lead to a condition called "inbreeding depression" upon repeated self-breeding or inbreeding.

Inbreeding depression is a reduction in vigor (or any other character) due to prolonged inbreeding. This can manifest as a reduction in potency or a decrease in yield or rate of growth. Progress of depression is dependent, in part, on the breeding system of the crop. Earlier, when we discussed dioecy, we said cannabis is an outcrossing or cross-pollinating species. Cross-pollinated crops usually exhibit a higher degree of inbreeding depression when "selfed," or inbred, than do selfing crops. For example, tomato (an inbreeding or selfing species) can be selfed for 20 generations with no apparent loss in vigor or yield, whereas some experiments have shown that the yield of corn per acre is decreased quite dramatically when inbred for 20 generations.

In cross-pollinated crops, deleterious genes remain hidden within populations, and the negative attributes of these recessive traits can be revealed or unmasked via continual inbreeding. Inbreeding depression can be apparent in S1 populations after a single generation of self-fertilization. When breeding cannabis using small populations, as is often the case with continual 1:1 mating schemes, inbreeding depression typically becomes apparent within three to six generations. To deal with this problem, breeders often maintain separate parallel breeding lines, each of which are selected for similar or identical sets of traits. After generations of inbreeding, when each of the inbred lines, or selfed populations, begin to show inbreeding depression, they are hybridized or outcrossed to each other to restore vigor and eliminate inbreeding depression while preserving the genetic stability of the traits under selection.

The vast majority of texts written to date on the subject of breeding cannabis have espoused 1:1 mating strategies, much to the detriment and health of cannabis germplasm. Sadly, this is the preferred breeding scheme used today by the majority of commercial seed banks. These breeders don't realize that cannabis is naturally an out-crossing or cross-pollinating species and existed in wild breeding populations of hundreds if not thousands of individuals. Within these many individuals lies a wide range of versions of different genes. When we select only one or two plants from this vast array as our breeding population, we drastically reduce the genetic variability found in the original population (a genetic bottleneck). This variability is lost from the populations, and unavailable to future generations.

Outbreeding

Outbreeding is the process of crossing or hybridizing plants or groups of plants with other plants to which there is no, or only a distant, relation. Any time a breeder is hybridizing using plants that reside outside of the family, group, or variety, hybrid seed is produced. For example, an F1 hybrid seed is the first generation off-

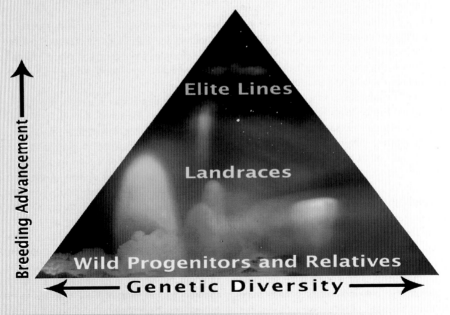

This pyramid shows the evolution of breeding cannabis.

spring resulting from a cross of two distinct true-breeding plants or populations. Each of the parent populations were hybridized (outcrossed to each other) to produce the new generation, which is now comprised of genetics from both parental populations. Outcrossing results in the introduction of new and different genetic material to each of the respective pools.

Filial Breeding - A type of breeding system where siblings of the same progeny lot and generation are intermated to produce new generations. The first hybrid generation of two distinct true-breeding lines is denoted the F1 generation (F, filial). If two F1 siblings are bred, or the F1 population is allowed to be open pollinated, the resulting generation is labeled F2.

Mating siblings chosen from the F2, results in the F3 population. F4, F5, F6 generations, etc., are obtained in the same manner, by crossing plants of the same generation and progeny lot. Note that as long as any number of siblings of a generation (F[n]) are mated, the resulting generations is denoted (F[n+1]).

Filial inbreeding with selection for specific traits is the most common method for establishing a pure or a true-breeding population, when breeding cross-pollinated species such as cannabis.

Backcross Breeding - A type of breeding that involves repeated crossing of progeny with one of the original parental genotypes; cannabis breeders most often cross progeny to the mother plant. This parent is known as the recurrent parent. The nonrecurrent parent is called the donor parent. More widely, any time a generation is crossed to a previous generation, it is a form of backcross breeding. Backcross breeding has become one of the staple methods clandestine cannabis breeders use, mainly because it is a simple, rapid method when using greenhouses or growrooms, and requires only small populations. The principal goal of backcross breeding is to create a population of individuals derived mainly from the genetics of one single parent (the recurrent parent).

The donor parent is chosen based on a trait

Sprayed with `Stamen-It!' from PG-Solutions, this plant that started out as a female is now expressing only male flowers.

of interest that the recurrent parent lacks; the idea is to introgress this trait into the backcross population, such that the new population is comprised mainly of genetics from the recurrent parent, but also contains the genes responsible for the trait of interest from the donor parent.

The backcross method is a suitable scheme for adding new desirable traits to a mostly ideal, relatively true-breeding genotype. When embarking on a backcross breeding plan, the recurrent parent should be a highly acceptable or nearly ideal genotype (for example, an existing commercial cultivar or inbred line). The ideal traits considered for introgression into the new seed line should be simply inherited and easily scored for phenotype. The best donor parent must possess the desired trait, but should not be seriously deficient in other traits. Backcross line production is repeatable, if the same parents are used.

Backcross breeding is best used when adding simply inherited dominant traits that can easily be identified in the progeny of each generation (Example 1). Recessive traits are more difficult to select for in backcross breeding, since their expression is masked by dominance in each backcross to the recurrent parent. An additional round of open pollination or sib-mating is needed after each backcross generation, to expose homozygous-recessive plants. Individuals showing the recessive condition are selected from F2 segregating generations and backcrossed to the recurrent parent (see Example 2).

Example 1- Backcrossing: Incorporating A Dominant Trait

Step1 - Recurrent Parent × Donor Parent

|

V

F1 Hybrid generation

Step 2 - Select desirable plants showing dominant trait, and hybridize selected plants to recurrent parent. The generation produced is denoted BC1 (some cannabis breeders break from botanical convention and denote this generation B×1. [BC1= B×1]).

Step 3 - Select plants from BC1 and hybridize with the recurrent parent; the resulting generation is denoted BC2.

Step 4 - Select plants from BC2 and hybridize with the recurrent parent; the resulting generation is denoted BC3.

Example 2 Backcrossing: Incorporating A Recessive Trait

Step1 - Recurrent Parent × Donor

|

V

F1 Hybrid generation

Step 2 - Select desirable plants, and create an F2 population via full sib-mating.

Step 3 - Select plants showing the desired recessive trait in the F2 generation, then hybridize selected F2-recessive plants to the recurrent parent. The generation produced is denoted BC1.

Step 4 - Select plants from BC1, and create

a generation of F2 plants via sib-mating; the resulting generation can be denoted BC1F2.

Step 5 - Select desirable BC1F2 plants showing the recessive condition, and hybridize with the recurrent parent; the resulting generation is denoted BC2.

Step 6 - Select plants from BC2, and create an F2 population via sib-mating; denote the resulting generation BC2F2.

Step 7 - Select plants showing the recessive condition from the BC2F2 generation, and hybridize to the recurrent parent; the resulting generation is denoted BC3.

Step 8 - Grow out BC3, select and sib-mate the most ideal candidates to create an F2 population, where plants showing the recessive condition are then selected and used as a basis for a new inbred, or open-pollinated, seed line.

This new generation created from the F2 is a population that consists of, on average, ~93.7% of genes from the recurrent parent, and only ~6.3% of genes leftover from the donor parent. Most importantly, one should note that since only homozygous-recessives were chosen for mating in the BC3F2 generation, the entire resulting BC3F3 generation is homozygous for the recessive trait, and breeds true for this recessive trait. Our new population meets our breeding objective. It is a population derived mainly from the genetics of the recurrent parent, yet breeds true for our introgressed recessive trait.

Backcross-derived lines are expected to be well-adapted to the environment in which they will be grown, which is another reason backcrossing is often used by cannabis breeders who operate indoors. Indoor grow rooms are easily replicated all over the world, so the grower is able to grow the plants in a similar environment in which they were bred. Progeny therefore need less extensive field-testing by the breeder across a wide range of environments.

If two or more characters are to be introgressed into a new seed line, these would usually be tracked in separate backcross programs, and the individual products would be combined in a final set of crosses after the new populations have been created by backcrossing.

The backcross scheme has specific drawbacks, however. When the recurrent parent is not very true-breeding, the resulting backcross generations segregate, and many of the traits deemed desirable to the line fail to be reproduced reliably. Another limitation of the backcross is that the "improved" variety differs only slightly from the recurrent parent (e.g., one trait). If multiple traits are to be introgressed into the new population, other techniques such as inbreeding or recurrent selection, may be more rewarding.

Selfing

Selfing is the process of creating seed by fertilizing a plant with pollen obtained from itself. The result of a self-cross is a population of plants that derive from a single individual. The first generation population derived from selfing an individual is called the S1 population. If an individual is chosen from the S1, and again selfed, the resulting population is denoted the S2 generation. Subsequent generations derived in the same manner are denoted S3, S4, etc.

Traits for which the plant is homozygous remain homozygous upon selfing, whereas heterozygous loci segregate, and may demonstrate novel expressions of these characters.

We know homozygous loci remain homozygous in future generations upon selfing, but what about the heterozygous loci? Each selfed generation leads to an increase in homozygosity by 50% for each heterozygous locus, and each subsequent generation, derived from selfing an S1 individual, is 50% more homozygous than the parent from which it was derived. Repeated selfing, or single-seed descent, is the fastest way to achieve homozygosity within a group or family. Again, the more plants grown from a selfed population, the better probability a breeder has of finding selfed progeny that show all of the desired traits.

Single-seed descent - A plant is self-fertilized and the resulting seed collected. One of these seeds is selected and grown, again self-fertilized, and seed produced. All progeny and future generations have descended from a single ancestor, as long as no pollen from an external family is introduced. Each generation is the result of selfing one individual from the previous generation.

After six generations of selfing without selection, 98.44% of the genes of an individual are homozygous–this refers to genes, not the number of plants that are homozygous.

Recurrent Selection - Any breeding program designed to concentrate favorable genes scattered among a number of individuals by repeated cycles of selection for favorable traits.

Step 1- Identify superior genotypes for the trait under selection.

Step 2 - Intermate the superior genotypes and select improved progeny.

Step 3 - Repeat steps 1 & 2 over a series of generations.

Pedigree Selection - A system of breeding in which individual plants are selected in the segregating generations from a cross on the basis of their desirability, judged individually, and on the basis of a pedigree record.

Ploidy - Cannabis plants are, by nature, diploids with twenty chromosomes. At meiosis, each parent's gamete contributes ten chromosomes to the zygote they have formed. Cannabis cells may be haploid (have 1 copy of each chromosome set) as in gametes, or diploid (2 chromosome sets per cell).

Some researchers have wondered whether triploid, or tetraploid cannabis (cells with either 3 or 4 chromosome sets respectively) are agronomically important. In some species, polyploid plants grow bigger, yield more, or outperform typical diploid members of the same species. Some early reports touted polyploid cannabis as being more potent. This research was flimsy and unscientific at best, and ever since this report, many cannabis growers have attempted inducing polyploidy in many varieties, none leading to agronomic success.

Diploid plants are considered normal and have one set of chromosomes, which occur in pairs within each plant cell. Polyploid plants have more than one set of chromosomes per cell. Polyploid plant chromosomes occur in groups of 3-4 instead of in pairs. Tetraploid plants groups occur with four chromosomes in each cell.

At one time, breeders believed that polyploid and tetraploid plants would produce a superior resin-packed plant.

The polyploid characteristic can be induced with an application of colchicine. Just remember, colchicine is a poison, and polyploid plants do not contain more THC-potent resin.

Mutagenesis–Inducing Variation

If variation does not exist for the trait or traits of interest, or cannot be found in other populations, it is theoretically possible to induce variation by exposing seeds or other tissues to radiation, alkylating agents, or other mutagens such as colchicine or EMS (ethylmethylsulfonate). These treatments cause changes at the DNA level that have the remote potential to result in desirable, novel phenotypes.

There is much rumour and speculation about this technique amongst breeders and growers. It's a common myth that treating seeds with colchicine and growing the plants results in more potent cannabis plants. Let's put this myth to rest; it is completely untrue. While the possibility does exist on a theoretical level, no valid experiments have ever shown this to be true. Potential breeders would be better off using their time and space for selecting better plants than trying this technique as a method for improving plant stock.

That being said, let's take a look at the theory behind the concept.

Imagine you have a population of plants which, when grown from seed and inbred within the population, consistently produces high-THC plants. It is theoretically possible to treat many of these seeds with a mutagen, grow and inbreed the seeds, and find plants in subsequent generations that produce no THC. These mutagens can destroy genes along a chromo-

some, and when copies of this chromosome are inherited by future generations, a new or "novel" phenotype can appear. In our example, the no THC condition is the novel phenotype.

These mutations, however, occur at random and are extremely unreliable. The probability of finding plants which have a desired mutation in the gene of interest is very low. A breeder may treat many thousands of seeds, grow 100,000 plants, and still not see the desired altered phenotypes. This technique is costly in both time and space. It is often used in the breeding of "legal plants" when growing out thousands of individuals and searching for these novel phenotypes is not problematic. Performing such population screens in cannabis is not practical, especially for clandestine breeders. The potentially hazardous nature of these mutagenic agents is another very good reason to choose other breeding options. Inducing variability is likely not the best option, at least for the hobby breeder.

If you are serious about breeding cannabis, check out *Marijuana Botany, An Advanced Study: The Propagation and Breeding of Distinctive Cannabis*, by Robert Connell Clarke, Ronin Press. Using understandable scientific detail, Clarke discusses genetics and breeding, chemistry, and much more of interest to the budding breeder. This book is worth its weight in 'Haze' buds. If you can't find it at the bookstore, check out our web site: www.marijuana growing.com .

Conversion Charts and Tables

Carbon Dioxide Facts and Figures

molecular weight = 44 grams/mole
sublimes (solid to gas) at 78.5°C at 1 atmosphere - air density = 1.2928 grams/liter (i.e., at equal temperatures and pressures carbon dioxide is heavier than air, and CO_2 will fall to the bottom of an air/ CO_2 mixture.

psi = 1 atmosphere

Physical properties of Propane:

specific gravity of gas (air = 1)	1.50
pounds per gallon of liquid @ 60°F (15°C)	4.23
gallons per pound of liquid @ 60°F (15°C)	0.236
Btu per cubic foot of gas @ 60°F (15°C)	2488
Btu per pound of gas	21548
Btu per gallon of gas @ 60°F	90502
cubic feet of gas per gallon of liquid	36.38
octane number	100+

Combustion Data:

cubic feet of air to burn 1 gallon of propane	873.6
cubic feet of CO_2 per gallon of Propane burned	109.2
cubic feet of nitrogen per gallon of propane burned	688
pounds of CO_2 per gallon of propane burned	12.7
pounds of nitrogen per gallon of propane burned	51.2
pounds of water vapor per gallon of propane burned	6.8
1 pound of propane produces in kWh	6.3
Btu's per kW hour	3412

1 Therm	100,000 Btu	Specific gravity of liquid	0.509
1 cubic foot natural gas	1000 Btu	Vapor pressure (psig) 00F	23.5
1 pound steam	970 Btu	Vapor pressure (psig) 700 F	109
1 kilowatt	3413 Btu	Vapor pressure (psig) 1000 F	172

Calculations for Metric Users

1 cubic meter = 1 m × 1 m × 1 m = 1000 liters
fans are rated at liters per minute or liters per second

cubic feet = L × W × H
cubic meters = L × W × H

Buy a fan that will clear the grow room volume of air in one to five minutes. Run the fan for twice the time to theoretically clear the grow room of air.

Work out the amount of CO_2 gas to add:

For example, if you want 1500 ppm and ambient CO_2 is 350 ppm, you will need to add: 1500 ppm minus 350 ppm = 1150 ppm CO_2.

A poorly sealed grow room can have 20 percent leakage which should be added to the amount of CO_2 required.

For example, to get the desired 1500 ppm of CO_2 for a grow room with 21.6 cubic meters, add: 21.4 × 1150 = 24.61 liters × 1.2 = 29.53 liters.

This information tells you to set the flow meter to 6 liters per minute and run the gas for 5 minutes.

Leave the gas-enriched air for 20 minutes and exhaust the air from the garden room.

Metric Conversion Chart - Approximations

When You Know	Multiply by	To Find
Length		
millimeters	0.04	inches
centimeters	0.39	inches
meters	3.28	feet
kilometers	0.62	miles
inches	25.40	millimeters
inches	2.54	centimeters
feet	30.48	centimeters
yards	0.91	meters
miles	1.16	kilometers
Area		
sq. centimeters	0.16	square inches
square meters	1.20	square yards
square kilometers	0.39	square miles
hectares	2.47	acres
sq. inches	6.45	sq. centimeters
square feet	0.09	square meters
square yards	0.84	square meters
square miles	2.60	sq. kilometers
acres	0.40	hectares
Volume		
milliliters	0.20	teaspoons
milliliters	0.60	tablespoons
milliliters	0.03	fluid ounces
liters	4.23	cups
liters	2.12	pints
liters	1.06	quarts
liters	0.26	gallons

cubic meters	35.32	cubic feet
cubic meters	1.35	cubic yards
teaspoons	4.93	milliliters
tablespoons	14.78	milliliters
fluid ounces	29.57	milliliters
cups	0.24	liters
pints	0.47	liters
quarts	0.95	liters
gallons	3.790	liters

Mass and Weight
1 gram = 0.035 ounces
1 kilogram = 2.21 pounds
1 ounce = 28.35 grams
1 pound = 0.45 kilograms

1 inch (in) = 25.4 millimeters (mm)
1 foot (12 in) = 0.3048 meters (m)
1 yard (3 ft = 0.9144 meters
1 mile = 1.60937 kilometers
1 square inch = 645.16 square millimeters
1 square foot = 0.0929 square meters
1 square yard = 0.8361 square meters
1 square mile = 2.59 square kilometers

Liquid Measure Conversion
1 pint (UK) = 0.56826 liters
1 pint dry (USA) = 0.55059 liters
1 pint liquid (USA) = 0.47318 liters
1 gallon (UK) (8 pints) = 4.5459 liters
1 gallon dry (USA) = 4.4047 liters
1 gallon liquid (USA) = 3.7853 liters

1 ounce = 28.3495 grams
1 pound (16 ounces) = 0.453592 kilograms

1 gram = 15.4325 grains
1 kilogram = 2.2046223 pounds

1 millimeter = 0.03937014 inches (UK)
1 millimeter = 0.03937 inches (USA)
1 centimeter = 0.3937014 inches (UK)
1 centimeter = 0.3937 inches (USA)
1 meter = 3.280845 feet (UK)
1 meter = 3.280833 feet (USA)
1 kilometer = 0.6213722 miles
1 cm = 0.001 meter
mm = 0.0001 meter
nm = 0.000 000 001 meter
gm = grams
sq = squared

EC = electrical conductivity
ppm = parts per million
Celsius to Fahrenheit
Celsius temperature = (°F - 32) × 0.55
Fahrenheit temperature = (°C × 1.8) + 32

Light Conversion
1 foot-candle = 10.76 = lux
1 lux = 0.09293
lux = 1 lumen/square meters
lumens per square foot = lumens per meter squared

cfm (cubic feet per minute) = liters per hour
Inches of rain = liters per meter squared
psi (pounds per square inch) = kg per square meter

1 liter = 1 kg (of pure water)
1 kilometer = 1000 meters
1 meter = 100 centimeters
1 meter = 1000 millimeters

Cannabis Seed Companies
Many companies were not included in this abridged list because they do not have catalogs and were too difficult to contact.

Almighty Seeds
www.almightyseeds

.com

BC Bud Depot
No catalog
www.bcbudonline.com

Black Label Seeds

www.highqualityseeds.nl

British Colombia Seed Co.
No catalog
www.thebcsc.com

Kannabia

www.kannabia.net

Chimera

www.chimeraseeds.co.uk

DJ Short
No catalog. No website

Dutch Passion

www.dutch-passion.nl

Flying Dutchmen

www.flyingdutchmen.com

Good House Seeds

www.goodhouse seeds.com

Greenhouse

www.greenhouse seeds.nl

Hemcy

www.hemcy.com

High Quality Seeds

www.highquality seeds.nl

Homegrown Fantaseeds

www.homegrown fantaseeds.com

Legend Seeds

www.legendsseeds.com

Magus Genetics

www.magusgenetics .com

Mandala Seeds

www.mandalaseeds .com

Mr. Nice-Swiss

www.mrnice.co.uk

Nirvana

www.nirvana.nl

No Mercy Supply
No catalog
www.nomercy.nl

Owl's Production

Website: None

Paradise Seeds

www. paradise-seeds.com

Reeferman Seeds

www.reefermanseeds.com

Sagarmatha
www.
highestseeds
.com

Sensi Seeds
www.
sensiseeds.
com

Serious Seeds
www.
serious
seeds.com

Soma Seeds - No catalog
www.somaseeds.nl

Spice of Life
www.spiceoflife
seeds.com

THSeeds

www.thseeds.com

Valchanvre

www.valchanvre.ch

Willy Jack - No catalog
www.willyjack.com

World Wide Seeds
No catalog
www.world wideseeds.com

Glossary

absorb: to draw or take in: Rootlets absorb water and nutrients.

AC (alternating current): an electric current that reverses its direction at regularly occurring intervals: Homes have AC.

acid: a sour substance: An acid or sour soil has a low pH.

active: a hydroponic system that actively moves the nutrient solution

adobe: heavy clay soil that drains slowly: Adobe is not suitable for container gardening.

aeration: to supply soil and roots with air or oxygen

adventitious roots: roots that grow from unusual spots, as on the (stem) pericycle or endodermis of an older root. Auxin level may influence this type of root growth.

Adventitious roots

aeroponics: growing plants by misting roots suspended in air

aggregate: a substrate that is of nearly uniform size and used for the inert hydroponic medium

agronomically: having to do with the economics of agriculture

alkaline: refers to soil, or any substance, with a pH over 7

alkylation: a process in which an alkyl group is substituted or added to a compound

alleles: two genes, each of which occupies the same position or locus on two homogenious chromosomes

amendments: can be either organic or mineral based: Amendments change the texture of a growing medium.

ampere (amp): the unit used to measure the strength of an electric current: A 20-ampere circuit is overloaded when drawing more than 16 amps.

androecious: a plant having staminate (MALE) flowers: An androecious population consists of only males, sometimes called all-male.

anemophilous: pollinated by wind-dispersed pollen

annual: a plant that normally completes its entire life cycle in one year or less: Cannabis is an annual.

arc tube: container for luminous gases; houses the arc in an HID lamp

asexual propagation: reproducing using non-sexual means such as taking cuttings from a parent plant: will produce exact genetic replicas of the parent plant

auxin: classification of plant hormones: Auxins are responsible for foliage and root elongation.

bacteria: very small, one-celled plants that have no chlorophyll

bag seed: the common term given seed of unknown origin that was found in a bag of cannabis

ballast: a stabilizing unit that regulates the flow of electricity and starts an HID lamp: A ballast consists of a transformer and a capacitor.

beneficial insect: a good insect that eats bad, marijuana-munching insects

biodegradable: to decompose through natural bacterial action. Substances made of organic matter can be broken down naturally.

biosynthesis: the production of a chemical compound by a plant

bleach: household laundry bleach is used in a mild water solution to sterilize grow rooms and as soil fungicide

blood meal: high-nitrogen organic fertilizer made from dried blood: Dogs love blood meal!

bloom: to yield flowers

blossom booster: fertilizer high in phosphorus and potassium that increases flower yield and weight

bonsai: a very short or dwarfed plant

bract: small spur-like foliage that grows from the stem at the point from which flowers emerge

breaker box: electrical circuit box having on/off switches rather than fuses: The main breaker box is also called a "service panel."

breed: to sexually propagate cannabis under controlled circumstances

bud: 1. a small, undeveloped stem or shoot. 2. a collection of (flowering) calyxes on a branch

bud blight:: a withering condition that attacks flower buds

buffer: a substance that reduces the shock and cushions against fluctuations: Many fertilizers contain buffer agents.

bulb: outer glass envelope or jacket that protects the arc tube of an HID lamp

bulbous trichome: ball-shaped, resin-producing plant hair without a stalk

callus: tissue made of undifferentiated cells produced by rooting hormones on plant cuttings

Callus

calyx: the pod harboring male or female cannabis reproductive organs

cambium: layer of cells which divides and differentiates into xylem and phloem and is responsible for growth

Cannabaceae: scientific family to which Cannabis (marijuana) and Humulus (hops) belong

cannabinoid: a hydrocarbon unique to cannabis

cannabinoid profile: proportional ratio and levels of major cannabinoids found in cannabis being tested

Cannabis: scientific name for marijuana specifying genus

capitate stalked trichome: resin-producing plant hair without a stalk, high in THC content

carbohydrate: neutral compound of carbon, hydrogen, and oxygen, mostly formed by green plants: Sugar, starch, and cellulose are carbohydrates.

carbon dioxide (CO_2): a colorless, odorless, tasteless gas in the air; necessary for plant life

caustic: a substance that destroys, kills, or eats away by chemical activity

CBD: cannabidiol: CBD usually prolongs the high.

CBC: cannabichromene: second most abundant cannabinoid in drug-type cannabis

CBDV: cannabidiverol

CBG: cannabigerol

CBN: cannabinol

CBNV: cannabiverol

CBT: cannabitriol

CCY: cannabicyclol

cell: the base structural unit of plants: cells contain a nucleus, membrane, and chloroplasts

cellulose: a complex carbohydrate that stiffens a plant: Outdoor stems contain more stiff cellulose than plants grown indoors.

Outdoor Plant

Indoor Plant

centigrade: a scale for measuring temperature where 100 degrees is the boiling point of water, and 0 degrees is the freezing point of water

cfm: cubic feet per minute; measures air velocity. Ventilation or extraction fans are measured in the cfm of air they can move.

chelate: combining nutrients in an atomic ring that is easy for plant to absorb

chimera (also chimaera)**:** 1. a plant or organism with tissues from at least two genetically distinct parents 2. A fire-breathing female monster most often portrayed as a lion, goat, and serpent composite.

chlorophyll: the green photosynthetic matter of plants: Chlorophyll is found in the chloroplasts of a cell and is necessary to photosynthesis.

GLOSSARY

chlorosis: the condition of a sick plant with yellowing leaves due to inadequate formation of chlorophyll: Chlorosis is caused by

Chlorosis

a nutrient deficiency, often iron or imbalanced pH.

chromosomes: microscopically small, dark-staining bodies visible in the nucleus of a cell at the time of nuclear cell division; the number in any species is usually constant. Chromosomes contain the genetic material of a species. Cannabis has 10 pairs of chromosomes.

circuit: a circular route traveled by electricity from a power source, through an outlet, and back to ground

clay: soil made of very fine organic and mineral particles: Clay drains slowly and is not suitable for container gardening.

climate: the average condition of the weather in a grow room or outdoors

clone: 1. a rooted cutting of a plant 2. asexual propagation

CO_2 enrichment: used to augment grow room or greenhouse atmosphere to speed growth

cola: Mexican and North American slang word for a marijuana flower

Cola

top: Cola in Spanish actually means tail.

colchicine: poisonous alkaloid from the autumn crocus, used in plant breeding to induce polyploid mutations

cold: for cannabis, air temperatures below 50°F (10°C)

cold frame: an unheated outdoor structure usually clad in glass or clear plastic, used to protect and acclimatize seedlings and plants

color spectrum: the band of colors (measured in nm) emitted by a light source

color tracer: a coloring agent that is added to many commercial fertilizers so the horticulturist knows there is fertilizer in the solution: Peters has a blue color tracer.

compaction: soil condition that results from tightly packed soil which limits aeration and root penetration

companion planting: planting garlic, marigolds, etc., along with cannabis to discourage pests

compost: mixture of decayed organic matter, high in nutrients: Compost must be well-rotted before use. When too young, decomposition uses nitrogen; after sufficient decomposition, compost releases nitrogen.

core: the transformer in the ballast is often referred to as a core

cotyledon: seed leaves, first leaves that appear on a plant

creeper: marijuana high in CBD having psychoactive qualities that sneak up on smoker: The creeper high usually lasts longer.

critical daylength: maximum daylength which will bring about flowering in cannabis

cross-pollination: fertilizing a plant with pollen from an unrelated individual of the same species

crystal: 1. appearance resin has when found on foliage 2. fertilizers often come in soluble crystals

cubic foot: volume measurement in feet: width × length × height = cubic feet

cultivar: a contraction of "cultivated variety," a variety of plant that has been intentionally created or selected; not naturally occurring

cure: 1. slow drying process that makes marijuana more pleasant and palatable to smoke 2. to make a sick plant healthy

cuticle: thin layer of plant wax (cutin) on the surface of the aboveground parts of plants

cutting: 1. growing-tip cut from a parent plant for asexual propagation 2. clone 3. slip

cytokinins: plant hormones that promote cell division and growth and delay the aging of leaves

damping-off: fungus disease that attacks young seedlings and clones causing stem to rot at base: Over-watering is the main cause of damping-off.

DC (direct current): a continuous electric current that only flows in one direction

decompose: to rot or decay, etc., through organic chemical change

dehumidify: to remove moisture from air

dehydrate: to remove water from foliage

deplete: to exhaust soil of nutrients, making it infertile: Once a soil is used to grow a container crop, it is depleted.

desiccate: to cause to dry up: Insecticidal soap desiccates its victims.

detergent: liquid soap concentrate used: 1. as a wetting agent for sprays and water 2. pesticide, Note: detergent must be totally organic to be safe for plants.

diapause: A period of plant dormancy during which growth or development is suspended or diminished

dioecy: a condition where separate sexes occur on separate individuals; each plant displays a single gender

dioecious: a population consisting of gynoecious and androecious plants

disease: sickness of any kind

dose: amount of fertilizer, insecticide, etc., given to a plant, usually in a water solution

double potting: a two-pot transplanting technique that minimizes root disturbance

drainage: to empty soil of excess water. Good drainage: water passes through soil, evenly promoting plant growth. Bad drainage: drainage water stands in soil, actually drowning roots.

drip (irrigation) system: efficient watering system that employs a main hose with small water emitters (tiny holes) which meter out water one drop at a time at regular, frequent intervals

drip line: a line around a plant directly under its outermost branch tips: Roots seldom grow beyond the drip line.

The drip line.

dry ice: cold, white, solid substance formed when CO_2 is compressed and cooled: Dry ice changes into CO_2 gas at room temperatures.

dry soil pocket: small portion of soil that remains dry after watering: Dry soil pockets may be remedied by adding a wetting agent (soap) to water and/or waiting 15 minutes between waterings.

dry well: drain hole filled with rocks, to receive drainage water

electrode: a solid electric conductor used to establish electrical arc between contacts at either end of an HID lamp

elongate: to grow in length: Cannabis stretches from three inches to a foot when flowering is induced.

embolism: bubble of air in the transpiration stream of a cutting; blocks uptake of water and nutrients

emit: to give off, send out (as light or sound, etc.)

embryo: a young plant, developing within the seed: In cannabis, an embryo is derived from a fertilized ovule.

Encarsia formosa: a parasitic wasp that preys on whiteflies

envelope: outer protective bulb or jacket of a lamp

Epsom salts: hydrated magnesium sulfate in the form of white crystalline salt: Epsom salts add magnesium to soil.

equinox: when sun crosses the equator and day and night are each 12 hours long: The equinox happens twice a year.

essential oils: volatile oils that give plants their characteristic odor or flavor; contained in the secreted resins of plants

ethane methyl sulfonate: a mutagenic chemical that causes changes at the DNA level; induces genetic mutations

etiolation: growth of a plant in total darkness to increase the chances of root initiation

Etiolation

F1: first filial generation, the offspring of two P1 (parent) plants

F1 hybrid: heterozygous first filial generation

F2: second filial generation, resulting from a cross between two F1 plants

fan leaves: large, fan-like marijuana leaves: Fan leaves are usually low in potency.

female: pistillate, ovule, seed producing

fertilize: 1. to apply fertilizer (nutrients) to roots and foliage 2. to impregnate (unite) male pollen with female plant ovary

fertilizer burn: overfertilization; first, leaf tips burn (turn brown), then leaves curl

FIM pruning: acronym for "Fuck, I missed!" pruning method. See page 64 for more information.

flat: a shallow container used to start seedlings or clones

flower: blossom, a mass of calyxes on a stem, top, or bud

foliage: the leaves, or more generally, the green part of a plant

Flat of clones.

foliar feed: misting fertilizer solution, which is absorbed by the foliage

foot-candle (fc): one fc is equal to the amount of light that falls on one square foot of surface located one foot away from one candle

fritted: to fuse or embed nutrients with a glass compound: Fritted Trace Elements (FTE) are long lasting and do not easily leach out of substrate.

fungicide: product that destroys or inhibits fungus

fungistat: product that inhibits fungus

fungus: a lower plant (lacking chlorophyll) that may attack green plants: Mold, rust, mildew, mushrooms, and bacteria are fungi.

fuse: an electrical safety device made of a metal that melts and interrupts the circuit when overloaded

fuse box: electrical circuit box containing circuits controlled by fuses

ganja: slang term for cannabis, from the Indian (Hindustani) word for marijuana

gametes: a reproductive cell specialized for fertilization, having the haploid number of chromosomes: a mature pollen grain or ovule capable of fusing with a gamete of the opposite sex to produce the embryo

gene: part of a chromosome that influences the development and the potency of a plant: Genes are inherited through sexual propagation.

gene pool: collection of possible gene combinations in an available population

genetic makeup: the genes inherited from parent plants: Genetic makeup is the most important factor dictating vigor and potency.

genotype: specific genetic makeup of an individual, which determines the physical appearance of that individual

germplasm: the sum total of the genetic or hereditary materials in a species

gibberellin: a class of plant growth hormone used to promote stem elongation: Gibberellic acid is a form of gibberellin.

girdling: removing a strip of bark or crushing the stem of a plant. Girdling limits the flow of nutrients, water, and plant products, which can kill the plant.

glandular trichome: plant hair gland which secretes resin

gpm: gallons per minute

green lacewing: insect that preys on aphids, thrips, whiteflies, etc., and their larva and offspring

greenhouse: a heated structure with transparent/translucent walls and ceiling which offer some environmental control to promote plant growth

guano: dung from birds, high in organic nutrients: Seabird guano is noted for being high in nitrogen, and bat guano is high in phosphorus.

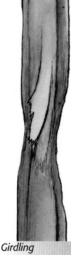
Girdling

gynoecious: an individual plant having all pistillate flowers: in reference to a population, all-female

gynoecium: female part of a flower that consists of one or more pistils

halide: binary chemical compound of a halogen(s) with an electropositive element(s)

halogen: any of the non-metallic elements fluorine, chlorine, bromine, iodine, and astatine existing in a free state: Halogens are enclosed within the arc tube of a metal halide lamp.

hardening-off: gradual adaptation of indoor or greenhouse plants to an outside environment

hashish/hash: a psychoactive drug formed of compressed resin heads of glandular trichomes shaken, washed, or rubbed from cannabis foliage

hash oil: solution of tetrahydrocannabinol with a high THC content; made from cannabis

hemp: fibrous cannabis low in THC, used to make a menagerie of products from textiles to automobiles

hermaphrodite: an individual having flowers of both sexes on the same plant. Hermaphrodites are more correctly referred to as "intersex."

Hertz (Hz): a unit of a frequency that cycles one time each second: A home with a 60 hertz AC current cycles 60 times per second.

heterosis: hybrid vigor such that an F1 hybrid falls outside the performance range of the parents with respect to some character or characters: usually applied to size, rate of growth, or general vigor

heterozygous loci: regions along homologous chromosome that have different alleles

HID: High Intensity Discharge lamp: This is the type of lamp used in many indoor grow rooms.

homologous chromosomes: members of paired chromosomes in non-gametic cells; homologous chromosomes are similar in size, shape, and, supposedly, in function. One of each of the homologous chromosomal pair is derived from the male parent, the other from the female.

honeydew: a sticky honey-like substance secreted onto foliage by aphids, scale, and mealy bugs

hood: the reflective cover of a lamp

HOR: the abbreviation stamped on some HID bulbs meaning they may be burned in a horizontal position

hormone: chemical substance that controls the growth and development of a plant: Root-inducing hormones help clones root.

horticulture: the science and art of cultivating plants

hose bib: water outlet usually found outdoors that contains an on/off valve

hostile environment: environment that is unfriendly and inhospitable to pests and diseases

humidity, relative: ratio between the amount of moisture in the air and the greatest amount of moisture the air could hold at the same temperature

Hybrid vigor.

humus: dark, fertile, partially decomposed plant or animal matter: Humus forms the organic portion of the soil.

hybrid: an offspring from two plants of different breeds, variety, or genetic make-up

hybrid vigor: greater strength and health or faster rate of growth in the offspring resulting from the cross-breeding of two gene pools

hybridizing: see cross-pollination

hydrogen: light, colorless, odorless, highly flammable gas: Hydrogen combines with oxygen to form water.

hydroponics: growing plants in nutrient solutions without soil, usually in an inert soilless mix

hygrometer: instrument for measuring relative humidity in the atmosphere: A hygrometer will save time, frustration, and money.

IAA: Indol-eacetic acid, a plant hormone that stimulates growth

IBL: inbred line

inbreeding: the process of breeding solely within the seed lot with no external pollen inputs

induce: to effect, cause, or influence via stimulation: A 12-hour photoperiod stimulates flowering.

inductive photoperiod: daylength required to stimulate flowering

inert: a substance that will not chemically react. Inert growing mediums make it easy to control the chemistry of the nutrient solution.

inflorescence: a cluster of flowers

insecticide: a product that kills or inhibits insects

intensity: the amount or strength of light energy per unit or area: Intensity decreases the further away from the source.

intersex: a single individual expressing both staminate and pistillate flowers

intersexual: having sexual characteristics of both the typical male and typical female plants

introgress: to incorporate or add a trait to a given population, without otherwise altering the significant characteristic of the population

jacket: protective outer bulb or envelope of lamp

kif: Moroccan word for cannabis plants and flowers. It is also the Moroccan term for a mix of tobacco and cannabis which is smoked. Kif does not mean Moroccan hash.

Kilowatt hour (kWh): measure of electricity used per hour: A 1000-watt HID uses one kilowatt per hour.

landrace: is a (wild) cannabis variety that is not improved by humans

leach: to dissolve or wash out soluble components of soil by heavy watering

leader: see meristem

leggy: plant that is abnormally tall, with few leaves: usually caused by lack of light

life cycle: a series of growth stages through which cannabis must pass in its natural lifetime: The stages are seed, seedling, vegetative, and floral.

light mover: a device that moves a lamp back and forth or in a circular path across the ceiling of a grow room to provide more balanced light

Inductive photoperiod 12 hours day/night.

limbing: cutting off lower, secondary plant branches to encourage primary growth

lime: calcium compounds such as dolomite or hydrated lime that determine or alter soil pH level

litmus paper: *Limbing* chemically sensitive paper used to indicate pH levels in colorless liquids

loam: organic soil mixture of crumbly clay, silt, and sand

locus: a position on a chromosome where a specific gene is located. Plural: loci

lumen:

measurement of light output: One lumen is equal to the amount of light emitted by one candle that falls on one square foot of surface located one foot away from one candle.

macronutrient: one or all of the primary nutrients N-P-K (nitrogen, phosphorus, or potassium) or the secondary nutrients Mg (magnesium) and Ca (calcium)

manicure: trim leaves and large stems from buds with scissors or fine pruners so the most THC-potent portion remains

marijuana: cannabis; illegal drug in many countries, ingested for its THC content

meristem: 1. plant tissue from which new cells are formed; 2. the active growing tip of a root or stem

meristem pruning: cutting away the growth tip to encourage branching and limit height

micron: one-millionth of a meter. The symbol "μ" is used to denote micron.

micronutrients: trace elements necessary for plant health, including S, Fe, Mn, B, Mb, Zn, and Cu

millimeter: 0.04 inch

mist: to manufacture rain with the help of a spray bottle

moisture meter: electronic device that measures the moisture content of a substrate at any given point

monoecious: having male and female reproductive systems or flowers on the same plant

monoecious: an individual plant having both staminate and pistillate flowers. A monoecious population consists of plants expressing flowers of both genders.

monochromatic: producing only one color: LP sodium lamps are monochromatic.

morphology: the study of the form and structure of animals and plants

Mother Nature: the vast outdoors and all she holds: The indoor horticulturist assumes the role of Mother Nature.

mother plant: female marijuana plant held in vegetative state and used for cutting (cloning) stock: A mother plant may be grown from seed or be a clone.

mulch: a protective covering for the soil of compost, old leaves, paper, rocks, etc.: Indoors, mulch keeps soil too moist and possible fungus could result. Outdoors, mulch helps soil retain and attract moisture.

mutation: an inheritable change in genetic material

mycelium: the mass of strands that form the root-like part of fungi, often submerged in soil or a host body

nanometer (nm): 0.000000001 meter, one billionth of a meter, nm is used as a scale to measure electromagnetic wavelengths of light: Color and light spectrums are expressed in nanometers.

necrosis/ necrotic: localized death of a plant part due to injury or disease

nitrogen (N): essential element to plant growth; one of the three major nutrients N-P-K

Necrosis

node: 1. a joint; 2. the position on a stem from which leaves, shoots, or flowers grow

N-P-K: nitrogen, phosphorus, and potassium: the three major plant nutrients

nursery: gardening business that grows plants for sale or experimentation: A nursery is a great place to gather information.

Node

nutrient: plant food, essential elements N-P-K as well as secondary and trace elements fundamental to sustaining plant life

Ohms Power Law: a law that expresses the strength of an electric current: Volts × Amperes = Watts.

open pollination: pollination that occurs naturally, as opposed to controlled pollination, no effect of selection from human interference

optimum: 1. the most favorable condition for growth and reproduction 2. peak production

organic: 1. made of, derived from, or related to living organisms: Growers of organic cannabis use fertilizers and insect control methods of animal or vegetable origin. Unaltered rock powders are also considered organic.

osmosis: the equalizing movement of fluids through a semi-permeable membrane, such as in a living cell

outbreeding: breeding between individual cannabis plants that are not closely related

outcross: the process of breeding using individuals outside of the family, population, or group

overload: load to excess: An electrical circuit that uses more than 80 percent of its potential is overloaded. A 20 amp circuit drawing 17 amps is overloaded.

ovule: egg which contains the female genes and is found within the plant ovary: When fertilized, an ovule will grow into a seed.

oxygen: tasteless, colorless, odorless element: Plants need oxygen in the soil in order to grow.

parasite: organism that lives on or in another host organism without benefiting the host: Fungus is a parasite.

passive: hydroponic system that moves the nutrient solution through absorption or capillary action

pathogen: a disease-causing micro-organism, especially bacteria, fungi, and viruses

peat: partially decomposed vegetation (usually moss) with slow decay due to extreme moisture, cold, and acidic conditions

perennial: a plant, such as a tree or shrub, that completes its life cycle over several years

perlite: amendment of sand or volcanic glass expanded by heat, which aerates the soil or growth medium

pH: a scale from 0-14 that measures a growing medium's (or anything's) acid to alkaline balance: a pH of 7 is neutral, lower numbers indicate increasing acidity, and higher numbers increasing alkalinity: Cannabis grows best in a 6.5 to 8 pH range.

pH tester: electronic instrument or chemical used to measure the acid or alkaline balance in soil or water

phenotype: the outward form, characteristic, and appearance of a plant, determined by the interaction of the individual genotype with the environment

phloem: the food- and water-conducting tissue of vascular plants

phosphor coating: internal fluorescent bulb coating that diffuses light and affects various color outputs

phosphorus (P): one of the macronutrients that promote root and flower growth

photoperiod: the relationship between the length of light and dark in a 24-hour period; affects the growth and maturity of cannabis

photosynthesis: the building of chemical compounds (carbohydrates that plants need for growth) from light energy, water, and CO_2

Photosynthesis

phototropism: the environmental response movement of a plant part toward or away from a light source

phyllotaxy: the arrangement of leaves on a stem, and the principles that govern such arrangement

phytotoxic: substance that is toxic to plants normally burning the leaves.

phytotron: a completely enclosed indoor area with extensive environmental controls for the experimental growth (and study) of plants

pigment: the substance in paint or anything that absorbs light, producing (reflecting) the same color as the pigment

pistillate: female; having pistils but no functional stamens

pistils: small pair of fuzzy white hairs extending from top of female calyx: Pistils catch pollen and channel it into contact with the ovule for fertilization.

pod, seed: a dry calyx containing a mature or maturing seed

pollen: fine, yellow, dust-like microspores containing male genes

pollen sack: male flower containing pollen

pollination: the transfer of male pollen from the anther to the stigma of the same or a different flower to fertilize ovules which produce seeds

polyhybrid cross: a hybrid plant crossbred for more than one trait

pot: 1. container for growing medium 2. American slang word for marijuana

potbound: root system that is bound, stifled, or inhibited from normal growth by a too-small container

potassium (K): one of the macronutrients necessary for plant life

potent: capable of wielding strong physiological or chemical effects: marijuana rich in THC that provides a desirable psychoactive effect

power surge: interruption or change in flow of electricity

predatory insect: beneficial insect or parasite that hunts down and devours harmful insects

primordia: belonging to or characteristic of the earliest stage of development of an organism or a part

progeny: 1. one born of, begotten by, or derived from another; an offspring or a descendant: 2. offspring or descendants considered as a group

propagate: 1. sexual propagation: to produce a seed by breeding a male and female plant 2. asexual propagation: to produce a plant by cloning

pruning: trimming branches or parts of plants to strengthen those that remain, or bring shape to the plant

Punnett square: a tool developed by British geneticist, Reginald Punnett, used by biologists to predict the probability of possible genotypes of offspring

PVC (polyvinyl chloride) pipe: plastic pipe that is easy to work with, readily available, and used to transport liquid and air

pyrethrum: natural insecticide made from the blossoms of various chrysanthemums

RH: relative humidity: see humidity, relative

radicle: the part of a plant seedling that develops into a root, the root tip

recovery: hydroponic system that reclaims the nutrient solution and recycles it

rejuvenation: a mature plant, having completed its life cycle (flowering) that is stimulated by a new 18-hour photoperiod, to rejuvenate or produce new vegetative growth

resin glands: tiny pores that secrete resin

retting: to moisten or soak in order to soften and separate the fibers from the woody tissue by partial rotting

root: 1. the underground part of a plant: Roots function to absorb water and nutrients as well as anchor a plant in the ground. 2. to root (start) a cutting or clone

root hormone: root-inducing substance

rootbound: see potbound

roguing: to weed out inferior, diseased, or undesirable plants from a crop, field, or population area

salt: crystalline compound that results from improper pH or toxic

Root bound plant.

build-up of fertilizer: Salt will burn plants, preventing them from absorbing nutrients.

scion: the shoot (containing buds) that is used for grafting

SCROG: screen of green: a growing method which involves training cannabis shoots onto a net, trellis, or chicken wire

scuff: to scrape and roughen the surface: Seeds with a hard outer shell germinate faster when scuffed.

Seal-a-meal: airtight sealer for plastic baggies used to seal in freshness of pungent marijuana

Sea of Green (SOG): a method of growing tightly spaced cloned plantlets. The clones are flowered almost immediately after rooting for a small yield per plant, but no wasted space.

secondary nutrients: calcium (Ca) and magnesium (Mg). Ca and Mg are considered to be primary nutrients by some sources.

seed: the mature, fertilized ovule of a pistillate plant, containing a protective shell, embryo, and supply of food: A seed will germinate and grow, given heat and moisture.

selfing: to fertilize with pollen from the same flower or plant; self-pollination

senescence: the (declining) growth stage in a plant or plant part from its prime to death

sexual propagation: in plants, the reproduction by means of seed following fertilization

shake: slang term for "Bunk," lower growth, or least potent portion of harvest: small particles of cannabis broken off the main "nug" inside a bag due to rough handling: Many times, shake is flaked or powder-like and used for cooking.

short circuit: condition that results when wires cross and form a circuit. A short circuit will trip breaker switches and blow fuses.

sinsemilla: two Spanish words: sin = without, semilla = seed, combined into one word by Americans: Sinsemilla describes potent marijuana from flowering female cannabis plants kept seedless by preventing pollination in order to promote a high THC content.

Sea of Green.

soap: 1. cleaning agent 2. wetting agent 3. insecticide: All soap used in horticulture should be biodegradable.

socket: threaded, wired holder for a light-bulb

soilless mix: a growing medium made up of mineral particles such as vermiculite, perlite, sand, pumice, etc.: Organic moss is often a component of soilless mix.

soluble: able to be dissolved in liquid, especially water

solution: 1. a mixture of two or more solids, liquids, or gases, often with water 2. answer to a problem

sponge rock: large pieces of perlite, a light, mineral soil amendment

spore: seed-like offspring of certain bacteria, fungi, algae, and some nonflowering plants

sprout: 1. a shoot of a plant, as from a recently germinated seed 2. small, new growth of leaf or stem

square feet (sq. ft.): length × width; a measurement of area

stagnant: motionless air or water: for healthy cannabis growth, water must drain and not become stagnant

stamen: the male floral organ, bearing the anther, which produces pollen to fertilize female flowers

staminate: male, pollen-producing flower having stamens but no pistils

sterilize: to make super clean by removing dirt, germs, and bacteria; disinfect pruning tools to avoid spreading disease

stigma: the tip of the flower's pistil, which receives the pollen

stigmatic: the portion of the pistil on which the pollen germinates

stipule: one of a pair of small, leaf-like appendages found at the base of the leaf-stalk of many plants

stomata: small mouth-like or nose-like openings on leaf underside, responsible for transpiration and many other life functions: The millions of stomata must be kept very clean to function properly.

strain: 1. ancestry, lineage, phenotype, a particular type of cannabis having the same characteristics

stress: a physical or chemical factor that causes extra exertion by plants, usually by restricting fluid flow to foliage: A stressed plant will grow poorly.

substrate: the medium on which an organism lives, as soil, soilless mix, rock, etc.

sugar: food product of a plant

sump: a reservoir that receives drainage; a drain or receptacle for hydroponic nutrient solutions used for growing cannabis

super bloom: a common name for fertilizer high in phosphorus and potassium that promotes flower formation and growth

synthesis: the production of a substance, such as chlorophyll, by uniting light energy, elements, or chemical compounds

taproot: the main or primary root that grows from the seed: Lateral roots will branch off the taproot.

taxonomy: classification of plants and animals according to their family relationships

Teflon tape: tape that is extremely useful to help seal all kinds of threaded pipe joints. I like Teflon tape better than putty.

Terminal bud.

tepid water: lukewarm 70-80°F (21-27°C) water: Always use tepid water around plants to facilitate chemical processes and ease shock.

terminal bud: the growth tip of main stem or branch

terpene: hydrocarbons found in essential oils (resins) produced by plants; gives the resin a strong aroma

testa: the hard outer covering of a seed

THC: tetrahydrocannibinol: physiologically active ingredient which is the primary intoxicant in marijuana

THCV: tetrahydrocannabivarol: a psychoactive chemical found in cannabis

thermostat: a device for regulating temperature: A thermostat may control a heater, furnace, or vent fan.

timer: an electrical device for regulating photoperiod, fan, etc.: A timer is a must in all grow rooms.

toxic life: the amount of time a pesticide or fungicide remains active or live

transformer: a device in the ballast that transforms electric current from one voltage to another.

transpire: to give off water vapor and by-products via the stomata on leaves

transplant: to uproot a plant and root ball and replant it in new soil

trellis: a frame of small boards (lattice) that trains or supports plants

trellising: method of restricting plant growth or altering its shape and size by tying plant to lattice work or wire screen

trichome: resin-secreting plant hair

triploid: having three sets of chromosomes within each cell, may contribute to increased vigor

tungsten: a heavy, hard metal with a high melting point that conducts electricity well: Tungsten is used for a filament in tungsten halogen lamps.

ultraviolet: light with very short wavelengths, out of the far blue visible spectrum

variety: distinct strain, phenotype (see strain)

vascular: referring to a plant's circulatory system which carries sap throughout the body of the plant

vector: 1. an organism (as an insect) that transmits disease, a pathogen 2. an organism that transmits genes, a pollinator

vegetative: growth stage in which cannabis rapidly produces new leafy growth and green chlorophyll

vent: an opening such as a window or door that allows the circulation of fresh air

ventilation: circulation of fresh air, fundamental to a healthy indoor garden: An exhaust fan creates ventilation.

vermiculite: mica processed and expanded by heat: Vermiculite is a soil amendment and medium for rooting cuttings.

vitamin B1: vitamin that is absorbed by tender root hairs, easing transplant wilt and shock

weed: 1. slang word for marijuana 2. any undesirable plant: One person's weed is another person's flower!

wetting agent: a compound that reduces the droplet size and lowers the surface tension of the water, making it wetter: Liquid concentrate dish soap is a good wetting agent if it is biodegradable.

whorl: where three or more leaves or petals arise from the same point and form a circle around it

whorled phyllotaxy: three or more leaves or branches located at each node along the branches and stems: People often confuse the term whorled phyllotaxy with the condition, triploidy (a chromosomal anomaly).

wick: the part of a passive watering system the nutrient passes up to be absorbed by the medium and roots: A passive hydroponic system uses a wick suspended in the nutrient solution.

wilt: 1. to become limp from lack of water 2. plant disease/disorder

wire ties: paper-coated wire ties are excellent for tying down or training plants

xylem: vascular tissue that transports water and minerals from the roots throughout the stems and leaves

Air-cooled lighting covers this indoor garden with plenty of light, and little excess heat. The strain is 'Sour Bubble.'

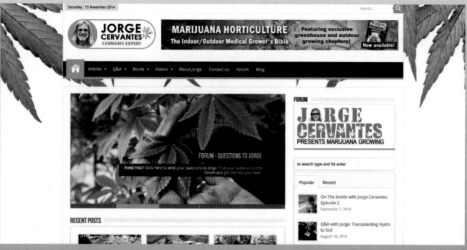

www.marijuanagrowing.com

www.youtube.com/user/jorgecervantesmj

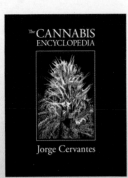

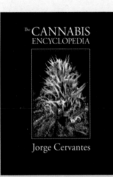